BACK CHANNEL TO CUBA

BACK CHANNEL TO CUBA

THE **HIDDEN HISTORY** OF NEGOTIATIONS BETWEEN **WASHINGTON** AND **HAVANA**

William M. LeoGrande
& Peter Kornbluh

THE UNIVERSITY OF NORTH CAROLINA PRESS CHAPEL HILL

This book was published with the assistance of a grant from American University and the assistance of the William Rand Kenan Jr. Fund of the University of North Carolina Press.

Jacket illustrations: Richard Nixon and Fidel Castro, 1959 (Cuban Revolution Collection, MS 650, Manuscripts and Archives, Yale University Library); telephone cord (© depositphotos.com/kiss 777); Barack Obama and Raúl Castro, 2013 (Chip Somodevilla/Getty Images).

Library of Congress Cataloging-in-Publication Data
LeoGrande, William M.
Back channel to Cuba : the hidden history of negotiations between Washington and Havana / William M. LeoGrande and Peter Kornbluh.
pages cm
Includes bibliographical references and index.
ISBN 978-1-4696-1763-3 (cloth : alkaline paper) —
ISBN 978-1-4696-1764-0 (ebook)
1. United States—Foreign relations—Cuba. 2. Cuba—Foreign relations—United States. 3. Negotiation—United States—History. 4. Negotiation—Cuba—History. 5. Reconciliation—History. 6. United States—Foreign relations—1945–1989. 7. United States—Foreign relations—1989–
I. Kornbluh, Peter. II. Title.
E183.8.C9L384 2014
327.7307291—dc23
2014013123

18 17 16 15 14 5 4 3 2 1

To the memory of friends and colleagues Robert A. Pastor,
Saul Landau, Viron P. "Pete" Vaky, Barry Sklar, William D. Rogers, and
Patricia Cepeda, who worked conscientiously for reconciliation between
Cuba and the United States but, sadly, did not live to see it

CONTENTS

ILLUSTRATIONS

ACKNOWLEDGMENTS

Authors invariably accumulate many debts as they write a book. We are grateful to everyone who agreed to be interviewed, especially our Cuban colleagues who trusted two North Americans to present their side of the story fairly. We especially appreciate those who participated in this rich history of dialogue and diplomacy between the United States and Cuba and were willing to share their memories and contemporaneous notes: Peter Bourne, Bernardo Benes, Alfredo Durán, Kirby Jones, Max Lesnick, Abraham Lowenthal, John Nolan, Richard Nuccio, Governor Bill Richardson, and John J. "Jay" Taylor. Robert Pastor, who traveled to Cuba with President Jimmy Carter in 2002, provided us with a large cache of documents from the Carter administration that were declassified for that trip. Dan Fisk, who worked for Senator Jesse Helms, provided us with another file of documents declassified for one of the senator's congressional inquiries. William D. Rogers worked closely with the National Security Archive to obtain the declassification of his "Special Activities" file on the secret talks with Cuba. Piero Gleijeses generously shared some of the documents he obtained from Cuban archives during his own pathbreaking research on Cuban policy in Africa.

A number of individuals took a special interest in this project and provided us with invaluable guidance and support. To Fulton Armstrong, Lars Schoultz, and Julia Sweig, we owe a sincere debt of gratitude. Special credit goes to Philip Brenner and James G. Blight, who were early collaborators on charting this history.

We also received invaluable assistance from many archivists, including César Rodríguez, curator of the Latin American Collection, and Judith Ann Schiff, chief research archivist, at the Yale University Library; Claryn Spies, Manuscripts and Archives Division at the Yale University Library; Carol A. Leadenham, assistant archivist for reference at the Hoover Institution Archives; Suzanne Forbes at the Kennedy Library; Regina Greenwell at the Johnson Library; and Donna Lehman at the Ford Library.

During the course of this project, we were fortunate to have the support of some outstanding research assistants, including Kimberly Moloney, Marguerite Rose Jiménez, and Luciano Melo at American University. At the

National Security Archive, Marian Schlotterbeck, Michael Lemon, Andrew Kragie, Erin Maskell, Carly Ackerman, and Tim Casey provided extraordinary assistance. A special thanks to Joshua Frens-String for his contribution.

As an institution dedicated to obtaining the declassification of documents on Cuba policy, the National Security Archive deserves a special thanks. William Burr offered invaluable Kissinger memoranda and telephone conversation transcripts. Svetlana Savranskaya shared her revealing research from the Russian archives. Longtime archive friend and associate Jim Hershberg shared his extraordinary work on Brazil. Sue Bechtel was consistently and cheerfully helpful. Tom Blanton, as always, provided his substantive support, creative ideas, and infectious enthusiasm.

The Arca Foundation hosted a conference at its Musgrove meeting center that enabled us to bring together more than a dozen former U.S. policy makers and participants in U.S.-Cuba diplomatic contacts to share their experiences and draw lessons from them; we are grateful for the support of Anna Leffer-Kuhn. American University provided research support to help finance our investigations. Mario Bronfman of the Ford Foundation, Andrea Panaritis and the late Robert Vitarelli of the Christopher Reynolds Foundation, and Dick and Sally Roberts of the Coyote Foundation provided generous support to the National Security Archive's Cuba Documentation Project that sustained this historical inquiry from start to finish.

Two anonymous readers for the University of North Carolina Press provided close and thorough reviews. Their detailed comments demonstrated an impressive knowledge of the history of U.S.-Cuban relations, and the final result is better for having had their input. We also want to thank our editors, Elaine Maisner, Ron Maner, and Brian MacDonald for their professionalism, understanding, and advice. With infinite patience, Elaine helped us shape this project from the outset and deftly guided us through the challenges, choices, and decisions that inevitably confront coauthors.

In addition we benefited from the guidance and support of family and friends. Peter Kornbluh gratefully thanks Joyce Kornbluh for her copyediting and proofreading talents, Gabriel Kornbluh for his technical skills, David Corn for his steady encouragement, and Gabriela Vega for her consistent interest, support, and sage advice. William M. LeoGrande thanks Marty Langelan for her encouragement, understanding, and unfailingly good editorial judgment.

Finally, we are especially grateful to Jimmy Carter and Fidel Castro for taking time to talk with us about a unique history that they helped to create.

ABBREVIATIONS

ASNE American Society of Newspaper Editors
BTTR Brothers to the Rescue
CANF Cuban American National Foundation
CDA Cuban Democracy Act
CFC Cuban Families Committee for the Liberation
of the Prisoners of War
CIA Central Intelligence Agency
CORU Coordinación de Organizaciones Revolucionarias Unidas
(Coordination of United Revolutionary Organizations)
DAI Development Alternatives Inc.
DAR Daughters of the American Revolution
DAS deputy assistant secretary of state
DEA U.S. Drug Enforcement Administration
DGI Dirección General de Inteligencia (Cuban Directorate of
Intelligence)
DIS Drug Interdiction Officer at the U.S. Interests Section in
Havana
DOD U.S. Department of Defense
DOS Department of State
ExComm Executive Committee (Kennedy administration)
FBI U.S. Federal Bureau of Investigation
FNLA Frente Nacional de Libertação de Angola (National Front for
the Liberation of Angola)
GOC Government of Cuba
GTMO Guantánamo Naval Station (aka Gitmo)
IADC International Association of Drilling Contractors
ICE U.S. Immigration and Customs Enforcement
INCSR International Narcotics Control Strategy Report
INDER Instituto Nacional de Deportes, Educación Física y Recreación
(Institute of Sport, Physical Education, and Recreation, Cuba)
INS U.S. Immigration and Naturalization Service
IRI International Republican Institute

MemCon Memorandum of Conversation
MINFAR Ministerio de las Fuerzas Armadas Revolucionarias de Cuba
(Ministry of the Revolutionary Armed Forces)
MININT Ministerio del Interior de Cuba (Ministry of the Interior)
MINREX Ministerio de Relaciones Exteriores de Cuba (Ministry of
Foreign Relations)
MPLA Movimento Popular de Libertação de Angola (Popular
Movement for the Liberation of Angola)
MRBM medium range ballistic missile
NCPAC National Conservative Political Action Committee
NGO nongovernmental organization
NID National Intelligence Daily
NIE National Intelligence Estimate
NPP national policy paper
NSC National Security Council
OAS Organization of American States
OCB Operations Coordinating Board (Eisenhower administration)
OFAC Office of Foreign Assets Control, U.S. Department of the
Treasury
ONDCP Office of National Drug Control Policy
OSS Office of Strategic Services
PRC Policy Review Committee (Carter administration)
SALT Strategic Arms Limitation Treaty
SWAPO Southwest African People's Organization
UN United Nations
UNDCP United Nations International Drug Control Program
UNITA União Nacional para a Independência Total de Angola
(National Union for Total Independence of Angola)
USAID U.S. Agency for International Development
USG United States Government
USINT U.S. Interests Section
USSR Union of Soviet Socialist Republics

BACK CHANNEL TO CUBA

REBUILDING BRIDGES

Our relations are like a bridge in war-time. I'm not going to talk about who blew it up—I think it was you who blew it up. The war has ended and now we are reconstructing the bridge, brick by brick, 90 miles from Key West to Varadero beach. It is not a bridge that can be reconstructed easily, as fast as it was destroyed. It takes a long time. If both parties reconstruct their part of the bridge, we can shake hands without winners or losers.

—Raúl Castro to Senators George McGovern and James Abourezk, April 8, 1977

In early April of 1963, during talks in Havana over the release of Americans being held in Cuban jails as spies, Fidel Castro first broached his interest in improving relations with the United States. "If any relations were to commence between the U.S. and Cuba," Castro asked U.S. negotiator James Donovan, "how would it come about and what would be involved?"[1]

Sent to Cuba in the fall of 1962 by President John F. Kennedy and his brother Robert to undertake the first real negotiations with Cuba's revolutionary regime, Donovan had secured the freedom of more than one thousand members of the CIA-led exile brigade that Castro's forces had defeated at the Bay of Pigs. In addition to the prisoners, Donovan also secured Castro's confidence. Through trips in January, March, and April 1963, he built on that confidence to negotiate the freedom of several dozen U.S. citizens detained after the revolution. In the respectful nature of their talks, Castro found the first trusted U.S. representative with whom he could seriously discuss how Havana and Washington might move toward restoring civility and normalcy in the dark wake of the Bay of Pigs and the Cuban missile crisis. "In view of the past history on both sides here, the problem of how to inaugurate any relations was a very difficult one," Castro observed.

"So I said, 'now do you know how porcupines make love?'" Donovan remembered responding. "And he said no. And I said well, the answer is 'very carefully,' and that is how you and the U.S. would have to get into this."[2]

As Donovan pursued his shuttle diplomacy during the spring of 1963, some Kennedy administration officials sought to use his special relationship

1

with Castro to begin a dialogue toward ending hostilities with Cuba. Within the CIA, however, others saw a different opportunity—an opportunity to use the negotiations, and the negotiator, to assassinate Fidel Castro. Knowing that Donovan planned to bring a scuba diving suit as a confidence-building gift for the Cuban leader, members of the covert "executive action" unit developed a plot to contaminate the snorkel with tubercle bacillus, and poison the wetsuit with a fungus. "They tried to use him as the instrument . . . the lawyer who was negotiating the liberation of the Playa Girón prisoners!" Castro exclaimed years later.[3] Only the intervention of Donovan's CIA handlers, Milan Miskovsky and Frank DeRosa, prevented him from becoming an unwitting, would-be assassin.[4]

The CIA's infamous assassination plots—exploding conch shells, poison pens, poison pills, sniper rifles, toxic cigars—are the stuff of legend in the history of U.S. policy toward the Cuban revolution. Washington's efforts to roll back the revolution, through exile paramilitary attacks, covert action, overt economic embargo, and contemporary "democracy promotion" programs, have dominated and defined more than a half century of U.S.-Cuban relations. What Henry Kissinger characterized as the "perpetual antagonism" between Washington and Havana remains among the most entrenched and enduring conflicts in the history of U.S. foreign policy.

The Untold Story

There is, however, another side to the history of U.S.-Cuban relations, far less known but more relevant today: the bilateral efforts at dialogue, rapprochement, and reconciliation. Every president since Eisenhower has engaged in some form of dialogue with Castro and his representatives. Some talks have been tightly circumscribed, dealing only with specific, narrow issues of mutual interest, such as immigration, air piracy, and drug interdiction. Others have been wide-ranging, engaging the full panoply of issues at stake between the two sides. Some episodes of dialogue produced tangible agreements, formal and informal; others sputtered to a halt with no discernible result. But every U.S. president, Democrat and Republican alike, has seen some advantage in talking to Cuba.

Indeed, both Democratic and Republican administrations have engaged in little-known efforts to arrive at a modus vivendi with the Cuban revolution. After authorizing a paramilitary invasion to overthrow Castro by force and implementing a full trade embargo to cripple the Cuban economy, John F. Kennedy ordered his aides to "start thinking along more flexible lines" in negotiating a state of peaceful coexistence with Castro. During Gerald Ford's presidency, Henry Kissinger directed his aides to "deal straight with Castro" and negotiate improved relations like "a big guy, not like a shyster." Jimmy Carter actually signed a presidential decision directive to "achieve normalization of our relations with Cuba" through "direct and confidential talks."[5]

Given the domestic political sensitivity surrounding any hint of better relations with Havana, these talks, and many other contacts with Cuba, have often been conducted through secret, back-channel diplomacy. To maintain plausible deniability, U.S. presidents have turned to third countries, among them Mexico, Spain, Britain, and Brazil, as hosts and facilitators. To limit the political risk of direct contact, Washington and Havana have developed creative clandestine methods of communication—deploying famous literary figures, journalists, politicians, businessmen, and even a former president of the United States as interlocutors. When face-to-face talks have been necessary, Cuban and U.S. officials have met furtively, in foreign cities such as Paris, Cuernavaca, and Toronto, or in private homes, crowded cafeterias, prominent hotels, and even on the steps of the Lincoln Memorial in Washington, D.C. On several occasions, White House and State Department officials have secretly traveled to Havana to negotiate face-to-face with Fidel Castro.

Not surprisingly, this rich history of U.S. back-channel diplomacy with Cuba has been shrouded in secrecy, buried in thousands of classified files that record the internal debates, meetings, agendas, negotiations, arguments, and agreements that have transpired over more than half a century. In the absence of an accessible historical record, scholarship and analysis on U.S.-Cuban relations has largely focused on the more prominent and visible history of antagonism, skewing the historical debate over whether better ties were possible—or even desirable. The dearth of evidence on the many efforts to find common ground has empowered the "anti-dialogueros," as one U.S. official called them, to cast serious diplomacy with Cuba as an oxymoron at best, a heresy at worst. Long after the end of the Cold War, talking with Cuba remained a delicate and controversial political proposition—even as the benefits have become increasingly obvious to both countries.

Back Channel to Cuba

This book presents a comprehensive chronicle of the history of dialogue between the United States and Cuba since 1959. The pages that follow are an attempt to assess this historical record of negotiations—both secret and open—at a time when that record is especially pertinent to the political discourse over U.S. relations with Cuba. Both Barack Obama and Raúl Castro publicly declared their desire to move beyond the past half-century's legacy of hostility. Both Washington and Havana appeared to realize that international, national, and mutual interests would be advanced by a successful negotiation of normal bilateral ties. But as the history of dialogue shows, having the intention to improve relations and actually accomplishing it are two different things. Between intention and realization lies a long road of negotiation on complex problems.

But the past holds lessons for contemporary policy makers on how to navigate that road. How have previous talks evolved between Washington and Havana? Why have some succeeded and others failed? What does this history tell policy makers, scholars, and concerned citizens about the potential for rapprochement between two nations that have been "intimate enemies" for more than half a century?[6] These are among the key questions explored in this volume.

To reconstruct this history, we have spent more than a decade unearthing the classified files—through the Freedom of Information Act, mandatory declassification review, and archival research—on multiple episodes of dialogue between Washington and Havana. These include the State Department's file, "Efforts at Negotiation with Cuba," from the Eisenhower administration; "Contacts with Cuban Leaders" records compiled during the Kennedy and Johnson administrations; the "Special Activities" file kept by Henry Kissinger's office on his top secret attempt to negotiate normal relations; the Carter administration's road map to normalization and memoranda of conversations with Fidel Castro himself; and internal papers from the Clinton White House on engagement with Havana. These records, along with hundreds of others, shed new light on the policies, strategies, and interplay of both governments in their pursuit of better relations.

With the documents in hand, we interviewed a broad array of the surviving policy makers and negotiators who drafted the documents and participated in talks—Fidel Castro and former president Jimmy Carter among them—along with the intermediaries who carried messages back and forth between Washington and Havana. Their firsthand accounts bring the documentary record to life, adding a critical human dimension to the story. Indeed, in many ways, this book chronicles the tenacious efforts of key official and nonofficial policy actors who, for more than fifty years, challenged the national security managers in successive administrations to consider the options of dialogue and engagement over the dominant U.S. approach of antagonism and estrangement.

The perennial conflict between U.S. officials who advocated punishing Cuba to force its compliance and those who argued for diplomacy is a recurrent theme of this history. Every administration has had its "hawks" and "doves" on Cuba. How they interacted depended, to some degree, on the domestic and international circumstances of the time. At every juncture, efforts at dialogue—and their success or failure—were a product not only of the state of relations between Washington and Havana but also of the balance of domestic political forces in the two capitals. To the extent possible given space limitations, this book provides and analyzes the political circumstances and context within which bilateral talks took place.

Although Fidel Castro's preeminence and dominance meant that policy making in Havana was less fractious than it was in Washington, the pages that follow reveal that there were debates on the Cuban side as well. Cuban policy was hardly static; Fidel's attitude toward the United States evolved over time. Raúl Castro's succession introduced yet another factor—his determination to resolve the revolution's critical outstanding problems, among them relations with the United States, before passing the baton to the next generation of Cuban leaders.

For more than half a century, the history of talks has been inextricably intertwined with, and overshadowed by, the more infamous history of acrimony and distrust in U.S.-Cuban relations. *Back Channel to Cuba* aspires to give the history of dialogue its due. This history provides strong evidence that, despite proceeding "very carefully," both the United States and Cuba have long recognized that negotiation and cooperation offer potential benefits over a perpetual state of antagonism and aggression. "Our interest is in getting the Cuban issue behind us, not in prolonging it indefinitely," one SECRET memo written almost thirty years ago to Henry Kissinger stated clearly.[7]

"Our relations are like a bridge in war-time," Raúl Castro observed shortly thereafter, describing the damage done by years of hostility. "It is not a bridge that can be reconstructed easily, as fast as it was destroyed. It takes a long time. If both parties reconstruct their part of the bridge, we can shake hands without winners or losers."[8]

1. EISENHOWER
Patience and Forbearance

During the first nine months of my stay in Cuba, I did my best to convince Castro and many of his personal advisers of our good intentions. . . . It was not until November of 1959 that I was finally convinced that we could not expect to reach any sort of understanding with him. But even after that, I was in favor of maintaining all possible contacts and exploring all possibilities of negotiation.

—Ambassador Philip Bonsal, letter to Arthur Schlesinger Jr., November 13, 1962

Fidel Castro, in his olive green fatigues, and Acting Secretary of State Christian A. Herter, in his three-piece suit and bow tie, made an incongruous couple. Castro, on his first trip to the United States since the triumph of the revolution, met Herter for lunch in the Pan-American Room of Washington's luxurious Statler Hilton Hotel on April 16, 1959. Sitting in front of a large primitive art mural of a Latin American peasant tilling the soil, they engaged in animated conversation. When Castro pulled out a cigar, Herter lit it for him.[1]

Fidel's mood was buoyant. Just four months earlier, he had led an army of bearded guerrillas in the Sierra Maestra of eastern Cuba; now he was Cuba's new prime minister, having lunch with the one of the most powerful officials in the United States government. Events had moved fast in those intervening weeks—certainly faster than Washington had anticipated. Eager to tell Cuba's story and certain he could sway U.S. opinion by the force of his own conviction, Fidel told Herter of his plans for Cuba and admitted his frustration at his own lack of experience in the practical affairs of governing. He made a plea for patience while he worked to restore order in the aftermath of the revolution.[2]

Herter, more than twice Fidel's age, was a seasoned diplomat intent on taking Castro's measure and persuading him that good relations with the United States were in Cuba's best interests.[3] What impressed Herter most was Castro's youthful immaturity. He reported to Eisenhower that he was

Fidel Castro chatting with Acting Secretary of State Christian A. Herter on April 16, 1959. Castro was a guest at a luncheon given in his honor by Herter here in the Pan-American Room of the Statler Hilton Hotel in Washington, D.C. (© Bettmann/CORBIS)

sorry the president had not had a chance to meet Castro, who was "a most interesting individual" but "very much like a child in many ways."[4] One of the most startling sights, he added, was Castro's eight "wild-eyed" armed bodyguards, who swept into the Pan-American Room and sat down on the floor to wait while the official delegations ate lunch.[5] The patrician Herter was not comfortable with the disarray of revolutionary change, and in this, he would prove to be a faithful representative of his government.

During lunch, William Wieland, director of the Office of Caribbean and Mexican Affairs, was introduced to Castro as the State Department official "in charge of Cuban affairs," to which Fidel replied, "And I thought I was in charge of Cuban affairs."[6] It was a clever joke but fraught with symbolism.

For half a century, a parade of U.S. presidents and their representatives had acted as if the United States was in charge of Cuban affairs. Fidel, with a smile, was serving notice that this, too, was about to change.

Prologue to Revolution

Herter's lunch with Castro displayed in microcosm some recurring features of the many dialogues to come between U.S. and Cuban officials. Talks were often guarded, undertaken with a certain reticence because neither side trusted the other's intentions. Sometimes those suspicions were enough in themselves to derail the process. On the U.S. side, positions often reflected an arrogance born of Great Power hubris and a presumption that U.S. priorities should naturally take precedence over Cuba's. On the Cuban side, positions often reflected a stubborn pride, born of a half century of domination, that made resistance to U.S. demands a virtue in its own right. One hundred years of tumultuous relations between the two countries weighed heavily on both.

During the nineteenth century, Washington openly coveted Cuba and saw its acquisition as inevitable. As John Quincy Adams famously said in 1823, "If an apple severed by its native tree cannot choose but fall to the ground, Cuba . . . can gravitate only towards the North American Union."[7] Although Cuba remained a Spanish possession, its economy and social life were already gravitating toward the United States. Economic ties produced a free flow of people in both directions, carrying with them the artifacts and values of their respective cultures. The culture and national identity of modern Cuba were shaped by this encounter with the United States. "The North American presence was ubiquitous, expanding in all directions at once," wrote historian Louis Pérez Jr. "At every point that this presence made contact with the prevailing order of Cuban life—almost everywhere—it challenged, it contested, it changed."[8]

This pervasive U.S. influence eroded Spanish colonial control and laid the cultural foundation for Cuba's independence movement. But it also posed a threat to Cuba's aspiration to become a free and independent country, as José Martí, the father of Cuban independence, foresaw. Shortly before riding into battle against the Spanish, and to his death, Martí wrote: "Every day now I am in danger of giving my life for my country and my duty . . . in order to prevent, by the timely independence of Cuba, the United States from extending its hold across the Antilles and falling with all the greater force on the lands of our America. All I have done up to now and all I will do is for that."[9]

In 1898 the United States intervened in Cuba's three-year-old war of independence, quickly defeated the Spanish, and occupied the island until 1902. As the price of independence, Cubans were forced to accept the Platt Amendment to their constitution. It gave the United States the right to intervene in Cuba to protect its independence, required Cuba to sell or lease land to the United States for naval bases (the origin of Guantánamo Naval Station), and prohibited Cuba from signing treaties with any other foreign governments to provide them with bases. Not surprisingly, the Platt Amendment was anathema to Cuban nationalists.[10]

Over the next two decades, U.S. troops returned to Cuba several times to halt outbreaks of political violence. Treaties and laws promulgated by the U.S. military governors gave U.S. businesses unmatched advantages in the Cuban market, and U.S. investment flowed freely. By the 1930s, U.S. interests owned most of the sugar industry—the heart of the Cuban economy—most of the tobacco industry, the banks, and public utilities. The power and influence of U.S. investors over Cuba's economy came to rival the power and influence of U.S. diplomats over its political affairs.[11]

Cuba's politics during the early decades of the century were marked by corruption, both financial and electoral. In 1933, Gerardo Machado's dictatorship was overthrown by a coalition of university students, organized labor, and noncommissioned military officers, which established a revolutionary government promising social reform. Worried that these progressives threatened U.S. interests, Washington conspired with the head of the armed forces, Fulgencio Batista, to engineer a coup just three months after the revolutionaries took office.[12] With U.S. support, Batista ruled Cuba, either directly or indirectly, until 1944, when, after a reasonably free election, he turned power over to the opposition. But in 1952, Batista emerged from retirement and organized a military coup to return himself to power.

The United States was not deeply troubled by Batista's seizure of power, suspension of constitutional rule, or flagrant corruption, including deals with the Mafia. He had long been a faithful ally, siding with Washington internationally and safeguarding U.S. interests. Even as opposition to Batista mounted and police repression grew more brutal, Washington continued to support him.[13] Ambassador Arthur Gardner, a political appointee, was such an ostentatious booster that even Batista was embarrassed by the slavishness of his praise. "I'm glad Ambassador Gardner approves of my government," Batista quipped, "but I wish he wouldn't talk about it so much."[14]

Fidel Castro, then a young lawyer, emerged as the leader of the opposition by organizing an audacious but unsuccessful assault on the army's

Moncada Barracks in Santiago, Cuba, on July 26, 1953—the date for which his revolutionary movement would later be named. Defending himself during his trial for sedition, Castro argued eloquently that insurrection against Batista's unconstitutional regime was justified, famously closing with the words, "Condemn me. It does not matter. History will absolve me." Distributed nationwide in pamphlet form, the speech made him a national figure.[15]

Inspired by the writings of José Martí, Fidel Castro was a fervent nationalist; he could quote key passages from Martí's work from memory. Having grown up in rural Cuba where poverty was stark, he had a visceral understanding of the deep inequality of Cuba's social order and an instinctive sympathy for the poor. Castro's original political program was radically reformist, calling for social programs to fight poverty, agrarian reform, and greater Cuban autonomy from U.S. influence.[16] Washington saw Castro as a dangerous radical.[17]

As the revolutionary movement gathered force, the Eisenhower administration was torn between its instinct to support the reliable but increasingly unpopular Batista and the dawning realization that Batista could not survive. But efforts to distance the United States from the tottering regime were ineffectual. To many Cubans, the long-standing ties between Batista and the United States made it impossible for Washington to escape its role as Batista's patron. As Batista's armed forces collapsed in the final months of 1958, Washington tried to engineer a transition, replacing Batista with military officers willing to continue the fight against Castro's Rebel Army. The maneuver failed; on January 1, 1959, Batista fled into exile. Fidel Castro's forces occupied the eastern city of Santiago, and a day later rebel troops led by Ernesto "Che" Guevara entered the city of Havana. Despite Washington's desperate last-minute maneuvers, the revolution had triumphed.

Cubans were full of hope and anticipation at the fall of the dictator, and Washington was full of trepidation about the shape of things to come. How should the United States deal with this brash young band of revolutionaries and the potential challenge to U.S. hegemony they represented—not just in our own backyard but right on the back porch. How would Cuba's new leaders deal with the Colossus of the North, whose dominance they resented but on whom Cuba remained deeply dependent? Could the two sides reach a modus vivendi? Would they want to?

The "Soft Glove" Approach

Ambassador Philip W. Bonsal arrived in Havana on February 19, 1959, determined to break the mold of previous U.S. ambassadors who so often acted like proconsuls. For the next twenty months, Bonsal would work tirelessly to build a constructive relationship with Cuba's new revolutionary government, keeping open the channels for negotiation as long as he could while struggling against obstacles in Washington as well as Havana. The relationship between Cuba and the United States was changing radically as a result of the revolution. The paternalism that had marked relations since 1898 had become an anachronism, but Bonsal was convinced that he could navigate the transition to a new, more equal relationship by engaging Cuba's revolutionary leaders in dialogue.

Bonsal came well-equipped for the challenge. Unlike his two predecessors, political appointees Arthur Gardner and Earl E. T. Smith, Bonsal was a professional Foreign Service officer who had lived in Latin America most of his adult life. Patrician in bearing, gentlemanly in demeanor, Bonsal had a reputation as a liberal reformer. He disdained as shortsighted Washington's proclivity to tolerate dictators who claimed ideological kinship with the United States. He favored support for social change, even when it infringed on the interests of U.S. investors. As ambassador to Colombia, Bonsal's meetings with democratic opponents of General Gustavo Rojas Pinilla so angered the dictator that Bonsal had to be recalled. From there he was sent to Bolivia, where his policy of constructive engagement helped steer a revolutionary government toward moderation.[18]

Good relations, Bonsal believed, would be grounded in the economic "mutuality of interest" between Cuba and the United States. Rhetoric and youthful exuberance aside, Castro and his *barbudos* (bearded guerrillas) would eventually realize that economic ties between the two countries were so intricate that neither would be well served by rupturing them. This, in turn, would "exercise a stabilizing and moderating influence" on the new government.[19]

Official Washington distrusted Fidel and his rebel army commanders, however. "I was impressed by the reserve with which Castro was viewed," Bonsal wrote of his State Department colleagues. "They accepted the Cuban reality as it then appeared and were determined to develop productive relations with the new government . . . [but] they had no enthusiasm for Castro."[20] U.S. officials suspected that Castro was dangerously radical, even if he was not a communist. His nationalism and commitment to social change were bound to conflict with U.S. interests on the island, where U.S. investors had more than a billion dollars in assets.[21]

In April 1959 the Latin American bureau of the State Department held a Caribbean chiefs of mission conference in San Salvador to brief U.S. ambassadors on Cuba policy. Bonsal held center stage, arguing that Castro's policies were "reformist, nationalistic, and somewhat socialistic and neutral-ist" but nevertheless that the trajectory of the regime was malleable. More-over, Bonsal pointed out to skeptical colleagues, the revolution was a fait accompli. Castro was firmly in power—the quintessential charismatic leader, so popular that everyone called him Fidel, even his enemies. Polls showed backing for the new government exceeding 90 percent. Washington had lit-tle choice but to deal with Castro, so Bonsal argued for a policy of "patience and forbearance."[22] In private, Bonsal told his colleagues that Cuba needed a revolution, and Castro was not as bad as he seemed. If Washington followed a "soft-glove" approach, Bonsal was confident he could handle Castro.[23]

The rebels of Castro's 26th of July Movement distrusted the United States because of its dominance of the Cuban economy, its history of interfering in Cuban politics, its friendship with Batista, and its eleventh-hour maneuvers to keep Castro from coming to power. Before Bonsal even landed in Havana, relations were marred by vocal criticism in the U.S. press and Congress over summary trials and executions of several hundred police and military of-ficials from the old regime—what Senator Wayne Morris (D-Ore.) called the "bloodbath" in Cuba.[24] Cubans were flabbergasted at this sudden eruption of concern for human rights. There had been no comparable outcry during Batista's reign of terror, which took the lives of thousands. The Americans seemed to be "defending their old friends," recalled Carlos Franqui, editor of the daily newspaper, *Revolución*.[25]

All across the island, clandestine cemeteries were being exhumed, reveal-ing the gruesome handiwork of Batista's police. "Hardly a Cuban does not have a relative who was killed during the Batista terror," wrote *New York Times* reporter Ruby Hart Phillips.[26] "Many of those executed were well known to the populace as thugs and assassins of the worst type," the U.S. Consulate in Santiago reported to Washington. "There is little doubt but that a number would have faced the possibility of capital punishment in any state having . . . war crimes trials."[27]

Fidel Castro saw U.S. criticism of the trials as a cynical "campaign of lies" to defame the revolution and a harbinger of U.S. hostility. He reacted defi-antly. On January 21, hundreds of thousands of Cubans rallied at the Presi-dential Palace to support the trials and to listen as Castro blasted the United States for its aid to Batista, its refusal to extradite his cronies and return the millions they stole from the Cuban Treasury, and the bombing of Hiroshima and Nagasaki.[28] In this first skirmish between the United States and Cuba's revolutionary government, the U.S. charges infuriated Castro, and his harsh anti-American rhetoric in response angered U.S. officials.

Nevertheless, Bonsal arrived at his new post confidant that an enlightened U.S. attitude combined with ties of economic interdependence would be a sufficient foundation upon which to build friendly relations. He told every Cuban minister he met that Washington hoped to have good relations with the new government, sympathized with many of its promised social reforms, and was eager to help.[29]

Bonsal had his first audience with Fidel on March 5, 1959, on the veranda of Castro's villa in the suburb of Cojimar, about fifteen miles outside Havana. Speaking with intensity, Fidel leaned forward on the edge of his patio chair, as if to physically drive home his points. Gesturing exuberantly, cigar in hand, he described his plans for agrarian reform, rent reductions, low-cost housing, and industrialization—what he called the "vital elements" of the revolution.[30]

He was "in an effusive mood," the ambassador reported to Washington. "I endeavored to convey to Castro the goodwill and hopefulness with which my government envisaged the relations between our two countries." He reminded Castro that U.S. investors had made important contributions to Cuba's economic development and could make further contributions under the right conditions. He gently pointed out that people in the United States were as proud of their country as Cubans were of theirs and equally sensitive to "misinterpretations" of their actions—an oblique reference to Castro's frequent anti-American gibes. But, Bonsal said, he hoped they could "maintain a frank cordial relationship . . . even on matters on which there may be disagreement." After their private meeting, they smiled for the photographers and parted warmly.

At a press conference the next day, Castro described the meeting as a "cordial and friendly conversation." His verdict: "A good ambassador."[31] Yet despite this promising first meeting, Bonsal would find it exasperatingly difficult to arrange future meetings with Cuba's "maximum leader." To Castro, Bonsal's expressions of concern, no matter how diplomatically delivered, cast the ambassador with "the demeanor of a proconsul." Later Castro would recall that he avoided Bonsal intentionally: "This gentleman's statements were simply intolerable."[32] Castro's message was clear: the U.S. ambassador was no longer, as former ambassador Smith liked to say, "the second most important man in Cuba; sometimes even more important than the president."[33]

Fidel's Goodwill Tour

The day after meeting Bonsal, Castro announced he had accepted an invitation by the American Society of Newspaper Editors (ASNE) to visit the United States in April 1959. The trip was "unofficial," which suited Castro

U.S. ambassador Philip W. Bonsal meeting Fidel Castro for the first time on the veranda of Castro's villa in the Havana suburb of Cojimar, March 5, 1959. (Andrew St. George Papers, Manuscripts and Archives, Yale University Library)

just fine; he was loathe to be seen as a typical Latin American leader, going to Washington hat-in-hand for help.[34] Nevertheless, his visit offered an occasion for senior U.S. officials to meet Castro, and for midlevel officials from both governments to discuss relations. Castro brought a large retinue, including most of his top economic advisors.

In retrospect, this trip may have been the best opportunity the two governments had to avoid a break in relations. The Eisenhower administration, though deeply suspicious of the guerrilla leader, had not yet decided that U.S. national interest demanded his removal. Castro, though deeply suspicious of Washington, had not yet decided that his revolution required a complete break with the United States. "At that time, we believed the revolutionary project could be carried out with a great deal of comprehension on the part of the people of the United States," Castro later told Lee Lockwood. "[I went] precisely in an effort to keep public opinion in the United States better informed and better disposed toward the Revolution."[35]

"Fidel went to the United States full of hope," recalled his press secretary, Teresa Casuso. "He was in a good mood."[36]

Intent on using the eleven-day trip to the best advantage, the Cubans hired a public relations firm, Bernard Relin and Associates, Inc. Although they ignored the firm's advice to shave their beards and exchange their olive green uniforms for business suits, they nevertheless made a good impression. Everywhere Fidel went he was met by cheering crowds. Fifteen hundred were on hand when he arrived at Washington's National Airport; two thousand greeted him at New York's Penn Station; ten thousand turned out to hear him speak at Harvard; and thirty-five thousand attended his outdoor address in Central Park. Fidel was delighted. "This is just the way it is in Cuba," he marveled, wading into the crowds to shake hands.[37] At the Bronx Zoo, in a display of youthful exuberance, Castro jumped over the guardrail and stuck his hand into the tiger cage, playfully taunting the big cats. It was quintessential Fidel—boldly courting danger, fearless to the point of recklessness—a style not unlike his approach to dealing with the United States.[38]

In Washington, Castro met for an hour and a half with members of the Senate Foreign Relations Committee and the House Foreign Affairs Committee. At every opportunity, he spoke to the press—in imperfect English— hoping to dispel the negative image left by the war crimes trials. He went on NBC's Meet the Press, fielding reporters' questions for half an hour. He spoke at Columbia, Princeton, and Harvard. At Princeton University, Castro happened to meet former secretary of state Dean Acheson at a reception hosted by New Jersey governor Robert Meyner. To Acheson, Castro came across as smart and levelheaded. "This fellow Castro really knows what he is doing," Acheson told a colleague shortly after the meeting. "He is going to cause us some problems down the road."[39] In Cambridge, Castro had dinner at the Faculty Club with Dean of Arts and Sciences McGeorge Bundy, who then introduced him to an adulatory crowd.[40] Two years hence, as President John F. Kennedy's national security advisor, Bundy would plot Castro's ouster.

Everywhere he went, Fidel patiently answered questions about the alleged communist infiltration of his government, the executions of Batista's henchmen, and his attitude toward the United States.[41] Despite the "most impertinent questions, [Fidel] never lost his temper, always kept his good humor," Carlos Franqui marveled. Castro was, as the State Department put it, "a man

Fidel Castro waves to cheering crowds in New York during his April 1959 trip to the United States. (© Roberto Salas, Havana)

on his best behavior."[42] And he was very effective. His exuberance, relaxed informality, and somewhat broken English were a thoroughly winning combination. "The reception Premier Castro received here was so friendly that he will surely return feeling better about the United States than when he arrived," the *New York Times* editorialized. "By the same token, it seems obvious that Americans feel better about Fidel Castro than they did before."[43]

If the unofficial part of Fidel's visit was a roaring success, the official part was not. President Eisenhower "was more than irritated" when he first got word of the trip. "I inquired whether we could not refuse him a visa," he recalled. Advised that such a snub would only strengthen Castro's hand by rallying nationalist opinion behind him, Eisenhower relented, but "I nevertheless refused to see him."[44] Instead, Ike went golfing in Augusta, Georgia, a slight not lost on the Cuban leader. (Months later, after U.S.-Cuban relations had deteriorated, Castro would go golfing with Che Guevara and invite the international press. "The golf game was a photo opportunity," Fidel recalled. "The real purpose was to make fun of Eisenhower.")[45]

The State Department had higher hopes for Castro's trip. His entourage included many of his government's most prominent pro-American moderates. The presence of National Bank president Felipe Pazos, Minister of the Treasury Rufo López-Fresquet, and Minister of Economy Regino Boti suggested that Castro wanted to open serious discussions about economic cooperation—a conclusion reinforced by the fact that Pazos submitted in advance a memorandum outlining an agenda for "talks regarding financial assistance and cooperation."[46]

What followed, however, was a minuet of reticence. Before arriving in Washington, Castro stunned members of his economic team by telling them not to ask for aid. Wasn't that the whole reason for the trip?, asked López-Fresquet. "Look, Rufo," Fidel replied, "I don't want this trip to be like that of other new Latin American leaders who always come to the U.S. to ask for money. I want this to be a goodwill trip. Besides, the Americans will be surprised. And when we go back to Cuba, they will offer us aid without our asking for it."[47]

Sure enough, at his first press conference upon arrival, reporters asked Castro if he had come to request U.S. aid. "No," he replied, "we are proud to be independent and have no intention of asking anyone for anything." He repeated that refrain in his speech to the newspaper editors, declaring, "I did not come here for money. You should not think of our country as a beggar." In private, he repeatedly ordered his economic advisors not to ask for anything.[48]

U.S. officials were puzzled. On the basis of exchanges with the Cubans prior to the trip, they expected the issue of aid to be high on the agenda. They hinted at Washington's willingness to provide assistance, trying to get the Cubans to begin the conversation. Secretary of the Treasury Robert Anderson told his counterpart López-Fresquet that the United States wanted to help. Assistant Secretary of State for Inter-American Affairs R. Richard Rubottom explicitly asked the Cuban economists how the United States could cooperate in addressing Cuba's most pressing economic needs. "We were prepared to offer them a loan of $25 million then and there," said a State Department official who was in the meeting.[49]

"The attitude of the U.S. was that of a most willing lender," Felipe Pazos recalled.[50] But the Cubans obeyed their commander in chief and responded noncommittally to all inquiries. In the end, the Cubans wouldn't ask, and the

Americans didn't offer. "Fidel was hoping for offers which he never received," Teresa Casuso wrote, and not receiving them "vexed him greatly."[51]

If the lack of discussion about economic aid was a missed opportunity, Fidel's two and a half hour meeting with Vice President Richard M. Nixon was an opportunity gone horribly wrong. "The meeting between Fidel and Nixon was an out-and-out disaster," according to *Revolución* editor Carlos Franqui, who accompanied Fidel on the trip. "Their mutual dislike would be long-lived."[52] The two met in Washington for two and a half hours on April 19 at Nixon's office in the Capitol, because he didn't want to host Castro at the White House or "entertain" him at the vice president's residence. Nixon talked to Castro "just like a father," the vice president told his aides immediately afterward, although he felt that Castro had not listened to him.[53] He presumed to give Castro advice about how to govern, warning him of the growing influence of Communists in his government. "He was incredibly naive with regard to the Communist threat," Nixon wrote in a memo summarizing the meeting. Castro's skepticism about the efficacy of elections, his distrust of private capital, and his failure to share Nixon's obsession with the international communist menace, led the vice president to conclude that Castro was inimical to U.S. interests. But Castro was an adversary to be reckoned with. "The one fact we can be sure of is that he has those indefinable qualities which make him a leader of men," Nixon concluded. "Whatever we may think of him he is going to be a great factor in the development of Cuba and very possibly in Latin American affairs generally. . . . Because he has the power to lead, to which I have referred, we have no choice but at least to orient him in the right direction." This tutorial approach proved short-lived. Within weeks, Nixon became an advocate for overthrowing Castro.[54]

Castro emerged from the meeting unimpressed and insulted. "This man has spent the whole time scolding me," Fidel complained.[55] Personally, he thought Nixon was "superficial," uninterested when Fidel tried to explain Cuba's wrenching economic and social problems.[56] "When Nixon started to talk, nothing could stop him," Castro recalled. Nearly half a century after their encounter, Nixon's patronizing lecture still rankled. "Not even an elementary school student would hope to receive so many lessons."[57]

Meeting the CIA

Castro would have an even stranger encounter on his trip—a secret meeting with the CIA. While he and his entourage were in Washington, a U.S. official approached López-Fresquet to arrange a meeting between Castro and

Vice President Richard Nixon and Cuban prime minister Fidel Castro leave Nixon's Capitol Hill office April 19, 1959, after a closed-door chat lasting two hours and twenty minutes. The meeting had been listed on Castro's program as a fifteen-minute visit. (AP Photo)

the "highest authority of American intelligence on the Communists in Latin America." At first, Castro was reluctant, but he finally agreed to a private meeting in New York.[58]

Although the CIA had conspired to keep Fidel from coming to power during the final weeks of the Batista dictatorship, relations between the CIA and the 26th of July Movement had not been entirely bad. CIA officers in the U.S. Embassy knew better than most the depths of Batista's brutality and had little use for him. More than once they made formal inquiries to Batista's police about the status of captured rebels, knowing that the mere fact of the inquiry would likely prevent the prisoner's disappearance. Ambassador Earl E. T. Smith thought the CIA station in the embassy was pro-Castro.[59] Even in

Washington, CIA officials following events in Cuba had a certain admiration for the young revolutionaries' courage and sense of mission. "In those days, we were all Fidelistas," recalled Robert Reynolds, then head of the Caribbean Desk in the CIA's covert operations branch, the Directorate of Plans.[60]

In August 1958 the chief of the CIA's Paramilitary Division Political and Psychological Staff, Alfred Cox, recommended abandoning Batista and secretly supplying Castro with arms and money. "A practical way to protect US interests in this matter," Cox suggested, "would be to make secret contact with Castro, assure him of the U.S. sympathy with some of his objectives and offer him support."[61] That did not happen, but as the Batista regime crumbled, the CIA station chief in Havana endorsed a quiet proposal from the city's archbishop that the United States "discreetly" open a dialogue with Castro. An "operation of this nature could pay big future dividends," the chief of station cabled headquarters on December 18, 1958, less than two weeks before the triumph of the revolution. "Regardless how we may feel about Castro and his movement, both will be important political forces for a long time to come."[62]

At the same time, Castro was trying to open a dialogue with Washington. In mid-December, he told journalist Andrew St. George that he would welcome having a U.S. representative visit him in the Sierra Maestra to discuss "a number of important political issues."[63] All these tentative efforts to open a dialogue were overtaken by the sudden collapse of the Batista regime on January 1, 1959.

Castro's April visit to the United States provided the CIA with its first real opportunity to communicate with Cuba's new leader. Fidel agreed to meet the CIA emissary at the New York Statler Hilton Hotel, where the Cuban delegation was staying. The CIA sent Gerry Droller (aka Frank Bender, the pseudonym he used as chief of political action for the Bay of Pigs invasion). Bender, a German immigrant and veteran of the OSS, was new to the Latin American division and did not speak Spanish. His attitude was cavalier—"breezily aggressive," according to fellow spy Howard Hunt.[64] He spent three hours with Fidel, smoking cigars, and instructing the *comandante* on the dangers of international communism. The Cuban Communist Party, Bender warned, was an agent of this international menace and a threat to Castro's leadership.

Fidel countered that Cuba's Communists were a minority, and he could handle them. The United States, he said, was overly concerned with communism. The best bulwark against its spread would be for the United States to stop neglecting Latin America's social and economic problems. Nevertheless, Bender felt that Fidel had received the briefing on international communism "seriously and in good faith." He "listened intently and reacted favorably, [and] was eager to accept suggestions that information on international communism be channeled to him in the future." Castro agreed to establish a secret back channel to the CIA and designated López-Fresquet as the Cuban contact.[65] Bender emerged from the meeting exultant. "Castro is not only not a communist," he assured López-Fresquet, "but he is a strong anti-communist fighter." A month later, the U.S. Embassy activated the secret channel by sending a message to Castro, but he never responded, and no further messages followed.[66]

The Eisenhower administration was no more enamored of Fidel after his visit than before. Acknowledging that the trip was a public relations triumph, the State Department's assessment nevertheless concluded, "There is little probability that Castro has altered the essentially radical course of his revolution. . . . While we certainly know him better than before, Castro remains an enigma and we should await his decisions on specific matters before assuming a more optimistic view . . . [regarding] the possibility of developing a constructive relationship with him and his government."[67]

On balance, Castro's trip to the United States was a missed opportunity. Fidel saw it as chance to appeal directly to U.S. public opinion, countering the lies in the press about the trials of Batista's henchmen. The moderates in his entourage saw it as an opportunity to improve ties with the United States, countering the radical influence of Raúl Castro and Che Guevara.[68] Bonsal and his embassy staff hoped the trip would open the discussion of U.S. aid, thereby reinforcing the economic ties binding Cuba to the United States. But in the end, Castro's fear of looking like a supplicant outweighed his need for assistance, and Washington's disdain for the revolution's unorthodox politics outweighed Bonsal's strategy of engagement. As writer Hugh Thomas put it, "Each side, proud and suspicious, held back."[69]

The Cubans left empty-handed, but they got an earful about communism. Castro went away convinced that Washington was obsessed with it. Senators interrogated him about it. Nixon lectured him on it. The CIA tried to recruit him to fight it. The message was clear: Cuba was not free to choose its own path if that path was regarded as communist by the United States. What the Eisenhower administration failed to grasp, however, was that Cuba's Communists were not some alien force, but an essential part of Castro's revolutionary coalition—allies he was not about to betray to curry favor with the United States.[70]

Prompt and Adequate Compensation

On May 17, just days after Castro's return to Havana, the Revolutionary Government promulgated the first agrarian reform law. It nationalized most estates in excess of one thousand acres, which affected only about 10 percent of farms but 40 percent of the arable land. Some of the expropriated estates were broken up into small family farms, but others—especially the sugar plantations—were run as cooperatives or state enterprises. Compensation would be based on assessed value for tax purposes and paid with twenty-year bonds yielding 4.5 percent interest.[71]

Agrarian reform was bound to impact U.S. interests since many of Cuba's largest plantations were foreign-owned. Initially, the U.S. government seemed to take the reform in stride. Bonsal was instructed to tell Castro that the United States recognized Cuba's sovereign right to expropriate land, was "not opposed to sound land reform," and would even be willing to provide aid to implement a well-designed program. The proposed law, however, had "greatly concerned and disturbed" U.S. investors, and Washington expected "prompt, adequate, and effective compensation." Moreover, if the reform so damaged sugar production that Cuba could not meet its contractual obligations, Washington would have to act to guarantee supply—a thinly veiled threat that Cuba's portion of the sugar import quota could be reduced. (By law, Cuba was allowed to sell a set amount of sugar to the United States at a subsidized price.)[72]

Bonsal never got to deliver the message directly because Fidel refused to see him. Giving up in frustration, Bonsal finally recommended that the U.S. reaction be delivered in a formal diplomatic note. The State Department delivered the note on June 11, 1959, and simultaneously released it publicly, a signal that Washington was losing patience.[73] The note prompted a quick response; Castro called Bonsal to a meeting the next day to reassure the ambassador that he was not opposed in principle to foreign investment and that he recognized Cuba's obligation to pay compensation. "He was relaxed and friendly," Bonsal reported to Washington, "and showed no signs of being upset at our note." However, Castro pointed out, Cuba could not afford to pay in cash as the U.S. note implicitly suggested it should by citing a provision of the Constitution of 1940 specifying cash compensation for nationalizations. Bonsal left the meeting hopeful that the interests of U.S. investors could be protected.[74] Decision makers in Washington were less sanguine.

The controversy over the agrarian reform marked a critical turning point in U.S.-Cuban relations, not so much because the reform itself was especially radical (it was not, compared to reforms President John F. Kennedy would soon support through the Alliance for Progress) or because the issue of compensation was so nettlesome (both sides purported to be willing to negotiate a compromise). Rather, Washington saw the law as a bellwether of the revolution's radical direction. It was written not by the Ministry of Agriculture or the cabinet, but by Fidel's inner circle—a group of confidantes, most of them *comandantes* who had fought with him in the Sierra. This inner circle, which included Raúl Castro and Che Guevara, was markedly more radical than the cabinet, to which the law was presented as a fait accompli.[75] Ministers who protested—five of them, moderates all, including Foreign Minister Roberto Agramonte—were fired the same evening the U.S. note was delivered. This confirmed the suspicions of Washington conservatives that Castro was committed to radical social reform and that the moderates in his government—in whom Washington had invested its hopes for a pro-American Cuba—had been eclipsed.

Within the Eisenhower administration, attitudes were hardening. Bonsal's policy of patient watchful waiting had not shown any tangible results. Castro's anti-American rhetoric had not subsided, his radical domestic policies and partnership with Cuba's Communists showed no signs of abating, and his support for revolutionary expeditions abroad threatened to destabilize the Caribbean. The agrarian reform was the proverbial straw that broke the back of "patience and forbearance" because it added to this list of grievances a new threat to U.S. investors.

In late June and early July, key officials in the Eisenhower administration reached the conclusion that the continued existence of Fidel Castro's government conflicted with U.S. interests. Policy shifted from a cautious willingness to seek a constructive relationship to a clear determination to bring about Castro's demise. The initiative came from Assistant Secretary Rubottom, who had originally backed Bonsal despite his own skepticism. Rubottom gave up on constructive engagement after the agrarian reform and removal of the moderates from the cabinet. "These were all indications . . . that Castro was not a man with whom the United States could work," Rubottom explained.[76]

On July 8, Rubottom and Deputy Under Secretary of State for Political Affairs Robert D. Murphy took the issue of rolling back the Cuban revolution to a luncheon meeting of Eisenhower's Operations Coordinating Board (OCB)—an interagency group comprising senior officials who met weekly to discuss major foreign policy issues. It was time, Rubottom argued, for policy to shift "from the testing phase in which Castro had failed practically every test we had given him to the pressure phase."[77] This was followed by another meeting on July 15, with Murphy and CIA director Allen Dulles. "I told them that I felt the time had come when the United States should give some consideration to supporting the anti-Castro people, that this man was a clear-cut threat to the United States," Rubottom recalled.[78] Together, they convinced Secretary of State Herter, and planning for a new policy commenced.[79]

Rubottom described the policy change to the National Security Council a few months later: "The period from January to March [1959] might be characterized as the honeymoon period of the Castro Government. In April a downward trend in U.S.-Cuban relations had been evident. . . . In June we had reached the decision that it was not possible to achieve our objectives with Castro in power. . . . In July and August, we had been busy drawing up a program to replace Castro." The Central Intelligence Agency was tasked to develop plans to support Castro's domestic opponents, weaken his regime, and culminate in regime change before the end of Eisenhower's presidency.[80] The final decision to implement the plan, however, was delayed by a fresh flurry of diplomacy from Cuba's new foreign minister, Raúl Roa.

Quiet Diplomacy

Raúl Roa had been a revolutionary in his youth during the 1930s struggle against dictator Gerardo Machado, so he felt a kinship with Fidel Castro and his *comandantes*. A respected intellectual, Roa had been dean of social sciences at the University of Havana and, since January 1959, represented Cuba in the Organization of American States (OAS). He was unquestionably more radical than his predecessor, Roberto Agramonte, but he seemed sincere in his desire to reverse the deterioration of U.S.-Cuban relations. Before Roa headed back to Cuba from his United Nations post, Rubottom hosted a lunch for him at the State Department. Rubottom immediately raised the issue of expropriations, saying that he felt "grave and real fears" that "drastic measures" like the agrarian reform threatened "the very basis, the roots, of this Cuban-American special economic and political relationship."

Roa replied that Cuba "has no desire or intent to change the bases of the U.S.-Cuban relationship." But it was a mistake, he added, for Washington to have made its diplomatic note about the agrarian reform public. "It would be better if our differences could be discussed in private through normal diplomatic channels." Rubottom agreed.[81] In a private "off the record" conversation with Rubottom's deputy assistant secretary, William Wieland, Roa hinted that public rebukes simply antagonized Castro. "He gave me the impression that he was trying to say that if we avoided rubbing Castro in public the wrong way, he felt that sufficient internal pressures would be built up to cause Castro either to yield with the adoption of a more moderate program or to face the collapse of his government," Wieland reported. "Of course, he did not say this in as many words."[82]

In Havana, Roa suggested to Bonsal that the two governments try to resolve their differences through quiet dialogue. Good relations with the United States were not incompatible with the goals of the revolution, he insisted, and he proposed that the two of them meet regularly to work on improving bilateral ties.[83] Roa also assured Bonsal that the Cubans were prepared to work out the issue of compensation. U.S. companies whose premises had been "intervened" (seized) suddenly found the government more forthcoming in private discussions about compensation.[84] A confidential source in Havana suggested a motive behind the new Cuban peace offensive: Castro, the source told the embassy, "has [a] strong belief the U.S. [is] probably planning secretly to bring about his overthrow." He was prepared to come to terms with Washington if this could be done "without sacrificing Cuba's sovereignty."[85]

The new dialogue had barely gotten under way, however, when it was complicated by the defection of Pedro Díaz Lanz, chief of the Cuban air force. Díaz Lanz, who ran guns for the Rebel Army during the insurrection, fled to Miami in June 1959 after Fidel rebuked him for complaining publicly about communist "indoctrination" in the air force. The real trauma, however, came two weeks later when Díaz Lanz testified before the Senate Internal Security Subcommittee, claiming that Castro and virtually every senior official in his government were communists.[86] In a speech on July 11, Castro denounced Díaz Lanz as "Cuba's Benedict Arnold," and attacked the United States more severely than at any time since his April trip.[87]

A week later, just as the Díaz Lanz storm was clearing, a new one broke—the forced resignation of President Manuel Urrutia. Urrutia, a distinguished jurist, had been designated president by the 26th of July Movement before the triumph of the revolution, but his role in the new government was largely ceremonial, especially after Castro became prime minister in February. In late June and early July, Urrutia also spoke out publicly against communists in the government. On July 17, Castro abruptly resigned as prime minister, telling the nation that he could no longer work with Urrutia, whose anticommunism had aligned him with enemies of the revolution, foreign and domestic. Crowds poured into the streets demanding Urrutia's resignation, and the president complied.[88] Castro resumed office, having shown that the legitimacy of the regime rested not with any institution or office but with him personally.

Roa's efforts to improve bilateral relations continued nonetheless. On July 30, he met with Bonsal and reiterated Cuba's desire to improve relations despite Castro's harsh anti-American rhetoric surrounding the Díaz Lanz and Urrutia incidents. He also promised to arrange a meeting for Bonsal with Fidel, although it took more than a month.[89] Finally, in September, Roa hosted a private dinner at his home for Castro and Bonsal. The conversation stretched into the wee hours of the morning. Bonsal recounted the litany of U.S. concerns: the unceasing barrage of anti-American rhetoric, the growing communist influence in the government, and the nationalizations of U.S. property. Castro was conciliatory. He regretted some of his own harsh public jabs at the United States, he said, and recognized the positive contributions U.S. investors had made to Cuba's development. As to the Cold War, he professed to have no interest in it; Cuba was too busy instituting sweeping domestic changes. The best international strategy for the United States, Castro argued, would be a massive economic assistance program for Latin America, including Cuba.[90]

Castro's call for a Latin American Marshall Plan echoed a proposal he had made to the OAS in Buenos Aires in May. When Roa repeated the proposal publicly at the United Nations three weeks later, Bonsal urged Washington to be ready to respond positively to a Cuban request for bilateral aid, "if and when the climate between the two countries improves."[91] The Cubans wanted aid, Bonsal was certain, but pride prevented them from asking directly. He wanted to send a signal that a request would be met with a favorable response.[92]

It was too late. In Washington for consultations the following week, Bonsal could sense that support for his policy of patience had evaporated. "We have all been staunch advocates of extending the hand of friendship to Cuba and adopting a patient, tolerant attitude," William Wieland, Rubottom's deputy, told the ambassador, "but we cannot continue this policy much longer without some positive achievement to show in its justification."[93] Nevertheless, Wieland supported Bonsal's argument in favor of bilateral aid.

Rubottom, however, did not. The political climate in Washington would not allow it. "We would be tossed out," for proposing such a thing, Rubottom warned. "We have to walk a tightrope," he continued. "While trying to keep up a semblance of good relations with the present regime, we must, at the same time, try to keep alive any spark of opposition and to let the opposition know we are aware of its existence and not committed to Castro."[94] As he departed for Havana, Bonsal registered his disappointment by asking that he be instructed in writing on how he should respond to a Cuban request for aid and that he be advised if the State Department came to the conclusion "that the Castro Government is a hopeless proposition."[95] When Bonsal next met with Roa in early October, he informed him that it was "up to Cuba to take the initiative" if it wanted improved relations. Months of anti-American rhetoric had taken their toll, Bonsal warned, and the deterioration of relations was the "unfortunate harvest which Cuba is now gathering from attitudes, statements and actions of her rulers since January 1."[96]

Patience Runs Out

Bonsal's efforts to make progress through quiet dialogue with Roa came to a loud, public end in October. The tumult began with a gaffe. On October 16 a State Department official mistakenly revealed that the United States had urged Great Britain not to deliver jet aircraft originally purchased by Batista. To Castro, this was proof of Washington's perfidy in claiming to want better relations. The news, Roa told Bonsal, seriously damaged their dialogue.[97] Publicly, Washington insisted that its opposition to the aircraft sale was simply part of its general policy to limit arms imports to Latin America. Privately, Allen Dulles told the British ambassador that he hoped to force Castro to buy arms from the Soviet bloc because, in the case of Guatemala, it had been a shipment of Soviet arms that had "created the occasion for what had been done" (the CIA's overthrow of the Guatemalan government) and "the same might be true in the case of Cuba."[98]

Four days after the aircraft story broke, *Comandante* Huber Matos, the 26th of July Movement commander in Camagüey province, resigned over what he saw as growing communist influence in the government. Earlier that fall, he had begun speaking with other Rebel Army veterans about how to put a stop to it.[99] Raúl Castro's appointment in October as minister of the Revolutionary Armed Forces brought the issue to a head and prompted Matos, along with more than a dozen other officers in Camagüey, to resign. Matos was immediately arrested for plotting against the government, tried for sedition, and sentenced to twenty years in prison.[100] On the very day Matos was arrested, Pedro Díaz Lanz reentered the picture, "bombing" Havana with anti-Castro leaflets. Anti-aircraft fire went astray causing several dozen casualties and creating the impression that Lanz's plane dropped bombs. The day after Lanz's flight, *Revolución's* banner headline read, "The Planes Came from the United States."[101]

To Castro, these disparate events belied a pattern. Exiles were attacking Cuba with impunity from airfields in Florida, Washington was blocking Cuba's ability to acquire the weapons it needed to defend itself, and Díaz Lanz's brazen attack on Havana coincided with Matos's abortive mutiny. In a speech on October 26, to more than 300,000 people rallying in defense of the revolution, Castro compared Díaz Lanz's flight to the attack on Pearl Harbor and accused the United States of "foreign aggression" for giving the "war criminals" a safe haven from which to attack.[102]

Castro's rhetoric was "as strongly anti-American as anything he has ever done," Bonsal advised the State Department—so harsh that even the stoic ambassador recommended a public response.[103] Washington delivered its reply the following day in a public note decrying the "deliberate and concerted efforts in Cuba to replace the traditional friendship between the Cuban and American people with distrust and hostility." Castro's charges were "utterly unfounded." The note went on to assure Cubans that the United States was adhering to a policy of nonintervention, had nothing to do with the Díaz Lanz incident, and was working "diligently" to halt illegal flights against Cuba.[104] None of these claims was strictly true.

The harsh rhetorical flurries of October led to Bonsal's recall and gave administration hard-liners the impetus they needed to push a formal change in U.S. policy through the bureaucracy. The informal consensus to oust Castro reached over the summer led to a September draft policy paper, classified SECRET, spelling out Washington's new objectives. It argued that the Cuban government's behavior was incompatible with U.S. policy objectives in Latin America and that Bonsal's policy of "overt sympathy and forbearance" toward Castro should be replaced by "a policy of overt pressure."[105] A revised version of the new policy statement, "Current Basic U.S. Policy," was finalized in the State Department on October 23 and approved by President Eisenhower on November 5.[106]

"The immediate objective of the United States with respect to Cuba," the new policy statement declared, "is the development of a situation in which, not later than the end of 1960, the Government then in control of Cuba should, in its domestic and foreign policies, meet . . . the basic United States policy objectives for Latin American countries." As Rubottom explained in his cover memo, this meant overthrowing Castro. "The policies and programs of the Castro government . . . are inconsistent with the minimal requirements of good Cuban-U.S. relations," he wrote, ". . . and will not be satisfactorily altered except as a result of Cuban opposition to Castro's present course and/or a change in the Cuban regime."[107]

Given Castro's widespread popularity in Cuba and Latin America, U.S. officials regarded this new policy of hostility as extremely sensitive. Washington would maintain a public facade of proper relations while working secretly to destabilize Cuba's government. As Rubottom explained, "The approved program authorized us to support elements in Cuba opposed to the Castro government while making Castro's downfall seem to be the result of his own mistakes."[108]

A covert policy required covert implementation, so the CIA took the lead. The agency had been developing plans for Cuba since the summer, providing assistance to prominent defectors, including Pedro Díaz Lanz, and to selected domestic opponents of Castro.[109] In December, the CIA developed the first plan for paramilitary action in Cuba, the seed from which the Bay of Pigs operation would eventually grow, and J. C. King, chief of the Western Hemisphere Division for covert operations, first recommended that "thorough consideration be given to the elimination of Fidel Castro" in order to "greatly accelerate the fall of the present government."[110]

The Argentine Ambassador Intercedes

Rubottom delayed informing Bonsal that the administration had given up on his strategy of patience and forbearance and was now bent on overthrowing Castro. "With considerable reluctance we have found ourselves forced closer and closer to the realization and frank recognition of the fact that it may be unduly optimistic and even unrealistic to assume that we shall ever be able to do business with the Castro Government," he wrote in a personal letter almost a month after the key decisions had already been taken.[111]

In reply, Bonsal acknowledged his own frustration. "The efforts of our Government to create an atmosphere of good will and good faith have certainly not found an echo," he admitted. "The situation is, however, fraught with all sorts of dangers."[112] On the ground in Cuba, Bonsal was keenly aware that Castro's popular support was broad and deep and that there was no significant organized opposition to the revolutionary government. He saw little prospect of Washington's new strategy being effective, so he refused to give up hope that some sort of accommodation might be found. In this hope, he was encouraged by continuing assurances from Foreign Minister Roa and others that the Cubans did, indeed, want to continue a dialogue on outstanding bilateral issues.[113]

The last serious effort to negotiate a modus vivendi began, ironically, as the unintended consequence of a diplomatic shouting match. Campaigning in Miami on January 16, 1960, Vice President Nixon warned that Cuba's hostility toward U.S. investors risked damaging the Cuban economy, deterring future investment, and perhaps provoking Congress to cut Cuba's sugar quota. Castro responded angrily to the implied threat and denounced the U.S. Embassy for plotting with traitors to subvert the revolution.[114] He continued his tirade on a television program the following day, accusing the Spanish ambassador, Juan Pablo de Lojendio, of improprieties as well. Insulted, Lojendio came directly to the studio, interrupted the program on the air and demanded the right to defend himself. This led to shouting, a brief scuffle, and Castro's declaring the ambassador persona non grata on the spot.[115]

Castro's personal attack on Bonsal led the Department of State to recall him again, over his objections. But the recall proved fortuitous. Back in Washington, Bonsal convinced Secretary Herter and President Eisenhower to offer Castro one last olive branch. It was not an easy sell. Meeting with Bonsal on January 25, the president remarked that Castro was acting like a "mad man," and that perhaps the U.S. Navy should be deployed to "quarantine" the island. "If they [the Cuban people] are hungry, they will throw Castro out," the president surmised.

"We should not punish the whole Cuban people for the acts of one abnormal man," Bonsal replied, and the president relented.[116] Instead, he approved a new statement of U.S. policy that Bonsal had drafted, opening the door to renewed dialogue. On January 26, Eisenhower released the statement to the press. He expressed concern about the poor state of relations with Cuba but acknowledged Cuba's right to undertake social, economic, and political reforms. Most importantly, the president called for negotiations to settle bilateral differences and concluded that there were "reasonable bases for a workable and satisfactory relationship between our two sovereign countries."[117]

Coincident with Eisenhower's statement, Bonsal instructed Chargé d'Affaires Daniel M. Braddock in Havana to approach the Brazilian and Argentine ambassadors to ask for their good offices in initiating a U.S.-Cuban dialogue. The ambassadors, both known for having good personal relationships with senior Cuban officials, were asked to advise their Cuban contacts that Eisenhower's statement represented a real desire by the United States to negotiate, and that the Cubans should "react soberly and calmly to what may be [the] final opportunity [to] avoid serious consequences."[118] The Brazilian ambassador applauded the U.S. initiative but lamented that he had little contact with Cuban leaders. "They don't want any advice," he told Braddock.[119]

The Argentine ambassador, Julio A. Amoedo, responded more energetically. He spent the whole day on January 26 trying to track down Fidel, finally catching up with him that evening at the house of his aide, Celia Sánchez. Amoedo outlined the U.S. proposal: if the Cubans would stop vilifying the United States in public, Bonsal would return to Havana and meet with Castro to establish a formal mechanism for negotiations. Looking ahead, Amoedo said, the United States was disposed to provide Cuba with assistance for its economic and social reforms. The promise of aid was something the ambassador threw in on his own initiative, hoping to make the offer more attractive.[120]

According to Amoedo, Fidel's initial reaction was "entirely negative." As it happened, Amoedo arrived just as Castro was reviewing his reply to Eisenhower, slated to run as an editorial in *Revolución* the next morning. It "categorically and brutally rejected" the U.S. statement, Amoedo recalled. Convinced the die was cast, Amoedo rose to leave, but Castro bid him stay. After talking about the U.S. proposal for more than an hour, Castro called the offices of *Revolución*, had the editorial pulled, and ordered that no further attacks on Washington be published.[121] "He agreed the differences with the U.S. should be discussed," Amoedo recalled, "and told me that Dorticós would make a statement to that effect."[122]

Speaking the next day, President Osvaldo Dorticós did not back away from Cuba's complaints against Washington, but his statement was conciliatory enough that the U.S. Embassy concluded it "contained some ground for optimism in that it affirmed the Cuban government's desire for friendly relations with the United States and its willingness to negotiate differences."[123] Braddock met with Roa on February 4, to reiterate that Washington wanted to open a dialogue, but expected a retraction of Castro's public charges that Bonsal had encouraged counterrevolution. While negotiations were under way, Braddock added, both sides should pledge to "maintain an atmosphere free of public accusations and recriminations." Roa replied that Cuba also wanted a resumption of normal relations. Two weeks later, the Cubans agreed to Washington's conditions: they formally notified Washington that they had no charges to make against Ambassador Bonsal, and they agreed to maintain a constructive atmosphere while talks were under way.[124]

Just as it seemed that Bonsal's strategy was about to pay off, Cuba added a condition of its own. On February 22, just four days after accepting Washington's proposal, the Cubans declared that a commission of Cuban negotiators was prepared to begin talks in Washington on the condition that, while talks were under way, neither the Eisenhower administration nor the Congress would undertake any action "which might . . . cause harm to the Cuban economy or people."[125] This demand was a clear reference to pending legislation on the sugar quota and the ongoing debate in Washington over whether Cuba's portion of the quota should be cut or suspended. Washington's reaction was decidedly negative. Bonsal thought the new demand had been "advanced for propaganda purposes."[126] Moreover, the administration could hardly bind the Congress from acting on the sugar quota, unless the president vetoed the legislation. Secretary of State Herter rejected the Cuban demand but reaffirmed Washington's desire to negotiate. The embassy reported that the Cuban reaction to the U.S. note was "heated" but that the Cubans would probably go ahead with the talks regardless.[127]

The fragile dialogue initiated by Amoedo's good offices might still have blossomed into formal negotiations had not other events intervened. On March 4, the French freighter *La Coubre*, unloading an arms shipment from Belgium, exploded in Havana harbor, killing seventy-five dock workers and wounding more than two hundred.[128] Forty years later, Castro's recollection of the carnage was still vivid. "I was at the main office of the National Institute of Agrarian Reform," he recounted. "All of a sudden, we heard a very strong explosion and the building itself was shaken. . . . Minutes after, there was a second explosion. . . . When we arrived at the docks, there was a crowd of people, wounded wandering around, people trying to help. We could hear the sirens of the police and ambulances coming to pick up the wounded and the dead. I can still see the scene as if I were looking at it now. The impact was huge."[129]

Castro was utterly convinced the CIA was responsible.* He knew that Washington had blocked the British delivery of jet fighters to Cuba and had tried unsuccessfully to talk the Belgians out of delivering the munitions on *La Coubre*. "We must look for the guilty ones among those who did not want us to have these weapons," he said at the funeral for those killed in the explosion. "We have the right to think that those who through diplomacy tried to prevent us from getting this equipment, could certainly have tried to achieve the same objective by other methods." Comparing the destruction of *La Coubre* to the sinking of the U.S. battleship *Maine* in Havana harbor in 1898 which precipitated the Spanish-American War, Castro warned Washington not to make the mistake of thinking that it could once again send troops to abort Cuba's struggle for true independence. "We are not in the 1910s or 1920s or 1930s. Cubans today, the Cubans of this generation . . . will fight, if they attack us, to the last drop of blood. . . . Our choice would be *patria o muerte* [homeland or death]."[130]

---

* Years later, at a conference on the fortieth anniversary of the Bay of Pigs in 2001, Robert Reynolds, who had been deputy chief of the CIA's Cuba Task Force, assured Castro, "We did not plan, or sponsor, or support that tragic accident." While accepting Reynolds's honesty, Castro questioned whether Reynolds might have been unaware of the operation. "I don't consider that the issue has been completely concluded," he said (Transcript, panel one, Bay of Pigs Forty Years Later conference, Havana, Cuba, March 22–24, 2001, NSA Cuba Collection). In 2007, writing about the explosion in one of his "reflections," Castro reiterated his conviction that the CIA blew up the ship ("Reflections of President Fidel Castro: World Tyranny: The Basics of the Killing Machine," *Granma International*, July 9, 2007).

Washington called Castro's accusation of sabotage "unfounded and irresponsible." The Cubans rejected the U.S. protest as "insulting."[131] Three days after Castro's funeral oration, Deputy Chief of Mission Braddock cabled Washington that the Embassy Country Team, which had backed Bonsal's diplomatic efforts consistently and loyally, had now unanimously concluded, "There is no hope that U.S. will ever be able to establish a satisfactory relationship with the Cuban Government as long as it is dominated by Fidel Castro, Raúl Castro, Che Guevara, and like-minded associates." In the wake of the explosion, Braddock wrote privately to Bonsal, "I cannot help feeling this case will be a cause célèbre in the history of U.S.-Cuban relations."[132]

Another event also undercut Washington's interest in talks—the February visit to Cuba of Soviet Vice President Anastas I. Mikoyan. Although Castro's tolerance of Communists in his government had been an irritant for Washington since early 1959, Castro showed no special affinity for the Soviet Union during his first year in power, despite some behind-the-scenes contacts.[133] The initial Soviet reaction to the Cuban revolution was diffident, but in late 1959 Castro invited a Soviet trade mission in Mexico to visit Cuba, and Mikoyan arrived with it on February 4, 1960. The ten-day visit concluded with a trade agreement and $100 million in credit for Cuba. Shortly thereafter, Soviet premier Nikita Khrushchev began to publicly praise the Cuban revolution.[134]

Wayne Smith, then a junior Foreign Service officer in the Havana embassy, recalled the impact Mikoyan's visit had on U.S. attitudes. "Based on the warmth of the welcoming speeches, the degree to which the proverbial red carpet was rolled out for Mr. Mikoyan . . . our conclusion was that Prime Minister Castro had made his decision that Cuba was going to become a close ally of the Soviet Union." After that, Washington doubted the sincerity of Cuba's calls for negotiations. "We quite frankly thought it was a stalling tactic. The U.S. government was no longer interested. Thus, we didn't explore the possibilities."[135]

In the aftermath of the *La Coubre* explosion, a semiprivate feeler was sent out by a Cuban businessman with close ties to the CIA. Mario Lazo, legal advisor to the U.S. Embassy, approached Treasury Minister López-Fresquet, confiding that the U.S. government was prepared to work aggressively to halt the exile flights from Florida that were burning Cuban sugar cane fields. Washington wanted to know if the Cubans, in return, would be prepared to engage in serious talks on a broad range of issues. López-Fresquet immediately transmitted the query to Castro, who remarked, "What an interesting thing this international chess game is." Fidel took the proposal under advisement. Two days later, on March 17, President Dorticós informed López-Fresquet that Fidel had decided not to respond. "We don't trust the U.S.," Dorticós explained. "We think that what they want us to do is contradict ourselves. Once we admit publicly that they are on the level and friendly to us, they will not give Cuba anything."[136]

Fidel's instincts were right. As State Department official William Wieland told his friend, Adolf Berle, Washington's proposals to negotiate were intended to "slowly . . . close in on Castro—by offering to negotiate everything and then taking him up on his desire to be clear of the United States."[137] On March 17, the same day Dorticós rejected Lazo's feeler, Eisenhower signed a top secret authorization for "A Program of Covert Action against the Castro Regime," giving the CIA the green light to begin covert paramilitary operations to roll back the Cuban revolution.[138]

Things Fall Apart

Bonsal returned to Havana on March 20, but there was little left for him to do. He conferred regularly with Ambassador Amoedo, who doggedly continued his mediation efforts, beseeching Castro at every opportunity to make peace with Washington. At a dinner party Amoedo hosted for Latin American ambassadors in April, Castro admitted he might have made some errors in dealing with the United States and purported to be willing to negotiate. Roa followed up with a formal proposal for talks soon thereafter, but nothing came of it. In reward for his efforts, however, Amoedo requested and received a signed photo of President Eisenhower to hang in his home.[139]

Bonsal would never again meet with Fidel. Castro didn't invite him, and Bonsal didn't ask. "Fidel has insulted and offended our government on numerous occasions," Bonsal wrote to Rubottom. "If he wants to see me . . . he can let me know."[140] Nevertheless, Bonsal continued to argue that Washington should adhere to his policy of patience despite Cuba's intransigence. This would demonstrate to Latin America that the United States was not hostile to social change and that the breakdown in relations was Havana's fault. Moreover, Bonsal argued, if the United States exhibited overt hostility to the Cuban revolution, it would rally nationalist sentiment behind Castro.[141] Despite the accuracy of Bonsal's premises, he was essentially recommending that the United States do nothing in the face of Castro's defiance. For a superpower long dominant in its own sphere of influence, such a notion was anathema. Patience would be mistaken for passivity, and passivity for weakness—weakness that would encourage other nationalist forces across Latin America to challenge U.S. security and economic policy and interests.[142] Moreover, 1960 was an election year, and as Bonsal knew full well, "The American posture of moderation in the face of Castro's insulting and aggressive behavior was becoming a political liability." For an administration whose vice president was in the race, silently enduring Castro's attacks became untenable. "If you can't stand up to Castro, how can you be expected to stand up to Khrushchev?" Kennedy taunted Nixon on the campaign trail.[143]

As spring gave way to summer, the conflict between Cuba and the United States shifted from the diplomatic arena to the economic. Administration hard-liners like Nixon and Assistant Secretary of State for Economic Affairs Thomas C. Mann had been arguing since the fall of 1959 that Washington should cut Cuba's sugar quota. In 1960, Cuba held one-third of the total U.S. sugar import quota and was paid two cents per pound above the world market price. To threaten Cuba's sugar quota was to threaten to demolish the Cuban economy.

Bonsal and the State Department team working on Cuba vigorously opposed cutting the quota, which they called "the ultimate weapon." Such a move would be counterproductive, they argued. It might cripple the Cuban economy, but it would not dislodge Castro's government. On the contrary, it would "rally Cuban nationalist sentiment around Castro," allowing him to "shift the blame for their economic and other troubles . . . to the United States." Cutting the quota would inflict further political harm on Castro's opponents by placing them "in the difficult position of seeming to side with the United States in measures taken against the interests of all Cubans." On the basis of this analysis, a State Department working group convened to explore options for economic sanctions recommended against them all.[144] Even Rubottom's most conservative deputy, John Calvin Hill, worried that overt sanctions would strengthen Castro. "We cannot expect patriotic and self-respecting Cubans, no matter how distasteful Castro's policies may be to them, to side with the United States," Hill cautioned, "if we go so far along the lines of reprisals that the quarrel no longer is between Castro and the real interests of the Cuban people but a quarrel between the United States and their country."[145]

These arguments carried the day so long as Washington was intent on hiding its hostility behind a facade of diplomatic propriety. But as relations deteriorated and Castro's rhetoric became more heated, the arguments for restraint sounded increasingly hollow. Once the administration had settled on a strategy to remove Castro from power, the employment of economic sanctions seemed a logical complement to the CIA's covert support for the domestic opposition and paramilitary training of an exile force. "It was silly," Eisenhower wrote later, "to continue to give Cuba favored treatment."[146]

Bonsal's view was more strategic. He regarded Cuba's economic ties to the United States as a limiting condition on Castro's apostasy. When the fever of revolution finally broke, Cuba's economic dependency would force the government to come to political terms with Washington. If the United States, in a fit of pique, ruptured those ties of its own initiative, it would squander the best leverage it had over the future direction of the revolution.[147]

The casus belli that ignited the economic war between Cuba and the United States proved to be Soviet oil rather than Cuban sugar. As part of the trade agreement Mikoyan and Castro signed in February 1960, the Soviets sold Cuba crude oil in exchange for sugar. The first tanker of Soviet oil arrived on April 19 and was sent to refineries owned by Standard Oil, Texaco, and British-Dutch Shell. Although the companies were uncomfortable departing from their normal procedure of refining their own crude, they were willing to cooperate rather than risk confrontation. But when they sought counsel from Treasury Secretary Robert B. Anderson, he told them, to their surprise, that refusing to accept Soviet oil would be "consistent with U.S. policy," and he promised they would have the support of the U.S. government.[148]

The Cubans "will no doubt treat this as a serious challenge and a test of strength, as indeed it will be," Bonsal warned when he heard of the decision. "Drastic measures can be anticipated."[149] When the oil companies refused to accept the Soviet crude, the Cubans seized the refineries. If the United States declared economic war against the revolution, Castro warned, he would nationalize everything the Americans owned in Cuba, "down to the nails in their shoes."[150]

The seizure of the refineries gave administration hard-liners the perfect excuse to cancel the sugar quota. Secretary Anderson compared the seizures to Iran's nationalization of the oil industry in 1951. The CIA argued that economic sanctions were necessary to undermine Castro's popular support and boost the morale of his pro-U.S. opponents. Nixon argued for sanctions as a public rebuke to the Cubans "in order to indicate that we would not allow ourselves to be kicked around completely," lest Uncle Sam be labeled "Uncle Sucker."[151]

On July 3, 1960, Congress passed a law giving the president discretionary authority to reduce Cuba's sugar quota. The Cubans countered with a law authorizing Castro to nationalize U.S. property, stipulating that compensation would be paid from a fund derived from sugar sales to the United States. No sugar, no compensation. That same day, July 6, Eisenhower made the announcement that everyone was expecting: the United States would buy no more Cuban sugar in 1960.[152]

Denouncing U.S. "economic aggression," Castro retaliated by nationalizing most major U.S.-owned businesses on the island, worth a total of more than $600 million.[153] Two months later, Washington escalated the economic war, prohibiting exports to Cuba except for food and medicine, thereby laying the foundation of the economic embargo that would be the central issue of contention in U.S.-Cuban relations for the next half century. Castro countered by expropriating the remaining U.S. properties in Cuba, worth an additional $250 million.[154]

As U.S.-Cuban relations disintegrated, Soviet-Cuban relations blossomed. Within days of Eisenhower's decision to cut the Cuban sugar quota, Khrushchev wrote to Castro pledging that the Soviet Union would buy the sugar that the United States had refused. Privately, the Soviet premier was confident that U.S. hostility would drive Cuba into the Soviet camp "like an iron filing to a magnet."[155] In September, Fidel Castro returned to the United States to speak at the General Assembly of the United Nations. When Nikita Khrushchev stopped by to pay his respects, a photographer caught Castro enveloping the diminutive Russian in an enormous bear hug. The photo, which ran in major papers across the nation, symbolized perfectly Cuba's defection from the Western camp.[156]

By the fall of 1960, there was no disposition in Washington to reverse the decay of U.S.-Cuban relations. When Mexico, Brazil, and Canada approached the United States offering their good offices, Rubottom argued against it on the grounds that the Mexicans identified too closely with Cuba, seeing a parallel between the Cuban revolution and their own; the Brazilians were too enmeshed in their own domestic politics to be an honest broker; and the Canadians simply did not share Washington's concern about communism in Cuba. "Finally," Rubottom added, "the initiative for good offices may have come from Cuba itself," a fact he saw as disqualifying rather than hopeful. The initiative was rebuffed, as was another conciliatory signal from Havana sent through the Chilean government.[157]

When Bonsal suggested testing the diplomatic waters by opening discussions with Cuba over the sugar quota for 1961, Rubottom's successor as assistant secretary, Thomas Mann, killed the idea. There would be no improvement in U.S.-Cuban relations, Mann said, until Cuba cut its ties to the Sino-Soviet bloc and halted the export of revolution. "The prospects that Castro will take action along this line seem to me to be very dim, if not nonexistent," he concluded. "Our best bet is to wait for a successor regime."[158]

Bonsal's tenure as ambassador to Cuba ended shortly thereafter, not with a bang but a whimper. In October 1960, the day after Washington imposed the export embargo, Bonsal was unceremoniously recalled from Havana for "extended consultations." He had lost the confidence of senior officials, who had long-since given up on coexisting with Cuba and were tired of his incessant efforts to find a diplomatic path back from the precipice. The embassy was left open as a listening post from which CIA officers could maintain contact with the internal opposition.[159]

On January 2, 1961, speaking at a rally to celebrate the second anniversary of the triumph of the revolution, Castro denounced the embassy as a "nest of spies," and demanded that the staff be reduced from eighty-seven to eleven within forty-eight hours. Eisenhower's response, on January 3, was to break relations.[160] The final break came as a surprise to no one. The trajectory of relations had been leading inexorably toward it. U.S. dependents had been evacuated and sensitive documents shipped back to Washington months earlier. On January 4, the embassy staff left by ferry. "When the break came," diplomat Wayne Smith recalled, "we merely packed our bags, turned out the lights, and were ready to go."[161] Getting back to Havana would prove to be a lot harder.

The Failure of Diplomacy: Could the Break Have Been Avoided?

The official breach in relations left Cuba and the United States in a state of undeclared war, with little means or inclination on either side to address their differences. In the years to come, diplomats would face major challenges trying to reopen the channels of communication through which the two governments could begin to reengage. Cold War confrontations, Havana's revolutionary ideology, and Washington's hegemonic arrogance all conspired against attempts to bridge the deep divide between the two countries. The road back to normal diplomatic relations would prove long and treacherous.

With perfect hindsight, the United States and Cuba might have found enough common ground to preserve their core interests while maintaining normal relations, but this would have required a radical change in the historical relationship between the two countries, far beyond what U.S. officials could imagine at the time. To Washington, Cuba was a reliable ally and business partner with more U.S. investment per capita than any other country in Latin America. To Cuban nationalists, Cuba was a pseudo-republic whose independence from Spain had been short-circuited by U.S. military occupation and the imposition of the demeaning Platt Amendment. Fidel Castro came to power in 1959 with two broad goals for his revolution: to win, once and for all, Cuba's independence from U.S. domination, and to radically change Cuban society in pursuit of greater social justice.[162] Inevitably, both these goals brought him into conflict with the United States.

Bonsal's declarations of goodwill notwithstanding, Castro knew Washington was covertly supporting his enemies. Dozens of Batista's henchmen were given refuge in the United States—some with the CIA's help—and Washington refused to extradite them. They began launching raids against Cuba almost immediately, and the United States did virtually nothing to stop them. CIA officers at the embassy in Havana met with disgruntled moderates, supported their opposition activities, and helped smuggle them into exile when the time came.

In Washington, the issue most galling to U.S. officials was the least substantial: "anti-Americanism"—Fidel's incessant, harsh rhetoric directed at the United States. U.S. officials understood that the rhetoric was partly, if not primarily, for domestic consumption. After an early speech at a massive rally defending the "war crimes" trials, Castro seemed genuinely surprised that U.S. chargé Daniel Braddock would interpret it as hostile to the United States. At a public rally, "certain points of view" needed to be expressed, Castro explained, but he had "intended no hurt to the United States."[163]

Intended or not, U.S. officials took offense, and their reaction was visceral. It rankled to have Castro incessantly lambasting the United States, not just for its current policy but for the whole long history of its relations with Cuba. Turning the other cheek was not the preferred response of a Great Power when challenged in its own backyard. Castro's rhetorical salvos made it especially difficult for Bonsal to sustain the policy of patience and forbearance.

Because of Castro's anti-American rhetoric, "there was a general reluctance on the part of the U.S. government . . . to throw itself wholeheartedly into the job of winning Castro over to our side with the carrot," a White House post-mortem on the break in relations concluded. "The U.S. government, in the face of Cuban ungratefulness and ungentlemanly antics, generally limited its cooperative investment to bland, oral extensions of goodwill; concrete offers of aid were generally held in abeyance until the Cubans 'shaped-up' or swallowed their nationalist pride and asked for aid."[164]

Domestic politics was an important factor on the Cuban side as well. In the months after January 2, 1959, the broad, multiclass coalition that overthrew Batista began to unravel over the future course of the revolution. Relations with the United States became a focal point of this internal struggle.

Moderates like Agramonte, Urrutia, Pazos, and López-Fresquet hoped for friendly relations with Washington, combined with reformist domestic policies that would give Cuban capitalism a human face. The radicals of the 26th of July Movement, like Raúl Castro, Che Guevara, and ultimately Fidel himself, wanted to free Cuba from the political and economic orbit of the United States and build socialism. Relations between Havana and Washington soured in tandem with the fading political fortunes of the moderates, who one U.S. official called "the best vehicles for maintaining U.S. interests in the island."[165]

The negotiation in late 1959 and early 1960 ultimately came to naught because neither side felt compelled to drive them to a successful conclusion. The United States did not believe it needed to make any major concessions to Castro because it did not believe his government could survive the combined force of economic sanctions and covert political and paramilitary pressure. For the next half century, the impetus to find common ground would have to compete in Washington with the hope that the revolution might be reversed.

On the Cuban side, the advantages of coexistence were more substantial but the grounds were narrow. Unless Castro was willing to betray his own vision of a Cuba free from Washington's dominance, coexistence would be possible only if Washington willingly allowed Cuba to escape its orbit. That it would not do. Once the Soviet Union stepped in to provide economic and military assistance to cushion Cuba's separation from the United States, Castro had the means to realize his vision and had no compelling reason to make concessions at the bargaining table. Even after U.S. influence was eliminated, Cuban leaders remained ambivalent about restoring normal relations, weighing the advantages against the fear that Cuba might be pulled back into subordination.

Looking back, most U.S. officials who dealt with Cuba during 1959–60, concluded that the break was inevitable. "I do not believe . . . that Castro, in spite of the statements he allowed Dorticós and Roa to make from time to time, ever contemplated meaningful relations with the United States," Bonsal wrote to Arthur Schlesinger Jr. in 1962, a letter Schlesinger passed to President John F. Kennedy. "He equated the success of his revolution with the complete destruction of U.S. interests in Cuba."[166]

But other U.S. officials blamed Washington as much as Havana. "We mistakenly looked at Cuba through traditional eyeglasses and mistakenly regarded it as controllable," concluded the White House post-mortem in 1964. "We were probably so used to thinking in the standard stereotyped terms of 'immense reservoirs of good will' toward the U.S. [and were] so fully persuaded of Cuba's total dependence on the U.S., that we could not recognize the force of Cuban nationalist pride, and apparently found it difficult to take Cuba or Castro seriously."[167]

Raúl Castro also thought the break in relations was unavoidable because Washington would never accept the revolution's challenge to its dominance. "The 1959 land reform was the Rubicon of our revolution—a death sentence for our U.S. relations," he told actor Sean Penn in 2008. "At that moment, there was no discussion about socialism, or Cuba dealing with Russia. But the die was cast."[168]

Fidel himself evinced less certainty about the inevitability of the split. "I must acknowledge that I may have had some responsibility for our first divorce—I as well as the United States," Castro admitted in 1978. "In retrospect, I can see a number of things I wish I had done differently. We would not in any event have ended up close friends. The United States had dominated us too long. The Cuban revolution was determined to end that domination. There was, then, an inherent conflict of interest. Still, even adversaries find it useful to maintain bridges between them," Fidel reflected. "Perhaps I burned some of those bridges precipitously; there were times when I may have been more abrupt, more aggressive, than was called for by the situation. We were all younger then; we made the mistakes of youth."[169]

For the next half century, diplomats in both capitals would struggle to rebuild the bridges between these two near neighbors, so divided by ideology and interests.

2. KENNEDY
The Secret Search for Accommodation

The President does not agree that we should make the breaking of Sino/Soviet ties a non-negotiable point. We don't want to present Castro with a condition that he obviously cannot fulfill. We should start thinking along more flexible lines. . . . The above must be kept close to the vest. The President, himself, is very interested in this one.

—TOP SECRET/EYES ONLY Memorandum for the Record on negotiating with Castro, March 4, 1963

On November 22, 1963, the French journalist Jean Daniel was in Cuba to transmit a message of potential reconciliation from President John F. Kennedy to Fidel Castro—"a gesture," as Castro would describe it years later, "an indication of a desire to establish contact . . . to establish a certain kind of communication."[1] At a government protocol house in Varadero Beach, local fishermen had brought a big, fresh fish for lunch as "a homage to Fidel," Daniel recalled. In the middle of the meal, as he and Castro were discussing Kennedy's secret "feeler" about the possibility of better relations, the phone rang and Fidel received the shocking news that the president of the United States had been shot in Dallas. "This is an end to your mission of peace. This is an end to your mission. . . ." Castro told Daniel. "Everything has changed."[2]

John F. Kennedy's abbreviated presidency ended with an effort to reconcile with Cuba, but it did not begin that way. As a candidate, Kennedy tacked to the right of Vice President Richard M. Nixon, accusing the Eisenhower administration of abandoning Cuban "fighters for freedom"—the exiles who sought to roll back the Cuban revolution. As president-elect, he was briefed by the CIA on Eisenhower's covert paramilitary project to invade Cuba with an exile brigade. As president, he ignored the entreaties of several Latin American governments that, at Cuba's behest, tried to intercede at the last minute to broker a U.S.-Cuban dialogue before the Bay of Pigs invasion.[3] Instead, Kennedy gave the green light, sending a CIA-led paramilitary exile force ashore at Playa Girón on April 17, 1961, in the hope that the invaders would somehow spark a popular uprising. They didn't, and within seventy-two hours, the brigade's beachhead had collapsed; more than twelve hundred of them were taken prisoner. "Victory has a thousand fathers, and defeat is an orphan," said Kennedy as he publicly acknowledged his personal responsibility for one of the great debacles in the history of U.S. foreign policy. "I am the responsible member of government."[4]

"We were hysterical about Castro at the time of the Bay of Pigs and thereafter," former secretary of defense Robert McNamara later testified before Congress.[5] Indeed, the trauma of defeat and humiliation at the Bay of Pigs spurred both President Kennedy and his brother, Attorney General Robert F. Kennedy, to focus exceptional attention on how to "redress" the "insult" of their defeat. The president soon tasked his brother to oversee "Operation Mongoose," a massive, multifaceted campaign of overt diplomatic and economic pressure to isolate and impoverish the island, and covert paramilitary operations to overthrow the Communist regime. President Kennedy imposed a full economic embargo in February 1962, which has remained the central pillar of a hostile U.S. policy for more than five decades. And during Kennedy's abbreviated tenure as president, the CIA escalated its "executive action" efforts to kill Castro. An internal TOP SECRET CIA history on assassination attempts against the Cuban leader noted an extraordinary coincidence: "It is likely that at the very moment President Kennedy was shot, a CIA officer was meeting with a Cuban agent in Paris and giving him an assassination device for use against Castro."[6]

Yet, at that very same moment, Jean Daniel was in Cuba extending President Kennedy's olive branch of reconciliation. Indeed, while the history of Kennedy's thousand days is dominated by infamous acts of aggression against Cuba, his administration also secretly explored the alternative of accommodation. As more aggressive options proved unequal to the task of ousting Castro and the missile crisis dramatically demonstrated the dangers of hostility, the more civil option of trying to domesticate him through dialogue gained adherents—including the president himself. "We wanted to make a reality check on what could or could not be done with Fidel Castro," McGeorge Bundy explained in an interview shortly before his death in 1996. The president "clearly thought this was an exploration worth making because it might lead to something."[7]

Amid economic destabilization, covert operations, and assassination plots, the Kennedy administration secretly but actively began to pursue what classified National Security Council (NSC) and CIA records referred to as "the rapprochement track" with Cuba. Since "we had no department of 'peaceful tricks,'" Bundy recalled, the key problem was "finding a way to do it" that was "secret, secure and reliable."[8] To a policy built upon "overt and covert nastiness," as one TOP SECRET White House memorandum characterized U.S. operations, Kennedy's aides cautiously added "the sweet approach"—the possibility of "quietly enticing Castro over to us."[9]

First Talks: "Below-ground Dialogue"

The first opportunity for talks between a high-ranking Kennedy administration official and a high-ranking leader of the Cuban revolution came at the founding meeting of the Alliance for Progress in Punta del Este, Uruguay. Spontaneous and informal, the encounter in the early morning hours of August 18, 1961, came at the initiative of Ernesto "Che" Guevara. During the conference, Guevara saw a young White House aide named Richard Goodwin smoking a cigar across the room. He sent an Argentine diplomat named Horacio Rodríguez Larreta to convey this dare: "I bet he wouldn't smoke Cuban cigars." As Goodwin recalled his response, "I said, 'Hell I'd smoke them in a minute but I can't get them at home any more.' Next day in my room there was a box of Cuban cigars with a handwritten note from Che Guevara."[10]

The note and the Cohibas—delivered in an ornate mahogany box inlaid with the seal of the Republic of Cuba—were for President Kennedy. They represented Cuba's first real diplomatic gesture toward the United States in the aftermath of the Bay of Pigs invasion. "To write to the enemy is difficult," Che's message read. "I limit myself to extending my hand."

Guevara proposed a meeting. But the head of the U.S. delegation, Treasury Secretary Douglas Dillon, vetoed the idea after Guevara's harsh criticism of the United States in his speech to the conference. Not to be deterred, Guevara tracked Goodwin down at a private party in Montevideo at 2:00 A.M. on the last night of the conference. "While all the women at the party swarmed around him," Goodwin later reported to President Kennedy, Che sent a message over with the Argentine diplomat Rodríguez Larreta and Brazilian ambassador Edmundo Barbosa da Silva that he "had something important to say to me." Goodwin remembered, "I was very curious."

Accompanied by the Argentine and Brazilian diplomats who acted as interpreters, Guevara and Goodwin went into a small side room. With just a couch and one chair in the room, Guevara immediately sat down on the floor in front of the couch; Goodwin sat himself down on the floor in front of the chair because "I was not going to let him out proletarianize me." Although

Goodwin would report to President Kennedy that he broke up the conversation "after 20–40 minutes," years later he recounted that their meeting continued "until dawn had lighted the Montevideo skies."

Guevara thanked Goodwin for the Bay of Pigs. "Their hold on the country had been a bit shaky," he explained, "but the invasion allowed the leadership to consolidate most of the major elements of the country around Fidel."

"Perhaps, I answered, they would return the favor and attack Guantánamo."

"Oh, no," Guevara laughed. "We would never be so foolish as to do that."[11]

From there, the conversation took a more serious turn. "I had the definite impression that he had thought out his remarks very carefully. They were extremely well organized," Goodwin wrote in his secret report.[12] High on Guevara's agenda was disabusing the United States of any false assumptions about the nature of the Cuban revolution: the revolution was "irreversible." It could not be overthrown internally, and the United States should not engage the myth that Fidel was a moderate "surrounded by a bunch of fanatic and aggressive men." The revolution was strong, Guevara told Goodwin. The Bay of Pigs invasion "transformed them from an aggrieved little country to an equal."

Empowered as an "equal," Che pressed for a dialogue toward some type of coexistence with Washington. "They would like a modus vivendi—at least an interim modus vivendi," Goodwin reported. "Of course, he said, it was difficult to put forth a practical formula for such a modus vivendi—he knew because he had spent a lot time thinking about it." Guevara proposed a formula for negotiations in which Cuba would offer five concessions: (1) While Cuba would not return expropriated properties, it could commit to paying for them through trade; (2) Cuba would agree to forgo a political alliance with "the East" even though the revolution's "natural sympathies" lay in that direction; (3) Cuba would have free elections, but only after the "institutionalization of the revolution" and creation of a one-party state; (4) Cuba would be willing to address its activities in other Latin American countries; and (5) "of course, they would not attack Guantánamo."

In conclusion, Guevara made a pragmatic suggestion—one that Cuba would invoke again and again in pressing for diplomatic dialogue over the next five decades. "He knew it was difficult to negotiate these things but we could open up some of these issues by beginning to discuss secondary issues [such as airplane hijackings] . . . as a cover for more serious conversation." And Che made a final point that would become a fixture of Cuba's negotiating position in all future talks: Cuba "could discuss no formula that would mean giving up the type of society to which they were dedicated."[13]

"Any negotiation between the two countries was likely to be impossible given the irreconcilable differences that exist between the two," Goodwin told Che, according to a summary of the meeting by the Brazilian ambassador.[14] Goodwin nevertheless promised Guevara that he would report the conversation to "the highest level of his government." Both agreed to keep their meeting a secret.[15]

When Goodwin returned to Washington, he went directly to the White House to brief Kennedy and give him Guevara's box of cigars. This gift represented Cuba's first attempt—although certainly not its last—at cigar diplomacy. The cigars certainly caught JFK's attention, as Goodwin put them on his desk in the Oval Office: "He opened them and he says, 'Are they good?' And I said, 'Good, Mr. President!' I said, 'No they are the best,' whereupon he immediately took one out of the box, bit off the end and lit it up. Then he turned on me and said, 'You should have smoked the first one.' I said, 'Too late now, Mr. President.'"*[16]

Following that meeting, Goodwin drafted a pivotal memo to the president evaluating what he called Cuba's "below-ground dialogue" with the United States and its implications for U.S. policy.[17] Cuba "desires an understanding with the United States," Goodwin surmised, because it was "undergoing severe economic stress" and because "the Soviet Union is not prepared to undertake the large effort necessary to get them on their feet." Since Guevara was one of the most committed communists in Cuba, in Goodwin's analysis, there were probably "others in the Cuban government even more dedicated to an accommodation with the United States."

Although he recommended that the United States avoid "the impression we are obsessed with Castro," most of Goodwin's action options focused not on exploring the diplomatic opening from Cuba but rather on escalating U.S. operations to undermine the revolution. Economic warfare should be quietly intensified, psychological and propaganda operations escalated, and covert subversion and sabotage stepped up. Only at the very end of his memo did Goodwin suggest that the administration "seek some way of continuing the

---

* A few months later, before signing the executive order that banned trade with Cuba, Kennedy sent his press secretary, Pierre Salinger, on a late-night shopping trip around Washington to buy up as many Cuban cigars as he could find for Kennedy's private stash. When Salinger told the president the next morning that he found twelve hundred cigars, "Kennedy smiled, and opened up his desk," Salinger recalled. "He took out a long paper which he immediately signed. It was the decree banning all Cuban products from the United States. Cuban cigars were now illegal in our country" (Pierre Salinger, "Kennedy, Cuba and Cigars," *Cigar Aficionado*, November–December 2002).

below-ground dialogue that Che has begun. We can thus make it clear that we want to help Cuba and would help Cuba if it would sever communist ties and begin democratization. In this way we can begin to probe for the split in top leadership which might exist." To pursue that option, Goodwin tasked the CIA with finding what he described as a "precise, covert procedure for continuing below-ground dialogue with the Cuban Government"—an "operational technique" that would allow the administration to secretly talk to Fidel without having to look over its shoulder at the impact on domestic politics.[18]

But nothing came of Guevara's initiative. Within days of their meeting in Montevideo, Goodwin was assigned to head a Cuban Task Force made up of White House, CIA, Defense, and State Department officials dedicated to intensifying covert operations against Cuba to roll back the revolution. Within several weeks, he would draft the initial strategy paper for Operation Mongoose—the most extensive and expensive U.S. effort to overthrow Castro since the Bay of Pigs—which President Kennedy authorized on November 30, 1961.

Years later, Goodwin would reflect on the lost opportunity to continue the "low-level dialogue" he had started with Che Guevara in 1961. "It wasn't a bad deal," he wrote, "and given what was to come later, a detached analyst might urge that it be pursued. But the mood in America was not one of detachment. The emotion that had always surrounded the 'problem' of Cuba had, if anything, been heightened by our defeat at the Bay of Pigs. To make a deal with Castro, any kind of deal, would have been politically difficult, perhaps impossible." Since the Kennedy White House chose to ignore Guevara's proposal, Goodwin concluded, "We will never know."[19]

First Negotiations: The Bay of Pigs Prisoners

While the Bay of Pigs spawned the Kennedys' animus toward Fidel Castro, it also provided the opportunity for the first substantive U.S.-Cuban negotiations since diplomatic relations were severed in January 1961. President Kennedy's deep sense of angst and obligation over the capture and imprisonment of 1,214 members of the exile brigade led him to authorize a major behind-the-scenes negotiation to obtain their release. "They trusted me. And they're in prison now because I fucked up," Kennedy told Goodwin. "I have to get them out."[20]

Within a week of the invasion, Cuban officials signaled a deal might be possible. President Osvaldo Dorticós told foreign diplomats in Havana that his government wanted to "find a solution to the tension which exists between the two countries and which will lead to a form of peaceful co-existence, diplomatic and even friendly relations, if the government of the United States so desires."[21] Releasing the prisoners suited Castro's purposes—albeit in a way that underscored Cuba's historic victory over the Colossus of the North. Executing the captured brigade members would be politically damaging (though Fidel threatened to do it); imprisoning them indefinitely would be costly and become a permanent focal point of international pressure. Far better to barter them for what Fidel called "indemnification" from the United States and use the process to generate positive propaganda, as well as perhaps create an opening for broader talks with Washington.

Speaking to an audience of small farmers on May 17, 1961, Castro proposed an exchange: "the imperialist soldiers" for U.S.-built tractors. "The Pentagon, the Central Intelligence Agency, and all who sent them on that adventure love them so much. Very well, let them send 500 bulldozers and we will return them."[22] He was willing to negotiate with Kennedy administration officials, members of Congress, or prominent private citizens to make the necessary arrangements. And he would release a ten-member delegation of the prisoners to go to the United States and begin negotiations. Now, Fidel said, it was up to Kennedy: "Ahora, el señor Kennedy tiene la palabra."[23]

To avoid the high political costs of government-to-government talks with Castro, Kennedy personally recruited four prestigious citizens—former first lady Eleanor Roosevelt, United Automobile Workers leader Walter Reuther, Milton Eisenhower (brother of the former president), and Joseph Dodge (President Eisenhower's budget director)—to create a front group, the "Tractors-for-Freedom Committee." On May 22, the newly formed committee met at the Statler Hilton Hotel in Washington with the delegation of prisoners sent by Castro to present his demands for five hundred Caterpillar D-8 large tread-type tractors, or comparable machines, and five years worth of spare parts.

Faced with right-wing political attacks charging that the heavy tractors could be used for military construction, the committee organized a team of agricultural specialists to evaluate Cuba's needs; it then decided Castro's plans for agricultural reform did not require the powerful D-8 tractors. On June 2, the committee cabled Havana, offering 50 tread-type tractors and 450 smaller rubber-tire tractors—which Castro disparaged as "ridiculous little toy tractors."[24] The committee dictated how many tractors would be delivered and how many prisoners would have to be released with each delivery. And it gave Castro a June 7 deadline to accept their proposal.

Predictably, Castro rejected this patronizing position. "Your committee has not taken really practical steps to bring negotiations to immediate positive results," he wrote on June 6, and added the warning, "Cuba has the right to impose exemplary punishment on those who have committed against their own country a crime of high treason while they were acting under the orders of a foreign government."[25] Rather than abandon the dialogue, however, Castro invited Eleanor Roosevelt or Milton Eisenhower to come to Havana and continue the negotiations face-to-face.

Ignoring Castro's request, the committee sent its team of agricultural specialists to Havana with instructions to avoid political issues and focus on equipment. When Castro met with them on June 14, he expressed his disappointment that no senior member of the committee had come; he wanted to discuss a wider political agenda. Instead, he and the specialists spent three and a half hours debating the merits of the larger bulldozers versus smaller farming tractors. Finally, Fidel declared he would compromise on the type of machinery; or accept credits totaling $28 million; or, alternatively, exchange the brigade members for political prisoners in Europe instead of tractors. "We must talk openly and frankly," he told the delegation. "We want to release tension, we would like to have a change of relations."[26]

But the committee rejected Castro's alternative proposals and refused to negotiate further. At the secret instruction of the White House, the committee reiterated its original proposal to Castro—and gave him until June 23 to take it or leave it.

Castro dismissed their demand but continued to pursue the possibility of a deal. Publicly, he again dispatched the prisoner delegation to Florida to convey Cuba's counterproposals. Privately, he passed a message through *New York Times* reporter Tad Szulc to White House aide Arthur Schlesinger Jr. that "a successful negotiation on the rebels-for-tractors affair could lead to further U.S.-Cuban negotiations." Cuba "would be interested in the resumption of some form of relationship" with the United States if Kennedy would "quit trying to 'destroy' his revolution," Szulc reported. "The impression is he would like to reopen the door a bit."[27]

In November, Attorney General Robert Kennedy arranged for Szulc to brief the president. For an hour and a half, Szulc sat in the Oval office while President Kennedy, in his rocking chair, peppered him with questions, mostly about how Castro's government could be overthrown. But he also asked about Szulc's conversation with Castro in June. "Is it possible, in your judgment, for the United States and Cuba to establish some kind of dialogue?" Kennedy inquired. Szulc replied that Castro had told him he did not regard Kennedy as his "enemy" and that "if there was anyone in the United States government . . . with whom he, Castro, could come to terms and establish a dialogue, it would be President Kennedy." The president told Szulc, off-handedly, that if he spoke with Castro again, he should tell him that Kennedy, too, hoped that "some way could be found somewhere along the line to establish an understanding."[28]

In reality, dialogue was not a high presidential priority. Kennedy's feelings of personal responsibility for the Bay of Pigs prisoners notwithstanding, he placed greater importance on demonstrating U.S. resolve against Cuba and insulating the White House from conservative charges that his administration was soft on Communism. Not ready to openly negotiate for the brigade prisoners, the White House abandoned the Tractors-for-Freedom Committee to "ridicule and misunderstanding" by the public and the conservative press, according to Milton Eisenhower. "The public should have been told from the first, and should even now be told that the foreign policy decision was governmental," he told the president in what he later called "the bitterest letter I ever wrote."[29] Only six weeks after Kennedy had secretly created it, the committee disbanded on June 23. The Bay of Pigs prisoners would remain in Cuban jails for another eighteen months.

Project Mercy

After the talks broke down, the prisoner delegation and families of the brigade members formed a new organization, the Cuban Families Committee for the Liberation of the Prisoners of War (CFC), to raise the $28 million that Castro had demanded to purchase the tractors. Their campaign took on new urgency when Cuba put the prisoners on trial for treason, after which the prisoners and their relatives fully expected that some if not all of them would be sentenced to the firing squad. Working through a personal contact with Celia Sánchez, Fidel's chief of staff and confidante, the CFC launched a desperate, last-ditch effort to convince Castro that an exchange was still possible. Simultaneously, the group turned to the U.S. government for help in raising the necessary funds. When neither the brigade's CIA contacts in Miami nor the Cuba desk at the State Department would assist the organization, some frustrated CFC representatives impulsively marched into Robert Kennedy's office at the Justice Department and demanded an audience. To their surprise, the sympathetic Attorney General agreed not only to see them but to actually help them. "I give you my word we will do everything possible to keep them from being shot," he pledged.[30]

Kennedy referred the CFC delegation to Richard Goodwin, who then wrote a SECRET action paper for National Security Advisor McGeorge Bundy, outlining a plan to convince Castro not to execute the prisoners. "We are considering an approach to Castro—through intermediaries—to make a deal for the life of the prisoners; offering money or food to spare their lives," Goodwin reported. "This would probably be carried out, if it is carried out, through voluntary relief agencies."[31] Instead of execution, however, the brigade prisoners were found guilty and sentenced to thirty years in prison, or fines totaling $62 million. That was now the price of their freedom, Fidel told the CFC members during a meeting in April at the home of Berta Barreto de los Heros, the mother of one of the prisoners and the committee's liaison in Cuba. When the CFC members raised the idea of an exchange for foodstuffs, Castro replied that he would "probably find acceptable a formula for releasing the remaining prisoners based on $26 million in foodstuffs and medicines and the balance of the $62 million in cash," Secretary Rusk reported to the president. "Castro told the Committee not to be discouraged" and that "he was confident something could be worked out within ninety days."[32]

As a good faith gesture, Castro agreed to release sixty sick and wounded prisoners as long as the CFC pledged to pay their fines of $2.9 million later. Harry Ruiz-Williams was one of those prisoners. He developed a close personal relationship with Attorney General Robert Kennedy and would eventually become a key liaison between the White House and exile operatives working to overthrow Castro. In June 1962 he approached Robert Kennedy for support in finding a chairman for the CFC who could lead a fundraising drive. Kennedy told him to seek out "a man who knows how to deal with Castro"[33]—at the time, the most famous international negotiator in the United States, if not the world, James B. Donovan.

A Harvard law school graduate, Office of Strategic Services (OSS) veteran, and assistant prosecutor at the Nuremberg trials, Donovan gained fame as the man who arranged the dramatic February 1962 prisoner exchange of convicted Russian spy Rudolf Abel for the captured American U-2 pilot Frances Gary Powers. Donovan's success in negotiating this East-West spy swap—he personally escorted Abel to the middle of the Glienicke Bridge between East Berlin and Potsdam and then returned with Powers—earned him distinction as a "meta-diplomat."[34]

In June 1962, Donovan agreed to publicly represent the CFC and, privately, the U.S. government.[35] Before traveling to Havana to begin talks with Castro, Donovan met twice in Washington with Robert Kennedy and once with CIA director John McCone. "Mr. McCone's judgment is that I should immediately proceed to attempt to open negotiations with the Castro government, with the twin objectives of 1) lowering the minimum figure demanded by Castro and 2) arranging that a substantial part of this sum would be payable in food and medicine," as Donovan recorded his instructions.[36] At McCone's direction, the CIA established a safe house in Miami for Donovan to use in his trips back and forth to Havana. A secret code was designed for phone communications while Donovan was in Havana. The CIA even provided his mission with an operational codename: "Project Mercy."

Donovan made his first trip to Havana on August 30 and met with Castro for four hours the next day. The U.S. negotiator set a positive tone by immediately agreeing to call the process an "indemnity" rather than a humanitarian exchange—something Castro had demanded previously as an acknowledgment that Cuba deserved compensation for the costs of the invasion. Their negotiations began around Donovan's proposal to provide Cuba $5 million in cash or $20 to $25 million in food products. Fidel rejected this offer as humiliating—far below the court-imposed fines of $62 million. He insisted that the only cash he wanted was the $2.9 million the CFC had agreed to when he had released sixty prisoners in the spring. He would consider foodstuffs and other goods with a value commensurate with the $62 million in fines and would submit a list of what Cuba wanted.

Cuba's position enabled Donovan to focus on substituting medicines and drugs for foodstuffs; they were smaller in size and higher in value than food and would require lower shipping costs. Throughout September, Donovan made arrangements with the Kennedy administration to give tax write-offs to drug manufacturers who donated supplies for Cuba from older inventories. He also arranged a letter of credit from the Bank of Canada to cover delivery and shipping costs. He then returned to Cuba on October 3 to continue talks with the Cuban authorities.[37]

The second negotiating session did not go smoothly. Donovan endured a hostile meeting with Cuba's vice minister of the interior, Captain José Abrantes, and then a hellish drive over unpaved, pothole-riddled roads to Varadero Beach to meet Castro at the Dupont Estate. The talks became contentious over a number of points: whether the retail value or the wholesale value of the goods would be used to calculate the $62 million; Cuba's demand for a letter of credit of at least $16 million to guarantee the delivery of the goods; and whether Castro would release all the prisoners when the first shipment arrived or release them in stages corresponding to arriving shipments. "Absolutely no dice on releasing these boys in groups. They all have to come out as soon as the initial delivery is made," Donovan argued, and then dangled a carrot for Castro: "You'll just have to rely on the fact that among other things, the relationship created here could open a channel of communication that might be of mutual benefit to all parties concerned."[38]

Donovan returned to Miami and, over a secure phone, reported optimistically to his CIA contact on the progress in the negotiations. On the basis of that report, CIA director John McCone convened a special Saturday afternoon meeting at the State Department on October 8 to brief high-level officials that an agreement was imminent. The CIA had contracted with Pan Am for planes to "bring the prisoners out commencing today or tomorrow if all goes well," according to McCone, and Donovan would "return to Havana and fly out with the last group." President Kennedy also received a briefing that day and "approved the general conclusions" of the arrangement and plans—including that the U.S. government would admit publicly "without details" to being behind the negotiations.[39]

On October 10, Donovan shuttled back to Havana with an approved draft Memorandum of Agreement reflecting the terms he and Castro discussed at Varadero. But the meeting did not go well. Castro balked at Donovan's retail pricing numbers, and still refused to release all the prisoners after only the first shipment. He also wanted to revise the list of goods Cuban officials had previously provided to include baby food and different kinds of drugs.

Donovan reacted with controlled anger over Castro's apparent retreat from their tentative agreement. What, exactly, did Castro think he could do with the prisoners? "You can't shoot them," Donovan pointed out. "If you want to get rid of them, if you're going to sell them, you've got to sell them to me. There's no world market for prisoners." If Castro had decided he did not want to go through with the deal, Donovan declared, "there is not much point in my staying here. I will go home."[40]

Negotiations broke off on October 11, 1962, with an assumption on both sides that they would soon resume. Four days later, however, analysts at the CIA's National Photographic Interpretation Center examining reconnaissance pictures taken by a U-2 spy plane spotted clear evidence of the installation of Soviet nuclear-capable medium-range ballistic missiles (MRBMs) on the island. The Cuban Missile Crisis had begun.

Crisis Communications

On October 16, the day the CIA briefed the President on the U-2 intelligence, Kennedy gathered a select group of advisors, officially known as the "ExComm" (Executive Committee), to decide on a strategic response.

His Secretary of Defense, Robert McNamara, presented him with three basic options: the political option of "approaching Castro" and "approaching Khrushchev," a naval blockade to stop Soviet ships carrying weapons to Cuba, and "military action directed against Cuba." Fearing that a U.S. assault on Cuba could escalate into the ultimate doomsday scenario—nuclear Armageddon—the president chose option two to buy time to negotiate a resolution of the crisis with Khrushchev. But as the risk of war between the superpowers mounted over the next thirteen days, Kennedy also authorized a complicated clandestine approach to Castro. Washington's communications with Cuba, undertaken through Brazilian intermediaries, became the most enduring secret of missile crisis—an untold story until it was uncovered by historian James G. Hershberg forty years later in the foreign ministry archives of Brazil.[41]

Since the breach in U.S.-Cuban relations, Brazil had tried to position itself as a regional broker for rapprochement. During an April 1962 state visit to Washington by the new Brazilian president, João Goulart, his foreign minister, Francisco San Tiago Dantas, raised the possibility of approaching Castro on Washington's behalf. The time was right, Dantas urged Secretary of State Rusk, because Castro and hard-line Communists in his government were engaged in a power struggle. Brazil, Dantas suggested, was "in a good position to follow and influence [the] situation." If Castro became a Caribbean Tito, would that be acceptable to the United States?

Rusk responded that "from the U.S. viewpoint two things are not negotiable: (1) the direct Cuban ties with Moscow . . . ; and (2) Cuban subversive actions elsewhere in the hemisphere." But if Cuba would break with Moscow, "this would create a new situation."[42]

There was nothing to lose from Dantas's initiative, Rusk assured CIA director John McCone, who was the administration's leading opponent of any rapprochement with Castro: "Since we could try it without commitment, he might as well play his hand and see what happens."[43] A third-party interlocutor could be useful, Rusk argued presciently, if only to establish a channel of communication with Castro, "as the ability to reach him might be important at some future time."[44]

On April 22, the Brazilian ambassador in Havana, Luis Bastian Pinto, met with Castro to suggest that Cuba distance itself from Moscow and to offer help mediating the conflict with the United States since Brazil represented the "only significant channel left for Cuba to [the] West." Fidel was noncommittal; he thanked the Brazilian for the offer of assistance and promised to get back to him soon with "concrete suggestions," but he never did.[45]

Although the Brazilian diplomatic effort produced no results, the Kennedy administration continued to reach out to Castro about Cuba's potential return to the Western orbit. In an amazing coincidence, just hours before the White House learned of the existence of Soviet missiles on the island, the president sent a message to Castro through Algerian leader Ahmed Ben Bella, who was visiting Washington on October 15, 1962. With Ben Bella headed to Havana the next day, Kennedy seized the opportunity to discuss U.S.-Cuban relations. The United States had no intention of invading Cuba, Kennedy assured the Algerian leader, and reconciliation would be possible if Castro left his Latin American neighbors in peace. The United States could tolerate a "national communist" regime in Cuba as long as it did not serve as a spearhead of Soviet military power.

"Do you mean by this, Mr. Kennedy, a Yugoslavia or a Poland?" Ben Bella asked, to be sure he understood.

"Yes," Kennedy answered.[46]

Ben Bella arrived in Havana on October 16 and dutifully recounted this conversation to Castro. But by then Kennedy's message had been overtaken by the unfolding missile crisis. In Cuba, Soviet and Cuban personnel were laboring round the clock to make the missile sites operational. In Washington, Kennedy was holding his initial meetings with the ExComm and weighing a massive military attack on the island.

At the very first meeting of the ExComm on October 16, Secretary Rusk suggested that Washington transmit a message calling on Castro to break with the Soviets and include a *New York Times* article quoting a Soviet official as saying, "We'll trade Cuba for Berlin." The idea was to coax Castro to eject the missiles along with the Soviets by offering him a return to the West as an alternative to U.S. military intervention and regime change. As Rusk reiterated at the second evening meeting of the ExComm: "This might be the issue on which Castro might elect to break with Moscow if he knew that he were in deadly jeopardy." Rusk instructed his assistant secretary for Inter-American Affairs, Edwin Martin, to draft a possible "message to the bearded one."[47] The subsequent TOP SECRET letter to "Mr. F.C." warned that unless he quickly communicated to Washington that he would "not tolerate this misuse of Cuban territory, measures of vital significance for the future of Cuba will have to be initiated."[48]

These early ExComm meetings focused not on diplomacy, however, but on military options to take out the missiles: an invasion, a blockade, or a more limited air strike coupled with a blockade. During the first several days of the crisis, military officials and Secretary of Defense McNamara opposed any form of communication to either Castro or Khrushchev that would give away the element of surprise. "I don't think the message to Castro's got much in it," President Kennedy concluded as he considered the options.[49]

Nevertheless, the concept of communicating with Castro kept coming up during the ExComm's deliberations. In a memo to the president the next day, UN ambassador Adlai Stevenson urged Kennedy to have "your personal emissaries deliver your messages to C and K."[50] Martin proposed trying to negotiate a "co-existence pact" with Cuba if Castro ejected the Soviets. At a meeting on October 19, the ExComm briefly considered the idea of sending the U.S. ambassador to Mexico "as a secret emissary to see Castro and try to persuade him that letting the Soviets set up missile bases in his country was a suicidal act."[51]

In one of the most dramatic presidential addresses ever given to the nation, on October 22, Kennedy disclosed the discovery of the Soviet missiles in Cuba and the U.S. response. In announcing the imposition of a "strict quarantine" of all Soviet ships carrying "offensive military equipment" to Cuba, Kennedy promised both patience and resolve toward forcing the Soviets to dismantle the installations. "We will not prematurely or unnecessarily risk the costs of worldwide nuclear war in which even the fruits of victory would be ashes in our mouths—but neither will we shrink from that risk at any time it must be faced."[52]

As U.S. and Soviet naval forces approached one another on the seas off Cuba and the danger of a superpower confrontation escalated by the hour, the idea of a back-channel approach to Castro finally caught the president's interest. On October 24, the NSC outlined a four-point communication:

(a) Point out to him that just as the Soviets lied to us, they lied to the Cuban people; they are not going to bail him out.
(b) He, therefore, is under an obligation only to the Cuban people.
(c) There is only one course open to him—to expel the Soviets and their weapons, and make his peace with the Organization of American States (OAS) under its terms.
(d) He has only a short time to act.

A handwritten note by a member of the NSC staff succinctly summed up the approach: "Get word to Castro once ships turn back that if he kicks out Sovs we can live w. [with] him."[53]

As U.S. military planners pressed the president to set a date to attack Cuba, Kennedy instructed the ExComm to revisit "alternative courses of action."[54] In response, the State Department compiled a TOP SECRET options paper outlining a "Political Path" to resolving the crisis. One option was an "Approach to Castro," to be made "through a Latin American representative in Cuba, probably the Brazilian ambassador." The message would warn Castro that failure to expel the Soviets and their missiles would "result in the overthrow of his regime, if not its physical destruction." If he cooperated, however, an alternative message would be sent: "We would have to give some assurances, regardless of whether we intended to carry them out, that we would not ourselves undertake to overthrow the regime or support others trying to do so."[55]

At the ExComm meeting the next day, President Kennedy approved sending Castro a message, albeit disguised as a Brazilian communiqué. Once again, CIA director McCone objected, on the grounds that such a deal "would sort of insulate Castro from further actions." But the president overruled him. "I think we ought to concentrate on the missiles now," he determined. Kennedy's secret White House taping system captured his pessimism about this initiative. "It probably won't get anyplace" he mused, but "time is running out for us."[56]

In a TOP SECRET/EYES ONLY cable sent to Ambassador Lincoln Gordon in Rio de Janeiro, Rusk stated that it was time to "discuss with Castro alone RPT [repeat] alone" a way out of the missile crisis. He instructed Gordon to meet with Brazil's new prime minister, Hermes Lima, and ask him to have Brazil's ambassador to Havana, Luis Bastian Pinto, transmit this message to Castro as if it were a Brazilian initiative: "The action of the Soviet Union in using Cuban soil as sites for offensive nuclear missiles capable of striking most of the Western Hemisphere has placed the future of the Castro regime and the well-being of the Cuban people in great jeopardy." The Brazilian intermediary would then offer the carrot of better relations with the United States and the rest of Latin America if Castro would expel the Soviets and stop supporting revolutionaries in Latin America: "From such actions many changes in the relations between Cuba and the OAS countries, including the US, could flow." Finally, Bastian Pinto would tell Castro that "time was very short" for him to decide "whether to devote his great leadership abilities to the service of his Cuban peoples or to serving as a Soviet pawn."[57]

To disguise the origins of this message, U.S. Embassy officers translated it into Portuguese and typed it on plain paper. Ambassador Gordon then passed it to Brazil's foreign minister at a midnight meeting on October 27, emphasizing the "extreme importance of avoiding any indication that this [is] our idea." Gordon described the message as an "extremely important and sensitive diplomatic initiative . . . requiring utmost secrecy, with perhaps vital bearing on peace."[58]

But this peculiar back-channel effort did not go as planned. In addition to transmitting the U.S. message, President Goulart added a message of his own—that Brazil was "astounded and dismayed by [the] way in which Fidel had put Cuba in position of being mere merchandise of USSR to be traded for Turkish bases regardless of Cuban sovereignty."[59] And, instead of allowing Ambassador Bastian Pinto, who had previously dealt with Castro, to transmit the special message, the Brazilian courier, General José Albino da Silva, met with Fidel himself. Finally, by the time General Albino arrived in Havana on October 29, the Soviets had already announced they were withdrawing the missiles. Castro was openly incensed at Nikita Khrushchev for negotiating a deal to end the crisis without even consulting him.

On the morning of October 29, the angry Cuban leader went to the Brazilian Embassy to hear what General Albino had to say. He listened "with close attention and a certain degree of receptivity," Albino reported, as the Brazilian emissary presented proposals to move beyond the crisis into a new era of relations with the United States and Latin America.[60] The government of Brazil, Albino told him, "saw three essential conditions to passing through [the] crisis in Cuban relations with rest of hemisphere and normalizing them: "A) Demilitarization in sense of destruction of types of offensive weapons, bases, et cetera, which might be [a] base for Cuban armed attacks on neighbors; B) agreement to stop receiving arms which might accumulate war material exceeding needs for Cuban defense; C) abstention by Cuba from acting as [a] base for ideological aggression through export of propaganda, funds, et cetera."

In response, Castro had one demand: that the United States abandon its base at Guantánamo as a "condition of success in any set of negotiations for normalizing Cuban relations with the Hemisphere." Built at the turn of the century, the base had no real military relevance for the United States, Castro argued, and it was "humiliating for Cubans." In Ambassador Gordon's report to Washington on the talks, he noted that "injection of Guantánamo into discussions at this time would rule out any serious negotiation."[61]

With the protracted tensions in November and December over removing the Soviet missile systems from Cuba, this back-channel initiative went nowhere. Moreover, the Kennedy administration quickly soured on Brazil as a neutral intermediary, starting with Goulart's indiscreet leak of the initiative to the *New York Times*. The article, "Brazilian Reports Success in Cuban Conciliation Talks," quoted Albino as stating that his mission had been a "complete success" that saved Cuba from U.S. intervention and contributed "to the preservation of peace."[62] By trumpeting its role, the Goulart administration had violated its assurances that the mission would remain secret, Ambassador Gordon noted in an angry demarche to Prime Minister Lima several days later. The publicity could only "add to Castro's prestige and perhaps fortify his intransigence."[63]

Metadiplomacy: Donovan Returns

In the aftermath of the missile crisis, some hard-liners in the Kennedy administration saw an opportunity for the United States to get rid of Castro once and for all. CIA director John McCone and others lobbied hard—and successfully—for the president to forgo signing any UN agreement that would formalize the noninvasion pledge Washington made to end the crisis. For them, the latitude to overthrow the Cuban regime was more important than a formal, codified resolution to the most dangerous international crisis of the twentieth century.[64]

But while the CIA saw an opportunity to overthrow Castro, other officials saw an opportunity to reach an accommodation with him. They understood that the deal to end the crisis significantly raised the threshold of justification for any future invasion and that CIA covert operations were unlikely to bring about regime change. By January 1963, Bundy advised Kennedy that there was "well nigh universal agreement that Mongoose is at a dead end."[65] Indeed, the National Security Council would soon close it down. These policy makers noted that the breakdown in relations between Moscow and Havana had left Castro less intransigent and more inclined to reconsider his ties to the USSR—and to Washington. "The Soviet refusal to run the quarantine and its acquiescence in withdrawing the missiles shook the foundation of Cuban foreign policy," a State Department intelligence report, "Future Relations with Castro," concluded several months later. "Castro has indicated, sometimes vaguely, sometimes rather clearly, through various channels, public as well as private, that he is interested in an accommodation with the United States," the report continued. "His immediate disillusion over the Soviet missile crisis posture probably prompted him to grope for a policy which would diminish his dependence upon the Soviet Union."[66]

James Donovan was the first private channel through which Castro passed that indication. On November 20, 1962, Donovan reported to Attorney General Robert Kennedy that "Castro was anxious to conclude the transactions" over the Bay of Pigs prisoners.[67] The attorney general immediately moved into high gear to organize the government and the private sector to assist Donovan's negotiations, and he assigned a Kennedy associate, John Nolan, to help facilitate the terms of an agreement. Kennedy instructed Donovan to return to Cuba and finalize the deal for their release by Christmas day.[68]

When Donovan arrived in Havana on December 18, the Cubans received him with something akin to the red carpet treatment. The foreign minister greeted him at the airport and told him a special wood humidor filled with cigars awaited him as a gift from Fidel Castro. Castro met Donovan soon after he arrived and immediately agreed that Christmas seemed an appropriate deadline.

As final negotiations got down to the nuts and bolts, however, complications arose. Despite Donovan's efforts to substitute food and medicine for the $2.9 million in cash that Castro had demanded for releasing the original sick and wounded prisoners, the Cuban leader refused to budge. The Cubans judged the list of goods that Donovan had assembled to be unacceptable. Donovan was forced to arrange for the immediate trip of former U.S. surgeon general Leonard Schecle to Havana on December 20, to help Cuban officials understand the nature of the pharmaceuticals the United States proposed to ship. When Castro expressed considerable skepticism about the size of the first shipment that had already been loaded onto a freighter called the *African Pilot*, Donovan arranged a clandestine night visit of three Cuban Red Cross members to inspect the cargo. The whole prisoner release deal almost fell apart when the three Cubans deemed specific items on board to be unacceptable and demanded they be removed. Only when Nolan threatened to expose their presence in Miami to the anti-Castro exile community did they abandon their efforts to hold up the shipment.[69]

On December 21, Cuban officials and members of the Families Committee finally signed a memorandum of agreement for the release of the prisoners. The agreement assured the delivery, in stages, of $53 million in foodstuffs, medicines, and related equipment by July 1, 1963, with the prisoners being released "upon delivery of the first shipment covered by the letter of credit." When the *African Pilot* docked in Havana Harbor on December 23, the first airlift of prisoners began to leave from the San Antonio de los Baños airport. A second airlift scheduled for Christmas Eve was almost canceled when Castro demanded the $2.9 million that the Families Committee had committed to when the initial sixty prisoners had been released the previous April. In less than twenty-four hours, Robert Kennedy personally secured the money from two donors and the evacuation continued.[70]

How Porcupines Make Love

The successful liberation of the captured Bay of Pigs brigade set the stage for extended talks between Donovan and Castro that increasingly focused

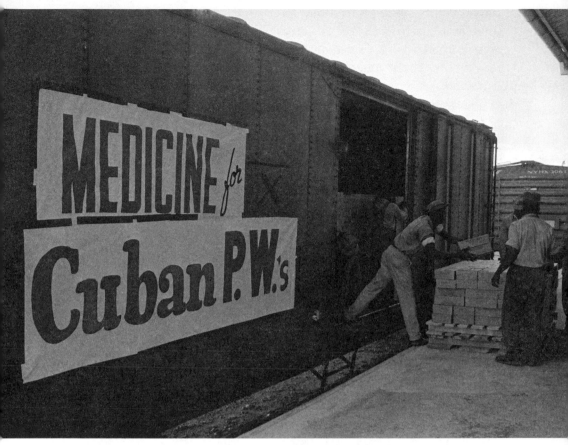

Longshoremen unload food and medicine bound for Cuba in the Bay of Pigs prisoner exchange, December 20, 1962. The deal was negotiated with Fidel Castro by New York attorney James Donovan, secretly acting on behalf of the U.S. government. (AP Photo)

on improving U.S.-Cuban relations. Donovan laid the groundwork for future negotiations by asking Castro "to offer me a Christmas present"—the release of several dozen U.S. citizens arrested as spies and saboteurs after the revolution. (The Cuban government considered all of them CIA operatives; three of them actually were.) At the eleventh hour of the Bay of Pigs prisoner talks, the CIA had asked Donovan to add the U.S. prisoners to his negotiating agenda with Castro. "Jesus Christ," Donovan complained to Kennedy associate John Nolan when he got the request. "I did the loaves and fishes, and now they want me to walk on water, too!"[71]

Castro demurred on releasing the U.S. prisoners along with the brigade members, but he left the door open for future talks if the shipments of food and medicines continued smoothly. "You and I have always dealt together in good faith," Castro said. "For this reason, you are entitled to say that if the present negotiation is carried out in good faith, you have my pledge of an early review of every American case for amnesty in the near future."[72]

In their last substantive conversation before Donovan returned to the States, the two again expressed their mutual respect. "I want you to know that I appreciate your cooperation in many things throughout our negotiations," Donovan told Castro. He then paid a high compliment to Cuba's maximum leader: "You have been very correct in your dealings with me." Fidel returned the favor, telling Donovan that he was more than a skilled negotiator; he was an American from whom Castro could learn. He invited Donovan to come back over the winter with his family for a vacation in a Varadero villa. "I would like to come out and you, Vallejo and I . . . will discuss the entire future of Cuba and Latin America and their relations with the United States," Castro continued. "I believe that we want the same things, and the question is how to accomplish this."[73]

On January 25, Donovan returned to Cuba for what he described as "the most cordial and intimate meeting to date" with Castro. Indeed, Castro welcomed him as a friend and a hero. During a visit to a medical school, Fidel led three hundred students in chanting "viva Donovan."[74] The two agreed to a prisoner exchange: Castro would release the U.S. citizens, and in return the U.S. would release four Cubans—one convicted of second-degree murder in the accidental shooting of a nine-year-old Venezuelan girl during a melee with anti-Castro Cubans in September 1960, and three arrested in the fall of 1962 on charges of plotting acts of sabotage in New York.

Castro invited Donovan to return to Cuba in March to finalize the exchange and indicated that "he wished to talk at length . . . about the future of Cuba and international relations." As Donovan boarded his plane to Miami, Fidel's aide de camp, René Vallejo, provided a clue as to what was on Castro's mind. Vallejo, Donovan reported to the State Department and the CIA the next day, "broached the subject of re-establishing diplomatic relations with the U.S."[75]

The debriefing report on Donovan's trip "looked interesting," President Kennedy remarked when he read it.[76] Castro's clear readiness to discuss better bilateral relations, and the evident rapport between him and Donovan, caught the attention of Kennedy and his top aides. As Donovan prepared to pursue his shuttle diplomacy in the spring of 1963, U.S. officials began evaluating the potential for using him as an intermediary to talk to Castro about broader U.S.-Cuban relations.

As the agency most responsible for handling Donovan's mission, the CIA drafted its own proposed "Instructions for James Donovan."[77] The United

States had missed its opportunity to overthrow Castro by force during the missile crisis "when the provocation was obvious and clearly demonstrable to the world," the CIA lamented, and Castro was too strong to be overthrown by exiles without direct U.S. military intervention. Therefore, "political warfare to persuade Castro to break with the Communists and restore some form of relations with the United States" had become an obvious option. "There seems to be some possibility that Castro might be weaned away from the Communists if his idealism, his nationalism and his vanity were all properly catered to," according the CIA drafters. "This is where Donovan comes in." His "time with Castro will provide the United States Government an invaluable opportunity to affect the course of events in Cuba." The CIA's instructions addressed three "potentialities of the Castro discussions":

First, Castro should be told that he must get the Russians out of Cuba lock, stock and barrel. This theme which should bear some success with Castro because he is beyond question disillusioned with his Soviet friends as a result of their removing the missiles and bombers, apparently without consultation or notice.

Second, Castro must agree to stop all Communist subversion efforts directed at Latin America. There is hope in this line also. At his last meeting he told Donovan that he thought there was the possibility of reform in Latin America without revolution between now and 1970. He must recognize that the Alliance for Progress has many of the same objectives as his revolution. . . .

Third, Castro should be persuaded to throw the Communists out of his government and to renounce his "Marxist-Leninist" thesis. As far as getting rid of his Communist associates is concerned, there are some indications that there are splits in the Cuban hierarchy. Further, Castro can be given plenty of illustrations of the dangers of his position and the fact that if he doesn't get rid of the others, they will inevitably get rid of him.[78]

If Castro agreed to all these things, the CIA instructed, Donovan could make the vague suggestion that Washington would consider softening its hostile policies toward Cuba. But if the carrots did not work, Donovan could always return to the threat of the stick. The CIA recommended that he "paint for Castro a glowing picture of what could be done for Cuba as a friend of the United States in contrast with the permanently black picture that will prevail—with only one ultimate result—if Cuba continues to make the United States her enemy."[79]

Both the State Department and the White House also took up the issue of Donovan's instructions. The State Department's Cuba desk officer, Robert Hurwitch, suggested that Donovan go to Cuba "for a week-long walk on the beach with Castro," with the following instructions: "Only two things are non-negotiable, 1) Cuba's ties with the Sino-Soviet bloc, and 2) Cuba's interference with the hemisphere." Hurwitch's concept, as Gordon Chase reported to McGeorge Bundy, was that Donovan would act as "a transmitter to the U.S. Government of any proposals Castro might make in response to this line."[80]

But when Bundy briefed the president on this strategy, Kennedy overruled it as too stringent. He wanted a more flexible approach. "The President does not agree that we should make the breaking of Sino/Soviet ties a non-negotiable point," stated a March 4, 1963, memorandum from Bundy recording Kennedy's reaction. "We don't want to present Castro with a condition that he obviously cannot fulfill. We should start thinking along more flexible lines." In addition, Kennedy recommended giving Donovan "some flies to dangle in front of Castro." The president's surprising position "must be kept close to the vest," the TOP SECRET/EYES ONLY memo advised. "The President, himself, is very interested in this one."[81]

The President's interest was held so close to the vest that Donovan apparently never received the green light to fully engage Castro on broader talks; the historical record reveals no indication that he was briefed on President Kennedy's desire for a more "flexible" approach. Instead, on March 12, Donovan received "negotiating instructions" from Robert Kennedy to "obtain the release of all US citizens in prison" but to avoid raising broader U.S.-Cuban relations. "You should *not* initiate any discussions of a political nature with Castro," the attorney general told Donovan. "Should Castro initiate such discussions, you should listen carefully, but reply only the minimum that common courtesy would dictate."[82]

When Donovan returned to Havana on March 14, his talks with Castro focused on the fate of nine additional imprisoned U.S. citizens—hapless skin divers whose life raft had washed up on a Cuban beach after their boat sank. If Donovan could convince him that they were not saboteurs, Castro said, he would let them go. In their negotiations, they agreed to avoid defining the exchange as a prisoner swap. Castro would grant clemency to the American prisoners in recognition of the final April shipments of medicine from the Bay of Pigs deal; the United States would subsequently release the four Cuban prisoners, also as an act of clemency. When Donovan left, Castro allowed him to take two American women—Geraldine Shamma and

Fidel Castro and James Donovan on a fishing trip at the Bay of Pigs, April 8, 1963. In 1962 Donovan successfully negotiated with Castro for the release of Bay of Pigs prisoners, and shortly after this meeting they agreed to an exchange of U.S. citizens held in Cuba for Cubans jailed in the United States. (Courtesy of John Donovan)

Martha O'Neal, who both had been jailed in 1960 for counterrevolutionary activities—back to Miami, as a gesture of goodwill.

Donovan returned to Havana on April 5. In hopes of finalizing the prisoner exchange, he brought three diplomatic props: his teenage son, who he hoped "would inspire confidence and make a favorable impression on Castro"; the now famous scuba-diving wetsuit (that the CIA's directorate of operations had wanted to contaminate with a toxic poison) as a gift for Castro; and the page proofs of a forthcoming article in the *Nation* magazine titled "How Metadiplomacy Works: James Donovan and Castro" which highlighted the potential for the prisoner exchange to set the stage "for some sort of conciliation between the American and Cuban people."[83] Castro responded positively. During their four-day visit he took Donovan and his son on a fishing expedition to the Bay of Pigs—Fidel personally speared fifteen fish, one of them a forty-pounder—gave them a tour of a new crocodile farm nearby, and arranged for them to attend a baseball game.

The negotiations also progressed. Despite his instructions not to raise the broader issue of bilateral ties, Donovan deftly used the *Nation* article to dangle the prospect of normalization of relations if the prisoner release succeeded. During a discussion with Castro that lasted from 2:15 to 6:30am, Donovan actually read the *Nation* story out loud—with René Vallejo translating.[84] Written by a veteran *New York Times* magazine reporter Gertrude Samuels, it quoted Donovan as stating, "I do believe that in these negotiations there does lie the greatest hope of creating some equitable solution to the problems now affecting relations between the two countries."[85] The article, along with others in *Look*, *Life*, and the *Saturday Evening Post*, Donovan suggested to Castro, reflected a shift in American attitudes toward the Cuban revolution in the aftermath of the missile crisis. The average citizen, Donovan said, "simply could not see involving the U.S. in nuclear warfare to vaguely restore Cuba to Batistaville." Castro was "extremely interested," Donovan later recounted in his CIA debriefing. He "thought that this article was excellent, that it showed wisdom."[86]

Their discussion of the *Nation* article led to the first serious conversation about how to restore relations between Washington and Havana. For the first time, Fidel Castro personally expressed his interest directly to a U.S. representative. He suggested that "perhaps the time was here for the Kennedy administration to adopt . . . a more statesman-like approach" to Cuba policy. "If any relations were to commence between the U.S. and Cuba," Fidel wanted to know, "how it would come about and what would be involved?"

In his debriefing at the CIA, Donovan noted his candid, and blunt, response:

> I told him that I was sure that if anything such as this occurred that just as no one in the U.S. wanted to see him as a satellite of Russia and wind up as another Bulgaria or Romania, so too I didn't think that the people of the U.S. were intent on his being a satellite of the U.S.; that the integrity of the revolution would be respected as long as his every effort was dedicated to the betterment of the Cuban people and not being a pawn of Russia and not trying to ferment internal conflict in the other Latin American countries.[87]

Castro then returned to his central concern: "He said, well, in view of the past history on both sides here, the problem of how to inaugurate any relations was a very difficult one." Donovan replied: "So I said to him, well, do you, are you familiar with porcupines, and this had to be translated by Vallejo, but they finally agreed that he did understand porcupines. So I said, now do you know how porcupines make love? And he said no. And I said well, the answer is 'very carefully,' and that's how you and the U.S. would have to get into this."[88] As Donovan told Castro, "I think an accommodation of views could be worked out."

In the end, the Cuban leader seemed convinced by Donovan's arguments that the prisoners created a stumbling block to better relations with the United States. "Now that you've shown me the article in *The Nation*," Castro told Donovan, "I'm prepared to take a chance on your analysis of the situation and your prophecies on what should happen." Holding the Americans as "a bargaining asset" was not in Cuba's interest, he conceded, because "perhaps it's preventing something more constructive from being accomplished."[89] He agreed to immediately free the nine skin divers and one U.S. missionary for Donovan to take back to Florida. As for the remaining American prisoners, Castro promised that if Donovan returned on April 22, "I'll release all of them to you."[90]

Two weeks later, Donovan returned to Havana one last time. As promised, Castro released twenty-seven more U.S. citizens; twenty-one of them, including the three CIA agents, returned with the U.S. negotiator to an Air Force base near Miami. The same day, Kennedy's Justice Department released the four Cubans in New York "in the national interest."[91] They were flown to Florida and then repatriated to Havana.

In all, Donovan's protracted negotiations with Castro yielded impressive results: the release of 1,113 Bay of Pigs prisoners—along with several thousand of their relatives—and thirty-nine U.S. citizens, among them three CIA agents. More importantly, he established himself as the first U.S. emissary to win Castro's trust and respect, personally creating a foundation for future dialogue between Havana and Washington. And during the last hours of his last trip, Donovan inadvertently set the stage for another cycle of back-channel talks between Cuba and the United States: he introduced Fidel Castro to a striking blonde reporter from ABC News named Lisa Howard.

The Lisa Howard Initiative

Lisa Howard was the Barbara Walters of her day—a gender barrier–breaking correspondent for ABC News with a special forte for obtaining exclusive, publicity-generating interviews with world-class political leaders. Her rise to stardom began as a Hollywood actress, known for roles as the vixen in a variety of movies and television shows, including CBS's popular soap operas, *Edge of Night* and *As the World Turns*. In 1953 *People Today* dubbed her TV's "first lady of sin." According to the prefeminist-era profile, "though a looker (5'3; 109 lbs; 35-23-35 from bust to hips), Miss Sin prefers to think of herself as the 'sensitive-intellectual type' who is 'going places.'"[92] Indeed, a far different profile of her ten years later in *Time Magazine* reflected how far she had traveled. "Lisa Howard has become television's first and only woman with her own network news show. Lisa has achieved this distinction by scrambling harder than six monkeys peeling the same banana," *Time* reported. "Political leaders, domestic and foreign, have learned there is no dodging Lisa Howard."[93]

Nikita Khrushchev became the first world leader to learn that lesson. After Howard emerged on the media scene as a volunteer stringer for the Mutual Radio Network in 1960, she became the first U.S. journalist to score a substantive interview with the Soviet premier by sneaking into the Russian mission in New York disguised as a washer woman and then following Khrushchev out to his limousine to convince him to grant her an exclusive. She then covered the 1960 Democratic National Convention, obtaining a major interview with the young senator from Massachusetts, John F. Kennedy. Since she already knew Kennedy and Khrushchev—more importantly, they knew her—ABC News hired her as their first female correspondent to cover the 1961 Vienna Summit. There, she ambushed Khrushchev in a public park, thrust a microphone into his face and, with the cameras rolling, grabbed Foreign Minister Andrei Gromyko to translate for the Soviet leader. As a reward for her success, ABC promoted her to anchor her own television news program—"Lisa Howard and News with a Woman's Touch."[94]

In 1962 Howard set her sights on another world-famous communist leader, Fidel Castro. She began peppering Cuba's UN mission with requests to go to Havana: "I am the girl who interviewed Khrushchev," she reminded Cuban officials. The American public wanted to know more about the Cuban revolution, she wrote; an ABC interview with Castro would serve the interests of both countries.[95]

In April 1963, Howard finally received permission to bring a TV crew to Cuba. But for several weeks, Castro ignored her. In desperation, she prevailed on Donovan, who was in Havana on his last trip, to arrange an introduction. Howard "begged me to use my influence with Castro to gain an interview for her," Donovan recalled in his unpublished memoir. "I went about it by whetting Castro's natural masculine curiosity and vanity. I told him there was a beautiful blonde dish of a reporter wanting to interview him and would he give her some of his time."[96] Castro did. He granted Howard an exclusive televised interview at the Hotel Riviera—his first with a U.S. network since 1959, and a major journalistic coup for ABC News.

When Howard's hour-long TV special, *Fidel Castro: Self Portrait*, aired on May 10, 1963, it generated instant headlines across the nation. "Castro Applauds U.S. 'Peace Steps,'" was the title of the *New York Times* front-page story, "Castro Makes Overt Hints He Wants Kennedy Parlay," the *Chicago Sun Times* announced. "Castro Would Like to Talk with Kennedy," blared the headline of the *Cleveland Plain Dealer*. During the interview, Fidel pointed to the prisoner negotiations with Donovan as "a beginning point for discussions. If the United States wants it, it is the beginning of better relations." A rapprochement was "possible if the United States government wishes it," Castro told Howard on camera. "In that case we would be agreed to seek and find the basis" for normalizing relations.[97]

Publicly, Lisa Howard pushed this angle of her interview. The press materials distributed to promote the broadcast stated that "the interview indicates that there is a possibility of a fresh dialogue between the United States and Cuba, however limited and tentative it may be in this highly inflammatory corner of the Cold War." In a subsequent cover story, "Castro's Overture," for the liberal journal *War/Peace Report*, Howard wrote that in eight hours of private conversation Castro had been "even more emphatic about his desire for negotiations with the United States. In our conversations he made it quite clear that he was ready to discuss: the Soviet personnel and military hardware on Cuban soil; compensation for expropriated American lands and investments; the question of Cuba as a base for Communist subversion throughout the Hemisphere." She urged Kennedy to "send an American government official on a quiet mission to Havana to see what Castro has to say." A country as powerful as the United States, she concluded, "has nothing to lose at a bargaining table with Fidel Castro."[98]

Privately, Howard fully committed herself to bringing those negotiations to fruition. To Castro, she conveyed this commitment in an extraordinary letter—"a little keepsake," she called it—written to him on Hotel Riviera stationary on April 27, after their interview. In her letter, Howard spoke to Castro candidly about her disagreement with the communist direction he had chosen. "I disapprove of much of your revolution as it exists today, and wish with all my being that events could have taken a different course." Still, she believed that Castro was among a rare group of men "who point the way" toward "the betterment of the human condition." Howard then made Fidel an offer. "And if in some small way, I can be privileged to help you play out that role I shall do all in my power to achieve this end," she wrote. "I am going to talk to certain people when I return to the States. I am going to tell them many things. I do not overestimate my influence. But I shall try to help."[99]

Ironically, the "certain people" Howard decided to talk to were Castro's archenemies inside the U.S. government—the CIA. Immediately upon returning from Cuba on April 30, the CIA debriefed her in Miami on Castro's views.[100] In a SECRET memorandum given to President Kennedy on May 1, CIA deputy director for plans Richard Helms reported on Howard's conclusion that "Fidel Castro is looking for a way to reach a rapprochement with the United States." Howard already had a list of acceptable intermediaries—Donovan and UN ambassador Adlai Stevenson among them—to pursue a dialogue, and offered to "arrange a meeting for any U.S. government spokesman with Castro through Vallejo, who will be the point of contact." Helm's report concluded, "Howard definitely wants to impress the U.S. Government with two facts: Castro is ready to discuss rapprochement and she herself is ready to discuss it with him if asked to do so by the U.S. Government."[101]

CIA director John McCone adamantly opposed this approach to Cuba, as he had opposed all previous initiatives, arguing that it would leak and compromise CIA operations against Castro. A secret letter rushed to the White House the next day conveyed McCone's recommendation that the "Lisa Howard report be handled in the most limited and sensitive manner" and "that no active steps be taken on the rapprochement matter at this time." McCone urged only the "most limited Washington discussions" on accommodation with Castro, and only in the context of "the rapprochement track being explored as a remote possibility and one of several alternatives."[102]

Exploring the "Sweet Approach"

Despite McCone's opposition, senior White House officials were already evaluating the "rapprochement track" as an alternative to overthrowing Castro. The catalyst for this debate was Bundy's young NSC deputy for Latin America, Gordon Chase. On April 11, in a TOP SECRET/EYES ONLY memo to his boss, Chase made an articulate pitch for what he called a "quiet policy turn-around" on Cuba. "We are all concerned about solving our Cuba problem," his memo began, "but so far, we have been looking seriously at only one side of the coin—ways to hurt Castro by varying degrees of overt and covert nastiness."

> We have not yet looked seriously at the other side of the coin—quietly enticing Castro over to us. If the sweet approach turned out to be

feasible and, in turn, successful, the benefits would be substantial. In the short run, we would probably be able to neutralize at least 2 of our main worries about Castro—the reintroduction of offensive missiles and Cuban subversion. In the long run, we would be able to work on eliminating Castro at our leisure and from a good vantage point.

Such a radical reconsideration of U.S. policy toward the Cuban revolution would not be easily achieved, Chase acknowledged. But "while the practical obstacles to this sort of approach may be immense," he concluded, "they may not be insuperable." With Kennedy's hawkish aides pushing him to toward "more violent solutions to the Cuban problem," Chase suggested, the president might also want to consider the "feasibility" of a "policy turn-around."[103]

Just ten days after receiving Chase's memo, Bundy launched a major review of policy toward Cuba. Washington, he argued, had essentially three options: overthrow Castro, which would probably require direct intervention; contain Castro, while trying to extract major concessions from him by pressure; or develop "some form of accommodation with Castro." In a memorandum titled "The Cuban Problem," Bundy provided the rationale for accommodation:

> Faint hints of this possibility appear in Donovan explorations and elsewhere. There is always the possibility that Castro or others currently high in the regime might find advantage in a gradual shift away from their present level of dependence on Moscow. In strictly economic terms, both the United States and Cuba have much to gain from reestablishment of relations. A Titoist Castro is not inconceivable and a full diplomatic revolution would not be the most extraordinary event in the 20th century.[104]

By June the CIA had accumulated intelligence from at least a half-dozen sources besides Lisa Howard "suggesting Cuban interest in a rapprochement with the United States," according to a SECRET memorandum from Deputy Director for Plans Richard Helms.[105] On June 6 the "Special Group"—the high-level interagency committee responsible for covert action against Cuba—"discussed various possibilities of establishing channels of communication to Castro" and agreed it was "a useful endeavor."[106] The CIA's sources indicated that James Donovan would be acceptable to the Cubans as a negotiator, but Washington would have to take the first step. "The U.S. does not understand that Latin pride will not permit Cuba to humiliate itself in the eyes of the world by making the first overture," another diplomatic source indicated, but the United States could "afford to be charitable and take the initiative."[107]

Most members of Kennedy's national security team were not feeling charitable toward Cuba, however. As they debated Bundy's options during the spring, few of them found the "sweet approach" very attractive. Secretary of Defense McNamara argued that "the elimination of the Castro regime was a requirement" and that, if "our present policy would not result in its downfall, we should develop a program for approval which would produce changes acceptable to us." Robert Kennedy agreed, calling for "a program with the objective of overthrowing Castro in eighteen months."[108] McCone argued that Castro's trips to Moscow in April and May had repaired the breach in relations caused by the missile crisis, so there was no longer any opening for negotiations to exploit. Any rapprochement that retained Soviet troops in Cuba and maintained Cuba as a closed society "could not be acceptable to the U.S.," McCone declared. It would be "out of the question."[109]

The Latin American bureau at the State Department was equally recalcitrant. Any accommodation would require the United States to accept the permanence of Castro's communism. "The precedent would be established for other communist regimes in the hemisphere and the whole effort to keep them out of this area and to establish its special status would fall to the ground," the bureau warned apocalyptically. "It could mean the death of the Inter-American System." Besides, Assistant Secretary of State Edwin Martin explained, it was no use trying to wean Cuba from Moscow by offering him inducements because Castro would "make promises and not keep them. . . . He did not stay bought."[110]

Through meeting after meeting of the NSC Standing Group, Bundy kept putting the negotiations option back on the table, with some support from Rusk, but he could get no traction with other senior officials. In June, the review of Cuba policy concluded with the approval of a new set of covert paramilitary plans to harass Castro—"Autonomous Operations" in which exiles would essentially conduct their own sabotage operations with U.S. financing but not control—even though no one believed they would topple the regime.[111]

With the Kennedy White House unwilling to take action on Castro's feelers for a dialogue, Lisa Howard stepped forward and seized the initiative herself. She instigated the first face-to-face meeting between U.S. and Cuban officials in the United States—with such diplomatic dexterity that each side believed the other had made the first overture.

In September, Howard developed her own trustworthy back channel into the administration, through a fellow journalist-turned-diplomat, William

Attwood. As the former editor of *Look Magazine* who had once interviewed Castro himself, Attwood knew Howard and shared her belief that improved U.S.-Cuban relations were possible and—from the perspective of U.S. national interests—preferable. At the United Nations, where he was special advisor to Ambassador Adlai Stevenson, Attwood had heard that Castro was unhappy with his Soviet satellite status and would go to some length to obtain normalization of relations with the United States. Howard's *War/Peace* article, which Attwood read, seemed to convey the same sentiment. On September 12, Attwood and Howard discussed the article on the phone—and Howard convinced him that the Cubans were interested in talks with Washington. The two then hatched a plan to initiate a discreet, secret dialogue between Washington and Havana.[112]

Over the next six days, Attwood drafted a two-page "Memorandum on Cuba," for Ambassador Stevenson and Undersecretary of State W. Averell Harriman that laid out the rationale for a low-profile contact with Cuban authorities. The impact of present U.S. policy, he wrote, "is mainly negative: a. It aggravates Castro's anti-Americanism and his desire to cause us trouble and embarrassment; b. In the eyes of the world largely made up of small countries, it freezes us in the unattractive posture of a big country trying to bully a small country." Since the United States was not going to overthrow Castro by overt force, why not explore a dialogue? "It would seem that we have something to gain and nothing to lose by finding out whether in fact Castro does want to talk and what concessions he would be prepared to make," Attwood concluded.[113]

Stevenson liked Attwood's proposal, though he had doubts about whether it would fly. "Unfortunately," he told Attwood, "the CIA is still in charge of Cuba." But when Stevenson spoke to Kennedy about the idea in New York on September 20, the president authorized Attwood to contact Cuban officials at the UN. "I then told Miss Howard to set up the contact, that is to have a small reception at her house so that it could be done very casually, not as a formal approach by us," Attwood would later recall.[114] In the middle of the UN delegates lounge on September 23, Howard approached Cuba's UN ambassador Carlos Lechuga and, according to his recollection, said that Attwood "wanted to talk to me and that it was urgent." Howard invited Lechuga to come to a party at her Central Park apartment that very evening to meet Attwood.[115]

In the midst of cocktails, finger foods, and several dozen members of New York's high society, the first bilateral talks on the potential for a U.S.-Cuban accommodation took place. Standing in a corner of Howard's spacious living room, Attwood and Lechuga conferred on the interest of their respective leaders in what Attwood called "an exchange of views." Castro, Lechuga told Attwood, "had hoped to contact or get in touch with President Kennedy in '61 and then came the Bay of Pigs and that was that." But Lechuga "hinted that Castro was indeed in the mood to talk," Attwood recalled, and "thought there was a good chance I might be invited to Cuba if I wished to talk to Castro." As Lechuga remembers the conversation, it was Attwood who suggested going to Havana, stating that he was about "to request authorization from the President to go to Cuba to meet with Fidel Castro and ask about the feasibility of a rapprochement between Havana and Washington."[116]

The next day, Attwood met with Robert Kennedy in Washington, D.C., and reported on the cocktail party dialogue. The attorney general reacted positively if cautiously. "If the United States could get something going of a positive nature with Cuba, that would lift the burden of the Bay of Pigs and the whole Cuban mess off of the Administration, that would be a plus," Attwood recalled him saying. "But it had to be Castro's initiative. It could not look as though the United States was seeking an accommodation."[117] Kennedy worried "that the trip to Cuba . . . would be rather risky, said it was bound to leak and said it might result in some Congressional investigation or something," Attwood later testified. "Anyway, it might be a problem. But he did think the matter was worth pursuing."[118]

So did the White House. Throughout the fall of 1963, a small group within the Kennedy administration explored this new back-channel dialogue with Cuba. "This whole operation was very closely held," Attwood recalled; besides himself, only the president, Attorney General, Bundy, Chase, Stevenson, and Harriman knew of it.[119] Bundy designated Chase to be Attwood's direct contact. Attwood was instructed to tell Lechuga that a meeting in Havana would be "difficult . . . in light of my official status," but that he was authorized to meet a high-level Cuban emissary at the UN. Lisa Howard offered her home as a communications center for Attwood to send a message, via phone, directly to Castro through his aide de camp, René Vallejo. On October 20, she placed a call to Vallejo "to make certain that Castro knew there was a U.S. official available if Castro wanted to talk."[120]

On October 31, Vallejo reached Howard and conveyed Castro's interest in proceeding. "Castro would very much like to talk to the U.S. official anytime and appreciated the importance of discretion of all concerned," Attwood wrote in his notes on Howard's report on the conversation. "Castro would therefore be willing to send a plane to Mexico to pick up the official and fly him to a private airport near Varadero where Castro could talk to him alone." To Vallejo, Howard voiced her doubts that a U.S. official would risk going to Cuba; she urged him to consider coming to the UN or arranging to meet in Mexico. "Vallejo replied that Castro wanted to do the talking himself, but did not completely rule out this situation if there was no other way of engaging a dialogue."[121]

Castro's invitation set off a flurry of discussion inside the administration, including the Oval Office. On November 5, Bundy briefed President Kennedy on Castro's meeting proposal. "Bill Attwood has partly generated, and partly responded to feelers from Castro and now has an invitation to go down and talk to Fidel about terms and conditions in which he would be interested in a change of relations with the U.S.," Bundy told the president. "Normally I would not recommend someone so close to us, but Bill does have the advantage that he knows Castro." Kennedy's taping system recorded his concern about how the secret mission would stay secret. "How can Attwood get in and out of there very privately," the president asked. "Can we get Attwood off the payroll before he goes?" Bundy and Kennedy then discussed the need for a "cover plan" if the trip leaked to the press, and the possibility of "sanitizing" Attwood—retiring him from his UN post for at least "a month or two"—before undertaking the secret dialogue.[122]

Despite the political sensitivity, Kennedy wanted to move forward, albeit cautiously. As Bundy told Attwood, "The President was more in favor of pushing towards an opening toward Cuba than was the State Department, the idea being—well, getting them out of the Soviet fold and perhaps wiping out the Bay of Pigs and maybe getting back to normal."[123] However, it "did not seem practicable" to send him to Cuba "at this stage." The White House preferred to begin with a meeting between Vallejo and Attwood at the United Nations and expected Vallejo to speak to a change in Castro's position on the issues that concerned Washington—an end to Soviet influence and Cuban subversion in the region. As Bundy indicated in a SECRET/SENSITIVE memorandum for the record dated November 12, "Reversals of these policies may or may not be sufficient to produce a change in the policy of the United States, but they are certainly necessary, and without an indication of readiness to move in these directions, it is hard for us to see what could be accomplished by a visit to Cuba." Attwood summarized the impasse: "The President decided it might be useful for me to go down to Cuba and see Castro, but first we'd have to know what the agenda was."[124]

Again, Lisa Howard played the role of facilitator. On November 14, she told Vallejo that the U.S. preferred a preliminary meeting in New York to set the agenda for any substantive secret dialogue in Havana. She then arranged for Vallejo to talk directly to Attwood on the evening of November 18. That night, Attwood came to Howard's apartment at midnight. The two spent a couple of hours drinking bourbon, listening to jazz, and talking about Camus as Howard telephoned Havana at least a half dozen times trying to locate Vallejo. Finally after 2:00 A.M., she reached him at his home and handed Attwood the phone. As Attwood reported to the White House:

> I told him Miss Howard had kept me informed of her talks with him and that I assumed he knew of our interest in hearing what Castro had in mind. Vallejo said he did, and reiterated the invitation to come to Cuba, stressing the fact that security could be guaranteed. I replied that we felt a preliminary meeting was essential to make sure there was something useful to talk about, and asked if he was able to come to New York. Vallejo said he could not come "at this time." However, if that's how we felt, he said that "we" would send instructions to Lechuga to propose and discuss with me "an agenda for a later meeting with Castro." I said I would await Lechuga's call.[125]

When Attwood passed this information on to Bundy later that day, he was told that when the agenda was received, "the President wanted to see me at the White House and decide what to say and whether to go [to Cuba] or what we should do next."

"That was the nineteenth of November," Attwood recalled, "three days before the assassination."[126]

Kennedy's Last Effort

In the seventy-two hours before his death, President Kennedy himself sent two messages to Castro. The first came in the form of a speech before the Inter-American Press Association in Miami on November 18. Cuba had become "a weapon in an effort dictated by external powers to subvert the other American republics," Kennedy stated. "This and this alone divides us. As long as this is true, nothing is possible. Without it, everything is possible."[127] According to White House aide Arthur Schlesinger Jr., who helped write the speech, Kennedy's language was intended to convey to Castro the potential for normalization.[128] But like so much of Kennedy's Cuba policy, the suggestion of reconciliation came packaged in tough rhetoric. The olive branch was so well camouflaged that the *Los Angeles Times* headline the next day read, "Kennedy Urges Cuban Revolt."[129]

Kennedy reinforced his indirect message of possible détente with a more explicit one delivered by French journalist Jean Daniel. Daniel met privately with Kennedy in late October on his way to Havana—a meeting arranged by Attwood to focus the president's attention on Cuba.[130] Kennedy shared with

Journalist Jean Daniel with Fidel Castro on the eve of President John F. Kennedy's assassination. Daniel was carrying a message from Kennedy offering the possibility of reconciliation between Cuba and the United States. (Magnum Photos/Marc Riboud)

Daniel the point he would make in the speech—the trade embargo could be lifted if Castro ended his support for leftist movements in the hemisphere. The president also expressed some empathy for Castro's anti-Americanism, acknowledging that the United States had committed a "number of sins" in prerevolutionary Cuba, including turning the island into "the whorehouse of the U.S."[131]

"Now," Kennedy acknowledged, "we shall have to pay for those sins."

Daniel observed that the president seemed to be "seeking a way out" of the poor state of relations with Cuba. Kennedy asked him to "come back and see me" after conferring with Fidel. "This conversation will be much more interesting when you return."

"When I left him," Daniel recalled, "I had the impression I was a messenger of peace."

Daniel passed Kennedy's message to Castro during their first meeting on November 20, and the two discussed it again as they sat down to lunch on a beautiful day in Varadero Beach on November 22. "He listened to me intently. He was drinking my words," Daniel recalled in an interview forty years later. "Clearly he was happy about the message I was delivering. Sometimes he would say, 'Maybe he has changed. Maybe things are possible with this man.'" Kennedy could become "the greatest president of the United States, the leader who may at last understand that there can be coexistence between capitalists and socialists, even in the Americas," Fidel exclaimed. He asked Daniel to take a message back. "So far as we are concerned, everything can be restored to normalcy on the basis of mutual respect of sovereignty."

In Daniel's estimation, both Kennedy and Castro "seemed ready to make peace." Then, Castro received the news that Kennedy had been shot in Dallas. "This is terrible," Castro exclaimed. "They are going to say we did it." On a radio in the house, the two finally found a Florida station to listen to the reports of the assassination. Angry and shocked, Castro railed about the "disgusting" and indecent details being broadcast of Kennedy's blood running on his wife's stockings. He turned to Daniel and acknowledged the obvious: "This is the end of your mission of peace."

"I was thinking the same thing," Daniel recalled. "If I could not go back and tell Kennedy about my mission, [then] there was no mission."

3. JOHNSON
Castro Reaches Out

Tell the President (and I cannot stress this too strongly) that I seriously hope that Cuba and the United States can eventually sit down in an atmosphere of good will and of mutual respect and negotiate our differences. I believe that there are *no* areas of contention between us that cannot be discussed and settled within a climate of mutual understanding. . . . Tell the President that he should not interpret my conciliatory attitude, my desire for discussions as a sign of weakness. Such an interpretation would be a serious miscalculation.

—Secret message from Fidel Castro to Lyndon Johnson, February 1964

Just seventy-two hours after the death of President Kennedy, White House aide Gordon Chase typed out a TOP SECRET briefing paper on the opportunity that had been destroyed by an assassin's bullet. "President Kennedy could have accommodated with Castro and gotten away with it with a minimum of domestic heat," he wrote. Unlike Kennedy, however, Lyndon Johnson had "no background of being successfully nasty to Castro [during the missile crisis], and would probably run a greater risk of being accused, by the American people, of 'going soft'" on communism. In addition, Chase pointed out, the fact that Lee Harvey Oswald had been identified as "a pro-Castro type" made a rapprochement with Cuba far more difficult. "The events of November 22," Chase concluded, "would appear to make accommodation with Castro an even more doubtful issue than it was."[1]

The specter of a Cuban connection to the Kennedy assassination hovered over the new administration. To dispel the growing clamor about an international communist conspiracy, Johnson moved quickly to appoint a presidential commission to investigate whether Lee Harvey Oswald had acted alone. "Now these wild people are charging Khrushchev killed Kennedy and Castro killed Kennedy," Johnson told Supreme Court chief justice Earl Warren, whom he personally convinced to chair the investigation. "But the American people and the world *have got to know* who *killed* Kennedy and *why*."[2]

Johnson's political instincts lent themselves to a hard line on Cuba—particularly in an election year in which he expected his Republican opponent to be a hawkish Cold Warrior such as Richard Nixon or Barry Goldwater. The Cuban situation was "one that we could not live with and we had to evolve more aggressive policies," he instructed CIA director John A. McCone at the end of his first week in the White House.[3] In a December 2 phone conversation with Senator J. William Fulbright—captured by Johnson's secret taping system—the president made it clear that he did not want a repeat of the Bay of Pigs fiasco. "I'm just asking you what we ought to be doing to pinch their nuts more than we're doing."[4]

A number of the programs Johnson inherited from the Kennedy administration—covert sabotage, exile paramilitary operations, and the trade embargo—would be tools in such "pinch" policies, as the new administration moved to step up economic and diplomatic pressures to isolate Cuba in the region. But despite crises over Cuban involvement in Latin America, confrontation over seized fishing boats, U.S. efforts to regionalize the embargo, and the U.S. invasion of the Dominican Republic to prevent "another Cuba," the back-channel communications with Castro continued, eventually reaching into the Oval Office. Despite the new president's disinclination to pursue his predecessor's talks with Cuba, Kennedy's initiative took on a life of its own as Havana and Washington sustained an ongoing dialogue through intermediaries and third countries. Under Johnson came the first review of the merits and effectiveness of a hostile Cuba policy. Indeed, following the death of Che Guevara in 1967, U.S. officials would begin actively considering options for an alternative, more conciliatory approach to Cuba.

Keeping Kennedy's "U.S./Cuba Line" Open

For U.S.-Cuban relations, the murder of the president could not have come at a worse moment. As Kennedy lay dying at Dallas Memorial Hospital, the Cuban diplomatic pouch was on its way to New York, containing Castro's agenda for a secret meeting on rapprochement, as requested by the White House. "Castro's reply came through the day after [Kennedy] died, proposing an agenda and suggesting these talks," William Attwood recalled.[5] In the turmoil following the assassination, however, there was no mechanism to transmit this message to the Oval Office, and no U.S. policy team prepared to receive it.

Only McGeorge Bundy's young national security aide for Latin America, Gordon Chase, seemed able to focus on the potential opportunity for better relations that had been set in motion during the last days of the Kennedy administration. Still unaware that Castro's response had arrived, on November 25 Chase sought to prepare Bundy—and through him President Johnson—for the possibility of a meeting between Attwood and Cuban UN ambassador Carlos Lechuga to explore Cuba's agenda. "We have little or nothing to lose and there will be some benefits; at a minimum, we should get a valuable reading as to what Castro regards as negotiable (e.g. the Soviet tie-in) and a hint as to how he views the effect of November 22 on Cuban/U.S. relations."[6]

In fact, Castro viewed the assassination and its impact on Cuba with serious alarm. As his prophesy of "they will say we did it" appeared to be realized, he understood the dangerous implications for Cuba. "The death of President Kennedy can have very negative repercussions for the interests of our country," Castro stated in a televised speech on November 24, adopting a decidedly moderate tone as world leaders gathered in Washington for the state funeral. "But in this case it is not the question of our interest, but of the interests of the whole world."[7]

In New York, Ambassador Lechuga told Lisa Howard that he had received a letter of authorization to discuss an agenda for talks with Attwood. Howard passed the information along to her contacts in the new administration. On December 2, Attwood and Lechuga crossed paths in the UN Delegates Lounge; Lechuga reiterated that he had "been authorized to have a preliminary discussion" and "wondered how things now stood."[8]

This was the moment the Kennedy team had worked toward—to find out if common ground existed for a modus vivendi between the United States and Cuba. Attwood's request for instructions set off an internal discussion on how to proceed. "The ball is in our court; Bill [Attwood] owes Lechuga a call. What to do?" Chase asked Bundy. On the one hand, "We have nothing to lose in listening to what Castro has to say; there is no commitment on our side," Chase suggested. On the other hand, even such a low-level meeting had become politically perilous. "Things are different now, particularly with this Oswald [pro-Castro] business."[9]

On the morning of December 3, Chase conferred with Bundy about how to move forward. A meeting with Lechuga might be possible, Bundy said, but secrecy was paramount and a "foolproof denial" was needed if it leaked. Later that day Chase provided the national security advisor with a TOP SECRET scenario whereby Attwood would get Lechuga to divulge Fidel's instructions and position without actually presenting a U.S. response:

> Bill Attwood should call Lechuga and make an appointment to see him. At the meeting he should say the following:
>
> (a) The new Administration has not yet had an opportunity to examine the Cuban question in detail.
>
> (b) However, in deference to the late President's judgment that it is worthwhile to hear what is on Castro's mind, and in view of the fact that what Castro says may have a bearing on the new Administration's eventual assessment of the Cuban situation, I am authorized to hear you out.
>
> (c) (After hearing Lechuga's story.) You can rest assured that the information will be passed on to the proper people. If we are interested in further talks, I will let you know.[10]

The next day, Lechuga again approached Attwood, telling him "he now had a letter directly from Castro approving detailed talks and an agenda." Still lacking instructions, Attwood was forced to put him off. "This went on," Attwood recalled years later. "I kept seeing Lechuga and Lechuga would say he was waiting for an answer, and I kept saying well the door isn't closed, I just don't know." From the White House, Chase told Attwood that a decision would take time because all U.S. policies, including Cuba, were under review.[11]

As President Johnson prepared to travel to New York on December 17 to address the UN General Assembly, he read Attwood's comprehensive chronology of the "discreet contacts" with the Cubans in the fall of 1963.[12] At a luncheon at Ambassador Adlai Stevenson's apartment in the Waldorf Astoria, Attwood recalled, the president "told me that he'd read my chronological account of the Cuban initiative 'with interest.'" But Attwood received no executive direction on pursuing the talks.[13]

Two days later, Johnson convened his first national security meeting to review the status of anti-Castro operations. In preparation, McGeorge Bundy briefed the president on "our Cuban problem—where we have been since January, 1963; where we are now; and where we seem to be heading."[14] The minimum objective of U.S. policy was to prevent Cuba from being a Soviet satellite or a threat to its neighbors. Toward those ends, United States had pressured the Soviets to withdraw the majority of their military personnel and was enlisting other Latin American nations to oppose Cuban subversion. The discovery, in early December, of a cache of arms in Venezuela that was traced back to Cuba gave Washington new ammunition to press the

OAS to isolate Cuba diplomatically and commercially on the grounds that Castro was fomenting subversion. The CIA was engaged in a series of covert operations designed to stimulate an internal coup against Castro, destabilize the economy, and provide secret support for "autonomous" exile actions of infiltration and sabotage that would begin in January 1964. In theory, Bundy reported, these operations could lead to "a degree of disorganization, uncertainty, and discontent in Cuba" such that Castro would be overthrown.

But Bundy's briefing also highlighted another potential eventuality: "Accommodation with Castro on U.S. Terms." U.S. operations against Cuba, Cuba's isolation in the region, and distrust of the Soviets could convince Castro that he has "no choice" but accommodation. "Castro may already be thinking along these lines," Bundy argued to the new president: "In the past few months he has made a number of accommodation noises and since he undoubtedly has a pretty good reading of our minimum terms, these noises could conceivably indicate he is willing to go a long way toward meeting them."[15] A message to Castro, he suggested, could read like this:

> Fidel, we are content to let events continue on their present course. We intend to maintain, and whenever possible, to increase our pressures against you until you fall; we are pretty certain we will be successful. . . . However, we are reasonable men. We are not intent on having your head per se; neither do we relish the suffering of the Cuban people. You know our central concerns—the Soviet connection and the subversion. If you feel you are in a position to allay these concerns, we can probably work out a way to live amicably together and to build a prosperous Cuba. If you don't feel you can meet our concerns, then just forget the whole thing.[16]

There were certain to be problems with this approach, particularly with a skeptical American public and, of course, hard-line conservatives. But arguments against coming to terms with Castro could be rebutted, Bundy noted in relatively firm language. "Accommodation remains a distinct possibility, if not now then for later."

Amid lengthy discussion of CIA sabotage operations and pressure on the OAS to cut off economic and diplomatic relations with Cuba, the issue of the talks with Castro did come up at the December 19, 1963, national security briefing. There had been "very tenuous, sensitive, and marginal contacts," Bundy noted obliquely. Washington now faced "a decision as to whether or not we are prepared to listen to what Castro has to say."[17] Other than Under Secretary of State George Ball, who noted that U.S. contacts with

Cuba could have an "unsettling effect" on Cuba's relations with the Soviets, nobody voiced support or opposition to continuing the communications.

Nevertheless, President Johnson decided to shelve the back-channel talks. The president did "not want to appear soft on anything, especially Cuba," Bundy told his aides several days later. The Cuba contacts "would be put on ice for a while," Attwood recalls being told in late December. "While the door was not closed on further contact with Lechuga, the timing was not now considered right," Chase informed Attwood.[18] In his memoir, *The Twilight Struggle*, Attwood recalled Chase telling him, "It doesn't look like it's going to be continued now because it's an election year. We'll keep it in mind but that it was a dead issue."[19]

For the first time, but certainly not the last, electoral political considerations undercut an initiative to improve U.S.-Cuban relations. But the "U.S./Cuba line" started during the Kennedy administration remained open. Key U.S. policy actors led by Gordon Chase and Adlai Stevenson refused to let it close. Castro himself continued to pursue it, and secret intermediaries like Lisa Howard, Jean Daniel, and various Latin American governments continued their attempts to broker a rapprochement throughout the Johnson years.

The Return of Lisa Howard

With Kennedy's death, Jean Daniel's role as an "unofficial envoy" ended; he then reverted to his profession as a journalist and broke the news of the late president's secret message to Castro in a front-page story in the *New York Times*, and a two-part series in the *New Republic*.[20] His meetings with the two leaders, Daniel wrote in the *Times* on December 11, had established "in effect a dialogue between President Kennedy and Premier Fidel Castro."[21] When told of Kennedy's perspective on Cuba and U.S.-Cuban relations, Daniel reported in the *New Republic*, Castro suggested that Kennedy had "the possibility of becoming, in the eyes of history, the greatest President of the United States, the leader who may at last understand that there can be coexistence between capitalists and socialists, even in the Americas."[22]

In Cuba, Castro also sought to call attention to the aborted talks with Kennedy—without actually revealing that they had taken place. In a speech on January 2, marking the fifth anniversary of the revolution, the Cuban premier softened his renowned anti-U.S. rhetoric and highlighted the potential for "peaceful coexistence." His "discussion of the subject of 'normalizing' U.S.-Cuban relations was more extensive than in any prior public speech by Castro," according to CIA analysts, who noted its "generally conciliatory tone."[23] Had

JFK lived, Castro predicted, "an eventual normalization of relations with the Kennedy Administration was possible." In a forceful rebuke from Washington, Secretary of State Dean Rusk responded that it was "not true" that Kennedy planned for any early reconciliation between Cuba and the United States.[24]

Undeterred, Castro returned to this theme both publicly and privately. In February, the CIA obtained intelligence from a source close to Cuban foreign minister Raúl Roa that Castro believed "President Kennedy would have gone on ultimately to negotiate with Cuba," not because of any "love for Cuba" but rather because of a practical acceptance of the Cuban revolution as a "fait accompli." According to Roa, they believed that Johnson "is unaware of his predecessor's activities in this matter, and for this reason is not continuing President Kennedy's policy."[25]

To encourage Johnson to finish what Kennedy had started, Castro turned to the back-channel intermediary who had worked so hard to bring Washington and Havana together in the fall of 1963. He invited Lisa Howard to revisit Cuba. In late January, Howard contacted Gordon Chase at the White House to say she was returning to Cuba to do a second major ABC News special on the Cuban revolution. Did the White House want to take the opportunity to send a message? Given Johnson's disinclination to dialogue with Castro, Chase declined. But, he told her, U.S. officials would be interested in anything Castro had to say.

With a camera crew in tow, Howard spent ten days filming in Havana and the Cuban countryside. At Fidel's direction, Che Guevara granted Howard a rare and exclusive interview for the news program *Issues and Answers*. "Major Guevara," she asked, "Fidel Castro has often stated he favors normal relations with the United States. Are you also in favor of normalized relations?"

"Absolutely," Che responded, noting that as minister of industry, normal trade ties would be particularly beneficial to him. "On the basis of principles of total equality, the normalization of relations would be ideal for us."

What did he want from the United States? she asked. Puffing methodically on his cigar, Che replied, "Perhaps the most frank and objective response would be: Nothing. Nothing for or against us. Just leave us alone."[26]

Fidel Castro spent several days with Howard while she was there, leading her on tours of agricultural farms, allowing her to film him playing baseball, and even breaking news to her that he intended to turn off the water at the Guantánamo Bay naval base in response to the U.S. Coast Guard's seizure of four Cuban fishing boats and their crews. He agreed to a lengthy on-camera interview, filmed in her hotel suite in the early hours of the morning on February 13, 1964.

Journalist Lisa Howard with Fidel Castro in February 1964. During the Kennedy and Johnson administrations, Howard served as a private channel of communication between Castro and the U.S. government. During this trip, Castro gave Howard a personal message for President Johnson promising not to cause problems during the 1964 presidential election campaign. (Magnum Photos/Elliott Erwitt)

As the interview got under way, Howard posed a question to which only she, Fidel, and a few others inside the U.S. and Cuban governments already knew the answer: "You said at one point after President Kennedy's death that you believed that under Kennedy it was going to be possible to normalize relations between Cuba and the United States. What leads you to believe that?" In halting English, Castro answered with careful diplomatic discretion:

> After three years as president of the United States, Kennedy had much more experience than he had at the beginning, and I think he had a better understanding of the world problems, and about Cuba. My opinion is that he was in the way of persuading himself of his mistakes about Cuba. . . . We had some evidence that some change was taking place in the mind of the government of the United States . . . a new situation . . . and we had evidence I do not want to speak about now.[27]

Off camera, Castro conferred privately with Howard about sustaining the secret communications with the United States he and she had initiated the year before. He shared his perspective that at some point the U.S. government would have to recognize the reality of the Cuban revolution and come to the negotiating table. During a long discussion before she returned to the United States, the two worked out a "verbal message" to President Johnson to encourage him to pick up where Kennedy left off.[28]

This secret communiqué covered four basic points. First, Castro wanted to convey to Johnson that he understood that Cuba would become a political football in the 1964 election and was willing to play along if Johnson assumed a rhetorically hard-line position and even took hostile actions—if they were for domestic political purposes. "Please tell President Johnson that I earnestly desire his election to the Presidency in November," the message began with a touch of humor. "But if there is anything I can do to add to his majority (aside from retiring from politics), I shall be happy to cooperate. If the President feels it necessary during the campaign to make bellicose statements about Cuba or even to take some hostile action—if he will inform me, unofficially, that a specific action is required because of domestic political considerations, I shall understand and not take any retaliatory action," Castro promised.

Then he tackled the issue of whether Johnson was aware of the dialogue that the White House was pursuing through William Attwood and Lisa Howard at the end of the Kennedy administration. His message recounted what had transpired and reiterated that Cuba remained hopeful that the two nations would eventually resume the secret talks:

> I'm aware that pre-electoral political considerations may delay this approach until after November. Tell the President (and I cannot stress this too strongly) that I seriously hope that Cuba and the United States can eventually sit down in an atmosphere of good will and of mutual respect and negotiate our differences. I believe that there are no areas of contention between us that cannot be discussed and settled in a climate of mutual understanding.

But Castro wanted to make sure Johnson did not misinterpret Cuba's interest in talks. "Tell the President he should not interpret my conciliatory attitude, my desire for discussion as a sign of weakness. . . . We are not weak . . . the Revolution is strong. . . . And it is from this position of strength that we wish to resolve our differences with the United States." Finally, Castro concluded the message with a pledge of discretion. "Tell the President I realize fully the need for absolute secrecy, if he should decide to continue the Kennedy approach. I revealed nothing at that time. . . . I have revealed nothing since. . . . I would reveal nothing now."[29]

Castro's communiqué was one of the most sensitive ever transmitted to the U.S. government. (It would remain secret for thirty-five years.) Howard agreed that she would personally courier the message to the president of the United States. When she returned from Havana, however, Howard discovered that the door to the Oval Office was closed to her. Given the political sensitivity of talks with Cuba, as well as Jean Daniel's front-page stories, White House officials perceived as folly a high-profile journalist ferrying messages directly from the Cuban premier to the U.S. president. In a "Lisa Alert," Bundy characterized Howard as "an extraordinarily determined and self important creature [who] will undoubtedly knock at every door we have at least five times" and warned his colleagues against "letting her play this game with us."[30]

To obtain Castro's message, however, Gordon Chase adopted a more conciliatory approach. In February, Chase replaced Attwood—who was appointed ambassador to Kenya—as Lisa Howard's primary contact in the U.S. government. Like Attwood, he shared her interest in improving U.S.-Cuban relations. As White House point man on Cuba, he refused to abandon the possibility of a bilateral accord that would benefit both nations. On Saturday, March 7, Chase traveled to New York for a private debriefing on Howard's trip. The two spent several hours at Howard's East Central Park apartment discussing in great detail Fidel's attitudes and positions, as well their mutually shared goal of convincing Castro to publicly reject the Soviets and return to the Western camp.[31]

For Howard, the meeting offered an opportunity to press her case that the Johnson administration should communicate with Castro. If there was a scenario in which the United States could live with Fidel, she strongly advised, then that message should be conveyed to him—preferably through her. Castro was convinced, she said, that the United States would "not be content until we destroy him," and therefore he acted accordingly. "Implicit in his present state of mind is the belief that the only alternative he has to the Russians is destruction," she told Chase. A promise of peaceful coexistence, on the other hand, would provide him with a basis for ending his security relationship with Moscow.

At the end of their meeting, Chase asked for Fidel's note. Howard refused to give it to him. She would be breaking faith with Castro if she divulged it to anyone but President Johnson, she said. If Fidel has something to say to us, Chase prodded her, then "he had apparently not picked a very good messenger." Despite his efforts, Chase left New York City empty-handed.

Chastened for undermining her own cause, Howard called Chase the next day to say that she had basically shared "the guts" of the message to the president—which she described as "a firm confirmation of Fidel's eagerness to negotiate a settlement for better relations." While the message did not contain any "terms of a rapprochement," she said, "Castro obviously had to be aware that negotiations implied a willingness on his part to give something up."[32]

In his TOP SECRET report back to the White House, Chase summed up the central point: "Mrs. Howard said that Fidel very much wants an accommodation with the U.S. It is even conceivable that he would kick the Russians out of Cuba if he thought that he could get assistance from us and a credible guarantee that we would not try to destroy him." It was a long shot, Chase argued to Bundy, but this approach could "bring about, over time, one of the truly great victories of the twentieth century—the ejection of the USSR from the W. Hemisphere."[33]

Energized by his meeting with Howard, Chase began peppering Bundy with detailed position papers on pursuing a diplomatic dialogue with Castro. On March 11, he recommended an approach to Castro before the November elections, returning to the theme of casting accommodation as a defeat for the Soviets. "Obviously, the President could not live with a headline which reads 'U.S. Accommodates with Castro,'" Chase argued. "On the other hand, he might live superbly with a headline which reads 'USSR Ejected from Cuba' or 'USSR/Cuba Tie-Line Broken.'"[34] Two days later, Chase sent his boss a TOP SECRET memo, "Negotiations with Castro—Possible Scenario First Steps," recommending another approach to Lechuga. The U.S. intermediary would reiterate the administration's position: "We only want an end to Cuban subversion and an end to Cuban dependence on the Bloc," and would also solicit Cuba's position. "What does Castro want? We are reasonable men and are willing to listen." If Castro proved to be interested, Chase recommended, "we should keep the negotiations going at a slow pace [unless] it appears we are going to hit the jackpot (ejection of the Russians)."[35]

In mid-April, Chase combined all his arguments into a concise two-page TOP SECRET/EYES ONLY memorandum for the record titled "Talks with Castro." He listed three reasons why Washington should pursue "a deal that would constitute a magnificent victory for the U.S.":

> First, while it is obviously a long shot, Castro could conceivably buy accommodation on U.S. terms. There is a substantial body of evidence which points to Castro's unhappiness with the present state of affairs and to his eagerness to negotiate a settlement. Presumably, he realizes that he will have to give us something substantial to get such a settlement. Second, talks with Castro will tend to intensify Cuban/ Soviet tensions. Third, the disadvantages of talking to Castro appear minimal. There will probably be no leakage in view of the fact that it is also in Castro's interest to keep quiet. If there is leakage, we can probably deny it credibly—e.g. "this is too funny for words."[36]

For those administration officials who would argue that talks were politically risky during an election year, Chase had a ready answer. If Castro felt invested in a dialogue with the United States, he would refrain from brazen action in the region. "U.S./Cuban talks will tend to keep Castro cool during a time when we want the noise level low," he argued. "From past experience it is fair to say that Castro will probably act with a certain amount of restraint if he feels there is a chance we might come to terms with him."[37]

"Black Channels"

Chase's depiction of dialogue as a tool for crisis prevention was an attempt to turn necessity into a virtue. In the spring of 1964, Washington policy makers faced a series of real and potential conflicts with Cuba. The few advocates of accommodation found little support among other officials and agencies that were intent on a more aggressive approach. Drawing on evidence of

Cuban support for armed revolution in Venezuela and Brazil, the State Department, led by hard-line Assistant Secretary of State for Inter-American Affairs Thomas Mann, was mobilizing to pressure the OAS to cut off all regional diplomatic and commercial ties with the island. Isolating Castro, Mann argued to President Johnson, "is a hell of a lot better than taking him into our bosom."[38] The Defense Department was consumed by a standoff with Castro over its naval base at Guantánamo Bay. The CIA's focus was on its "autonomous operations" program of covertly supporting exile sabotage operations. Most ominously, CIA director John McCone perceived a growing threat that Cuba might shoot down a U-2 spy plane, which could escalate into a major military confrontation.

The crisis at Guantánamo evolved out of the Coast Guard's seizure of four Cuban fishing boats in U.S. territorial waters near the Dry Tortugas on February 2, 1964. The Cuban fishermen were first held at a U.S. naval base and then dumped into a small Florida jail in Key West. Cuba immediately protested what it termed "the unprecedented, arbitrary and illegal jailing of the Cuban crewmen . . . piratically kidnapped by the North American government."[39]

Privately, President Johnson fumed that it was "a damn fool thing to pick them up. . . . They been fishing there up till the last few years, constantly, [and] nobody bothered them."[40] Publicly, however, the president had to flex Washington's muscles. After Castro announced on February 6 that he was cutting off the water to Guantánamo until the fishermen were released, Johnson retaliated by firing, in phases, most of the twenty-five hundred Cubans who worked on the base. Eventually the fishing crews were released, the captains fined, and the boats returned to Cuba.

But the fishing boat flap gave way to a potentially more dangerous situation: Castro's threat to fire on U-2 reconnaissance planes conducting surveillance flights over the island. In March, a few weeks after the Cuban fisherman were detained, the White House received a CIA intelligence report that "one of the things [Castro] thought of doing was to shoot down one of our U-2 planes in retaliation," Bundy told President Johnson. This was "extremely interesting and disturbing" and underscored the need to "warn Castro" on the dangers of interfering with U.S. surveillance aircraft. On March 6, Johnson instructed Secretary of State Dean Rusk to come up with a plan for "appropriate, strong, high-level warnings" regarding Castro's "itchy finger on the trigger of the surface-to-air-missiles in Cuba."[41]

The form and transmission of such a warning became the subject of intense debate inside the administration. Should the warning be public or discreet, direct or through intermediaries? Should the Soviets be enlisted to reinforce the message to Castro? "Castro scares me because I think he is a man who can regard a threat as credible but still disregard the consequences if his honor and emotion are involved," Gordon Chase argued. "We are most likely to prevent a shoot-down if our note to Castro is buttressed by a good strong pitch from Khrushchev."[42] But the leading Soviet expert in the administration, Ambassador Tommy Thompson, argued that the Soviets would be forced to formally back Cuba's right to defend its airspace, and any prior notice to Moscow would transform a conflict from "a purely United States/Cuban affair" into another superpower confrontation. Bundy found this argument persuasive.[43]

Secretary Rusk came up with his own recommendations for using indirect channels to alert both the Cubans and the Soviets. The message, in the form of a diplomatic note to Castro, would be sent through the Czech ambassador to Washington. "Using this method and channel we can be sure that the Soviets will also get the message without our incurring the disadvantage of making a special direct approach to them." In addition, Rusk recommended using "black channels" to send Castro a message that could not be traced back to the United States. The "black channel" message, Rusk suggested, would make three points: "(a) we have taken very careful note of his recent public statements on overflights; (b) we interpret these statements as a threat to shoot down our surveillance flights; and (c) we would like nothing better, and we are prepared to react immediately to such an eventuality."[44]

On March 27, the United States passed the diplomatic message to Czech ambassador Karel Duda along with the admonition to "make sure that there is no misunderstanding about our continuing position on this matter."[45] Secretary Rusk himself raised the issue with Soviet ambassador Anatoly Dobrynin in late April, explaining that the United States had continued to conduct overflights of Cuba after the missile crisis because Moscow had not been able to obtain Castro's permission for on-the-ground inspection for nuclear weapons. Rusk emphasized that "he was mentioning these matters out of a desire to avoid a major crisis with Cuba" and "hoped that the Soviet Government will caution Castro not to inflame the situation into a major crisis."[46]

Several weeks later, the CIA's Western Hemisphere division implemented Rusk's "black channel." On May 8, a case officer from the CIA's Western Hemisphere division met with an asset in New York, code-named JMINDIGO. They discussed how to pass a message covertly to Castro that "the United States government is serious about the U-2 flights over Cuba and intends to continue the flights indefinitely. There will be no change in this policy after the November elections."

This message would be sent to Castro through one of the more circuitous forms of communication in the annals of U.S.-Cuban dialogue. According to a secret memorandum to CIA's deputy director for plans, Richard Helms, JMINDIGO would exploit his "very close personal" friendship with an attorney named Michael Standard who worked at the New York law firm of Boudin and Rabinowitz, which represented Cuban interests in the United States. "JMINDIGO will give the above-quoted message to Standard on 9 May, doing in such a way that it does not appear to be the reason for the meeting and making it clear to Standard that the information is being given in confidence," stated the report to Helms. "JMINDIGO is certain that Standard will immediately give the information to [Cuba's UN ambassador] Lechuga, who will, of course, relay it to Castro."

To verify that, in fact, the communication made it to Cuba, JMINDIGO planned to meet several days later with Lechuga, under the pretext of arranging to take a trip to Cuba. The CIA asset would then give Lechuga an opportunity to ask him about the U-2 flights. He would confirm that there was reason to believe that the U-2 flights would continue. "By giving the information to Standard, a friend, in confidence, and by only half-confirming it later to Lechuga," the report to Helms noted, "JMINDIGO will have made the information believable to the Cubans and will not have placed himself under as much suspicion."

"If in the future there is any need to pass additional information via this channel," the memo concluded, "JMINDIGO would be in the position to do so."[47]

The Lisa/Castro/Stevenson/Johnson Line

In the end, it was not the CIA's circuitous, clandestine "black channel" but a high-level back channel between Castro and Johnson that resolved the threat of a shoot-down. This new communications channel was provided by the indefatigable Lisa Howard, who finally achieved at least indirect access to the Oval Office.

As she continued to try to present Fidel's "Verbal Message" directly to President Johnson, Howard did battle with the national security bureaucracy to keep her hand in the game of clandestine diplomacy. In April and May, she frequently made late night calls to Gordon Chase, whom she correctly perceived as an ally in the cause of normalization, to report on her upcoming

ABC television special on *Cuba and Castro Today* (which aired on April 19) as well as her conversations with Fidel and his top aide, René Vallejo, about the undelivered message to Johnson. On May 1, she called to say that Fidel was "very angry these days and that probably one of the reasons was that he has never received any response to his message to President Johnson," Chase reported to Bundy.[48] "Lisa Howard called to needle me about her desire to see the President," Chase reported again on May 4. "She went through her routine about the President not wanting to see her. I went through my routine about the fact that she had every opportunity to give her message to me and that her refusal to do so was indefensible." On May 15, Howard called yet again and "roundly scolded me and the White House for taking her message from Fidel to the President as a joke," Chase reported. "I assured her we didn't."[49]

Stymied at the White House, Howard turned, once again, to the United Nations, communicating directly with UN ambassador Adlai Stevenson, who had played a pivotal part in initiating the talks between William Attwood and Ambassador Lechuga nine months earlier. In early June, she convinced Stevenson to deliver to President Johnson the lengthy, typed message from Castro that she had carried back from Havana in February. Stevenson attached a cover memo to the president, dated June 16 and stamped TOP SE-CRET, describing the talks that had started under Kennedy and suggesting that some form of dialogue could be renewed outside of normal channels. Howard, Ambassador Stevenson advised, "is convinced that [Castro] sincerely wants some channel of communication. If it could be resumed on a low enough level to avoid any possible embarrassment, it might be worth considering."[50]

In a follow-up memo to the president on June 24, marked SECRET AND PERSONAL, Ambassador Stevenson passed along an important message from Castro about the U-2 overflights: "Nothing will happen to our planes and we do not need to send him any warnings," it stated. Indeed, Castro pledged that "there will be no crisis until after the November elections," Stevenson reported. "He will use utmost restraint and we can relax." Castro felt that "all of our crises could be avoided if there was some way to communicate. [Castro] assumed that he could call [Howard] and she call me and I would advise you."[51]

When a Marine at Guantánamo shot a Cuban guard, Castro used this back channel to inquire if the incident had been an isolated act or a provocation. After discussing the issue with President Johnson, Bundy authorized Stevenson to tell Howard to tell Castro that there was "no U.S. Government plan to provoke incidents at Guantánamo." The episode was contained.[52]

MEMORANDUM

~~TOP SECRET~~
~~EYES ONLY~~

July 7, 1964

MEMORANDUM FOR MR. BUNDY

SUBJECT: Adlai Stevenson and Lisa Howard

DECLASSIFIED
E.O. 12356, Sec. 3.4
NIJ _94-231_
By _ng_, NARA, Date _7-12-95_

Here are some thoughts on the above subject.

1. I think we should be clear that the latest developments add at least two new factors to the situation which make Lisa Howard's participation even scarier than it was before. One, for the first time during the Johnson Administration, Lisa has been used to carry a message from the U.S. to Cuba. Before this, the Johnson Administration had relatively little to fear from Lisa since, essentially, we were just listening to her reports on and from Castro. Two, Lisa's contact on the U.S. side is far sexier now (Stevenson), than at any time in the past (Attwood and then Chase).

2. While I'm in favor of having a channel to Castro, I would feel somewhat safer if we could find a way to remove Lisa from direct participation in the business of passing messages (a view which I have held for some time -- e.g. see attached memo). Accordingly, you might want to consider the desirability of calling Stevenson to make such points as the following:

   (a) Lisa Howard's participation in the U.S./Cuba channel, understandably, makes us nervous -- the more so now, since communications are passing and may pass, in the future, from the U.S. to Cuba. Also, the name of Lisa's new American contact, Adlai Stevenson, is not an unsexy one from a public media point of view.

   (b) We would appreciate it if you would give some thought to ways and means of retaining a channel to Castro but removing Lisa from direct participation.

   (c) One possibility might be to shift the channel to Lechuga, the channel which had been set up just before President Kennedy died. With Bill Attwood gone, perhaps you could have Sid Yates (Attwood's nominee) pass Lechuga in the corridor periodically to exchange whatever messages may need to be exchanged.

   We doubt that Castro would object to a change in channels. In your memo of June 26 you note, "that for want of anything better, he (Castro) assumed that he could call her and she call me and I would advise you."

   (d) We recognize that it won't be easy to extricate Lisa from the operation. One way to do it might be to simply tell her that we have nothing further to say;

~~TOP SECRET -- EYES ONLY~~

Memorandum from National Security Council staff member Gordon Chase to National Security Advisor McGeorge Bundy expressing growing concern about journalist Lisa Howard's role carrying messages back and forth between the White House and Fidel Castro. (LBJ Presidential Library)

Now, for the first time in the post-revolution history of U.S.-Cuban relations there was a functioning back channel between the Oval Office and Castro's office—that Chase dubbed the "Castro/Lisa Howard/Stevenson/President line" of communication. But Howard's singular success in creating a secret bridge between the highest levels of the U.S. and Cuban leadership proved to be short-lived.[53] In a memorandum to Bundy on July 7, Chase laid out a comprehensive argument for removing her from this sensitive role. "We should be clear that the latest developments add at least two new factors to the situation which make Lisa Howard's participation even scarier than it was before," Chase wrote:

> *One*, for the first time during the Johnson administration, Lisa has been used to carry a message *from* the U.S. *to* Cuba. Before this, the Johnson Administration had relatively little to fear from Lisa since, essentially, we were just listening to her reports on and from Castro. Two, Lisa's contact on the U.S. side is far sexier now (Stevenson), than at any time in the past (Attwood and then Chase).[54]

"While I'm in favor of having a channel to Castro, I would feel somewhat safer if we could find a way to remove Lisa from direct participation in the business of passing messages," Chase noted. He recommended that Bundy authorize a message to Stevenson stating that future messages to and from Cuba should be passed not through Howard but directly from Stevenson's office to Lechuga. From that point onward, Howard participated in no further transmission of messages between the White House and Fidel Castro.

Castro Reaches Out

In the early summer of 1964, Fidel Castro took steps to address a looming threat to any positive change in U.S.-Cuban relations: the pending publication of the Warren Commission report on the assassination of John F. Kennedy. Fearing that the commission would accept allegations that Cuba was somehow involved, Castro secretly sent a message to Washington that he wanted to meet before the report was finalized. "The whole thing was hush-hush," recalled former secretary of transportation William T. Coleman Jr., then a young lawyer on the commission staff who was chosen to undertake the highly sensitive, secret mission of meeting Castro on his yacht off the coast of Cuba.

For three hours they had what Coleman described as "a pretty animated conversation"—a conversation kept secret for almost half a century—during which he grilled Castro on any possible Cuban complicity, which Castro denied. When Coleman returned to Washington, he briefed Chief Justice Earl Warren. "I came back and I said I hadn't found out anything that would cause me to think there's proof he *did* do it," he reported.[55]

As the summer progressed, Castro escalated his efforts to reach out to the Johnson administration. On July 5, 1964, the Cuban leader initiated what the State Department's Bureau of Intelligence and Research described as the "strongest bid to date for a U.S.-Cuban rapprochement." In an interview with *New York Times* reporter Richard Eder, Castro proposed "extensive discussion of the issues" dividing Havana and Washington. He offered to halt assistance to Latin American revolutionaries if the United States halted exile operations; to release political prisoners; and eventually indemnify U.S. corporations for expropriated properties—if an accommodation could be reached. Fidel even accepted his share of the blame for the breakdown in U.S.-Cuban relations. "There was the passion and extremism that characterizes the initial phase of any revolution on our part," he told Eder. "Look, the truth is that neither of the two countries, neither the United States nor us, did very much to prevent things having gotten to this point."[56]

Two weeks later Raúl Castro reinforced this message, holding a rare news conference in which he declared that Cuba might consider dropping its precondition that the embargo be lifted before a dialogue with Washington could take place. "Despite our repeated announcements of our desire to discuss problems, so far we haven't received any definite answer from the United States." Cuba, he said, was willing to meet the U.S. negotiators any place to discuss improving relations, "even the moon."[57]

Castro's decision to reach out reflected his heightened concern over the inherent danger of conflict with the United States. In February he passed an extraordinary proposal to Swiss ambassador Emil Stadelhofer to send to Washington: "The Cuban Government is willing to release twenty thousand political prisoners in exchange for a pledge from the United States Government that there will be no invasion of Cuba and that Cuba will not be molested by the United States." Stadelhofer asked Gustavo de los Reyes, a recently released prisoner who was going into exile, to courier this message to State Department officials. According to the memorandum of conversation of Reyes's meeting in Washington, he reported that he asked Stadelhofer "why Castro wanted such a pledge" since President Kennedy had made such assurances at the end of the missile crisis. "Stadelhofer replied that the Cuban Government did not know whether this 'assurance' carried over to the Administration of President Johnson."[58]

In March the CIA reported on intelligence from a source inside the office of Foreign Minister Raúl Roa that Castro "sincerely desires to enter into negotiations with the United States with the aim of reducing tensions between the two countries." Castro had held a meeting with ambassadors from other Latin American countries in Havana, in which he proposed to halt involvement "in any revolutionary plots in or against Latin American countries," if "the Latin American countries would stop 'conspiring' against him."[59] Castro seemed ready to deal.

To assure that Washington got the message, Castro also made this commitment to Britain's ambassador to Havana, Adam Watson. In July 1964 Castro took Watson and his wife to visit farms in the Cuban countryside. The two talked specifically about how to arrive at a relaxation of tensions with the United States. Castro voiced the opinion that Lyndon Johnson was a "moderate and realistic man" and that world peace depended on his election in 1964 over Barry Goldwater. Toward that goal, he had made the gesture of moving Cuban troops back from the periphery of Guantánamo to avoid any petty clashes. After the elections, he noted, "it ought to be possible to arrange for further unilateral gestures by both sides which would lessen tension. . . . it ought to be possible to arrive at a position where [the Americans] did not object to their friends improving their relations with Cuba, and indeed saw advantages for themselves in this." Castro specifically asked Watson to report his views to the British government, including his recognition that he would have "to reduce or give up those of his international activities which were particularly upsetting to the U.S."[60]

In August, Watson submitted an eight-page report laying out his assessment that Castro seemed ready to negotiate a modus vivendi with Washington:

> I regard it as quite wrong to say that Castro would only like to normalize relations on his own terms. On the contrary, he has been making very serious efforts through diplomatic and other channels to find out what the American terms may be after November. I believe that he is getting himself ready to swallow as much of them as he can, bitter though they may be.
>
> Castro does not seem to be thinking in terms of a treaty or pact. Not only would such a contract be almost impossibly difficult to negotiate; it would be still harder to verify and lead to endless recriminations. . . . I think Castro would like to proceed as he sees Mr. Khrushchev and President Johnson proceed, by a series of parallel unilateral actions.

I have the impression that he would like an understanding that both sides would reduce their activities directed against the other's position until such activities have substantially ceased.[61]

The British Foreign Ministry forwarded this communication to Washington. But the NSC and the State Department discounted Watson's report, as well as Fidel and Raúl's public statements. "We cannot accept Castro's promise that he will stop his subversion," Bundy's NSC aide, Robert Sayre, advised. "His whole record is one of broken promises and duplicity. We do not believe a Communist will renounce the world revolution." Moreover, he added, Castro's interest in improving relations with Washington to ease Cuba's economic woes "is further evidence that inter-American policy on Castro has been effective."[62]

U.S. officials also dismissed Castro's peace proposals as a crass effort to undermine momentum for an impending OAS resolution being pushed by the United States and Venezuela, which would regionalize the U.S. diplomatic and economic embargo. Responding to the discovery of a cache of arms that was traced back to Cuba in December 1963, Venezuela had filed a formal request for a meeting of consultations to sanction Cuba. Throughout the spring and early summer of 1964, the State Department aggressively pushed for a harsh condemnation and regional sanctions. At the July 26 meeting of Latin American foreign ministers, the OAS voted 15 to 4 to terminate diplomatic and commercial relations with Cuba. Castro responded that same day in his annual July 26 speech with the "Declaration of Santiago," affirming Cuba's right to support revolutionary movements "in all those nations which engage in similar intervention in the internal affairs of our country" by supporting U.S. sanctions.[63]

Chile, Uruguay, Bolivia, and Mexico voted against the OAS resolution, but only Mexico refused to abide by it and break relations with Cuba. In Havana, Mexico was heralded for standing up to U.S. pressure. But the Mexican government's move to resist the U.S.-orchestrated sanctions was not quite the nationalist, maverick decision it seemed. Since late 1960, the Mexican government had pursued a dual-track policy toward Cuba. The strength of the Mexican Left and its solidarity with the Cuban revolution, President López Mateos explained to CIA director Allen Dulles during a secret meeting in January 1961, compelled Mexico to maintain economic and political ties to Cuba and not take any overt effort to undermine or overthrow the regime. But, he promised, Mexico also would be willing to work with the United States "beneath the table."[64]

Secretly, Mexico supported the Bay of Pigs operation by briefly lending its territory as a staging ground and allowing the CIA to house the political leaders of the exile brigade in its capital city. At the same time, the Mexican government tried to broker a modus vivendi between Havana and Washington before the attack. Mexico would "not cease in its efforts" to bring "peace and harmony" to the hemispheric family "in which Cuba rightfully holds a place of distinction," López Mateos declared in September 1960.[65] On at least three subsequent occasions, his government extended offers to Presidents Kennedy and Johnson to act as an interlocutor for better relations with the Cuban revolution.

As the United States organized the regionwide embargo of Cuba at the OAS, Mexico pressed for a deal to safeguard its position as a regional broker and bridge to the island. Just before the OAS vote, the United States, Brazil, and Mexico made a "secret pact" to assure that one OAS country—Mexico— would maintain relations with Cuba. Not even President Johnson knew that Secretary of State Rusk had orchestrated an exception to the regional isolation of Cuba. In November 1964, when Johnson was preparing to meet Mexico's new president-elect, Gustavo Díaz Ordaz, he asked Rusk whether he should complain about Mexico's decision to maintain relations. "Oh, I would not play that up very much," Rusk responded. "The background on that is that during our foreign ministers' meeting in late July, a number of us—Brazil and others—talked about the practical desirability of having one Latin American embassy there if possible. And so the hemisphere is fairly relaxed about the Mexicans staying there."

"All right, that's good," President Johnson responded.[66]

Che Guevara Comes to Town

In the aftermath of the OAS vote, the prospects for a U.S.-Cuban dialogue seemed nonexistent. Now that Latin America had joined the U.S. embargo, the Johnson administration focused its attention on further tightening the economic screws by pressing European allies to reduce or terminate their commercial relations with Cuba.[67]

U.S. efforts to undermine and overthrow Castro, however, suffered a major international embarrassment on September 14, 1964, when the lead exile paramilitary group in the CIA's "autonomous operations" program, the Movimiento Revolucionario Rebelde, attacked the Spanish freighter *Sierra Aranzazu* off the coast of Cuba, mistaking it for the Cuban merchant ship *Sierra Maestra*. The attack killed the captain, first mate, and chief engineer and injured eight other crewmen. It created a significant diplomatic scandal and generated a major reevaluation within the administration of the wisdom of continuing the CIA's clandestine support for paramilitary operations. Indeed, the "Aranzazu incident," as it was referred to in secret NSC records, marked the beginning of a slow, protracted, shutdown of active CIA support for violent anti-Castro exile activities.[68]

Faced with pressure to reduce its core sabotage programs, the agency conceived the concept of a clandestine set of messages to top Castro officials. During a meeting with NSC and Pentagon aides on November 10, CIA operations director Desmond Fitzgerald suggested a "black channel" approach to Cuban president Osvaldo Dorticós, in an effort to drive a wedge between him and Castro. The idea was to get a message to Dorticós in "an unattributable, deniable fashion" that there could be no modus vivendi with Castro, but the United States "might well be able to live with Dorticós." According to Fitzgerald, "a move like this could conceivably produce a big dividend. At best it will start Dorticós plotting; at worst (if Castro finds out), it will help to sow some seeds of dissension and distrust."[69] The CIA planned to bring the communications proposal to the "Special Group"—the high-level interagency committee that approved clandestine operations.

Fidel had his own creative ideas about communicating with the Johnson administration: use the occasion of Che Guevara's visit to the United States to transmit a message of interest in better relations. On December 9, Guevara arrived in New York to give a major speech before the UN General Assembly. His presentation was fiery, forceful, and very anti-imperialist, denouncing the United States for creating "an International of Crime" throughout Latin America and intervening throughout the Third World.[70] While Che was speaking, a team of Cuban exiles fired a bazooka at the UN building from a small boat in the Hudson River. The assassination attempt only added to the caché of Che's visit.

Over the next five days, Guevara took New York City by storm. He did several major media interviews, including an appearance on the CBS news show, *Meet the Press*. With his entourage, he went to the theater to see a new film on the presidency of John F. Kennedy. And he attended an Upper East Side soirée held in his honor at the home of Lisa Howard.

For Howard, Che's visit represented the final opportunity to reinsert herself as an intermediary and advance her quest to bring Cuba and the United States together. On the morning of December 15, she placed an excited phone call to Gordon Chase at the NSC. "Che Guevara has something to say to us," and Howard was "in a position to arrange a meeting." She pressed

Chase to jump on a plane and rush to New York, but he demurred. The Johnson administration, he responded, "would be interested in hearing what Che had to say . . . outside of the public limelight."[71]

Howard's offer to arrange a meeting with Guevara set off a substantive, high-level discussion inside the administration about whether and how to respond. Under Secretary of State George Ball, Assistant Secretary of State Thomas Mann, his deputy John Crimmins, and Chase conferred on three problems: how to ascertain if "this is Lisa Howard building bridges" or a real interest from Guevara to talk; how to meet with him secretly and securely; and how to circumvent Howard, who Chase felt was "so subjectively wound up in rapprochement that one would never know what Guevara is saying and what Lisa is interpreting."

"This could be a Lisa-generated operation," Chase told State Department officials, but he laid odds, "probably 7–5," that "Guevara, in fact, would like to talk to us." The mechanics of talking to Guevara would be the tough part. "He is a real center of attention in New York (e.g. police, crowds) and it would be extremely awkward to try and get together with him privately."[72]

U.S. officials settled on a convoluted scheme to use a British diplomat at the UN to approach Guevara on December 16 using this script: "An American colleague informs me that a press source has told him that you have something to say to an American official; my American colleague is not at all sure of the accuracy of this report"; and, finally, "is it true?" If Che answered no, then the issue was over. But if he answered yes, then the British official would convey the U.S. interest in setting up a meeting by saying: "I got the distinct impression that my American colleague is willing to listen to what you say, but I would have to check back with him to make sure." The State Department would then set up a safe and secure meeting at the UN between Guevara and one of Ambassador Stevenson's deputies. "The approach is worth it only if it can be done without showing eagerness," Chase reported to Bundy. "My own guess is that there is little that Guevara has to tell us that we don't already know—but a listening session might be interesting."[73]

On December 16, Lisa Howard returned to her use of "cocktail diplomacy"—throwing a reception at her East 74th Street apartment for Guevara. The soirée drew the denizens of New York's literati, including Norman Mailer, who arrived noticeably intoxicated. "All the women were sitting at Guevara's feet," recalled one partygoer, as Guevara waxed eloquently about socialism and revolution.[74]

Among the invitees was the liberal Democratic senator from Minnesota, Eugene McCarthy. As the crowd thinned late in the evening, Guevara and

McCarthy sat down to talk privately. McCarthy listened as Guevara described the economic and political situation in Cuba, Cuban support for revolution in Latin America—"a necessary mission for the Cuban government since revolution offered the only hope of progress"—and Cuban views on the United States. By the time the evening was over, the senator left with the impression that Che's overall interest was to establish better relations with the United States.[75]

The next morning, Howard called Adlai Stevenson at the UN and suggested that he talk privately with Guevara. Stevenson "was all hot to go on this," Chase reported. Under Secretary Ball, however, refused to authorize the meeting. After learning about the Che-McCarthy cocktail encounter, the State Department also canceled the British approach to Guevara to set up a clandestine meeting.[76]

Later that day, Senator McCarthy came to the State Department to be debriefed by Ball and Assistant Secretary Mann on what Che had to say. According to a classified summary of their meeting, the senator "believed the purpose of the meeting was to express Cuban interest in trade with the US and US recognition of the Cuban Regime." But U.S. officials appeared more preoccupied with chastising the senator for talking to this prominent Cuban representative without authorization. Ball "emphasized the danger of meetings such as that which the Senator had had with Guevara," because there was "a suspicion throughout Latin America that the U.S. might make a deal with Cuba behind the backs of the other American states" and that "could provide a propaganda line useful to the Communists." It was essential, Ball admonished, "that nothing be publicly said about the McCarthy-Guevara meeting."[77]

With that, the U.S.-Cuba contacts first initiated under the Kennedy administration came to an anticlimactic end.[78]

The Camarioca Crisis

Throughout 1964, the Johnson administration continued to press forward on efforts to "pinch" Cuba economically, diplomatically, and militarily. In early 1964, the administration tightened the embargo, curtailing the sale of food and medicine by requiring exporters to get licenses from the Commerce Department, few of which were ever granted. The move to limit food sales came in response to a political attack launched by the conservative senator from New York, Kenneth Keating, against Cuban efforts to purchase $2 million worth of lard. The sale, Keating claimed, would have "a significant impact upon the foreign policy and international interests of the United States."[79] National Security Advisor McGeorge Bundy's office asked the Department of Agriculture to provide an analysis of the "uses of lard" in hopes that some ominous strategic purpose could explain U.S. action to block the purchase. "Cuba could be expected to use 100 percent of any lard it gets for edible purposes," an aide reported back. "It would probably not be credible to take the line that we have decided to stop shipments of lard because it is not solely a food."[80]

The administration also took steps to crack down on travel to Cuba, pressing Latin American nations to prohibit their citizens from going to the island, and, for the first time, prosecuting U.S. citizens who had violated the travel ban initiated just after Washington broke diplomatic relations in January 1961. The prosecutions generated a significant internal debate over the freedom to travel, pitting the attorney general of the United States, Robert Kennedy, against the State Department and the White House.

For Kennedy, prosecuting idealistic students who were hell-bent on traveling to Cuba seemed both impractical and un-American. There was no way to really stop U.S. citizens from traveling to Cuba, he warned Secretary of State Rusk; eventually the Justice Department would face prosecuting hundreds of America's youth. Moreover, restricting Americans' right to travel went against the freedoms that he had sworn to protect as attorney general. Lifting the travel ban, he argued, would be "more consistent with our views as a free society and would contrast with such things as the Berlin Wall and Communist controls on such travel."[81]

Kennedy's position won support at the State Department legal office. "The present travel restrictions are inconsistent with traditional American liberties," two of the department's leading lawyers submitted to Rusk. But other State Department officials opposed lifting the ban because the United States would appear hypocritical in its efforts to isolate Castro in the region.[82]

The debate ended with the president. In May 1964, Bundy presented Johnson with an options memo to decide the fate of travel to Cuba. There were "two distinct schools of thought" on the travel issue: Robert Kennedy's desire to end controls on the basis of "our libertarian tradition and the difficulty of controlling travel," and current U.S. policy to enlist other Latin American nations to isolate Cuba politically and culturally and to "prevent their nationals from going to Cuba." Johnson chose to sustain the ban and to prosecute those who violated it.[83]

Tightening the embargo damaged the Cuban economy, reducing the standard of living and prompting a new wave of migration. During the

1962 missile crisis, the United States terminated all flights to and from the island; thereafter, Cubans had no safe, legal, organized way to leave. Instead, they were forced to either hijack boats or risk their lives crossing the Florida Strait on rickety rafts. Hijackers received a U.S. Coast Guard escort when they arrived in U.S. waters and a hero's welcome at the docks of Key West and Miami. Rather than establish a legal immigration process—which would require negotiations, agreement, and cooperation with the Cuban government—the Johnson administration preferred to promote the image of Cuba as a repressive regime by leaving Cuban migrants no option but illegal departure.

Castro responded on September 28, 1965, by unleashing an exodus from the port of Camarioca—the first of several immigration crises he would generate over the years. Any Cuban who wanted to could leave, he announced dramatically, and boats from Florida could come to pick them up at Camarioca. In a direct challenge to Washington to negotiate normal immigration procedures, he declared: "Now the imperialists have the word. We are going to see what they do or say."[84]

U.S. officials attempted to punt the issue back to Castro. If the Cuban leader "has any serious proposal to make, there are diplomatic channels readily available," declared the State Department on September 30.[85] Behind closed doors, the White House considered options on how to respond. Castro's "vague and ambiguous" proposal to allow people to leave by boat, State Department officials warned Bundy, was an attempt to "turn the propaganda tables upon us" because of Washington's reluctance to accept massive numbers of refugees. But the United States could still win the propaganda war, Cuba desk officer William Bowdler advised Bundy. If the exodus was large enough, it would have a disruptive effect on the regime economically and politically, and Washington could point to the vast numbers of people wanting to flee the island to tarnish the image of the revolution. Moreover, by accepting tens of thousands of Cubans, "we will preserve our image as a haven for oppressed people," he wrote.[86]

President Johnson agreed. Signing a new immigration bill at the foot of the Statue of Liberty on October 3, Johnson announced an open-ended embrace of Cuban refugees—a policy that would remain unchanged for three decades. "We Americans will welcome these Cuban people," stated the president. "For the tides of history run strong, and in another day they can return to their homeland to find it cleansed of terror and free from fear."[87]

Only three days later, Bundy authorized a diplomatic note to Cuba "to kick off the negotiations on modalities." Swiss ambassador to Havana Emil

Stadelhofer would act as the go-between. The administration proposed to provide transportation for several thousand refugees a month, starting with immediate relatives of Cubans already in the United States, then political prisoners, and then "all other persons in Cuba who wish to live in the United States." With hundreds of small boats already traversing the Florida Strait toward Camarioca, the Johnson administration suggested that both governments discourage the disorderly movement of individuals during the negotiations.[88]

The Cuban government countered with an October 12 diplomatic note calling for a flow of twelve thousand refugees a month. Castro roundly rejected Washington's effort to place political prisoners on the list of eligible refugees. Indeed, Cuba rejected the very concept of U.S. lists; Cuba would determine who would be allowed to leave. Havana identified the airfield at Varadero Beach as suitable for a refugee airlift and noted that "the Cuban side is ready to begin at any moment."[89]

On the evening of October 14, Castro met with Ambassador Stadelhofer and raised a series of issues that U.S. officials labeled "more communications hanky-panky."[90] The Cuban leader was concerned that the U.S. Coast Guard was detaining boats returning from Cuba with refugees, discouraging the sealift that Cuba had set in motion. He also wanted the immigration accord to establish a legal deterrent to illegal immigration involving the theft of boats.

The State Department drafted a series of responses for Stadelhofer to present to Castro, focusing on stopping the small-boat traffic as a "disorderly, irregular and dangerous method of transportation" and blaming Cuba's "propaganda broadcasts" for continuing to stimulate it.[91] The talks almost broke down on October 19, when Castro sent an angry diplomatic note to the Swiss Embassy blasting the administration for "resorting to imputations and insinuations that are an open affront to Cuba" and warning that Cuba would consider it "useless to continue an exchange of notes that give promise of no practical solution."[92]

By then, the sealift from Camarioca had escalated dramatically, with some three hundred Cubans arriving daily in Florida. The dramatic exodus mobilized the Johnson administration to propose an agreement providing a safe, legal means of departure for émigrés. The U.S. proposal reiterated a refugee level of three thousand to four thousand a month, leaving through an airlift at Varadero, regulated by checklists and immigration inspectors, to be continued indefinitely.[93] After conferring with Castro on October 27, Ambassador Stadelhofer cabled the State Department that the agreement was "practically accepted by the Cubans."[94]

The next day, the Cuban Interior Ministry announced that the port of Camarioca would close that very night to further refugee traffic. But closing the port created a new humanitarian problem: more than four hundred boats and two thousand refugees were left stranded at Camarioca. On the morning of November 5, Bowdler reported to the White House, Cuban foreign minister Raúl Roa asked Stadelhofer "for us to bail them out of their problem."[95] Later in November, the remaining refugees were extracted from Camarioca via an official U.S. government sealift.

The 1965 migration agreement marked the first formal diplomatic accord negotiated between Washington and Havana since the revolution. As such, the State Department suggested it should handle the rollout—to downplay its importance. "There is considerable speculation that the agreement on refugees may presage a thaw in US-Cuban relations," McGeorge Bundy advised President Johnson's press secretary, Bill Moyers. "I think the noise level on this kind of accommodation speculation will be lower if State releases the notes."[96] On November 6, however, the White House announced the agreement on the Cuban Refugee Airlift. "I am pleased with the understanding which has been reached," read the statement from President Johnson.[97]

Starting on December 1, the U.S. government initiated two daily flights, five days a week, between Miami and Varadero. During their first year of operation, the flights carried 45,000 Cubans to the United States. By the time the airlift ended in April 1973, a total of 260,737 Cubans had safely immigrated under the November 1965 immigration accord.[98] Within a year of arriving, all of them were eligible to become permanent U.S. residents under the Cuban Adjustment Act—a special immigration law passed on November 2, 1966, assuring that all Cubans would be granted U.S. residency and hence a path to citizenship.

Third-Country Intermediaries

In April 1967 Secretary of State Dean Rusk met with Chilean foreign minister Gabriel Valdés at an economic summit held in Punta del Este, Uruguay. During a recent trip to Cuba, Valdés said, he had noted "differences of view in Havana" about relations with the United States "which might be open to probing." Rusk reiterated the U.S. position that Cuba "could find its way back to the Hemisphere" by severing military association with Soviets and ending interference in the affairs of other Latin American states. The "internal organization" of Cuba was not the crucial obstacle. "I told Valdés I saw no objection to any most secret probes which he might wish to undertake and that if he got anything of interest coming back we would be glad to know about it," the secretary cabled his ambassador in Santiago, Ralph Dungan, to alert him to the discussion. "I further said that I would set up this special channel between you and me in order to assure maximum secrecy and that he could be entirely frank in passing on to you, and to you alone, anything that develops."[99]

In the mid-1960s, various countries played the role of assertive intermediaries between Washington and Havana. At times, they pressed the United States government on their own initiative; at other times, Castro used friendly nations to pass along messages of conciliation. Washington also used third countries. Besides Mexico, Great Britain, Canada, and Franco's Spain offered their good offices to bring Washington and Havana closer together.

As a follow-up to British ambassador Adam Watson's extensive discussions with Fidel Castro in October 1964, Foreign Minister Patrick Gordon Walker quietly offered to "act as a middle man for a dialogue between the U.S. and Cuba." The White House resisted the British offer, but Her Majesty's government persisted. In March 1965 London sent instructions to its Washington embassy to feel out the Johnson administration on joint U.K.-Canadian-U.S. talks about Cuba policy that would examine options open to the West. "They may regard the talks as the first step in a process to move us toward a relaxation of current pressures on Cuba," Cuba desk officer John Crimmins reported to Assistant Secretary Mann.[100]

The talks took place on March 17 and 18, 1965. The British representatives forcefully advanced the argument that Castro would end his subversive practices in Latin America "if he got something meaningful in return." The British advocated offering increased contact with the West in exchange for Castro's good behavior. But the Johnson administration refused to budge. Gordon Chase, John Crimmins, and William Bowdler presented the counterargument: relaxation would reduce pressures on Cuba to break with the Soviets, give Cuba political and economic respectability, and demonstrate to Latin American nations that the Cuban model was worthwhile after all. "The meetings gave us an opportunity to educate the British and Canadians to our side of the story," Chase reported to Bundy, "and, hopefully, to persuade them that we are really not madmen when it comes to Cuba."[101]

Spain also offered its good offices. Despite its fascist ideology, the Franco regime maintained strong economic, political, and cultural ties to Castro's Cuba. Between 1964 and 1967, the Spanish Foreign Ministry undertook a series of clandestine efforts to facilitate talks between Washington and Havana.

In the spring of 1964, Castro's representatives approached officials in Spain for assistance in arriving at a "modus vivendi" with the United States. Soon thereafter, Spanish diplomats in Paris arranged for one of the more bizarre secret meetings to ever take place between U.S. and Cuban officials. At a Parisian café on April 22, two CIA officers, a Spanish official, and Cuba's ambassador to France, Antonio Carrillo, sat down to talk. Carrillo presented himself as a personal representative of Fidel Castro, empowered to discuss the possibility of a rapprochement. "His government was willing to discuss issues with the U.S. when we felt we could do so," according to a report on the conversation. The CIA's main interest in Carrillo was as a potential defector; the agency informed the White House that "they were not pushing for action on the rapprochement issue." But they also advised that if the president wanted to pursue rapprochement talks "via the Paris route," the White House should make the decision soon "while the [Carrillo] contact was still warm."[102] Before any follow-up could occur, however, the story of Cuba's efforts to enlist the Franco government as an intermediary leaked to the *New York Times*. On May 22, the *Times*'s Madrid bureau reported that "Cuba is putting out feelers for an 'arrangement' with the U.S." Based on anonymous sources, the article cited hints from Cuban diplomats in Madrid that Castro wanted an improvement in Cuban-U.S. relations.[103] The same day, ABC News ran a story citing a document ostensibly being circulated by Cuban diplomats that outlined the contours of a rapprochement: the United States would close Guantánamo; Cuba would commit not to intervene in revolutionary struggles in Latin America; the United States would make a nonintervention pledge and cut off support for violent exiles; Cuba would open negotiations on compensation for expropriated property; the United States would lift the blockade; and the United Nations would oversee implementation of these accords.

The leak generated serious concern among senior White House aides and quickly curtailed CIA contacts with Carrillo. "This leak seems to confirm my own previous hunch that the Paris activity is not the safest way to do business; we may want to consider drying it up now," Chase reported to Bundy. "If we want to continue, we should consider using the Lechuga channel which could easily be opened up again. Generally speaking," he added, "I think we should lie low for a while."[104]

Three years later, in the fall of 1967, it was the Johnson administration that took the initiative to enlist Spain to ferry a message to Cuba. During a meeting with Spanish foreign minister Fernando María Castiella in mid-November, Secretary of State Rusk raised the issue of Spain's direct access to Castro. It "would perhaps be beneficial," Rusk suggested, "if they were to remind Castro that there are only two issues in our relations with Cuba which we regard as non-negotiable: 1) Cuban intervention and guerrilla activities in Latin America, and 2) the presence of Soviet arms on Cuban soil. The U.S. had no interest in interfering in Cuba's internal political situation," Rusk stated clearly.[105] As Castiella reported back to Madrid in a cable stamped ESTRICTAMENTE CONFIDENCIAL and titled "Secretaria de Estado Dean Rusk Sugiere Gestion Espanola Cerca de Fidel Castro," Rusk then paused and added, "Perhaps Castro would want to reconsider these questions."[106]

Spanish Embassy officials understood Rusk's suggestions to be an official request to assume the role of intermediary. Their understanding was explicitly reinforced by a follow-up conversation between the Spain and Portugal desk officer, George Landau, and a Spanish Embassy attaché. This was the first time the secretary of state had formally expressed this idea, Landau said. Rusk had been motivated to make this suggestion by the "discretion, tact, and generosity with which Spain could undertake such a delicate mission to approach, in the service of peace, countries with which she is a reliable friend."[107]

Back in Madrid, however, the Foreign Ministry decided to ask Ambassador Merri del Valle to reaffirm that Washington actually intended for this sensitive message to be brought to Havana. The embassy received confirmation from Rusk's office that it should proceed. To assure there was no misunderstanding, on November 18, Deputy Under Secretary of State for Political Affairs Foy D. Kohler cabled his counterpart in the Spanish Foreign Ministry: "We confirm, repeat, confirm, the intention of [Rusk's] words with respect to Cuba. Mr. Rusk would appreciate it if, at a time and manner that seems most opportune, you could pass his statements on the American position to the Cuban Prime Minister."[108]

In late November, Franco's Foreign Ministry sent a secret envoy, veteran diplomat Adolfo Martín-Gamero, to Havana to deliver this "special message" to Castro. For three and a half hours, they talked over dinner at a protocol house in the Havana neighborhood of Vedado. The message "was accepted with evident interest," the envoy reported in his first dispatch, "and has had an undoubtable effect as we predicted." Castro expressed his "profound thanks" to the Spanish government for this "friendly gesture." He promised to keep the mission and the message absolutely secret.[109]

The two also spent the next day together, riding around the countryside in Castro's jeep. "From our conversations, it is clear how surprised and interested [Fidel] is," Martín-Gamero advised in a second report. Castro said he "wanted to analyze carefully the motives and timing of the message before responding, but promised to maintain discretion," and to use the same channel for any response he may decide to make."[110]

On December 22, the Spanish report on the "special message" reached President Johnson's desk. In a cover memo, Special Presidential Advisor Walt Rostow both minimized and misrepresented the nature of the State Department overture, blaming Spain for being overzealous: "The Spaniards have taken what Secretary Rusk intended to be a low-key reminder to Castro of our position and, for self-serving reasons, escalated it to a special message delivered by a special envoy," he complained. If it leaked out "that the U.S. has taken the initiative in putting out accommodation feelers to Castro, it may prove embarrassing to us in Latin America and on the domestic political front." But "as long as there are no leaks," Rostow noted, "this may prove to be an interesting and useful exercise."[111]

But the "special message" yielded no further results. On July 15, 1968, Spanish foreign minister Castiella and his envoy Martín-Gamero personally briefed Secretary Rusk on the status of the mission. Castro had been "pleased with the information," Martín-Gamero related, but "said he would have to wait for some signs from the U.S." When Rusk asked what kind of signs Castro expected, Martín-Gamero responded that Castro had not provided any specifics. Since the message was delivered, "nothing had been heard from the Cubans," Castiella noted. Rusk then suggested that Spain might take steps to find out if the Cubans "consider this issue still alive."[112] Only one day later, however, the Johnson administration called off the Spanish overture. An aide to Rusk, Robert Sayre, met with a Spanish official, Nuño Aguirre de Cárcer, and informed him that the United States "did not believe it would be useful for the Spanish to hold any further conversations or make any further approaches at this time."[113]

Positive Containment: Rethinking U.S. Policy

Secretary Rusk's recruitment of Spain to carry a feeler to Castro followed, by only a few weeks, a rare but significant victory in Washington's ongoing low-intensity war against Cuba. In early October 1967, the CIA and a U.S.-trained special unit of the Bolivian military captured and executed Che Guevara in a mountainous region of southern Bolivia where he had been leading a small band of insurgents. "We are 99% sure that Che Guevara is dead," Rostow reported in a SECRET memorandum to the president on October 11. The elimination of Guevara, he informed Johnson, would "have a strong impact in discouraging would-be guerrillas" in Latin America.[114]

Indeed, the loss of Guevara undercut his model of insurgent warfare in Latin America and led to a hiatus in Cuba's active role in region. "Che Guevara's death was a crippling—perhaps fatal—blow to the Bolivian guerrilla movement and may prove a serious setback for Fidel Castro's hopes to foment violent revolution in 'all or almost all' Latin American countries," noted the State Department's Bureau of Intelligence and Research.[115] At a national memorial service for his fallen comrade, Castro angrily declared that "those who sing victory" over Guevara's death would be "mistaken" to think "that his death is the defeat of his ideas, the defeat of his tactics, the defeat of his guerrilla concepts."[116] But not until the Sandinista revolution in Nicaragua more than a decade later would Cuba again provide significant support to another Latin American insurgency.

Cuban "subversion" was one of the two major issues that, as Secretary Rusk had told the Spanish, "were non-negotiable" in U.S. policy toward Cuba (the other being Havana's military ties to the Soviet Union). Guevara's fatal failure could not help but create an opening for proponents of a different policy approach to Cuba. Moreover, Che's demise corresponded with evolving international circumstances that forced a change in the administration's focus on the island.

By mid-1967, the domestic and foreign catastrophe known as Vietnam had begun to overwhelm Washington. As the war effort faltered and public pressure mounted on President Johnson to reduce America's overt military presence in Vietnam, the CIA received orders to dramatically escalate its covert operations in Indochina. The reprioritization of the CIA's mission, budget, and manpower meant that it would have to close its largest and most expensive outpost in the world—the CIA station in Miami. Although it would take five years to fully dismantle the station, the decision to do so meant that the heyday of CIA-sponsored exile operations against Cuba was over.

Nor were there any prospects of Castro being overthrown by internal forces. "Organized internal resistance to the Castro regime has been eradicated and, aside from an occasional isolated act of sabotage, internal security has ceased to be a serious problem," declared a 1966 *Current Intelligence Weekly Special Report*. "Barring Castro's death or disability, the present regime will maintain an unassailable hold on Cuba indefinitely."[117]

Faced with these realities, the Johnson administration undertook the first substantive Cuba policy review since the regimen of covert operations, trade sanctions, and multilateral efforts to isolate the island had been put in place by Presidents Eisenhower and Kennedy. "After six years it is only prudent to ask whether this policy will be the best means of advancing our national interests," the State Department's Policy Planning Council advised Secretary of State Rusk. "A review of our Cuba policy seems very much needed."[118]

In mid-May 1967, Rusk authorized a national policy paper (NPP) on strategy toward Castro's Cuba. Over the next fourteen months, the NPP Working Group on Cuba—made up of analysts from the State Department, CIA, NSC, and Department of Defense (DOD), and chaired by Deputy Assistant Secretary of State for Inter-American Affairs Viron P. ("Pete") Vaky—conducted a wide-ranging comprehensive evaluation of current and potential approaches to dealing with the Castro regime. Among the "potential" alternatives that the review seriously examined was "the opportunities and risks involved in seeking some accommodation."

Officially titled "National Policy Paper—Cuba: United States Policy," the review presented a logical, step-by-step analysis that contradicted both the popular wisdom and the propaganda of the era. "Castro is in full control and Cuba is still a one-man show," the study acknowledged. But, since the "Guevara fiasco," he had shown little public interest in the export of revolution. Moreover, relations with the Soviet Union "were not good." Fidel Castro, these analysts understood, "has no intention of subordinating himself to Soviet discipline and direction and he has increasingly disagreed with Soviet concepts, strategies and theories."[119]

Even so, as long as Castro needed security against "feared U.S. intervention," it would be hard to wean him away from Soviet support. "Castro deeply mistrusts and fears the U.S. and sincerely believes that the U.S. is implacably hostile to him and bent on his eventual overthrow," the authors reported. "Accordingly, Castro's reflex is to view the U.S. and anything it does in the worst light and with the greatest suspicion."

In this context, Washington's preconditions for improving relations—that Cuba terminate ties with Moscow and end support for revolutionary groups in Latin America—had no chance of being met. It was "unrealistic to expect Castro, unilaterally and in advance, to change policies and orientation so fundamentally, as it would be to expect the U.S. to do the equivalent in reverse," the authors pointed out. "As long as Castro remains convinced that the U.S. is his major enemy bent on his destruction he is unlikely to take any such major steps voluntarily." So, unless the Johnson administration wanted to overthrow Castro by force, it needed to exchange its punitive policy for a more effective approach.

To determine what that approach should be, the task force posed five policy questions:

1) Is Castro's overthrow indispensable to achievement of vital U.S. objectives, or could these be met even though the Castro regime survives indefinitely?
2) Is Castro's overthrow possible without U.S. action? If not, is the U.S. prepared to use force?
3) Is an accommodation on terms satisfactory to the U.S. possible or worth seeking, or is hostile coexistence the only feasible modus vivendi?
4) What would be the minimum which U.S. interests would require for a tolerable modus vivendi? . . .
5) Are there any still good reasons to retain the present isolation/ economic denial policy?

On the first question, the analysts were unequivocal: eliminating Castro was "not indispensible" to U.S. interests. Cuba's activities in the hemisphere did not represent a mortal national security threat, nor were they likely to "become an unmanageable problem." On the second question, the lack of wisdom of continuing attempts to overthrow Castro by force was self-evident. Years of CIA covert and paramilitary operations had failed to do anything but further entrench the regime. Ever bigger sabotage missions ran the risk of escalating into open warfare, which could lead to a superpower confrontation with the Soviets "and a serious increase in world tension." The United States would be condemned around the world for unprovoked aggression. Finally, the Cuban people would reject U.S. intervention and rally to the nationalist cause of the revolution. "It is frankly very questionable whether the U.S. can achieve satisfactory long-range rehabilitation of Cuba by coercion from the outside," the study candidly acknowledged.

Since the regime was not going to collapse on its own, and open intervention would be too costly, the United States faced two basic policy options: continuing a static state of perpetual hostility or pursuing a modus vivendi. Continuing the policy of what the study termed the "hostile adversary concept" meant that Washington would maintain its policies of diplomatic isolation, economic denial, and maximum external pressures to foster internal upheaval. But in an argument repeated throughout the study, the authors noted that Washington's power to isolate Cuba politically and economically had diminished and would diminish further. Forewarning the eventual rebellion of European and Latin American allies against the embargo, the authors noted that "the political cost to the U.S. of discouraging other nations from trading with Cuba is increasing while its ability to convince them to follow that course is lessening." The current policy "is a negative and reactive one which merely holds the line and offers limited promise of encouraging desirable change in Cuban policies."

As an alternative to "passive containment," the analysts recommended "positive containment"—an effort to create a more "relaxed atmosphere" through threat reduction, diplomatic engagement, and various carrots to persuade Fidel to modify his bad behaviors and meet U.S. interests. Under the "positive containment" scenario, the United States would maintain the trade embargo as a bargaining chip and continue efforts to stem Cuban subversion in the region. But to those sticks would be added "the controlled relaxation of U.S. pressures" and other carrots with the goal of fostering "a more constructive modus vivendi." Positive containment would advance "the economic and cultural magnetism of the U.S. and the promises of economic/political benefits which Cuba could gain from more rational behavior." For the first time, U.S. government officials suggested a "people-to-people" strategy, noting that "consideration should be given to increasing selectively non-official contact with Cuban society" and to project "patience and friendliness toward the Cuban people."

The United States would drop the demands for Castro to sever ties with the Soviets and cease revolutionary activities in Latin America as preconditions for talks. Instead, those demands would become longer-term goals to be arrived at through a succession of quid pro quos that both countries would undertake—essentially a form of what the Clinton administration would, years later, call "calibrated response." According to the policy paper, a series of "parallel steps"—each side moving on its own but in response to the other—in the coming months and years could evolve like this:

CASTRO'S QUIDS	U.S. QUOS
Continued repatriation of U.S. citizens	Grant licenses for commercial shipment of drugs and pharmaceuticals on a more lenient basis
Tone down anti-U.S. propaganda and attitude	Tone down hostile propaganda; selective relaxation of travel ban both ways

Release political prisoners	Permit U.S. foreign subsidiaries to trade
Begin cessation of support to insurgents in Latin America, and effective evidence of this	Permit full commercial trade in drugs and pharmaceuticals, possibly foodstuffs; public declaration by U.S. officials that the U.S. will not intervene in Cuba
Stop guerrilla training in Cuba	Permit additional U.S. trade in consumer goods and some industrial equipment; propose to OAS that relations be renewed
Willingness to enter talks on indemnification of U.S. business interests	Willingness to unfreeze Cuban assets and relax all restrictions on financial transactions
Willingness to break military tie with Soviets	Offer nonaggression pact; accept back into OAS; facilitate equipment of Cuban armed forces with U.S. or European equipment

Using positive containment to foster a more "relaxed atmosphere" in U.S.-Cuban relations had a number of policy advantages. If Washington extended the olive branch, Fidel would be put on the defensive and no longer able to "use the U.S. as a scapegoat for his regime's problems." Indeed, even if Castro proved unresponsive, Washington could dangle these carrots in front of members of the top echelon of his regime "to convey the idea to such elements that it would be in their interest to effect a switch in policy that could make possible a thaw with the U.S. under the terms envisaged." These approaches would be made quietly, and "in more specific form covertly."

The National Policy Paper finished with a series of "taskers" to the CIA, DOD, State Department, and U.S. Agency for International Development (USAID), to implement the new strategy. These agencies would begin to "create the general atmosphere for subsequent probes" and avoid any new manifestation of an abrasive attitude toward Havana. They would foster the message, through subtle propaganda, that Washington was not hostile toward the Cuban revolution, only its "aggressive external conduct." The State Department would use foreign diplomatic channels to assure Castro that the United States would be willing to reach a reasonable accommodation. Finally, contingency plans would be drawn up for lifting the trade embargo and reintegrating Cuba into the OAS.

This was the "preferred strategy," the study concluded. It offered a far better chance of advancing U.S. national security interests than continuing the hostile, adversarial policy toward Cuba in place since the beginning of the 1960s.

A Policy Vacuum

These were radical recommendations—a true departure from the conventional wisdom of how to rid the hemisphere of Fidel Castro and his revolution. Predictably, those who supported the status quo of sticks over carrots quickly tried to stymie any new approach. After a draft of the national policy paper began to circulate in June 1968, Assistant Secretary of State for Inter-American Affairs Covey Oliver sent a memorandum to the Chairman of the Policy Planning Board Henry D. Owens cautioning against implementing most of its recommendations. Cuba's economy was deteriorating, he argued, and the regime faced growing external and internal pressures. With "real doubts as to the viability" of Castro's future, Oliver advised, now was not the time to "convey a seeming signal that we have finally accepted the permanence of the Castro regime."[120] The State Department's Office of Inter-American Political Affairs also weighed in, arguing that "this is not the most propitious moment to embark on such a program, as Cuba's present economic straits and the signs of growing discontent would indicate that the pinch of isolation is having a real effect."[121]

Over at the CIA, officials sought to appropriate the task force's recommendations of communications with top Cuban leaders to advance their institutional interest in regime change. At an August 15, meeting, the top CIA officers on Latin America, including Western Hemisphere Chief William Broe and veteran Cuba operative David Atlee Phillips, suggested a covert approach to "Cuban leaders around Castro to assure them the U.S. had no wish to abrogate or wipe out the gains of the Cuban revolution." The CIA would then offer to "support them in any post-Castro regime" if they would "take timely action that would expedite the removal of Castro as the regime's leader." Both Viron Vaky and Covey Oliver objected that the discussion of "Castro's removal" was "not appropriate."

But the meeting continued to focus on the issue of negotiating with Cuba. "There was a world-wide impression that secret negotiations were in fact going on between Cuba and the United States," Phillips reported. He noted that the CIA had maintained a secret "facility"—presumably in a third country—that could be used in future communications with the Cubans. "Should we attempt to open up and pursue a dialogue or should we close it down immediately?" Phillips asked. Assistant Secretary Oliver responded that "a freeze should be put on any further talk and that it merely be indicated to the Cubans that the channel should be kept open for their use if they so desired." If asked by Cuban intelligence officers, Oliver suggested, the CIA should say that "the ball was in the Cuban court and that channels for negotiation existed."[122] At the end of the meeting, the CIA and the State Department decided to create a small study group to "consider the question of what exactly we should do next about Cuba."

In the waning months of the Johnson administration, Cuba policy was in a state of flux—"both confused and becalmed," as Phillips described it. Major covert operations were being dismantled, secret messages were still being passed through various channels, and an internal effort to reframe the overall policy approach toward Cuba from "passive" to "positive" containment was under way. But the dramatic planning paper for moving toward a more enlightened diplomatic posture was "never formally processed for approval," a State Department memorandum noted only a few days before the November 1968 presidential election. Instead, "it was decided that it should be considered by the new administration."[123]

4. NIXON AND FORD

Kissinger's Caribbean Détente

It is better to deal straight with Castro. Behave chivalrously; do it like a big guy, not like a shyster.

—Secretary of State Henry Kissinger to his aides, April, 1975

At 2:32 P.M., on April 24, 1974, Secretary of State Henry Kissinger took a phone call from Frank Mankiewicz, a longtime Democratic Party operative. "That trip I told you about is now on . . . to the Caribbean," Mankiewicz said as Kissinger's secret taping system recorded his cryptic remarks. "I told you I might be doing a television interview with . . ." Kissinger immediately understood: "Yes, yes, I know exactly—of course. Good. Then I want to see you. . . . I must see you before you do that."[1] Nine weeks later, when Mankiewicz and two colleagues, Saul Landau and Kirby Jones, traveled to Cuba, they carried with them a short, handwritten, unsigned note from Kissinger to Fidel Castro. ("This is the way I did it with Chou En-lai," Mankiewicz remembers Kissinger saying when he gave him the letter.) The message stated that the secretary of state was anxious to discuss bilateral issues and that such discussions should be held discreetly, through intermediaries.

"This is a very serious communication and we will, of course, consider it very carefully," Castro said after reading the message in his study. When Mankiewicz returned from Cuba, he carried a secret reply from Castro as well as a box of premium Cuban cigars—Fidel's official gift for the U.S. secretary of state.[*2]

So began the most serious effort to normalize relations between the United States and Cuba since Washington broke ties with Havana in January 1961.

---

* When a U.S. Customs officer tried to confiscate the cigars as contraband, Mankiewicz issued a stern warning: "Son, this box of cigars is a personal gift for Secretary of State Henry Kissinger. Are you sure you want to take them away?" Kissinger got his cigars—though he didn't smoke (Mankiewicz interview, June 5, 1994).

Kissinger's message set in motion a protracted effort to achieve an "opening" to Cuba comparable to the opening to China—an effort to extend the Nixon-Kissinger strategy of détente with the Soviet Union to its Communist ally in the Caribbean. Over the next eighteen months, emissaries traveled back and forth between Washington and Havana, and Kissinger's deputies quietly met with Cuban officials in airport lounges, New York hotels, and private homes to discuss the issues that divided the United States and Cuba. "It is better to deal straight with Castro," Kissinger instructed his assistants, taking a position on Cuba that had not been heard before from a high-ranking U.S. policy maker. "Behave chivalrously; do it like a big guy, not like a shyster. Let him know: We are moving in a new direction; we'd like to synchronize; . . . steps will be unilateral; reciprocity is necessary."[3]

Nixon and Castro

Kissinger chose to initiate contact with Cuba during the waning weeks of the Nixon administration—when all attention was on Watergate. "I don't think I even told President Nixon," he would later admit, because Nixon "disliked Castro intensely."[4] As vice president in April 1959, Nixon was the highest U.S. official ever to meet with Castro. But although Nixon's report to President Eisenhower made it clear that he was impressed with Fidel's charisma and leadership qualities, Nixon would later write in his memoirs that he emerged from that meeting as the leading advocate for overthrowing Cuba's revolutionary regime.[5]

As president, Nixon took a hard line toward Cuba. When a prominent exile attempted to contact the new president only eleven days after the inauguration, Kissinger sent Nixon a memo suggesting that the State Department handle all meetings with the exile community. "I disagree," Nixon wrote at the bottom of the memorandum. "State has handled this with disgusting incompetence. Their careerists are Pro-Castro for the most part."[6] Early in his first term, Nixon specifically directed the CIA to come up with a new plan to put "paramilitary pressure" on Cuba. When the agency resisted such operations as unfeasible, Nixon sought to unleash the violent exiles running raids into Cuba from the shores of Miami. "We should not inhibit Cuban exile activity against their homeland," he wrote in the margin of an article about Coast Guard action to arrest members of the terrorist exile group, Alpha 66, effectively ordering U.S. law enforcement agencies to ignore the Neutrality Act.[7] "I had the distinct impression from the president," CIA director Richard Helms reported to Attorney General John Mitchell, "that he rather favors some anti-Castro activity by this Alpha-66 group."[8]

Despite Nixon's known antipathy for dealing with Cuba, in February 1969, Castro initiated a discreet approach to the new administration through the good offices of Switzerland's embassy. Only ten days after Nixon's inauguration, the Cuban leader called in Swiss ambassador Alfred Fischli for a forty-minute meeting. Cubans were illegally leaving the island through the U.S. base on Guantánamo, Castro said. He did not want to "build a Berlin wall around the base," and implied that he hoped the Nixon administration would block this avenue of escape. He asked Ambassador Fischli if he thought Washington would be willing to cooperate with Cuba in thwarting plots by Cuban exiles to introduce hoof-and-mouth viruses into the Cuban cattle industry. He complained about U.S. intervention in Latin America but offered a hint that Cuba was willing to curb its support for revolutionary movements by noting that "we should all stop interfering." As Fischli told Secretary of State William P. Rogers in Washington on March 11, Castro asked him to "convey a message that he was interested in establishing a discussion of such issues, presumably with the view toward edging toward a detente."[9]

Castro's exploratory effort set off the first policy discussion within the Nixon White House on dialogue with Cuba. Cuba's initiative was an opportunity, Kissinger's NSC deputy, Viron "Pete" Vaky, advised: "Other recent Cuban actions reflect a more moderate attitude toward the U.S. than has been the case, and there definitely appears to be an overall pattern suggesting a bid for a detente."[10]

On April 4, in a SECRET "action" memo to the president titled "Cuba—Message from Castro Suggesting a Desire for Detente," Kissinger made the first effort to convince Nixon that "a cautious probe" could benefit the administration. "In fact," Kissinger told the president, "putting out a feeler to Castro now would keep open the option of a dialogue, should you wish to use that approach at a later time." Nixon, however, refused to check either "Approve" or "Disapprove." Instead he scrawled at the bottom of the document: "a *very, very* cautious probe."[11]

With this restrictive approval, the State Department drafted a short response for Ambassador Fischli to give to Castro: "It would be appreciated if the Ambassador could ask Castro to explain more precisely 1) what he may have in mind as regards the parameters or nature of any contact or dialogue; and 2) whether he has in mind specific or limited subjects."[12] Typed on plain paper, this message was passed to the Swiss ambassador to Washington, Felix Schnyder, on April 11. Meeting with Under Secretary of State U. Alexis Johnson and Viron Vaky, Schnyder reported on additional meetings between

Fischli and President Osvaldo Dorticós in Havana. The two had discussed issues of concern to both Cuba and the United States, among them plane hijackings, Guantánamo, and some twenty U.S. citizens held in Cuban prisons. According to Schnyder, the Cubans "seemed pleased" with this ongoing interchange and "considered the Swiss a desirable channel through which to establish a dialogue."[13]

But this promising start was cut short by Nixon's opposition. In September, Kissinger convened an NSC task force to review options on Cuba policy, among them force, isolation, carrot and stick, and "normalization." The normalization option of seeking negotiations "without preconditions on a wide-ranging improvement in U.S.-Cuban relations" was immediately ruled out because of, as Kissinger reminded top CIA, DOS, DOD, and NSC officials, "the overture through the Swiss which the President stopped."[14] So, too, were the options of using a proactive carrot and stick for "constructive change" in relations (as Vaky's national policy paper had recommended at the end of the Johnson administration).

During a meeting with his top aides at Camp David on September 27, Nixon reiterated that "he wanted to follow a very tough line on Cuba . . . and he did not want to hear press speculation that we were considering a new policy."[15] When such speculation arose in the international media several months later, the White House had the State Department send a cable to U.S. embassies in Latin American to squash the "rumor-mongering" about an accommodation with Cuba: "[Cuba] policy remains unaltered. There are no rpt [repeat] no conversations underway or contemplated between the USG and the Cuban Government concerning a modification of the present relationship."[16]

In March 1970 Nixon called both his national security advisor and his CIA director, Richard Helms, to the Oval office. To Helms, Nixon posed the question of whether he should change Cuba policy. The president "pointed out that he was under pressure from Canada and certain other countries to ease up on Castro and possibly to enter into diplomatic relationships somewhere down the road," Helms recorded in his notes. Nixon went on to say that the State Department "was advocating some change of policy such as this." Helms reinforced Nixon's hard-line instinct: "I told the President that I thought we should continue the present policy of keeping Castro isolated and of applying economic sanctions against his country. I pointed out that Cuba was costing the Soviet Union a million dollars a day and that if indeed the President wanted to cause the Soviet Union headaches . . . this was one [way] he had within his power by doing nothing."

"You have convinced me," Nixon declared.[17]

Six months later, when Socialist Salvador Allende was elected president of Chile, Nixon and Helms revisited the question about whether, as Nixon put it, "we should hold course on Cuba or should we start being nice to Castro." The president made his preference clear. "My conviction is very strong that we cannot relent in our policy towards Cuba," Nixon insisted. "If we throw in the towel on the Cubans, the effect on the rest of Latin America could be massive, encouraging them, encouraging Communists, Marxists, Allende, or call it what you will, to try for revolution.[18]"

For most of his first term, Nixon forcefully held the U.S. government to that uncompromising position. His hand was strengthened by the short-lived superpower confrontation in the fall of 1970, with distinct echoes of the 1962 Cuban Missile Crisis, over Soviet efforts to build a support base in Cienfuegos Bay that could service Soviet nuclear-armed submarines. But even after Kissinger deftly resolved that conflict diplomatically, the issue of better relations with Cuba continued to surface, put on the agenda by other Latin American nations.

In December 1971, as Nixon prepared for a private meeting with Brazilian president Emilio Medici, Kissinger briefed him on Brazil's request to be alerted to any future dialogue with Castro that might portend a different U.S. approach toward Cuba. "I'm not going to change the policy," Nixon vehemently responded during this conversation, recorded by his secret taping system:

NIXON: I've said I'm not going to change the policy.
KISSINGER: I know.
NIXON: I'm not changing the policy towards Castro as long as I'm alive.
KISSINGER: All right. Well then . . .
NIXON: That's absolute. Final. No appeal whatever. I never want you to raise it with me again.[19]

The Hijacking Accord

Nevertheless, the national interest in fighting terrorism in the skies would compel Nixon to communicate, negotiate, and cooperate with Cuba. During his presidency, "skyjacking" emerged as a significant problem. Between 1961 and 1967, 17 planes were hijacked to Cuba; in 1968 alone, the number jumped to 29, with 19 of the flights originating in the United States. Between 1968 and 1972, the number of plane hijackings worldwide rose to 325. Of those, 173 were diverted to Cuba.[20]

Since the early years of the revolution, the Cuban government had worried that air piracy would become a bilateral issue between Washington and Havana. In his August 20, 1961, meeting with Richard Goodwin in Montevideo, Che Guevara noted that Cuba had not been responsible for the spate of U.S. planes commandeered to Cuba by political sympathizers of the revolution. "He is afraid that if these thefts keep up it will be very dangerous," Goodwin reported. For its part, Cuba wanted the United States to return exiles who used violence to hijack planes and boats to escape the island. In an exchange of diplomatic notes in July and August of 1961, the Cuban government first proposed a mutual accord to return all hijackers to their country of origin. The Kennedy administration rejected this petition.[21]

Eight years later, with a dozen hijackings to Cuba in the first two months of 1969 alone, the new Nixon administration secretly approached Cuba about returning the perpetrators to the United States. Quietly, Cuba began to expel some hijackers to third countries, and encourage others to leave. But the global epidemic of air piracy put Cuba in the international spotlight as a destination for plane pirates. On September 19, the Cuban government announced a new law: Cuba would now prosecute or extradite all foreign hijackers. Extradition, however, would take place only with countries that had negotiated a bilateral antihijacking accord with Cuba.[22]

The highly publicized law "appears to be a major gambit by Cuba," Viron Vaky advised Kissinger, "not only with respect to the hijacking situation but perhaps in terms of relations with us as well." Cuban vice president Carlos Rafael Rodríguez had referred to the new law as an opportunity to build "a new modus vivendi" between the two countries. "The quid pro quo which Castro presumably intends to exact is not clear and may give us trouble," Vaky noted, referring to Cuba's demand for reciprocity. That meant the United States would have to treat Cuban exiles who had hijacked planes and boats as criminals and return them to the island. "However, we believe the Cuban decree could represent a significant step and are considering how best to respond to it."[23] Soon the Department of State was sending secret diplomatic notes through the Swiss Embassy trying to find a "neutral" solution to returning U.S. hijackers from Cuba. But Nixon refused to budge on what Kissinger termed the "troublesome reciprocal elements"—Castro's demand that the United States return Cuban hijackers. The 1969 effort to arrive at a formal antihijacking accord ended without resolution.

In both word and deed, however, Cuba continued to signal its willingness to find a solution to airline hijackings. "Cuba has now become one of the best behaved of the hijacking states, since it immediately allows the planes and passengers to return and often jails the hijackers," the NSC reported in October 1970. "It recently returned its first hijacker, and offered to return all hijackers provided we do the same (a commitment we cannot make because of the political asylum aspect)."[24] After a particularly violent set of criminal skyjackings in October and November 1972, including one in which a guard was killed and the hijackers extorted $2 million from Southern Airways, Fidel Castro again took the diplomatic initiative. On November 15, Radio Havana announced that the Cuban government was "ready to take such steps which might lead to the adoption of a broad agreement" with the United States to deter future hijackings.[25]

Within a day, Secretary of State William P. Rogers replied: The U.S. government was "prepared to negotiate an arrangement regarding hijacking and other serious crimes which may be committed in the future." It would also "consider favorably any arrangement and location for such talks that would expedite agreement."[26] The Cubans reacted expeditiously; nine days later, Cuban officials met with the Swiss ambassador and formally presented a draft treaty on hijackings. "On the basis of equality and strict reciprocity," it read, both governments would punish with ten to thirty years of imprisonment any person who "seizes, takes control of, appropriates, or diverts" an aircraft or other vessel. In a clause on violent exile operations in the United States, the draft accord also obliged both countries to pursue and severely punish those persons who were using its territory to promote or plan "acts of violence or depredation against aircraft or vessels of any type."[27]

Over the next eight weeks the Swiss Embassy in Havana conveyed messages back and forth, and by mid-February the two countries had arrived at a formal agreement. Hijackers and anyone engaging in violence against planes or vessels would be either prosecuted or extradited, as the Cuban draft had proposed. The one exception, insisted on by the United States, was for political refugees who commandeered a vessel without engaging in violence.[28]

For Fidel, signing the antihijacking treaty served multiple interests. The hijackings put Cuba in a negative international spotlight as a haven for terrorists. Forcing the United States to prosecute or return Cubans who hijacked boats or planes could serve as a deterrent for violent seizures of Cuban vessels. Moreover, counterterrorism cooperation could address Cuba's leading national security concern: violent counterrevolutionary operations by the anti-Castro exile community in the United States. Finally, as Che Guevara pointed out to Richard Goodwin in August 1961, an agreement on air piracy was one of those "subordinate issues" that could pave the way for talks on a modus vivendi between Washington and Havana.

But President Nixon explicitly opposed any possibility of improved relations. Indeed, from the start of the talks, Nixon feared that an antihijacking
accord would be interpreted as a change in Washington's overall posture of
hostility toward Cuba. On February 13, 1973, as Secretary Rogers presented
the president with the final language of the accord, Nixon's secret Oval Office taping system picked up his continuing anxiety about this issue:

NIXON: Does it get into anything in terms of normalization of relations
because that's the only thing that would concern me. If you could
cover that because I don't want the Cuban community to go up in a,
up in a . . .
ROGERS: What I would say is that it doesn't change any policy as far as
Cuba's concerned.[29]

Two days later, as Rogers announced the new accord, he went out of his
way to state that cooperation on hijacking did not signal a thaw in relations.
The bilateral agreement, he explained to reporters, "does not foreshadow a
change of policies as far as the United States is concerned."[30]

Kissinger's Cuba Initiative

Increasingly, Henry Kissinger came to disagree with that position. His assessment of Cuba policy evolved from his first months in office as national security
advisor when he tacitly sided with Nixon's hard-line approach, to mid-1973,
when Kissinger became secretary of state and found the Cuba controversy
high on the agenda of the U.S. Congress and the inter-American community.
In 1969 he was skeptical of the claim that "the benefits of our present policy
are declining because of rising costs." By 1973 he was convinced of it.[31]

Quite simply, the new secretary of state realized that sustaining an outdated U.S. approach to Cuba created far more policy problems for Washington than advantages. At home, public support for continuing sanctions
was waning, and the U.S. Congress was threatening to pass legislation lifting
the embargo. Domestically, the Cold War consensus to sustain a hard-line
posture against Cuba had unraveled, due in no small measure to the dramatic Nixon-Kissinger opening to Communist China. If the United States
could have diplomatic relations with a faraway power such as China, why
not have relations with a small island off its coast? A Harris opinion poll
taken in the spring of 1973 showed that 51 percent of the American public
favored normal relations while 33 percent opposed.[32] Key Democrats, as well
as Republicans, openly questioned the wisdom of the embargo and pressed

the administration to change what they considered to be an anachronistic and self-defeating policy.

As early as January 1973, a caucus of moderate Republicans (including then Representative Gerald Ford) known as the Wednesday Group, issued a report entitled "A Detente with Cuba," which urged Nixon to consider normalizing relations.[33] In April 1974 the Senate passed a resolution, sponsored by Senators Claiborne Pell and Jacob Javits, calling for a full congressional and executive branch review of Cuba policy. In September, Javits and Pell became the first senior senators to travel to Cuba to meet with Fidel Castro. "The Castro Government interpreted our trip as an opening—a positive step on the long road back to a normalization of relations," the senators concluded after a three and a half hour dinner with the Cuban leader and his aides. "A propitious moment has arrived in United States–Cuban relations when it is possible to begin to talk. The time is ripe for beginning the process of normalization."[34]

Internationally, the White House faced even greater demands for normalization. A rebellion was brewing against the OAS diplomatic and trade sanctions adopted under U.S. pressure in 1964. In the spring of 1970, Chilean president Eduardo Frei announced that his country would break the OAS embargo and restore trade with Cuba. Diplomatic relations were renewed in November by newly elected president Salvador Allende. Peru reopened an embassy in Havana in 1972. Argentina restored diplomatic ties in 1973. More importantly, Argentina demanded that the Argentine subsidiaries of U.S. automakers sell vehicles to Cuba, and, along with Peru, proposed that the OAS formally lift sanctions and allow member states to restore ties and trade, ending Cuba's political and economic isolation. Several key countries were "quietly going AWOL from the 1964 sanctions—and use our evident intransigence on Cuba to play to the[ir] domestic left," Kissinger's aides reported. "In most of these countries, U.S. movement on Cuba would be a considerable plus in our relationship."[35]

As secretary of state, Kissinger found that the issue of Cuba dominated meetings with his Latin American counterparts. As the OAS initiative to lift sanctions against Cuba advanced through various regional meetings in 1974 and 1975, he held extensive behind-the-scenes discussions with Latin American foreign ministers. "Let me be very frank with you," Kissinger told Argentine foreign minister Alberto Vignes at a September 16, 1974, meeting discussing the OAS initiative. "Cuba can do very little for us. From the foreign policy standpoint it would help remove anomalies in our relations with other countries. Cuba in and of itself is not very important to the United

States. . . . The Cuba issue is significant only as it affects our relations with other Latin American countries."

But President Gerald Ford's new administration faced domestic political constraints on its ability to change the framework of U.S.-Cuban relations, Kissinger explained to Vignes. "We have a full quota of domestic opposition and we are not looking for more." At the same time, Kissinger noted that the U.S. position was evolving now that Nixon was gone. "How far the situation will evolve depends on the United States domestic scene and it depends upon how the Cubans behave."

Foreign Minister Vignes pressed Kissinger on whether there "would be bilateral contacts between the United States and Cuba" in the aftermath of the OAS vote to rescind sanctions. "That has occurred to me," Kissinger replied. "We have no contacts now with Cuba."[36]

The Secret Talks

Kissinger was lying to Vignes. By then, his office was already in direct contact with the Cubans. Only eight weeks before, on July 18, 1974, Frank Mankiewicz had delivered Kissinger's initial message to Castro. After reading it, Castro asked, "Will you take back a letter?" When Mankiewicz returned, he brought Kissinger a handwritten note from Castro accepting the U.S. offer to initiate a dialogue.[37] Kissinger then asked Mankiewicz to help facilitate secret talks with the Cubans.

On September 14, Mankiewicz traveled to New York to meet with Teofilo Acosta, chargé d'affaires at the Cuban mission at the United Nations. The ostensible purpose of the meeting was to arrange another TV interview for Fidel Castro—this time with Dan Rather of CBS News. But Mankiewicz told Acosta that he would be bringing another message from Kissinger. Two weeks later, as Castro prepared for the CBS interview, Mankiewicz met with him privately and briefed him on Kissinger's new communication. Kissinger had chosen his deputy, Lawrence Eagleburger, as his representative in the clandestine talks, Mankiewicz said. Castro responded that he would appoint a veteran diplomat and member of the Cuban Communist Party, Ramón Sánchez-Parodi, to represent Cuba. When he returned to Washington, Mankiewicz passed this information on to Kissinger's office.[38]

As an intermediary, Mankiewicz provided a degree of plausible denial. He was a prominent liberal, particularly on the issue of Cuba. His distance from a Republican administration "made him an ideal emissary," Kissinger wrote

From right to left, Frank Mankiewicz, Kirby Jones, and Saul Landau deliver a message to Fidel Castro from Secretary of State Henry Kissinger, proposing negotiations to normalize U.S.-Cuban relations, July 1974. (Courtesy of Frank Mankiewicz)

in his memoirs.[39] "He could convey a message, but he could not drag us into anything irrevocable." If the story leaked, U.S. officials could simply say that Mankiewicz had acted on his own.

Indeed, even by Kissinger's standards of furtive diplomacy, this "special project" was shrouded in extreme secrecy. "There was total secrecy about this," recalled his deputy, William D. Rogers, who became a key player in, and advocate of, the clandestine talks with Cuba. Kissinger kept his secret diplomacy tightly guarded, out of sight of the National Security Council and away from his own State Department. "Only Kissinger, Eagleburger and myself knew about this initiative," noted Rogers. "We were afraid of leaks; we were dealing with dynamite."[40]

Not even President Ford, it appears, was fully briefed. "We need to talk about Cuba," Kissinger informed the new president on August 15, 1974, six days after Nixon resigned. Yet he did not tell Ford about the initial exchange of messages with Castro. When Ford asked if "you have any suggestions for a Cuban policy change," Kissinger responded, disingenuously: "There have been many appeals from Cuba. Castro wants to meet with me. . . . The issue is the trade embargo," he noted. "We need to loosen up or we isolate ourselves."[41]

A month later, Kissinger informed Ford, "We are being moved into relations with Cuba. But it should not appear to the American people that it is being forced on us. So I would hold tough at the OAS," he recommended. "But we should start with low-level talks with the Cubans to see what we can get for it."[42] In late September, as Mankiewicz got ready to deliver a second message to Castro, Kissinger obliquely informed Ford about the feeler to Fidel. "On Cuba, our policy is to give grudgingly in the OAS and send a message to Castro to see what we could get bilaterally." But, Kissinger told the president, "We can't let that pipsqueak drive us."[43]

Throughout the fall of 1974, Mankiewicz remained Kissinger's "special channel." He continued to ferry messages to Castro, and returned to New York in November and December to meet with officials at Cuba's UN mission, arranging for Cuba's emissary, Sánchez-Parodi, to be given a multiple entry visa to enter the United States. These efforts set the stage for a series of secret talks in 1975 and early 1976—the first direct dialogue between Washington and Havana aimed at restoring relations since their rupture in January 1961.

Yet the sour state of U.S.-Cuban relations almost sabotaged the first clandestine meeting. Despite Eagleburger's directive to the U.S. consulate in Mexico to provide Sánchez-Parodi with a special visa, a consular officer placed him on a list of designated threats to U.S. national security. When Sánchez-Parodi arrived at JFK airport, an immigration official intercepted him. "The INS official saw the visa, issued me a red card and sent me to a closed room," Sánchez-Parodi recalled.[44] Waiting for him outside, Néstor García, first secretary of Cuba's UN Mission, realized there was a problem. "As soon I knew what was going on, I called Eagleburger at the State Department," he recounted. Eagleburger acted quickly to rectify this diplomatic insult.[45] "I was in the room for a few minutes until some guy came, apologized, and released me," remembers Sánchez-Parodi.[46]

On Saturday morning, January 11, Eagleburger and Mankiewicz flew into New York on the Eastern Airlines shuttle to meet Sánchez-Parodi and García. Their first secret meeting took place in the most public of places: a bustling cafeteria at La Guardia airport. After Mankiewicz made the necessary introductions, the four men held "exploratory talks" on how to engage in a substantive dialogue on U.S.-Cuban relations. At one point, an indigent blind man who was hawking ballpoint pens interrupted their conversation. "He tossed a bunch of pens on the table," García recalls. "The only way we could get rid of him was to buy some, so we did. As he left, we were thinking that there were microphones hidden in some, or all, of the pens that could record our conversation—a possible sign of the presence of the CIA or FBI."[47]

Kissinger's office devoted extensive preparations to this meeting. On January 2, Assistant Secretary Rogers presented Kissinger with a comprehensive "check list" of issues. From Cuba, Washington would want compensation for expropriated properties; payments on defaulted bonds and postal debt; the release of U.S. political prisoners; improvements on human rights; a halt to "mischievous involvement" in the Puerto Rico issue; restraint on support for Latin American insurgents; and preservation of "the principle that Cuba will not be a base for 'offensive' weapons." From the United States, Cuba would want an end of economic sanctions; removal of U.S. restrictions on third-country shipping and aviation connections; a halt to aerial surveillance; a cessation of violent exile operations; the return of Guantánamo; and at least tacit support for lifting the 1964 OAS sanctions, allowing Cuba's reintegration into inter-American economic and political institutions.[48]

"I think we should avoid large issues like Guantánamo, trade and expropriation payments in the beginning," Rogers argued in a SECRET/NO DIS/ EYES ONLY cover memo to Kissinger. "The early meetings should be limited to questions which will test whether this is the time and place for major progress."[49] Rogers also provided Kissinger with the first draft of an aide-mémoire for the Cubans on the general U.S. position on talks toward better relations. "Such meetings as these," it began, "can define the matters on both sides which our governments may determine should be discussed." Kissinger ordered substantial rewrites of this document, which would determine the tone with which the U.S. negotiators would open the talks. Indeed, Rogers wrote three more drafts before Kissinger gave it to Eagleburger the night before the meeting with the Cubans. "We are meeting here to explore the possibilities for a more normal relationship between our two countries," stated the final document that Eagleburger provided to the Cubans at La Guardia airport. It contained no demand for internal changes to Cuba's political system. In "both thought and language," Eagleburger told Sánchez-Parodi and García over coffee, the two-page document reflected Kissinger's conception of détente and the congenial diplomatic tone the United States wanted for the talks with Cuba:

The ideological differences between us are wide. But the fact that such talks will not bridge the ideological differences does not mean that they cannot be useful in addressing concrete issues which it is in the interest of both countries to resolve. The United States is able and willing to make progress on such issues even with socialist nations with whom we are in fundamental ideological disagreement, as the recent progress in our relations with Soviet Union and the People's Republic of China has shown.[50]

The Cuban emissaries responded that they had no instructions to actually negotiate—that their task was "to listen and report back to their authorities in Havana." Sánchez-Parodi did, however, offer what he termed "personal comments" on U.S.-Cuban relations and the need to lift the embargo before other issues could be addressed.[51] "With the blockade in place," he stated, "no aspects of normalizing relations could be discussed." The meeting seemed to grow tense when Eagleburger warned that, "for us, this problem is not the most important in our foreign policy."

Sánchez-Parodi responded by noting that Cubans "were not Chinese, and did not look like Chinese. But we can have more patience than the Chinese."[52]

Nevertheless, Eagleburger stressed that the United States wanted to continue the dialogue and meet again. To facilitate covert communications, he provided García with a contact sheet—names, pseudonyms, telephone numbers, and coded language to use. Eagleburger himself would use the codename "Mr. Henderson." The conversation code the Cuban and U.S. officials were to employ for future telephone communications read like this:

How is your health? (We want to meet.)
I have a slight headache, but otherwise I am well. (Agreed.)
I don't feel well. (I will report on this and call you back.)
How is your sister? (Where)
How is your wife? (Washington, at Eagleburger's home) or
How is your brother, Henry? (New York, La Guardia)
Do you like New York? (When)
It's nice except for X months during the year (X days from now)
I have to go out now. I'll call you again at X time. (X time)

In the aftermath of the first meeting, Kissinger's office moved quickly to build a good-faith foundation for further talks. Assistant Secretary Rogers wrote to the Inter-Departmental Committee for Internal Security, chaired by the Justice Department, to request that the 25-mile travel restriction on

Cuban diplomats at the United Nations be expanded to a radius of 250 miles so they could travel to Washington.[53] Several days later, the State Department arranged a multiple entry visa for Cuba's deputy foreign minister, José Viera—Sánchez-Parodi's designated alternate if a meeting was scheduled when he could not attend. At the same time, Rogers ordered a reconsideration of U.S. prohibitions against trade with Cuba by U.S. corporations through foreign subsidiaries. That review led to a decision, announced February 12, to license Litton Industries of Canada to export $517,000 in office furniture to Cuba.[54]

To make sure that the Cubans understood the diplomatic significance of these actions, Eagleburger contacted Néstor García. When a major snow storm prevented Eagleburger from flying to New York for a face-to-face meeting, García called him from a public pay phone near Yankee Stadium to receive a briefing on the U.S. "gesture of good will." Three times, García had to ask Eagleburger to stop dictating when his pen froze. (The two joked that these were the pens García bought from the blind man at La Guardia.[55])

To assure that Fidel himself understood, in late January, Kissinger again used Mankiewicz as his private courier to send another secret message to Castro describing the steps the United States had taken and reiterating U.S. interest in continuing the talks. "The United States is taking these steps as an expression of its interest in exploring the normalization of relations," according to a draft of the note. The January 11 meeting "was useful," the secret message continued, "and a further meeting of officials is now appropriate."[56]

Rogers hoped that the next meeting might soon take place in Panama. "I am going to Panama for a Canal Company Board meeting on Friday, January 31," he reported to Kissinger. "Larry could be there in a few hours. . . . Larry can arrange a meeting easily through his special channel [with García]." Rogers's memo indicated the expectations the U.S. side carried into the talks with Cuba:

> We suggested in the message which Mankiewicz is now carrying to Havana that we meet again. They have had time to digest the earlier message which Larry gave them, that we need a *quid pro quo*. The Cubans had nothing to say at the earlier meeting beyond the tired precondition that the blockade be ended. I think we can properly expect something substantive now. And Larry needs the sun.[57]

But Kissinger preferred to leave the ball in Cuba's court. "Panama just involves one more country," he scrawled on Rogers's memo. "Let Cuba make the next move."[58]

Fidel Castro evidently noted the significance of these early U.S. gestures and responded with gestures of his own. Meeting with Mankiewicz at the end of January, Castro reacted positively to Washington's suggestion that he allow family visits to and from the island. Rather than make this an official U.S. demand, Mankiewicz had been instructed to raise the possibility of family visits as his own idea. That way, as a memo from Rogers to Kissinger put it, he would "emphasize to the Cubans the importance of the human rights issue to the normalization process, in a way that will permit Castro to move" without feeling Washington was intervening in Cuba's internal affairs.[59]

Significantly, the Cubans also softened their long-standing demand that the trade embargo be lifted before any negotiations could take place. In an interview with *Le Monde*, Cuban deputy prime minister Carlos Rafael Rodríguez made conciliatory remarks about the Ford administration, noting that while ending the U.S. embargo remained Cuba's condition for normalizing relations, lifting it "could comprise various phases and assume various forms."[60] In January, the Cuban government also offered to exchange its most famous American prisoner, Larry Lunt, a CIA agent captured in 1965, for the Puerto Rican nationalist, Lolita Lebrón. In addition, Rogers reported to Kissinger that Cuban intelligence officials had contacted CIA station chiefs in several countries indicating that "Cuba is prepared to consider better relations."[61]

But the Cubans made no move to set up another negotiating session with the United States, nor did they take what U.S. officials considered to be a truly substantive "responsive gesture," such as releasing American prisoners, or allowing family visits. As the winter of 1975 progressed, Assistant Secretary Rogers became concerned that the window of opportunity for the executive branch to seize the initiative was closing as congressional pressure for changing U.S. policy mounted and the OAS moved toward lifting multilateral sanctions. "The Cuban nettle gets pricklier all the time," he wrote in a SECRET February 20 memo to Kissinger. "Pressures to move . . . are going to increase considerably over the next few months. And our bargaining strength with the Cubans will decline accordingly."[62]

Rogers recommended a four-step "interrelated strategy" to position the United States in Latin America and with the Cubans:

1) Over the next two months we begin to indicate that we can support a change in 1964 voting procedures [that would allow sanctions to be lifted] at the May OAS meeting.

2) That we in the meanwhile relieve some of the pressure, both from the U.S. private sector and from friendly governments by dropping the ban on third-country subsidiary trade in non-U.S. goods with Cuba. This will be taken as an important gesture by the Latins. It will avoid conflict with Canada, and hopefully with Mexico. But it will be seen everywhere as a promise of more to come.

3) That between now and the May meeting we begin to explore whether we can come up with something with the Cubans on the big issues between us, particularly expropriation and blocked assets.

I urge we do this before, not after, the OAS meeting. I do so because I think our bargaining power, whatever it may be now, will be less in June.

Finally, Rogers recommended that the U.S. attempt to "strike an interim deal of prisoners for baseball."[63]

Using "Baseball Diplomacy" to advance relations with Cuba—the same way the sport of Ping Pong had contributed to the U.S. opening to China—represented a potentially dramatic move by Washington. A few weeks before, at a Christmas party in New York City, the commissioner of baseball, Bowie Kuhn, had approached Kissinger about taking a team to Cuba in March 1975 for a series of exhibition games that would be broadcast on U.S. television. Kuhn followed up on January 14 with a letter stating that he would soon be meeting with the head of Cuba's National Institute of Sports, Physical Education and Recreation (Instituto Nacional de Deportes, Educación Física y Recreación) to finalize the details and that "Premier Castro favors this project."[64]

A baseball series between the two nations would be a major diplomatic opening, Rogers reported to Kissinger on February 13. "The announcement that a major league squad was to play in Cuba in late March would have a symbolic significance not limited to the sports pages," Rogers argued. "In Latin America, the move would also reawaken memories of your China moves." But Rogers cautioned that the Cubans had done nothing "so far that could be taken as a move to which the baseball trip might be considered a responsive gesture. This may be due to the stickiness of our communications techniques," he noted, or "it may be that the Cubans just have not been able to bring themselves to decide to do anything."[65]

Now, a week later, Rogers recommended that the United States specifically offer to trade a baseball game for the release of three U.S. citizens languishing in Cuban jails for counterrevolutionary activities. This would show if the Cubans were serious about negotiations. "I would test the negotiating water by telling the Cubans that we want them released," he advised Kissinger, "that we have already done a great deal and that we cannot let the baseball team play the exhibition game until we see some movement on the Cuba side like this."[66]

But Kissinger rejected baseball diplomacy with Cuba.[67] Instead, on March 1, he opted to send the Cubans a very public message that the United States was willing to reassess its policy of hostility if Cuba was willing to reciprocate. In a major speech on Latin America in Houston, Texas, Kissinger stated that if the OAS lifted multilateral sanctions against Cuba, the United States would consider changes in its bilateral relations. "We see no virtue in perpetual antagonism between the United States and Cuba," the secretary of state declared:

> Our concerns relate above all to Cuba's external and military relationships with countries outside the hemisphere. We have taken some symbolic steps to indicate we are prepared to move in a new direction if Cuba will. Fundamental change cannot come, however, unless Cuba demonstrates a readiness to assume the mutuality of obligation and regard upon which a new relationship must be founded.[68]

Clear as it was, Kissinger's Houston speech failed to illicit a response from Cuba.

Restarting the Dialogue

As a vote in the OAS loomed to repeal the 1964 sanctions, the State Department conducted a major policy review in the spring of 1975 to prepare for the post-sanctions era and for the possible restoration of U.S.-Cuban relations. In late March, Rogers's deputy, Harry Shlaudeman, completed a study, "Normalizing Relations with Cuba," laying out challenges for U.S. policy makers and negotiation scenarios toward that "ultimate goal." The main problem Shlaudeman identified was that Castro "holds most of the cards." With the OAS set to remove regional sanctions in July, Cuba had "already succeeded in breaking the inter-American blockade without making a single significant concession and without ever having to deal with us. [Castro] may believe that a little patience will bring him the same happy result with respect to U.S. sanctions."[69]

Washington, the study argued, needed a "reappraisal" of what it could reasonably expect from Castro and what it could give him in return. "Our interest is in getting the Cuba issue behind us, not in prolonging it indefinitely," Shlaudeman argued. "If there is benefit to us in an end to the state of 'perpetual antagonism' it lies in getting Cuba off the domestic and inter-American agendas—in extracting the symbolism from an intrinsically trivial issue."[70] Moreover, there was urgency to the Cuba situation, Shlaudeman reminded his superiors. Time was running out on Washington's diplomatic poker game with Havana. As he wrote in the cover memo: "We have a poor hand to play and should ask for a new deal before we lose our last chip."[71]

Drawing on Shlaudeman's admonitions, Rogers stepped up his efforts to resume contacts with the Cubans. "It is evident that our earlier effort with the Cubans is dead in the water," he wrote in a memo to Kissinger on April 25. "We think we should approach the Cubans once more" with the following message:

> We would say that we took several symbolic steps but that we have seen no response. Is this intended? We would say that the first purpose of the meeting would be to determine if we have read the Cubans wrong. Do they mean for us to understand that they will not respond with symbolic steps?
>
> Secondly, we would point out that we are considering how the OAS sanctions may well be lifted, and that this step would remove the Cuba issue from the multilateral agenda. Each country would be free to determine its own relationships. How and in what way—if at all—would Cuba anticipate that the issues between the U.S. and Cuba should be addressed. Only directly, through second-hand reporting of gestures and signs? Or by informal and unofficial contacts?[72]

Rogers sought Kissinger's authorization for what he called "a secret advance probe"—reaching out to their Cuban contacts in New York before the OAS meeting in July. In a pair of lengthy option papers containing "illustrative scenarios for establishing bilateral relations," he sought to play on Kissinger's worst fear—the loss of executive branch prerogative in the making of foreign policy. A "stand pat policy," Rogers argued, "would cede to Congress the initiative and risk leaving to the Executive Branch the only option of accepting or vetoing ham-handed legislative repeals of the trade restrictions." There was momentum in Washington for improving relations, he warned. "If the Executive does not take the initiative, Congress, which has already grabbed for it, will keep it."[73]

In May, Castro sent some signals that strengthened Rogers's hand. During a visit by Senator George McGovern in Havana, Castro agreed to return two million dollars in ransom that had been paid to three American hijackers who commandeered a Southern Airways plane to Havana in 1972. He also agreed to allow the parents of major league pitcher Luis Tiant to leave Cuba. McGovern reported that Castro was puzzled by the suggestion that his regime had not made sufficient gestures. Cuba did not want to be seen as a supplicant. Nonetheless, "Castro is reaching out to improve relations with the U.S.," McGovern told Rogers in a confidential telephone call when he returned to Washington on May 12. His "primary objective at this time is to normalize relations with the United States."[74]

At a meeting with the secretary of state on June 9, Rogers and Eagleburger presented their case for recontacting the Cuban negotiators. They wanted to be authorized to meet with the Cuban emissaries *before* the OAS met in San José, Costa Rica, in order to have as strong a bargaining position as possible. "We have few cards to play now," Rogers reminded Kissinger; "after San Jose, we'll have fewer."

"The Cubans have never replied to the message [we sent] to a diplomat in New York," Eagleburger reminded them.

Kissinger did not seem surprised. "The Chinese played with exchanging messages for a year," he reminded his aides.

"There have been four messages to the Cubans and no reply," Eagleburger continued.

Kissinger was not convinced they should take the initiative to restart the talks. "I don't see what we gain tactically by a probe."

"The cards in our hands are declining in number. The point is that our position is being continually chiseled away by Congress," Rogers replied, playing on Kissinger's dislike of congressional meddling in foreign policy.

"Don't let them," Kissinger countered. "This should be easy."

"A Kennedy bill to abolish all the sanctions could pass," Rogers warned.

"That would be a great one to veto," Kissinger replied.

"Or you could hold your nose and let it go through," Eagleburger suggested.

By the end of the meeting, Kissinger recognized the diplomatic logic of meeting with the Cubans before the OAS vote. "I favored a probe with Cuba last year but there was no answer; what new now can be said?" Kissinger observed. "They treat us with contempt. But since all these things are going to happen, we might as well start a dialogue: Just before San Jose; do it in four weeks," he instructed Eagleburger and Rogers. "Do a message to Castro, but get it up to me before it leaks; as it usually does before I get it."[75]

Kissinger's new message to Castro stated simply that the United States had noted "recent evidences" that Cuba "is interested in exploring ways to move in a new direction in its relations with the United States." The United States would be supporting the OAS initiative to lift multilateral sanctions, it stated. "We think it would be highly useful, before the San José meeting takes place, to reestablish our confidential bilateral meetings in order to permit a further government-to-government exchange of views."[76] Eagleburger and Rogers passed this note to Néstor García during a 10:00 A.M. meeting at Washington's National Airport on June 21. García agreed to send his superiors the U.S. proposal for another negotiating session at the venerable Pierre Hotel in New York, before the OAS meeting on July 29.

When García returned to Washington several days later to deliver Castro's written response, the clandestine diplomacy took a comic turn. García called Eagleburger's house to arrange the meeting and asked to speak to "Mr. Henderson," following the code they had agreed to use. "You have the wrong number" Eagleburger's wife responded, and hung up. When García called again, she hung up immediately. Realizing that Eagleburger had failed to brief his wife on the code names for communications with the Cubans, the third time García called, he simply asked for Mr. Eagleburger.[77]

At a meeting at Eagleburger's home with Assistant Secretary Rogers, the three officials reviewed Cuba's agreement to hold formal, secret talks on July 9 at the Pierre Hotel on Fifth Avenue (chosen because it was near Cuba's UN mission and because "it could be entered without going past the desk," Rogers wrote in an internal memo).[78] At one point, Rogers suggested that both sides create a list of issues on which an exchange of viewpoints would be productive. But García demurred. In the short period of time between now and the meeting at the Pierre, he would not be able to create such a list. "List or no list," he suggested, "if an issue came up that one or the other party was not ready to discuss, in that case it just wouldn't be discussed." As García left to return to the airport, Mrs. Eagleburger reminded him that now that she understood the diplomatic situation, he could call again for "Mr. Henderson" anytime.[79]

The Pierre Meeting

Over a banquet-style lunch in suite 727 at the Pierre Hotel on July 9, the United States and Cuba held their very first formal negotiating session on how to normalize relations.[80] At the outset, Eagleburger told the Cubans that he had met with Kissinger the night before and that the secretary of state was disposed to meet with the Cuban foreign minister during the UN General Assembly meetings in September. From that positive icebreaker, the talks turned to what Rogers described as "a series of ideas for a reciprocal, across-the-board improvement of relations" leading to full bilateral ties—a "package deal" was the phrase the Cubans remember him using. As a major gesture, Washington would support lifting multilateral sanctions at the OAS, Rogers began. Thereafter, the United States would begin to dismantle the trade embargo, piece by piece, in response to a series of gestures from the Cubans which Rogers laid out:

- The release of U.S. nationals held in Cuban jails
- Exit permits for some 800 Cubans with dual U.S. citizenship
- Contributing to family unification by permitting up to 100 family visits a week to and from the United States
- Curtailment of Cuba's military relations with the USSR
- Restraint in promoting Puerto Rican independence
- A pledge of nonintervention in the Western Hemisphere
- Movement to settle compensation claims of U.S. citizens for expropriated properties

These steps would be linked to steps Washington would take to ease the embargo, Kissinger would later write, making normalization of relations "a two-way street" that "would occur at the end of the process, not as a precondition for it."[81] There would have to be a "balance of actions" on both sides for the process to succeed, Eagleburger reiterated after Rogers had finished his presentation.[82]

Sánchez-Parodi had come from Havana with what he described later as "a long list of issues to discuss." But the rest of the meeting was spent responding to the points raised by the U.S. side. A series of quid pro quos would not work, he informed Rogers and Eagleburger, because Cuba's precondition for talks was the lifting of the embargo. "We cannot negotiate under the blockade," he insisted. "We are willing to discuss issues relating to the easing of the embargo but until the embargo is lifted, Cuba and the United States cannot deal with each other as equals and consequently cannot negotiate."[83]

The Cuban negotiator then proceeded to go point by point through the demands the U.S. side had made. First, Cuba would gladly consider compensation for expropriated properties, if the United States would accede to a formula to compensate Cuba for the losses and damages from the embargo and the acts of aggression since 1959. Cuba was disposed to analyze the situation of U.S. citizens whom Washington considered political prisoners and would evaluate the idea of dual citizenship, although Cuba did not recognize that legal status. Cuba was even more disposed, "in principle," to address the

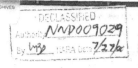

DECLASSIFIED
Author: *NND009029*
By *WJB* NARA Date *7/27/06*

SECRET/~~SENSITIVE~~

MEMORANDUM OF CONVERSATION

Participants:

    U.S.:   Deputy Under Secretary for Management
                   Lawrence S. Eagleburger

                   Assistant Secretary for Inter-American Affairs
                   William D. Rogers

                   Wesley W. Egan (notetaker)

    Cuba: First Secretary of the Cuban Mission to the
                   United Nations, Nestor Garcia

                   Mr. Sanchez Parodi

Date, Time,   July 9, 1975, 1:30 p.m. to 4:30 p.m.
Place: Pierre Hotel, New York City.

                   Prior to the official discussions Mr. Eagleburger
mentioned that if Cuba thought it was appropriate,
the Secretary would consider meeting with a senior
official in New York during the upcoming UNGA
session. The Cubans responded that they would
take the suggestion back and both sides were
clear that such a meeting did not preclude further
discussions at the working level. They were close
to enchanted that the Secretary would consider
coming into the picture.

                   Assistant Secretary Rogers began the substantive
discussion with a presentation based on the talking
points prepared beforehand. He noted that the
process of discussion must be reciprocal, that we
recognized the recent gestures made by Cuba, and
that we were prepared to allow the baseball visit
and to support movement at San Jose. He noted that
hostility is not a permanent feature of our nature
and that these talks should examine a number of
issues. He then touched on the nine points (talking
points attached) as follows:

First page of the Memorandum of Conversation between U.S. and Cuban diplomats
at the Pierre Hotel in New York, July 9, 1975. This meeting was the first formal negotiating session about normalizing U.S.-Cuban relations. (National Archives and Records
Administration)

issue of family travel from Cuba to the United States, and from the United States to Cuba within certain limits.

Sánchez-Parodi took a much harder line, however, on the demand that Cuba should modify its relations with the Soviet Union at the behest of the United States. "The Cubans had no intention of telling the U.S. how to regulate its relations with other nations, and could not permit that [the United States] try to regulate Cuba's," he argued. Nor would Cuba cease its efforts on Puerto Rico because "we believe that Puerto Rico has a need for independence and self-determination." As to the rest of Latin America, he noted, Cuba would pledge its respect for nonintervention if the United States would acknowledge its own covert and overt intervention in the region. "For example, Chile and the Dominican Republic. We must have assurances that what has happened in the past will not happen again."[84] Following up on that line of argument, Sánchez-Parodi noted that his government wanted to put a cessation of CIA operations against Cuba on the negotiating table. Finally, the Cubans wanted a complete withdrawal of U.S. personnel from Guantánamo.

By now the meeting had lasted almost four hours and Eagleburger began to look at his watch. Both Sánchez-Parodi and García seemed to take offense at the idea that U.S. officials had not allotted sufficient time to discuss these complex issues. "Four hours was very little time to cover the presentations of both sides," García would write in his memoir.[85] "Eagleburger was obviously in a hurry," Sánchez-Parodi later observed. "It seemed to me that he was more interested in not missing his shuttle flight than in discussing issues standing in the way of the normalization of U.S.-Cuban relations."[86] Nevertheless, the meeting ended on a relatively amicable note, with Rogers suggesting that both sides take a week to evaluate the information from this conversation before fixing a date for another session. The Cubans agreed.

In the weeks that followed, the momentum for improving relations seemed to build on both sides. On July 29, 1975, the United States voted along with the OAS nations to lift multilateral trade and diplomatic sanctions against Cuba. The State Department then announced publicly that the United States was prepared to open "serious discussions" with the Cubans on normalizing relations.[87] Two days later, Eagleburger called García in New York and gave him a short message in both Spanish and English: "We are ready to continue when you are ready to meet again."[88] In early August, the Cubans returned the $2 million in ransom money to Southern Airways, as Castro had promised McGovern—a move praised by the chairman of the Senate Foreign Relations Committee, John Sparkman (D-Ala.), as "very solid evidence that the Cuban government is genuinely interested in pursuing a policy of improved relations with the United States."[89]

Indeed, Kissinger felt positive enough about the momentum to brief President Ford in detail on the talks. "You know we have been talking with the Cubans," he told the president in the Oval office on August 7. "You know we said we were willing to move on the basis of reciprocity. I said we would get in touch with them, but I have now said that the next move is up to them." Kissinger then sought Ford's approval for a major escalation in the talks: "Maybe I could meet with the foreign minister if he comes up for the UN session."

"It would be all right if they have made some moves and if you can do it privately," Ford said approvingly.

"It might leak," Kissinger warned.

"Maybe not," the president replied. "They have been good so far."

Kissinger and Ford then discussed the challenge to the U.S. ban on third-country subsidiary trade with Cuba. "We now have little reason for it," Kissinger admitted to the president. "We could either change the rule or grant item-by-item exceptions." The president's position was that it was "better to change the rule than do it one by one."[90]

Twelve days later, Kissinger formally recommended ending the punitive policy of banning third-country subsidiary trade with Cuba. "These steps will be recognized as constructive ones by Castro," Kissinger wrote, "and will put the onus on him to take the next conciliatory gestures towards us."[91] On August 21, the State Department announced three changes in the embargo law: the licensing of subsidiaries of U.S. companies in foreign countries to do business with Cuba, abolition of foreign aid penalties on countries trading with Cuba, and allowing ships engaged in Cuban commerce to refuel in U.S. ports. On August 22, Castro publicly characterized this move as "a positive gesture" and declared that there could be "negotiation on how to negotiate" further changes in the embargo.[92]

The Puerto Rico Obstacle

The warm summer of U.S.-Cuban détente soon gave way to a chilly autumn of disagreement and tension. During an increasingly contentious political campaign in the United States in which Ronald Reagan challenged Ford for the Republican nomination, Castro made two foreign policy decisions that U.S. officials perceived as deliberately provocative, undermining the process of normalization.

First, Cuba took a very public position on Puerto Rico at the United Nations in August calling for Puerto Rican independence and hosting the World Peace Council International Conference of Solidarity with the Independence of Puerto Rico in early September. On August 25 Eagleburger called García and arranged for a typed message to be brought to the Cuban mission at the UN. The U.S. note was blunt: it reviewed the progress in the talks and the steps the United States had taken to "contribute to an improvement in the atmosphere in which those talks take place." Cuba's actions on Puerto Rico, in contrast, were "wholly inconsistent" with that effort, the note warned. "Continuing efforts by the Government of Cuba to play upon the Puerto Rico issue in public must be considered by the United States Government as anything but a 'positive step' in keeping with the relationship we have both been trying to develop, and as harmful to a further improvement of relations between our two countries."[93]

The Cubans responded with their own diplomatic note, which García passed to Rogers at a bar in La Guardia airport on September 6. The communiqué applauded the positive steps that had accompanied the talks so far but reiterated Cuba's historical position on Puerto Rican independence. Cuba's support for Puerto Rico, the note stated, was not intended to disrupt the course of the diplomatic talks over normalizing relations.[94]

Kissinger did not see it that way. At a press conference in early September, he declared Cuba's sponsorship of the Puerto Rican Solidarity Conference to be "an unfriendly act and a severe setback" to the prospects for improving relations.[95] "We were neuralgic on Puerto Rico," recalled Eagleburger.[96] Nevertheless, in early October Eagleburger met with Frank Mankiewicz and pressed him to use his Cuban contacts to pass the message to Castro that Washington was anxious to continue the negotiations toward better relations. A few days later, Eagleburger met with Mankiewicz's colleague, Kirby Jones, who was on his way to Cuba, and asked him to press the Cubans for a humanitarian gesture such as allowing family visits. President Ford, Eagleburger said, had become sensitive to attacks by Ronald Reagan that Ford was "soft on Communism." Kissinger himself met with Mankiewicz on October 14 and reiterated the message that he was willing to meet with a designated Cuban official in New York.[97]

In November, Fidel Castro sent a message through Kirby Jones—who had replaced Mankiewicz as the secret courier between Havana and Washington—that Cuba was ready to permit a limited number of family visits on a humanitarian basis and that arrangements could be made through the "special channel."[98] By then, however, Castro's audacious decision to send combat troops into the civil war in Angola had become a major impediment to normalizing U.S.-Cuban relations.

The Angolan Obstacle

Cuba's bold military foray into Africa began in April 1975 with a request for help from António Agostinho Neto, the leader of the Popular Movement for the Liberation of Angola (MPLA), the anticolonial party that had led the fight for independence from Portugal. With the date for Angolan independence approaching, the MPLA came under attack by two rival movements, the National Front for the Liberation of Angola (FNLA) and the National Union for Total Independence of Angola (UNITA), both supported covertly by the United States and South Africa. Initially, Castro responded to Neto's request by sending hundreds of Cuban military advisors. After the Ford administration escalated the CIA's paramilitary program in July and South African troops invaded Angola in October, Cuba launched a massive air and sealift with Soviet logistical support, deploying thirty-six thousand troops to prevent the Angolan capital of Luanda from falling to South African forces. The Cuban troops halted the South African advance, and on November 11, 1975, Angola became an independent country under the leadership of the MPLA. "The Cuban role in Africa was unprecedented," Piero Gleijeses notes in his definitive book, *Conflicting Missions: Cuba, Africa, and the United States.* "What other Third World country had ever projected its power beyond its immediate neighborhood?"[99]

Kissinger was apoplectic. How could this "pipsqueak," as he repeatedly referred to Castro during meetings with President Ford, challenge the United States of America on the world geopolitical stage? U.S. analysts had never anticipated that Cuba had the capabilities for a long-range military incursion and believed (incorrectly) that Castro was acting as a surrogate for the Soviets. This was the type of threat to U.S. interests that Kissinger had hoped the prospect of better relations would mitigate. In his mind, Cuba was thumbing its nose at the United States at precisely the moment that Washington had offered the olive branch of normalization.

Initially, Kissinger responded by publicly threatening to terminate the process of normalization—a nebulous threat since the Cubans had never responded to Eagleburger's call in August for a follow-up to the Pierre Hotel meeting. When a reporter asked Kissinger on November 11 "when you might deliver us a Cuban cigar" as a symbol of a successful rapprochement, he replied, "We were making progress earlier this year in improving relations with Cuba. But in recent months, Cuba has taken some actions, such as their pressure for the independence of Puerto Rico . . . and by its interference in conflicts in areas thousands of miles away, such as Angola, that have given us some pause."[100]

Two weeks later the secretary of state used even sharper language. "In recent months the United States has demonstrated, by deed as well as word, its readiness to improve relations with Cuba," he said in a speech in Detroit on November 24. "But let there be no illusions: a policy of conciliation will not survive Cuban meddling in Puerto Rico or Cuban armed intervention in the affairs of other nations struggling to decide their own fate." But then he added, "The process of improving relations depends on Cuba conducting a responsible foreign policy," leaving the door to better relations ajar if Cuba altered its conduct abroad. "If it does not, we cannot continue the process we have started."[101]

On December 20, however, President Ford effectively closed the door on continuing talks. "The action by the Cuban government in sending combat troops to Angola destroys any opportunity for improvement of relations with the United States," he told reporters. Cuba's decision "to involve itself in a massive military way in Angola," the president stated bluntly, "ends, as far as I am concerned, any efforts at all to have friendlier relations with the Government of Cuba."[102]

But even after President Ford's unambiguous declaration, Kissinger's team pragmatically pursued the diplomatic back channel they had set up almost a year earlier. On December 24, Eagleburger and Rogers sent the secretary of state a SECRET/NO DIS/EYES ONLY memorandum and draft of talking points for another meeting with their "special channel." Rogers and Eagleburger recommended that the United States deliver a "strong message on Angola. . . . There is no basis for such reciprocal conversations until Cuba is prepared to withdraw its troops." Kissinger approved the meeting but vetoed that message as "much too strong." Instead, he requested a communiqué that "expresses appreciation re: Kirby Jones message [on family visits] and asks for clarification, [and] indicates that no fundamental improvement is possible in our relations under present conditions."[103]

Rogers passed this message to García on January 12, 1976, during a forty-five-minute meeting at Washington's National Airport. On the issue of Cuban family visits, they found common ground. "Cuba [is] ready for family visits now," García informed Rogers. The two discussed how visitors would be selected and what kind of public announcement would be made. The Cubans preferred an early announcement, García said, but they understood it might be delayed because of U.S. domestic politics. "He is sensitive to the March 9, Florida primary," Rogers reported to Kissinger.

Then the discussion turned to the acrimonious issue of Angola. García took notes as Rogers "slowly and deliberately" read Kissinger's authorized talking points, writing down, word-for-word, the final paragraph: "Cuba's dispatch of combat troops to take part in an internal conflict between Africans in Angola is a fundamental obstacle to any far-reaching effort to resolve the basic issues between us at this time."[104] Rogers was far less diplomatic when he departed from reading Kissinger's position paper. "Néstor, sorry for the word, [but] you fucked it up," García recalls being told. "You are in Angola, Néstor. You fucked it up."[105]

García was not ready, or instructed, to discuss Angola, Rogers noted with chagrin in his report on the meeting. The Cuban emissary responded that Castro had recently stated Cuba's position on Angola, and García "would not have much to add." There was, according to Rogers, "nothing in his manner or in his words which betrayed a sensitivity to the recent developments in Angola, and Cuba's admittedly decisive role. For my part, I admit, the irony hung heavy. Not, evidently, for him."[106]

For U.S. officials, it seemed inconceivable that Castro would pass up a chance to finally reestablish normal relations with the United States in order to support an anticolonial struggle in distant Africa. For the Cubans, it seemed only natural that they would refuse to compromise their independent foreign policy. In a news conference three days after the Rogers-García meeting, Castro reiterated both Cuba's interest in talks with the United States and its independence of action. "It is not that Cuba rejects the ideal of improving relations with the United States—we are in favor of peace, of the policy of détente, of coexistence between states with different social systems," Castro asserted. "What we do not accept are humiliating conditions—the absurd price which the United States apparently would have us pay for an improvement in relations."[107]

Nevertheless, Cuba kept the door open by sending instructions for García to meet again with his U.S. contacts to discuss family visits. On Sunday morning, February 7, García took the Eastern shuttle to National Airport and met one last time with Eagleburger. Reading from a typed set of talking points, García presented the Cuban government's position on the visits: up to sixty people, from ten families in the United States, would be permitted a ten-day visit to the island. Preference would be given to the aged or ill, or to family members visiting older or sick parents or grandparents. No one involved with counterrevolutionary activities would be permitted to come.

Contrary to the Ford administration's hopes for ongoing family travel that would bring up to one hundred people to and from the island weekly, this was to be a one-time-only arrangement because "conditions are not favorable to starting a continued flow of visits to Cuba, much less the establishment of a regular airlift," García told Eagleburger.

"This is our stand," the Cuban talking points concluded: "It constitutes a gesture which indicates that, on the part of Cuba, there is not an attitude of permanent hostility toward the United States."[108] When the meeting ended, Eagleburger accompanied García to the gate for his plane back to New York. "Given the way we both acted," the Cuban diplomat would later write, "we did not have even the remotest idea that this would be the last meeting we would have."[109]

"Clobbering" Cuba: Contingency Planning for Retaliation

With the 1976 U.S. presidential campaign season under way, Cuba policy became a political hot potato, with the predictable impact on any progress toward rapprochement. Facing intense criticism over Kissinger's policy of détente from Ronald Reagan, President Ford tacked to the right on Angola. "Let me say categorically and emphatically," Ford declared during a February campaign stop in Florida seeking the Cuban American vote, "the United States will have nothing to do with Castro's Cuba—period." Visiting Miami again two weeks later, the president called Castro "an international outlaw" guilty of "flagrant aggression" in Angola. In an April speech commemorating the Bay of Pigs, Castro responded by calling Ford "a vulgar liar" for criticizing Cuba's overt involvement in Angola while concealing the CIA's covert assistance to UNITA and the FNLA.[110]

Kissinger shifted his strategy from using the bait of better relations as incentive for Cuba to quit Angola, to making public and private threats of U.S. retaliation if the Cuban incursion expanded to other areas. "I think we are going to have to smash Castro. We probably can't do it before the elections," he told President Ford in the Oval Office on February 25.

"I agree," the president responded.[111]

In another Oval Office meeting on March 15, the president and secretary of state discussed "clobbering" Cuba. "I think sooner or later we are going to have to crack the Cubans. . . . I think we have to humiliate them," Kissinger argued. "If they move into Namibia or Rhodesia, I would be in favor of clobbering them. That would create a furor . . . but I think we might have to demand they get out of Africa."

"What if they don't?" asked Ford.

"I think we could blockade," Kissinger responded.[112]

In a speech before the World Affairs Council in Dallas on March 22, Kissinger publicly warned that the United States "will not accept further Cuban military adventures abroad." After the speech he reiterated to reporters: "We have pointed out the dangers to Cuba. We are serious about what I have said." To underscore his point, later that day the Pentagon announced that it would review contingency planning for military action against Cuba.[113]

This was no idle saber rattling. On March 24, Kissinger convened a small, elite team of national security officials known as the "special action group." Among those in attendance were Secretary of Defense Donald Rumsfeld, the CIA's Deputy Director Vernon Walters, and National Security Advisor Brent Scowcroft. "We want to get planning started in the political, economic and military fields so that we can see what we can do if we want to move against Cuba," Kissinger announced at the outset of the meeting. "In the military field there is an invasion or blockade."[114]

During the meeting, Kissinger laid out a veritable domino theory of why Cuba needed to be stopped in Africa. "If the Cubans destroy Rhodesia then Namibia is next and then there is South Africa. It might only take five years." Coming at the same time as the loss of Vietnam, Cuba's challenge took on even greater strategic importance in Kissinger's worldview. "If there is a perception overseas that we are so weakened by our internal debate so that it looks like we can't do anything about a country of eight million people, then in three or four years we are going to have a real crisis," Kissinger warned. Turning to General George Brown of the Joint Chiefs, he declared that "if we decide to use military power it must succeed. There should be no halfway measures—we get no reward for using military power in moderation."[115] To maintain total secrecy, Kissinger instructed that only a select few officials from each department work on this "special action" project. At the same time, he wanted the Cubans to have something to worry about. "They should know we plan to do something."[116]

Drafted by mid-April, the U.S. plans "to do something" ranged from punitive economic and political measures to acts of war such as mining Cuba's harbors and launching airstrikes "to destroy selected Cuban military and military-related targets." The comprehensive planning papers ordered by Kissinger—a set of secret reports titled "Cuban Contingencies"—outlined optional measures, including "Deterrence," "Cease and Desist," "Interdiction," and military "Retaliation," as responses to any expansion of Cuban intervention in Africa or Latin America. "Our basic objective is to prevent the creation of a pattern of international conduct in which Cuba and the USSR arrogate to themselves the right to intervene with combat forces in local or regional conflict," stated a summary of the contingency plans.[117]

Any use of force, however, portended a potentially dangerous confrontation with Cuban or Soviet troops. Indeed, there would be an "extremely high" threat of a superpower conflagration—once again over the little island of Cuba, the contingency planners noted. But the 1962 missile crisis would "be a misleading analogy," because world conditions and power relations were "vastly different" in 1976, and "a new Cuban crisis would not necessarily lead to a Soviet retreat."[118] Indeed, Kissinger's aides warned ominously, "A Cuban/Soviet response could escalate in areas that would maximize US casualties and thus provoke stronger response. The circumstances that could lead the United States to select a military option against Cuba should be serious enough to warrant further action in preparation for general war."[119]

The U.S. pursuit of a Caribbean détente with Cuba had clearly come to an end.

Assessing the Failure

On March 9, 1976, Assistant Secretary William D. Rogers met with Kirby Jones to discuss the collapse of the secret initiative to normalize relations. Rogers was perplexed that the Cubans had not shown more interest. Why hadn't they responded to Washington's repeated messages to reconvene after the Pierre Hotel meeting, and to Kissinger's offer to meet face-to-face with Cuba's foreign minister? "He thought things could have moved very fast nine months ago if the Cubans had responded to the willingness to meet," Jones wrote afterward.[120]

"Nine months ago," Rogers asked Jones, "why didn't the Cubans indicate what they might have been prepared to do if we had started the lifting of the blockade?" The State Department, he said, would have been "satisfied with an indication" that the Cubans were ready to discuss compensation for expropriated properties and other issues that needed to be resolved for a return to normalcy. A deal was possible in 1975, Rogers was certain. "We would have been able to fix something up to make everyone happy and could have moved very fast."[121]

Clearly, U.S. officials had taken significant steps toward a rapprochement. Kissinger had personally initiated contact with Castro. The secretary of state had set a tone for those talks with a carefully worded aide-mémoire assuring the Cubans that ideology and their political system did not stand in the way of better ties. In a series of escalating gestures, U.S. officials moderated travel restrictions on Cuban diplomats, arranged special visas for Cuban negotiators, licensed the sale of specific goods to Cuba, lifted the ban on third-country subsidiary trade, and actually voted in favor of the OAS decision to rescind multilateral economic and diplomatic sanctions.

To be sure, some of these changes were forced on the administration by domestic and international pressures. What made the Kissinger effort at a Caribbean détente unique, however, was that he and his top deputies used those pressures as an opportunity to try to end what Kissinger called "the perpetual antagonism" in relations with Cuba. Publicly, the secretary of state announced that the United States was "prepared to move in a new direction if Cuba will."[122] Privately, his office passed the unprecedented message to the Cubans that Kissinger was willing to meet with a high Cuban official, or even Fidel Castro himself, to reframe U.S.-Cuban relations. "I thought we made them an offer they couldn't refuse," Rogers recalled many years later. "But they did."[123]

The Cubans certainly recognized these signals and made gestures of their own. Castro returned the Southern Airways ransom, allowed Luis Tiant's parents to immigrate to the United States, and agreed to a small number of exile family members to visit their relatives on the island. Rhetorically, Fidel echoed the call for better relations. "We wish friendship," he told American reporters during the visit of Senator George McGovern in May 1975, speaking in English for maximum effect. "We belong to two different worlds but we are neighbors. One way or another we owe it to ourselves to live in peace."[124]

But Castro wanted at least part of the embargo dismantled before truly engaging in full-fledged negotiations. Specifically, he called for the United States to show "a small sign" of goodwill by lifting the ban on trade in food and medicine. "We would prefer the lifting of the entire embargo," he stated in May 1975, "but we are talking about the need for a gesture."[125] However Cuba would not compromise its foreign policy principles in the Caribbean and Africa for the sake of rapprochement with Washington.

Years later, Kissinger would profess not to be surprised at the way the Cubans negotiated. "I felt that the Cubans had gone to school in Hanoi in their way of dealing with the U.S.," he recalled, "which is to ask for ninety percent of what you want at the start. They simply didn't understand our position; they didn't go to school in Beijing."[126] But his aides remained mystified and chagrined that the Cubans never really responded to U.S. entreaties to keep talking, never made a substantive reciprocal gesture indicating a real desire to normalize relations, and sacrificed the process in favor of a military incursion in Africa. "Angola was fatal," Rogers reflected. "But I also believe that the Cubans were never really serious about this." The United States, he reiterated in an interview with the authors, was "very serious" about pursuing Kissinger's conception of détente in the Caribbean. "We'd begun with China and the Soviet Union," he said. "Cuba was the next step."[127]

In many ways, the Cubans approached the talks with the United States just as the CIA predicted they would. In a classified July 1975 Intelligence Memorandum, "Cuba's U.S. Policy: Ready for a Change," CIA analysts noted that "Fidel Castro wants to negotiate an improvement in relations with the U.S." The assessment stated, however, that

- he is in no hurry to restore full ties;
- he will accept no loss of prestige in negotiating an improvement;
- his demands will be stiff;
- he expects the US to make the first formal move.

The CIA suggested that Cuba would essentially play hard to get. Havana would avoid the impression that it was anxious for reconciliation. Eagerness would imply the existence of an exploitable weakness. It would also undercut Cuba's policy of maintaining an aura of confrontation between the United States and Latin America. Moreover, it might alarm the more nationalistic Cuban leaders who feared a recrudescence of U.S. influence in Cuba. Presciently, the CIA predicted that Cuba would "not sacrifice its revolutionary bona fides for the sake of detente."[128]

Fidel himself said as much to Bulgarian leader Todor Zhivkov just after the final round of secret talks with Washington ended. "It will take a long time before our relations with the United States begin to improve," Castro said. "The problem is that we live in a region of the world where the conflicts between the nations and the United States are constantly increasing. . . . What are we to do in such a situation? Shall we remain neutral or shall we adopt a friendly attitude towards the Americans? The latter is practically impossible. The peculiar situation we have found ourselves in makes the normalization of our relations difficult to achieve."[129]

Cuba's reluctance to take clear steps toward better relations collided with a domestic political need in the United States for some symbolic peg on which to hang the contentious issue of normalizing ties. In a candid moment of conversation with President Houari Boumediene of Algeria in October 1974, Kissinger admitted that domestic politics played a considerable role in

Washington's latitude to lift the embargo. "In principle, if we can normalize relations with Peking, there is no reason we cannot do it with Cuba," Kissinger said.

"The problem is the blockade," Boumediene reminded him.

"A solution could be found if [Castro] is flexible," Kissinger answered. "As far as I am concerned, it is a question of domestic politics. We have to show something he's doing, to justify the lifting," the secretary explained. "There is not much he can do for us. All we want is an independent foreign policy. . . . We need something we can use to explain this domestically."[130]

Clearly, Cuba's military foray into Angola was not the type of domestic explanation Kissinger sought. "If it was politically difficult before, it became impossible after Angola," Eagleburger recalled. Kissinger came to the same conclusion: "There was absolutely no possibility we could tolerate the Cubans moving into a new theater, becoming a strategic base in the Cold War, and still improve relations."[131]

The Perpetual Hostility Continues

As 1976 progressed, relations between Washington and Havana deteriorated even further, undermined by exile terrorism designed to sabotage any improvement of bilateral ties. In June, violent exile groups gathered in the Dominican Republic to create the Coordination of United Revolutionary Organizations (Coordinación de Organizaciones Revolucionarias Unidas, CORU), which the FBI described as "an anti-Castro terrorist umbrella organization." CORU planned a series of attacks throughout the Caribbean region targeting travel agencies engaged in business with Cuba, Cuban diplomatic facilities and personnel, and the consulates of countries that had restored relations with Cuba. On July 17, the Cuban Embassy in Bogotá, Colombia, was attacked with machine gun fire; on July 22, hit men shot and killed a Cuban official in Merida, Mexico; on August 9, CORU claimed credit for the kidnapping and disappearance of two Cuban consulate security agents in Buenos Aires; on August 18, the office of Cubana airlines was bombed in Panama City, Panama; and on September 1, a bomb destroyed the Guyanese Embassy in Port of Spain, Trinidad and Tobago. On September 21, Cuban exiles, collaborating with Chilean secret police operatives, detonated a car bomb in downtown Washington, D.C., killing former Chilean ambassador Orlando Letelier, and his young colleague, Ronni Karpen Moffitt.

This summer of violence culminated on October 6, 1976, with the midair bombing of Cubana airlines flight 455, killing all seventy-three passengers and crew, among them the entire Cuban Olympic fencing team. CIA and FBI intelligence reporting indicated that the plane bombing had been planned in Caracas by the head of CORU, Orlando Bosch, and a former CIA operative, Luis Posada Carriles. "We are going to hit a Cuban airliner and Orlando has the details," one TOP SECRET CIA report quoted Posada as saying only days before the jet exploded just after takeoff from Barbados.[132]

Stunned by the worst pre-9/11 act of aviation terrorism in the Western Hemisphere, Fidel Castro reacted with extreme anger. In a major speech during a ceremony for the Cubana 455 victims on October 15, he linked the bombers to the CIA and blamed the United States for harboring terrorists and sponsoring such atrocities. "Who, if not the CIA, with the sanctuary of established imperialist domination and impunity in this hemisphere, is capable of such deeds?" he declared. In retaliation, Castro announced that he was abrogating the 1973 antihijacking accord until Washington put a stop to terrorist attacks against Cuba launched from the United States. "There can be no collaboration of any kind between an aggressor country and a country under attack."[133]

By the end of the Ford administration, relations with Cuba had regressed into the dark, mutual hostility that had characterized them since the early 60s. For all its efforts, the Kissinger initiative had produced no real narrowing of the deep chasm between Washington and Havana. The Ford administration's extraordinary, behind-the-scenes effort at détente in the Caribbean had failed.

Yet, Kissinger's unsuccessful secret diplomacy did yield one important result: it set the stage for a new Democratic administration to pick up where its Republican predecessor had left off.

5. **CARTER**

Close, but No Cigar

I always had a high opinion of Carter as a man of honor, an ethical man. . . .
Carter was a man who wanted to fix the problems between the United States
and Cuba.

—Fidel Castro to biographer Ignacio Ramonet, 2008

"I have concluded that we should attempt to achieve normalization of our
relations with Cuba," President Jimmy Carter ordered in Presidential Directive NSC-6, just weeks after his inauguration. "To this end, we should
begin direct and confidential talks in a measured and careful fashion with
representatives of the Government of Cuba."[1] No president before or since
has made as determined an effort to normalize U.S.-Cuban relations. Carter's
personal belief in civil relations with friend and foe alike, Cuba's reduced
support for Latin American revolutions, and détente between the superpowers all led Carter toward normalization. "I felt then, as I do now, that the best
way to bring about a change in its Communist regime was to have open trade
and commerce, and visitation, and diplomatic relations with Cuba," he told
the authors in an interview at the Carter Center.[2]

Despite this clear presidential directive, the road to better relations was
neither straight nor smooth. From the outset, senior U.S. officials were of
two minds about the value of improving relations with Havana. And for
Fidel Castro, improving relations with Washington was just one of several
competing foreign policy objectives. At the National Security Council, a
young new Ph.D. from Harvard, Robert A. Pastor, had just taken a job as
National Security Advisor Zbigniew Brzezinski's director for Latin America.
In a briefing paper on Carter's decision to normalize relations, Pastor wrote
that senior officials were focused on the question of how to get the process
moving. "That is the easy question," Pastor warned. "The more difficult and
important one . . . is not how to start the process, but rather how to manage
it and keep it from getting stuck."[3] He could not have been more prescient.

(EHC)

THE WHITE HOUSE
WASHINGTON
March 15, 1977

7707356 L

Presidential Directive/NSC-6

Jimmy Carter

TO:
      The Vice President
      The Secretary of State
      The Secretary of Defense

ALSO:
      The Secretary of the Treasury
      The Attorney General
      The Secretary of Commerce
      The United States Representative to
         the United Nations
      The Director of Central Intelligence

SUBJECT: Cuba

After reviewing the results of the meeting of the Policy Review
Committee held on Wednesday, March 9, 1977, to discuss U.S. policy
to Cuba, I have concluded that we should attempt to achieve normalization of our relations with Cuba.

To this end, we should begin direct and confidential talks in a
measured and careful fashion with representatives of the Government of Cuba. Our objective is to set in motion a process which
will lead to the reestablishment of diplomatic relations between the
United States and Cuba and which will advance the interests of the
United States with respect to:

-- Combating terrorism;

-- Human rights;

-- Cuba's foreign intervention;

-- Compensation for American expropriated property; and

-- Reduction of the Cuban relationship (political and military) with
   the Soviet Union.

DF

Presidential Directive NSC-6, signed by Jimmy Carter on March 15, 1977, directing his government to work toward normalizing relations with Cuba. (Jimmy Carter Library and Museum)

Signals

During the transition, Frank Mankiewicz met with President-elect Carter at Blair House and briefed him on Kissinger's secret talks with Havana. "He was very interested," Mankiewicz recalled, "and sent me to brief [incoming secretary of state] Cyrus Vance."[4] Even before the inauguration, the new administration began signaling its intentions to pick up where Kissinger left off. At his confirmation hearing on January 11, Vance called the trade embargo ineffective and added, "If Cuba is willing to live within the international system, then we ought to seek ways to find whether we can eliminate the impediments which exist between us and try to move toward normalization."[5]

In late January, the Cubans sent a proposal through Swiss diplomats in Havana for talks on fishing and maritime boundaries, and Washington accepted.[6] Both countries had adopted a two-hundred-mile commercial fishing zone; with Cuba just ninety miles from Florida and Cuba's large commercial fishing fleet plying the waters off the U.S. Atlantic coast, talks were imperative. The State Department also announced that it hoped to discuss other issues, including renewal of the antihijacking treaty, which Cuba had abrogated after the terrorist bombing of Cubana flight 455.[7]

Less than a month after inauguration, Carter suspended reconnaissance flights over Cuba by SR-71 spy planes. Halting the flights did not seriously impair U.S. intelligence gathering—technological advances made it possible keep an eye on Cuba from satellites and offshore flights—but it was an important gesture to the Cubans, whose national dignity was offended by the routine violation of their airspace.[8] In March, the State Department gave permission for basketball players from the University of South Dakota and South Dakota State University to travel to Cuba for exhibition games. Shortly thereafter, Secretary Vance allowed the ban on travel to Cuba by U.S. residents to expire (along with the ban on travel to three other countries).[9]

"The minuet begins," said a U.S. official.[10]

In an interview with journalist Bill Moyers, Castro said that Carter struck him as a man with "a sense of morals" and that Cuba and the United States did not have to "live constantly as enemies." Cuba, he declared, was ready to improve relations. Nevertheless, Castro held to his traditional stance: before negotiations could commence, the United States would have to lift the embargo. Cuba could not negotiate, as he often said, with "a dagger at our throat."[11] This posed a dilemma, since the embargo provided Washington's main leverage in any negotiation. To give it up at the outset, getting nothing in return, was impractical. To circumvent the problem, Castro indicated he was ready for secret "discussions"—rather than negotiations—on a range of issues.[12] There seemed to be a new readiness on both sides to move forward. Still, Castro was cautious, skeptical that Carter, despite his best intentions, would be able to deliver on normalization during his first term. "I am not pessimistic. I think it will take time," Fidel said in April 1977, during his meeting with Senators George McGovern (D-S.D.) and Jim Abourezk (D-S.D.). "What will prevail," he mused, "the idealism of President Carter or the reality of the United States?"[13]

A few months later, Castro told Senator Frank Church that he understood Carter was preoccupied with winning ratification of the Panama Canal Treaty, predicting this would delay improving relations with Cuba. "He can't do both at once."[14] Having jousted with Washington for the better part of two decades, Fidel may have had a better appreciation for Washington's political realities than the newly arrived governor from Georgia.

Carter's determination to normalize relations was not unconditional. Three issues stood as obstacles: Havana's support for revolution in Latin America, its military deployments in Africa, and the detention of thousands of political prisoners. "If I can be convinced that Cuba wants to remove their aggravating influence from other countries in this hemisphere, will not participate in violence in nations across the ocean, will recommit the former relationship that existed in Cuba toward human rights, then I would be willing to move toward normalizing relationships with Cuba," Carter said in his first major statement on the subject.[15]

Of the three issues, Africa would prove to be the toughest. Cuba's active assistance to revolutionaries in Latin America had waned in the 1970s, for lack of effective movements to support (though this would soon change with the eruption of revolution in Central America). The Africa problem appeared manageable, too, at first. Cuban troops had been withdrawing from Angola since March 1976, with the Cuban force declining from a peak of some thirty-six thousand to a low of about twelve thousand by early 1977.[16] Castro told Senators McGovern and Abourezk that the drawdown would continue and that he did not envision any other military deployments in Africa. The withdrawals, combined with Castro's assurances that the Angolan intervention was unique, led Carter to regard Cuba's expeditionary force in Angola as a problem that was solving itself.[17] At a press conference on January 31, Vance was asked whether the new administration would adhere to Henry Kissinger's demand that the Cubans withdraw troops from Angola before relations could be normalized. "I don't want to set any preconditions at this point," he replied. Acknowledging that the troops in Angola were "not helpful," he nevertheless affirmed that the administration hoped to "begin the process of moving toward normalization."[18]

Brzezinski was not entirely comfortable with this, but he kept his counsel. Whereas Vance thought the policy of hostility toward Cuba was ineffective and counterproductive, Brzezinski, like Kissinger before him, saw Cuba in the global context of the U.S.-Soviet rivalry. His strategic goal was to pry Cuba from the Soviet orbit, turning Fidel into a Latin Tito: "I didn't object to it if we could suck him away," he said of the decision to normalize relations. "I was somewhat skeptical as to whether this would work," he added, "but I felt there was no harm in trying."[19] Nevertheless, in March, just two months into the administration, he had Bob Pastor task the CIA to assess the effect of delaying normalization. The CIA replied that a delay "would not have any significant effect on U.S. political or economic interests."[20]

Measured and Reciprocal Steps

As the new administration prepared for talks with Havana, the National Security Council undertook a formal review of Cuba policy. Carter's foreign policy team was candid about the real conflicts of interest between the United States and Cuba, and the difficulties in reaching a modus vivendi, right from the SECRET policy review's opening paragraph:

> There are many compelling reasons why the US should move toward the normalization of relations with Cuba. However, the difficulties in achieving full normalization of relations should not be minimized. The issues involved are extremely complex and nettlesome. Fidel Castro is a wily and tough negotiator committed to some goals that are antithetical to those of the United States. The process of resolving differences with Cuba will be difficult and tensions and problems will remain even after relations have been restored.[21]

Nevertheless, it concluded, normalization would serve the long-term interests of the United States, which included reducing Cuba's dependence on the Soviet Union, giving Cuba incentives to cease its foreign interventions, improving human rights, obtaining compensation for nationalized U.S. property, reestablishing a U.S. presence in Cuba, opening up trade opportunities in this natural market, and demonstrating Washington's willingness to tolerate regimes of different political philosophies.

The State Department expected Cuba to be flexible on family reunification but to reject any discussion of political prisoners "as an infringement of national sovereignty." Convincing Cuba to reduce its military ties to the Soviet Union was not directly negotiable either, although better relations with Washington might make Cuba feel less need for such ties. "Realistically . . . this is not likely to be possible until a new U.S.-Cuban relationship is achieved and consolidated several years from now," the review acknowledged.

On Angola, "Castro understands that further military intervention in Africa or elsewhere would have a sharply negative effect on relations with the U.S.," and thus new adventures were unlikely. Nevertheless, the Cuban presence in Angola would not be ending any time soon. "Cuba probably cannot withdraw its forces entirely from Angola without risking the collapse of the MPLA regime," the report concluded.

Negotiations on compensation for nationalized U.S. property "will be protracted and difficult," the report predicted, both because Cuba did not have the hard currency reserves necessary to pay any substantial claim and because Cuba had counterclaims for the damage done by the embargo and the CIA's covert war in the 1960s. "Cuba apparently perceives the gains from renewed trade with the United States to be great, and it may therefore be willing to makes some significant non-economic concessions in return." For that reason, "The embargo is the major U.S. bargaining chip." Although Cuba's tangible interest in better relations was economic, the policy report concluded, the symbolism of normalization was even more important "because it would be seen as a symbol of our acceptance of the Cuban Revolution as a *fait accompli* which we are willing to live with." All in all, the policy review would prove to be an impressively accurate indicator of both the critical issues and the stumbling blocks that lay ahead.

The NSC's Policy Review Committee (PRC), one of the two top-level interagency committees in Carter's NSC system, met on March 9, 1977, and recommended moving toward normalization. It approved a "step-by-step" negotiating strategy proceeding on "a measured and reciprocal basis," beginning with negotiations on fisheries and maritime boundaries.[22] The U.S. delegation would use the opportunity to raise other issues, such as cultural exchanges, family reunification, and the hijacking agreement. If the Cubans responded positively,

> We would continue periodic meetings to discuss reciprocal gestures that could be taken over several months to improve the climate. . . . As areas of agreement emerge we would probe the Cubans on other major issues, including those they say are not negotiable. . . . A variant on this strategy could be to establish packages and package deals that would

have to be resolved before any final agreements are concluded. We would seek to coordinate reciprocal gestures as part of these packages in order to sustain momentum and build public support. We would not give up the embargo chip and reestablish embassies unless and until Cuba has made a draw down of its forces in Angola, demonstrated its restraint on further overseas adventures, and made important gestures on human rights.[23]

To begin the dialogue, Vance chose his new assistant secretary for inter-American affairs, Terence A. Todman. One of the few African Americans of ambassadorial rank in the Foreign Service, Todman had served mainly in Africa, although he led the embassy in Costa Rica just prior to his appointment. When Vance interviewed him for the post, Todman told the secretary, "We had been going the wrong way on Cuba for a number of years," and that it was "important for us to open up to Cuba—very important."[24]

The first round of talks with the Cubans on fishing and maritime issues began at the Roosevelt Hotel in New York on March 24. The Cuban delegation was headed by Deputy Foreign Minister Pelegrín Torras. "We felt we were about to begin a process of perhaps sweeping consequences," recalled Wayne Smith, who had served as a junior Foreign Service officer in Havana under Ambassador Philip Bonsal and was soon to be named coordinator for Cuban affairs at State. Todman broke the initial tension by apologizing to the Cubans for the wintry cold weather and saying he hoped the "the warmth of our meeting" would compensate for it.[25] The atmosphere at the talks was friendly and open, although it quickly became apparent that the U.S. side was ready to move ahead more quickly than its counterpart. The Cubans seemed genuinely surprised at Todman's opening remarks, in which he reviewed a wide range of bilateral issues. Torras replied that the Cuban side had instructions to discuss only fishing and maritime boundaries but that the U.S. delegation should not mistake this for disinterest. From there, the talks lapsed into a highly technical discussion that consumed the next four days.[26]

With an agreement nearly complete, Torras invited the U.S. delegation to Havana for a second, final round of talks. Todman thought this was Cuba's way of asserting its diplomatic equality, since the outstanding issues could have been quickly and easily resolved without recourse to another meeting. He was stunned, however, when Secretary Vance told him President Carter did not want the U.S. delegation to travel to Havana. "Zbig had convinced the president I shouldn't go," Todman recalled, allegedly for fear the Cubans would somehow exploit the visit for political gain. Incensed, Todman told Vance that if the president did not have confidence that he could go to Cuba and effectively represent the interests of the United States, then they had the wrong person in the job. "I would have quit over it," Todman said, looking back on the incident. Vance communicated Todman's insistence to the president, who relented.[27]

The spat over going to Havana was symptomatic of growing U.S. disappointment that the Cubans had not responded more vigorously to U.S. overtures, such as ending SR-71 overflights and lifting the travel ban. "I must register my general feeling that so far we seem to be taking more initiatives toward Castro than he is towards us," Brzezinski wrote in a memo to Carter in late April.

"I agree," Carter wrote in the margin.[28]

Vance agreed, too, and instructed Todman to tell the Cubans that Washington was looking for reciprocal gestures, such as reinstating the antihijacking agreement, releasing several U.S. citizens held since the 1960s as CIA agents, allowing Cuban American family visits, and allowing U.S. citizens in Cuba to repatriate with their Cuban families if they so desired.[29]

The U.S. delegation departed for Havana on April 25 and after two days signed a fishing and maritime boundaries agreement. "The fishing agreement was easy," Todman recalled. "The Cubans needed our fish and we really wanted a maritime boundaries agreement."[30] Once again, however, the Cuban delegation was not ready to broaden the agenda. Although the formal negotiations stuck to fishing, Todman had two private meetings with Cuban foreign minister Isidoro Malmierca, which Todman described as "conversations" rather than "negotiations."[31] He listed the full range of bilateral issues Washington hoped to discuss and offered several specific proposals. The United States would lift the embargo on food and medicine if Cuba would take humanitarian measures such as releasing U.S. prisoners and dual nationals and perhaps freeing Cuban political prisoners—though Todman was careful to note that this last suggestion represented "in no way any interest in interfering in Cuba's internal affairs." If Cuba would reactivate the antihijacking agreement, "the United States would be disposed to make declarations from the highest levels reiterating its position condemning all terrorist actions and give assurances that they will be suppressed," Todman promised, according to the secret Cuban transcript of the meeting.[32] Washington wanted to normalize relations, and Cuba should regard the lifting of the travel ban and the end of SR-71 overflights as "gestures that indicate the attitude of the United States."

"Relations between Cuba and the United States should be normal," Malmierca agreed. "The situation that has existed for many years should not be everlasting." Lifting the embargo on food and medicine "would be a very important step." But Cuba would not reinstate the antihijacking agreement in exchange for mere promises. "More than declarations are required," he insisted. "Up to now, there are no indications that the counterrevolutionary groups have encountered any obstacles in developing their activities," he said, reminding Todman of the links between some of the groups and the CIA. Nor would Cuba negotiate its presence in Angola.

Todman tried to end on a positive note by endorsing a recent statement by Raúl Castro that U.S.-Cuban relations were like a bridge blown up in wartime that had to be rebuilt, brick by brick. "It is necessary to build the bridge from both sides," Todman said. "The distance that separates us, the gap that has existed for many years, is very large. We can't build this bridge from just one side."

Malmierca agreed: "For our part, we did not think we would just sit and wait for the bridge to be finished."

During the fishing negotiations, Todman suggested opening Interests Sections in Washington and Havana staffed by Cuban and U.S. diplomats. Since the break in relations in January 1961, Cuban and U.S. affairs had been handled by the Czech and Swiss embassies respectively. By opening Interests Sections staffed by Cuban and U.S. diplomats, the two governments would gain most of the advantages of having embassies in each other's capitals, even though they did not have formal diplomatic relations. "The Cubans had a presence here [at the United Nations], but we had none there," Todman reasoned. It made sense for Washington to get people back in Havana.

Taking a major step toward more formal diplomatic ties intrigued the Cubans; Malmierca asked Todman for a formal proposal. Shortly thereafter, Culver Gleysteen, State's coordinator for Cuban affairs, presented a draft agreement to Néstor García at Cuba's UN mission. The Cubans accepted it almost unchanged. "We had a very easy negotiation," recalled Todman's deputy, William H. Luers, who met with Vice Minister Torras in New York on May 30, to formally sign the agreement to open Interests Sections on September 1. After the signing, Luers and Torras smoked cigars together; "Fidel told me to get a deal," Torras confided."[33]

At the end of the Havana round of fishing talks, the Cubans invited Todman to meet with Castro. Perhaps sensitized by Brzezinski's objections to his trip, Todman feared that the Cubans might be playing a game of diplomatic one-upmanship, so he declined. Nevertheless, he was optimistic about the future. The "chances are good" for further improvements in relations, he told the press.[34] Carter was upbeat, too. Speaking to reporters on May 31, the day after the Interests Sections agreement was signed, Carter praised the "good progress" made in the negotiations with Havana. "We still have a lot of differences between us, but I have been encouraged," adding that a normal friendly relationship was "my ultimate goal."[35] A few weeks after the Todman trip, Cuba announced that eighty-four U.S. citizens residing in Cuba would be allowed to leave for the United States with their Cuban families. Castro also told Senator Frank Church that he would consider releasing seven CIA agents (though the last of them would remain in prison for another two years).[36]

Deciding on Next Steps

The next logical step for Washington was to partially lift the embargo, enabling Castro to gracefully back off his traditional posture that there could be no negotiations with the embargo still in place. Castro argued that the embargo had been imposed unilaterally and therefore had to be removed unconditionally. Viewed from Washington, the nationalization of U.S. property in 1960 was the proximate cause for imposing the embargo, so it could not be lifted until the compensation issue was addressed. In practice, of course, the Cubans had been willing to discuss a range of bilateral issues, including migration, hijacking, fishing, and maritime boundaries. But the Cuban precondition loomed as an obstacle to negotiations on normalizing relations.

Even before Carter's inauguration, the Cubans began suggesting that the way out of this catch-22 might be to lift the embargo on food and medicine. Vice President Carlos Rafael Rodríguez said as much to visiting former U.S. government officials in late 1976. In February and March, Castro explicitly proposed this approach to Congressman Bingham and to Senators McGovern and Abourezk.[37] Upon his return from Havana, McGovern asked Carter if he would oppose legislation to lift the ban on trade in food and medicine. "A Congressional initiative would not cause me concern," Carter replied.[38] Shortly thereafter, McGovern introduced legislation to do just that. But upon reflection, Carter had second thoughts. Sugar, after all, was food. To allow Cuba to sell sugar to the United States meant opening the U.S. market to Cuba's principal export, with no countervailing concession. A partial lifting of the embargo was a good idea to "help move the process along," Secretary Vance advised Carter. But "a partial lifting of the embargo *should not* include Cuban sugar imports to the U.S. . . . . To give him [Castro] access to the U.S. sugar market at the beginning of the process would be to give away most of our bargaining position."

"I agree," Carter wrote in the margin of Vance's memo.[39]

When Bob Pastor was unable to get McGovern to exclude sugar from his proposal to allow two-way trade in food and medicine, administration officials expressed "skeptical neutrality" toward it. Culver Gleysteen told the Senate that approval of the bill would demolish U.S. leverage in any negotiation. As a result, the Senate Foreign Relations Committee rejected McGovern's proposal, adopting instead a provision for one-way trade only, allowing Cuba to buy food and medicine in the United States but not sell it.[40] That was not the gesture the Cubans were looking for. Castro had warned McGovern in March that one-way trade "did not make much sense." In public, he was more adamant, telling Barbara Walters that if Washington allowed only one-way trade, "We would not buy anything at all in the United States, not even an aspirin for headaches, and we have a lot of headaches."[41] In June, McGovern allowed the one-way trade provision to be dropped from the Senate bill as fruitless. The road to normalization was going to have some potholes.

Presidential Directive NSC-6, which set the normalization process in motion, called for the National Security Council to recommend to the president how to proceed after "an exploratory round of discussions." Conclusion of the agreements on fishing, maritime boundaries, and Interests Sections seemed an opportune time to take stock and decide on next steps. In preparation for an NSC Policy Review Committee (PRC) meeting in early August 1977, Pastor warned Brzezinski against trying to directly negotiate foreign policy concessions from Cuba. "We will not affect Castro's desire to influence events in Africa by trying to slow or halt the normalization process," he wrote. "It is the wrong instrument, and it will have no effect other than to halt the normalization process and preclude the accumulation of sufficient influence by the U.S. over Cuba which might eventually factor into Cuba's decision-making." The way to mitigate Cuban behavior, whether in Africa, Latin America, or in relation to the Soviet Union, was to ensnare the Cubans in a web of economic and diplomatic relations with the United States that would provide Washington with some future leverage over Cuban behavior.[42] Pastor would prove to be right about Castro's intransigence when it came to negotiating away his foreign policy. But his recommendation to avoid this trap by not demanding such concessions struck Brzezinski as soft. "He would always sort of playfully—or unplayfully—stick needles in me about being pro-Cuban," Pastor recalled.[43]

The PRC convened on August 3, 1977, to discuss the same options considered when the White House decided to normalize relations in March.

Option one simply continued the "step by step" approach, looking for more discrete areas where the two countries might hammer out agreements. The second option called for stepping up the pace by trying to negotiate "limited packaged deals"—for example, "a partial lifting of the embargo in return for a number of Cuban steps in the human rights area." The third option, which Brzezinski denigrated as the "full swoop," was to move directly to a full normalization of relations.

The PRC readily agreed to continue step-by-step discussions with the Cubans for the next two months to see if agreements could be reached on law enforcement cooperation, family visits, cultural exchanges, and the release of U.S. prisoners. If these exploratory discussions went well, the next step would be "packaged deals." To start, Washington would propose to lift the ban on sales of food and medicine to Cuba and allow limited Cuban exports to the United States in exchange for the release of U.S. prisoners, the repatriation of U.S. citizens and their Cuban families, and visits of divided families—the same package Todman had offered Malmierca in Havana.

But the PRC meeting deadlocked over whether to make these negotiations contingent on Cuba reducing its military presence in Africa. Brzezinski, increasingly skeptical of normalization, joined with the Defense Department and Joint Chiefs to insist on conditionality. "NSC, DOD, and JCS feel that for international and domestic reasons we should not lift *any* part of the embargo until Cuba demonstrated also some tangible restraint on its activities in Africa," Brzezinski wrote to Carter. "State, Treasury and Commerce believe that at the beginning of the talks we should state that we *assume* Cuba will show restraint in its military activities in Africa. . . . Progress toward normalization would be inhibited if this *assumption* did not hold" (emphasis in the originals). Brzezinski recommended that Carter condition partial lifting of the embargo on the Cubans taking "some visible and concrete steps toward restraining and reducing their activities in Africa." Carter checked the box agreeing with Brzezinski's recommendation.[44] Just how far Washington would go to improve relations with Cuba while Cuban troops remained in Angola was resolved in favor of hard conditionality.

Shortly after the PRC meeting on Cuba policy, Carter's Special Assistant for Health Issues Peter Bourne wrote a memo to the State Department arguing that they should allow the sale of medicine to Cuba. On the basis of his conversations with Cuban minister of health José Antonio Gutiérrez Muñiz at the World Health Assembly in Geneva in May, Bourne believed a U.S. offer would help sustain momentum toward better relations.[45] He received no immediate response, but the idea resurfaced in September when Bourne encountered Gutiérrez Muñiz again at a diplomatic reception in Washington for the Pan American Health Organization. The Cuban minister buttonholed Bourne to ask whether Washington would be willing to sell Cuba certain drugs that could not be obtained elsewhere. "I'd be happy to talk to you," Bourne replied, "but this reception probably isn't the place to go into the details. Why don't you come to the White House tomorrow?"

"I did that with some naïveté," Bourne admitted later, not realizing at the time that Gutiérrez Muñiz's visit to the White House the next day was the first for a senior Cuban official since 1959. "It was seen as an extraordinary breakthrough by the government in Havana," Bourne said ruefully. The symbolism of the meeting also caught the attention of Brzezinski, who scolded Bourne for not coordinating with the NSC staff. "He was always pissed off that I was getting into what he considered foreign policy stuff, which was not part of my brief."[46]

At the White House, Gutiérrez Muñiz presented Bourne with a list of seventy-two drugs that Cuba would like to buy, twenty-two of which were manufactured only in the United States. To Bourne, allowing the Cubans to buy the drugs seemed like a good way both to improve relations and to fulfill a humanitarian need. But when he pitched the idea to Brzezinski's office a few days later, Pastor reacted unenthusiastically, telling him, "The time was not ripe" for such a gesture.[47] Bourne would not relent, however. "I was totally committed to having it happen."[48]

To pacify Bourne, Pastor tasked the State Department to investigate the idea. The Cubans were correct that none of the twenty-two drugs could be purchased outside the United States; moreover, the Food and Drug Administration judged eighteen of them to be "lifesaving." On October 13, State convened an interagency meeting to consider Bourne's proposal and recommended that Cuba be licensed to make a one-time purchase of the eighteen lifesaving drugs. Deputy Secretary of State Warren Christopher sent the group's recommendation forward to Brzezinski, arguing that the sale was "a measured gesture in response to recent Cuban actions," which included allowing the departure of U.S. citizens with their Cuban families and releasing one of the U.S. prisoners. "Licensing a shipment of lifesaving medicines . . . is a small concession we could make at no great political cost. . . . It would be well-received by the Cubans and might produce further gestures on their part."[49] Writing on Christmas Eve, Pastor sent Brzezinski a memo entitled "'Tis the Season," arguing that in the spirit of the holidays, they should approve the drug sale.[50]

The president did eventually approve the limited one-time sales in February 1978. By then, the internal haggling over the Cuban request had taken five months. Insulted, the Cubans refused to purchase the medicines on a one-time basis.[51] In March, when U.S. surgeon general Julius Richmond visited Cuba to promote cooperation on health issues, Minister Gutiérrez Muñiz renewed the request to buy at least the twenty-two drugs unavailable outside the United States. Lyle Lane, the chief of the U.S. Interests Section in Havana, endorsed the idea in a cable to Washington, arguing that such a small sale would not poke much of a hole in the embargo. "Such a limited gesture would appear responsive to Cuban political prisoner release," Lane added, "and might create a more propitious atmosphere for releasing political prisoners or other steps."[52] Washington, however, held firm to the one-time-only license and the deal was never consummated. The Cubans took the rejection of the medicine request as an indication that Washington was not really serious about improving relations. As Vice President Carlos Rafael Rodríguez told U.S. diplomats in a private meeting months later, "We found your attitude in regard to the freeing of sales of certain medicines to be petty."[53]

Africa, Again

As Carter was deciding to make normalization contingent on Cuba's reducing its involvement in Africa, events on the ground were moving in the opposite direction. Two incidents in early 1977 led Havana to halt troop withdrawals from Angola and send reinforcements. In March, several thousand Katangan exiles invaded Zaire's Shaba Province (formerly Katanga) from western Angola. During the Angolan civil war the Katangans had received both arms and military training from the Cubans. Zaire immediately charged that Angola and Cuba had staged the Shaba invasion. Castro, in the middle of an eight-nation Africa tour, denied categorically that there was "a single Cuban" in Zaire or that Cuba had trained or armed the Katangans for the invasion; in fact, Havana was just as surprised by the invasion as Washington.[54] Washington responded with surprising equanimity. Both Vance and Carter acknowledged that there was no evidence of Cuban involvement.[55] By April, the Katangans had been driven back across the Angolan border, but the clash increased the threat of war between Angola and Zaire, thus aggravating Angola's security problems.

The second event that ended Cuban troop withdrawals was a challenge to President António Agostinho Neto's leadership from within his own party.

In May, a pro-Soviet faction staged a coup attempt. The conspiracy had at least tacit Soviet support, but Cuban troops joined with forces loyal to Neto to suppress it.[56] Confronted with an insurgency by Jonas Savimbi's guerrillas, the persistent danger of South African intervention, the threat of war with Zaire, and his government's own internal divisions, Neto requested Cuban reinforcements. "The Angolan government didn't feel terribly safe after that," Fidel later explained. "If we had continued to withdraw at that point, Angola would have been invaded by Zaire and South Africa."[57] Over the ensuing months, the number of Cuban troops in Angola increased by some 20 percent to approximately nineteen thousand men.[58]

While the Cubans were shoring up Angola's deteriorating security, they were also being drawn into the Byzantine geopolitics of the Horn of Africa, where two nominally Marxist-Leninist governments were facing off over traditional ethnic animosities and contested borders. Somalia's leader, Siad Barre, was stoking unrest among ethnic Somalis living in Ethiopia's Ogaden region. Ethiopia's radical military government led by Mengistu Haile Mariam faced not only the Ogaden insurgency but another separatist uprising in Eritrea and armed resistance within Ethiopia itself. In March 1977, during his trip to Africa, Castro tried unsuccessfully to mediate the Ogaden conflict.[59] The fighting escalated in May when several thousand insurgents entered the Ogaden from Somalia, and in July forty thousand regular Somali troops invaded the region. The Soviet Union and Cuba responded by increasing their aid to Ethiopia. By the fall, the number of Cuban military advisors had climbed to several hundred.[60]

The Cuban role had crossed a threshold for President Carter. On November 11, he blasted their involvement in Africa in unusually harsh terms: "The Cubans have, in effect, taken on the colonial aspect that the Portuguese gave up in months gone by," Carter said. "They are now spreading into other countries. . . . We consider this to be a threat to the permanent peace in Africa."[61]

Brzezinski fired an even bigger rhetorical gun a few days later on November 16, at the "Sperling Breakfast," a venerable not-for-attribution press backgrounder organized by *Christian Science Monitor* reporter Godfrey Sperling. Brzezinski claimed that a new intelligence study had found a surge in Cuban combat troops in Angola since July, a buildup of advisors in Ethiopia, and military missions in ten other countries. "We have to be seriously disturbed by the implication of the growing military presence in Africa and raise a warning flag about it," Brzezinski declared. And, he added, it made normalizing relations "impossible."[62]

Brzezinski's press briefing took the State Department by surprise. Wayne Smith, who had replaced Gleysteen as coordinator for Cuban Affairs, first heard about it on his car radio. When he got to the office, Smith called Pastor to get an explanation. "What the hell is this?" he demanded. Pastor insisted that Brzezinski had done nothing more than reaffirm the president's oft-stated concern about Cuban involvement in Africa, so there was no need to clear the briefing with State. "But he is saying that this will affect the possibility of moving ahead with the dialogue and towards normalization," Smith countered. To Smith, it looked like Brzezinski was changing policy singlehandedly.[63]

Although he did not let on, Pastor was just as surprised as Smith. "I learned about it in the *New York Times* that morning, too," he said later. But Pastor defended his boss. The aim of both the president's November 11 speech and Brzezinski's briefing was to warn the Cubans that Washington was seriously unhappy with their buildup in Ethiopia. "Both the President and Zbig felt very strongly that we needed to send a very strong signal. Carter was not going to tolerate any further expansion of the Cuban military presence in Africa."[64]

Brzezinski, for his part, was unperturbed by the State Department's ruffled feathers. "I'm sure there were people at the State Department howling that I had a press briefing," he told the authors, adding, "If the president told me to give a briefing, I did not have to clear it with Secretary Vance."[65] The fall of 1977 was a period of "growing disagreements with State," Brzezinski acknowledged. "I was becoming increasingly concerned over the longer-term implications of the Soviet strategic buildup and by the growing Soviet-Cuban military penetration of the Horn of Africa."[66]

There was at least one other senior official who shared Brzezinski's concerns: the president. "I felt that this was a test case for Castro," Carter recalled, "and I let Castro know very firmly that his involvement in Ethiopia and earlier Angola—but Angola was secondary—was a test case of whether we should proceed with normalization."[67] The reinforcement of Cuban troops in Angola and the deployment of advisors to Ethiopia made Castro's previous assurances that he was drawing down in Africa seem disingenuous. "The president feels that Castro has been something less than straight on this issue," a senior official told the press.[68]

If Brzezinski's press briefing was intended to send the Cubans a clear warning not to expand their involvement in Africa, it simply confused them. Ramón Sánchez-Parodi, chief of the Cuban Interests Section in Washington, asked Wayne Smith what was going on. "We understand this is a matter of concern to you," Sánchez-Parodi acknowledged. "We accept that. But if you thought we were building up in Angola, why did you not raise the question with us through the diplomatic channels we now have? . . . We thought it was for situations like this that you wanted to have them."[69]

In Havana, Vice President Carlos Rafael Rodríguez summoned Lyle Lane to ask for an explanation of Brzezinski's public attack. Was the administration trying to act tough in order to win conservative support for the Panama Canal treaties? Was Washington confused about Cuba's intentions in Africa? Or had the Carter administration decided it was no longer interested in improving relations? "We wanted to clarify what was going on," Rodríguez said later. "If Jimmy Carter needed to recapture an image he had lost of antileftism, we could sympathize with his political predicament, but we did not like to be used."[70]

On November 13, 1977, the day after Brzezinski's incendiary press briefing, Somalia severed diplomatic relations with Cuba and expelled the Soviet military mission, hoping this would entice Western nations to come to its aid.[71] Instead, the expulsions only served to clear the way for a full Soviet and Cuban commitment to Ethiopia. Over the next three months, the Cuban presence expanded from four hundred advisors to some seventeen thousand regular troops.[72] The Somalis, short on supplies, proved no match for the Cubans. By early March, they had fallen back across the border.

The West never came to Somalia's aid because it was the clear aggressor in its attempt to incorporate the Ogaden into a "Greater Somalia," thus violating a cardinal principle of African politics: the permanence of existing borders.[73] As NSC aide Paul Henze wrote to Brzezinski, "The Soviets and Cubans have legality and African sentiment on their side."[74] Nevertheless, the Ogaden war opened a deep fissure in Carter's foreign policy team. Brzezinski thought the deployment of Cubans to Ethiopia required a tough response. "I became personally of the opinion that we weren't going to get anywhere with these guys simply by trying to get an accommodation," he said later. "We had to concentrate on making it too costly for them to pursue this policy." He proposed expanding covert U.S. assistance to Jonas Savimbi's UNITA guerrillas in Angola, to pin down the Cubans and bleed them. (Despite the 1976 Clark Amendment prohibiting such aid, Washington had been secretly channeling it through other countries in violation of the spirit if not the letter of the law).[75]

Vance believed that Washington had let the superpower rivalry distort its relations with the Third World, to the detriment of the national interest. Aiding Somali was a losing proposition, both politically and militarily, because it was the aggressor. Moreover, the more threatened the Angolans felt, the less likely they were to ask the Cubans to go home.[76] The fight over the Horn of Africa badly damaged relations between the secretary and national security advisor. "Ethiopia was really the decisive issue that separated Vance and Brzezinski," Robert Pastor recalled. "It split them apart."[77]

However justified Castro felt his actions in the Horn were, they proved fatal to the process of normalizing U.S.-Cuban relations. At the August 1977 PRC meeting on next steps toward normalization, even Vance had agreed that any new Cuban adventures in Africa would scuttle the process. "The president and his national security team had decided consciously not to let Angola impede the progress," Pastor told the authors, "but everybody also agreed that any Cuban military action beyond that would make normalization impossible."[78] Cuba's intervention in Ethiopia convinced U.S. policy makers that Angola had not been an anomaly, that Cuba had adopted an aggressive foreign policy in sharp conflict with U.S. interests in the Third World. Carter acknowledged that after the Ogaden war, he "gave up" on normalizing relations with Cuba in the short term. "The turning point for me was in Ethiopia."[79]

Shaba II

On May 11, 1978, the Katangan gendarmes launched another assault across the Angolan border into Zaire. Dubbed "Shaba II" by the media, it was a carbon copy of the 1977 attack in every respect but one—the U.S. response. In 1977 Washington accepted Cuba's claims of innocence. In 1978, the invasion set off a public shouting match between Fidel Castro and Jimmy Carter. Once again, Zaire charged that Cuban troops accompanied the invasion force, which prompted an unusual diplomatic initiative from Castro. At eight o'clock in the evening on May 17, he summoned the chief of the U.S. Interests Section, Lyle Lane, to his office. It was Lane's first audience with the Cuban leader.[80] Castro told Lane he had a message for Secretary Vance and President Carter: "There is not even one Cuban with the Katangan forces in Shaba," Castro said. "Cuba has had *no* participation either directly or indirectly in the Shaba affair. Cuba has provided *no* weapons or other materiel to the Katangan forces. Cuba has *not* trained the Katangan forces." In fact, Castro continued, Cuba had not had any contact with the Katangans since the end of the war in Angola at least two years before. Cuba opposed the Katangans' action because it risked sparking a war between Angola and Zaire.

"It is obvious he attached great importance to getting the above message about the Shaba crisis to the highest levels of the USG [U.S. Government]," Lane cabled Washington.

Vance replied that Washington had "noted" Cuba's assurances that it was not involved in Shaba. "We trust that this is the case, since such involvement would be viewed with the gravest concern here."[81] On the same day that Vance sent his reply, the New York Times published the details of Lane's meeting with Castro and his categorical denial of any Cuban involvement. That morning, at an interagency group chaired by Brzezinski's deputy, David Aaron, the CIA representative claimed to have new evidence that Cubans had trained the Katangans more recently than Castro acknowledged, suggesting that his denials were disingenuous.[82] Aaron instructed State Department spokesman Tom Reston to note the Cuban involvement at the department's noon briefing. "It is now our understanding," Reston told the press, "that the insurgents in Shaba Province have been trained recently by Cubans in Angola and that they are employing Soviet weapons." At the White House, Press Secretary Jody Powell made a similar statement.[83]

The Cuban reaction was swift and furious. Lyle Lane was summoned to a meeting with Deputy Foreign Minister René Anillo. "It is truly irritating that after leaking the news about Comrade Fidel's words to you, there should now appear a public declaration making these imputations," Anillo scolded. By leaking Castro's assurances and immediately contradicting them, Washington was, in effect, publicly calling Castro a liar. "We consider the declarations of Reston absolutely dishonest and an act of bad faith," Anillo continued. "We cannot understand why a constructive gesture on our part should be met in this way."[84]

The answer was geopolitics. The Shaba II invasion followed close on the heels of the Cuban intervention in Ethiopia, which had sharply altered U.S. perceptions of Cuban and Soviet intentions. The circumstances of the Ogaden war prevented any effective U.S. response, but Shaba II gave Brzezinski an opportunity to vent his frustration over Cuba's African policy and to frame Washington's support for Zaire as a tough rebuke to Soviet and Cuban adventurism.[85]

The first casualty was Vance's hope of reenergizing the normalization process. Vance had requested a secret meeting with Cuban vice president Carlos Rafael Rodríguez during the May UN General Assembly meeting. "Vance hoped at least to begin getting the process of improving relations . . . back on track," wrote Wayne Smith, who prepared Vance's briefing materials.[86]

Unbeknownst to Vance, the afternoon he was slated to speak with Rodríguez, President Carter began a press conference in Chicago by escalating the charge that Cuba was responsible for the Shaba invasion. "We believe that Cuba had known of the Katangan plans to invade and obviously did nothing to restrain them from crossing the border." He went on to say that it was a "joke" to call Cuba a nonaligned nation. "They act as a surrogate for the Soviet Union."[87]

That evening, Vance met Rodríguez at the Waldorf Astoria residence of the U.S. ambassador to the UN, Andrew Young. An angry Rodriquez took issue with Carter's remarks in Chicago. Vance, taken aback and red-faced, turned to Young and asked, "Andy, is this true?"[88]

"Vance was obviously unaware of these statements," recalled Rodríguez's foreign policy aide, Carlos Martínez Salsamendi. Despite Vance's impending meeting with Rodríguez, Brzezinski's office had not briefed him on what the president planned to say in Chicago.[89] Rather than clearing the air for a resumption of discussions about normalization, as Vance had hoped, the meeting diverged into a debate about Shaba. In subsequent public statements, Rodríguez was scathing, calling the U.S. accusations "absolutely false" and "based on impudently repeated lies."[90]

By questioning Castro's honesty, the White House had thrown down the gauntlet. Fidel was quick to pick it up. Meeting for nine hours on June 13 with visiting Congressmen Stephen J. Solarz (D-N.Y.) and Anthony C. Beilenson (D-Calif.), two hours of which included reporters, Castro ripped into the U.S. administration. The claim that Cuba had any role whatsoever in the Shaba invasion was a personal insult to him and a lie. "It is not a half lie. It is an absolute, total, complete lie," Castro said with obvious anger. "It is not a small lie, it's a big lie. It is not a negligible lie, it is an important lie . . . a lie manufactured in Brzezinski's office." He portrayed Brzezinski as a Svengali who had "confused and deceived" the president. "Carter is an honest man," Castro offered, but he had been "caught up by these deceits and lies."[91]

For Carter, this public face-off with Castro turned into a political embarrassment because the evidence that the Cubans had facilitated the Shaba invasion was scanty and unreliable. Administration officials themselves disagreed about it. An intelligence community source said the evidence was "too flimsy" to stand up to close scrutiny.[92] The president himself, looking back on the Shaba crisis, had second thoughts. "I think now that I overreacted, maybe based on incorrect intelligence," he told the authors. "I think that Castro's assurances to me about his limited role [in Shaba] were probably more truthful than I thought at the time."[93]

The damage, however, was done. "The opportunity to [re]start negotiations had passed," Rodríguez later recalled.[94]

Private Emissaries

As relations deteriorated over Ethiopia and Shaba, both Havana and Washington sought to open back-channel communications to explore whether normalization was still possible. At the height of the Ethiopian crisis in December 1977, two congressmen, Richard Nolan (D.-Minn.) and Frederick W. Richmond (D-N.Y.), told the administration of their impending trip to Cuba, and were briefed separately by Vance, Brzezinski, and President Carter himself. The congressmen wanted to jump-start normalization by telling Castro that Washington was still interested and by offering cultural exchanges. "We got the green light to go ahead," Nolan recalled, provided Castro understood that Washington would be watching for reciprocal actions on his part. As examples of reciprocity, the congressmen would propose the release of the five remaining CIA prisoners, the release of Cuban political prisoners, exit visas for dual nationals and their families, and a drawdown of Cuban forces in Angola. Vance also asked the congressmen to gauge Castro's interest in establishing contact through a high-level U.S. emissary to help work through the obstacles to normal relations. Brzezinski and Carter focused more on Africa, adamant that Nolan and Richmond clearly convey to Castro that a reduction of Cuban military involvement had become a precondition for further progress. Carter's message was blunt: "Just tell them to get out of Angola."[95]

In Havana, Nolan and Richmond met with Castro for almost eight hours, starting at eleven o'clock on the night of December 5 and lasting until dawn. "He's a night person," Nolan quipped. The congressmen laid out their proposals for cultural and educational exchanges in the arts, agriculture, and tourism. Castro favored them all, but he balked at the reciprocal steps they wanted. He agreed to allow dual nationals to emigrate, but the issue of the CIA prisoners was thornier. These people had conspired to overthrow his government, even plotting against the lives of Cuban leaders, Castro pointed out. He compared them to the four Puerto Rican nationalists jailed in the United States for opening fire on the House of Representatives from the visitors' gallery in 1954 and for trying to assassinate President Harry S. Truman at Blair House in 1950. He suggested an exchange.[96]

Castro's proposal was, in actuality, a response to a letter Carter had sent him privately via Senator George McGovern, who visited Cuba just a few days before Nolan and Richmond. Urging Castro to release the U.S. prisoners, Carter wrote, "Now it is necessary that both our countries put aside the difficulties of the past and create a new relationship based upon mutual trust and equality." He went on to solicit Castro's thoughts on how to resolve the prisoners issue. Replying via Nolan and Richmond, Castro revived a proposal he first made in January 1975 and repeated to Barbara Walters in early 1977—to swap the CIA agents for the Puerto Rican nationalists.[97] On the issue of Cuban prisoners, Castro was noncommittal. He acknowledged holding about three thousand opponents, which was, he said, about 20 percent of the number held previously. Nevertheless, he was reluctant to release people who might go to Miami and join exile terrorist groups.[98]

Angola was "the biggest irritation" to President Carter, the congressmen explained, and "some indication of a willingness to de-escalate Cuban involvement" was necessary for normalization. They cajoled Fidel to give them something to take back, even a statement in principle that Cuba intended to draw down. But Castro was as adamant as Carter. Cuban troops were in Angola at the request of its government, to defend it against the threat of foreign aggression from Zaire and South Africa. "The Angolans still do not feel safe," he explained. Cuba would not negotiate its support for Angola with Washington, betraying the Angolans' trust. "No country that respected itself would do this." Moreover, it was "not equitable" for Washington to make such a demand as a condition of normal bilateral relations. Should Cuba demand that the United States close its bases in Turkey or Spain?[99]

"He felt very, very strongly about it and argued his case quite well," Nolan recalled.[100]

As the meeting came to a close, Castro reiterated his desire to improve relations but not at the expense of principle. "If the issue of Cuban-American relations is placed in the context of Africa, the restoration of relations will not advance," he said flatly. "I am not willing to enter into any kind of compromise on Angola. Please convey this."[101] To be sure his message got across, Fidel repeated it immediately at a press conference. "Our relationship with Africa—that, we can't discuss, that we can't negotiate," he insisted. Castro had heard the message loud and clear that Africa had become the critical stumbling block. Asked about the prospects for normalization, Castro replied that if the reporter lived to be ninety, "then you may live to see the normalization between our two countries."[102]

A few weeks later, in February 1978, Jimmy Carter turned to an old friend and political supporter, Coca-Cola CEO J. Paul Austin, to conduct a bit of private diplomacy. Austin had been angling since the mid-1970s to get Coke back into Cuba, where it had had a lucrative $27.5 million business before Fidel Castro nationalized it in 1961. In 1976, when Cuban diplomats in Mexico and Colombia hinted to Coke representatives that the Cubans would be interested in Coke's return to Cuba, Austin sent attorney Joseph Califano to seek Kissinger's approval for a trip to Havana. "We'd be violently against it," Kissinger replied, still fuming over Cuba's intervention in Angola. "I don't want him to go. It will give all the wrong signals."[103]

Austin's trip to Havana had to wait until his friend Jimmy Carter became president and lifted the travel ban. He finally went in June 1977 and met with Fidel Castro to discuss the possibility of opening a Coca-Cola bottling plant in Cuba.[104] On his return, he spent half an hour in the Oval Office briefing the president on his conversations. Austin "was favorably impressed with Castro's attitude toward me and eventual lifting of the trade embargo and normalizing relationships with Cuba," Carter recorded in his diary.[105] Cuba was not the only country to which Austin traveled as an informal diplomat for Carter. In early 1977, he held wide-ranging talks with Egyptian president Anwar Sadat and reported back to the White House.[106]

In February 1978, with the State Department and NSC battling over how to respond to the escalating crisis in Ethiopia, Carter called on Austin for a confidential mission. The president asked him to carry a personal letter to Castro and engage him in discussions about reviving the dimming prospects for normalization. "As you know," Carter wrote to Castro, "I have hoped it would be possible for you and me to move towards full normalization of relations, and I would like to see progress made in removing the obstacles that impede forward movement."[107]

"I asked Paul to go down as my emissary," Carter told the authors. "I felt that this would be a good way for me to have a direct assessment of what Castro's commitment was." With Cuban troops and Soviet advisors pouring into Ethiopia, Carter thought that Castro was caught between his desire to improve relations with Washington and the demands of his Soviet patrons to support them in the Horn of Africa. "I wanted to let Castro decide once and for all: do you want to normalize relations with the United States or not? And that was the basic message that I wanted to send through a non-governmental emissary."[108]

Unfortunately, Austin's failing health compromised his mission. Unbeknownst to Carter, he had begun to show the early symptoms of Alzheimer's disease. To the Cubans, he proposed a wild scheme in which Castro would travel to Washington for a summit with Carter and then spend Christmas with the Carters at their home in Plains, Georgia. The Cubans seemed to sense there was something amiss. After a brief meeting with Fidel, Austin was sent back to Washington carrying a warm but noncommittal reply. When Carter and Brzezinski met with Austin in the Oval Office to hear his trip report, they were aghast at what Carter characterized as his "incoherence."[109]

"We just didn't know what the guy was talking about," Brzezinski recalled. "What we asked him to do became something much more. It was a good lesson not to rely on non-professionally trained people to conduct private negotiations because there was a real disconnect between what the guy was sent to talk about and what he came back with."[110] Yet despite Austin's unauthorized summit proposal, the president would send him back to Cuba in September 1980 to open a dialogue on the Mariel crisis, paving the way for a settlement.

The Peripatetic Banker

Meanwhile, the Cubans were cultivating their own back channel. In August 1977, they singled out a prominent Cuban American, Bernardo Benes, to serve as a secret emissary, not only for dialogue with the U.S. government but also to build a bridge to the Cuban American community. Benes was vacationing with his family in Panama when, during breakfast at the Hilton Hotel, a waiter approached him with an urgent phone call from a friend who told him, "There are some Cubans here who want to see you. Can you have lunch with us today?"[111]

Over lunch and far into the evening, Benes met with José Luis Padrón, a former colonel in Cuba's special forces, and his deputy, Antonio "Tony" de la Guardia. Their lengthy conversation covered Benes's opinions about the Cuban revolution, Miami politics, and U.S. policy. Castro's men, it seemed, were sizing him up. "The Cuban officials," Benes recalled, "thought I would be a good contact to carry to the United States administration the reconciliation offers they wanted to show."[112]

"He had influence and connections in the administration," recalled Cuban diplomat Ramón Sánchez-Parodi when asked why Cuba selected Benes, "and he had been important in the election."[113]

As an interlocutor with Washington and the Miami community, Benes seemed a perfect pick. He originally supported the revolution and even briefly worked in the Treasury Ministry in 1959 until Castro expropriated his father's factory. In November 1960, with only $215 dollars hidden in his sport coat, Benes left Cuba for Miami. There, he became a leading entrepreneur, rising to become vice chairman of the board of Continental National Bank of Miami and establishing himself as a high-profile member of Miami's civic society. At the time the Cubans picked him as a secret intermediary, Benes was what journalist Mirta Ojito described as "a walking billboard for the success of the Cuban exile community."[114]

In the mid-1960s, Benes helped finance violent exile operations against Castro, but by 1975 he had become disillusioned with the prospects for rolling back the revolution by force. He began concentrating on family reunification and the plight of political prisoners. When Carter ran for president on a human rights platform, Benes used his position as chairman of Florida's Hispanic Committee to organize financial and political support.

The first thing that Benes did after returning from Panama was to call veteran CIA case officer Lawrence Sternfeld. It took the agency less than eight hours to identify the Cubans Benes had met as Castro's personal representatives—used for his most important political missions. Sternfeld described Padrón as "Fidel's proxy around the world." When Benes asked for instructions on how to proceed, Sternfeld told him to "keep the contact. You have the green light for further meetings."[115]

José Luis Padrón served in Cuba's intelligence service in the Ministry of the Interior. More importantly, he had been a friend of Fidel Castro for years and had his trust. When Castro decided to send Cuban troops to Angola in 1975, Padrón was deputy commander of the first special forces units deployed and his distinguished service raised his status further. Padrón became involved in the U.S.-Cuban dialogue almost by accident. He was in Panama working with the government of Omar Torrijos (with which Cuba had friendly relations) when he found out that Benes was visiting. For several months, the Cuban government had been putting out feelers to moderate Cuban Americans, hoping to open a dialogue with the exile community. Padrón cabled Havana for instructions on whether to approach Benes. "The response was, 'Yes,'" Padrón recalled, "and that's how the dialogue started." Castro assigned Padrón to represent him in the talks with Benes and subsequently with the United States, but the *Comandante* was never far from the scene. "My work was under the explicit orders of Fidel," Padrón told the authors. "Fidel wanted to keep tight control over this." After every meeting, Padrón prepared detailed reports for Castro.[116]

The Cubans gave Benes the code name "Benito," and the Cuban consulate in Kingston, Jamaica, became his designated point of contact. Throughout the fall of 1977, he traveled to Jamaica to confer with Padrón and de la Guardia. Other meetings took place in Panama, Mexico, and New York. After every meeting, Benes reported to an Hispanic FBI official known to him as

"Mr. Taco."[117] To have a second person to back him up in this extraordinary operation, Benes enlisted a Cuban American friend and business partner, the chairman of the board of Continental National Bank of Miami, Charles (Carlos) Dascal.

On February 12, 1978, Benes and Dascal flew to Jamaica where Padrón and de la Guardia were waiting for them. Two days later, they flew to Cuba, where a caravan of Mercedes whisked them to the Palace of the Revolution for a private meeting with Fidel Castro. Their meeting represented Castro's most serious effort to engage with an emerging moderate sector of the exile community. Castro had developed a more nuanced view of Miami, once seen as simply a hotbed of *gusanos* (worms), the epithet Castro had used to characterize the exiles since the earliest years of the revolution. The vise grip on power held by the hard-liners in the exile community might be loosened if enlightened civic leaders like Benes emerged with evidence of Havana's interest in a rapprochement. At the very least, Carter would find stronger allies and weaker opponents in his effort to change the hostile framework of U.S. policy. For Benes, the meeting with Castro represented the chance to undertake what he called a "'Mission Impossible' of reality"—a humanitarian effort to liberate thousands of political prisoners from Cuba's jails, facilitate travel to and from the island, and reunify Cuban families separated by exile.[118]

After joking that he had come to collect the $1 million that Cuba owed him and his family for expropriating their textile factory, Benes accompanied Castro to his private office. From ten o'clock that night until five in the morning, they discussed virtually every issue of concern to the exile community and to the U.S. government. On political prisoners, Castro was ready to deal. He expressed "his sympathy" on this issue, Benes remembered.[119] On family reunification, Castro took the position that unrestricted travel would necessitate lifting the U.S. embargo. He seemed very committed, however, to making substantive gestures and concessions to restart the normalization process. He acknowledged that normal relations would "imply compromises" on Cuba's latitude to act freely around the world, and that he was ready to consider those compromises. He was even willing to discuss Cuban policy in Africa. If the embargo were lifted, he said, Cuba would immediately welcome renewed trade and investment. To advance the goal of better relations, Castro stressed to Benes, his government wanted to keep "an extra-official communication channel" open with the U.S. government.

Fidel gave Benes his blessing to be that "extra-official" channel. This initial seven-hour meeting was the first of fifteen lengthy conversations Benes would hold with Castro over the next year, conversations in which Benes

Cuban American banker Bernardo Benes (center) meeting with Fidel Castro in 1978 to discuss the release of Cuban political prisoners. At the right is Orlando Padrón, a member of the Committee of 75 organized by Benes. As a result of Benes's efforts, more than three thousand prisoners were released and allowed to emigrate with their families to the United States. (Miami News)

more than held his own. "Benes is the only person where Fidel can't get a word in," said one of Castro's aides.[120] Benes's secret dialogue would eventually produce the release of more than three thousand political prisoners—the most significant gesture Castro had made toward the Cuban American community and the U.S. government since the release of the Bay of Pigs prisoners in 1962.

More immediately, Benes's meeting with Castro opened the door for a direct dialogue between U.S. and Cuban officials, though getting the process started proved to be difficult. On March 9, Benes and Dascal traveled to Washington to brief Brzezinski on their conversation with Castro. The meeting did not go very well. "I just wasn't convinced that he was reliable," Brzezinski told the authors.[121] Brzezinski directed the CIA chief of station in Mexico to discourage Benes from "using the Agency to circumvent official Government to Government channels."[122] Benes, however, was not easily discouraged.

Nor were the Cubans. Five weeks after Benes first spoke with Castro in Havana, Padrón asked Benes to meet him in Mexico City. During twenty hours of talks between March 20 and 22, they discussed concretely what Fidel was willing to negotiate with the United States. Padrón gave Benes a message from Castro to Brzezinski, more detailed than the initial offer to start a dialogue. Padrón dictated a series of talking points: Castro had changed his position "180 degrees" regarding relations with the Miami community and Washington. He was "very interested in establishing communication channels to exchange ideas and opinions." He was prepared to release hundreds of political prisoners and grant permission for exile travel to visit relatives on the island. Cuba wanted "mutual cooperation" with Washington on fighting terrorism. Cuba would provide some compensation for expropriated properties. Castro considered Jimmy Carter a person of "high religious and moral principles" and wanted a face-to-face meeting with him before his term in office ended.[123]

Benes traveled to Washington to personally deliver Padrón's message. On March 27, Benes provided Brzezinski with a memorandum he himself had written, entitled "Message from President of Cuba Fidel Castro, to President Carter and/or Dr. Z.B.," summarizing the positions Padrón had voiced in Mexico. Benes's memorandum also noted that the Cubans were prepared to hold secret talks in New York City, Mexico City, Panama City, or Kingston, Jamaica. It contained the surprising offer to arrange "a direct phone communication of F. Castro with President Carter or Dr. Z.B." In a personal comment, Benes called Castro's initiative "the most positive thing coming out of Cuba in [the] last 20 years. . . . The opportunity to solve the Cuban problem is *now*."[124] By the end of the meeting, however, Benes was convinced that Brzezinski had little interest in a quick resolution to the Cuban problem. He did not appear to appreciate this opportunity to advance the cause of human rights in Cuba and change U.S.-Cuban relations. As Benes later wrote in an unpublished memoir, "I realized those documents were going to die in a drawer."[125]

Despite Brzezinski's skepticism, Benes was wrong. Brzezinski forwarded the documents to his deputy, David Aaron, asking for recommendations for follow-up. But his real concern, according to a TOP SECRET cover memo he dictated, was to get Benes "out of this, because he seems to me to be a self-starter, and I do not know what he is saying to the Cubans. . . . We certainly did not commission him to say anything." Brzezinski instructed Aaron: "Have someone, preferably someone like Bob Gates [career CIA officer Robert M. Gates, then serving on the NSC staff] phone Benes and simply tell him that we thank him for the information and that the matter will be taken on from here by us."[126] Thus began a series of secret bilateral meetings between U.S. and Cuban officials that stretched out for almost a year.

La Côte Basque

Following up on Benes's message, the NSC staff arranged for David Aaron and Robert Gates to meet secretly with Padrón on April 14 in New York. The FBI outfitted Gates with a wire to record the meeting, taping the recorder to his back and running microphones over both shoulders. "He was not exactly one of those operational guys at CIA," Aaron recalled with some amusement. "It was quite an experience for him."[127] Wired for sound, Gates rendezvoused with Aaron and Padrón at La Côte Basque, across from the stately St. Regis Hotel. Famous for its haute cuisine and celebrity clientele, the restaurant provided the setting for patron Truman Capote's infamous 1975 tale of high-society gossip, "La Côte Basque." It was, by Aaron's reckoning, one of the "toniest" French restaurants in New York. With its classical decor and floor-to-ceiling murals of the Basque countryside, La Côte was an incongruous venue for a clandestine meeting between senior U.S. officials and a top Cuban intelligence officer—cloak and dagger amidst Manhattan's ladies-who-lunch.

Both sides approached the meeting warily, not sure what to expect. "I don't think he had much of an idea who I was, nor did I of him," Aaron said of Padrón. "He was quite tense at the beginning. I think, being a security guy, he probably noticed a couple of guys having lunch around us who didn't look like they could afford to be there. I think he suspected he was surrounded by FBI, which he was." Aaron and Gates were on guard, too. "We weren't too sure what they had in mind," Aaron recalled. "We didn't know whether it was a provocation. Was it entrapment? We didn't know what the hell it was." To break the ice, they began by talking about baseball. Padrón, as it happened, was an avid New York Yankees fan. Eventually, Aaron steered the conversation to the issue at hand, and Padrón got to the point. The Cubans wanted to know whether there was some way to resuscitate the normalization process. To facilitate that, Cuba was prepared to release a large number of political prisoners.[128]

Following his talking points, Aaron responded that he had not come to undertake negotiations on specific issues but rather to explore "the larger framework which is necessary for any improvement in relations." Cuban military intervention in Africa was "the principal obstacle to an improvement." Washington did not object to Cuba sending civilian advisors abroad, "but we cannot accept Cuban combat forces operating at will in Africa or elsewhere." Further Cuban military intervention in southern Africa would not be tolerated and would have "the most serious adverse consequences for direct U.S.-Cuban relations," Aaron warned.[129] Aaron asked Padrón three questions: "What was the prospect of their troops leaving Ethiopia and Angola; In this connection, what did the Cubans have in mind in asking about assurances regarding Ethiopian and Angolan territorial integrity; What assurance could we have that the Cubans would not intervene militarily in Namibia and Rhodesia?"[130] Continuation of a dialogue would depend on a demonstrable Cuban response to U.S. concerns, Aaron concluded.

It was a succinct statement of Brzezinski's position: no normalization unless the Cubans made concessions in Africa. Padrón did not appear taken aback by Aaron's hard line. He stuck to Cuba's position with equal tenacity: although Cuba wanted better relations with Washington, its involvement in Africa was not open to negotiation. After three hours of sparring, the lunch came to an inconclusive end. The spy-diplomats adjourned, leaving La Côte Basque to its society matrons. "The initiative had been worthwhile," Gates concluded, "but had failed utterly." Further meetings would be pointless, he thought, and he recommended against them.[131]

Padrón did not think the meeting had gone very well either. When there was no follow-up from Washington, the Cubans turned to Benes to try another tack. Benes and Dascal returned to Washington on May 17 to brief Congressman Dante Fascell (D-Fla.) on the Cuban initiative and the unresponsiveness of the NSC. Fascell, whose Florida district included a growing Cuban American constituency, immediately called Secretary Vance and urged him to meet with Benes.[132] "I better see this guy," Vance remarked to his special assistant, Peter Tarnoff, when he got off the phone. Vance met with Benes and Dascal at five in the afternoon that same day and assigned Tarnoff to follow up on the Cuban initiative.

"I had no experience in Latin America," Tarnoff recalled. "I was there simply as Vance's guy." Vance and Tarnoff both thought it was "interesting and exciting that Cuba would take the initiative to have a dialogue over a small part of the relationship," Tarnoff said, referring to the proposed prisoner release. "If this was real, it sounded worth pursuing."[133] He did not know it at the time, but he was about to become one of the most important secret liaisons between the U.S. and Cuban governments, a role he would play through two Democratic administrations.

The State Department's Channel

While Vance wanted to pursue the opening to Cuba, Brzezinski did not. "The NSC was quite reluctant to have this dialogue go forward because of everything else that was going on in the world," Tarnoff recalled. Finally, Vance and Brzezinski agreed on a two-track approach, which the president approved. The NSC would keep open its channel to discuss broad political issues with the Cubans, and the State Department would open a separate channel to explore Cuba's offer to release political prisoners and to discuss the operational details of admitting them to the United States.[134]

Vance sent his under secretary for political affairs and diplomatic troubleshooter David Newsom to New York to meet with Padrón on June 15, at the St. Regis Hotel. Newsom, a career diplomat, had a reputation as thoughtful, polite, and skilled at finding workable solutions to complex problems. "He has a way of squaring circles that others don't," said a colleague.[135] Although Newsom was supposed to focus narrowly on the prisoners issue, he was well prepared to talk with the Cubans about Africa. He had been assistant secretary of state for African affairs from 1969 to 1974 and had been working for Vance on diplomatic solutions for two volatile southern African issues—Namibian independence and majority rule in Zimbabwe (Rhodesia).

José Luis Padrón came accompanied by Tony de la Guardia, whom Fidel had designated as his liaison with the Cuban American community.[136] "Benes and Dascal have been very constructive in making us aware of the importance of finding a constructive solution to the prisoners problem," Padrón began. He wanted to let Washington know that his government had already begun releasing political prisoners and would allow them to leave along with their families if Washington would take them. "The decision has been made," he explained. "There is nothing to negotiate. . . . We are asking for nothing in return." Nevertheless, Cuba hoped Washington would agree to receive the ex-prisoners. "We look at this as something that can improve the climate between the U.S. Cuban community and Cuba. . . . I also look at it as a gesture consistent with President Carter's projected policy [on human rights]." Without making a firm commitment, Newsom suggested that Washington would be willing to facilitate an orderly exodus. He promised a more definitive answer at their next meeting.

Padrón then turned to Africa, responding to the questions that Aaron had posed two months earlier at La Côte Basque. "We . . . do not want any supranational war in Africa," Padrón said. "We think that a constructive and satisfactory solution can be found for both sides. . . . We are prepared to work toward peace anywhere where we can play an active and effective role." However, the atmosphere toward Cuba fostered by a "big public campaign," like the one blaming Cuba for the Shaba II crisis, "is not the kind of climate that can promote satisfactory solutions."

Newsom countered that Washington perceived Cuba's military role in Africa as "making an African solution more difficult and as supporting an outside influence unfriendly to the United States." The United States wanted good relations with Africa governments of all ideological hues, Newsom explained. But, he continued, referring to Cuban support for pro-Soviet regimes, "It is not in our interest to see an Eastern European colonialism [in Africa]." Sensing the sharp disjuncture between their two positions, Newsom added, "I assume you wanted me to deal frankly and honestly with the problem."

Padrón did not shrink from the debate. The Cubans were in Angola because their ally was under external attack. And according to press reports, Padrón pointed out, some Carter officials were proposing covert assistance to UNITA to aggravate Angola's insecurity. "Now if these problems were merely internal, if there was no real possibility of an invasion from outside, then neither Neto nor Cuba would be interested in maintaining Cuban troops there." But if Washington thought it could pressure Cuba into withdrawal by escalating the fighting, Padrón noted, "This would be a grave error."

Padrón then opened a door that had not been opened before. "If Carter's intentions are to bring a peaceful solution to southern Africa, we should sit down in all frankness and define concrete steps to be taken," Padrón proposed. "There is no miracle solution," he acknowledged. "The most important thing is to initiate the dialogue." Cuba, he reiterated, was not interested in a wider war in Africa. "We are prepared to contribute to a solution satisfactory to the interests of both sides." For months, Castro had been insisting that Cuba's Africa policy was not subject to negotiation with the United States. Now Padrón was saying that Havana would be willing, confidentially, to talk with Washington about ways to deescalate African tensions. Havana's allies would have to be involved in any final solution, of course—Cuba could not make decisions without consulting them. But if they were given adequate guarantees against external threats to their security, "the necessary basis will immediately be established for the final return of all Cuban troops to Cuba. I think anything is possible—it just depends on our deciding to do it." Unbeknownst to the United States, Cuba was actually eager to resume withdrawing its forces from Angola, but the Angolan government, unable to defend itself against South Africa, would not agree.[137]

The atmosphere at this meeting was more relaxed than it had been at La Côte Basque. "What struck me . . . was the closeness of the ties," Newsom recalled. "One of them had a grandmother living in Brooklyn. Padrón wanted to get all the baseball scores. They were very much into the American scene both by family and by interest." During a coffee break, the two sides talked baseball, and Padrón discovered in Newsom a fellow New York Yankees fan. "If the Yankees ever play in Havana," Padrón joked, "then we *will* have a problem of internal order."[138]

When they broke for lunch, Newsom thought it best that they have food brought in. "I was told by the department that I could cover the cost of coffee and sandwiches. I made a fatal error and asked for room service," he recalled ruefully. "Room service comes in with the St. Regis menu. The Cubans eyes lit up. They ordered a five course meal with steak and everything else, and I had to explain it to the State Department accountant."[139]

At the close of their meeting, Padrón and Newsom agreed to establish a secure phone link to coordinate future meetings and allow quick, high-level communications between the two governments. Peter Tarnoff, Vance's special assistant, took responsibility for managing the link and became a participant in the dialogue.[140]

Reporting to President Carter on the meeting, Vance recommended that the released Cuban prisoners be paroled into the United States, and that the dialogue be kept going. "If Padrón can be taken at face value, it would seem worthwhile to continue to explore with him Cuban policies. . . . With your permission, I will be talking to Zbig on how we conduct future conversations with the Cubans on political issues and in particular how we respond to the latest conversation with Padrón."[141]

Padrón's offer to begin bilateral discussions on Africa was a potentially important opening in the Cuban position, but Brzezinski was not eager to follow up. "I am still not clear from Padrón's conversation with Newsom whether the Cubans are prepared to talk seriously about these issues, though they apparently wish to continue to talk," Brzezinski wrote in his report to the president. "I am concerned that talk for its own sake will be misinterpreted or possibly exploited by the Cubans."[142] Despite Brzezinski's skepticism, the president decided to keep the dialogue going.

For the third meeting, on July 5, Padrón and de la Guardia came to Washington, D.C. Tarnoff picked them up at the Madison Hotel downtown and drove them to Newsom's home, a stately French chateau–style house on a tree-lined street in northwest Washington's Woodley Park neighborhood, just behind the National Cathedral. The quiet residential setting created a relaxed atmosphere.[143] "We had the group for lunch, and my wife, my daughter and her boyfriend from Stanford served the meal," Newsom recalled. After the dishes were cleared, the diplomats stayed around the dining room table to conduct business. Newsom began by informing the Cubans that the United States would agree to accept the political prisoners Castro planned to release, albeit after a case-by-case review by the Justice Department.[144]

Padrón reported that Cuba had decided to also allow the exit of all the dual nationals and their families on the most recent list provided by the State Department, and that travel restrictions on Cuban Americans would soon be relaxed, allowing them to visit the island. With these decisions, Cuba had delivered on most of the issues on the "step by step" agenda the Carter administration had outlined back in August. Only the CIA prisoners remained. From there, the conversation turned to broader issues. Padrón raised the embargo, noting that Cuba accepted the principle that compensation was due to U.S. citizens whose property was expropriated and "was willing to discuss the modalities of such compensation."

Did Cuba expect reciprocal compensation for the costs of the embargo and acts of sabotage carried out in the 1960s? Newsom asked.

Yes, Padrón acknowledged, that was part of the equation.

Newsom and Tarnoff made clear that they had no instructions to discuss the embargo, but Padrón pressed on. He emphasized that lifting the embargo was not a precondition to reaching agreements on other issues. He suggested that future talks take up the question of Cuba's stance on Puerto Rican independence at the United Nations (which continued to vex Washington), and that they return to the issues of Cuban policy in Africa and compensation for nationalized property. He invited them to Cuba for the next round of talks so President Castro could join in.[145]

"Padrón stated clearly that Castro is interested in pursuing with us a discussion of broader political subjects," Vance reported to Carter. "Padrón maintained that Castro wants to learn in detail our concerns about Cuban policy in Africa, and he volunteered Castro's willingness to discuss ways to find peaceful and negotiated solutions to the problem areas in Africa on a country-by-country basis."[146]

Whose Channel Is It?

The Cubans' proposal to broaden the agenda of the secret talks touched off a battle within the Carter administration over who should conduct the dialogue. Immediately after the meeting at Newsom's house, Secretary Vance proposed that the NSC channel be closed and that future contacts with the Cubans be handled through the State Department. "I believe that we should accept the Cuban offer to discuss our concerns about Cuban policies in specific areas," Vance wrote to the president, recommending that "you authorize us to inform the Cuban government that Newsom and Tarnoff would meet further with Padrón to discuss some broader political issues."[147]

Not surprisingly, Brzezinski objected. He reminded Carter that he had already decided to keep two channels open—the State channel to negotiate the specifics of the prisoner release and the NSC channel to discuss broader political issues. To turn the whole discussion over to State was "clearly not a good idea," Brzezinski insisted.[148] As the debate heated up, each side began to denigrate the negotiating skills of the other. Vance castigated Aaron over how he handled his meeting at La Côte Basque, and Aaron in turn accused Newsom of deviating from policy in his conversations with Padrón.[149] By talking with the Cubans about Africa rather than sticking to prisoners, "Newsom exceeded his mandate," Aaron charged (although it was Padrón who raised Africa in order to answer questions that Aaron himself had posed at the first meeting). In short, Aaron concluded, "We . . . had a much more satisfactory discussion than Newsom did. . . . I don't think we should be penalized for doing a good job."[150]

The real issue, of course, was not the relative diplomatic skill of Aaron and Newsom, both of whom were experienced negotiators. The real issue was the festering division between Vance and Brzezinski over whether there was anything to be gained by talking to the Cubans at all. Vance continued to believe that improved relations could pay dividends in Africa and elsewhere.[151] Brzezinski thought the Cubans were so wedded to the Soviets that any improvement of relations would appear to reward bad behavior, making it harder to restrain Soviet actions elsewhere. The solution Carter settled on was to combine the NSC and State Department channels, so that from mid-1978 until the fall of 1980, the U.S. delegation always included representatives from both agencies.[152] "We thought they were playing good cop, bad cop," Padrón recalled, "but bit by bit we understood that we were in fact seeing two positions that were to some extent in conflict with one another."

Meeting with East German leader Eric Honecker in 1980, Castro described how the Americans distrusted one another. "Every time they sent a contact group to us . . . this group consisted of two men. The first belonged to the State Department, the other to the National Security Council."[153]

"How right he was," Newsom reflected.[154]

Soon after the meeting at the St. Regis, Newsom and Tarnoff briefed Coordinator for Cuba Affairs Wayne Smith on the secret dialogue and enlisted him to prepare background materials for the fourth round, scheduled for August in Atlanta, Georgia. Smith suggested that Washington could improve the atmosphere by making a small gesture in advance of the Atlanta meeting—allowing the Cubans to buy medicine in the United States. The NSC refused to agree, on the grounds that Washington had already offered a one-time sale in February, which the Cubans had rejected. "There were to be *no* steps on our side," Smith recalled.[155]

In advance of the Atlanta meeting, Padrón met again with Benes and Dascal to register Cuba's concerns that the talks with Washington were not making much headway. The processing of released political prisoners into the United States was too slow, the administration was lobbying nonaligned countries to move the 1979 Nonaligned Movement summit away from Havana, and Carter had done nothing positive in response to Cuban overtures. Padrón told Benes and Dascal that the upcoming meeting in Atlanta was "very important" as an indicator of U.S. seriousness. Summarizing the report of the meeting that Benes and Dascal gave him, Tarnoff wrote, "In speculating about the alleged 'U.S. slowness' in responding to Cuban overtures on political and prisoner release subjects, Padrón wondered whether the USG [U.S. Government] was buying time or was not interested in real progress or saw no hope of reaching a significant understanding with the Cuban Government. He further speculated that the American reluctance to move ahead rapidly might be caused by the November elections in the U.S. If this was a real consideration, he asked that the U.S. representatives tell him openly that such was the case."[156] Brzezinski's skepticism was coming to be matched by Padrón's.

The meeting in Atlanta on August 8 was the first in which the United States sent a joint delegation, with Newsom representing the State Department and Aaron representing the NSC. Havana sent Padrón and de la Guardia, along with a new player, José Antonio Arbesú, an expert on the United States from the Communist Party Central Committee staff. Arbesú was a smart, ideologically committed, and tough-minded negotiator. "He's a guy who can discuss 1937 musicals and talk about Senate votes, not only how the vote went but why various senators voted the way they did," Wayne Smith observed.[157]

Originally, the two delegations intended to take in an Atlanta Braves baseball game after their daylong negotiation, but the FBI committed an error in making the arrangements—the Braves were playing on the road in Cincinnati. The agenda for the Atlanta meeting was to finalize arrangements for the United States to accept released Cuban political prisoners and to again broach the politically sensitive issues of Cuban policy toward Africa and Puerto Rico.[158] Aaron began by openly questioning the utility of continuing the talks. President Carter wanted to know if the Cubans were "serious," Aaron told Padrón. The Cubans took offense at what they regarded as Washington's arrogance. "Of course we are serious," Padrón replied. He was "a bit surprised that the president should question or doubt [our] real intentions."

But from the outset, the talks appeared to be at an impasse. The U.S. side urged the Cubans to refrain from stoking anti-American sentiment at the United Nations over Puerto Rico, and the Cubans explained once again that their historic ties to their sister island required them to defend the principle of Puerto Rican independence. When Newsom asked about releasing the CIA prisoners, Padrón repeated the offer to trade them for the imprisoned Puerto Rican nationalists, promising to keep any agreement on an exchange absolutely confidential. "There will never be a leak from our side," Arbesú interjected. But Washington still would not make a deal.

The U.S. side repeated its objections to Cuba's Africa policy, and the Cubans repeated their defense of it, while insisting that it should have no bearing on bilateral relations. "Where do we go from here?" Aaron asked. "What can we expect in terms of Cuba's military presence in Africa?" The United States worried that Cuban troops might intervene in Namibia or Rhodesia, and he accused Cuba of keeping troops in Angola and Ethiopia for "internal security" rather than to defend them against external aggression, despite Padrón's repeated declarations to the contrary.

Padrón countered by reminding the U.S. diplomats that Cuba was in Africa "on the decision and invitation of legally constituted governments . . . in response to external aggression," which the United States had helped instigate. "We desire a peaceful solution to all the conflicts in southern Africa," Padrón declared, "But it does not all depend on us."

When Padrón tried to get the U.S. delegation to discuss the embargo and Guantánamo, he got nowhere, and his frustration began to show. "We have not dealt with the blockade, and it is our impression that you are avoiding the issue. . . . For us it is totally unacceptable for the United States to ask for a constructive and positive position from us on problems vital to its interests, and for it to not respond at all with any constructive gesture on the points Cuba considers vital." The two sides, he warned, were headed for a "vicious circle," with each demanding actions the other deemed unacceptable.

As the talks wound down, both sides noted that their positions were not moving any closer. "Both of us have been very frank," Aaron observed, "but I have the impression that solutions are a long way down the road." Padrón agreed.

While the conflict between the State Department and the NSC over who should talk to the Cubans had been settled by merging the two channels, the policy differences between the two agencies had been papered over rather than resolved, and it was visible in the different tone that Aaron and Newsom took during the dialogue—Aaron, brusque and aggressive; Newsom diplomatic and reassuring. "Brzezinski regarded Cuba as one of the erogenous zones of American foreign policy—that was the phrase he liked to use, meaning that it caused a lot of excitement but it didn't really matter very much," Aaron recalled. "He was skeptical and doubtful about the dialogue. He gave me very tough instructions. . . . We made pretty substantial demands."[159]

"If there was one constant theme," Newsom said, "it was the Cuban desire to talk about the embargo and the strict instructions that we were under to discuss no bilateral relations issues unless we got a commitment from the Cubans to withdraw their troops from Angola." That was the condition Brzezinski imposed for continuing with the dialogue. "The Cubans always replied that was none of our business," Newsom added. "My personal feeling was that there might have been a chance to make some progress on other issues if we had been permitted to take a somewhat different tack. . . . But our hands were pretty well tied."[160]

For the fifth meeting, everyone traveled to Cuernavaca, Mexico, for the weekend of October 28–29. "The Cubans insistently wanted us to come to Havana, and Cuernavaca was a final compromise, getting out of the United States but not going to Havana," Newsom recalled.[161] The two teams set up at the Hotel Villa del Conquistador. With lush, spacious grounds and small cabins behind the main hotel, the venue was well suited for informal conversation outside the formal negotiating sessions. The U.S. delegation had cabins on one side of the grounds, the Cubans had cabins across the way.

The U.S. delegation reiterated the same basic positions it had laid out in Atlanta. "My instructions were to say, 'Well, we're happy to consider normalizing relations, but you have to do two or three things,'" Aaron related. "'One of them is to get out of [Ethiopia], the other is to get out of Angola.'" Washington would have lifted the embargo on sales of medicine and nickel smelting technology after the Atlanta meeting, the Cubans were told, if Havana had responded to U.S. concerns on Africa or Puerto Rico. The Cubans found this tactic of dangling benefits just out of reach offensive. They reiterated that Cuba's policy in Africa was not negotiable.[162]

The U.S. side again raised the issue of the CIA prisoners in Cuba, urging their release as a humanitarian gesture that would improve the political atmosphere for dialogue. Padrón responded that the release of the U.S. prisoners was a sensitive political issue in Cuba. Only Fidel could change that policy, just as only Fidel could speak authoritatively about Cuban policy in Africa. They should hold the next meeting in Cuba, so that the U.S. team could meet with Fidel himself. "There is no substitute for direct contact with our leaders," Padrón argued. "It would be very constructive and positive for some if not all of you to go to Havana."[163]

There would need to be "more progress" on the Cuban role in Africa before a meeting in Havana would be possible, Newsom replied. Padrón found it unreasonable that they could meet in the United States and in Mexico without preconditions but that Cuba would have to make concessions before they could meet in Havana.

Cuba had already made important concessions, Padrón noted, releasing dual nationals and some three thousand political prisoners, and Washington had made no reciprocal gesture. The embargo was "the main obstacle" to better relations. Newsom responded that the issue of the embargo could be taken up only if Cuba demonstrated "some movement . . . relating to Cuba's policy and presence in Africa."

That, said Padrón, was not a constructive approach. "The blockade is still a political weapon that the United States . . . is using to try to force decisions which fall within the purview of Cuban sovereignty," he charged. The U.S. position was "unacceptable" and "almost amounts to political blackmail." In light of that, "I do not see the possibility of much progress towards substantive agreements with the United States," he concluded. The meeting ended with little accomplished and no follow-up meeting scheduled.

Aaron had the impression that the Cubans were getting tired of repeating the same arguments at every negotiating session, with no apparent progress, and had decided that the process was reaching a dead end. "Before we even had much of a discussion, it seemed pretty clear that they were sort of backing away from this thing," Aaron recalled. "I went for a long walk with

[Arbesú]. He made some complaint about how we had asked for an awful lot, and I said, 'Yeah, but I get the sense that you're not interested in doing anything.'

"And he said, 'No, I think that time has passed; we're probably moving in another direction.'

"We had tough demands," Aaron reflected, "and they had come to the conclusion that this wasn't going to work out."[164]

Despite the stalemate, the negotiators had met together so often they had developed a certain rapport. One evening, as the two delegations sat down to dinner at separate tables, the Cubans saw the Americans singing Happy Birthday to translator Stephanie van Reigersberg. After the meal, Padrón and de la Guardia scoured the town looking for a florist so they could buy Stephanie flowers. Finding none open, they settled on a wreath from a funeral parlor. The Cubans apologized for the origin of the blossoms and insisted that they did not mean to leave a macabre impression. Van Reigersberg thought the gesture was sweet. "I said, 'This has got to be the most wonderful birthday present that I have ever gotten,'" she recalled. "And they said, well, they had to do something to remember my birthday."[165]

Although the Cubans took away no concessions from the U.S. side, they took away something else. No sooner had the Cuban delegation departed the hotel than the U.S. team was visited by the hotel management. "The chief housekeeper came to me and said, 'Who's going to pay for the towels and linen? Your friends on the other side have just left and they've taken all the towels and linens with them,'" Newsom remembered.

"See," David Aaron quipped, "the embargo is working!"[166]

Back in Washington, Aaron was convinced that there was nothing to be gained from continuing the dialogue. "The private meeting with the Cubans resulted in a complete impasse," he reported to the president. "The Cubans were on a very tight leash and spoke largely for the record. . . . Our assessment is that the Cubans are preparing to increase their presence in Southern Africa and that they have, therefore, decided that this channel should go dormant until the issue of Africa is no longer an obstacle to normalization."

In the margin of Aaron's memo, next to the sentence reporting that no new meeting had been scheduled, Carter wrote, "Do not plan another."[167]

Benes's Encore

While the secret dialogue between Havana and Washington sputtered, Castro's overture to the Cuban American community was proving more successful, thanks to the indefatigable Bernardo Benes. Once Cuban and U.S. officials began talking directly, Benes's services as intermediary were no longer needed, and he was cut out of the government-to-government dialogue. Both governments were wary of Benes's tendency to exaggerate. "Bernardo Benes was a promoter of Bernardo Benes," Newsom ventured. "He had a tendency to portray to the Cubans that greater progress was being made than was in fact the case."[168] When Padrón met Newsom at his home in Washington in July 1978, Newsom warned the Cubans against "excessive optimism" about the prospects for bilateral relations based on Benes's "exuberance and enthusiasm." Padrón understood and said he had "no intention of getting carried away."[169] The Cubans were just as leery of Benes. Padrón later described Benes's approach as a "filosofía boniatillo," meaning he "sweetened everything" in order to move the talks along. Padrón acknowledged that the Cubans "came to realize that Benes wasn't telling it quite like it was."[170]

As Benes's role in the government-to-government dialogue diminished, he turned his attention to bridging the chasm of animosity between Fidel Castro and the exile community. Benes pulled together a group of moderate Cuban Americans, dubbed the Committee of 75, to engage the Cuban government over prisoner releases and the right of exiles to return for visits. The group traveled to Havana for its first session with Castro on November 20–22, 1978. At the conclusion, Castro announced formally that he would free all remaining political prisoners except those who had engaged in terrorist violence. He also agreed to allow Cubans abroad who had left after January 1959 to return for visits beginning in January 1979.[171] At a second meeting with an expanded group of 150 exiles on December 8–9, Castro signed an agreement committing his government to the prisoner releases and family visits. The group returned to Miami with 70 prisoners and 107 family members.[172]

Castro thought that his outreach through Benes had forged a channel to maintain the dialogue with the exile community, but that proved overly optimistic. The Committee of 75 was too diverse ideologically to act as a group and dissolved in disagreement almost immediately. Participants also came under intense pressure in Miami, where they were vilified as traitors. Two participants, Carlos Muñiz Varela and Eulalio J. Negrín, were murdered by anti-Castro terrorists. As the leader of the dialogue, Benes was threatened and ostracized by the much of the community. Even some of the prisoners who owed their freedom to Benes denounced him. He was stunned; he had expected to be treated as a hero for securing the release of long-suffering prisoners. Instead, the fact that he negotiated with Fidel Castro was seen as treasonous.[173] Once a philanthropic and business leader in the Cuban

American community, Benes all but abandoned public life. "I became a pariah in Miami," he said looking back. "I have lived a very private, secret life in the last 21 years."[174]

Our Men in Havana

President Carter's decision to break off the secret dialogue sparked renewed debate over Cuba policy. At the State Department, Vance defended the dialogue and the possibility of better relations. Knowing the importance of human rights to Carter, Castro had released thousands of political prisoners in hopes of reviving prospects for normalization. In response, Washington had done nothing.[175] If the administration hoped to win further concessions, the State Department argued, it would need to demonstrate some reciprocity. "We could respond with a similar humanitarian gesture by lifting the U.S. trade embargo on medications or restoring commercial air service or formalizing cultural exchanges," one official suggested. Moreover, State pointed out, although the Cubans refused to make any formal commitments regarding Africa, they had not obstructed Western diplomatic initiatives on Namibia, and they helped the Angolan government disarm the Katangans so there would be no repetition of the Shaba incursion.[176]

Brzezinski remained skeptical. "By then, I must say, I was somewhat ticked off in general about this whole dialogue because it seemed to me it was dragging on and the State Department insisted on pursuing it because it was given a mission," he recalled. "The purpose of diplomacy is not just to conduct diplomacy."[177] On the key strategic issue of concern to Brzezinski—Cuban troops in Africa—Castro still refused to budge.

In a classic bureaucratic compromise, State lost the argument for a U.S. gesture in response to Castro's prisoner release but won the argument for resuming the dialogue. Washington acceded to Padrón's repeated requests to meet in Havana, in the hope that this would lead to the release of the CIA prisoners.[178] Brzezinski opposed sending the delegation to Havana, just as he had opposed sending Todman to finalize the fishing treaty the year before. It was some sort of political trap, he insisted, although how the Cubans could manipulate such a sojourn to their advantage was never clear. Brzezinski failed to understand that meeting in Havana, not just in New York and Washington, was for the Cubans a symbol of their equality—not to mention that it let Fidel Castro get in on the action. In the end, Brzezinski agreed to a compromise to "downgrade the delegation," as Pastor put it, sending him and Tarnoff instead of Aaron and Newsom. "David Aaron's position and mine were too high in diplomatic terms, which would have indicated a level of engagement that the White House didn't want to make," Newsom recalled, "One of the few times that either of our positions was considered too elevated!"[179]

Before Pastor and Tarnoff left for Havana, however, U.S.-Cuban relations took a decided turn for the worse. At the end of October, the press broke the news that the Soviets had sent Cuba about a dozen MiG-23 fighter-bombers to replace its aging MiG-21s. In some configurations, the MiG-23 was capable of carrying nuclear weapons. When news of the delivery became public, conservatives tried to spin it as equivalent to the 1962 missile crisis—despite the fact that there was no evidence the Cuban MiG-23s were nuclear-capable or that there were any nuclear weapons in Cuba.[180] Carter resisted calls to reenact the 1962 confrontation, accepting Soviet assurances that the MiGs were not nuclear-capable. But shortly thereafter, he ordered a resumption of SR-71 overflights of Cuba—flights he had halted in early 1977 as a gesture to improve relations. The overflights were intended to send both Havana and Moscow the message that Washington was not passively accepting their increased military cooperation. Almost simultaneously, the United States and Great Britain launched large-scale naval exercises just off Cuba's coast. "We wanted to show the Russians we could wax them in our own backyard," one official explained.[181] Washington did not follow the normal courtesy of notifying Havana of the exercises in advance.

The confluence of events left the Cubans puzzled. "It was difficult for us to understand why you had responded to a positive overture [releasing political prisoners] with a punitive threat," an aide to Castro told Wayne Smith. "It was as though you wished to punish us for acceding to your wishes. And that you chose to do so just at the moment you were asking us for still another concession, the release of the four Americans, puzzled us further."[182]

In this atmosphere, prospects for the Havana round of talks were not auspicious. Tarnoff and Pastor arrived on December 2, 1978, met at the airport by their Cuban counterparts, Padrón, Arbesú, and de la Guardia. Two new "impeccably polished Mercedes" drove them to their protocol house, a beautiful villa complete with swimming pool. "Where did the revolution go?" Pastor teased the Cubans.

Cuba's revolution was a "revolution without vengeance," de la Guardia replied with good humor, aiming "to preserve what was beautiful before."

Pastor found Havana fascinating. It was "frozen in 1959," he reported to Brzezinski after the trip. "The great majority of the cars on the roads are American—pre-1959. And they're still working. . . . The effect of the embargo is as clear as the Havana skyline." To Pastor, the scarcity of modern conveniences and consumer goods posed an opportunity for the United States. "There is no question in my mind that the Cuban people and economy are open, eager, and vulnerable to U.S. culture and consumer goods," he concluded. "I don't know how Castro thinks he will be able to deal with the inevitable onslaught of Yanqui consumerism. He doesn't have to look much further than Padrón's French ties."[183]

Late that afternoon, Tarnoff and Pastor were driven to the Palace of the Revolution, where they met with Vice President Carlos Rafael Rodríguez. Tarnoff got right to the main reason for their trip—the hope that Cuba would free the four remaining CIA prisoners. President Carter was still not willing to release the Puerto Rican prisoners in exchange, Tarnoff explained, but Washington hoped nevertheless that Cuba might make a unilateral gesture by releasing the Americans.[184]

Rodríguez was not encouraging. "We have not closed the door on the subject," he said, but why should Cuba make such a concession? Gestures such as prisoner releases depended upon the overall state of bilateral relations. Castro had decided to release the Cuban political prisoners because the Carter administration began with a more constructive attitude than any since Kennedy's. Recent events, however, had raised doubts about U.S. intentions. The SR-71 overflights caused "much bitterness" among Cubans. "The plane is not only offensive and illegal, but it also broke many windows and eardrums across Cuba," Rodríguez explained. Finally, Rodríguez could not fathom why Carter was unable to see the parallel between the imprisoned Puerto Rican nationalists and the imprisoned Americans. "I do understand why there should be no exchange, but you could free the Puerto Ricans now and in three months we would free the American citizens. It could be a gentleman's agreement between us."

From there, the conversation turned to Africa. Tarnoff reiterated the negative impact that Cuban military involvement had on bilateral relations. "We understand that you are not disposed to negotiate your Africa policy with the United States," Tarnoff concluded. "But it is no secret that the fact of your Africa policy is very central to the relations between our two countries. This is a political fact in the United States." Then Tarnoff struck out in a direction that differed from Aaron's approach in Cuernavaca, where he had pressed the Cubans to commit themselves to troop withdrawals from Angola and Ethiopia.

"We are not seeking formal negotiations or commitments from you, but what we are seeking are acts in the diplomatic and military field," Tarnoff explained. After Newsom had asked Padrón in New York if Cuba would encourage the Southwest African People's Organization (SWAPO) to cooperate with Western efforts to find a diplomatic path to Namibian independence, Washington noticed a positive change in Cuba's position. "We are not asking you if there was a cause and effect relationship," Tarnoff continued. "It is sufficient that we saw peaceful improvements. Therefore, we are interested in actions, not words and commitments."

This was an important point, Rodríguez noted, because a formal commitment to the United States limiting Cuba's options in Africa was "impossible both in principle and for practical reasons." However, Fidel himself had said publicly that Cuba supported peaceful solutions to the problems of Namibia and Rhodesia. "Without arrogance, I can assure you that we would never decide anything as a function of a precondition imposed by the United States," Rodríguez concluded. "The pride of small countries, which can even push them to make the wrong decision at times, and their feelings of dignity and sensitivity must be borne in mind."

Here, then, was a sliver of common ground. If Cuba did not obstruct diplomatic settlements in Namibia and Rhodesia, its policies would not directly conflict with Washington's unless diplomacy failed and armed conflict ensued. There might even be potential for cooperation in moving diplomatic solutions forward, so long as Washington did not expect Cuba to make any formal commitments limiting its right to support its allies. Combined with Padrón's earlier suggestion that Cuban and U.S. diplomats discuss ways to cooperate in fostering diplomatic solutions in Africa, this indicated more Cuban flexibility on Africa than they had expressed previously.

After some five hours, with a break for dinner, the conversation concluded with the core issue for Cuba—the embargo. Rodríguez repeated Cuba's long-standing position. The "blockade," as the Cubans referred to it, had to be removed unconditionally. Tarnoff tried to explain that, since the embargo had been in place for many years, "it is a political fact that to remove it would not be seen as redressing an unfair balance, but it would be seen as a positive move toward Cuba." Moreover, the embargo was the product of a complex web of executive orders and laws that would have to be dismantled. "If I let my imagination run free, this late at night, and I imagine how the lifting of the embargo might be approached," Tarnoff mused, "I imagine a piece-by-piece review. . . . I also imagine some relationship, although not a formal one, with progress made on issues not subject to negotiations or preconditions but as governments judge overall relations." He reassured Rodríguez that the Carter administration had not given up on its initial aim of achieving normal relations and that Washington understood full well that the embargo was a critical element.

Rodríguez was glad to hear that normalization was still on Carter's agenda, but he evinced some skepticism. Carter had begun his term by creating "a good atmosphere," but things had been going downhill. "Every time problems have arisen, they have always been exaggerated, and false information has been given to the media against Cuba," Rodríguez complained. Most recently, Washington had staged the naval exercises. "We saw on our radars a naval mobilization. . . . You can well understand that at that point, we didn't think that the resumption of relations and the lifting of the embargo were very close at hand."

Meeting Fidel

The following evening, Tarnoff and Pastor were summoned to meet with Castro. As they stood waiting to be ushered into his office, Pastor turned to Padrón and said that he had an important issue to take up with Castro, but first he wanted to ask Padrón if he could raise it.

"The *Comandante* wants you to know you can raise any issue you want," Padrón replied.

"In the interest of the professional friendship we've established over time," Pastor continued, "I feel compelled to mention one issue we want to raise."

"No, no, you don't need to," Padrón insisted.

"Yes, I do," Pastor said seriously. "We want to tell the *Comandante* we were asked by the Hotel Conquistador whether we can bring back the towels you took."

For an instant, Padrón looked shocked and stricken, until he realized Pastor was joking. Then everyone had a good laugh. "How did you know about that?" Padrón asked.

"That's what we have the CIA for," Pastor quipped. Then, the tension of the moment broken, they went in to meet Fidel—the first senior U.S. officials to meet with him in eighteen years.[185]

Castro had been well briefed on their meeting with Rodríguez, and he seemed to think that Carlos Rafael had been too diplomatic. "I don't want you to go back to the United States with any illusions that things can be easy in relations between the United States and Cuba," he began. "The United States has had the wrong approach in regard to Cuba, it has had a wrong approach historically, which has not yet changed. I am not very optimistic that things can improve."[186]

At first, President Carter had "created a favorable atmosphere," but then "someone got the idea of fomenting agitation in regard to the presence of Cuban military and civilian personnel in Africa," Castro complained. "This was deliberate propaganda. . . . Most of it was exaggerated and mendacious." That was followed by the false accusations of Cuban involvement in the Shaba II incursion. "This hurt us very much," Castro lamented. Then came the SR-71 overflights and the naval maneuvers. "We were working on the premise of the possibility of improving relations with the United States. Now these premises have been refuted by the facts I have mentioned. . . . There should be no mistake—we cannot be pressured, impressed, bribed or bought."

Although Fidel spoke softly, he spoke with great intensity and power. "This was the first meeting he had with U.S. officials since the ties had been broken, and he just vented all of the anger," Pastor recalled. "I felt like I was being run over by a train."[187]

Replying to Castro's opening sally, Tarnoff stuck to his instructions. "Africa is central to our concerns," he began, and Cuba's increased military presence in Africa made diplomatic solutions in the region more difficult. "We wish to make it very clear that we are not interested in negotiating our Africa policy with you and we understand that you are not interested in negotiating yours with us," Tarnoff stipulated. But 70 percent of the time spent in secret talks since April had focused on Africa as the two sides tried to gauge one another's intentions. Clearly the two countries were still far apart on the issues. "I would ask you if you believe these talks have been of any use or have served any purpose," Tarnoff said, challenging Fidel's pessimism. "Given the differences, do you feel that our talking is still worthwhile?"

"Yes, I think they are useful," Fidel conceded. "Otherwise we would not have agreed to exchange views and opinions." On Africa, Castro reiterated his often-articulated position that it was none of Washington's business if Cuba supported its friends in Africa. "We have never discussed with you the activities of the United States throughout the entire world," he pointed out. "Perhaps it is because the United States is a great power, it feels it can do what it wants. . . . Perhaps it is idealistic of me, but I never accepted the universal prerogatives of the United States. I never accepted and never will accept the existence of a different law and different rules."

Castro's position on the embargo was also unchanged. It was not right for Washington to tie lifting the embargo to Cuban policies in Africa. The embargo was a unilateral imposition by Washington, and Cuba would make no concessions to have it removed. "Maybe you have gotten to like the blockade. Maybe

Robert A. Pastor, National Security Council director for Latin America, meeting with President Jimmy Carter in 1977. Pastor played a central role in Carter's policy toward Cuba. He and Peter Tarnoff, special assistant to Secretary of State Cyrus Vance, were the first U.S. government officials to meet with Fidel Castro since the break in diplomatic relations in January 1961. (Courtesy of the Pastor family)

you have gotten fond of it; you always have a different pretext for using it against us," Fidel mused. "We will never surrender to it, we are determined," he warned the Americans. "We are prepared to bear our cross as long as necessary."

As the conversation headed into its fifth hour, Tarnoff raised the issue that had prompted the administration to send him and Pastor to Havana in the first place—the imprisoned CIA agents. With Cuba freeing thousands of its own citizens jailed for political reasons, could not the four remaining U.S. prisoners be freed as well?

"It is not possible now," Castro said flatly. "I don't have enough confidence in the relationship." He had already freed several Americans along with the several thousand Cuban prisoners but "we have had no gesture from the United States in exchange." Nevertheless, the possibility of an informal exchange for the release of the Puerto Rican nationalists was still on the table. "I do not understand why you are so tough on the Puerto Ricans," Castro said in exasperation. "The U.S. could make a gesture and release them, then we would make another gesture—without any linkage—just a unilateral humanitarian gesture, and the U.S. does not do it! . . . But if you do something for them, we will do likewise," he promised. As the meeting concluded at 3:00 A.M., Castro seemed more sanguine about the dialogue than he had been when the conversation began. "I have the impression that this has been a very fruitful exchange," he said, and proposed that the dialogue continue.

The bottom line, however, was that Tarnoff and Pastor returned to Washington empty-handed—without the U.S. prisoners and without any Cuban policy concessions on Africa. In his report to Carter, Brzezinski argued that the two sides were at an impasse. "We reiterated our position that the embargo was related to their military activities in Africa and they completely and unequivocally rejected that," Brzezinski wrote. "We should have no illusions about their intentions in Africa. They will not be helpful; they do not view developments in Africa as we do; they probably define their interests in Africa differently than we do. They want to play an important role in Africa, and if that means they will have to live with the embargo, they are reconciled to it."[188] Brzezinski's assessment that there was no possibility of common ground in Africa was wrong, but it would be almost a decade before another U.S. administration was able to identify and build on the convergence of U.S. and Cuban interests that Padrón, Rodríguez, and Castro himself hinted at. Brzezinski was right about one thing, though: Cuba's policy in Africa was more important to Fidel Castro than normal relations with the United States.

For Washington, Castro's tough message and his refusal to release the U.S. prisoners marked the final failure of the secret talks. Looking back, there were threads of the conversations that, had the two sides grasped them firmly, might have helped unravel what Fidel called the "tangled ball of yarn" of bilateral relations.[189] Padrón's suggestion to Newsom in New York that Washington and Havana should discuss ways of cooperating to secure diplomatic solutions to African problems was an opportunity missed. Another was Tarnoff's assurance to Carlos Rafael Rodríguez that Washington did not expect or need Havana to make formal commitments to the United States limiting its options in Africa, but rather the United States would simply watch for and respond to constructive Cuban behavior. A third was Castro's aside, in his meeting with Tarnoff and Pastor, that while "overall relations cannot get any better" with the embargo in place, progress might still be made on specific bilateral issues. All of these exchanges hinted at some flexibility compared to the more rigid public positions of the two sides, but they were roads not taken. In the end, the talks accomplished very little besides the release of the Cuban political prisoners (which was Castro's gambit to get the talks started rather than a product of the dialogue) and a degree of confidence building among the negotiators which would prove important when they met again across the bargaining table in the future.

Years later, Newsom still thought the discussions could have been more fruitful. "I've often felt that if we'd been able to say, we are prepared to discuss these other issues but you [Cubans] have to understand that there's a very serious political issue that we have to face in any agreements we would reach, and that's the issue of the Cuban troops in Africa—that would have been a somewhat different approach." Newsom did not gainsay the depth of the "very, very, very profound difference" between the U.S. and Cuban positions, but he viewed them with a diplomat's eye. "The State Department's approach was to try to start with a potentially manageable issue and see if we couldn't get some solution to it and then kind of go from there, maybe take other steps that would be mutually beneficial and hopefully end up in some more normalized relationship," he explained. "Zbig's approach was much more strategic; he wanted to have the kind of meeting with the Cubans that Kissinger had with the Chinese, you know, which was a strategic discussion of where are we going . . . whose interests are what, and what are the big issues. Can we make any progress on those, because they are the ones that are really important. And those are two totally different concepts."[190]

As epilogue to the secret talks, the exchange of the CIA prisoners for the Puerto Rican nationalists came to fruition after all. A few weeks after meeting with Tarnoff and Pastor, Castro hosted ten members of Congress and repeated his proposal for a reciprocal prisoner release. On the delegation was Congressman Benjamin Gilman (R-N.Y.). A year earlier, Gilman had played a central role in constructing a three-way prisoner exchange involving a Soviet spy convicted in the United States, an American prisoner in East Germany, and an Israeli businessman jailed in Mozambique. Gilman had worked with East German attorney Wolfgang Vogel on that exchange. At the time, Vogel gave Gilman a Cuban proposal to trade Puerto Rican nationalist Lolita Lebrón for CIA agent Larry Lunt. Gilman, in turn, had passed the offer to Carter officials.[191] Nothing came of the Cuban feeler, however, because President Carter was unwilling to grant clemency to Lebrón or the other imprisoned

Puerto Ricans. A year later, energized by his trip to Cuba, Gilman turned his attention to freeing the CIA prisoners by lobbying the Carter administration to accept Castro's "reciprocal humanitarian gesture."[192]

At the NSC, Pastor thought the trade for the CIA agents in Cuba made good sense, so long as there was no explicit quid pro quo. Public sentiment in Puerto Rico favored clemency for the nationalists, most of whom were eligible or nearly eligible for parole anyway. Brzezinski asked the Justice Department to report on the pros and cons of granting clemency, but Justice responded that the issue was a domestic matter and therefore none of the NSC's business.[193] Months passed with no further word until suddenly, "out of nowhere," Pastor recalled, the Justice Department leaked the story that the attorney general had recommended clemency for the Puerto Ricans and the president would announce it shortly. And so he did, on September 6, 1979. Eleven days later, good to his word, Castro ordered the release of the four remaining CIA prisoners—Larry Lunt, Juan Tur, Everett Jackson, and Claudio Rodrígues Morales.

Cool but Communicative

The end of the secret dialogue in December 1978 left the Carter administration without a clear policy direction. If movement toward normalization was premised on Cuban concessions in Africa, and they refused to make any, what should Washington do next? In preparation for an interagency meeting to review Cuba policy in May 1979, the State Department prepared a briefing paper laying out three options: (1) "Dialogue with increased engagement," which was essentially a return to the early 1977 policy, before Brzezinski convinced Carter to condition further progress on Cuban withdrawals from Africa; (2) "Punitive measures against Cuba," which involved rolling back some of the bilateral agreements already reached and imposing new sanctions; and (3) "Containment," which focused on "denying to Cuba targets of opportunity in Africa and in this hemisphere," by strengthening U.S. allies through increased foreign assistance.

State favored the first option, arguing that Brzezinski's conditionality "so far has been ineffective and it has at the same time deprived us of bargaining quids in other areas of interest to us. . . . Thus we find ourselves at a sterile impasse." State's position paper went on to suggest lifting the embargo on the sale of medicine and resuming regular air service to Cuba in order to facilitate the emigration of Cuban ex-prisoners and family visits by Cuban Americans. These low-cost concessions could be used to restart talks with the Cubans on areas of interest to Washington, including Africa and Central America, where U.S.-backed governments were facing a rising tide of popular opposition. The briefing paper sidestepped the main argument against this strategy—that Washington had already held six rounds of talks with Havana since April 1978 and made essentially no progress on the issues of principal concern. The second option was a poor alternative because there was not much Washington could do to Cuba by way of sanctions. "A basic problem with such an approach is that short of acts of war, such as a naval blockade, it is not likely to have any appreciable effect," State argued. However, it would, in all probability, push Havana and Moscow closer together.[194]

At the NSC, Robert Pastor prepared a briefing paper for Brzezinski countering State's menu of alternatives. He titled it, "Putting the Cubes on Ice," and began with some stark truths: "Since 1970, in our 'relationship' with Cuba, American policy has been driven out of unmitigated frustration to adopt some of the most ineffective and immoral policies in U.S. history. This frustration is a function of three simple facts, which are still valid: (1) Cuba causes us terrible problems; (2) Cuba is a little country, and we are a superpower; and (3) We have almost no leverage or influence over the Cubans." Despite the disparity in power between the two nations, there was no way for Washington to make Cuba behave. Thus, whatever the interagency meeting decided to do, Pastor concluded, it "can only affect Cuba on the margins."

Pastor proposed his own bundle of policy initiatives, which he dubbed "cool but communicative." Washington should maintain channels of communication with Havana, "but at the same time we should seek to tighten the wall around the Cubans." That meant urging Western nations to cut off financial credits to exacerbate Cuba's debt problems; undercutting Cuba's leadership in the Third World by emphasizing its dependence on the Soviet Union; and "lobbying hard" against Cuba's bid for a seat on the United Nations Security Council.[195] Pastor, who began as a believer in normalization, had become disillusioned by Cuba's activist policy in Africa. "I ended up at a very different place than I began," he acknowledged.[196]

Pastor's policy bundle amounted to a slightly refurbished version of the policies of diplomatic isolation and economic denial that Washington had followed without much success since 1960s. Indeed, it was the unwillingness of U.S. allies to continue cooperating with such measures that first led Kissinger to contemplate normalizing relations with Cuba. Now, policy was coming full circle back to where it had been in 1973.

Brzezinski chaired the interagency meeting on Cuba on July 20, the day after the triumph of the Sandinista revolution in Nicaragua—not an auspicious moment for improving U.S.-Cuban relations. Vance argued for State's option of renewed dialogue; Brzezinski argued for Pastor's "cool but communicative" strategy of isolation. Neither gave any ground. The participants "explored different strategies for the U.S.," the meeting summary read, "but we did not reach any conclusions." The group agreed only that Washington should continue to encourage moderate voices in the Nonaligned Movement to resist Cuban efforts to radicalize it and should share evidence of Cuba's military buildup with friendly governments.[197]

The Soviet Combat Brigade

In the spring of 1979, Brzezinski tasked the intelligence community to prepare an assessment of Cuban-Soviet military cooperation around the world.[198] The National Security Agency concluded in June that there was evidence of a Soviet ground force unit in Cuba—a "brigade" separate from the military advisory group.[199] On August 28, with most of official Washington out of town on vacation, the National Intelligence Daily (NID), which compiled key intelligence information for more than four hundred clients in executive agencies and Congress, reported on maneuvers by the Soviet unit and labeled it a "combat brigade." The phrase was chosen arbitrarily by the author of the NID, who simply assumed that if the brigade was not part of the Soviet training mission, it must be intended for combat. Within days, the NID was leaked to a reporter at *Aviation Week* magazine.[200]

Senior administration officials were well aware of the political firestorm that could ensue from news of Soviet combat troops in Cuba. "Secretary Vance's primary concern was the impact on SALT [the Strategic Arms Limitation Treaty], already encountering heavy weather in Congress," recalled David Newsom. Vance pulled together his senior aides to devise a damage control strategy. State would contact both the Soviets and the Cubans to warn them of U.S. concerns about the brigade and seek an explanation for its presence. With luck, they might resolve the incident through quiet diplomacy before the news broke in the mainstream press, just as Henry Kissinger had defused a potential crisis over construction of a Soviet nuclear submarine base at the Cuban port of Cienfuegos in 1970. Newsom was tasked to brief key congressional leaders so they heard the news from the administration before they read it in the morning paper.[201]

The next day, Newsom began calling majority and minority leaders in both the House and the Senate, along with the chairs and ranking members of the foreign affairs committees. All reacted calmly to the news, except for Senator

Frank Church, chairman of the Foreign Relations Committee. Church was facing a tough reelection fight, having been targeted by the National Conservative Political Action Committee (NCPAC), for being soft on communism. His 1977 trip to Cuba, in which he spent three days traveling the island with Fidel Castro, became a political albatross when Republicans circulated campaign ads featuring Church and Castro smoking cigars together. Seeing an opportunity to seize the initiative, Church called a press conference to announce the discovery of the brigade and demand that it be removed.[202]

In a press conference of his own on September 5, Vance began by saying the brigade was "a very serious matter" but that it had no air- or sealift capacity to enable it to strike outside of Cuba.[203] Asked by a reporter if Washington would demand removal of the brigade, Vance tried to avoid committing himself to any specific action by saying, "I will not be satisfied with the maintenance of the status quo." But calling the status quo unacceptable locked the administration into a policy of insisting that it be changed, and the Soviets would prove to be much less accommodating than Vance hoped. "In hindsight," Vance wrote in his memoirs, "I regret not having used words less open to misinterpretation."[204]

A central problem for the administration was the paucity of its real knowledge about the brigade. "We're still not sure of all our facts," an intelligence official told the New York Times on the same day Vance held his press conference. "We don't know how far back this goes, and not knowing that, we don't know why they are there."[205] When Vance asked Soviet ambassador Anatoly Dobrynin to withdraw the brigade, Dobrynin insisted that the mission of the force was training, they had every right to be in Cuba, they had been there for years, and they posed no threat to the United States. The crisis was an artificial one created by the United States and would have to be solved by the United States.[206]

For Brzezinski, the brigade provided an opportunity to demonstrate Washington's toughness in the face of the Soviet Union's strategic advances in Africa and Latin America. He advocated threatening unspecified military action if the Soviets did not withdraw it. Vance wanted to contain the brigade issue, appealing to Moscow's desire to salvage SALT as the lever to win concessions. Brzezinski was contemptuous of Vance's refusal to see the brigade in a wider strategic context. Vance and Newsom, he said later, were "weak people when it came to dealing with the Soviets."[207]

Brzezinski took his case directly to the president. He often used his weekly NSC report as a vehicle for raising broader strategic issues.[208] In the midst of the brigade crisis, he entitled one report, "Acquiescence vs. Assertiveness."

Public opinion in the United States and the world at large viewed the administration as "perhaps the most timid since World War II," he began. The problem was a perception that "in the U.S.-Soviet relationship, the Soviet side is the assertive party and the U.S. side is more acquiescent." The perception was not wrong, Brzezinski wrote. "In tone and occasionally in substance, we have been excessively acquiescent," and the State Department was the principal culprit. "Today," Brzezinski warned, "much of the world is watching to see how we will behave on the Soviet/Cuban issue. . . . Failure to cope with it firmly can have the effect of vitiating your foreign policy accomplishments and conclusively stamping the administration as weak." On the surface, Brzezinski's report exemplified the sort of broad strategic thinking that Carter found so attractive in his national security advisor. But, it was also a not-too-veiled appeal to what David Halberstam, in *The Best and the Brightest*, called the "manhood" argument. Atop the memo, Carter wrote a single word: "Good."[209]

After Vance's fifth inconclusive meeting with Dobrynin, Carter wrote directly to Soviet president Leonid Brezhnev via the hotline. The presence of the brigade was a matter of "genuine and deep concern to the U.S. government and the American public," he wrote. "This concern is not an artificial creation." He appealed for a positive Soviet response to resolve the crisis and preserve the SALT agreement.[210] Brezhnev responded two days later, offering only assurances that the Soviet forces were part of a training center, and would remain so. This was substantially what the Soviets had been saying all along, but it could be fashioned into a plausibly successful outcome, which Carter announced to the nation in a televised speech on October 1.[211]

The ill-timed tempest over the brigade did nothing to improve U.S.-Cuban relations. Wayne Smith had only just arrived in Cuba to take over from Lyle Lane as chief of the Interests Section when the Soviet combat brigade crisis broke. On August 29, he received instructions to notify Cuba of Washington's concern over the Soviet brigade and suggest it be withdrawn. Vice Minister Pelegrín Torras replied that Soviet military personnel in Cuban were none of Washington's business.[212] When Vance and Carter said the status quo was unacceptable, Smith quickly cabled Washington that they should not repeat such a declaration unless they were prepared for a confrontation. "Whatever Soviet inclinations might be, I wrote, the Cubans definitely would not agree to withdrawal of the brigade, and in this instance the Soviets were unlikely to ignore Cuban views."[213] Smith was right, but for reasons even he did not fully understand.

Carter's Republican critics were quick to compare the Soviet combat brigade crisis to the 1962 missile crisis, despite the fact that the brigade posed no plausible threat to the United States.[214] Their overheated rhetoric obscured the real echoes of 1962. During the missile crisis, Nikita Khrushchev, looking into the abyss of nuclear war, negotiated a way back from the brink without even informing the Cubans until after an agreement had been reached. Castro was so angry that he came close to breaking off his romance with the Soviets. To reassure Castro that the Soviet Union was still committed to the defense of the revolution, Khrushchev agreed to leave a small contingent of troops on the island when the units guarding the missiles were withdrawn. "We pressured the Soviets to leave a combat brigade here," Castro told the authors. "We wanted them as a symbol of the Soviet commitment to Cuba."[215] It was precisely this symbolic Soviet presence that Washington rediscovered in June 1979 and dubbed the "Soviet combat brigade." For the Soviets to acquiesce to U.S. demands that the troops be withdrawn would have been to relive the public humiliation of the missile crisis and to once again betray Cuba's trust by reneging on a solemn promise of military support. This the Soviets would not do, even at the price of SALT.

Castro believed the Carter administration had intentionally concocted the crisis to sabotage the Nonaligned summit just then convening in Havana. For more than a year, Washington had been waging a behind the scenes diplomatic battle to encourage pro-Western states in the Nonaligned Movement to oppose Cuba's efforts to steer the movement toward the socialist camp. Bob Pastor managed the campaign. Pastor was on his honeymoon on the Salmon River in Idaho when the brigade crisis went public. A forest ranger tracked him down, and he was summoned back to Washington. "I didn't really think that justified interrupting my honeymoon, but Brzezinski disagreed," Pastor recalled with a smile. "I immediately thought, Fidel is going to think we've come up with this as a way to undermine the summit. And it turns out that was exactly what he thought, because later he told me so."[216]

In Castro's assessment, the Carter administration's internal divisions had killed any prospect for improved relations. "I believed that there were people in the United States who favored the improvement of relations with Cuba, and that there were people who opposed the improvement of relations," he told the press. "Unquestionably . . . those who have been struggling against the improvement of relations have won." There was no other way to interpret the constant stream of false accusations and phony issues—Shaba II, the MiG-23 flap, and now the brigade crisis.[217]

Castro was right. Brzezinski had, indeed, won the war with Vance. Vance had insisted that the State Department rather than the NSC manage the combat brigade crisis, and he had handled it poorly. He set the terms of the political debate when he called the status quo unacceptable, and then Carter was forced to accept it. The fiasco of the Soviet combat brigade broke the stalemate between Vance and Brzezinski over Cuba policy. On October 4, 1979, just days after Carter addressed the nation on the Soviet brigade, he approved Presidential Directive (PD)/NSC-52, outlining a new policy, the purpose of which was to "contain Cuba as a source of violent revolutionary change." It spelled out a program of economic and military assistance for the Caribbean and Central America to reduce opportunities for Cuban subversion, a program of diplomacy and propaganda to build opposition to Cuba's role as Nonaligned chair, continued efforts to restrict European financial credits to Cuba, and warnings to the Soviet Union that its support of Cuban activism would damage détente. It was, in short, the policy Brzezinski had been pushing for more than a year.[218]

PD/NSC-52 also included one immediate goal: "to press vigorously to preclude Cuba from gaining a seat on the UN Security Council." Traditionally, the chair of the Nonaligned Movement was easily elected to the Security Council. To foil Cuba's bid for the Latin American seat, Washington recruited Colombia as an alternate and lobbied Latin American delegates and Nonaligned moderates. "We went full tilt to block them," Pastor recalled.[219] Voting began in late October 1979, and through a record 154 ballots, Cuba held a simple majority but could not win the required two-thirds. Then, just after Christmas, the Soviet Union invaded Afghanistan. The invasion was a diplomatic catastrophe for Cuba. Coming only months after the Havana Nonaligned Summit, the Soviet invasion of a Nonaligned member state demolished the Cuban claim that the Soviets were "natural allies" of the Third World. If Cuba were elected to the Security Council, it would be presiding in January 1980, when the council took up the issue of the Soviet invasion. For many members of the Nonaligned Movement, this was too much— especially since the Cubans refused to publicly condemn the Soviet attack. As new instructions from governments around the world arrived in New York, Cuba's majority evaporated, and Colombia pulled into the lead. Rather than face the ignominy of defeat, Cuba accepted a compromise, withdrawing in favor of Mexico.[220]

Return to Havana

In late December 1979, Bernardo Benes approached Peter Tarnoff to suggest another high-level meeting between U.S. and Cuban officials. Tarnoff assumed that Benes was conveying a proposal from the Cubans, as he had the year before. In fact, Benes had not met with Castro for months, and the Cubans had sent no such message. When the State Department (with Carter's approval) contacted Havana to arrange a meeting, Castro assumed the initiative was coming from Washington. The confusion was not dispelled until the meeting was under way.[221]

Peter Tarnoff and Bob Pastor received their instructions in the Oval Office from President Carter personally. "I . . . instructed them to warn Castro about subversion in Latin America, to reemphasize the requirements we would have for improved relations with Cuba, and primarily listen to what he had to say," Carter noted in his diary. The president also told them to see if they could convince Castro to publicly criticize the Soviet invasion of Afghanistan.[222]

Much of the January 16, 1980, discussion in Havana focused on the deteriorating international situation.[223] The demise of détente left Fidel Castro deeply pessimistic about the prospects for Third World economic development and palpably worried about the danger of armed conflict between the superpowers. Events drove home to him how much Cuba remained at the mercy of global forces beyond its control. "We are small," Fidel said with uncharacteristic humility. "We are really like a grain of sand and cannot really contribute very much to resolving the many events which have been unleashed." The invasion of Afghanistan had taken Cuba by surprise. "Why things happened the way they did, I do not understand," Castro confessed. The Soviets had neither forewarned him of the invasion nor briefed him about it.[224]

Unquestionably, Cuba's bid for the UN Security Council seat had been hurt by the invasion, Castro acknowledged, and it had greatly complicated Cuba's position as leader of the Nonaligned Movement. "We are playing two roles," he explained. "We are playing the role of the revolutionary and we are also playing the role of the member of the Nonaligned Movement. It's not easy." He disapproved of the invasion, but Cuba would not publicly join with the United States to criticize the Soviet Union. Cuba's disagreements would be expressed privately. Soviet assistance had been "a matter of life and death in our confrontation with the United States," Castro pointed out. "We are not opportunists nor are we ingrates. We cannot improve relations with the United States by becoming enemies of the Soviet Union." And why should they have to? The Cold War put small countries like Cuba in a vise between the superpowers. "We cannot conceive that friendship with the United States has to imply a break with the Soviet Union," he said plaintively.

Tarnoff and Pastor raised the issue of Cuban support for revolution in Central America and the Caribbean as an obstacle to improving bilateral relations. Castro was adamant that Cuba's aim was not to cause Washington problems. In Panama, he pointed out, he had urged General Omar Torrijos to avoid a confrontation with Washington over the canal and instead seek a diplomatic settlement. "In Nicaragua, we favor a moderate government and a multi-party system, and we are not interested in causing conflict with the United States," he continued. But in El Salvador and Guatemala, revolutionaries were fighting against murderous reactionary regimes, and Cuba would not repudiate its right to help them.

Reviewing the situation in Africa, Tarnoff noted diplomatic progress toward an independent Zimbabwe under the auspices of the Lancaster House accords, and Castro expressed Cuba's support for the accords as well. Turning to Namibia, occupied by South African troops who staged periodic attacks across Angola's border, Tarnoff asked Castro directly: "If there is a resolution of the Namibian question, would Cuban combat forces be withdrawn from Angola?"

"We will be happier than you when we can withdraw our forces," Fidel replied. "It is easier to put troops in than to take them out." Cuba had already withdrawn about 30 percent of its troops from Ethiopia, he noted, and he wanted to resume withdrawals from Angola as well, but the Angolans would not agree to it because of ongoing South African incursions from Namibia. "When Namibia is resolved," Fidel said, "we will have good arguments to reduce our troops strength, not unilaterally, but based on discussions with them."

As the ten-hour conversation was winding down, they turned to the issue of Cuban political prisoners, where a serious logistical snafu had arisen. Cuba had released some thirty-nine hundred prisoners in 1978, of whom twenty-five hundred wanted to emigrate to the United States along with their families. Processing of the prisoners by U.S. immigration officials had been extremely slow, as the Justice Department insisted on meticulously reviewing every individual case. Washington had also agreed to take another one thousand ex-prisoners who had been released previously. But several thousand other ex-prisoners were still in Cuba, and the proposed U.S. limits would leave them and their families stranded there. The United States could not absorb them, Tarnoff explained.

Fidel seemed taken aback. "What are you going to do with the rest of the ex-prisoners who hope to go to the United States? Are you just going to leave them here?" Although he didn't say so, Castro suspected that Washington's aim was to stoke political discontent by marooning the ex-prisoners in Cuba.[225] Washington had agreed in 1978 to take the prisoners and their families. Now it was reneging.

Yet when Cubans hijacked boats, they were greeted in Florida with great fanfare as heroes, thereby encouraging acts of violence. "That's an absurd situation," Castro scolded the Americans. "You must do something to discourage these people. You cannot leave us with the job if you yourself do nothing." He did not want to unleash a flood of migrants as in the past, but he would not sit still if Washington blocked legal migration while at the same time encouraging illegal departures. "Either you take measures," he warned, "or we should be free of any obligation to control those who want to leave illegally." It was a warning that Washington did not take seriously enough.

The Havana conversation, like those in 1978, did not lead to any breakthrough. Both sides expressed their views on the issues, clarifying the scope of their disagreement. But on no issue did either side offer any real concessions, so the gulf between their positions remained unbridged. "There was some marginal interest in what Castro was saying," Tarnoff recalled, "but the Cuban relationship became hostage to the deteriorating relationship with the Soviet Union."[226] After Afghanistan, Carter's foreign policy hardened into familiar Cold War patterns, and the idea of improving relations with Havana was simply submerged by larger geopolitical forces. "In that scale of things," Brzezinski told the authors, "the whole business of Castro seemed to me to be a piddling affair. In my job, it was a damn nuisance."[227]

Mariel

In 1979–80, the Cuban economy suffered a serious recession. A third of the sugar crop and the entire tobacco crop were lost to disease. Swine flu decimated the pig population, producing shortages of pork, a staple in the Cuban diet. Nickel exports fell short of planning targets, and the adoption by many countries of the two-hundred-mile commercial fishing limit banished the Cuban fleet from its traditional haunts.[228] The resulting shortages of consumer goods coincided with an influx of Cuban American visitors. During the 1978 dialogue with the Committee of 75 organized by Bernardo Benes, Castro had agreed to allow exiles to visit the island. In 1979, more than one hundred thousand Cuban Americans did. Almost all of them, even those with modest incomes, brought gifts for friends and family—gifts that were lavish by Cuban standards. By bringing goods that were hard or impossible to come by in Cuba, the returning exiles were making an implicit statement that their decision to emigrate had been the right one. They had prospered, while those who stayed behind languished. The contrast between the prosperity of those who had left and the austerity endured by those who stayed was palpable. "The government made a mistake allowing them to return," explained one Cuban woman. "We could see they were well!"[229]

Cuba's recession and the invidious comparison between living standards in Cuba and in Miami increased emigration pressure. Since the end of the Freedom Flights in 1973, the only Cubans who had been able to emigrate legally to the United States were those who met the same strict criteria as aspiring immigrants elsewhere. However, Cubans who made it to the United States illegally—by sailing across the Florida Strait, for example—were routinely granted permanent residence under the 1966 Cuban Adjustment Act. Beginning in late 1979, there was a surge in the number of small boats being stolen or hijacked in Cuba for the trip across the strait. As Castro complained to Tarnoff and Pastor, the perpetrators were welcomed in Miami as heroes; not one was ever prosecuted, even when they resorted to violence.

Fidel's complaint about the paradox of U.S. immigration policy was just one of several warnings preceding the migration crisis that unfolded over the summer of 1980. The first formal Cuban protest came several months earlier, in October 1979, when Wayne Smith was called to the Foreign Ministry over a boat hijacking. "We aren't asking you to return the hijackers to Cuba," the Cuban official told Smith. "We understand that wouldn't be politically feasible, and it isn't necessary anyway. What is necessary is that your government reaffirm its intention to uphold the law with respect to hijackings. That will help discourage what might become a very dangerous practice." In reporting to Washington, Smith recommended a strongly worded public statement affirming U.S. intentions to prosecute hijackers. He received no response. "My follow-up cables also disappeared into the Washington void."[230]

Over the ensuing months, four more boat hijackings prompted Cuban diplomatic protests, and following each one Smith cabled Washington urging action. Still, nothing happened. In February, after armed Cuban hijackers diverted a Liberian freighter to Florida and were released by U.S. authorities, Carlos Rafael Rodríguez issued an unambiguous warning. "I hope, Smith, that you are emphasizing to your government the gravity with which mine views this situation. Our patience is running out. If your government wants people in small boats, we can give you more than you bargained for."[231]

A few weeks later, on March 8, 1980, Castro reiterated the warning publicly. "They encourage the illegal departures from the country, the hijacking of boats, practically receiving those who hijack a vessel as heroes," Castro said of the U.S. government. "We have protested and have warned them." If Washington continued to look the other way, "We might also have to take our own measures. . . . We once had to open the Camarioca port," he reminded the United States. "We hope we don't have to take such measures again."[232]

In Washington, there was no sense of urgency. "The Castro regime may again resort to large-scale emigration to reduce discontent," the CIA's Cuba Analytic Center warned in late January, but the State Department's Bureau of Legal Affairs did not get around to acting on Smith's October 1979 cable until February 1980.[233] As the number of hijackings mounted, however, the issue went to the White House, and the president endorsed Smith's recommendation. "We should restrict these maritime hijackings by law if possible," Carter wrote. "Use public warnings and cooperate with Cuba." Even this presidential dictum did little to grease the wheels of the bureaucracy, however. Five weeks later, the State Department and Justice Department were still trading memos about what ought to be done.[234] By then, it was too late.

One way disaffected Cubans sought to emigrate in the spring of 1980 was by claiming political asylum at the embassies of other Latin American governments. In Havana, asylum seekers had to run the gauntlet of Cuban guards outside embassy gates. The early months of 1980 witnessed a rash of gate-crashers, and the governments concerned refused to turn them over to the Cuban police. To Fidel Castro, the behavior of the embassies was exactly parallel to Washington's. The Latin American countries would not accept Cubans who sought to emigrate legally, but they encouraged violence by accepting anyone who broke into their embassy grounds by force.[235]

On April 1, six Cubans hijacked a bus and crashed through the gates of the Peruvian Embassy. Cuban guards fired on the bus, and one of them was killed in the crossfire. "When we told the *Comandante* of the policeman's death, his face turned deep red," one of Castro's aides told Wayne Smith. "I have never seen him so angry."[236] On Fidel's orders, the police tore down the barriers and guard posts outside the Peruvian Embassy, leaving the grounds unguarded. "We cannot give protection to embassies that do not cooperate with that protection," explained a front-page editorial in *Granma*.[237] The ploy, according to Cuban officials, was to make Peru an object lesson. They expected several hundred migrants to seek refuge at the embassy, creating a logistical nightmare for the staff and making other embassies think twice about accepting future gate-crashers.[238] But Castro had miscalculated.

Within 72 hours, more than ten thousand people poured into the Peruvian Embassy grounds—so many that there was literally no room for people to lie down to sleep. "There are people in the branches of the trees, on top of the destroyed iron grating, and even on the roof of the embassy," a Peruvian official said, describing the scene.[239] The humanitarian crisis was so acute the Cuban government had no choice but to provide food, water, and sanitation for the crowd and to promise them safe passage off the island if they would just go home. Yet at the same time, *Granma* denounced the asylum seekers as "delinquents, lumpenproletarians, antisocial and parasitic elements."[240] Most of the refugees at the embassy were afraid to leave, and many of those who did were confronted at home by angry neighbors who denounced them as traitors and, in some cases, assaulted them.

For the Cuban government, the entire episode was a huge embarrassment that it wanted to bring to a quick conclusion. Cuba initially agreed for the refugees to be flown to a reception center in Costa Rica, from which they would continue on to various destinations. This might have resolved the problem, but President Carter and Costa Rican president Rodrigo Carazo could not resist the temptation to exploit Castro's predicament. Carazo made it a point to greet the Cuban refugees as they disembarked in Costa Rica, drawing media attention to their stories of misery. Cuban vice minister of foreign relations Ricardo Alarcón confronted Costa Rican foreign minister Carlos Aguilar about the media circus, demanding, "Why do you have to make such a spectacle out of this?"[241]

At a White House reception on April 9, Carter described Cuba as a Soviet puppet, adding, "We see the hunger of many people on that island to escape political deprivation of freedom and also economic adversity. Our heart goes out to the almost 10,000 freedom-loving Cubans who entered a temporarily opened gate at the Peruvian Embassy."[242] The following day, *Granma* denounced the speech and Carter personally, calling him an "insolent person" who had "reached the peak of shamelessness" by expressing his sympathy for the "criminals" at the embassy.[243]

On April 18, Castro suspended the refugee flights to Costa Rica. On April 21, an editorial in *Granma* invited Cuban Americans to come pick up refugees from the Peruvian Embassy or their relatives, and two days later, the paper directed would-be emigrants to congregate at the port of Mariel, where U.S. vessels could come get them. The State Department tried to deter Cuban Americans from sailing south by warning that anyone aiding illegal immigration would be committing a felony. The warning had no impact.[244] "What I didn't realize, and what no one seemed to realize, was that events were rapidly moving out of our control," wrote Victor H. Palmieri, the State Department's coordinator for refugee affairs. "Miami Cubans who had never steered a boat before were puttering out to sea while the U.S. Coast Guard and Customs officials waved them on. . . . The flotilla was forming—the horse was leaving the barn!"[245]

In an uncanny act of political jujitsu, Fidel Castro turned Cuba's embarrassment over how many of its citizens wanted to leave into Washington's embarrassment over its inability to control its own coast. By the end of April, over a thousand boats were anchored in Mariel harbor, taking on refugees as fast as Cuban officials could process them. After a four-hour meeting on April 23, Carter's domestic policy staff settled on a two-pronged policy of stepping up efforts to deter boats from going to Mariel by threatening the operators with fines and possible imprisonment, while continuing to welcome into the United States the refugees they brought back. Palmieri dubbed this policy "get tough but remain compassionate," neatly capturing U.S. ambivalence.[246]

A few days later, the tension between Havana and Washington escalated. On May 2, a crowd of about eight hundred ex-political prisoners gathered in front of the U.S. Interests Section on Havana's seaside boulevard, the Malecón, to apply for visas to enter the United States. As they waited, dozens of government supporters armed with bats, bricks, and chains converged on the building and attacked the ex-prisoners. During the ensuing riot, some four hundred Cubans took refuge inside the Interests Section. Despite Cuban government promises that they would not be arrested, most refused to leave.[247] For the next several days, Wayne Smith negotiated with the Cuban Foreign Ministry, urging it to simply allow the United States to fly the ex-prisoners out of Cuba. Since the Cuban government had already given them exit visas and wanted to be rid of them, it was an easy solution to a problem both governments claimed to want resolved. The Cubans, however, refused, arguing that if they allowed the ex-prisoners to leave, it would encourage others to break into diplomatic missions. Privately, Cuban officials acknowledged that they wanted to use the Mariel boatlift and the ex-prisoners as leverage to force Washington to negotiate on broader issues. "If we ever get back to negotiating anything," Alarcón told Smith, "it will have to be based on a step-by-step process based on reciprocity. . . . We aren't going to sit down with you to talk about stopping the Mariel operation and then have that be the end of it."[248]

Now dubbed the "Freedom Flotilla," the boatlift continued unabated. On May 14, Carter ordered the Coast Guard to seize boats ferrying Cubans to Florida illegally.[249] This directive would eventually slow the exodus, but it could not stop the boats already anchored at Mariel—more than a thousand of them—from returning laden with refugees. When Carter announced the tough new enforcement measures, forty thousand Cubans had been brought to south Florida. Before the boatlift finally ended, eighty thousand more would follow.

Crisis Dialogue

If Washington could not shut off the flow of refugees, the only option was to convince Castro to shut it off from the Cuban side. After Cuba rejected a Costa Rican proposal for multilateral talks aimed at ending the refugee crisis, Carter approved a bilateral approach.[250] Wayne Smith conveyed the proposal to the Cubans, who requested a full-scale negotiation led by Carter's new secretary of state, Edmund S. Muskie (Vance had resigned on April 28 in the wake of the failed mission to rescue the Iranian hostages). Washington countered by suggesting a new round of midlevel talks, with Tarnoff and Pastor traveling once again to Havana. The Cubans agreed.[251] "If we were to have any chance of getting the sea-lift closed down," Wayne Smith recalled, "we would have to present the negotiations . . . as just the start of a dialogue that would carry us, issue by issue, to the discussion of all the other problems between us." The negotiating position Tarnoff prepared struck just the right note, Smith thought. It demanded an end to the exodus but at the same time offered to resume discussions on the full range of bilateral issues. Tarnoff did not have the last word, however. The NSC refused to agree to a broad dialogue, insisting that the talks be restricted to the boatlift and the Cubans trapped in the Interests Section. "We had some other problems then—Afghanistan and Iran," Brzezinski said, looking back at the decision. "So it was not the time for what might appear to be one-sided concessions."[252]

When Tarnoff and Pastor arrived in Havana with their restrictive instructions, Smith demanded to know what had happened to the earlier plan. "We thought the other approach was too soft," Pastor explained.

"If this is the best you could come up with, you should have stayed home," Smith answered. "This will be a wasted trip."[253]

That afternoon, Tarnoff, Pastor, and Smith met with Padrón, Alarcón, and Arbesú at a government protocol house. Tarnoff opened the meeting, trying to put the best face possible on the U.S. position. He reiterated Washington's desire to eventually normalize relations and that "steps leading to such normalization not be delayed indefinitely." But the reason Washington had requested a new round of talks was its "pressing concern" over the migration crisis. "If we cannot resolve the manageable problems which arise, such as those of immigration and the Interests Section, the chances of a general improvement are even more remote." He went on to describe in detail the U.S. position on Mariel, the Cubans in the Interests Section, and maritime hijacking.[254]

When Tarnoff concluded, Padrón looked quizzically at the U.S. team. "Is that it?" he asked. "Is that all?"

"Yes, that's our position," Tarnoff replied.[255]

"I must tell you frankly that our feeling is one of dissatisfaction and frustration that the U.S. side is beginning these exploratory talks by dealing only with those issues which it labels 'pressing' and 'urgent,'" Padrón answered. "Unfortunately, once again the U.S. deals only with those matters which are in its own interests, ignoring those issues which are the essence of the problems between us." The Cuban side, Padrón made clear, was not disposed to even discuss immigration unless the U.S. side was willing to be more forthcoming about broader issues like the embargo. All Tarnoff could do was repeat the position U.S. negotiators had been articulating since David Aaron and Bob Gates first sat down with Padrón at the La Côte Basque two years earlier: a general improvement in relations depended on Cuba responding to U.S. concerns about its relationship with the Soviet Union and its role in Africa, Central America, and the Caribbean. As usual, the Cubans flatly rejected the idea that they should radically revise their entire foreign policy just to improve relations with the United States. Washington's presumption that it could stand as the "judge and arbiter" of Cuba's relations with others was "one-sided, unconstructive, and unacceptable," Padrón declared. The dialogue went downhill from there.

During a break, Pastor took Arbesú aside. "What I am about to tell you is personal; I am not representing the U.S. government, but just giving you the perspective of an American citizen," Pastor began. "Your behavior on this issue is doing more to strengthen Ronald Reagan's candidacy for president than anything you could possibly do." Arbesú didn't respond, but he understood the point and communicated it to Fidel. Eventually, Castro would come to the same conclusion—but not yet.[256]

Tensions rose as the two sides sparred with one another. As the evening wore on toward midnight, the negotiators, most of whom had been meeting on and off for two years, shifted from calling one another by their first names to using surnames. "I think we are going around in circles," Tarnoff said in frustration. "My impression of the results of this round of talks is one of great disappointment. . . . I think we have exhausted the usefulness of this round."[257] Tarnoff and Pastor flew back to Washington the next day, empty-handed. "The Cuban side was unusually polemical," they reported to Brzezinski and

Muskie. "It became clear to us that although these confidential talks have proven useful in helping us to understand Cuba's views on a wide range of issues, we have clearly reached a dead-end in terms of resolving problems."[258]

Blue Fire

In early July, Cuba and the United States came to the brink of open conflict. A large freighter, the *Blue Fire*, capable of holding some three thousand people, anchored at Mariel and began taking on passengers. If freighters rather than small pleasure boats began transporting Cuban refugees, the scale of the migration crisis would escalate dramatically. U.S. officials quickly decided that the *Blue Fire* had to be stopped, by military force if necessary. Naval forces were assembled and pre-positioned to blockade the port of Mariel. "We almost went to war over the *Blue Fire*," Robert Pastor recalled.[259]

Secretary of State Muskie insisted on trying to resolve the problem diplomatically before taking military action. Pastor suggested they approach Carlos Rafael Rodríguez, who had impressed him during the Havana negotiations as serious and levelheaded. "He was smart, he was on top of issues, he was not full of a lot of rhetoric. We immediately recognized that he was a critical person. I remembered that when we got into the *Blue Fire* crisis."[260] On July 3, Wayne Smith delivered a message from Muskie to Rodríguez warning that the United States had the gravest concerns about the *Blue Fire*. But the demarche held a carrot as well as a stick. Washington remained open to the possibility of improving relations, Muskie's note said, but if the *Blue Fire* sailed, that opportunity would be foreclosed. Reading the note, Rodríguez remarked that it had "some barbs" but was basically "constructive." He would have to consult with Fidel about the ship, but he could assure Muskie, "in the strictest confidence," that Castro had made a decision to do nothing that could be construed as deliberately provocative leading up to the U.S. elections.

Loading the *Blue Fire* "would definitely be construed in the United States as provocative," Smith warned.

"You can tell the Secretary I will see what I can do," Rodríguez replied. "Our relations are bad enough as it is without adding more complications. What we need is a truce, not escalation."

While the Cubans deliberated about how to respond to Muskie's message, another SR-71 overflew Havana. "Cubans will doubtless be angered over flight which resulted in loud sonic boom almost knocking members USINT from their chairs," Smith angrily cabled Washington. "Would it not have been advisable to hold off on overflight at least until we heard what Carlos Rafael Rodríguez had to say?" As Smith wrote later, "To send me in to ask the Cubans not to load the *Blue Fire*—in effect, to ask for a concession—and at the same time to do something that was bound to provoke them, struck me as utterly stupid."[261]

When Smith met with Rodríguez that evening, the vice president was more mystified than angry. "I don't understand what your government intended," he began. "The *Blue Fire* isn't going to load, but I don't mind telling you that the overflight today almost ruined everything. A few people in the meeting this afternoon wanted to retaliate by loading not only the *Blue Fire* but several other vessels as well. Fortunately cooler heads prevailed—this time."[262]

As summer turned toward fall, the socially disruptive consequences of the boatlift began to weigh more heavily on Cuban officials. Tens of thousands of citizens still hoped to leave, and social tensions between would-be emigrants and the revolution's loyal supporters were tearing apart local communities. And gradually, Castro's anger at Jimmy Carter was supplanted by his concern that the boatlift was hurting Carter politically, making the election of Ronald Reagan more likely. "We felt we let it go on too long," Carlos Rafael Rodríguez admitted, looking back.[263]

The boatlift gave Carter a huge political black eye. His inability to control the southern border—following the Soviet invasion of Afghanistan and the seizure of American hostages in Iran—reinforced the public's perception that the president was weak, incapable of defending the interests of the United States abroad. "Carter couldn't get the Russians to move out of Cuba," quipped Republican nominee Ronald Reagan, referring to the Soviet combat brigade, "so he's moving out the Cubans."[264]

In late August, José Luis Padrón contacted Peter Tarnoff using the communications back channel they had established when the dialogue first began in 1978. He invited Tarnoff to return to Havana to reopen the dialogue with an eye toward ending the migration crisis. Tarnoff asked Muskie if he could make the trip alone, and Muskie backed the idea, arguing to the president that the chances of success would be greater if the NSC staff was not involved. Brzezinski did not fight it. "By then I frankly didn't have much interest in this," he recalled. "I just didn't think it was leading anywhere and I had other fish to fry."[265]

Tarnoff traveled to Havana in early September with broader instructions than he and Pastor had carried three months before. Unlike June, when Castro had refused to meet with the U.S. delegation, he saw Tarnoff and Smith right away. "He was clearly willing to be helpful," Tarnoff recalled. "I was instructed to tell him that if the president was re-elected, he would do his best to have an expanded relationship that would address a broad range of issues." Castro agreed immediately to end the boatlift, but said he was doing so "unconditionally," without expecting any quid pro quo, and without demanding any promise of broader talks.[266] He also told Smith that he wanted to resolve the problem of the Cubans at the Interests Section, and gave his personal guarantee that they would be allowed to leave for the United States immediately.[267]

Upon Tarnoff's return, Carter insisted on a personal briefing. He was convinced that an end to the boatlift would boost his electoral prospects in Florida and Arkansas (where some of the refugees were being housed—a politically unpopular move that cost Governor Bill Clinton reelection and shaped his own views about Cuba). "Tarnoff reported very favorable results of his discussions with Castro," Carter wrote in his diary. Not only would Fidel close Mariel, but he also "refused to accept anything in return . . . and made it clear there was no quid pro quo involved."[268]

Secretary of State Muskie attended the Oval Office briefing but was especially anxious to get from Tarnoff a package of cigars that Fidel Castro had sent as a gift. Muskie opened the elaborate package as soon as the Oval Office meeting adjourned. "But he was disappointed when, under all the wrapping, it held just 100 cigars," Tarnoff recalled, "the legal limit for what could be brought into the United States!"[269]

Missed Opportunities

During the critical first year of his presidency, Jimmy Carter seemed uncertain about what he wanted from better relations with Cuba, and how great an impediment Cuba's role in Africa posed. He believed in principle that the United States should have normal diplomatic relations with adversaries whenever possible, yet he also shared Brzezinski's hope that normal relations might wean Cuba from the Soviets.[270] When Cuban troops were drawing down in Angola, they seemed to pose a fleeting problem, but when withdrawals stopped in the spring of 1977, the Angola problem loomed larger. When Cuba deployed troops to Ethiopia a few months later, followed by Carter and Castro's public shouting match over Shaba II, all forward momentum on normalization was lost. "I think Castro saw my confrontation with him both publicly and privately on Ethiopia as a turning point," Carter said reflecting back on that critical moment. "I think he kind of gave up, as did I, on the immediate prospect of full normal relations. So both of us kind of backed away from that."[271]

In Havana, the Cubans found Washington's stance confusing. On the one hand, Carter was clearly less hostile than any previous U.S. president and demonstrated his sincerity by taking positive initiatives in 1977. Yet Brzezinski seemed intent on stoking the coals of hostility. By the end of the year, Castro was convinced that normalization was in all likelihood stalled until Carter's second term.[272] Nevertheless, the Cubans did not give up hope. The release of thousands of political prisoners and the secret dialogue with Washington gave both sides a chance to refine their understanding of the issues separating them and to probe for points of agreement. But the talks produced little in the way of real progress. The informal exchanges that Carlos Rafael Rodríguez characterized as "talking about the conditions for talking" never matured into formal negotiations.[273]

Throughout the secret dialogue, Castro stood on principle. As much as he wanted normal relations with Washington, he was not prepared to sacrifice his global aspirations to achieve it, and he bristled at Washington's expectation that he should have to. Washington would never countenance a Cuban demand that it withdraw troops from Europe as a condition of establishing normal bilateral relations, so why should the United States expect Cuba to withdraw from Africa? While this may have been a defensible position in principle, it ignored the realpolitik of Cuba's role in the global rivalry between the superpowers. Cuban actions in Africa, undertaken in concert with the Soviets and subsidized by them, had real consequences for U.S. interests. Vance and Brzezinski might disagree over how serious a threat such actions posed and what remedy to prescribe, but no U.S. policy maker could ignore them.

Jimmy Carter aspired to be the first post–Cold War president in an era when the Cold War was not quite over. The fragile structure of détente erected by Kissinger buckled under the weight of superpower competition in the Third World, especially Africa. With his foreign policy team divided, Carter oscillated between his hopes for world peace and his fears of Soviet aggression. Vance urged the president to look beyond the "inordinate fear of Communism," toward a brighter post–Cold War future. Brzezinski kept reminding him the Cold War was not yet over.[274]

Looking back, Carter felt he missed an opportunity to cut the Gordian knot of U.S.-Cuban hostility. "It may be that we overemphasized the need for Cuba to make a dramatic break with the Soviet Union in Ethiopia," Carter reflected. "I think in retrospect, knowing what I know since I left the White House, I should have gone ahead and been more flexible in dealing with Cuba and established full diplomatic relations."[275] Defeated for reelection by Ronald Reagan, Carter had no second term, and no second chance to normalize relations.

6. **REAGAN AND BUSH**
Diplomatic Necessity

We are two neighbors who have had abominable relations. And unlike people, we aren't able to move away.

—Ricardo Alarcón, Vice Minister of Foreign Relations

"You just give me the word," Secretary of State Alexander M. Haig told President Ronald Reagan, "and I'll turn that fucking island into a parking lot."[1] In March 1981, just a few weeks after inauguration, Reagan's National Security Council began debating how to respond to the escalating civil war in El Salvador. Haig advocated "going to the source," telling his stunned colleagues they would have to invade Cuba and put an end to the Castro regime. The president seemed tempted, but to Haig's chagrin, no one else was eager to begin the new administration with a foreign war.[2]

Ronald Reagan entered the Oval Office in 1981 considering whether to invade Cuba, but by the time he left eight years later, his administration had negotiated major agreements on migration and southern Africa. The strange odyssey of Reagan's Cuba policy resulted not from a change of heart but from the recognition that the United States and Cuba had mutual interests that could only be advanced by cooperation—even in the midst of ongoing hostility. By the time Reagan's successor, George H. W. Bush took office, however, the crisis of European communism had changed the international landscape dramatically. The collapse of the Soviet Union left Cuba vulnerable, reviving dreams in Washington that had lain dormant since the 1960s—dreams of rolling back the Cuban revolution.

Central America: In Search of a Diplomatic Firebreak

At the outset, Reagan was determined to restore America's global stature by taking the offensive in the Cold War. Urged on by Haig, Reagan declared Central America the place to draw the line against the expansion of Soviet influence in the Third World. He blamed the Soviets, acting through their "proxy" Cuba, for the revolutionary turmoil engulfing Nicaragua, El Salvador, and Guatemala.[3] During the campaign, Reagan called repeatedly for a blockade of Cuba in retaliation for the Soviet invasion of Afghanistan.[4] Now, however, he was dissuaded from endorsing Haig's invasion proposal by other senior officials, who pointed out that the large and well-trained Cuban army could turn the country into another Vietnam. Still, the decision left Reagan frustrated. "Intelligence reports say Castro is very worried about me," he wrote in his diary. "I'm very worried that we can't come up with something to justify his worrying."[5]

The Cubans *were* worried. To avert a U.S. military attack, Havana pursued a two-track policy of strengthening its armed forces while trying to build a diplomatic firebreak against direct U.S. intervention. On the military front, Havana hoped to deter an attack by making certain that the direct cost and the risk of confrontation with the Soviet Union would be so high that policy makers in Washington would recoil at the price.[6]

On the diplomatic front, Cuba sought to defuse regional tension by supporting peace initiatives by Mexico, Venezuela, and others. Fidel Castro advised the Sandinista government in Nicaragua to be flexible in negotiations with Washington and urged the guerrillas in El Salvador to accept a negotiated end to the civil war. Havana also approached Washington directly. The first diplomatic signal came in February 1981. The Cubans reduced their arms shipments to the Salvadoran rebels and told Wayne Smith, chief of the U.S. Interests Section, that they wanted to contribute to a political solution to the conflict. They proposed bilateral discussions toward that end. Smith passed the message to Washington and heard nothing in reply. After a few weeks, he telephoned the State Department's coordinator for Cuban affairs, Myles Frechette. "Myles replied that no one was interested in that sort of approach. . . . He advised me to stop sending such recommendations."[7]

Meanwhile, the Cubans were sending the same message through private channels. In February 1981 columnist Jack Anderson set up a meeting between Bernardo Benes, interlocutor during the Carter administration, and Roger Fontaine, Reagan's new National Security Council director for Latin America. The Cubans, Benes said, were interested in a high-level dialogue. When Haig found out about Fontaine's meeting, he was livid. "We had spent three weeks putting fear into the hearts of the Cubans," he complained. "This diversion undermined the whole effort." Fontaine never followed up with Benes.[8]

Cuba also sent signals through Latin American heads of state. In July 1981 President José López Portillo of Mexico offered to mediate between Havana and Washington. Reagan's cabinet debated the offer but decided to test the Cubans first. Haig sent a message to Castro through Mexican foreign minister Jorge Castañeda Sr., asking Havana to take back the "excludables"— Cuban criminals who had come over on the 1980 Mariel boatlift. Castro told López Portillo that Cuba was willing to discuss the excludables and any other issue. Haig resisted talks as anathema to his strategy of raising Castro's level of anxiety. "There could be no talk about normalization, no relief of the pressure, no conversations on any subject except the return to Havana of the Cuban criminals and the termination of Cuba's interventionism," Haig wrote in his memoirs.[9]

By the fall of 1981, the deteriorating military situation in El Salvador had once again pushed Central America to the top of Reagan's agenda. Haig used the occasion to renew his advocacy for "going to the source."[10] He convinced the Pentagon to draw up plans for a range of military actions, including a full blockade of Cuba and a joint U.S.–Latin American invasion of the island—an old option Haig himself had suggested back in 1963 when, as a young lieutenant colonel, he served on a Pentagon task force on Cuba.[11] The Pentagon's final report outlined a series of escalating sanctions and threats designed both to punish Castro and to frighten him into a less activist foreign policy. In early September the administration tightened visa restrictions on Cuban officials traveling to the United States and announced plans to establish Radio Martí, a propaganda radio station modeled on Radio Free Europe and named after José Martí, the father of Cuban independence. Measures were also taken to tighten the economic embargo.[12]

Wayne Smith was appalled by the direction of U.S. policy. A twenty-year veteran of the Foreign Service, Smith had first served in Cuba during the late 1950s. He had seen it all: the insurrection against Batista, the deterioration of Washington's relations with the brash new revolutionary government, the Bay of Pigs, the missile crisis, and the CIA's secret war. By common agreement, Wayne Smith was the U.S. government's preeminent expert on Cuba. He knew Fidel Castro well enough to realize that threats would not work. Short of a direct military attack, there was nothing Washington could do that had not already been tried. "No matter to what levels we escalate tensions and uncertainty, the Cubans will *not*, as a result of our threats, moderate their behavior," Smith warned Reagan's new assistant secretary of state for Inter-American affairs Thomas O. Enders.[13] Smith was ignored. Knowledgeable though he might be, Smith had been sent to Havana by Jimmy Carter, and he favored improving relations with Cuba. In the Reagan administration, Smith was regarded as soft on Castro.

On October 22, 1981, the Mexican ambassador in Havana called on Smith to recount a conversation in which Castro affirmed Cuba's support for a negotiated settlement in El Salvador. If a ceasefire could be arranged that would assure the security of the guerrillas and their civilian supporters, and if fair elections could be assured, the war could be ended. Just to be sure the message had been received, Vice Minister of Foreign Affairs Ricardo Alarcón visited Smith the same day to repeat it. Smith sent word to Washington but again received no response.[14]

At the North-South Summit held at the Mexican resort of Cancun in October 1981, President López Portillo seized the opportunity to instigate a confidential U.S.-Cuban dialogue. Cuba had been involved in the preparatory meetings for the summit, and Mexican officials had hoped the gathering of world leaders might include a "discreet" meeting between Castro and Reagan. But, according to Mexican diplomat Andrés Rozental, U.S. officials balked when they learned Castro was scheduled to attend. "If Fidel came, Reagan wouldn't," Rozental recalled. López Portillo was forced to call Castro and disinvite him. "Castro understood immediately," Rozental remembers, "and graciously agreed not to make it an issue."[15] Instead, López Portillo invited the Cuban leader to a private presummit meeting on the island of Cozumel. There, the two talked about a potential U.S.-Cuban dialogue. Castro affirmed that he was willing to discuss all outstanding issues with Washington.

At the conclusion of the Cancun summit, during the limousine ride to the airport, López Portillo and Castañeda appealed directly to Reagan to open a dialogue with Havana. López Portillo asked Reagan to return Mexico's favor of disinviting Castro to Cancun by authorizing a U.S. emissary to meet secretly with Cuba's vice president, Carlos Rafael Rodríguez. Reagan readily agreed and directed Haig to undertake the mission.

Haig traveled to Mexico City in late November for his secret meeting with Rodríguez—the highest-level diplomatic meeting between the two countries since 1959. An unmarked car whisked Haig from the U.S. Embassy to Castañeda's spacious suburban home. The Mexican foreign minister introduced the two protagonists to each other in his library and then left them to talk privately. Haig began with a litany of U.S. complaints against Cuba, from its role in Africa to its support for revolutionaries in Central America.[16] "We have come to a crossroads which . . . even by a most modest appraisal, may be described as dangerous," he warned. Cuba's role in Nicaragua and El Salvador was simply "unacceptable intervention" and "a threat to our vital interests." If Cuba would halt such behavior and "turn away" from the Soviet

Union, Washington would normalize relations. If not, the consequences for Cuba would be dire.

Rodríguez replied that Cuba had every right as a sovereign country to assist Nicaragua, as it had assisted Angola and Ethiopia. The United States, he reminded Haig, claimed the right to support Jonas Savimbi's guerrilla war in Angola. "Frankly speaking, we do not understand why the United States, merely because it happens to be, at the present time, one of the most powerful states, can have a right which we, being a small country, do not have." Nevertheless, he reaffirmed Cuba's support for a negotiated settlement in El Salvador. Having normal relations with the United States would be good for Cuba, Rodríguez agreed, but Cubans would not "sacrifice our primary principles" to win Washington's favor. By these, he meant Cuba's sovereignty, its friendship with the Soviet Union, and its solidarity with other Third World nations. Cuba wanted to avoid a confrontation with Washington, "but neither are we afraid of a confrontation."

Haig implored and threatened; Rodríguez remained stoic. "It was not a conversation intended to reach conclusions," Rodríguez said later, "although we each presented our point of view very clearly."[17] They agreed only that the dialogue should continue. Haig suggested that roving Ambassador Vernon Walters travel to Havana for the next round of talks, but he warned that Washington was not interested in talks like those conducted during the Carter administration. "They were nothing but a series of delaying tactics, in order to prevent any progress. And nothing was achieved by that, not a thing," Haig said. "If you are prepared to speak seriously, we are also prepared. But we are in need of a prepared context for discussions and some kind of sign from your side that results will be achieved." Washington wanted actions, not words.

"We are prepared to search for a solution," Rodríguez affirmed.

Both the Mexicans and the Cubans believed a positive step had been taken. "We had accomplished what we wanted—to get them together," recalled Rozental. Face-to-face, the Cubans found Haig to be far more levelheaded, respectful, and reasonable than his vitriolic Cold War rhetoric had led them to expect. In Rodríguez's opinion, shared later with Mexican officials, Haig was "neither crazy nor stupid, but a reasonably intelligent, experienced person with whom conversation was possible." Haig had emphasized the need to make a supreme effort to settle issues through "la via pacífica"—the peaceful road.[18]

Haig, on the other hand, came away from the meeting convinced that U.S. pressure was working. The Cubans were "very anxious" about Washington taking military action against them, he concluded, but they were still not willing to make any significant concessions.[19] Haig missed the point of what Rodríguez said on several key issues. Cuba was willing to support a political settlement in El Salvador based on free elections, nominally the same outcome Washington itself was seeking. To be sure, the process for putting a ceasefire in place, assuring security for all, and actually conducting a free election would have been devilishly difficult, involving more actors than just Havana and Washington. But the two positions were close enough to merit exploration. In Africa, Rodríguez said, Cuba was willing to withdraw its troops from Angola as part of a negotiated settlement linked to Namibian independence. This, too, was consistent with Reagan's policy. Here, too, the details would prove so complex that it would take years to sort them out, but Reagan's assistant secretary of state for Africa, Chester A. Crocker, would eventually prove it could be done, and the Cubans, once brought into the process, would play a constructive role.

Within a month of Haig's meeting with Rodríguez, the Cubans provided the tangible sign of their seriousness that Haig had demanded. Although Rodríguez stoutly defended Cuba's right to aid Nicaragua in the face of Haig's insistence that such aid was "unacceptable," the signal Castro chose to send Washington was to halt arms shipments to the Sandinistas. "What I can say is that all shipments of military equipment from Cuba to Nicaragua have been suspended, and that we hope this improves the atmosphere for negotiations," Carlos Martínez Salsamendi, Rodríguez's chief foreign policy advisor, informed Wayne Smith in December. "We hope that this can lead to something positive."[20]

The Cubans were ready to deal on issues of real concern to Washington. They would not desert their Soviet friends in exchange for trade with the United States, but on the issues that had brought the two countries to the brink of war, the Cubans were signaling their willingness to compromise. Washington never responded to Salsamendi's signal, other than to continue its harsh anti-Cuban rhetoric. "The bottom line," Wayne Smith concluded, "was . . . that we weren't interested in talks and we weren't going to accept this as a gesture."[21]

"Everything Is Negotiable"

Once again, it was the Mexicans who got the diplomatic ball rolling. In a speech on February 21, 1982, President López Portillo offered a peace initiative to loosen the "three knots of tension" in Central America: El Salvador,

Nicaragua, and relations between the United States and Cuba. He repeated the warning, first given to Haig in November, that direct U.S. intervention would be a "gigantic historical error" provoking a "continental convulsion" of anti-Americanism.[22] The Nicaraguans and the Cubans accepted Mexico's proposal immediately. This posed a political problem for Reagan. If the White House dismissed the Mexican initiative too quickly, it would appear uninterested in diplomacy. Yet if Washington entered into negotiations, it would blunt Reagan's effort to forcefully "draw the line" against communism in Central America. "We were cool to the initiative from the beginning," explained one U.S. official, "but we were effectively ambushed by Congress and public opinion. We had to agree to negotiate or appear unreasonable."[23]

There was little likelihood, therefore, that anything positive would come of Ambassador Vernon Walters's trip to Cuba. On March 1, Walters met with Reagan to receive instructions. "He told me he wanted to find out from Castro whether we could stop the military aid he was sending to Nicaragua and the other leftist guerrillas in San Salvador," Walters recalled. Reagan directed him to tell the Cubans that they were "headed inexorably toward confrontation" and that Washington was prepared to use force. But the president also told Walters to hold out an olive branch of possible rapprochement if Cuba was willing meet four "indispensable" U.S. demands:

(a) your organizational, training and logistical support for military movements against organized governments in Central America and Colombia must end;

(b) your security and military assistance to Nicaragua—the advisers and the material—must be withdrawn;

(c) Cuban forces must be withdrawn from Angola; and

(d) you must take back the Cuban criminals unlawfully sent to the U.S. or we will be required to consider other means of returning them to Cuba.[24]

Walters himself was pessimistic about the prospects: "I thought that Castro was a true believer in all that Marxist claptrap." Haig, too, expected that the Cubans would prove inflexible, "but for the record he wanted it known that we had tried."[25]

On the morning of March 4, Walters flew by unmarked Lear Jet to Havana by way of Fort Lauderdale (so as not to attract attention in Miami). He was met at the airport by José Luis Padrón, and after lunch they went immediately to meet Fidel at the presidential palace. (It was an odd reunion. In April 1959, during Fidel's two-week trip to the United States, Walters, then a young military officer and an accomplished linguist, had been assigned as Fidel's translator.) Castro began the meeting by setting the parameters: "I hope we can reach some sort of agreement that will benefit both our countries," he affirmed. "But if you have come here to threaten me, you should know that I have been threatened by every president since Kennedy."

Walters replied that President Reagan had sent him not to threaten Castro but "to see if there is any sort of arrangement that can be reached between us that will put an end to the confrontation that has lasted for a quarter of a century." Washington felt Cuba was endangering its vital interests in Central America by supporting the Salvadoran guerrillas and the Sandinistas, Walters explained, and under such circumstances, "We are prepared to consider all options, without exceptions. Without exceptions."

Cuba would discuss any issue the United States wanted, Castro replied, but he refused in principle to agree to any preconditions. The matter of the Mariel excludables was one that the two sides could resolve. The Central American issues were "more difficult" because they involved other interested parties. Nevertheless, Castro pointed out, Cuba already had suspended military aid to both Nicaragua and the Salvadoran guerrillas and was willing to act constructively in support of López Portillo's plan for negotiations in El Salvador.[26] "Everything is negotiable," Fidel offered.

But they didn't negotiate. On the basis of Haig's meeting with Rodríguez in Mexico, the Cubans expected Walters would come to Havana with an agenda of issues on which the two sides could begin discussions. Walters, however, was not empowered to actually negotiate; his instructions were to simply communicate Washington's position and report back on Castro's response.[27] Walters repeated Haig's litany of complaints about Cuban behavior and told anecdotes about his colorful career as a translator. When Fidel tried to explain Cuba's policy, Walters interrupted to argue with him about Marxist philosophy. "The discussions with Walters were very difficult," recalled Rodríguez. "It was not a complete waste of time. We learned a lot of things about the life of Eisenhower, about DeGaulle and others chiefs of state Walters knew," Rodríguez said wryly. "But we went nowhere."[28]

Walters did not follow up by exploring either the terms under which the excludables might be returned or what the Cubans envisioned as next steps toward diplomatic solutions in Central America. Instead, he simply decided Castro was stalling in hopes of dragging out a dialogue to prevent military action. "Nothing Castro had said at any time during my visit gave me the impression that he was really prepared to negotiate seriously with us," Walters concluded. After just one substantive session with Castro, Walters flew back to Washington and reported to President Reagan. Had Castro given any indication that he was willing to stop aiding Central American revolutionaries, Reagan asked. "I heard nothing that could lead me to this conclusion," Walters replied.[29]

He hadn't listened. Walters went to Havana with a preconceived conviction that Castro's ideological commitment to communism foreclosed any prospect of compromise. When Castro offered compromise, it didn't register with Walters. Even Cuba's suspension of aid to the Sandinistas and the Salvadoran guerrillas was discounted as ephemeral. Wayne Smith believed the Walters visit was "a charade aimed at giving the impression of a willingness to talk where in fact no such willingness existed."[30]

After waiting about a month, the Cubans made one last effort to jumpstart negotiations. Vice President Rodríguez told a visiting group of U.S. foreign policy specialists that Cuba wanted to talk to Washington about reducing tensions in Central America.[31] The region had become the "focal point" of U.S.-Cuban conflict, pulling the two countries toward confrontation, Rodríguez said. "We think that is the first thing to avoid." Cuba was willing to join the United States in exercising "mutual restraint," but talks with U.S. officials had gone nowhere. "We are convinced that an important part of U.S.-Cuban differences emerge from misunderstandings," Rodríguez complained, evidently frustrated that both Haig and Walters had failed to grasp the concessions Cuba offered—or had chosen to ignore them. "To see Fidel Castro as a bomb thrower is unrealistic."

Acknowledging that Cuba had provided "material assistance" to the Salvadoran guerrillas in 1980 and early 1981, Rodríguez insisted that arms shipments had stopped more than a year before and that even military aid to Nicaragua had been suspended. "The United States has said that ending our aid to El Salvador is a prerequisite to normalization. We can affirm that for over a year, all our solidarity with El Salvador has been political solidarity, without any material element." Moreover, the guerrillas were seeking "a progressive democratic system, not socialism," Rodríguez explained. "If we understand this, many options for political solutions are possible."

While Cuba could not and would not negotiate over the heads of its Central American allies, it pledged to abide by any agreement the Central Americans could contrive. "Cuba will accept the solutions reached between the parties," the vice president promised. "Cuba will put an end to its solidarity with the guerrillas, but all sides must do the same." If this cleared the way for normalization of U.S.-Cuban relations, Rodríguez added, "We would impose certain restrictions on the behavior of Cuba," if the United States would do likewise. Rodríguez suggested to the visitors that Havana and Washington should resume discussions about Central America, Africa, and outstanding bilateral issues. "Life has created a need for us to begin discussions," he said philosophically.

All through the Carter years, Cuba had asserted its right and duty to assist its ideological allies. When Washington complained about this international solidarity, Cuba bristled, insisting that its relations with others were none of Washington's business. Now, fearing that Cuba and the United States stood at the brink of open conflict, Havana was offering to take a step back, acknowledging for the first time that Cuba's actions abroad did affect Washington's legitimate interests. If the breach in bilateral relations were healed, Cuba pledged to act with greater restraint in areas of concern to the United States, so long as Washington reciprocated. Perhaps the offer was merely a ploy to defuse the danger of the moment, but it was a stunning concession nonetheless—one the Cubans had never made before.

Shortly after the American delegation's visit, Rodríguez gave Wayne Smith the same message. "We want a peaceful solution in Central America," Rodríguez insisted. "We understand your security concerns and are willing to address them. If you are willing to meet us half way and deal on the basis of mutual respect, there is no reason we cannot at long last begin to put aside the unproductive animosity between us. We are as weary of it as you are."[32]

Haig dismissed the overtures. The Cubans were simply "trying to buy time for the Salvadoran guerrillas," he told the president. "There is basically no give in the Cuban position. . . . If the Cubans really want to accommodate our concerns, they will let us know privately. This is not such a signal."[33] On April 19, 1982, the administration announced new sanctions to punish Cuba for "increasing its support for violence in the hemisphere." It also reimposed restrictions on travel to Cuba that had been lifted by President Carter in 1977, closed down the only commercial air link between Miami and Havana, allowed a fishing agreement signed in the era of détente to lapse, and named Cuba to the official list of terrorist states. In an effort to impede Cuba's exports, the United States also warned its trade partners that they would have to certify that products sold in the United States contained no Cuban nickel.[34]

Over the next few months, the CIA prepared an intelligence assessment reviewing all the various Cuban offers to negotiate. It concluded that the Cubans were not serious. "We believe that Cuba's repeated offers to negotiate on Central America are an effort to buy time and gain a propaganda advantage," the key finding read. "They have not been accompanied by any

MEMORANDUM   2674

NATIONAL SECURITY COUNCIL

April 21, 1982

ACTION

MEMORANDUM FOR WILLIAM P. CLARK

FROM: ROGER W. FONTAINE

SUBJECT: Secretary Haig's Memo to the President
                on Recent Cuban Overtures

Secretary Haig has written the President a memorandum (at Tab A)
analyzing two recent "signals" from the Cubans involving the
possibility of negotiating a breakthrough on U.S.-Cuban relations.
Secretary Haig sees little new in this Cuban ploy and recommends
inferentially no response.

I strongly agree. Havana has played this game so often and so well
that the movements are as timebound in their preciseness as the
Bolshoi version of "Swan Lake." Still, it has the power to persuade
the young, the innocent, and the editorial board of the New York Times.
(Attached at Tab II are the Times and the Post responses to Cuba's
"signals.")

I would only add that a complete and effective answer to Havana's
ploy requires a carefully mounted public response which not only
announces no talks on Havana's terms but why no talks can take place.
We cannot afford for Havana to appear the reasonable side in this
matter.

At Tab I is your memorandum forwarding Secretary Haig's memorandum
to the President.

Recommendations

That you sign your memorandum forwarding Secretary Haig's memo
to the President at Tab I.

        Approve _____✓_____   Disapprove _____

That you approve addressing this topic at an early Core Management
Group Meeting.

        Approve ___✓___   Disapprove _____

Attachments
Tab I   Clark memo to President
         Tab A   Secretary Haig's memo to the President
Tab II   New York Times editorial of April 20, 1982 and Washington
         Post editorial of April 21, 1982.

DECLASSIFIED

Review on April 21, 1988

NLRR M259/5 #82563

BY KML NARA DATE 9/13/11

Memorandum recommending that President Reagan reject Cuba's repeated attempts in
late 1981 and early 1982 to engage the administration in a dialogue on Central America.
Reagan accepted the recommendation. (National Archives and Records Administration)

signs of a willingness to make concessions on the key issue of Havana supplying arms to insurgents." Moreover, support for insurgents abroad was "deeply rooted in the revolution's ideology," the report asserted, and on this "the Castro regime in 23 years has never demonstrated a readiness to compromise." And even if Cuba reduced its support for its Central American allies, that would represent no more than a temporary tactical shift. In conclusion, the report claimed, contacts with Cuba had produced "no credible evidence that Havana is ready to offer any significant concessions either to bring peace in Central America or to defuse its antagonistic relationship with Washington."[35]

The CIA report echoed Haig's and Walters's conclusions from their meetings with Cuban officials, and it suffered from the same preconceptions. Rather than actually test the sincerity of Castro's offer to restrain his actions in Central America, the CIA simply assumed that the "hard-line guerrilla veterans" running Cuba were irrevocably dedicated to "a policy of unyielding hostility toward the United States." Talking to them was pointless.

Straining to explain why they continued to refuse to respond to Cuba's diplomatic feelers, U.S. officials began claiming that they had tried and failed. The Cubans only wanted to talk about bilateral issues, not their role in Central America, a senior official told the press. "Our probing so far hasn't disclosed any change in that pattern," he said. "There isn't any give."[36] That, of course, was quite the opposite of what the Cubans were saying. "The administration simply lied," Wayne Smith wrote later. "It had no evidence that Cuban support for armed violence in Latin America was increasing, nor had the Cubans refused to discuss anything with us. Quite the contrary: the Cubans were willing to hold talks and the U.S. was refusing."[37] Smith was so disgusted at the mendacity of his own government that he turned down an ambassadorial appointment—it would have been his first—and retired from the Foreign Service.

Grenada: Blood on the Runway

In March 1979 Maurice Bishop's socialist New Jewel Movement seized power from the eccentric prime minister Eric Gairy on the tiny Caribbean island of Grenada, the world's foremost producer of nutmeg. By the time Ronald Reagan became president, Grenada was host to several hundred Cubans—doctors, teachers, technicians, two dozen military advisors, and about five hundred construction workers building a new airport that Washington worried could service Soviet bombers or Cuban troop transports on their way to

Africa. "It isn't nutmeg that's at stake in the Caribbean and Central America," President Reagan declared. "It is the United States' national security."[38]

In October 1983 a faction within the New Jewel movement overthrew the government, murdering Bishop and several members of his cabinet. The United States seized upon the disorder as an excuse to invade the island under the pretext of rescuing U.S. students at the medical school there. As an armada of U.S. war ships approached Grenada, Fidel Castro tried to head off the inevitable, sending Washington a message on October 22, that Cubans in Grenada were reporting no civil disorder. The note proposed that the two governments maintain contact to avert violence. To the Cubans in Grenada, Castro sent orders not to initiate combat with U.S. forces in the event of an invasion but to defend Cuban positions if attacked.[39]

Washington also wanted to avoid combat with the Cubans but could not tell Havana until the invasion was under way lest the defenders be forewarned. So Cuba's note went unanswered for three days, until U.S. troops went ashore on the morning of October 25. At 3:00 A.M., John Ferch, the new head of the U.S. Interests Section, received an urgent message from Washington to be delivered to the Cuban Foreign Ministry. "It said, 'We're not attacking you. Tell your troops to lay down their arms. If they stop shooting, they can keep their arms, they can keep their flags, and they can leave with honor,'" Ferch recalled. He delivered the message to Ricardo Alarcón at 8:30 A.M.[40]

Coincidentally, Ferch also had a 10:00 A.M. appointment with José Luis Padrón and delivered the same message to him. Ferch waited as Padrón relayed the message to Fidel Castro over the phone. When the call concluded, a shaken Padrón turned to Ferch: "The *Comandante* said, 'Tell Ferch his information has been overtaken. The Cuban troops have fought to the last man defending the flag. Just ask him to find out when the Yankee invaders will send the bodies back.'" There was not much to say in response to that, Ferch thought.[41]

Events had outrun diplomacy. Fighting between the invasion force and Cuban construction workers at the airport had begun an hour and a half before Ferch delivered Washington's note. Faced with overwhelming U.S. firepower and armed only with light weapons, the Cubans nevertheless put up fierce resistance throughout the day. That evening, Ferch delivered a second message in hopes of ending hostilities: "Cuban personnel stationed in Grenada are not the target of U.S. troop action there," the message read. "The United States is ready to cooperate with Cuban authorities in evacuation of its personnel to Cuba.... The United States does not want to portray the withdrawal [of] Cuban armed personnel as a surrender. Finally, it regrets the armed clashes . . . and considers that they have occurred due [to] confusion and accidents."[42]

A few hours later, Padrón replied that Cuba would cooperate to find "an honorable way to put an end to [the] battle."[43] A ceasefire ended the fighting, and Cuba accepted an offer from Spain and Colombia to mediate repatriation of the 784 Cubans in Grenada, 24 of whom had been killed in the battle, and 57 wounded.[44] At a moment of real crisis, the U.S. Interests Section had proved an invaluable channel of communication between the two governments, facilitating a quick end to the fighting and preventing the conflict from escalating.

Prisoners and Excludables: The Migration Talks

Although Central America dominated the agenda of U.S. relations with Cuba during Reagan's first term, migration issues were a persistent irritant. Cuba and the United States had been stalemated on migration ever since May 1980, when, in the midst of the Mariel boatlift, a government-inspired mob attacked prospective emigrants waiting for visas outside the U.S. Interests Section in Havana. The melee drove more than four hundred people inside the old embassy building, halting normal operations, including the processing of visas for several thousand former prisoners released as a result of negotiations in 1978.

Mariel also created another migration issue. Several thousand Mariel refugees were not eligible for admission to the United States because of serious criminal records. These "excludables" were detained pending their return to Cuba, but they could not be returned unless the Cuban government agreed to take them (notwithstanding Al Haig's proposal to put them on an old ship and anchor them in Havana harbor).[45] Shortly after the Mariel crisis ended, during the final months of the Carter administration, Wayne Smith had opened talks with the Cubans about returning the excludables. During two sessions in December 1980 and early January 1981, U.S. and Cuban negotiators hammered out the essential points of an agreement. Smith felt an accord could have been signed before Ronald Reagan's inauguration but the Cubans delayed. "Perhaps they calculated . . . they could take some of the confrontational wind out of the new administration's sails" by signing the migration agreement with Reagan rather than Carter, Smith thought.[46] If so, they miscalculated.

The new administration had no interest in talking with the Cubans about anything. In February 1981, when Cuba proposed a third round of migration talks, Washington rejected the overture.[47] Nor would Washington allow Smith to resume processing visas for the former prisoners, much to his surprise. "Here were anti-Communist dissidents—people who had opposed Castro and languished in prison because of it—and the previous administration had already said we would bring them to the United States," Smith wrote later. "Surely the Reagan administration would not welch on that promise. But it did."[48] Despite persistent entreaties, Smith was denied permission to resume visa processing because Washington had decided to link the prisoners' visas to the return of the excludables. The Cuban government wanted the former prisoners out of the country, lest they become a focal point for opposition. Getting rid of the prisoners was the only incentive the Cubans had to accept the excludables.[49] This linkage produced a catch-22 that left the former prisoners in limbo. Washington would process their visas only if Cuba agreed to take back the excludables, but return of the excludables could be achieved only by talking with the Cuban government, which Washington was unwilling to do.

George Shultz broke this stalemate after he replaced Haig as secretary of state in 1982. Shultz was more willing to negotiate with adversaries when it served U.S. interests. At the same time, pressure was building in Congress for the United States to keep its word to the former Cuban prisoners.[50] If Congress forced the administration to accept the former prisoners unilaterally, the Cubans would no longer have any incentive to accept the excludables. The only solution, therefore, was to negotiate an agreement with the Cubans on both issues before the Congress decoupled them.

On May 24, 1983, Assistant Secretary Enders summoned Ramón Sánchez-Parodi, the head of the Cuban Interests Section in Washington, to the State Department and handed him a diplomatic note asking Cuba to accept return of the excludables and proposing migration talks. No visas for Cubans to emigrate to the United States would be processed until the excludables were returned, Enders explained.[51] Sánchez-Parodi asked if other issues would also be open for discussion.

"No, sir," Enders replied. The meeting lasted no more than fifteen minutes.[52]

A few weeks later, the Cubans responded cautiously but positively. As a gesture of good faith, they also answered a long-standing U.S. request for information about hijackers who had commandeered U.S. aircraft to Cuba, providing a list of the hijackers and their prison sentences.[53] While the Cuban government certainly had an interest in normalizing migration to the United States, it also hoped successful talks on migration would lead to talks on other issues.[54]

The two governments exchanged another round of diplomatic notes, slowly moving toward talks, but their momentum was interrupted by the U.S. invasion of Grenada in October. As the U.S. presidential election campaign got under way in the spring of 1984, Washington again approached Cuba about starting migration talks, but the Cubans were wary. They had no interest in boosting Ronald Reagan's reelection prospects; they agreed to talk only after November. That stance changed, however, as a result of Democratic presidential candidate Jesse Jackson's trip to Cuba in June.[55]

At the State Department's request, Jackson agreed to ask for the release of Cuban political prisoners and to urge Castro to begin migration talks.[56] In discussions with Jackson, Castro was noncommittal on most foreign policy issues. Jackson, after all, could deliver nothing with regard to U.S. policy. Nevertheless, Jackson won the release of twenty-two U.S. citizens jailed in Cuba, mostly for drug trafficking, and twenty-six Cuban political prisoners. Castro also agreed to resume migration talks before the November election if both Democrats and Republicans promised not to make the talks a campaign issue.[57]

Despite having conveyed the administration's proposal to Castro and gotten a positive response, Jackson was publicly excoriated upon his return. Secretary Shultz and President Reagan both refused to meet with him to hear a report on his conversations with Castro. Shultz called his trip "scandalous" and "disruptive," while the president suggested it was a violation of the Logan Act, prohibiting private citizens from negotiating with foreign governments. "We don't see any basic movement in the Cuban government's position," said State Department spokesman John Hughes, ignoring the offer of migration talks.[58] The administration was nevertheless quick to follow up privately on the opening Jackson created. "Jackson was the catalyst," acknowledged Kenneth Skoug, State's coordinator for Cuban affairs. His trip "unlocked the door to negotiations."[59]

Migration talks convened on July 12, 1984, with the U.S. delegation headed by the State Department's deputy legal advisor Michael Kozak and the Cuban delegation headed by Vice Foreign Minister Ricardo Alarcón. The two teams met at a midtown Manhattan hotel, where the U.S. delegation registered under assumed names so as not to draw attention. Kozak had been part of the U.S. team during the 1980–81 migration talks at the close of the Carter administration, so he was familiar with the issues. Not prone to ideological diatribes, Kozak looked for practical ways to resolve the differences between the two sides. "He was very lawyer-like," Alarcón recalled.[60]

As the senior Cuban official most knowledgeable about the United States, Alarcón would be Castro's principal interlocutor with Washington for the next several decades. Skoug, a member of the U.S. team, remembered him as "a seasoned diplomat and skillful negotiator." Alarcón opened by taking such a tough position that the U.S. diplomats thought they had traveled to New York for nothing. He insisted that Cuba would accept the return of only people held in detention continuously since the Mariel boatlift, not those who had subsequently committed crimes in the United States that made them deportable. He demanded that Washington agree to accept thirty thousand Cuban immigrants annually and return anyone who left Cuba illegally. "The Cuban position on the first day seemed unreasonable, even as an opening gambit," Skoug recalled.[61]

The second day was better. Kozak outlined the U.S. position, explaining that the return of the excludables was a necessary condition for the United States to accept large numbers of former prisoners and their families. The Cubans agreed to accept the expanded U.S. list of excludables "for information purposes" and proposed a second round of talks in Havana. The U.S. delegation countered by proposing New York as the site, and the Cubans agreed. "The two delegations were establishing a rapport," Skoug thought.[62]

Between the two rounds of talks, both sides were busy sending signals. In Havana, Vice President Carlos Rafael Rodríguez told journalist Carl Migdail that Cuba was open to discussions with Washington on a whole range of issues, from migration to Central America.[63] In his annual state of the revolution address on July 26, Castro reiterated his willingness to negotiate. "Just as we are prepared to fight and die," he said, "we are not afraid to participate in talks or discussions." He specifically mentioned both migration and southern Africa.[64]

The Reagan administration responded with tantalizing signals of its own. In an interview, Secretary Shultz said that Washington would test Castro's sincerity in talks on migration, and if results were positive, "perhaps other things can be worked out."[65] A few weeks later, Kenneth Skoug gave a lengthy speech to the Americas Society in New York, in which he roundly criticized the Cuban regime but nevertheless declared Washington's willingness to engage with Cuba "on the basis of equality and mutual respect and to make concessions in order to resolve problems." He held out the possibility of dialogue on issues of mutual interest, including migration, radio interference, and "perhaps other issues of this nature."[66] U.S. officials sought to entice the Cubans into making concessions on migration in hopes that an agreement might be parlayed into broader talks. The Cubans, for their part, imagined that progress on migration would demonstrate their bona fides as responsible diplomatic partners and indefinitely delay the inauguration of propaganda broadcasts by Radio Martí, which had been approved but not yet gone on the air. They also hoped it would open the door to Cuban participation in the ongoing international discussions on southern Africa led by Washington.[67]

The second round of migration talks convened in New York in August, where the two sides reached agreement on the basic outline of an accord. The third round, held November 28 in the Pérez de Cuellar suite at the U.N. Plaza Hotel with its expansive view of the Manhattan skyline, proved decisive. After a week of discussion, several key issues remained unresolved. The Cubans, Alarcón announced, would have to return to Havana for consultations. Kozak, sensing that agreement was close and mindful that any number of external events might derail the talks before the two sides could reconvene, urged Alarcón to call Havana instead. Although it was well after midnight, Alarcón agreed to call Carlos Rafael Rodríguez. At 3:00 A.M., Alarcón awakened Kozak to tell him, "Carlos Rafael agreed with you." The talks continued and two days later, they reached agreement.[68]

After Reagan and Castro approved the final terms, the negotiators reconvened on December 13, at the Roosevelt Hotel to finalize the accord. But before signing, they spent a grueling eighteen hours comparing the names of the excludables on the U.S. and Cuban lists. In the middle of this marathon, a U.S. official read out the name "Nome Hodes," and the Cubans broke up laughing. Apparently, when asked his name by a U.S. immigration officer, one of the detainees replied, "No me jodes," ("Don't fuck with me"), which the U.S. interrogator dutifully recorded.[69] By the time the names had all been read, it was 1:40 A.M., and the State Suite where the delegations were meeting was a mess, littered with overflowing ashtrays and empty coffee cups, smelling of stale cigar and cigarette smoke. Olga Miranda, the legal advisor on the Cuban delegation, and Stephanie van Reigersberg, the translator for the U.S. side, couldn't stand the idea that the final agreement would be signed amid such filth. "Olga and I, the two of us, cleaned the place up," van Reigersberg recalled, "so that the agreement could be signed in a clean and decorous environment."[70]

As Kenneth Skoug later wrote, the migration agreement met "virtually every major U.S. objective." The Cubans agreed to take back 2,746 excludables, and Washington agreed to treat Cuba like any other country with regard to immigration quotas, which meant that up to twenty thousand Cubans annually might qualify. In addition, Washington agreed to accept the former political prisoners and their families who had been waiting since 1980.[71]

"It is important we do what we can to turn back on this road of tension," Alarcón told the press when the agreement was announced. "And to the extent that we can demonstrate that agreement can be reached—at least partially, in at least some aspect—it is a way of affirming the validity of negotiations. . . . We are two neighbors who have had abominable relations. And unlike people, we aren't able to move away."[72]

Castro praised Washington's "positive and constructive" approach and expressed his hope that "the same spirit that characterized these talks" might extend to discussions on other issues.[73] That same night at a diplomatic reception, Castro called aside John Ferch, the head of the U.S. Interests Section, to underscore the point. "I want the American people to know that I have undertaken a commitment," Castro said about the accord. "I am serious about this moral commitment; I want the American people to know. Ferch, tell the American people." Ferch was taken aback by the intensity of Castro's desire to convey his sincerity—and amused at the idea that a U.S. diplomat in Havana could tell the American people anything.[74]

Castro echoed these sentiments in January 1985, in marathon meetings with a congressional delegation. During thirty-seven hours of talks over six days, Castro told the legislators that Cuba would support a negotiated agreement in Central America to end the war in Nicaragua, and a U.S.-brokered agreement in southern Africa leading to Namibian independence. "Clearly Cuba is in a new mood for accommodation," said Congressman Jim Leach (R-Iowa) upon returning from Havana.[75]

Shortly after the congressional trip, Castro gave a five-hour interview to the *Washington Post*, touching many of the same themes. He praised the migration talks as "constructive and positive" and expressed the hope that they would be followed by talks on other bilateral issues such as Coast Guard cooperation, radio interference, hijacking, and fishing rights. He repeated Cuba's pledge to support peace accords in Central America and southern Africa. "I am speaking of a readiness to work, to strive in order to find solutions to the problem," he said.[76]

Washington did not share Cuba's enthusiasm for extending the dialogue into other areas. Just three days after the migration agreement was signed, Skoug gave another major address on Cuba at the Carnegie Endowment in Washington, emphasizing that the talks had been "strictly limited" to migration issues and that there was no basis for a broader improvement in bilateral relations. Such an improvement would require Cuba to meet two conditions: significantly reduce or sever its close ties to the Soviet Union, and halt its support for revolutionary movements and Marxist governments in Africa and Latin America. "However, Havana has made clear that its support for revolution, like the Soviet alliance, is not for negotiation."[77] So there was nothing more to talk about.

The administration's abrupt turnaround from earlier hints that progress on migration might lead to broader talks was intentional. "The speech in Washington deliberately did not mention, as did the one in New York in June, other possible areas of agreement between us," Skoug acknowledged. Having pocketed Cuba's concessions on migration, "Senior officials in the Reagan administration had no desire to move quickly to new areas of negotiation with Cuba." The White House's public response to Castro's overtures was dismissive. "We've heard this before," Reagan said. "Early in my administration there were signals sent of this kind, and we took them up on it. And we have tried to have some meetings with them, and nothing came of it. Their words are never backed by deeds."[78]

In February 1985 Skoug traveled to Cuba to discuss implementation of the migration agreement and had a series of meetings with senior Cuban officials, including Alarcón, José Antonio Arbesú, José Luis Padrón, and Fidel himself—Castro's first meeting with a U.S. official since Vernon Walters's visit in 1982. The Cubans proposed additional bilateral talks, and reemphasized Castro's public declarations that they would be willing to cooperate on reaching negotiated settlements in Central America and southern Africa. Skoug begged off any discussion of Central America or Africa on the grounds that he had no instructions. On bilateral issues he was noncommittal. Upon returning to Washington, he reported to Secretary Shultz and National Security Advisor Robert C. McFarlane that the Cubans had shown "no intention to alter Havana's basic approach to foreign policy."[79]

At the U.S. Interests Section in Havana, John Ferch responded more proactively to the Cuban signals. On his own initiative, he inquired whether the Cubans were serious about discussing a range of bilateral issues, and they replied affirmatively. When Ferch reported this exchange to Washington, Skoug opposed pursuing it. But senior State Department officials were not quite so closed-minded. Under Secretary for Political Affairs Michael Armacost and Secretary Shultz both concluded that negotiations on a limited number of bilateral issues might be fruitful. Ferch, who was due to rotate out as chief of mission, was instructed to suggest specific issues for discussion during his anticipated protocol departure meeting with Castro and was sent a memorandum to pass along to Padrón. Washington proposed that the two sides hold a review session on the implementation of the migration accord in June, which would afford an opportunity to begin exploring other issues.[80]

Before either of these meetings could occur, however, the diplomatic apple-cart was overturned by Radio Martí.

Back to Square One

Proposed originally by Reagan in 1981, Radio Martí had encountered significant congressional opposition for fear that Cuba would retaliate with high powered radio transmissions of its own, causing widespread interference with U.S. commercial stations. "We are going to broadcast back," Castro promised. "I think the Americans are going to be listening to a lot of Cuban music."[81] Concerns about Cuban broadcasts delayed legislation for Radio Martí until late 1983, and the launch was delayed further while the administration tried to craft a response to the anticipated Cuban reaction. "We're ready to go with Radio Martí," Reagan wrote in his diary in December 1984. "Cuba, however, threatens retaliation . . . jamming American radio stations all the way to the Midwest. . . . What to do? Right now, I don't know."[82]

On the diplomatic front, the State Department had been trying to smooth the way for Radio Martí by telling the Cubans not to overreact. After all, it was just a Cuban service of the Voice of America, they pointed out, and VOA had been broadcasting to Cuba for years. But the Cubans understood perfectly well that Radio Martí was designed with subversive intent, and naming it after José Martí, the hero of Cuban independence, added insult to injury.[83]

Castro thought that his concessions on the migration agreement and willingness to discuss other issues would lead Washington to shelve plans for the radio.[84] But Radio Martí was as much a product of domestic politics as of foreign policy. The station was the top priority of the newly formed Cuban American National Foundation (CANF), a lobbying group of wealthy Miami exiles created to assure that no U.S. president would make concessions to Castro's Cuba. During the 1980s and 1990s, it would become the most powerful domestic political voice on U.S.-Cuban relations, dominating the policy discourse, punishing its foes, and rewarding its friends with campaign contributions. Urged onward by CANF's founder and chairman Jorge Mas Canosa, Reagan decided on May 17, 1985, that Radio Martí should begin broadcasting forthwith.[85] It went on the air three days later, May 20, 1985, Cuba's Independence Day.

Havana's reaction was predictably angry. Castro was said to be personally insulted that the United States had launched the propaganda broadcasts despite his repeated overtures for better relations.[86] Instead of retaliating with radio broadcasts of his own, however, Castro canceled the migration agreement and halted Cuban American visits to the island. "No one in Washington had expected Cuba's response," Skoug admitted. "The Cubans had outsmarted us." Cuba also canceled the June meeting to review implementation of the migration accord, Ferch was disinvited from his farewell meeting with Castro, and couldn't even get Padrón to return his calls.[87] The agreement, which had taken over two years to negotiate, lasted just four months.

The public tone of relations turned poisonous as well. On May 29, just over a week after Radio Martí began broadcasting, Castro condemned U.S. policy in southern Africa, calling Reagan a liar and the United States an ally of apartheid. A few weeks later, Reagan railed against Cuba as part of a "new, international version of Murder, Incorporated." Cuba, Nicaragua, and others were terrorist states "engaged in acts of war" against the United States, he said. "We're not going to tolerate these attacks from outlaw states run by the strangest collection of misfits, loony tunes, and squalid criminals since the advent of the Third Reich."[88]

Not to be rhetorically outgunned, Fidel excoriated Reagan as "a madman, an imbecile and a bum . . . the worst terrorist in the history of mankind." Disappointed and perplexed at the sudden turn for the worse, the Cubans gave up hope of any bilateral improvement during Reagan's presidency. "This is definitely one of the worst moments in our relations," lamented a senior Cuban official.[89]

In May 1986, however, Washington received an indirect hint, through the Soviet Union, that the Cubans were rethinking their position on Radio Martí and the immigration accord. During a "regional consultation" on Latin America, Skoug asked Soviet diplomat Vladimir Kazimirov why the Cubans had suspended the migration agreement, which served their interests as well as Washington's. Kazimirov replied that the Cubans realized they might have acted in haste.[90]

Within days, Washington had an opportunity to take Havana's temperature on renewing the migration agreement. Gregory Craig, foreign policy aide to Senator Edward Kennedy (D-Mass.), was slated to travel to Cuba to accompany a released political prisoner to the United States. At the State Department's behest, Craig urged the Cubans to restore the migration accord. Castro responded with a proposal: Radio Martí would cease to be an obstacle if Cuba was granted an equivalent right to broadcast to the United States. Although the practical difficulties involved were enormous, Washington had previously told Havana it was not averse to the principle of equal access. Shultz took the Cuban proposal as a signal and proposed a negotiating session. The Cubans accepted.[91]

Convening at Cuba's embassy in Mexico City, the July 7–9, 1986, talks brought together the same principals who forged the migration agreement in the first place: Kozak and Skoug leading the U.S. side; Alarcón and Arbesú leading the Cubans. Each side had overestimated the other's need for success, however. "The U.S. delegation came to Mexico City believing Cuba wanted face-saving egress from a mutual dilemma," Skoug wrote of the meeting. "The Cubans came believing that the United States government, under siege from Cuban émigrés in Miami and desperate to rid itself of the Mariel criminals, might be ready (and able) to grant Cuba substantial concessions in broadcasting."[92] To the Cubans, equal radio access meant the ability to broadcast to the same percentage of the population in the United States that Radio Martí could reach in Cuba. Technically, that would have required forcing many U.S. broadcasters off the air, which the U.S. team was unwilling to countenance. In short order, the talks deadlocked and ended with no plans for further sessions. Another year would pass before the two sides returned to the bargaining table.

A difficult year it was. Washington launched the first of what would become an annual campaign in Geneva to have Cuba condemned by the UN Human Rights Commission for its treatment of political dissidents. In December 1986 a rare overflight of Cuban territory by an SR-71 reconnaissance aircraft prompted several days of massive demonstrations outside the U.S. Interests Section, following which Cuba prohibited cargo supply flights to the diplomatic post.[93] In February 1987 the head of the U.S. Interests Section, Curtis W. Kamman, was reassigned and not replaced for several months. In July the crisis culminated with Cuban charges that dozens of U.S. diplomats had engaged in spying—an accusation backed by hours of videotape of the diplomats dropping messages for their Cuban contacts, many of whom turned out to be double agents. "Our relations have dipped lower than what we thought could be the lowest point," Alarcón told Washington Post reporter Julia Preston.[94] For a time, it seemed as if the Interests Sections—the last vestige of President Carter's improvement in bilateral relations—might be closed. In reality, though, neither side wanted to lose these important listening posts. A series of meetings in Washington and Havana eventually led to a resolution of the supply flights problem.[95]

In September 1987, as temperatures cooled, the Cubans offered an olive branch of sorts. Alarcón informed John J. "Jay" Taylor, the new head of the U.S. Interests Section, that he would be willing to meet in Havana with Kozak "and anyone Kozak wants to bring along" to discuss a range of bilateral issues, including radio broadcasting. "Cuba does not wish to be like the bad neighbor who in an apartment building turns up his radio late at night and wakes everyone," Alarcón explained. Washington replied that talks would have to be in New York or on neutral ground, and the agenda would have to be the same as Mexico City in 1986—migration and radio issues. The Cubans agreed, and talks were set for November 4, 1987, in Montreal.[96]

As luck would have it, the flight carrying the Cuban delegation to Montreal was forced to make an unscheduled stop in New York, where the U.S. Immigration and Naturalization Service detained the Cubans for illegal entry and formally deported them. Such undiplomatic behavior might well have scuttled the talks before they began. That the Cubans took this misadventure with good humor boded well. After some preliminaries, Alarcón went straight to the point, suggesting a way to break the deadlock. Rather than hold the migration accord hostage to resolution of the radio broadcasting issue, why not restore the migration accord and simply agree to continue talking about radio issues. The U.S. side was taken aback. "This was in a few words the solution to the long struggle over the Migration Agreement," Skoug reflected. Kozak drafted the appropriate language for a new agreement, Alarcón edited it slightly, and the two teams took the draft back to their governments for approval.[97]

On November 19, the U.S. and Cuban delegations convened once again in Mexico City to formally sign the new accord. Arriving late at the U.S. ambassador's residence, the Cubans found the U.S. diplomats relaxing in the living room, with a fire in the fireplace and piano music in the background. Taking in the idyllic tableau, Alarcón quipped, "I feel like dropping concessions all around."[98] In truth, he had already dropped the big one in Montreal. The Cubans had accepted the U.S. position on migration with no tangible concession on radio broadcasting other than to discuss it further. In the end, as both sides must have surmised, further discussions produced no progress at all.

Cuba's willingness to give up the linkage between radio broadcasting and migration, thereby surrendering what leverage the migration accord gave them, had several sources. First, the migration accord was in Cuba's interest, not only because it enabled Castro to export former political prisoners to the United States but because it regularized normal migration and thereby reduced the pressure for socially disruptive and politically embarrassing bursts of illegal migration like Camarioca and Mariel. Second, Radio Martí had proved to be more annoyance than threat. Suspending the migration agreement had been an "angry reaction," a Cuban diplomat told the *New York Times* shortly before the migration talks resumed. "We are now more flexible in the way we see Radio Martí." Most importantly, however, another issue had risen to the top of both the Cuban and the U.S. agendas, overshadowing migration and radio broadcasting—southern Africa.[99]

Constructive Engagement, from Cape Town to Havana

In 1981, Ronald Reagan's policy toward southern Africa, like his policy toward Central America, focused on the East-West dimension of the conflict. He replaced Carter's policy of ostracizing South Africa with "constructive engagement." Secretary Haig described the policy as intended to "establish a new relationship with South Africa based on a realistic appraisal of our mutual interests in the southern African region," which he summarized as reducing Soviet influence by getting the Cubans out of Angola.[100]

To that end, Assistant Secretary of State for African Affairs Chester A. Crocker's strategy was to undertake an elaborate, multiplayer diplomatic process aimed at producing a quid pro quo: South Africa would comply with UN Resolution 435 by withdrawing from Namibia (Southwest Africa) and accepting the territory's independence, in exchange for the total withdrawal of Cuban troops from Angola. The negotiations Crocker hoped to broker were extraordinarily complex, involving not only the actors onstage—South Africa and Angola—but also those behind the scenes: Cuba, the Soviet Union, Namibia's independence movement (the Southwest African People's Organization, SWAPO), pro-Western guerrillas in Angola (Jonas Savimbi's Union for the Total Independence of Angola, UNITA), and the African "front line states" bordering South Africa (Botswana, Mozambique, Tanzania, Zambia, and Zimbabwe).

Yet despite the daunting nature of the task, Crocker's vision had a certain logic. The South Africans refused to get out of Namibia on the grounds that they needed a buffer between them and Cuban troops in Angola. The Angolans refused to send the Cubans home because they needed them to fend off the South African army on their southern border. A process linking Namibian independence to Cuban withdrawal would meet the nominal security concerns of both sides.[101]

By July 1981, Haig had extracted from South Africa an agreement in principle that it would implement Resolution 435 if the Cubans withdrew from Angola. Washington's engagement with Angola was less constructive. At first, the Angolans reacted badly to Crocker's linkage idea, seeing it as a threat to their security and a retreat from the UN commitment to unconditional independence for Namibia. A joint communiqué from Angola and

Cuba in February 1982 declared that the Cuban presence in Angola was a "bilateral matter between two sovereign states" and that a gradual drawdown of Cuban troops would commence only *after* Namibian independence. However, the Angolans did not close the door to further consultations with Washington, and gradually their position evolved. By April 1983, the Angolans had agreed that Cuban troop withdrawal could, in fact, be timed to specific benchmarks in the Namibian independence process.[102]

With this opening, Crocker thought the time had come to speak directly with Cuba. "There had been no contact with the Cubans since Dick Walters's tête-à-tête with Castro 18 months earlier," Crocker recalled. "The absence of such contact meant that we were flying partially blind."[103] Nothing came of the suggestion, however. Secretary Shultz, a stalwart supporter of Crocker's efforts, was in eclipse in mid-1983. Control over foreign policy had migrated temporarily to hard-liners in the NSC staff under National Security Advisor William P. Clark, who thought that talking to Cuba about Africa legitimized its presence there.

In 1984, as the pace of diplomacy quickened, the Cubans began signaling to Washington their desire to become involved directly. On February 22 the Cuban newspaper *Granma* ran an article characterizing the U.S. mediation effort as constructive—a sharp departure from Havana's usual polemics. "It was clear to me that this was a signal," John Ferch at the U.S. Interests Section recalled. He relayed the news to Washington.[104] A few weeks later, discussing Cuban troops in Angola with the *Washington Post*, Vice President Carlos Rafael Rodríguez said, "We have never envisioned an over-long presence of our forces. We are prepared for the moment when it is necessary and appropriate to begin the process of withdrawal."[105]

On April 17 Castro sent a message to the U.S. Interests Section proposing that Cuba and the United States maintain contact "for the purpose of exchanging views, perceptions, and information that could contribute to the peaceful solution of conflicts in the area." Washington responded immediately that "Assistant Secretary Crocker has considered it very important to maintain communication with Cuba on this problem." A few weeks later, in response to another Cuban diplomatic note, Washington suggested that if Cuba wished to elaborate its thinking on southern Africa, perhaps José Luis Padrón might serve as interlocutor.[106]

Shortly thereafter, in July 1984, Padrón contacted Ferch to probe the details of how Washington envisioned a southern African settlement. Padrón affirmed that Cuba expected to withdraw its troops from Angola in the context of a regional accord and suggested that Havana and Washington hold direct bilateral discussions to help move the peace process forward. "Clearly they wanted to have a dialogue," Ferch recalled. "They wanted to be part of the negotiations that Crocker had initiated."[107]

Washington still opposed giving the Cubans a seat at the table but hinted that a cooperative attitude from Havana would be rewarded in unspecified ways. Rather than opening a formal dialogue, the State Department proposed a "periodic exchange of views" about the talks through the Interests Section. Behind the scenes, the Cubans were trying to be constructive. In October 1984 the diplomatic process took a major step forward when the Angolans gave Washington a new proposal, crafted jointly with Cuba, outlining a timetable for Cuban troop withdrawal based on the implementation of Resolution 435. "This version had Cuban fingerprints all over it," Crocker recalled. It was not a proposal South Africa would accept, but it was a point of departure for the tough negotiations to come.[108]

In December the Angolans proposed that Cuba be brought into the talks. Once again Washington refused. The negotiation was already tremendously complex, and adding Cuba risked adding complications from the always-volatile U.S.-Cuban bilateral relationship. Moreover, the domestic politics of opening a dialogue with Cuba were still not fortuitous. Hard-line Republicans wanted Washington to embrace South Africa and UNITA without reservation, overthrow the Angolan government, and drive the Cuban expeditionary force into the sea.[109] To these partisans, negotiations with any outpost of the evil empire was tantamount to appeasement. "It was difficult enough sustaining our Africa policies in Washington," Crocker wrote, "without the added burden of having to meet some Cuban demand or to explain why we had 'legitimized' Castro's African policies." In retrospect, though, Crocker wondered if stonewalling Cuba in 1984 was a mistake: "A case can be made that we missed an important opportunity," he wrote later.[110]

Had the Cubans been more directly vested in the outcome of the diplomatic process, perhaps it would not have collapsed so disastrously in 1985. In quick succession, South Africa announced it would establish a government of its own choosing in Namibia, South African commandos were captured trying to sabotage Gulf Oil installations in Angola's Cabinda province, and the South African government responded to political unrest in its own townships with intensified repression. These events prompted the adoption of U.S. economic sanctions, which ruptured Washington's dialogue with Pretoria. In mid-1985, hard-liners in the Reagan administration won congressional repeal of the Clark Amendment that had prohibited CIA covert aid to UNITA, which ruptured Washington's dialogue with Angola.[111]

Coincidentally, relations with Cuba were soured by the advent of Radio Martí. Between February and May 1985, Castro went from calling Crocker's diplomacy "a positive influence" and offering Cuban cooperation to charging Washington with being an ally of South African apartheid unfit to mediate the region's conflicts.[112]

Crocker's negotiations remained stalled for two years. Then, on the eve of a visit to Havana by Angolan president Eduardo dos Santos in late July 1987, Castro sent a private inquiry to Washington through Peggy Dulaney, the daughter of international banker David Rockefeller. "I didn't want to use the Interests Section channel because I wanted to do this very discreetly," Castro explained to dos Santos, according to the declassified transcript of their summit meeting. "If you send something through the Interests Section, a month or two can go by without any response."

Cuba was prepared to facilitate a negotiated settlement in southern Africa but wanted a place at the bargaining table, since any accord involving Cuban withdrawal obviously had an impact on Cuban interests. "Cuba is ready to search for just political solutions to this problem," Fidel asserted in his verbal message, carried by Dulaney, "but we need the United States to respond concretely to a question: Will the US government accept Cuban participation along with Angola in the conversations taking place to search for solutions to the problem of southern Africa?" Dulaney conveyed the message in a meeting with National Security Advisor Frank Carlucci, Crocker, and several other officials. They responded positively, she reported back to Fidel. Crocker claimed that Cuban participation was up to the Angolans—a position that both Castro and dos Santos took as a good omen.[113] At the close of the Castro–dos Santos summit, the leaders issued a communique calling for the resumption of negotiations on Cuban withdrawal, and the Angolans followed up with a note to Washington demanding that Cuban negotiators be included.[114]

Castro's proposal set off a six-month battle inside the Reagan administration over whether to let the Cubans into the negotiating process.[115] Assistant Secretary for Inter-American Affairs Elliott Abrams resisted Cuban participation fiercely. "Aside from the fact that I have seen no evidence to subscribe to the notion that Cuban participation would be helpful on the substance of the negotiations," Abrams wrote to Jay Taylor at the U.S. Interests Section, "we have absolutely no desire to contribute to the enhancement of Cuba's stature by recognizing the role they have carved out for themselves by their military intervention in Africa."[116]

Over the ensuing months, Washington was pressured from several directions on the Cuba issue. The Angolans raised it in talks with Crocker in July and again in September. "The withdrawal of Cuban troops cannot be discussed without the participation of the sovereign state that sent these troops," Angolan foreign minister Afonso Van-Dúnem M'Binda insisted. "We are convinced that their participation will contribute in a constructive manner. . . . The moment has arrived to include Cuba in our discussions."[117] Soviet foreign minister Eduard Shevardnadze raised it with Shultz before the December 1987 summit between Reagan and Mikhail Gorbachev. In working-level meetings leading to the summit, the Soviets reiterated that the Cubans would accept total withdrawal as part of an agreement, but they needed to participate in the settlement.[118] The Cubans, too, kept pressing. In September, when Alarcón accepted a U.S. proposal that the two sides meet on migration and radio issues, he added that the Cubans would also like to have an "informal" dialogue about several other issues, including Angola. In Havana, Jay Taylor was not sure whether the Cubans were truly willing to contribute constructively to the southern Africa mediation, but he knew the Angolans would never accept an agreement the Cubans opposed. "Cuban cooperation, I believe, will be necessary not just in physically withdrawing its troops, but in deciding on the terms," Taylor advised Washington.[119]

Moreover, Taylor believed that the dramatic changes under way in the Soviet Union under Mikhail Gorbachev and the warming relationship between the two superpowers had convinced Castro to seek better relations with Washington. "The most important factor that impels Castro to favor a settlement in Angola is Castro's desire to normalize relations with the United States and his recognition that a settlement of the Angolan/CTW [Cuban Total Withdrawal] issue is a prerequisite," Taylor cabled Washington. "If he can withdraw honorably from Angola, he would do so, at least in part with the expectation that this could improve the prospects for a turn-around with the United States." Taylor concluded that there was "nothing to lose" by engaging in informal talks, as Alarcón had suggested.[120]

Abrams remained unconvinced. He wrote back blasting the Cubans for proposing "a grab bag of issues of interest to Cuba, to be discussed on Cuban terrain, as if we were suing for peace." Abrams feared the Cubans would somehow use the occasion of bilateral talks with Washington about Angola to some unspecified but perverse political advantage.[121] Nor was Taylor himself spared from Abrams's diatribe. Having just recently arrived in Havana to replace John Ferch, Taylor was not competent to judge Cuba's motives, Abrams upbraided him.[122]

Notwithstanding Abrams's fear that Cuba would sabotage the talks to spite Washington, the Cubans had good reasons to promote a settlement. Havana's self-interest mandated an honorable exit strategy from a war that had gone on far longer than expected. Moscow, Cuba's quartermaster in Africa, was trying to extricate itself from regional conflicts. Without Soviet logistical support, the Cuban military presence in Angola would be unsustainable anyway. And a settlement that assured both Namibian independence and the elimination of South African troops on Angola's border achieved the principal security aims for which Cuba had deployed troops in the first place. "We are . . . trying to join this international detente," Castro told his aides during a November 1987 review of Angola policy, as reported in a declassified transcript of the meeting. "We are trying because we, too, want to enjoy peace."[123]

The Africa bureau at State had no particular love for the Cubans, but it saw them as too influential to exclude. "Nobody liked the Cubans. Nobody trusted the Cubans. Nobody wanted to negotiate with them," recalled Larry Napper, one of Crocker's deputies "But we—the people in the Africa bureau involved with the negotiations—believed it was essential that the Cubans participate, because the Angolans were completely dependent on them."[124] At Crocker's insistence, Michael Kozak and Kenneth Skoug were finally authorized to speak with the Cubans about Angola during the Montreal migration talks, but strictly and only "informally" and "on the side"—that is, apart from the formal agenda.[125] Alarcón complained to them that Washington appeared to have decided to shut Cuba out of the southern Africa mediation. This was a mistake, he argued, because Cuba was interested in finding an honorable withdrawal, but only if given a place at the table.[126] Back in Havana, Alarcón made the same argument to Taylor over lunch at the U.S. residence. "Clearly, if the issue is Cuban troop withdrawal, Cuba must be involved," Alarcón reasoned. The lack of a civil dialogue with Washington on this important issue was "regrettable."

"I told him that once the Mariel agreement was restored, a discussion of broader differences would be possible," Taylor reported to Washington. "He noted that this point had been made in Montreal." With the Cuban concession on migration, Alarcón had expected Washington to reciprocate with movement on Angola. Taylor was impressed by Alarcón's straightforward avowal that Cuba would act constructively in southern Africa if given the opportunity.[127]

In Washington, the battle between Abrams and Crocker was heating up, fueled in part by Jay Taylor. Taylor had discovered that Abrams was not sharing Taylor's reporting on the Cuban attitude toward southern Africa with the State Department's Africa bureau. To Taylor, this was highly unprofessional. As it happened, Taylor had served in China with Chas Freeman, Crocker's principal deputy, who he now contacted directly. Armed with Taylor's reports, Freeman and Crocker were able to convince George Shultz that it was time to bring the Cubans into the game.[128]

On Christmas Day 1987, Taylor received instructions to meet with Jorge Risquet, a member of the Communist Party's Political Bureau and the senior official overseeing Cuban policy toward Africa. Taylor met in Risquet's office with Risquet and José Antonio Arbesú, a veteran of the 1978 talks between Cuba and the Carter administration. According to Risquet's declassified memorandum of the conversation, Taylor began by reading from an aide-mémoire that was not very conciliatory in tone, accusing Cuba of having "done nothing to contribute to achieving a settlement" and making matters worse by reinforcing its troops. "What are your intentions in Angola?" Taylor asked. "Is it Cuba's intention to facilitate or obstruct . . . a concrete and comprehensive schedule for the withdrawal of all Cuban forces?"

Risquet complained that Cuba still had not received a concrete answer as to whether the United States would agree to Cuban participation in the negotiations—a question raised during the migration talks in Montreal and Mexico City, and raised again in the message carried by Peggy Dulaney. In responding to the Dulaney message, the United States had suggested that Cuba could participate if Angola requested it, but the Angolans had requested it, and still the United States would not give a definitive answer.

"We are part of this conflict. We have the right to participate in these negotiations," Risquet declared. "We affirm once again that Cuba, like Angola, is disposed to negotiate seriously with the United States to find a solution." Cuba would not complicate the agenda, Risquet pledged. "The U.S. government fears that we will use these negotiations to raise issues about our bilateral differences. We assure you that is not our intention."

Signaling a major change in U.S. policy, Taylor replied, "We do not rule out the participation of Cuba in the conversations."[129]

The dialogue on Africa resumed on January 11, 1988, when Kozak, Skoug, Alarcón, and Arbesú met again in Mexico to review progress implementing the migration accord. To entice the Cubans into cooperating on Angola, the U.S. side held out a carrot: an accord on Angola "would contribute to improved U.S.-Cuban relations," the Cubans were told.[130] Over the ensuing months, the bilateral "conversations"—not "negotiations"—on Angola continued between Taylor, Risquet, and Alarcón, but the main arena of diplomacy became the multiparty talks. Shortly after the Mexico City meeting, the United States agreed to allow the Angolans to add a Cuban contingent to their negotiating team.

The first direct Cuban participation came on January 29, 1988, in Luanda, with Risquet leading the Cubans. Their participation produced quick results: for the first time, Cuba and Angola agreed in principle to *complete* rather than partial Cuban troop withdrawal. A second round of talks in March produced a Cuban-Angolan proposed timetable for withdrawal. Stretching over four years, it was too long, but it was a start.[131] Over the next nine months, diplomats from the three countries would meet twelve times with U.S. mediators, gradually hammering out a timetable for carrying out the Namibian track and the Angolan track simultaneously.[132]

In July 1988 Carlos Aldana Escalante joined the Cuban delegation. Aldana, also a member of the Communist Party's Political Bureau, was chief of ideological affairs and international relations for the party. Crocker had complained to the Angolans and Soviets that Risquet was too ideological and confrontational. Aldana, on the other hand, proved conciliatory and purposeful. A moderate reformer within the Cuban leadership who, by his own admission, found Gorbachev's reforms attractive, Aldana believed that Cuba's interests would best be served by repairing relations with the United States. As the Soviets disengaged from Third World conflicts and improved relations with Washington, Cuba would be wise not to get caught in the middle between the superpowers.[133]

"In one conversation over lunch, Aldana offered me an eloquent description of how much Cuba would gain from an honorable end to the conflicts in Southern Africa," Crocker recalled. He urged the Cuban to tell this to the South Africans, who still doubted Cuba's bona fides. "He went to the table and made a presentation which South African officials were still talking about three years later." Aldana argued that nothing could be more honorable for Cuba than withdrawal, "of our own free will and in the context of Resolution 435, so that a new nation is born." He called for a "peace without losers" in which each nation made a positive contribution to reaching accord. It was, Crocker thought, "a virtuoso performance" that changed the tenor of the talks.[134]

As one round of talks followed another, Crocker's respect for Cuban diplomacy grew. "To discover what the Cubans think is an art form," he cabled Secretary Shultz. "They are prepared for war as much as they are for peace. . . . We are witnesses to a great tactical virtuosity and a true creativity at the negotiation table."[135] Crocker soon realized that the Cuban position was being closely monitored and directed by Fidel Castro himself. Cuban technicians recorded every session for transmittal to Havana, and the Cuban delegation insisted on meeting only in locales where they had an embassy with secure communications. "Castro had the clearest strategy of any of the parties," and his determination to get an agreement "pulled [the Angolans] along in his wake," Crocker wrote. The Cubans were open to a much shorter time line for withdrawal than the Angolans, who feared for their security once the Cubans departed. "We might still be at the table today were it not for the Cuban factor," Crocker concluded.[136]

The final breakthrough came in round ten, in Geneva, in November 1988, just after George H. W. Bush's victory in the U.S. presidential election. Knowing that U.S. policy would soon come under review by a new administration and that diplomatic personnel would inevitably change, the parties had an incentive to finish their work before inauguration day. As the round opened, the South Africans proposed Cuban withdrawal over twenty-four months; the Cubans and Angolans held out for thirty. They agreed to split the difference at twenty-seven months, and the deal was done.[137]

On December 22, 1988, representatives of the four nations gathered at UN headquarters in New York to formally sign the three-party accord and a separate side agreement between Cuba and Angola spelling out the details of the Cuban withdrawal. Secretary of State Shultz praised the accord as a "momentous turning point in the history of southern Africa," but the discourse went downhill from there. Angolan Foreign Minister Afonso Van-Dúnem demanded an end to "foreign meddling in Angola's internal affairs," a reference to Washington's continued covert aid to Jonas Savimbi's guerrillas. Cuban foreign minister Isidoro Malmierca blasted the United States and South Africa for "causing enormous destruction and tens of thousands of deaths" in Angola. South African foreign minister Pik Botha shot back that he'd be happy to debate the relative merits of South Africa's and Cuba's human rights records. A surprised Secretary Shultz responded to Malmierca, adding that under the circumstances, it was "miraculous" that there was any agreement at all. In an aside to Crocker, Shultz added, "That's some bunch of characters you've been working with."[138]

George H. W. Bush and Castro's "Final Hours"

Fidel Castro expected that Cuba's cooperation on southern Africa would lead to better relations with Washington, just as U.S. diplomats had promised.[139] In Havana, Jay Taylor assumed George H. W. Bush's new administration would make good on that commitment. When the multiparty talks produced an agreement, Taylor began planning for an expanded bilateral dialogue. "I wrote a thought piece suggesting options on how we might follow up on our commitment to the Cubans that, if they cooperated in a positive outcome on Angola, this would result in improved U.S.-Cuban relations." He recommended discussing cooperation in areas of mutual interest such as migration and narcotics control and making some modest changes in the embargo, "letting it be known to the Cubans that this was the beginning step, that if there were more changes in Cuban behavior on Central America and human rights, then other things would follow."[140]

Taylor was stunned when Michael Kozak, now deputy assistant secretary of state for Latin America, replied that Washington had made no such commitment. "I got a cable from Mike . . . quite a strong cable. It was a zinger saying that I didn't know what I was talking about, and we never made any commitment to the Cubans about improving relations." To jog Kozak's memory, Taylor sent him the numbers of the cables describing the commitment, with the talking points that Secretary Shultz had approved and that Kozak himself had presented to the Cubans in Mexico City a year before. "I heard nothing further on the subject from him," Taylor recalled. "Needless to say, no consideration was given to following up our pledge. . . . I wondered what our reactions would have been if Castro had blatantly turned his back on a commitment made to us."[141]

In March 1989, just two months after inauguration, Secretary of State James Baker sent a confidential cable to all U.S. diplomatic posts explaining that the Bush administration would not improve relations with Havana, despite Cuba's withdrawal from Angola, "because Cuban behavior has not changed sufficiently to warrant a change in U.S. attitudes."[142]

"They saw Cuba's actions on the Angolan peace process . . . as a retreat which signified weakness," Taylor said of senior Bush officials. "Consequently, in their mind, the U.S. goal continued to be to isolate and weaken Castro as much as possible."[143]

Despite this refusal to honor Washington's pledge to Cuba, the Bush administration soon confronted the same imperative that drew the Reagan administration to the bargaining table. Secretary Baker's top priority in Latin America was to get the unpopular and divisive wars in Central America off Washington's policy agenda so he could focus on managing the end of the Cold War. For eight years, Reagan had pursued military solutions to these conflicts, to no avail. Bush was willing to accept diplomatic settlements, but that meant dealing with the Cubans, who were key players in Central America, just as they had been in southern Africa. Havana provided military aid and advisors to Nicaragua's Sandinista government and supported the guerrillas fighting the U.S.-backed government in El

Salvador. Fidel Castro could either foster or obstruct negotiations on both fronts.

Assistant Secretary of State for Inter-American Affairs Bernard Aronson authorized Taylor to open informal discussions with the Cubans about Central America. Once again, Carlos Aldana served as Taylor's principal contact. "Aldana seemed to believe that the new Bush administration might be amenable to a real break through in U.S.-Cuban relations," Taylor said. "But, he understood that for Washington, the test would be Central America."[144] Through 1989, Taylor and his political officer, Fulton Armstrong (a CIA analyst detailed to the Department of State), met frequently with Aldana and his assistant, Alfredo García Almeida. Cuba wanted to contribute to a political solution in Central America, as it had done in Angola, Aldana said. To that end, Havana would support the Esquipulas peace process, in which the five Central American presidents had agreed to hold free elections and end support for insurgents in neighboring countries. Cuba would also agree to accept the results of an election in Nicaragua. In the rapidly changing international environment, Aldana conceded, communism was not an appropriate model for Nicaragua. He also claimed Cuba had already halted arms flows to El Salvador and would not resume them if Havana was formally brought into the peace process.[145]

Gorbachev's Initiative

While Taylor conferred with Aldana, Washington focused on leveraging Soviet cooperation. At Baker's suggestion, President Bush decided to make Central America a test of Mikhail Gorbachev's new foreign policy. If the Soviets sincerely wanted to resolve regional conflicts, they should stop supplying economic and military aid to Nicaragua and Cuba. "We should subject the Soviets to Chinese water torture on this subject," Baker told the president. "We'll just keep telling them over and over—drop, drop, drop—that they've got to be part of the solution in Central America, or else they'll find lots of other problems harder to deal with."[146]

On March 27, 1989, just before Gorbachev traveled to Cuba, President Bush sent him a letter spelling out Washington's view. "It is hard to reconcile your slogans . . . with continuing high levels of Soviet and Cuban assistance to Nicaragua. . . ." Bush wrote. If this did not stop, it would "inevitably affect the nature of the [U.S.-Soviet] relationship." On a trip to Moscow that same month, Baker told Soviet foreign minister Eduard Shevardnadze that better relations between the superpowers were impossible unless the Soviet

Union stopped interfering in Central America. Shevardnadze suggested that Washington talk directly with the Cubans about their role in the region. "I'm afraid that doesn't work," Baker replied.[147]

Meeting in Havana on April 3, Gorbachev briefed Fidel Castro on Bush's letter and the two discussed how to respond. At Castro's suggestion, they agreed to make a sweeping proposal to Bush for "complete cessation of supplies of weapons" to Central America by all sides.[148] Gorbachev hoped that settling the Central America conflict might provide an opportunity to settle hostilities between Washington and Havana, as well. Castro was skeptical. He briefed Gorbachev in detail on Cuba's collaborative role in the southern African negotiations. The talks had been "very difficult," he noted, but Cuba had "persisted with firmness and flexibility." Washington had promised that if Cuba withdrew its troops from Africa, "then our relations would improve." Instead, in "a concession to the most reactionary circles in the United States," the U.S. administration was about to launch a new propaganda television station aimed at Cuba, TV Martí, which Castro characterized as "an aggressive act."

Gorbachev nevertheless suggested that they use Central America as an opportunity to widen the agenda. "We would go beyond the boundaries of the Central American problems, and present to Bush the collective platform of the Cuban leadership—how it sees the world today."

"Truly, this is an excellent idea," Castro replied. On April 5, as he accompanied the Soviet leader to the airport, Fidel asked Gorbachev to raise the possibility of improving U.S.-Cuban relations with Bush. "For us it is politically very important that you should try and influence Bush, at a time and form that you consider most appropriate."[149]

The time and place Gorbachev chose was during the Malta summit on December 2, 1989, when he met with Bush aboard the cruise ship *Maxim Gorky*. In private, Gorbachev related Castro's interest in better ties with Washington. "Castro essentially asked for our assistance with the normalization of relations with the U.S.," Gorbachev reported to Bush. "Perhaps we should think about some kind of mechanism to begin contacts on this issue. It seems to me that Castro understands how much the world has been changing. I felt it in my conversation with him. But he has a remarkably strong sense of self-esteem and independence."[150]

Bush asked Gorbachev if he could repeat Castro's proposal verbatim.

"His very words: 'Find a way to make the president aware of my interest in normalization.'"

Bush was dismissive. "Let's put all our cards on the table about Castro," he replied. "Castro is like a sea anchor as you move forward and the Western

Hemisphere moves toward democracy. He is against all of this. . . . We have had feelers from Castro, but never with an indication of a willingness to change."[151] Instead, Bush warned that continued Soviet support for Nicaragua and Cuba was "the single most disruptive element" in U.S.-Soviet bilateral relations. "Castro is embarrassing you," Bush scolded. "He's detracting from your credibility, violating everything you stand for. The one thing, sir, you must understand is that America cannot accept your support for Havana and Managua." Cut support for Cuba, Bush pressed, "so we are not on opposite sides."[152]

"I've told Castro that he's out of step with us and that he should be doing what the Eastern Europeans are doing," Gorbachev replied. "But he's his own man. . . . We cannot dictate to him."[153] If Washington wanted Cuban cooperation in Central America, it should open a dialogue with the Cubans directly. "Mr. Bush reacted very coldly to my proposal," Gorbachev recalled. "He indicated that the United States was not ready for any compromise in the matter."[154]

La TV Que No Se Ve

Back in Havana, the dialogue on Central America between Taylor and Aldana was complicated by the intrusion of a new issue—TV Martí. Just as Radio Martí derailed the 1985 migration accord, now U.S. plans to start television broadcasting to Cuba thwarted progress on Central America. TV Martí, like Radio Martí before it, was a pet project of the Cuban American National Foundation (CANF), not the State Department. "My reaction was that it was unwise to spend millions of dollars for an instrument that could easily be jammed by Cuba," Cuban Affairs coordinator Ken Skoug recalled. But the die was cast at a June 1988 meeting between U.S. officials and Cuban American supporters of TV Martí. Assistant Secretary Elliot Abrams and Skoug were carefully noncommittal until Vice President (and presidential candidate) Bush joined the group and gave TV Martí his unqualified endorsement.[155]

When Castro realized that Bush intended to go forward with the TV broadcasts, he warned that Cuba would "use all available means to respond."[156] On the one hand, Washington was seeking Cuban cooperation in Central America; on the other, it was preparing "to spit in Cuba's eye," Aldana privately complained to Jay Taylor. Cuba would take TV Martí as evidence of Washington's implacable hostility, Aldana warned, and simply jam it.[157] As an alternative, Aldana proposed opening Cuba to regular U.S. news broadcasts like CNN or PBS McNeil/Lehrer News Hour. "This seemed a rather remarkable proposal to be coming from a member of the Cuban Politburo," said Taylor, recalling his surprise. He cabled Washington, suggesting that the start of TV Martí be delayed while the United States explored these alternatives and continued discussions with the Cubans about Central America.

One of Taylor's frequent diplomatic contacts in Havana was Soviet Ambassador Yuri Petrov, who reportedly had close ties to Raúl Castro. Petrov wanted to promote better U.S.-Cuban relations in order to eliminate Cuba as a source of friction between Moscow and Washington. He assured Taylor that the Soviet Union was pressing the Cubans to support diplomatic settlements in Central America and that the Cubans were sincere when they said they would be prepared to cooperate. "Petrov kept pushing for the Cubans to play a Central American card with us, formalizing what they publicly said they were doing, supporting a regional peace accord," recalled Taylor's political officer, Fulton Armstrong. In December 1989 Petrov told Taylor that the Cubans would soon offer Washington a specific proposal on diplomatic cooperation in the region.[158]

Taylor returned to Washington for consultations. "I told Bernie [Aronson] that the Cubans wanted to know, if they played a positive role in Central America, could they really expect a new era of U.S.-Cuba relations?" Taylor, who thought the Cubans were serious, also advised Aronson that Castro could probably "throw the Nicaraguan election train off the tracks," if he chose to. Aronson instructed Taylor to tell the Cubans that Washington was open to hearing any specific proposal they might offer that would ensure free and fair elections in Nicaragua. "If their proposals seemed helpful," Taylor was instructed to say, "the Cubans could then be invited to participate in broader discussions, perhaps in the Esquipulas process, and this in turn would have consequences for their relations with the United States."[159] It was the same promise Washington had made to the Cubans—and reneged on—regarding cooperation in southern Africa.

TV Martí still had the potential to cut short this budding diplomatic opening, but Taylor was pleased to hear that an interagency study had concluded that TV Martí should be delayed while Washington explored Aldana's offer to accept a conventional broadcast alternative. Hopeful, Taylor returned to Havana on the evening of December 19 and immediately arranged to meet Aldana at his office the following morning to hear Cuba's proposal and deliver Washington's message.

That night, however, the United States invaded Panama to overthrow the government of General Manuel Noriega, whom Washington charged with conspiring to ship Colombian cocaine to the United States. "In the morning, tens of thousands of Cubans were 'spontaneously' demonstrating in front of the Interests Section," Taylor recalled. "A platform had been built overnight and loud speakers were broadcasting a steady stream of vitriolic speeches." Aldana's assistant, Alfredo García Almeida, telephoned to cancel Aldana's meeting with Taylor but asked if he could come by the Interests Section to convey a message. When he arrived, he had to push through the throng of protestors to get inside. It was, ironically, the first time a Cuban official had come to the Interests Section.[160]

García Almeida was ushered in to see Taylor, whose secretary offered the Cuban a cup of coffee. After adding several spoons of what he thought was sugar, García Almeida took a sip and gagged. "This coffee!" he sputtered. "What are you trying to do to me?!" By mistake, Taylor's secretary had brought out salt rather than sugar. "He expected to wake up in CIA headquarters in Langley or something," Taylor laughed.

Once García Almeida had been reassured that he was not being poisoned or shanghaied, the conversation got back on track. Because of the invasion of Panama, Taylor's meeting with Aldana would have to be postponed until things "cooled," García Almeida explained. But Aldana hoped to meet with Taylor early in the new year to present Cuba's proposal and resume the discussion on Central America.

Aldana never delivered the Cuban proposal. Events overtook it. On February 25, 1990, the Sandinistas lost the election in Nicaragua and agreed to turn over power to their U.S.-backed opponents. With that, the value to Washington of Cuban cooperation in Central America plummeted. "The Cuban card wasn't worth anything anymore," explained Armstrong. On February 9, the National Security Council decided to go forward with TV Martí, despite the unanimous interagency report against it. At 1:45 A.M. on March 27, it began broadcasting. The Cubans interpreted this as an insulting provocation that demonstrated a lack of U.S. interest in improving relations. In a heated denunciation of "this trash, this outrage, this insult to our country," Castro dubbed the broadcasts "tele-aggression." Cuba promptly jammed not only TV Martí but Radio Martí as well. "TV Martí was another nail in the coffin of cooperation on Central America," Armstrong recalled.[161]

The Cuban government jammed TV Martí so successfully that ordinary Cubans dubbed it "*La TV que no se ve*" (No See TV). Taylor and his staff traveled all around Havana and its suburbs to test reception and got nothing but static. Western journalists and Catholic priests reported the same result from across the island. But in Washington, TV Martí's patrons insisted that the vast majority of the Cuban population was watching the broadcasts, according to a dubious survey of newly arrived exiles.[162] Taylor, in Washington for consultations, invited the U.S. Information Agency officials responsible for TV Martí to come to Cuba to see for themselves. "Silence prevailed around the table," he recalled. "I don't think anyone there really believed TV Martí signals were being received in Cuba. It was a Kafkaesque moment—a true Orwellian experience, to see a room full of grown, educated men and women so afraid for their jobs or their political positions that they could take part in such a charade."[163]

Beyond Central America and TV Martí, broader international developments also diminished Washington's interest in dialogue with Havana. The collapse of communism in Eastern Europe, beginning with the Polish elections in June 1989, created a sense of triumphalism in Washington. Communist regimes were falling like dominoes. The United States had won the Cold War. Surely, Cuba's collapse could not be far behind. "Castro es el próximo," was the slogan in Miami: "Castro is next." Jorge Mas Canosa's Cuban American National Foundation wrote a constitution for a new government, which Mas Canosa himself aspired to lead.[164] The optimism was infectious. The CIA's National Intelligence Officer for Latin America, Brian Latell, believed the Cuban regime was riven by such serious divisions that Castro's imminent downfall was likely.[165] Assistant Secretary Aronson thought so, too, especially if Washington gave him a push. "Bernie's thought at this time was that somehow what happened in Nicaragua could be replicated in Cuba," according to one of his aides.[166] If Castro was truly a dead man walking, there was no reason to engage him in dialogue. The best policy was to simply wait for the successor regime. U.S. policy, focused since the 1960s on containing Cuba's international mischief, now reverted to the more ambitious aspiration of rolling back the revolution.

U.S. diplomats in Havana felt pressure to endorse these prognostications of Castro's imminent demise. But being on the ground in Cuba gave Taylor and Armstrong perspective on the regime's strengths as well as its weaknesses. "Our conclusion in 1989–1990 was that the crises at home . . . and abroad . . . constituted a serious blow to the government's credibility and to its previous image of near invincibility," Taylor recalled. "Nevertheless, we said, the government had substantial political assets remaining and had begun showing the flexibility to mount a strategy that could enable it to survive for years to come." He recommended that Washington ought to plan as if Castro would be around for another ten years. "Boy, that wasn't welcome," Taylor recalled.[167]

To help the process of regime transition along, Washington intensified its demands that Moscow cut economic and military aid to Havana. "If it turns out they are forced to swim without the Soviet life preserver, there is little doubt but that they will drown," explained a U.S. official. "It would only be a question of time."[168] In Moscow to meet with Shevardnadze in February 1990, Baker explicitly linked the prospect of economic aid from the United States to an end to Soviet aid for Cuba. Bush made the same argument at the June 1990 summit at Camp David. "We have no right to dictate to Fidel Castro how he should manage the affairs of his country," Gorbachev replied. Nevertheless, he tried to downplay Soviet assistance, assuring Bush that Soviet trade subsidies (exchanging Soviet oil at below market prices for Cuban sugar at above market prices) would end in the coming year.[169] Gorbachev again urged Bush to talk directly to the Cubans: "The moment you treated the Cubans as equal partners, they adopted a balanced and reasonable attitude." Bush replied that Washington would consider normalization only in the event of radical internal changes in Cuba.[170]

The failed coup against Gorbachev in August 1991 strengthened Washington's hand immensely. Many of Havana's best friends in the Kremlin, known collectively as the "Cuba Lobby," numbered among the plotters. Their disgrace left Cuba with few advocates.[171] Gorbachev, who had resisted Washington's demands that Moscow cut aid to Cuba, remained titular head of the Soviet state, but real power flowed to Boris Yeltsin, president of the Russian Republic. Yeltsin had no particular love for the Cubans. In September, James Baker made his first post-coup trip to Moscow to meet with both Yeltsin and Gorbachev. Loans from the United States would be easier to get, Baker reiterated, if the Soviet Union stopped subsidizing communism in places like Cuba, especially with military aid. Yeltsin promised that military aid to Cuba would end by January 1, 1992, and all Soviet military personnel would be withdrawn. In a separate meeting, Gorbachev reaffirmed that a Soviet military withdrawal would begin shortly. As they made their way to a post-meeting press conference, Baker asked Gorbachev if he would announce the withdrawal plans, "without expecting him to say yes." To Baker's surprise, Gorbachev agreed.[172]

In Havana, Fidel first learned of the planned withdrawal of Soviet troops from press reports of the Baker-Gorbachev news conference.[173] The Cuban Foreign Ministry issued an indignant rebuke to Gorbachev for making the announcement without prior consultations.[174] Two days later, *Granma* ran one of Fidel's signature editorials lambasting the Soviet "betrayal." The military contingent being withdrawn, the editorial noted, had been left in Cuba in 1962 as a symbol of the Soviet Union's commitment to Cuba's security. Now, as in 1962, Moscow had given in to U.S. demands "without even a single word spoken to our country" and, by so doing, had given the United States "a green light to carry out its plans of aggression against Cuba." Cuba, the editorial reminded Gorbachev, had always acted on principle, spurning Washington's blandishments to break with Moscow in exchange for better relations. The Soviets now repaid Cuba's loyalty by acquiescing to Washington's "hegemonic delirium."[175]

Castro had long feared that Gorbachev's "New Thinking" would sacrifice traditional allies to serve Soviet national interests. As the Soviet Union disengaged from regional conflicts and sought to end Cold War tensions, it was conceding to the United States the position of sole superpower, leaving former friends and allies like Cuba to fend for themselves.[176] "What will be Cuba's place in this world?" Castro plaintively asked Soviet Latin America specialist Yuri Pavlov.[177]

Cuba, Alone

Every president since Eisenhower had castigated Fidel Castro for presiding over a dictatorship, but none before Bush had demanded, as a condition of better relations, that Cuba undergo regime change. The issues on Washington's agenda had always emphasized Cuban foreign policy—Havana's support for revolution in Latin America and its expeditionary forces in Africa, as well as its strategic relationship with the Soviet Union. In early 1989, these were still the issues that Secretary Baker emphasized when he cabled U.S. diplomatic posts to deny rumors that Bush would improve relations with Cuba. By late 1989, however, Cuban troops had come home from Africa, Havana was normalizing relations with its Latin neighbors, and the Soviet Union was abandoning its strategic commitments abroad. The foreign policy issues had been rendered moot.

Yet better relations were still not in the cards. For Washington, the new international balance of forces revived the dream of rolling back the revolution. After the failure of the CIA's covert operations to unseat Fidel in the 1960s, regime change in Cuba was not a practical possibility. But as the collapse of European communism sent the Cuban economy reeling, that calculus changed, and Washington's demands changed with it. The United States, Bush declared, would normalize relations only if Cuba abandoned socialism and adopted multiparty electoral democracy. On May 20, 1991, Cuban Independence Day, Bush spelled out what he expected: "Our goals for the

Cuban nation, shared by Cubans everywhere, are plain and clear: freedom and democracy, Mr. Castro, not sometime, not someday, but now. If Cuba holds fully free and fair elections under international supervision, respects human rights, and stops subverting its neighbors, we can expect relations between our two countries to improve significantly."[178] In short, Cuba could have normal relations with the United States only if it capitulated.

7. CLINTON

From Calibrated Response
to Parallel Positive Steps

The embargo is a kind of Gordian knot, as complex as it is cruel. I'm not sure Clinton has Alexander the Great's sword to be able to cut it.

—Fidel Castro to Diane Sawyer, March 1993

In late August 1994, the Nobel Prize–winning novelist Gabriel García Márquez traveled to Martha's Vineyard for a private dinner with President Bill Clinton. "Gabo wanted to come and talk to Clinton about Cuba," recalled Rose Styron who, along with her famous husband, William, hosted the evening at their rambling island home.[1] But neither the Styrons nor the majority of the other luminaries at the dinner table—Mexican writer Carlos Fuentes and former deputy assistant secretary of state William Luers among them—knew that García Márquez was there as a secret emissary between Havana and Washington. While the guests gathered for fried chicken with rice and gravy, the writer presented the president with a private proposal from Fidel Castro to end the "*balsero* crisis"—the flood of Cubans taking to the sea in rickety rafts, inner tubes, and small boats to cross the Florida Strait. The next day, García Márquez left the Vineyard on a private jet provided by the Mexican government and flew on to Havana to report to Castro on President Clinton's response.

Like his predecessors, Clinton engaged in a range of secret talks with Cuba, although normalizing relations never made it onto the agenda because the president placed a higher priority on electoral votes in Florida than on relations with Havana. In his first term, the 1994 rafters migration crisis necessitated negotiations with Havana, resulting in two major migration accords. In his second term, he pursued dialogue on issues of mutual interest, including counter-narcotics and counterterrorism cooperation. Clinton was also more open to using soft power, actively fostering people-to-people ties for the first time since the 1970s. By improving the atmosphere of state-to-state relations and expanding societal engagement, the Clinton team consciously aimed to build a political constituency for improving relations—both in the United States and in Cuba.

Castro's decision to shoot down two small planes off the Cuban coast in February 1996, and Washington's reaction, fundamentally changed the parameters of U.S.-Cuban relations by inscribing U.S. economic sanctions into law. Nevertheless, creative White House strategists found ways to move relations forward. "We needed a dance, not to the same music but to a similar beat, where each side pursued interests independently," recalled a former White House official. "It's like a minuet, in which the partners do not touch each other much, but go through choreographed steps. We do things, they do things. But no one has to make concessions that cause political problems at home."[2]

Clinton's Campaign Calculus

Personally, Clinton understood the folly of a hostile U.S. policy toward Cuba. "Anybody with half a brain could see the embargo was counterproductive," he later told a confidante in the Oval Office. "It defied wiser policies of engagement that we had pursued with some Communist countries even at the height of the Cold War." Since the Reagan era, "Republicans had harvested the Cuban exile vote by snarling at Castro," Clinton noted, but "no one bothered to think forward about consequence."[3]

Politically, however, Clinton understood the imperative to snarl. In 1992, the electoral road to the White House ran through Florida. If Clinton could make inroads in the staunchly conservative Cuban American community, which normally voted Republican by overwhelming margins, he might carry the state. A consummate politician, Clinton was determined to appeal to Cuban Americans on the single issue that determined their votes: relations with Havana.

On April 23, 1992, Clinton attended a fundraiser at Victor's Cafe in the heart of Little Havana. Victor's large elegant dining room, with its high ceiling and terra cotta tile floor accented by tropical plants, made it a favorite venue for Cuban American political soirees. Some three hundred of Miami's wealthiest Cuban Americans were there, checkbooks in hand. Clinton did not disappoint. "I think [the George H. W. Bush] administration has missed a big opportunity to put the hammer down on Fidel Castro and Cuba," he told the largely Republican audience. "I have read the Torricelli-Graham bill and I like it."[4]

By intensifying U.S. economic sanctions, the Cuban Democracy Act (CDA)—the official title of the Torricelli-Graham bill—was intended "to wreak havoc on that island," according to its sponsor, Congressman Robert G. Torricelli (D-N.J.). It was Torricelli, Clinton's top campaign advisor on Latin America, who organized the fundraiser at Victor's Cafe. The congressman from New Jersey could turn out Miami's Cuban American elite because of his friendship with Jorge Mas Canosa, founder and president of the anti-Castro Cuban American National Foundation (CANF).

Torricelli and Mas Canosa were a political odd couple, drawn together by the mother's milk of politics—money. Although most Cuban Americans were Republicans, Mas Canosa and his Free Cuba political action committee always lobbied both sides of the aisle. When Torricelli became chairman of the House Subcommittee on Western Hemisphere Affairs in 1991, Mas Canosa and his friends began contributing to Torricelli's campaign coffers. Both men of outsized egos, intolerant of disagreement, and willing to flout convention to get their way, Mas Canosa and Torricelli hit it off right away. By 1992, only Congresswoman Ileana Ros-Lehtinen (R-Fla.), the first Cuban American elected to Congress, garnered more campaign contributions from Miami Cubans than Torricelli.[5] "Whatever the Foundation wants, the Foundation gets," Torricelli told his committee staff.[6]

On a yacht in Coral Gables, Torricelli and his new patrons drafted the Cuban Democracy Act in the summer of 1991.[7] The bill's intent was to tighten the U.S. economic embargo at a time when the Cuban economy was reeling from the collapse of the Soviet Union. It reinstated the ban on trade with Cuba by the subsidiaries of U.S. corporations abroad—a ban President Gerald Ford had lifted in 1975 to advance Henry Kissinger's secret dialogue with Havana. The Torricelli bill also banned vessels that traveled to Cuba from coming to the United States for 180 days and gave the president authority to cut foreign aid to any country aiding Cuba. Finally, the bill specified that the embargo should be lifted only in the event of democratic elections in Cuba. In addition to these "sticks," as Torricelli called them, the bill also included "carrots" authorizing increased people-to-people contact, humanitarian assistance, and sales of medicine.[8] Carrots notwithstanding, Torricelli's stated intention was unambiguous: "Castro must be brought to his knees."[9]

President Bush opposed the Torricelli bill at first. Its sanctions on U.S. companies operating abroad promised to cause diplomatic headaches with U.S. allies who saw it as an extraterritorial infringement on their sovereignty. In Bush's judgment, the incremental impact of tightening the embargo was not worth the cost.[10] But Bill Clinton's avid support for the bill forced Bush to endorse it. On October 24, 1992, the president flew to Miami and signed the Cuban Democracy Act into law in front of Mas Canosa and his CANF entourage.

Clinton's support for the Torricelli bill endeared him to the hard-line exile community. He raised some $275,000 in campaign contributions from Cuban Americans, several CANF directors among them.[11] Most importantly, he received Mas Canosa's political blessing. After meeting Clinton in Tampa just before the November election, Mas told the press that Cuban Americans "need not fear a Bill Clinton Administration."[12] Clinton won 22% of the Cuban American vote, more than any Democrat since Jimmy Carter—but not enough to carry Florida.[13]

Clinton's successful courtship of Mas Canosa proved to be a Faustian bargain. As quid pro quo, Mas expected to own the Cuba issue during Clinton's presidency, as the president-elect soon discovered. When Clinton nominated Mario L. Baeza, a black Cuban American corporate attorney from New Jersey, as assistant secretary of state for inter-American affairs, the White House thought the Cuban American community would be pleased. But Baeza was not part of what Fidel Castro disparagingly called the "Miami mafia." Baeza and his family had immigrated to the United States before the revolution so they were not exiles. He did not live in Miami and had no social or political ties to the community there. He was black, whereas most of Miami's Cuban American elite were white. Moreover, he had committed the unpardonable sin of traveling to Havana in June 1992, for a conference on foreign trade and investment opportunities.[14]

When word of Baeza's impending appointment leaked to the press, complaints poured in from Miami, orchestrated by CANF. Torricelli also announced his opposition because Baeza had once expressed concern that the Cuban Democracy Act might harm trade relations with European allies.[15] Faced with this pressure, the White House backed down; when Clinton sent a list of State Department nominees to the Senate in late January, Baeza's name was on it, but it had been crossed out.[16] Instead, the post went to Alexander F. Watson, a Foreign Service officer with long experience in Latin America, who happened to be the only senior career officer available.[17]

Pursuing a "More Enlightened" Policy

Not only did Torricelli and Mas Canosa sink Baeza's nomination, they also won an appointment for Torricelli's senior staff assistant, Richard A. Nuccio, as deputy assistant secretary of state. At the State Department, the career diplomats regarded Nuccio with suspicion, but his interest in Cuba and his willingness to work on it full-time gave him an advantage. Watson was happy to keep his distance from the issue. At the National Security Council, Richard Feinberg, the Latin America office director, decided early on that Cuba would be the black hole of Latin American policy, consuming all available time and energy unless he stayed away from it. "I didn't want to become the desk officer on Cuba," Feinberg explained.[18]

Torricelli and Mas Canosa trusted Nuccio, but unbeknownst to them, he regarded their "implosion model" of regime change in Cuba as "wrong" and "dangerous." The intent of the CDA, he told Watson, was "to maximize pressure and force an internal revolt" despite the potential for chaos and widespread violence. Rather than a "Romanian solution" ninety miles off the U.S. coast, Nuccio believed U.S. interests would be better served by an Eastern European–style "Velvet revolution" in Cuba. Pursuing a Caribbean Ostpolitik would be a far better strategy. "The principal instrument to promote change in Cuba that is more likely to be peaceful is to strengthen the civil society that has been so devastated by 30 years of dictatorship," he wrote to Watson. The lesson of the collapse of the Soviet bloc was that empowering artists, students, activists, and even military officers could create a "democratic core" for a post-communist transition.[19]

Nuccio opposed any accommodation with the Castro regime, but he supported strengthening the "carrots" in the CDA to build bridges to Cuban civil society—the people-to-people contacts known as "Track II" (which Nuccio suggestively referred to in secret memos as "penetrative programs")—even if that meant dialogue and collaboration with the government.* "The Cuban Democracy Act gives important flexibility to the new administration to adjust the balance between sticks and carrots in the law," Nuccio explained in a transition paper written during the campaign, "and, most importantly, provides the political cover necessary to carry out a more enlightened policy toward Cuba."[20]

Among the "enlightened" initiatives he recommended for "Clinton's First 100 Days" were to publicly reassure Havana that the United States posed "no military threat to Cuba" and had "no aggressive intentions." Such an announcement could be "one of several 'confidence building' measures." Another would be a concerted effort to prevent "armed attacks against Cuba

---

* Though Nuccio was probably unaware of it, Walter Rostow had proposed a "Track II" plan for Cuba in 1962, aimed at mobilizing the Cuban people to produce "the overthrow of Castro primarily from within rather than by invasion from without" (Memorandum, Martin to Johnson, "Track Two," October 12, 1962, NSA Cuba Collection).

by U.S. based groups" by vigorously enforcing the Neutrality Act. "Quiet consultation with the Cuban government," he noted, "may be necessary to carry out effectively this policy." To promote people-to-people contacts Nuccio recommended moving quickly to relax regulations on travel, modernize telecommunications, and expand family remittances. "This is worth doing," Nuccio wrote, "even if it requires negotiation with the Cuban government." After all, Nuccio added, "President Clinton ran for office on a theme of change. It would be ironic if Cuba policy were an area where his representatives were to argue for 'no change.'"[21]

In both tone and substance, the agenda Nuccio laid out shaped Cuba policy during Clinton's first year in office. On May 3, 1993, in his first major policy address on Latin America, Deputy Secretary of State Clifford Wharton declared, "The United States poses no military threat" to Cuba. "We hope the Cuban people will win their freedom through the kind of peaceful transition which has brought so many other nations into the democratic community."[22] To reinforce the point, U.S. officials began alerting Cuban authorities in advance of routine naval maneuvers near the island and opened low-level discussions on cooperation against narcotics trafficking.[23] U.S. officials also dialed back the anti-Castro rhetoric. "We weren't making these hysterical comments about Cuba," Richard Feinberg recalled. "We tried to lower the temperature a little bit."[24] In Havana, the Cubans recognized and appreciated the change in tone. "There is less verbal aggression this year in the White House than in the last 12 years," Raúl Castro told a Mexican reporter.[25]

In late May, U.S. Customs officials arrested nine members of the Alpha 66 paramilitary group on weapons charges as they prepared to sail for Cuba to incite an uprising. In a clear warning to Cuban exiles, the State Department announced that violations of the U.S. Neutrality Act would be vigorously prosecuted.[26] And, for the first time, Washington sought to discourage Cubans from using violence to flee the island. After a Cuban pilot commandeered a jet with fifty-two passengers aboard and flew it to Miami, the Justice Department invited Cuban security officers to come to the United States and testify before a grand jury weighing an indictment for air piracy. Although the case was eventually dropped, it represented one of the few U.S. attempts to prosecute Cuban hijackers—a failing the Cuban government had been complaining about since the late 1970s.[27]

In addition to promoting a more relaxed security atmosphere, the Clinton administration moved quickly to expand people-to-people contacts. In May 1993, the Treasury Department approved licenses for several U.S. physicians to travel to Cuba as part of an international team investigating the outbreak of a rare disease, optical neuritis, which had afflicted thousands of Cuban citizens. The Center for Decease Control and Prevention was then authorized to conduct a joint study with Cuba's Ministry of Health to identify the cause—a vitamin deficiency combined with cigar smoke.[28]

In June, the Treasury Department unveiled a new set of regulations licensing travel to Cuba for humanitarian, religious, and educational purposes, vastly expanding the number U.S. visitors. At the same time, the State Department began granting more visas to Cuban musicians, artists, and scholars for travel to the United States.[29] To handle the flow, the administration approved additional daily flights between Miami and Havana. In July, the State Department announced guidelines under which U.S. telecommunications companies would be allowed to upgrade the pathetically inadequate telephone service between Cuba and the United States. Using equipment that had not been updated since 1961, AT&T could route less than 1 percent of the 60 million calls originating annually in the United States. Because of the embargo, none of the revenue generated by the AT&T service had been paid to Cuba. The July guidelines provided that Cuba, for the first time, would share the revenue produced by the new service.[30]

The Cubans reciprocated with gestures of their own. In May the government released four prominent dissidents from prison. In July Castro announced that he would ease travel restrictions on Cuban American visits.[31] In September the Cubans handed over two cocaine traffickers captured when they sought refuge in Cuban territorial waters.[32] That same month, the two governments completed secret negotiations on an agreement in which Cuba would accept the return of fifteen hundred émigrés who had come to the United States during the Mariel boatlift and subsequently committed felonies.[33] Cuba came away from the accord with little more than a vague hope that its concession would set the stage for broader bilateral talks. Accepting the "excludables" was an unmistakable signal that Fidel Castro saw an opening for dialogue with this new, young Democratic president. Clinton reminded Fidel of JFK, the president he admired most, Castro told Diane Sawyer of ABC News. "I have no kind of personal conflict with Clinton," Castro noted with a hint of hopefulness. "It's a new administration."[34]

In August, Castro took the unusual step of personally calling for talks with Washington. "I think that in essence we should discuss any differences between the United States and Cuba," he told reporters. "It is a simple matter of being able to talk, negotiate, without any conditions. We do not place any conditions but we cannot accept impositions either. So, the only condition is that we talk and negotiate without any conditions."[35]

What U.S. officials called Castro's "charm offensive" fell on deaf ears in the White House. Even early in his first term, Clinton's reelection interests drove policy toward Cuba. The president's domestic political advisors lived in fear of how the Cuban American community would react to any hint of an opening to Havana. "It was just very clear that the political direction from the White House was that we don't want to be out front on this issue, and that we are very responsive to the Cuban American[s]," NSC official Richard Feinberg explained. "Clinton really wanted to carry Florida. That's what's driving this. That was *numero uno*."[36]

The White House routinely sought the advice of a small group of Cuban American Democrats and campaign donors whose entrée to the president was through Hillary Clinton's sister-in-law, Miami attorney Maria Victoria Arias. "Her faxes would go directly into the Oval Office," Feinberg recalled. The White House was so sensitive about keeping the group happy that when the NSC scheduler heard they were coming to Washington for a meeting, she ran into Deputy National Security Advisor Sandy Berger's office shouting, "The Cubans are coming! The Cubans are coming!"[37]

Apart from the politics of the issue, even people like Feinberg and Nuccio who favored a gradual relaxation of tensions doubted the utility of broad negotiations. "I didn't think Castro really wanted liberalization," Feinberg explained. In a memorandum in August 1993, Nuccio put the question rhetorically to Assistant Secretary Watson: "What do we have to dialogue about except the date of their departure?"[38]

The "Calibrated Response" Debate

Some officials, including Watson, had a more optimistic view of what might be possible. He penned a note to Nuccio—handwritten to keep it out of the computer system where other officials could access it—proposing a dialogue on democracy. "I have a simple but potentially explosive idea," Watson wrote. "Could we make a dramatic offer to enter into a dialogue with Castro focused on how we (and perhaps others) could help Cuba undertake the political and economic changes that are necessary? . . . perhaps devise schemes for bringing [democracy] about—set up an electoral regime, human rights ombudsman, farmers' markets, micro enterprise, privatization, etc. Of course, if changes are made, we could relax the embargo step by step as relevant to the specific changes."[39]

For Watson, a dialogue on democratic transition through a series of reciprocal initiatives—political reforms on the Cuban side and a piecemeal lifting of the embargo on the U.S. side—made perfect Washington sense. Such reciprocity was specifically authorized in a little-noticed clause in the CDA, section 1703, which simply stated: "It should be the policy of the United States to be prepared to reduce the sanctions in carefully calibrated ways in response to positive developments in Cuba."[40] The language had been conceived and drafted by Nuccio. "I invented the phrase 'calibrated response,' . . . as a way to offer to negotiate with the Cubans without giving them what they wanted—and domestic politics opposed—direct talks," Nuccio recounted. "We could do a shadow dance and perhaps move the relationship to a point where there might be enough incentive for an administration to take the risk of direct negotiations."[41]

But calibrated response could also operate within a framework of direct negotiations rather than preceding it, as Watson now envisioned. "Such an approach would meet to a large extent the concerns of our critics at home and abroad," he scribbled to Nuccio. "We'd take flack from the 'anti-dialogueros,' but they could not complain too much because we'd be focused on changing the system."[42]

Since the earliest dialogue between Richard Goodwin and Che Guevara in 1961, the Cubans had made it crystal clear that "changing the system" would never be on the negotiating table. Yet, in the wake of the collapse of the Soviet Union and the descent of Cuba's economy into a dire crisis known as the "Special Period," some U.S. officials speculated that Fidel Castro might be enticed to negotiate the denouement of Cuban socialism. All the European Communist regimes had collapsed; surely Castro would see the writing on the wall and opt for a peaceful transition into a new era of normal U.S.-Cuban relations. Castro "might agree to a democratic transition that he believed could preserve the gains of the revolution as he sees them and that offers him a graceful exit," noted one confidential State Department memo, "Seizing the Initiative to Promote a Soft Landing."[43]

Cuba was certainly reeling from the loss of Soviet aid. A CIA National Intelligence Estimate (NIE) circulated on August 1, 1993, concluded that "there is a better than even chance that Fidel Castro's government will fall within the next few years." Titled "The Outlook for Castro and Beyond" and classified SECRET, the NIE painted a grim picture of Cuba's crisis. Since 1989, the economy had contracted by more than 40 percent and would likely decline further. Approximately 85 percent of Cuba's trade had been with the Eastern bloc; after the collapse of communism, most of that trade evaporated. Soviet economic subsidies, some $4–5 billion annually, disappeared overnight, reducing Cuba's capacity to import by 75 percent. The inability to purchase raw materials such as fuel and fertilizer caused massive production losses in both manufacturing and agriculture, resulting in widespread unemployment. Electricity blackouts of ten to sixteen hours a day were commonplace in Havana. "The impact on the population already has been devastating," the intelligence analysts noted. "Food shortages and distribution problems have caused malnutrition and disease, and the difficulties of subsisting will intensify."[44]

According to the CIA, "regime-threatening instability" could occur at any time. And "serious instability in Cuba will have an immediate impact on the United States," warned the NIE, including massive, uncontrolled migration, the likely involvement of the exile community in the spreading civil strife, and "pressures for US or international military intervention."[45] Despite thirty years of efforts to destabilize Cuba's government, U.S. officials now realized that they were woefully unprepared for its demise. "The fundamental national security threat facing the United States from Cuba is of a societal collapse that leads to widespread violence," Nuccio wrote to Watson in August 1993.[46]

That was the ultimate "nightmare scenario," State Department official Philip Peters, a holdover from the Reagan-Bush years, argued to Watson shortly after the CIA estimate was distributed. "Given the situation on the island, I would argue that policy continuity, or even marginal change, is not a low-risk option. It's positively scary." If Cuba collapsed, U.S. policy makers would be asked, "Why, when the storm was gathering, were we spending our time on issues such as family remittances, airline charter applications, hotel package deals and telephone settlement rates? Where was the strategy?" Echoing Watson, Peters suggested a dramatic new initiative to promote a "dialogue for democracy," to be announced in a speech by Secretary of State Warren Christopher. "The purpose of the speech is to reframe the debate," Peters argued. "If ever a foreign policy case cried out for dramatic U.S. leadership, Cuba today is that case."[47]

Within the State Department, however, there were divergent opinions on how—and even if—Cuba policy should be reframed. Nuccio agreed with Peters that U.S. policy had been too timid while "a slow motion crisis" in Cuba gathered force, but he opposed any major new initiative. The embargo was a statement of "moral disapproval," Nuccio argued, and any relaxation of it would diminish Washington's moral stance. The "carrots" in the CDA were concessions enough. Nuccio also disparaged Peters's hint that perhaps Washington ought to take up Castro's offer of dialogue. "Is Fidel a reliable interlocutor?" Nuccio asked in a memo rebutting Peters's proposals. "Are we dealing with merely an unpredictable or possibly unstable leader? What is the mechanism or dynamic by which engagement with Fidel leads to a different outcome (democratic transition) than that which Fidel expects from such an engagement (validation of the revolution)?"[48]

Given the lack of consensus, the idea of a major policy speech was shelved, but the debate did not subside. Testifying on November 18, 1993, before the House Subcommittee on Western Hemisphere Affairs, Assistant Secretary Watson called attention to the potential for a "calibrated response"—lifting parts of the embargo under certain circumstances. "We are also willing 'to reduce the sanctions in carefully calibrated ways in response to positive developments in Cuba,'" he said, quoting the CDA. "To date," he hastened to add, "we have seen no movement towards democracy or towards respect for human rights."[49]

In late September 1993, Watson tasked Coordinator for Cuban Affairs Dennis Hays to convene a "Small Group" of officials from across the U.S. government to think strategically about Cuba policy. Secrecy was paramount; no formal minutes would be kept of the meetings and attendees were ordered not to use the word "Cuba" on their schedules. "We want to avoid giving the impression that our discussions on Cuba signal a policy review," Hays informed the officials from the NSC, CIA, Defense, Treasury and Justice departments who gathered for the first meeting. If word leaked out, they were to say they were meeting to develop contingency plans for another migration crisis.[50]

The SECRET agenda for the Small Group included contingency planning for various scenarios, including "broad policy guidelines on how to respond quickly and firmly to events before domestic political debate can paralyze governmental actions." The Small Group also looked at initiatives that would provide "benefits to Cuban people without helping the government," and state-to-state confidence-building measures. Finally, officials were tasked to prepare contingency plans for what to do if Castro died, resigned, or was overthrown; if civil war broke out in Cuba; or if widespread hunger and disease spread through the island.[51]

Over the next nine months, the agencies represented in the Small Group developed several contingency plans, entitled "Castro Death/Incapacitation," "Chaos/Civil War," and "Mass Exodus."[52] But few of the other initiatives gained any traction because of the acrimonious disagreement among midlevel State Department and NSC officials. There was "an internal war" inside State's Bureau of Inter-American Affairs, Nuccio recalled. "The Small Group was supposed to be a center for creative thinking, not paper production," he complained to Hays. If new and bolder initiatives were not taken, control of Cuba policy would "migrate away from us toward others on the NSC or the seventh floor."[53]

While NSC officials impatiently pressed the State Department to "think creatively and originally about Cuba policy," Hays and Michael Skol, Watson's principal deputy assistant secretary, opposed any new initiatives.[54] Easing the embargo or travel restrictions would put precious dollars into Castro's treasury at a time when he desperately needed hard currency to keep his economy afloat. Moreover, any relaxation of sanctions would cost Clinton his good standing with the Cuban American community, Hayes argued in a May 1994 memo to Watson, posing the question: "Why would he want to risk losing this support?"[55] On Cuba, the president "continues to speak the words we provide," Hays boasted, suggesting that Watson ignore the pressure from the NSC. "Only a few officials at NSC . . . are upset because we have to date thwarted their efforts to change U.S. policy."[56]

In the summer of 1994, those NSC officials moved to take Cuba policy out of the hands of the State Department bureaucrats. "I thought the notion that we had to wait until the Cuban regime collapsed before we engaged made no sense," Deputy National Security Advisor Samuel L. "Sandy" Berger told the authors. "Engaging with Cuba in some way was not only good for the Cuban people, but it would create a dynamic in Cuba that would lead to liberalization and would help shape the perceptions of the Cuban people towards us."[57] A "greater vigor" was needed in implementing exchanges, travel, and other civil society building measures, the NSC informed Watson.[58] Those measures included "increasing the flow of information and ideas into Cuba" through licensed "educational travel," expediting visas for Cubans to come to the United States for cultural and educational purposes, expanding Radio and TV Martí, and supporting independent groups on the island that could foster a culture of democracy. "The proposed program would go far towards exposing Cubans to Americans and to American ideas," stated a draft memorandum that National Security Advisor Anthony Lake prepared for the president. "We believe that initiatives can now be undertaken which will facilitate a non-violent transition to democracy in Cuba."[59]

As part of the planning for a new initiative on Cuba, the NSC also revived the concept of "calibrated response." A new staffer was tasked to develop a list of "tit-for-tats" with Cuba—which sanctions might be lifted or softened in response to clear steps toward democracy by the Castro regime. "My work on calibrated responses was an attempt to begin to be creative in exploring a new avenue in the U.S.-Cuban relationship," the official recalled. The idea was to "establish a new guideline for diplomacy and negotiations through which both sides could begin to make progress in improving the relationship."[60] In the late summer of 1994, the NSC also resurrected the concept of a presidential speech on Cuba. "Let me be specific," a draft of the speech read: "As the Cuban government implements concrete and verifiable measures to free political prisoners and protect human rights, to guarantee freedom of speech, of the press, and of assembly, and establish free farmers' markets and authorize small businesses, we will unilaterally reduce sanctions affecting trade and seek to improve the full range of relations with Cuba and its people."[61]

By then, however, efforts to reframe Cuba policy were being overtaken—indeed, overwhelmed—by the *balsero* crisis. As thousands of Cubans took to the seas on anything that would float, White House officials went into crisis management mode, shelving any new initiatives. Yet even as the new Cuban exodus gathered force, Secretary of State Warren Christopher, appearing on the CBS news program *Face the Nation*, dangled the carrot of calibrated response as an incentive for Castro. "If there are steps in a democratic direction in Cuba," Christopher said, "we'll respond in a carefully calibrated way."[62]

Secret Diplomacy and the *Balsero* Crisis

In August 1994 the "nightmare scenario" U.S. officials had feared became reality. Desperate for a full meal, reliable electricity, and simple economic security, Cubans began to flee the island by the thousands, many on home-made rafts (*balsas*). In 1990, the first year of the economic crisis Cubans called the "Special Period," 467 refugees had been picked up by the U.S. Coast Guard trying to cross the Florida Strait. In 1993 the first year of the Clinton administration, the number climbed to 3,656—even though such attempts at "illegal exit" were violations of Cuban law, subject to imprisonment.[63] "Economic desperation and Havana's faltering interception capabilities will drive greater numbers of Cubans to attempt to leave the country," a special CIA intelligence analysis, "Cuba: The Rising Specter of Illegal Migration," reported in May 1994. But the CIA also predicted that the "chances for another mass migration along the lines of the 1980 [Mariel] exodus remain slim."[64]

By midsummer, however, the number of Cubans setting sail for Florida on makeshift rafts and leaky boats was reminiscent of Mariel. Worse, some were resorting to violence. In July, armed gangs hijacked Cuban tugboats, ferries, and even navy ships, resulting in significant bloodshed. The most horrific episode took place on July 13, when a group of sixty-eight Cubans hijacked a tugboat and headed for Florida. Cuban police in three other boats pursued them. Whether intentionally (as the refugees believed) or unintentionally (as Cuban authorities claimed), the hijacked tugboat was rammed and sank. Thirty-seven people drowned, including women and children—a tragedy that caused the Castro government considerable embarrassment.[65]

On August 5 two policemen were killed when hijackers tried to seize a ferry in Havana harbor. The incident touched off widespread rioting along the waterfront, as hundreds of people chanted anti-Castro slogans, fought with police, and looted stores. It was the worst antigovernment demonstration in Cuba since 1959. That same evening, an angry Fidel Castro denounced Washington for encouraging hijackers by refusing to prosecute them and by limiting legal immigration. "We cannot continue to guard the coasts of the United States," he warned. Unless Washington changed its immigration policy, "we will stop blocking the departure of those who want to leave the country."[66]

The State Department warned Cuba that unleashing another uncontrolled exodus would have serious consequences. Other agencies put their contingency plan into action. On August 11 Attorney General Janet Reno announced that the Coast Guard would seize ships headed to or from Cuba for the purpose of picking up refugees and that any U.S. residents aboard would be prosecuted for smuggling illegal aliens.[67]

That same evening, following yet another hijacking in which a young naval officer was killed, Castro announced that Cuban police would no longer stop people trying to leave the island so long as they did not try to hijack boats or planes. He blamed the U.S. embargo for aggravating Cuba's economic problems, causing people to want to leave, and he blamed U.S. immigration policy for making it almost impossible for them to emigrate legally.[68] Now free to go, Cubans streamed to the beaches with small boats, rafts, inner tubes, and cars outfitted with pontoons in place of tires, to set out on the perilous ocean journey. Their numbers were staggering. On August 18 the U.S. Coast Guard rescued 535 rafters at sea; less than a week later, on August 23, the one-day number reached 3,253. The *balsero* crisis was under way.[69]

For the president, the crisis triggered a personal sense of déjà vu. Thirteen years earlier, when he was running for reelection as governor of Arkansas, rioting by Mariel refugees detained at Fort Chafee contributed to the one and only electoral defeat of his political career. He also recalled how weak and ineffective President Carter appeared during that mass exodus. "No new Mariel," White House aides repeated to one another as the Cuban crisis developed, "Remember Fort Chafee."[70]

The political risks posed by the crisis extended well beyond the White House. Florida's governor, Lawton Chiles, was locked in a tight reelection

Cubans set out for the United States on a raft made of old tires during the 1994 *balsero* crisis, as curious spectators along Havana's seaside boulevard, the Malecón, look on. Thousands of Cubans took to the sea on makeshift rafts like this one. (Magnum Photos/ Abbas)

race with Jeb Bush, son of the former president. The influx of refugees from Cuba, Haiti, and elsewhere had severely strained Florida's social services, and state politics were already roiled by an anti-immigration backlash. Governor Chiles declared a state of emergency and called on Clinton to take federal action to stem the human tide.[71] Chiles had an ally in Attorney General Janet Reno, former chief prosecutor in Dade County, Florida. Together, they convinced Clinton that the only way to staunch the flow of rafters was to "demagnetize" the United States by denying them entry.[72]

Contingency plans for a mass exodus called for the Coast Guard to intercept and turn back Cubans in boats, but in practice, the Coast Guard could not turn back rafts that were barely afloat. Once the refugees had been rescued, what should be done with them? If brought to the United States, they would aggravate Chiles's political problems, and more Cubans would be encouraged to follow. But they could not be sent back to Cuba without the Cuban government's consent to take them, and repatriation would be politically explosive. Cuban Americans would scream that Washington was delivering the freedom seekers back into the arms of Castro's totalitarian dictatorship.

At a high-level "principals" meeting of the National Security Council on August 18, NSC Senior Director for Democracy Morton Halperin came up with an interim solution: detain Cubans rescued at sea at the U.S. naval base at Guantánamo until they could be processed as legal immigrants or accepted into other countries. A similar detention policy had successfully ended a wave of Haitian rafters the previous spring. Still, the proposal effectively reversed twenty-eight years of leniency toward Cuban refugees, who had always been granted admission to the United States. No doubt the change would provoke howls of protest from Cuban Americans, Jorge Mas Canosa first among them. But "there was not any other option," Halperin recalled. "We had a very short meeting and I wrote a relatively short memo to the president that said, we met; we all agreed we have got to take them back to Guantánamo."[73] Clinton approved.

Once the detention policy had been announced, the White House's next priority was political damage control in Miami. Governor Chiles took on the role of mediator between the president and the exile community's self-appointed leader, Mas Canosa. "The reality was that if we were going to make an interdiction policy work, we couldn't do it without Mas," explained a senior aide to Chiles. "You couldn't have Mas outside the tent pissing in."

Mas made four demands as the price of his public support. The president would have to cut off family remittances to Cuba, sever air links, expand TV and Radio Martí, and impose a naval blockade on the island to topple the regime. The morning after Reno's late-night announcement, Chiles conveyed Mas Canosa's demands to the White House, along with the warning that if they were not met, Mas would publicly denounce the new policy. Chiles reported back to Mas that the White House was open to his first three demands, but not the blockade.[74]

That evening, Clinton interrupted his own forty-eighth birthday party in the White House to meet with Chiles, Mas Canosa, and several other Cuban American leaders who had flown to Washington on Mas Canosa's private jet to negotiate with the president. "You must kick out the last leg of the stool," Mas Canosa told Clinton, banging his fist on the table and demanding a naval blockade.[75] The president would not impose a blockade. But in what aides called "Operation Mollification," he did agree to impose the economic sanctions Mas demanded and to expand TV and Radio Marti.[76]

Not surprisingly, Fidel Castro reacted angrily. Halting the remittances, estimated at between $150 million and $500 million annually, was certain to damage the already deteriorating standard of living of thousands of ordinary Cubans. By making life more difficult, Washington was aggravating the very conditions that prompted migration in the first place. "We say that the blockade is the fundamental thing that encourages this, and the response is more blockade," Castro complained. "We say that the subversive broadcasts have been continuously encouraging illegal departures, and the response is more subversive broadcasts." But what galled Castro most was that Clinton appeared to have handed control of his Cuba policy to Mas Canosa. "No one would ever have believed it, that there would be Mafiosos of this type there in the White House discussing extremely important measures of an international nature," he complained.[77]

To the administration's chagrin, the new detention policy failed to stem the exodus. The rafters simply did not believe U.S. warnings that they would be detained indefinitely and never admitted to the United States. As Guantánamo rapidly filled up with thousands of *balseros* and hard-liners in the exile community clamored for more aggressive action, U.S. officials scrambled for a new approach. If Cuban refugees kept coming despite the detention policy, the only way to end the crisis was for the Cuban government to stop the rafters on the beaches. But the new sanctions gave Castro no incentive to help extricate Washington from its dilemma. "Coercive diplomacy against Cuba is not credible," Nuccio warned on August 21, and the use of force was "virtually unthinkable." Negotiations were a better option. Nuccio recommended opening "a private channel through a third country intermediary" to send a message "that we are prepared to listen to proposals from Cuban officials on migration, Gitmo, flights, remittances, food and medicine."[78]

At a White House press briefing the next day, veteran negotiator and Under Secretary of State Peter Tarnoff extended the olive branch of dialogue. "We are prepared to discuss legal emigration with the Cuban government," he declared, reminding reporters that the United States and Cuba had convened such talks a number of times since 1984. To allay exile fears that the talks would lead to broader negotiations on U.S.-Cuban relations, Tarnoff maintained that there was "no prospect of dialogue on other matters."[79]

As Tarnoff publicly called for talks to end the crisis, President Clinton undertook a more aggressive back-channel effort to open a dialogue. In an extraordinary historical coincidence, at the very same moment Fidel Castro also concluded that the time was ripe for a back-channel approach. On August 23 both leaders reached out to each other through separate, high-level intermediaries. With two phone calls, Clinton and Castro initiated what would become one of the most intricate episodes of secret talks in the history of dialogue between Washington and Havana.

Telephone Tree Diplomacy

The Cubans made the first call. At 11:00 A.M. August 23, one of Castro's closest comrades, filmmaker Alfredo Guevara, telephoned Max Lesnick, a prominent member of Miami's Cuban community. Lesnick had fought with Fidel in the Sierra Maestra, broken with him after the revolution, and fled to Florida in 1961. After supporting violent efforts to overthrow Castro in the 1960s, Lesnick became one of the leading voices of moderation in Miami. In conversations with Guevara as the rafters' crisis unfolded, Lesnick had urged a solution through "a mediation." Now Castro was using him to get a discreet message to a unique, high-level mediator—the thirty-ninth president of the United States, Jimmy Carter. "Transmit to Carter that we have no objection to whatever paradigm he wants to use in the search for solutions to the situation created between Cuba and the U.S.," Castro's initial message stated. "We think his presence as a serious, capable, and prestigious person could be constructive and useful."[80]

To establish a telephone chain for communications between Carter and Castro, Lesnick called his friend, Alfredo Durán. A Bay of Pigs veteran and prestigious Cuban American lawyer in Miami, Durán had served as chairman of the Florida Democratic Party during Carter's 1976 presidential campaign and he remained personally close to the ex-president. After talking to Lesnick, Durán called Carter and briefed him on Castro's interest in having him "act as a mediator" between Havana and Washington. Carter responded positively but cautiously. He "would do so only if there was no alternative," Carter remembered telling Durán, and if "my role would remain secret but approved in advance by both governments."[81]

Employing this cumbersome chain of communication—Castro-Guevara-Lesnick-Durán-Carter/Carter-Durán-Lesnick-Guevara-Castro—messages traveled back and forth between the United States and Cuba over the next five days. The first exchanges addressed Carter's request for a reaffirmation of his role from Castro. On August 25 Guevara called Lesnick from Castro's office and told him to pass the message to Carter that Cuba had "a great amount of confidence in your ability and honor." Carter then conferred with Under Secretary of State Peter Tarnoff and received authorization from the Clinton White House to act as an intermediary.[82]

As Carter understood them, the issues to be addressed were: Cuba's desire for talks on broader issues than migration; whether Washington would honor the 1984 immigration accord, which the Cubans interpreted as permitting twenty thousand migrants annually but which had yielded fewer than two thousand visas per year since it was signed; and whether Havana would allow detainees in Guantánamo to return home if they so desired. Tarnoff conveyed the U.S. reaction, which Carter described as "somewhat equivocal about Cuba's demands."[83] The former president forwarded Tarnoff's message to Durán, who passed it on to Lesnick for transmission to Havana.

Life-threatening squalls in the Florida Strait and Carter's own upcoming trip to Africa forced him to quicken the pace of the secret communications. On Friday, August 26, he placed a call directly to the Oval Office. "I outlined what I considered to be minimum concessions and offered to withdraw my involvement or to continue with his personal approval," Carter remembered telling President Clinton. "I needed some flexibility in dealing with Castro." Clinton put off an immediate decision, but Tarnoff soon called Carter back and reaffirmed the administration's "desire for me to continue my effort."[84]

Carter called Durán with this encouraging message: the White House now had "full knowledge" of Carter's proposals to resolve the crisis. Carter was ready to go to New York "to talk with someone who has Castro's trust" and who could arrange for Carter and Castro to confer directly. Later in the day, the telephone tree provided Carter with Castro's response: the Cuban ambassador to the UN, Fernando Remírez, was ready to talk to Carter in New York. Castro also offered, for the first time, to talk directly with the former president—he provided three private telephone numbers for Carter to use—and suggested some specific times over the weekend.[85]

That evening, Carter conferred at length with Ambassador Remírez. In his memoir, *Beyond the White House*, the former president described his proposal "that talks begin the following week in Washington or New York, that the agenda extend beyond immigration, that the outflow of boat people be stopped, that the U.S. immigration quota be raised to 28,000 annually, and that Cubans in Guantánamo desiring to return to Cuba could do so and not be punished."[86]

On August 27 Carter and Castro finally spoke directly. Castro asked Carter to relay to him the exact terms of the U.S. proposal. He then shared his reaction: Cuba was concerned about legal immigration levels, withdrawal of the new sanctions Clinton had just announced, and the future of U.S. hostility. Castro wanted talks not only about migration but about the embargo as well. Carter did not have all the answers Castro wanted but promised to convey his questions to the White House. Castro agreed that "he would send high-level officials to New York on Wednesday to negotiate in good faith."[87]

On August 28, however, as Carter worked to finalize planning for the negotiations, he received an unexpected phone call from Vice President Al Gore. Gore "expressed his thanks for what had been accomplished, said that an alternative communication channel had been established, and asked that I refrain from further participation," Carter recalled.[88] Clinton had effectively fired the former president as an intermediary.

"Top officials in Washington, who had approved previously, have now requested that I cease my communication with you, except to fulfill my promise of a response from last night," Carter informed Castro in his last communication—this one typed, signed, and passed to Cuba's UN mission. He then updated the Cuban leader on Washington's reaction to the issues Castro had raised in their phone conversation: "I am now informed that the Wednesday meeting will be confined more strictly to immigration matters than I had earlier believed. I was told that other avenues of communication (unknown to me), will be used to respond to the questions of a) rescinding recent actions by President Clinton if rafters are restrained and b) a confirmation of the non-aggression policy expressed by President Bush in May 1991." Carter expressed his "regret" for "this development" and offered Fidel his appreciation of "your frankness and constructive responses. . . . My hope is that you and American officials will be successful in finding some common ground on which to resolve the present crisis," Carter's message concluded, "and to prepare for a future resolution of long term differences."[89]

The Salinas–García Márquez Channel

The "alternative communication channel" that replaced Jimmy Carter was the president of Mexico, Carlos Salinas de Gotari. Salinas was "tight with Castro," Clinton explained, and gave the U.S. president his own communication channel "over the silent wall of non-recognition between the United States and Cuba."[90] Unbeknownst to Carter, the White House had been secretly using Salinas as a parallel interlocutor with Castro the entire time that Carter had been communicating with the Cuban leader. Now, with the talks set to begin and the Cubans demanding a broader agenda including

August 28, 1994   CONFIDENTIAL

To President Fidel Castro
through Cuban Office at the United Nations

Top officials in Washington, who had approved previously,
have now requested that I cease my communication with you, except
to fulfill my promise of a response from last night. Concerning
the issue of legal immigration levels, the number of 28,000 will
be honored. In fairness, I am now informed that the Wednesday
meeting will be confined more strictly to immigration matters
than I had earlier believed. Former Ambassador Mike Scole will
be heading the U.S. delegation. I was told that other avenues of
communication (unknown to me), will be used to respond to the
questions of a) rescinding recent actions by President Clinton
if rafters are restrained and b) a confirmation of the non-aggression policy expressed by President Bush in May 1991.

I regret this development, but want you to know that I have
been meticulous in speaking cautiously and only with authority.
Also, I appreciate your frankness and constructive responses, and
enjoyed our personal exchanges.

I will be leaving this evening for Africa and Russia, and
will send you a trip report when I return. My hope is that you
and American officials will be successful in finding some common
ground on which to resolve the present crisis and to prepare for
a future resolution of long term differences. Despite these
present restraints, I would like to stay in touch with you. You
have my telephone numbers both at home and at The Carter Center.

Sincerely,

Jimmy Carter

Jimmy Carter's final communication to Fidel Castro during the *balsero* crisis, August 28,
1994. Castro asked Carter to mediate the crisis, which he agreed to do until President
Clinton decided to rely instead on Mexican president Carlos Salinas. (National Security
Archive)

the embargo, Clinton decided to turn off Carter, whom he did not trust to act as a neutral intermediary. Working through Salinas made it "easier for [Clinton] to kick the can down the road," Peter Tarnoff recalled, referring to Castro's demand for broader talks. Salinas "was more desirable since he would not force policy on the administration," whereas "Carter would have pressed him aggressively if not emphatically to have a dialogue." Carter was "more than a conduit. He was someone who would have his own ideas."[91]

At half past eight on the evening of August 23, the same day Castro reached out to Carter, Clinton placed a phone call to Salinas at his Los Pinos residence in Mexico City. Clinton was worried about the flood of Cubans taking to the seas, he explained. The crisis carried serious repercussions for the United States, but the anti-immigration feelings it would unleash had implications for Mexican immigrants as well. Clinton asked Salinas "to find a way to establish direct contact with the Cuban government to better understand the Cuban government's position."[92]

"I needed a connection to the Cuban government, someone who would be completely discreet while having direct and immediate access to Fidel Castro," Salinas would recall. "Right from the start, I knew who the right person was. I telephoned Gabriel García Márquez." Within thirty minutes, the Nobel Laureate writer arrived at the presidential residence. Salinas briefed him on Clinton's request. García Márquez, an old friend of Fidel's, picked up the phone and called Havana. Soon thereafter, Salinas was on the line with the Cuban leader.[93]

Without mentioning President Clinton, Salinas conveyed his recent communications with the U.S. government about the *balseros*. The crisis was Washington's responsibility, Castro insisted. The exodus reflected "an untenable situation the Americans themselves had created by means of the economic blockade and the Torricelli bill [Cuban Democracy Act]." The United States had failed to live up to the 1984 migration agreement which provided for twenty thousand Cubans a year to migrate legally, Castro complained. Nevertheless, the Cuban leader was willing to enter into talks with Washington to seek a resolution, "but only so long as they would acknowledge the underlying cause, which was the blockade and its economic effect on the Cuban people."[94]

Clinton personally called again the next day to debrief Salinas on his conversation with Castro. Castro was willing to negotiate an end to the crisis but wanted an agenda for talks that included the blockade, Salinas reported. Clinton wanted a dialogue about migration, "not about other subjects." The embargo could be discussed at some future date, Clinton indicated, but "not under the present circumstances." According to Salinas, Clinton "insisted that it was advisable to sit down and solve the problem before the situation became unmanageable."[95]

Clinton's depiction of the conversation, as told to biographer Taylor Branch at the time, was less diplomatic. "He did not 'have a hard-on for Castro,'" Clinton said he told Salinas. "He did not want a fight. He was open to exploratory talks and exchanges on the side, but he served notice. . . . He would refuse to let Castro dictate the immigration policy of the United States."

"I don't care if I have to put fifty thousand Cubans in Guantánamo," Clinton warned.[96]

To convey Clinton's message, Salinas dispatched García Márquez to Cuba aboard the Mexican presidential plane. That night, and into the early morning of August 25, Salinas and Castro conferred for several hours by phone. In that pivotal conversation, Castro promised the Mexican president that he would reduce the departures of boats from Cuban beaches and accede to Clinton's wish that only migration issues be discussed in the initial meetings. "I understand the U.S. proposal. We can talk about immigration without mentioning other issues, because opening the dialogue to other matters could bring political problems in its wake," Castro told Salinas. "We will manage to talk without damage to the prestige of either party."[97]

Dinner Diplomacy

On August 27 Salinas spoke to Castro again, this time about taking advantage of a fortuitous opportunity: an upcoming dinner party on Martha's Vineyard that both Clinton and García Márquez would attend. With the Clintons vacationing near the estate of writer William Styron and his wife Rose, the summer gathering provided a perfect cover for García Márquez to carry a message from Castro directly to the U.S. president.[98]

Two days later, President Clinton wined and dined with García Márquez at the Styrons' home. The seating chart paired the author and the president at one end of a long, oval dinner table. Mexican writer Carlos Fuentes, Mexico's former foreign minister Bernardo Sepulveda, former U.S. deputy assistant secretary of state for Latin America William Luers, García Márquez's interpreter, Patricia Cepeda, and host Rose Styron were seated with them.

Over a sumptuous meal, García Márquez attempted to engage Clinton in a conversation about a new U.S. approach to Cuba. The writer provided an assessment of Fidel's psychology and how the president could appeal to

Guests at an August 1994 dinner party on Martha's Vineyard during which writer Gabriel García Márquez gave President Clinton a secret message from Fidel Castro about ending the *balsero* crisis. García Márquez played a key role as interlocutor during the crisis. From left to right: John O'Leary, Gabriel García Márquez, Rose Styron, Hillary Clinton, Bill Clinton, Patricia Cepeda, William Styron, and Carlos Fuentes. (Gabriela O'Leary)

it. He pointed out that over the years Washington had moved the goalposts on its demands: "Today it was democratization, before it had been breaking ties with the Soviet Union, getting the Cubans out of Angola and Ethiopia and Nicaragua." Over time, García Márquez suggested, Cuba had complied with these requests, but "the United States had not responded with even so much as an attempt at dialogue." Now there was another opportunity for talks and better bilateral ties. Washington's willingness to open up relations with Cuba would have a strong impact in the region, the Latin Americans at the table advised, rendering Castro's influence less relevant. "Try and come to an understanding with Fidel, as he has a very good opinion of you," García Márquez counseled Clinton.[99]

"Clinton was polite at the beginning, but he didn't bite," noted Luers, who was listening closely to the conversation. "When he realized he was being ambushed, he got less and less cooperative." The president "just turned off," recalls Rose Styron who was sitting next to Clinton. "We need to change the subject," Luers suggested to García Márquez in Spanish as the table talk grew tense. García Márquez immediately asked the president about what books he had been reading, and Clinton began talking energetically about a William Faulkner novel he had just finished. "This question opened Clinton up to one of the most interesting discussions about literature and ideas that I have heard," Luers remembers. There was no further discussion of Cuba over dinner.[100]

At some private point during the long evening, García Márquez shared Castro's message about the migration talks set to start the following week in New York. Clinton had a serious message of his own to convey to Castro: if the influx of *balseros* continued, Cuba would receive a "very different response" from the United States than it had during the Mariel boatlift when Jimmy Carter was president. Clinton reminded García Márquez that Mariel had hurt him politically when he was running for reelection as governor of Arkansas. "Castro has already cost me one election," Clinton warned. "He can't have two."[101]

At the end of the evening, the writer retired to his hotel room and worked with his interpreter, Patricia Cepeda, on a report for Castro. Leaving early the next day on a Mexican government plane provided to him by President Salinas, he flew back to Mexico and then onto Havana to brief Fidel on Clinton's reaction.

Resolving the *Balsero* Crisis

With U.S.-Cuba migration negotiations set to start on September 1, both sides used Salinas to communicate acceptable terms. On the eve of the talks, Clinton called from the Vineyard to say that the United States would offer "at least" twenty thousand annual visas to Cubans per year. Castro responded by pointing out that 160,000 Cubans were on the waiting list for visas because Washington had not honored the 1984 agreement; he wanted those Cubans added to the quota. At the end of the first day of talks, Clinton asked Salinas to reiterate to Castro that the United States would, in fact, allow a minimum of twenty thousand Cubans to emigrate legally each year if Cuban authorities quickly blocked any more rafters from leaving. The U.S. negotiators would also want assurances that Cubans housed at Guantánamo could return to their homes if they wanted to, without fear of persecution.[102]

This demand irked Castro, and he began to backtrack on his earlier concession to discuss only migration issues. The United States now wanted him to "sort out the mess they had created, without giving Cuba a chance to put any of its issues on the negotiating table," he complained. Cuba wanted a far-reaching solution to the pressures that spurred illegal migration; that meant discussing the embargo. The time to do that was now, particularly because Castro did not trust Clinton to follow through on his informal promise to discuss Cuba's concerns at a later date. The United States government had deceived him "more than once," he told Salinas, making promises for a dialogue that were not kept. Castro wanted some type of "link" from these talks to broader ones in the future, to assure that they would, in fact, take place after a migration accord was signed.

Shifting from interlocutor to mediator, Salinas assured Castro of Clinton's good faith. "We were facing a kind of 'ladder' with various rungs; the important thing was to take the first step, which meant sitting down and talking, even if only about the migration issue," Salinas advised. "If there was goodwill, that would create the political conditions for a future dialogue about other important matters."[103]

As Salinas and Castro privately addressed this contentious problem, the issue played out publicly at the talks in New York City. "We insist that there will be no solution as long as the embargo against Cuba, which is the cause of the whole problem, persists," declared the head of the Cuban negotiating team, former foreign minister Ricardo Alarcón.[104] For the first few days, the Cubans continued to press this issue. But the American delegation, led by Deputy Assistant Secretary of State Michael Skol, steadfastly refused to put it on the agenda. Even on the migration issue, the two sides were far apart at first. Washington offered to simplify and expand the mechanism for legal migration, assuring that at least twenty thousand Cubans a year would be admitted to the United States. The Cubans wanted the United States to take an additional one hundred thousand refugees immediately to clear up the backlog of people wanting to emigrate. The Cubans also insisted that Washington drop the new sanctions on travel and remittances that Clinton had imposed in August. The talks quickly stalled.[105]

Only the ongoing back-channel diplomacy enabled the two sides to find common ground. On September 5 Castro called Salinas with an urgent message for Clinton. The Cubans wanted two final guarantees: first, that the new agreement state clearly that the punitive measures Clinton had announced on August 20—termination of travel, telephone calls, and remittances—would be rescinded; and, second, that Clinton make a verbal commitment to Salinas for future talks on lifting the embargo. "Tell President Clinton to make a commitment with you, the President of Mexico, to sit down and talk about the economic consequences of the blockade," Castro told Salinas. "I'm not asking him to put it in writing. . . . I hope for Clinton's confirmation of this through you, to the effect that he's willing to discuss the economic causes as soon as possible. With that," Castro promised, "the problem will be solved."[106]

Clinton responded that since the United States had always taken the position that the migration talks were limited to the issues of migration, the final agreement could not include language on the August 20 measures. Nevertheless, Clinton promised to lift the restrictions within forty-five to sixty days and asked for Fidel to "trust his word."[107] On the guarantee for broader bilateral talks, Clinton finessed his answer. He would not make any public reference to such talks, but Salinas could inform Castro that "at some point in the future" the United States would be willing to discuss the broader bilateral relationship. "Similar discussions had already been held in the past," Clinton noted, "and this showed they could be repeated in the future." According to Salinas, Clinton "wanted Fidel to understand this so that the negotiations in New York could end on a positive note."[108]

In the evening on September 6, Castro called Salinas with his answer. "I'm going to say this very slowly so you can write down—as you told me you do—my answer to President Clinton's message," Fidel told him. "And my answer is this: We accept what he proposes and we trust him to keep his word."[109]

In New York, the two negotiating teams had spent a week trying to hammer out an accord, making little headway. On September 8, with the formal negotiations at an impasse, Alarcón flew to Havana for consultations. After receiving the assurances Salinas had relayed from Clinton, Castro stepped back from Cuba's demand for a broader dialogue. When Alarcón returned to the bargaining table, he was ready to accept Washington's proposal and finalize the accord. The United States would no longer automatically accept Cubans who arrived on its shores "in irregular ways." Those rescued at sea would be remanded to "safe havens" outside of the United States. The United States would now provide "at minimum" twenty thousand legal visas to Cubans seeking to emigrate each year. Pursuant to Cuba's demands, the United States agreed to provide six thousand additional visas to Cubans on the long waiting list. Cuba, in turn, would "take effective measures in every way possible to prevent unsafe departures" and allow those Cubans in Guantánamo who wanted to return home to do so. Both sides pledged cooperation in combating human trafficking and agreed to hold periodic consultations on implementation of the agreement.[110] "Although the blockade continues and although a hostile policy toward us persists, the truth is that as of tonight, in one area, in one zone of the relationship between the two countries, we have achieved normalcy," Ricardo Alarcón declared in announcing the successful conclusion of the talks on September 9. "It has been demonstrated that Cuba and the United States can reach agreement."[111]

The immigration accord finally stanched the flow of the *balseros*. As Cuban police began patrolling the beaches again and confiscating rafts, the number of refugees fell dramatically: on September 10 the Coast Guard rescued 1,004; on September 12, only 283; on September 14, just 17; and on September 18, none.[112]

Wet Foot–Dry Foot

Out of the turmoil and talks surrounding the *balsero* crisis came new momentum for changing U.S. Cuba policy. As the immigration agreement was about to be signed in New York, an editorial appeared on the opinion page of the *Washington Post* entitled "The Embargo Must Go." Co-authored by the chairmen of the Senate and House foreign relations committees, Claiborne Pell and Lee Hamilton, the article called on Clinton to lift key parts of the embargo, starting with the travel ban, and "open the door for a positive, rather than punitive, influence" on Cuba's future. "We may need to move gradually" on a new policy of engagement, they acknowledged, "but we need to move."[113]

At the State Department, Richard Nuccio launched an effort to rescind the August 20 sanctions as part of a new "package of initiatives" that included allowing communication between U.S. and Cuban military officers, authorizing news bureaus in Havana, and exploring future cooperation on narcotics interdiction and environmental issues.[114] To bolster his case in the face of resistance from opponents like Dennis Hays and Michael Skol, Nuccio had quietly encouraged Pell and Hamilton to publicly press for action.

Once again, Assistant Secretary Watson sought to promote a direct dialogue. "Can we fashion a strategy for dialogue with the regime that will advance our interests and gain international support without doing serious political damage in Florida?" he asked Nuccio. "It would show people we aren't petrified, it would pressure the regime, it would get international support if we do it right and—heaven forbid—if it worked, it would contribute to a peaceful transition."[115]

The new debate revived the idea of a major policy pronouncement built around the "calibrated response" concept. "With the Cuban rafters crisis under control," read an action memo drafted for National Security Advisor Anthony Lake in early October, "the time may be ripe to consider a more proactive approach." The memorandum, "A Calibrated Response to Cuban Reforms," listed potential reciprocal actions Washington could consider. If Cuba legalized farmers' markets and small private businesses, for example, the United States would begin selling fertilizers and farm implements to the island. If Cuba allowed independent political parties and scheduled municipal elections, the United States would remove the embargo against sales of food and medicine. And if Castro held internationally supervised free national elections, the United States would lift the embargo entirely and normalize relations. "A draft of a speech that spells this out in general terms is now under consideration to be given by the Secretary of State sometime in the near future," Lake was advised, "probably after the elections."[116]

But the speech was never given. In the November 1994 midterm elections, the Republicans won control of both the House and the Senate. The ultraconservative Jesse Helms (R-N.C.) took over from Pell as chair of the Senate Foreign Relations Committee, and the ultraconservative Dan Burton (R-Ind.) became chair of the House Subcommittee on Western Hemisphere Affairs. Helms and Burton soon began drafting new legislation, "The Cuban Liberty and Democratic Solidarity (Libertad) Act"—known simply as "Helms-Burton"—designed to globalize the trade embargo, further punish the Cuban economy, and block President Clinton from doing anything to improve relations with Havana.

Facing a hostile Republican Congress and more concerned than ever about Florida's pivotal role in the 1996 election, Clinton decided against any new Cuba initiative. But he could not ignore the growing humanitarian crisis at Guantánamo. Some twenty-one thousand intercepted rafters remained crammed into the makeshift detention center. Chief of the Atlantic Command General John J. Sheehan began sending alarming reports of mass frustration, violence, and even suicides among the Cuban inhabitants. Some of them were injecting diesel fuel into their veins, according to one report, in hopes of being transported to the United States for hospital care. If the base was not cleared soon, Sheehan warned, Guantánamo could erupt in rioting.[117]

Clinton's dilemma was stark. Holding the detainees indefinitely was proving to be impractical. Simply paroling them into the United States risked setting off another migration crisis, since the threat of indefinite detention would be hollow. Returning them to Cuba seemed politically impossible and, in any event, could not be done without the agreement of the Cuban government. At the NSC, Morton Halperin, who had advocated for the policy of detention in August, offered a possible solution: "The only way we could bring these people in [to the United States], I said, is if we announce that from now on we send people back to Cuba."[118]

But that, too, would require Cuba's agreement. And opening a dialogue with Havana about Guantánamo was fraught with problems. Initial consultations on implementing the September 1994 accord had gone poorly. The Cubans found the U.S. negotiator, Cuban Affairs Coordinator Dennis Hays, to be "rigid and arrogant, the worst kind of diplomat," according to Ricardo Alarcón who handled the migration talks for the Cuban side.[119]

Moreover, Castro was already angry that Clinton had reneged on his promise to rescind the August 20 sanctions. "The 45 days have gone by, the 60 days have gone by, two-and-a-half months have gone by and there is no news, there are no signs," Castro complained to President Salinas who, at Clinton's request, called Castro in late November to discuss the Guantánamo problem. "I am taking [the elections] into account, that is why we have not insisted," Castro noted. But "we have been waiting, trusting, naturally, in what was offered, what was promised."[120]

Nevertheless, senior U.S. officials began reaching out to the Cubans, using "cocktail diplomacy" to secretly talk about Guantánamo. In November 1994 Halperin met with Alarcón at the Georgetown mansion of Jennifer Cafritz and Laughton Phillips.[121] At the end of dinner, the other guests retired from the dining room to drink expensive brandy, leaving Halperin and Alarcón at the table to quietly discuss how to empty Guantánamo of its increasingly volatile inhabitants. Under the guise of attending another dinner party at the Foxhall Drive home of Tom Cohen and Lisa Fuentes, Halperin continued the dialogue with Cuba's UN ambassador, Fernando Remírez. Halperin came away from these conversations with the impression that the Cubans were willing to help Washington solve the problem.[122]

In the end, solving the Guantánamo problem fell to Peter Tarnoff. Since his key role in the secret dialogue during the Carter administration, Tarnoff had maintained close relations with Alarcón. During the 1980s, when Tarnoff served as president of the Council on Foreign Relations in New York and Alarcón was Cuba's vice minister of foreign relations, the two talked frequently by phone and met for martinis when Alarcón visited the UN. Over the years, they established a trusting camaraderie unique in the history of relations between the United States and revolutionary Cuba. Peter, Alarcón fondly observed, "was a good guy."[123]

On January 23, 1995, Tarnoff and Alarcón held their first secret negotiating session in New York. The clock was ticking on the refugee situation at

Guantánamo, Tarnoff explained. The Clinton administration needed Cuba's support and understanding to find a solution. The options were complicated. Efforts to relocate the refugees to third countries such as Panama and Belize were bogged down. Bringing everyone to the United States could set off another exodus. Could Cuba help the United States solve this problem and avoid another migration crisis? To Tarnoff's surprise, Alarcón "understood and accepted right away."[124]

On April 17, the thirty-fourth anniversary of the Bay of Pigs invasion, Tarnoff and Alarcón met again in the famous Oak Room bar in the Plaza Hotel. (They had intended to meet in the Tea Room, but Alarcón was not allowed to smoke his ever-present cigar there.) Alarcón was in New York for another consultation on implementing the 1994 migration agreement and was scheduled to meet the following day with the U.S. delegation, led by Dennis Hays. "Be sure you don't tell Dennis Hays about our talks," Tarnoff cautioned Alarcón.[125] Tarnoff outlined a U.S. proposal paroling Guantánamo detainees into the United States but also providing for the return to Cuba of new migrants intercepted at sea. Alarcón was "intrigued," Tarnoff recalls.

To finalize the details, Tarnoff and Alarcón met one more time in Toronto, over the weekend of April 29–30. Their meeting was ultrasecret, and White House officials took extensive steps to protect it from leaking. The National Security Agency was instructed to show any intercepts of Alarcón's phone calls only to the White House. At the NSC, Halperin drafted the negotiating instructions, which were then cleared by Deputy National Security Advisor Berger and the president himself. Halperin personally delivered the briefing book to Tarnoff to keep it secure. Nobody else but Secretary of State Warren Christopher knew where Tarnoff was going. As a cover story, he told his colleagues he and his wife were taking a short vacation.[126]

In Toronto, Tarnoff and Alarcón formalized an accord. The final language called for the "humanitarian parole" of Guantánamo detainees into the United States. To prevent future *balseros*, a section on "safety of life at sea" provided that the United States and Cuba would "cooperate jointly" on repatriating Cubans intercepted at sea or trying to cross onto the Guantánamo base. Both countries would "ensure that no action is taken against those migrants returned to Cuba." The statement reaffirmed a "joint commitment to take steps to prevent unsafe departures from Cuba which risk loss of human life and to oppose acts of violence associated with illegal immigration."[127]

Before the accord could be publicly announced, both Clinton and Castro had to sign off. Tarnoff and Alarcón worked out a plan to speak via phone at noon on May 1 "just to say, 'my guy's in, my guy's in,'" Halperin recalled. "I did a memo to the president early Monday morning; he approved it. I called Peter. He had his call with Alarcón. [Peter] called back and said, 'We are both in.'"[128] The "Joint Statement with the Republic of Cuba on Normalization of Migration" was announced the next day.

The new migration accord ended the thirty-year U.S. policy of encouraging illegal flight from Cuba. Cuban refugees could still win permanent resident status under the 1966 Cuban Adjustment Act but only if they actually reached the United States. Those intercepted at sea would go back to Cuba. On the basis of this distinction, the new policy came to be known as "wet foot–dry foot."

Predictably, the new agreement generated a storm of protest from the right—much of it focused on the secrecy of the negotiations and the implication that the talks portended a new era of cooperation between Washington and Havana. The new policy meant that "the United States will now be co-wardens of Castro's police state," CANF's Jorge Mas Canosa declared. Within days, the anti-Castro lobby was organizing angry protests in the streets of Miami's Little Havana—and in front of the White House gates.[129]

In damage control mode, Tarnoff met privately with Representatives Burton, Torricelli, Ileana Ros-Lehtinen (D-Fla.), Robert Menendez (D-N.J.), and Peter Deutsch (D-Fla.). He assured them that the Clinton administration still adhered to the Cuban Democracy Act and even shared the "overall objectives" of the draft Helms-Burton legislation. Secrecy had been necessary in the talks, he said, because "if word got out on the agreement, there could have been mass movements of people on water or over land to GTMO [Guantánamo] to beat the deadline."[130]

Their meeting on May 10 did nothing to mollify the anti-Castro legislators. On May 18 Tarnoff was hauled before Burton's Subcommittee, forced to testify under oath—a procedure rarely invoked with government officials—and publicly harangued for secretly talking to the enemy. Representative Ros-Lehtinen announced that she had 123 questions and then began asking them: "What did President Clinton know about the negotiations? Was there any promise given by the United States concerning relaxation of sanctions against Castro? Will the Clinton administration consider a naval blockade of Cuba if Castro violates this accord?"[131]

Representative Menendez attacked the very concept of secret talks: "Secret negotiations between the Castro dictatorship and Secretary of State Henry Kissinger under a Republican administration were wrong in 1974," he declared, "and those between the Castro dictatorship and Peter Tarnoff . . . under a

Democratic administration are wrong in 1995."[132] The Republican legislators also launched a McCarthy-like attack on Tarnoff's colleague, Morton Halperin. According to Burton, Halperin "supported the views of the leftist groups around the world." Ros-Lehtinen demanded to know: "Did Morton Halperin initiate the idea of holding secret talks?"[133]

To dampen opposition to the new policy, Clinton made Halperin the sacrificial lamb. Sandy Berger called him and broke the news. "I got canned," Halperin recalled. "The Miami exiles were very upset that they hadn't been consulted in advance on the accord and as part of reaching an understanding with the White House, I would no longer be working on Cuba policy."[134] A veteran voice for a rational policy was gone.

A shake-up also occurred at the Department of State. Angry at being kept in the dark about Tarnoff's secret negotiations, Cuban Affairs Coordinator Dennis Hays demanded to be reassigned. He was appointed ambassador to Suriname but, in 2000, left the State Department to work for Mas Canosa as head of CANF's Washington office. His colleague and ally, Deputy Assistant Secretary Michael Skol, also resigned his position in protest.

A New Policy Bureaucracy

As the political storm over the new accord subsided, the administration took the opportunity to restructure the Cuba policy-making process. On May 25 the White House announced that Richard Nuccio had been appointed "Special Advisor to the President and Secretary of State for Cuba." The position was a bureaucratic hybrid; Nuccio moved to a new office in the Old Executive Office Building adjacent to the West Wing but technically remained a State Department appointee, answering both to Under Secretary Tarnoff and Deputy National Security Advisor Berger. As "Cuba Czar," Nuccio would oversee new policy initiatives and chair a new Interagency Task Force on Cuba "responsible for implementation of all aspects of our Cuba policy." Nuccio wanted a policy that would be more "agile and creative," he told task force members when they first met on June 9. "I hope that we can demonstrate our ability to manage effectively what we currently do, so that we can then move forward aggressively to promote a peaceful democratic transition in Cuba."[135]

Throughout the summer of 1995, the Task Force worked to formulate a package of proposals for presidential consideration. These included establishing U.S. news bureaus in Havana, permitting U.S. nongovernmental organizations (NGOs) to work in Cuba, authorizing USAID funding to promote democracy, and easing restrictions on Cuban American travel, as well as educational, religious, and academic travel. There was also a series of "close-hold initiatives," as Nuccio reported to Tarnoff and Berger—"things we could/should be doing on Cuba policy that we cannot discuss publicly for a variety of reasons." Arranging for military-to-military contacts between the Cuban and U.S. armed forces was one creative but sensitive policy proposal. Counter-narcotics collaboration was another. The Task Force considered "a modest initiative to move beyond the existing cooperation on a case-by-case basis to a negotiated agreement that would involve DEA [Drug Enforcement Administration] and Coast Guard," Nuccio reported.[136]

In addition, the Task Force began to examine more significant initiatives— "offerings," as Nuccio remembered them, that "could be put on the table" if Cuba undertook major reforms. One was the return of Guantánamo, which would remove the imperial symbol of U.S. encroachment on Cuba sovereignty. Another was "getting Cuba off the terrorism list." Cuba was designated by the Department of State as a "state sponsor" of terrorism in 1982, because of Havana's support for revolutionaries in Central America. There was no longer any real reason for Cuba's designation, but the politics of removing Cuba from the list was complicated, Nuccio understood. He tasked State Department official Robert Gelbard to "do a reexamination of why Cuba is on the terrorist list."[137]

Looking back, Nuccio believed there were promising opportunities for new initiatives, especially with Tarnoff in charge of Cuba policy at the State Department. Tarnoff characterized his goal as "to move the relationship along, piece-by-piece," but he understood real change would be an uphill battle. Although Clinton had led Castro to believe that the United States would discuss the embargo after the migration issue was settled, "There was no energy in the administration to improve relations," Tarnoff recalled. Secretary of State Christopher "wouldn't put Cuba in the top twenty issues of importance, and Clinton wouldn't put it in the top 50." For Cuba policy, he said, "There was no rabbi on the issue to make it a priority."[138]

Military-to-Military Contacts: The Fence Line Talks

Little by little, however, relations did begin to change—in unexpected places. The 1994 rafters crisis produced a notable improvement in U.S.-Cuban military cooperation at Guantánamo Bay Naval Station. Under the 1903 Platt Amendment, the United States began leasing the forty-five-square-mile base, paying Cuba a nominal rent ($4,085 annually); a 1934 treaty gave the United

States basing rights in perpetuity. With the advent of the revolution, Fidel Castro demanded the United States return the base to Cuba. He stopped cashing the rent checks, collecting them in a drawer in his desk to show visitors.[139]

Guantánamo became a potential and perpetual flashpoint. In February 1964 Castro shut off the water supply in retaliation for the U.S. seizure of thirty-eight Cuban fishermen allegedly in U.S. waters. Johnson retaliated by cutting off the flow of dollars to Cuba by firing most of the base's three thousand Cuban employees.[140] While vowing that Cubans would "fight to the last man" defending their homeland, Castro moved to deescalate the crisis by assuring Washington that he would not initiate hostilities. Although Cuba wanted Guantánamo returned, it was "not an urgent question," he noted after the fishermen had been released, and could "takes years" to be resolved.[141]

Nevertheless, the risk of inadvertent conflict remained high. U.S. sentries reported that Cubans threw stones at them; Cuban sentries claimed that U.S. forces sometimes fired at them, killing or wounding several Cubans. In 1964 Castro took one of the first steps to reduce tensions at the base by ordering Cuban troops back from the base perimeter. Thereafter, relations between the U.S. and Cuban military units facing each other settled into wary routine.[142]

The land mines on both the sides of the fence separating the base from Cuban territory proved deadly dangerous to soldiers and civilians from both countries. In 1994, Marine Corps General John Sheehan, director of plans and policy (and later commander) of the Atlantic Fleet, decided to do something about it. "Under the framework of 'safety' I made the offer to the Cuban Border Guard commander to exchange information on minefield locations and agreed to a protocol for assisting people who might be caught in an active minefield," said Sheehan, recalling his first "confidence building" measure to reduce tensions at Guantánamo during the rafters crisis. As an act of "good faith," Sheehan provided the charts of the minefields on U.S. side of the fence.[143] His gesture prompted the local commander of the Cuban Border Guard to request a face-to-face meeting. Sheehan agreed. For an initial meeting, the two sides set up a tent on the "yellow line" separating the base from Cuban territory.

So began regularly scheduled monthly consultations, dubbed "the fence line talks" between the U.S. and Cuban local commanders—talks that continued after the migration crisis ended and evolved into one of the few channels for routine communication on crisis prevention. The agenda for the talks usually centered on information sharing about upcoming military maneuvers, troop movement around the base, migration issues, and responses to natural disasters—anything that could lead to potential misunderstanding and conflict. "The rule of thumb was 'no surprises,'" recalled General Sheehan, who headed the U.S. delegation in a half dozen of the early fence line talks.

For the U.S. military, dialogue with its Cuban counterpart made simple, common sense. The Cold War was over and the U.S. intelligence community had concluded that the debilitated Cuban military no longer represented a serious threat to the United States. "There was very much a sense among the military after the Cold War that the Cuban issue was literally obsolete and that policy needed to be changed," remembers Alberto Coll, who served as deputy assistant secretary of defense from 1990 to 1993. Officers who dealt with Cuba wanted "some form of engagement," even though the U.S. political leadership remained cautious.[144]

Given the sensitivities in Washington to any form of dialogue with Cuba, Sheehan and his colleagues understood the political risks of proceeding with the fence line talks. But the payoff was worth it, according to Sheehan, because "the potential of armed soldiers within rock-throwing range of each other making a mistake that could spiral out of control was very high." In addition, he told the authors, "I felt strongly that since the public rhetoric between the U.S. and Cuba was so political and ideologically charged, it was absolutely essential that a line of military-to-military communications should be opened as a potential vehicle for escalation management should it be required."[145]

This approach paid off, not only lowering tensions but essentially normalizing relations in a military zone of potential conflict. The U.S. and local Cuban commands established a "hot line" for emergencies and began conducting joint firefighting and hurricane evacuation exercises.[146] In 1996 President Clinton ordered that the U.S. minefield surrounding the base be dismantled, and over the next few years both sides withdrew their tanks and artillery.[147]

In 1999 the Clinton administration informed Cuba that it was contemplating using Guantánamo as a center for refugees from Kosovo. Although Cuba opposed the U.S. military role in the former Yugoslavia, it did not object and even offered medical assistance to the refugees if needed. In 2002, when President Bush ordered that Guantánamo be used as a detention center for prisoners in the war on terrorism, Cuba again lodged no complaint. Raúl Castro even told a reporter that if an Al Qaeda prisoner escaped, "He'll be caught and returned through the front doors of the U.S. base."[148]

"In 1994, the events concerning the Cuban and Haitian rafters created a situation that obliged us to cooperate," Raúl Castro explained, looking back at how military-to-military relations had developed. "Since then, there has been absolute calm here, appreciated by both countries. . . . There is an atmosphere of cooperation, of mutual respect and collaboration." Reflecting on what the fence line talks had achieved, Sheehan agreed. "By opening a discussion with the FAR [Revolutionary Armed Forces], an opportunity was created that allowed both sides to deal with practical issues that affected real people." Moreover, "there has also not been a serious fence line incident in over 25 years and we have not lost a single American Marine."[149]

Cubans saw the positive relations at Guantánamo as a model for U.S.-Cuban relations generally. "This minimum cooperation that exists here shows that we can do the same in many other things," according to Raúl Castro. "I believe that what has been achieved here, modestly, among persons who follow orders issued from above, has been to act rationally and with common sense."[150]

Brothers to the Rescue: A Back-Channel Failure

On October 3, 1995, more than a year after Bill Clinton secretly promised Fidel Castro that he would rescind his August 1994 sanctions in forty-five to sixty days, the president finally approved the restoration of Cuban American remittances and eased travel restrictions. It had taken three months to get the announcement cleared through the foreign policy bureaucracy. "The roll out must be well planned," a White House decision memorandum warned Clinton, "so that this action is, to the maximum extent, seen for what it is—reasonable humanitarian changes to the August 1994 controls plus pro-democracy moves, not anti-embargo or 'pro-Castro.'"[151]

Clinton announced the package of new initiatives three days later in a speech to the conservative NGO Freedom House. While promising to "tighten the enforcement of our embargo to keep the pressure for reform on," the president also sought to "promote the free flow of ideas" by licensing U.S. news bureaus in Havana, liberalizing religious and academic travel, granting a general license for Cuban Americans to visit once a year, and lifting the ban on family remittances imposed during the *balsero* crisis. Clinton also licensed NGO civic projects in Cuba "to promote peaceful change and protect human rights," and he announced that the first grant would go to Freedom House—$500,000 to purchase computer equipment, copiers, and fax machines for Cuban dissidents.[152]

As part of its rollout strategy, the administration worked overtime to assure the exile community and congressional Republicans that the new measures did not portend any opening to Cuba. U.S. policy, Richard Nuccio stated publicly, was to "maintain the existing embargo, the most comprehensive we have toward any country." Only if the Cubans took major steps toward democracy would the United States "respond appropriately," he said. "Big moves, big response." As Nuccio assured the hard-liners, "We don't have any secret negotiations going on."[153]

Nevertheless, within an hour of Clinton's announcement, Senate majority leader and Republican presidential hopeful Robert Dole declared that "all signs point to normalization and secret negotiations with Castro." The senator then announced that he would move the Helms-Burton legislation onto the Senate floor for immediate consideration. The bill, already passed by the House in September, prohibited U.S. assistance to Cuba until the advent of democracy and imposed sanctions against foreign countries and corporations that did business on the island. Among its many punitive measures, Helms-Burton allowed U.S. citizens to sue foreign corporations that "trafficked" in properties expropriated from wealthy Cubans or Americans following the revolution. Executives from these corporations would be denied visas to enter the United States. "It is time to tighten the screws," Senator Helms announced when he first presented the bill to the Senate Foreign Relations Committee. His cosponsor, Congressman Burton, predicted that passage would be "the last nail in [Castro's] coffin."[154]

Helms-Burton became a bitter battleground between the executive and the legislative branches. Not only did the bill "attack the President's constitutional authority to conduct foreign policy," according to a White House legislative strategy memorandum for Clinton, "Helms-Burton actually damages the prospects of a democratic transition in Cuba, and could conflict with broader U.S. interests, including compliance with major international trade agreements . . . and our commitment to respect international law."[155] The administration forcefully opposed the extraterritorial provisions of the bill, particularly Title III allowing lawsuits against third-country investors using expropriated properties in Cuba. Secretary of State Christopher threatened a presidential veto.

As the Helms-Burton legislation dominated public debate on Cuba policy in the latter half of 1995, a veritable Greek tragedy played out in the skies over Cuba's coast—a tragedy set in motion by repeated incursions into Cuban airspace by a group of Cuban American pilots known as Brothers to the Rescue (BTTR). Since 1991, the "Brothers" had been flying search missions for distressed Cuban rafters, notifying the U.S. Coast Guard whenever a small boat or raft needed rescue. But despite its humanitarian mission, BTTR's founder and director, Bay of Pigs veteran José Basulto, had a history of anti-Castro violence. In August 1962, he had positioned a boat with a 20mm cannon on its bow just off the coast of Havana and shelled the Hornedo de Rosita hotel, where he and his coconspirators believed Castro would be dining. "I was trained as a terrorist by the United States, in the use of violence to attain goals," said Basulto, but he claimed to have converted to nonviolence. "When I was young, my Hollywood hero was John Wayne. Now I'm like Luke Skywalker. I believe the force is with us."[156]

When the September 1994 immigration accord ended the flow of rafters in the Florida Strait, Basulto shifted BTTR's mission from rescue to provocation. "They started to redefine their mission as one of not helping innocent people at risk for their lives but to carry out a political agenda of harassing and threatening the Cuban government by overflights, dropping leaflets [into Cuba]," Nuccio explained.[157]

On November 10, 1994, Basulto dropped Brothers to the Rescue bumper stickers over the Cuban countryside. Repeatedly over the next eight months, BTTR planes violated Cuban airspace. Their most provocative act in 1995 came on July 13, when Basulto's Cessna Skymaster buzzed Havana, raining down thousands of religious medallions and leaflets reading "Brothers, Not Comrades" along the Malecón, Havana's broad seaside avenue. "We are proud of what we did," Basulto exalted after landing back in Miami, where footage of the mission taken by an NBC cameraman on the plane aired on local TV stations. "We want confrontation," Basulto declared. His bold incursion served "as a message to the Cuban people," he boasted. "The regime is not invulnerable."[158]

These overflights constituted a direct challenge to Cuba's national security and a flagrant affront to its sovereignty. "It was so humiliating," Castro later told *Time* magazine. "The U.S. would not have tolerated it if Washington's airspace had been violated by small airplanes."[159] Castro and his generals had long memories of the early years of the revolution when little planes would take off from Florida and drop incendiary devices over the Cuban countryside as part of the CIA's covert war of sabotage. (President Eisenhower posed the obvious question during an NSC discussion of the exile flights, wondering, "Why the Cubans don't just shoot the planes down?")[160] Given that dark history, Cuban officials made it clear to the Clinton administration that the incursions could not and would not be tolerated. As BTTR flights kept coming, the Cuban government used every channel of communication it could find—formal and informal, public and private, direct and through intermediaries—to press the U.S. government to clip Basulto's wings.

Officially, the Cubans filed one diplomatic protest after another. Following the July 13 incursion, their note contained a stern warning: Cuban security forces had a "firm determination to adopt whatever positions are necessary to avoid acts of provocation," and "any boat from abroad can be sunk and any airplane downed."[161] The Cuban Civil Aeronautics Institute sent a series of reports to the Federal Aviation Administration (FAA), along with evidence—copies of video radar and flight plans—it had accumulated on the violations of Cuban airspace. "I plead that you take actions necessary to avoid that these events repeat themselves," a Cuban official wrote to FAA administrator David Hinson in August as Basulto announced he was organizing another flight for early September.[162]

Given the clear and present danger of an international incident, the FAA's response seemed desultory at best and criminally negligent at worst. In late August, FAA officers met with Alfonso Fraga-Pérez, chief of the Cuban Interests Section in Washington, to review Cuba's complaint. The agency also issued a "Notice of Proposed Certificate Action" to suspend Basulto's piloting license for 120 days for violating Federal Aviation Regulations by "flying a Cessna 337 through Cuban airspace and over Havana"—a notice that did not, in practice, prevent him from actually flying. In Miami, FAA officials met face-to-face with Basulto before and after the July 13 incursion to warn him to stay away from Cuba. His actions made it clear that he would not comply.[163]

In August, Nuccio flew to Miami twice to meet with local FAA, FBI, Coast Guard, and Customs officials to press them to take quick enforcement action against Basulto and his pilots. Through diplomatic notes to Cuba, the State Department transmitted multiple FAA requests for "any evidence and identifying data" that could advance the agency's slow-moving investigation. State officials also used the notes to request that the Cuban government exercise "the utmost discretion and restraint and avoid the use of excessive force" in dealing with the incursions.[164]

"It was clear to everyone that we were playing with fire, and that we had a hose in our hand and refused to use it," recalled Fulton Armstrong, a CIA analyst detailed to the NSC in mid-1995 to work on Cuba.[165] As the bureaucracy dithered, BTTR and Basulto continued their provocations. Between August 1995 and February 1996, the Cuba government filed four more diplomatic notes protesting violations of its airspace—only to have the FAA request additional evidence for its plodding investigation. Emboldened by his seeming impunity, on January 13, 1996, Basulto again flew his planes over Havana, this time dropping a half a million leaflets exhorting the Cuban people to "Change Things Now." His ability to penetrate Cuban airspace, Basulto bragged to Radio Martí back in Miami, demonstrated that "Castro isn't impenetrable, that many things are within our reach to be done."[166]

Citizen Intermediaries

In Cuba, those who foresaw the coming confrontation resorted to back-channel diplomacy to reach the highest levels of the U.S. government. Ricardo Alarcón placed a series of secret phone calls to his friend and fellow negotiator, Peter Tarnoff, beseeching him to take action. "You say you want an accommodation, but you are letting this crap with the Brothers to the Rescue continue," as one White House official paraphrased Alarcón's angry message.[167] In response, Tarnoff brought the issue of how to ground the flights before the Interagency Task Force on Cuba. He also placed a call directly to Secretary of Transportation Federico Peña in an effort to light a fire under the bureaucracy. Tarnoff, who had private telephone numbers for Alarcón at his house, office, and even in the hospital room where his wife was convalescing, called to urge patience and assure him, "We are trying."[168]

Impatient, Alarcón turned to two intermediaries, Saul Landau and Scott Armstrong. Landau, a documentary filmmaker, had made two major movies about Fidel, written widely on U.S. policy, and traveled frequently to the island. Armstrong, a former journalist at the *Washington Post*, also had a long-standing interest in U.S.-Cuban relations. During the fall of 1994, they had played the role of citizen emissaries arranging Mort Halperin's secret dinner party meetings with Cuban officials to discuss Cuban refugees at Guantánamo.

Now, Landau and Armstrong were in Havana on a project to promote a baseball game between Cuban players and American major leaguers. Alarcón gave them a dire warning to take back to the White House: "The gravest consequences would occur" on the next BTTR flight into Cuban airspace. Upon their return to Washington, Landau and Armstrong contacted Halperin, who, although he was no longer the lead person on Cuba, was still on the NSC staff. "We saw Mort," Landau said, "and told him that the Cubans really meant business on this one. That the Administration couldn't fuck off anymore," Landau remembers. "He said he would take care of it."[169]

Using White House stationary for maximum authority, Halperin wrote to the head of the FAA, David Hinson, demanding that he revoke the licenses of

Basulto and his BTTR pilots "on the basis of their repeatedly filing false flight plans." Such pressure from the White House, Halperin believed—erroneously, as it turned out—would curtail the flights. Confident the issue had been resolved, Halperin's office asked Armstrong to transmit that message to Havana, which he did through the new head of the Cuban Interests Section, Fernando Remírez.

In fact, the issue was not resolved. The FAA office in Miami determined that Basulto could not be grounded until they had fully completed an enforcement investigative report. It refused to issue an Emergency Cease and Desist order, or take any steps beyond again warning Basulto not to violate Cuban airspace.

The Cuban military also tried to send a warning through private channels. At the Ministry of the Revolutionary Armed Forces (MINFAR) on February 8, 1996, a delegation of retired U.S. officers organized by the Center for Defense Information received a briefing on the BTTR overflights by Cuban Air Force Brigadier General Arnaldo Tamayo Méndez. "They have come here; they have violated our airspace, dropping leaflets and propaganda, which is a flagrant violation of our sovereignty," General Tamayo told the delegation, which included retired Rear Admiral Eugene Carroll and former U.S. ambassador to El Salvador Robert White. "We would like to see these acts of piracy against our country stopped," Tamayo continued. Cuba had the capability "to bring them down at any moment. We haven't done so precisely because we do not want to overheat the situation," Tamayo explained, "because then, of course, Cuba will be presented as a culprit, and the violators and those who stimulate these acts of piracy against us will get off scot free."[170] Privately, General Tamayo was even more blunt. In a side conversation with Ambassador White and Admiral Carroll, he made an extraordinary revelation: Castro had given a standing order to the Air Force to take all necessary steps to prevent another violation of Cuban airspace. "Are you going to wait until they drop a bomb on me before you take action?" Castro had asked his commanders in frustration.[171]

"What would be the reaction of your military if we shot down one of those planes?" Tamayo asked the visiting Americans, who were stunned by the question. "It was a calculated warning," Ambassador White recalled. "We were meant to take away the very clear impression that the Cubans had reached the limit of their tolerance."[172]

Back in Washington, the delegation arranged debriefings at both the Defense Intelligence Agency and the State Department.[173] The Cubans were "very upset about these over flights," Ambassador White related. "There was a sense they might take some kind of action." This did not seem to be news to U.S. officials.[174]

The Richardson Back Channel

The highest-level effort at secret diplomacy was undertaken by Fidel Castro himself. The Cuban leader seized the opportunity of a January 1996 visit by Bill Richardson to propose an unusual quid pro quo: political prisoners in exchange for grounding Basulto. Then a relatively unknown congressman from New Mexico with close ties to President Clinton, Richardson had developed a reputation for humanitarian missions abroad. In July 1995, he succeeded in talking Saddam Hussein into turning over two Americans who had crossed into Iraq from Kuwait and were being held on suspicion of espionage. Now he wanted to burnish his diplomatic credentials by getting political prisoners released from Cuba. With the assistance of Peter Bourne, a Castro biographer and former Carter White House official, Richardson arranged to meet Castro at a reception during the UN General Assembly meeting in late October of 1995. Castro was impressed with Richardson's Spanish, folksy charm, and connection to the White House; Fidel invited him to visit Havana.[175]

Richardson arrived in Cuba on January 17, 1996, only four days after Basulto's brazen airdrop of leaflets over Havana. The congressman carried a list of ten political prisoners he hoped Castro would release. He found Castro to be a "personable guy, engaging and humorous." Fidel gave Richardson the red carpet treatment, taking him to a baseball game, holding a lengthy nighttime meeting to discuss U.S.-Cuban relations, and giving him a box of premium Cuban cigars as a gift for President Clinton.[*]

When Richardson requested the release of the prisoners, "Castro said his top priority at that moment was the Brothers to the Rescue overflights," according to Peter Bourne, who was briefed on the talks after Richardson returned. If Richardson was as close to the president as he claimed, Castro said,

---

[*] Richardson passed the cigars to Richard Nuccio to give to the president, but Sandy Berger absolutely forbid it—worried, no doubt, about the political implications of Clinton receiving contraband Cuban cigars. The cigars stayed in Nuccio's office safe until one day the Secret Service showed up, confiscated them, crumbled them to pieces, and flushed them down a White House toilet while a disconsolate Nuccio watched. The president, who loved a good cigar, never knew about Fidel's gift (Nuccio interview, March 30, 2008).

"he should go back to Washington and get an assurance from Clinton that the flights would be stopped." Then "Richardson could come back in a month and two political prisoners would be released to him."[176] In a private memo to Richardson based on later conversations with Cuban officials, Bourne reported that "from their perspective, the deal was a clear quid pro quo."[177]

When Richardson returned to Washington on January 20, he contacted the White House. "I raised this with the President," Richardson told Bourne, "and he picked up the phone and called [Secretary of Transportation Federico] Peña . . . and said that he was very concerned about these flights and that they should be stopped."[178] This is the message that the Cubans heard when Richardson returned to Havana on February 9, to ferry three prisoners back to the United States. "Fidel felt you were telling him you brought Clinton's promise that he would not allow any further flights," Bourne reported to Richardson after speaking with Castro's aides. "They say Fidel told you, 'I am not releasing these prisoners for you, I am releasing them for President Clinton.'" Castro then told his aides that "he had a clear commitment from one head of state to another that the flights would be stopped."[179]

As he returned to Florida with the released prisoners, Richardson told CNN reporters that Castro had asked for nothing in exchange; two years later when a reporter for the New Yorker asked him about a quid pro quo, Richardson rejected it as a "total fiction, fantasy." Revisiting this episode in 2011, however, Richardson acknowledged that he had, in fact, approached the White House about the BTTR flights, although he could not recall to whom he had spoken.[180]

The Cubans never wavered in their conviction that, as Fidel Castro told the CBS News anchor Dan Rather, they had received assurances from the "highest levels" of the U.S. government that BTTR would cease its incursions.[181] Years later, after stepping down from power, Castro recalled that Richardson had "very earnestly told me, to the best of my recollection, the following: 'That will not be happening again; the President has ordered those flights stopped.'"[182] When the BTTR once again violated Cuban airspace only two weeks later, Bourne reported, "Castro was outraged and fuming over Clinton's behavior which, he felt, showed his word meant nothing."[183]

Countdown to Tragedy

In the weeks, days, and hours before the final confrontation in the skies off Cuba's coast, some U.S. officials sensed a calamity was coming. In January, U.S. military radar picked up evidence that the Cuban air force was practicing intercepting and firing on slow-moving aircraft.[184] Alarmed State Department officials peppered the FAA with requests for action. "State is increasingly concerned about Cuban reactions to these flagrant violations," wrote Cecilia Capestany, an official at the FAA's international aviation division, on January 22, 1996. "They are also asking from the FAA what is this agency doing to prevent/deter these actions. . . . Worst-case scenario is that one of these days the Cubans will shoot down one of these planes and the FAA better have all its ducks in a row."[185]

At the White House on the evening of February 23, Richard Nuccio received an alert that BTTR would be flying the next day. Alarmed, he fired off an urgent email to Deputy National Security Advisor Sandy Berger. "Previous overflights by José Basulto of the Brothers have been met with restraint by Cuban authorities. Tensions are sufficiently high within Cuba, however, that we fear this may finally tip the Cubans toward an attempt to shoot down or force down the plane," Nuccio warned.[186]

After conferring with his NSC colleague Robert Malley, Nuccio decided to instruct FAA officials in Miami to halt the flight on the basis of Basulto's past violations. To his surprise, they refused; they would agree only to "warn Basulto again about violating Cuban airspace."[187] Nuccio then asked the State Department to instruct Joseph Sullivan, chief of the U.S. Interests Section in Havana, to alert the Cuban government and urge "all possible restraint if any provocations occur." Word came back from Sullivan that any approach by him would be counterproductive. "These guys are in such a miserable, piss-angry mood," Sullivan replied by secure telephone, "that it may actually make things worse."[188]

There would be one other opportunity to alert the Cubans. By coincidence, that very evening Nuccio was scheduled to attend the performance of Cuba's Ballet Folklórico—a major cultural event at George Washington University's Lisner Auditorium made possible by Clinton's people-to-people initiative. Aware that the new chief of the Cuban Interests Section, Fernando Remírez, would also be attending, Nuccio decided the ballet would be a perfect cover for the two to meet, casually, for the first time. Peter Tarnoff had forbidden Nuccio to meet officially with Cuban diplomats, but an informal, accidental introduction could be useful in a future crisis. "I really just wanted to open a dialogue with Remírez," Nuccio told the authors. "I visualized someday having to be on the phone saying harsh things to this guy and I wanted him to know something about me."[189]

As the troupe danced its way through the rich history of Cuban music, Nuccio found himself in a "state of anxiety" over the BTTR flights. But when the chance came to meet Remírez at the post-performance reception, the two engaged in only perfunctory small talk. The most substantive exchange came as Remírez commented on the difficult state of U.S.-Cuban relations. Nuccio's Mexican-born wife, Angelina, then reminded him of a famous saying in her country: "So far from God, so close to the United States."

"Yes, that's it," Remírez replied. "You understand us exactly."[190]

As the pleasantries concluded, Nuccio faced a critical decision: whether to warn the Cuban official about the impending incursion. "I recall looking at Remírez as he moved toward the door and fighting with my impulse to pull him aside," Nuccio later wrote in an unpublished memoir. "I struggled with a gut instinct to appeal to the Cubans to exercise restraint in reacting to the flight and the worry that my remark would be misinterpreted if something tragic did occur." The security of silence prevailed. "As Remírez exited, I turned back to the bar and said nothing."[191]

At 1:15 P.M. the next day, Basulto's plane took off from Opa-Locka airport in Miami, accompanied by two other BTTR Cessnas. They filed a false flight plan with the FAA to patrol off the northern coast of Cuba in search of rafters. In reality, their mission was to again penetrate Cuban airspace as an act of solidarity with a Cuban dissident group called Concilio Cubano. In a crackdown on opponents, Castro's police had arrested dozens of Concilio members a few days before.

"Good afternoon, Havana Center," Basulto radioed Cuban flight controllers as the planes headed toward the island. "A cordial greeting from Brothers to the Rescue and its President José Basulto."

The Cuban controllers immediately warned him not to cross into their airspace. "I inform you that the zone north of Havana is active. You run danger by penetrating that side of North 24."

"We are ready to do it," Basulto responded with bravado. "It is our right as free Cubans."[192]

Acting on Castro's standing orders to prevent another penetration of Cuban airspace, two MiG-29 jets scrambled from their base at San Antonio de los Baños. The Cuban pilots followed none of the international protocols for warning, intercepting, and escorting unarmed civilian planes. Instead, at 3:19 P.M., a heat-seeking missile obliterated the first BTTR Cessna; at 3:26, the second was shot down.[193] The attack took the lives of four young Cuban Americans: Mario de la Peña, Armando Alejandre, Carlos Costa, and Pablo Morales. Only Basulto and his three crew members escaped back to Miami.

In Washington, the shoot-down generated a full-scale crisis. Within minutes, Nuccio was called into Sandy Berger's office and tasked to draw up "tough" options, including "military responses," for President Clinton's consideration. Nuccio cautioned against an overreaction. BTTR had "been playing with fire," he told Berger. "They got exactly what they were hoping to produce. If we respond militarily, they will have succeeded in producing the crisis they've been looking for." But the blatantly provocative nature of the BTTR flights no longer mattered. The United States, Berger told him, could simply not "stand by and let Castro kill American citizens."[194]

When President Clinton convened his top national security team in the White House Cabinet Room two days later, he weighed the option of a surgical airstrike or cruise missile attack on Cuba's MiG base. But the chairman of the Joint Chiefs of Staff, General John Shalikashvili, talked him out of it.[195] Instead Clinton ordered that a private warning be sent to Castro: "The next such action would meet a military response directly from the United States."[196] In addition, Clinton ordered a new ban on commercial flights between Cuba and the United States, restricted Cuban diplomats from traveling outside of their posts in New York and Washington, expanded Radio Martí's broadcast radius into Cuba, and authorized compensation for the families of the four BTTR victims from frozen Cuban bank accounts.[197]

More importantly, the president declared that he would "move promptly" to reach an agreement with Congress to pass the Helms-Burton legislation. "The shoot-down left the Clinton administration politically naked," Helms's top aide, Dan Fisk, observed.[198] Emboldened and empowered, anti-Castro forces in the Congress added a dramatic new clause to the bill—the codification of the embargo into law. No longer would it be a presidential prerogative to lift sanctions against Cuba; now it would take majority votes in Congress. The Clinton team, led by political advisor George Stephanopoulos, put up no objections. "The president has to sign the bill," he told National Security Advisor Anthony Lake and Chief of Staff Leon Panetta in a strategy meeting of senior staff. They agreed.[199]

Nuccio tried to object to this wholesale capitulation on Helms-Burton, only to be overruled. "Forget it," Tarnoff told him. "The decision's been made. It's over." That verdict was about more than just Helms-Burton, Nuccio knew. "He was saying that our gambit to improve relations was over, done." Shortly thereafter, Nuccio stepped down as White House special advisor on Cuba.

On March 12, 1996, with the families of the four BTTR pilots standing behind him, President Clinton signed the Helms-Burton bill into law as a "powerful, unified message to Havana." He then handed the pen to Jorge

Mas Canosa as a souvenir. With that, Clinton surrendered his presidential authority to make policy toward Cuba, and the authority of the presidents who would succeed him. Clinton understood what he had done. He felt "backed into a policy of proven failure," he lamented to a confidant in the Oval office, "closing off political engagement toward a peaceful transition in Cuba" for the sake of electoral expediency. "Supporting the bill was good election-year politics in Florida," Clinton conceded in his autobiography, "but it undermined whatever chance I might have had if I won a second term to lift the embargo in return for positive changes within Cuba."[200]

Clinton's Second Term: Changing the Paradigm

The passage of Helms-Burton, the Cuban Liberty and Democratic Solidarity (Libertad) Act, left Clinton's Cuba policy in shambles. By writing the embargo into law, the legislation took away most of the discretion on Cuba policy that presidents had enjoyed since Kennedy first imposed the full embargo in 1962. With the president prohibited by law from lifting sanctions piecemeal in response to Cuban actions, the core premise of Clinton's policy of calibrated response was vitiated. Quid pro quo was no longer a viable strategy because Washington could offer no quids for Cuban quos. That was precisely Helms's intention; he meant the law to be, in his words, "Clinton-proof."[201]

"The new law applied to Cuba a standard we set for no other nation and seriously limited what any administration could do to prepare for the day when Castro . . . finally departs the scene," wrote Secretary of State Madeleine Albright in her memoir. "We had no plan for dealing with the day after."[202] Faced with the constraints of the law, Sandy Berger, newly promoted to national security advisor, turned to his NSC staff to formulate options for a new approach. "After the Brothers were shot down, we regrouped," Berger told the authors. "We had to be as creative as we could because we were operating within a very difficult set of political constraints."[203]

"After Brothers to the Rescue, Berger asked me for a roadmap to get us out of shoot-down gulch," said Fulton Armstrong, who had served with Jay Taylor at the U.S. Interests Section in Havana and joined the NSC staff in 1995. "We were in a box after Helms-Burton and needed to poke holes in it."[204] Armstrong crafted an approach designed to "change the paradigm" by moving away from the quid pro quo strategy that had been at the heart of negotiations with Cuba ever since Henry Kissinger's initiative. Instead, Washington would take unilateral actions "based on national interests" and "based on the Cuban people rather than the old man," Armstrong said, referring to Castro. In addition to strengthening social and cultural ties between the Cuban and U.S. people, Armstrong also envisioned engaging the Cuban government "to build on areas of mutual interest," such as narcotics interdiction and counterterrorism.

To succeed, this strategy had to abandon the goal of regime change. "Who was going to let someone into their house if they think you are going to try to burn it down?" Armstrong asked pointedly. Moreover, the chances of U.S. policy unseating Fidel were nil. "Actuarial tables not embargo measures give us the best read as to how long he will remain in power," Armstrong wrote in a draft memo laying out his new policy proposals.

But negotiations with the Cuban government would come at the end of the process, not the beginning. "Most successful advances were not things that were negotiated, but things that came about through a long dance of steps, from which positive things happen," Armstrong explained. As a career CIA analyst, it galled Armstrong that the politics of the Cuba issue constantly got in the way of a policy that served the national interest, but he recognized the reality for what it was. "The quid pro quo approach is impossible because of the politics on both sides." Hard-liners would always work to block the quid and quos, derailing a gradual process.

This new approach of positive parallel steps was not an easy sell, especially in an election year. When Armstrong presented his ideas in a meeting of senior NSC staff, his colleagues objected that Miami would be apoplectic if the president took any new initiative on Cuba. They shot down each and every idea Armstrong presented. Finally, Berger interrupted: "Let's pretend we're the president's foreign policy advisors," he chided the naysayers. "Let's give the president the best foreign policy advice we can come up with, and leave the politics to his political advisors." Armstrong got a green light to move ahead.

In February 1997, after Clinton's reelection, the administration granted licenses for ten U.S. news organizations to establish permanent bureaus in Cuba. Fidel was wary about allowing news bureaus, but he had promised Ted Turner that Cable News Network could open one if it got a license, so CNN became the first, followed by Associated Press a year later.[205] The administration also quietly eased restrictions on visas for Cuban artists and musicians. In 1997, many of Cuba's top entertainers toured the United States.[206]

The Vatican's announcement that Pope John Paul II would visit Cuba in January 1998, created another opportunity. The administration relaxed travel restrictions temporarily so that Roman Catholics could go to Cuba to see the pope.[207] A few weeks later, in response to the pope's call for

"Cuba [to] open itself to the world and . . . the world [to] open itself up to Cuba,"[208] Clinton used his licensing authority to restore direct charter flights and ease restrictions on remittances. "We used the Pope's visit as a focal point for doing remittances and charter flights," Sandy Berger recalled. "My view was that engaging with the Cuban people would do a lot more to change Cuba than isolating them."[209] In a memo to the president recommending the new measures, Secretary Albright argued that the pope's trip to Cuba could catalyze an unraveling of the regime, just like his 1979 trip to Poland marked the beginning of the end of communism there.[210]

U.S. officials from the president on down were at pains to avoid sounding like the new measures were any sort of concession to Cuba. Such protestations notwithstanding, Fidel Castro hoped the new measures might, in fact, signal new flexibility in Washington. Upon hearing of the Clinton initiative, Castro sought out CNN's new bureau in Havana to register his approval, calling Clinton's actions, "a positive thing . . . which would be helpful and conducive to a better climate" in relations. Asked about the prospects for normalization, Castro sounded cautiously hopeful: "We trust that one day those relations will be improved. As far as we are concerned, we are willing to do whatever we can."[211]

Over the next few months, the momentum for a change in Cuba policy seemed to be building. The public war of words that so often characterized bilateral relations was replaced by polite compliments. Clinton praised Cuba's universal education and health care systems, and said he hoped to see relations improve. "Nothing would please me more than to see some rapprochement between the people of our two countries," he told reporters in July 1998, though he was careful to preface his comments by restating the need for Cuba to take steps toward democracy.[212] Fidel reciprocated by calling Clinton "a man of peace" who was pursuing "a program of social justice" and whose administration was on balance "positive." Clinton's "great error," Castro continued, was having caved in to "the Miami mafia" by signing the Helms-Burton legislation.[213]

The U.S. Chamber of Commerce organized a new organization, Americans for Humanitarian Trade with Cuba, an unusual alliance of some 600 business organizations and 140 religious and human rights groups dedicated to repealing the embargo on food and medicine.[214] By focusing specifically on food and medicine, this coalition was able to harness both the humanitarian impulses that arose in response to Cuba's economic hardship and the pecuniary interests of the business community—a combination that proved surprisingly powerful. In 2000, this coalition would finally succeed in repealing the embargo on the one-way sale of food to Cuba.[215]

Governments Need Political Space, Too

Despite the tight confines of Helms-Burton, Clinton officials hoped to build on the March 1998 measures with additional initiatives.[216] The venerable Council on Foreign Relations offered a vehicle for incubating new policy proposals—a task force on Cuba. The idea for the Cuba Task Force emerged from a meeting between council president Leslie Gelb and Sandy Berger in the spring of 1998. Gelb asked Berger what issues the council could take up that might prove helpful. One, they decided, was Cuba. To chair the task force, Gelb picked two former assistant secretaries of state for Latin America—William D. Rogers, who led Kissinger's opening to Cuba during the Ford administration, and Bernard Aronson, a Reagan Democrat who served in the Bush administration. Like all council working groups, the task force membership was a conspicuously bipartisan mix of former government officials, business people, and academics. Because Cuba was such a volatile domestic political issue, the task force also included an observers group of Clinton administration officials and congressional staff. Any new initiatives that could pass muster with both the members and the observers, so the thinking went, could be implemented with minimal political tumult.

Rather than challenge the Cuban Liberty and Democratic Solidarity Act and the Cuban Democracy Act head on, the task force's strategy was to focus on "provisions that call for increased contacts between Cubans and U.S. citizens, and other measures designed to encourage and support the growth of private enterprise and individual freedoms in Cuba."[217] This echoed Clinton's approach in the aftermath of Helms-Burton, and as the task force hammered out its recommendations, it became clear that they were very similar to proposals being developed inside the government.

"What we tried to do was find the wiggle-room in the embargo," explained Fulton Armstrong, who was an observer on the task force. "The Council came up with so many ideas like our own—a lot of their ideas made it into our package." Because the task force's membership was so bipartisan, its report provided political cover for Clinton's plans. "We needed political space. Governments need political space, too," Armstrong remarked.[218]

Armstrong worked closely with Julia Sweig, who provided staff support for the task force, on both the substance and timing of the task force report and the administration's new measures. "Fulton and I started talking on the phone all the time. We were on each other's speed dials," Sweig recalled. "He was letting me know we were on the same page, that we were on the right track. . . . I think that we reinforced their instincts and vice-versa," she continued. "It was unlike anything I've ever experienced since with any administration."[219] The Cuba Task Force recommended new initiatives in five areas ("baskets") intended to: (1) increase contacts between Cuban Americans and their families on the island; (2) increase people-to-people contacts; (3) increase humanitarian assistance; (4) open new U.S. private-sector activity in Cuba; and (5) foster government-to-government dialogue on issues of mutual national security interest.[220]

The timing of the council's final report helped push the review of the administration's new package of measures through the bureaucracy. On January 5, 1999, just days before the council report was released, President Clinton unveiled his new people-to-people initiatives, loosening license requirements for humanitarian and cultural travel, expanding direct flights from cities other than Miami, allowing remittances to anyone in Cuba (previously they were restricted to family members), offering to sell agricultural equipment to Cuba's private farmers, and proposing the restoration of direct mail service.[221] All of the new measures had analogs in the council report.

In contrast to Castro's benign reaction to the March 1998 measures, the Cuban government was more critical of the new package. In a long, caustic diatribe, National Assembly president Ricardo Alarcón called the January measures a "new stage in the war against Cuba." The regulations on remittances, in particular, meant that individuals or foundations in the United States could send money directly to Cuban dissidents. "What the hell is this?" stormed Alarcón. Such a regulation could have only "a clearly subversive, counterrevolutionary, interventionist purpose." The U.S. government was trying to turn religious and humanitarian institutions "into instruments of bribery, for buying consciences here in Cuba, in an effort to create traitors, people that would serve the interests of the United States against their own country of origin. Every American buy a Cuban!"[222]

The National Assembly responded with new legislation, the Law for the Protection of Cuban National Independence and the Economy (Law No. 88), making it illegal to disseminate subversive material from the United States, collaborate with foreign mass media for subversive purposes, hinder international economic relations, or receive material resources from the U.S. government, directly or indirectly.[223] That effectively meant that any Cuban involved with USAID's democracy promotion program was breaking the law.

Nevertheless, the Cuban government did nothing to limit the flow of remittances or restrict the accelerating pace of cultural and educational exchanges. "For the Cubans, accepting what we were doing was itself a concession," Armstrong noted. "We never had a single case of them refusing people on academic or people-to-people exchanges, and some of those religious people are pretty provocative."[224] During the last two years of the Clinton administration, more authentic people-to-people interaction took place than ever before, with steady flows of academics, artists, and sports teams moving in both directions. By the end of 2000, between 150,000 and 200,000 Americans were traveling to Cuba annually, and about a quarter of them were not Cuban Americans.[225]

Beisbol Diplomacy

Of all the social and cultural initiatives authorized by President Clinton on January 5, 1999, one in particular attracted the most public interest: baseball. The Baltimore Orioles would be licensed to play exhibition games with Cuba's national team. Two weeks later, Orioles owner Peter Angelos traveled to Havana to present Cuban officials with a formal proposal to "play ball" in the spring—one game in Havana, and one game at Camden Yards in Baltimore.[226]

The sportsmanship and universal appeal of baseball created a unique and level playing field to advance the cause of better U.S.-Cuban relations. Cubans are passionate about baseball—a sport popularized on the island by U.S. soldiers and sailors who brought bats, gloves, and balls during the occupation at the turn of the twentieth century. "Baseball was a common love between the two countries; it was true Americana," recalled Fulton Armstrong, the NSC official responsible for implementing this people-to-people goodwill gesture. The policy objective of the games was to "make a conscious effort after the BTTR shoot down and Helms-Burton to demonstrate that the American people did not have an aggressive intent toward Cuba—except to beat them at baseball."[227]

When the Orioles took the field in Havana on March 28, 1999, the game marked the culmination of almost twenty-five years of efforts to bring Cuba and the United States together on a baseball diamond. The idea for baseball diplomacy first surfaced in December 1974, when Commissioner Bowie Kuhn approached Secretary of State Henry Kissinger at a Christmas party to say that Major League Baseball was interested "in playing some games in Cuba."[228] The game would have "a magic value of projecting a positive image of the United States," Kuhn told Assistant Secretary of State for Inter-American Affairs William D. Rogers.[229] Rogers and Under Secretary Lawrence Eagleburger urged Kissinger to authorize the game. The public interest and goodwill it generated could support Kissinger's secret dialogue with Cuba that was just getting under way in early 1975. There would be an inevitable comparison with the Ping Pong diplomacy that had played a role in President Richard Nixon's opening to China. "The Chinese ping pong players were accepted by the U.S. public as a good way to break the ice between countries separated by decades of hostility," Kissinger's deputies noted. "Baseball with Cuba would serve a similar purpose."[230] Kissinger was not convinced; Commissioner Kuhn's effort was turned off.

Following Jimmy Carter's inauguration, Fidel Castro revived the idea. "I'd personally want to see our Cuban baseball team play the New York Yankees," he told Bill Moyers during a televised interview in February 1977. "I think we could beat the Yankees," Castro mused, savoring the symbolism. The Yankees promptly accepted the challenge, but other teams feared that the Bronx Bombers would take unfair advantage of the opportunity to scout Cuban talent.[231] Commissioner Kuhn vetoed the Yankee game in favor of his original plan to send an all-star team to Havana. Negotiations between Kuhn and Cuban sports officials continued into early 1978, but fell apart because Cuba refused to allow Major League Baseball to draft Cuban players. "Beisbol diplomacy" was an idea whose time had yet to come.[232]

More than twenty years later, bringing the Orioles to Cuba and the Cuban national team to Baltimore also proved to be a multiyear project. The games evolved out of a grant from the Arca Foundation to journalist Scott Armstrong and filmmaker Saul Landau to find new ways of building bridges between Cuba and the United States. During the famous baseball strike of 1994–95, Armstrong approached the players union with a proposal: since the players now had time on their hands, perhaps a group of them could be organized for a game in Cuba. In California, Armstrong shared this idea with actor Mike Farrell, who then introduced him to a well-connected "Jerry McGuire-type" sports agent named Richard L. Schaeffer. Schaeffer also believed that baseball could do for Cuba what Ping Pong had done for China. "You need a team. And of all the team owners, Peter Angelos is the real maverick who would do this," he advised Armstrong before setting up a meeting with the billionaire owner of the Orioles.[233]

"We met Angelos at his favorite Italian restaurant in Baltimore," Landau recalls. "He treated us to lunch and was very positive about the idea." Landau and Armstrong then took the concept to Cuban National Assembly president Ricardo Alarcón, who was also receptive.[234]

Convincing the Clinton administration, however, would take three years and a concerted lobbying effort that included some "skybox diplomacy." At one point in 1995, Schaeffer and Armstrong arranged for Peter Angelos to invite Clinton's National Security Advisor Anthony Lake to watch a game from the owner's box at Camden Yards—and to lobby Lake to support a game in Havana. "I'm to the right of Attila the Hun on Cuba," Lake said. "But I'm soft on baseball."[235]

The State Department played hardball, however, denying the Orioles a license to pursue the games in 1995, because the plan was deemed to be too high profile. The shoot-down of the Brothers to the Rescue planes in February 1996 and the subsequent passage of the Helms-Burton law cast a pall over U.S.-Cuban relations for the next two years. But in 1998, Scott Armstrong revived the proposal. Lake's successor, Sandy Berger, was also a baseball fan. "It was a great way of connecting with the Cuban people," he said of the games. "They're crazy about baseball. The more we could do to show the Cuban people who we were—that we were not just the Cuban American community, but that we were a diverse, generous people, a democratic people—the better. And what better way to do it than baseball? That was perfect."[236] Berger asked Fulton Armstrong (no relation to Scott) for a feasibility memo on the exhibition games. Baseball diplomacy, Fulton argued, fit nicely into the panoply of initiatives the White House was developing to move U.S.-Cuba policy forward.[237]

Even then, the State Department "created an obstacle course," Landau remembered. Secretary of State Albright infuriated the Cubans—and almost sabotaged the negotiations—by announcing publicly that the games were part of an initiative "to provide the peoples of Cuba with hope in their struggle" for democracy and that any proceeds from televising the games would go to the Cuban Catholic charity, Caritas. (The Cubans wanted the proceeds to go to the victims of Hurricane Mitch in Central America.) The State Department then issued a series of impractical conditions: the Cuban government could in no way profit from any television rights to the game; the Cuban government would not be allowed to sell tickets; the Orioles would be restricted from spending money for basic services in Cuba, such as translators and facilitators; and the Orioles delegation would be limited so as not to leave the impression that people were going to Cuba on a vacation junket.[238] For political reasons, the State Department did not want to use the word "agreement" to characterize the final terms under which the games

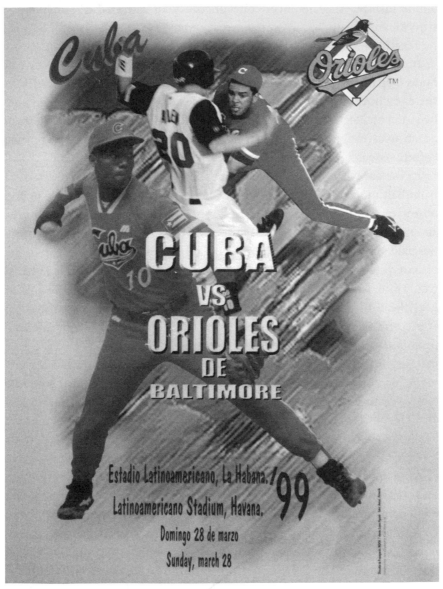

Poster advertising the baseball game between the Baltimore Orioles and the Cuban national team in Havana, March 28, 1999. The Orioles won, 3-2, in extra innings. The two teams played a second game in Baltimore, May 3, 1999, in which the Cubans evened the score by winning 12-6. (Courtesy of INDER)

would take place. "There were retrograde forces, entrenched bureaucrats, who were trying to find a way to make it impossible to pull this off," Schaeffer recalls.[239]

Indeed, during one protracted evening negotiating session between State Department officials and American League lawyers that lasted into the early hours of the morning, Peter Angelos became so exasperated that he stood up, declared "Fuck 'em," and walked out. It took a phone call from Scott Armstrong to Sandy Berger at two o'clock in the morning to resolve the impasse.[240]

In the early morning hours of March 26, 1999, a chartered jet lifted off from Baltimore-Washington International Airport carrying the Orioles and an entourage of some 150 others, including Major League Baseball Commissioner Bud Selig, a gaggle of journalists, and a team of kids from Elementary Baseball, an inner-city D.C. sports program. The day before the game, the Cubans feted the Orioles with an extravagant party on the patio of the historic Hotel Nacional. Behind the scenes, however, one final problem almost kept the team from taking the field: the refusal of the Cuban Institute of Sport, Physical Education, and Recreation (INDER) to provide four hundred promised tickets to the Orioles to distribute to ordinary Cuban fans. In a meeting with INDER officials, Major League Baseball's executive vice president for operations, Sandy Alderson, complained that the Castro regime had given tickets only to Communist Party apparatchiks, undermining the entire people-to-people concept that the game was designed to promote.[241] Saul Landau made a final plea to Alarcón, who arranged for the tickets to be provided.[242]

As members of Cuban officialdom made their way to the stadium in the early evening of March 28, diplomat Fernando Remírez got an urgent call on his cell phone from Michael Rannenberger, the State Department's Cuba desk officer. Two small planes had taken off from Miami, and the department was worried they might try to disrupt the game by dropping leaflets over the stadium. The Cubans were not about to let an exile stunt spoil their evening. "We can't do anything about it," Remírez told Rannenberger. "We're all at the ballgame."[243]

The game's most dramatic moment came before the first pitch was thrown. The teams lined up, facing each other on both sides of the mound, holding their respective national flags. With Fidel Castro, Peter Angelos, and Bud Selig standing behind home plate, the national anthems of Cuba and the United States played over the loudspeakers. The symbolism resonated through a stadium crowd of fifty-five thousand. "At that emotional moment, the utopia of fair play took over U.S.-Cuban relations," Rick Schaeffer recalled. Tied at 2-2 in the ninth, the game stretched into extra innings. Baltimore squeaked out a victory, 3-2, in the eleventh.

Five weeks later, the Cuban team traveled to Baltimore for a rematch, and revenge; they clobbered the Orioles, 12-6, in front of forty-eight thousand fans at Camden Yards. Diplomatic disagreements almost prevented that game from being played as well. The State Department refused to provide the number of visas requested by the Cubans—including one for Vice President José Fernández, on the grounds that he was a Communist Party leader and therefore a threat to U.S. security. Insulted, the Cubans threatened to cancel the game. After NSC officials intervened with the State Department, Peter Tarnoff telephoned his longtime partner in back-channel dialogue, Ricardo Alarcón, and worked out a final agreement on the makeup of the Cuban delegation, including the vice president.[244]

The goodwill engendered by the games proved to be temporary, but for the U.S. promoters, there was a sense of satisfaction. "For a brief moment there was a normal interaction between the Cuban and American people," noted Scott Armstrong, the individual most responsible for transforming the idea of beisbol diplomacy into a reality.[245] The view from the White House was similar. The games were "a successful implementation of the [people-to-people] policy," Fulton Armstrong remembers. To be sure, they represented more "symbolism" than substance, but symbols could be important. "All the Cuban kids who went to that game will never forget it. That's positive." Moreover, the United States and Cuba had often demonstrated "that we knew how to provoke each other," Armstrong added "The games demonstrated that we could become more civil—even if the prospect of normalization remained remote."[246]

Counter-Narcotics Cooperation

In addition to expanding people-to-people engagement, Clinton's foreign policy team envisioned increased cooperation with the Cuban government on several security issues, foremost among them narcotics interdiction. "That was the first thing we did that went beyond people-to-people, that was government-to-government," Berger explained to the authors. "It was a conceptual step, not just an incremental step."[247]

An incident just weeks before the 1996 presidential election signaled Cuba's willingness to cooperate. On October 1, the U.S. Coast Guard boarded a Miami-bound freighter, the *Limerick*, in international waters north of

Cuba. As the boarding party began to search for drugs, the ship's crew tried to scuttle the vessel. Everyone on board had to be evacuated as the *Limerick* listed to the side and drifted into Cuban waters. Although Cuban Border Guards denied the Coast Guard permission for hot pursuit, they towed the ship to Santiago de Cuba and began a search of their own. Aided by the U.S. Drug Enforcement Administration (DEA) and Coast Guard, Cuban authorities eventually discovered seven tons of cocaine hidden in secret compartments.[248] U.S. officials were invited to inspect the ship and gather evidence for prosecuting the smugglers. The U.S. Department of Justice requested that four Cuban officers provide testimony at the Miami trial of the *Limerick*'s captain and chief engineer, who were subsequently convicted of narcotics trafficking. "This was an important case," a senior Cuban Interior Ministry official told the authors. "We had the drugs and you had the traffickers." The experience with the *Limerick* convinced law enforcement officials on both sides of the Florida Strait of the potential for collaboration in the war on drugs. But despite this common interest, counter-narcotics cooperation, like all issues dealing with Cuba, proved fraught with politics.

Before there was cooperation between Cuba and the United States on drug trafficking, there was bitter acrimony. In the early decades of the revolution, Cuba was neither a producer nor a consumer of the marijuana and cocaine flowing northward from Latin America into the United States, so Fidel Castro was largely indifferent to the burgeoning drug industry. He shared the prevailing Latin American view that the scourge of drugs was a creation of U.S. consumers, not Latin American producers.[249] Although traffickers who strayed into Cuban territory faced harsh penalties, the Cuban Navy felt no obligation to help Washington police the Windward Passage. Because Cuba and the United States had no diplomatic relations, let alone any law enforcement or intelligence cooperation, Cuban waters offered a sanctuary for traffickers where the U.S. Coast Guard could not pursue them.

A significant number of traffickers were Cuban Americans. When arrested, some sought leniency by claiming that Cuban government officials were among their coconspirators. Such claims were largely uncorroborated and given little credence by U.S. authorities.[250] In 1982, however, U.S. officials for the first time openly accused Cuba of complicity in narcotics trafficking, claiming that Cuba hired Colombia narcotics trafficker Jaime Guillot-Lara in 1980 to smuggle weapons to the M-19 guerrilla movement in Colombia.[251] In November, a federal grand jury in Miami indicted fourteen people for trafficking, including Guillot-Lara and four senior Cuban officials. The Cubans' role, according to the indictment, was to provide "the protection and resupply" of Guillot-Lara's ships in Cuban waters.[252] Speaking to a Cuban American audience in Miami on May 20, 1983, Cuba's independence day, President Reagan said, "There is strong evidence that Castro officials are involved in the drug trade, peddling drugs like criminals, profiting on the misery of the addicted."[253]

When accounts of the Guillot-Lara case first began appearing in the press in early 1982, Cuban officials insistently and repeatedly denied any complicity.[254] Cuba also abrogated the 1978 Coast Guard agreement signed during the Carter administration, which had provided for limited narcotics interdiction and counterterrorism cooperation.[255] Shortly thereafter, José Luis Padrón, a confidante of Fidel Castro who led the secret talks with Washington during the Carter years, made an appointment with John Ferch, then head of the U.S. Interests Section in Havana. They met at Ferch's residence over coffee and cigars. "John, the *Comandante* has asked me to deliver a message," Padrón began. "When it comes to narcotics, we are revolutionaries. I want you to give a message to the president of the United States that you are barking up the wrong tree. You have my word, the *Comandante*'s word."[256]

Unbeknownst to Padrón, Ferch had firsthand knowledge of the Guillot-Lara case. He had been deputy chief of mission in the U.S. Embassy in Mexico when Guillot-Lara was arrested there in 1981. The U.S. and Cuban embassies in Mexico City had engaged in a behind-the-scenes diplomatic tug of war over Guillot-Lara—the U.S. diplomats trying to get him extradited to the United States, the Cubans trying to get him released. The Cubans won, and Guillot-Lara fled to Spain where he disappeared. When Ferch related this story to Padrón, the Cuban admitted that Guillot-Lara was not a stranger. "Well, yes, we know him, but we only deal with him when he is wearing his gun-running hat, not his narcotics hat."[257]

To signal his willingness to cooperate on drug interdiction, Fidel Castro began releasing and repatriating U.S. citizens held in Cuban prisons for narcotics trafficking.[258] In early 1985, buoyed by the successful negotiation of an immigration accord with Washington, Castro gave a series of interviews proposing talks on a range of issues, including counter-narcotics cooperation. "We said we were eager to stop airliner hijackings and we proved it," Castro told CBS News anchorman Dan Rather, referring to the 1973 antihijacking treaty. "We now say the same thing about drug traffic and we'll prove that too if we can get some truly international cooperation."[259] The Reagan administration spurned his overture.

In 1986 a Cuban American drug trafficker, Reinaldo Ruiz, made a business proposal to Tony de la Guardia, a senior official in Cuba's Ministry of the Interior (MININT). Ruiz needed a way station for moving cocaine from Colombia to distributors in the United States and would pay to establish a transit depot in Cuba. De la Guardia headed a secret MININT unit whose mission was to evade the U.S. embargo by smuggling goods from Panama and Miami. His men had their own fast boats, and could move in and out of Cuban ports without being stopped by the Border Guards. Ruiz and de la Guardia struck a deal; drug shipments began transiting Cuba in April 1987.

As the U.S. Coast Guard reported increased smuggling through Cuban waters and airspace, Jay Taylor, the new chief of the U.S. Interests Section in Havana, wanted to share the information with Cuban officials, but Washington rejected the idea. "It was assumed that Castro and his government were probably cooperating with the drug traffickers," Taylor recalled.[260] After the DEA arrested most of Ruiz's U.S. distributors in early 1988, Taylor was authorized to present Cuban authorities with evidence the island was being used as a way station. When he met with Carlos Aldana, a top official of the Cuban Communist Party, Aldana was skeptical. He blamed Miami exiles for "dragging Cuba into the story . . . to get lighter sentences," Taylor recalled. "But he promised to investigate."[261] Taylor began supplying Aldana with specific dates and times of airdrops into Cuban coastal waters.

Alerted by Taylor's information and by evidence from the trial of Ruiz's U.S. distributors, Cuban military investigators were able to trace the smuggling operation back to Tony de la Guardia. In June 1989, de la Guardia and thirteen other Cuban MININT and military officers were arrested, tried, and convicted of treason for having put Cuban security at risk by engaging in narcotics trafficking. De la Guardia and three others, including famed Division General Arnaldo Ochoa (a latecomer to the conspiracy), were executed.[262] The de la Guardia scandal was an enormous embarrassment to Fidel Castro, who had repeatedly declared that no Cuban officials were involved in the drug business and that U.S. charges to the contrary were nothing but imperialist slander—"lies from top to bottom," as he told NBC News reporter Maria Shriver in 1988.[263]

The revelation of drug trafficking among senior security officials prompted Cuba to take the danger of drug corruption much more seriously. As Castro said during the de la Guardia trials, the involvement of senior officials posed a national security threat by providing an excuse for U.S. intervention.[264] Just six months after the Cuban drug connection was revealed, the United States invaded Panama on the grounds that General Manuel Noriega's government was collaborating with Colombian drug cartels.

By 1993, Cuba had signed counter-narcotics cooperative agreements with Mexico, Colombia, Venezuela, Jamaica, and Guyana and was receiving assistance from France, Great Britain, and the United Nations International Drug Control Program (UNDCP). Exchanges of operational information between Cuban and U.S. authorities had become more routine, with Cuban air traffic controllers alerting U.S. controllers of suspicious flights, and Cuban Border Guards alerting the U.S. Coast Guard of suspicious ships. On one occasion in 1993, Cuba allowed the Coast Guard to enter Cuban waters in hot pursuit of traffickers, and when Cuban authorities captured them, they were turned over to the United States for prosecution.[265] Yet, still, Washington spurned Cuban offers to open a broader dialogue on counter-narcotics cooperation.

The *Limerick* case in 1996 proved to be a catalyst. "Cuba's conduct in that episode," the *Washington Post* reported, "whetted the appetite of American drug enforcement officials for making cooperation with Havana systematic and routine, not just a matter of occasional opportunity."[266] The U.S. Coast Guard, the DEA, the U.S. military's Southern Command, and the Office of National Drug Control Policy (ONDCP) all argued that Washington ought to expand cooperation. "From our point of view, the policy makes no sense," said a senior U.S. law enforcement official, complaining about the politically motivated limits on U.S. cooperation. "We can't close off the Caribbean [from drug traffic] without dealing with Cuba, and they have shown a willingness to cooperate with us by acting on all the information we pass on to them. It is a major hole that needs to be plugged."[267] The White House drug czar, General Barry McCaffrey, wanted to take Cubans up on their repeated offers to cooperate. "That dialogue might produce something useful," he said publicly. "I do not see any serious evidence, current or in the last decade, of Cuban Government overt complicity with drug crime."[268]

Fidel Castro himself reiterated Cuba's offer to cooperate to Senator Arlen Specter. "Please, ask the highest authorities in your country what level of cooperation they want, whether the present level, a higher level or the highest level possible. I simply say that we are ready for any of those degrees of cooperation. . . . It is silly not to reach a serious agreement for fear of the shouting in Miami."[269]

In the spring of 1999, the White House finally authorized negotiations with Cuba to expand counter-narcotics cooperation. That meeting took place in Havana on June 21. The U.S. delegation was led by the Department of State's deputy Cuba desk officer, Robert Witajewski, and included a drug specialist from State, two Coast Guard officials, and Michael Kozak, who had become head of the U.S. Interests Section in Havana. The Cuban team included Dagoberto Rodríguez, head of the Ministry of Foreign Relations U.S. section and a representative of the Cuban Armed Forces. The U.S. side offered four proposals: (1) upgrading the fax connection between the Coast Guard and the Cuban Border Guard to an actual telephone system to facilitate the exchange of real-time tactical information; (2) coordinating radio frequencies to facilitate ship-to-ship communications during interdiction operations; (3) stationing a counter-narcotics specialist at the U.S. Interests Section in Havana to coordinate with Cuban law enforcement; and (4) providing technical expertise to assist in joint boardings and searches of commercial vessels on a case-by-case basis. Within two weeks, the Cuban government accepted all four U.S. proposals. "The negotiations were absolutely painless," recalled Captain Randy Beardsworth, the Coast Guard representative at the meeting. "We outlined the four elements, Cubans said ok. It was that simple."[270]

The Cubans proposed regular consultative meetings on counter-narcotics cooperation, analogous to the semiannual consultations on migration, but Washington rejected the idea as too politically explosive.[271] Despite the modest nature of the agreement, the administration went to great lengths to play down the dialogue, insisting that it was nothing but a low-level technical discussion and did not represent any change in policy. The negotiations were defined as "conversations" conducted "at working level" and the delegation was referred to as very "low-level." References to "agreement," "accord," "collaboration," "training," or "equipment" were carefully omitted from official statements.

Nevertheless, as Castro predicted, the talks triggered shouting in Miami. Cuban American Congressman Lincoln Diaz-Balart (R-Fla.) accused Clinton of "appeasement and collaboration."[272] Dan Burton and Benjamin Gilman (R-N.Y.) introduced "The Cuba Drug Trafficking Act of 1999," requiring the president to make a determination as to whether Cuba should be classified as a "major drug trafficking" nation. The pressure from conservative Republicans in Congress caused the administration to blink, putting cooperation with Cuba on hold pending a full-scale intelligence community review of whether the Cuban government was complicit in drug trafficking, as the Republicans routinely charged.[273] In November 1999 the intelligence review concluded that there was no evidence of involvement in drug trafficking by senior Cuban officials or of sufficient trafficking through Cuba to justify including it on the "majors" list.[274] The new telephone link between the Coast Guard and Border Guard became operational in March 2000, and the Coast

Guard liaison was finally posted to Havana in September. Improved communication produced immediate results, leading to joint operations that intercepted several smugglers, according to the 2000 *International Narcotics Control Strategy Report (INCSR)*.[275]

Counterterrorism Cooperation

On April 12, 1997, a small bomb exploded in a discotheque in the Melia Cohiba hotel, the first of what would prove to be a wave of terrorist bombings targeting Havana's historic district and tourist hotels. On July 12, another bomb destroyed the men's room of the Hotel Capri, and a few minutes later, an explosive device detonated in the middle of the bustling lobby of the Hotel Nacional, seriously injuring five people. On August 22, the bombers hit the Hotel Sol Palmeras at Cuba's famous Varadero Beach resort. On September 4, a succession of four more explosions rocked Havana: one blew out the second floor walls of La Bodeguita de Medio, the famous restaurant frequented by Ernest Hemingway; another wrecked the lobby of the Hotel Miramar; a third damaged the Hotel Triton. A few blocks away, at the Hotel Copacabana, the fourth bomb exploded near the bar, killing thirty-two-year-old Italian businessman Fabio Di Celmo. It was the worst campaign of terrorist violence against Cuba since the 1970s.

The carefully planned attacks were orchestrated by Luis Posada Carriles, the leading purveyor of anti-Castro terrorism. Operating out of Central America, Posada contracted Salvadorans and Guatemalans to smuggle small devices filled with C-4 plastic explosive into Cuba to be planted in popular tourist destinations. To finance the bombing campaign, Posada raised money from Cuban American benefactors in Miami and New Jersey.[276] The purpose of the bombings, Posada explained in a candid interview with the *New York Times*, was "to make a big scandal so that the tourists don't come anymore." Opponents of the regime "need something to start the fire and that is my goal," he told the *Times*. "I sleep like a baby," he added without remorse. "That Italian was sitting in the wrong place at the wrong time."[277]

For the Cuban government, Luis Posada was public enemy number one. The official press often referred to him as "the Osama bin Laden of Latin America." Imprisoned in Venezuela for masterminding the October 6, 1976, bombing of a Cubana airlines flight that killed all seventy-three people on board, Posada escaped in 1985, reportedly with financial and logistical support from Jorge Mas Canosa.[278] Using the alias "Ramón Medina," he joined the Reagan administration's operation supplying arms to the Nicaraguan "contras" in violation of U.S. law. In the late 1980s, he worked as a security official for the Guatemalan government and began plotting a new campaign of violent attacks on Cuban targets. In February 1990, unidentified gunmen shot him twelve times on a street in Guatemala City; amazingly, he survived.

As part of Cuba's counterterrorism effort, in the mid-1990s the Cuban Directorate of Intelligence (DGI) infiltrated, one-by-one, fourteen spies into the Miami area. Known as La Red Avispa—the Wasp Network—the spies melted into the Cuban American exile community. Three of them focused on U.S. military installations but never managed to obtain any classified material. Most of the Wasp Network infiltrated exile groups they believed to be involved in violent operations against Cuba, including Brothers to the Rescue and the Cuban American National Foundation—which Cuban intelligence viewed as one of Posada's benefactors. From those operations the agents uncovered a number of violent plots, among them a plan to develop bomb-laden radio-controlled drones "to possibly kill Castro," and a plot, tied to Posada, to bomb another civilian airliner carrying tourists in and out of Cuba.[279]

In spite of Fidel Castro's long-standing suspicions of U.S. support for Posada's terrorist activities, the 1997 hotel bombings became the catalyst for a significant, albeit temporary, Cuban-U.S. collaboration to combat terrorism. There was some precedent for such cooperation. The Carter administration was the first to make a concerted effort to crackdown on exile terrorists, motivated in part by exile bombings in Miami (more than one hundred between 1974 and 1977) and by revelations that the CIA had shielded its former assets from arrest. In March 1977 Carter instructed the Justice Department to "take all necessary steps permitted by law to prevent terrorist or any illegal actions launched from within the United States against Cuba." After watching the CBS News documentary *The CIA's Secret Army*, which detailed the CIA's complicity in exile terrorism, Carter ordered an investigation by CIA director Stansfield Turner.[280]

In June 1977 the State Department for the first time passed word to Cuba that an exile group in Florida was plotting an attack on the Cuban coast using fast boats, and in August U.S. law enforcement officers arrested the plotters on state weapons charges and federal charges of violating the Neutrality Act. "I think a minimum of cooperation is in the reciprocal interests of trying to fight terrorist elements," Fidel Castro commented a few weeks later, adding, "It's the least the United States government can do."[281] In private, Castro told Senator Frank Church that, while he didn't think the U.S. government was behind terrorist attacks like the 1976 bombing of the Cubana airliner, "he thought it was done by terrorists who received their training at one time from the CIA," Church reported to the White House. "This is a monster that has been created and will be difficult to control," Castro told the senator.[282]

During both the Reagan and George H. W. Bush administrations, U.S. authorities continued to thwart exile plots launched from U.S. territory.[283] Reagan's Justice Department dismantled the most notorious exile terrorist group, Omega 7, arresting virtually its entire membership and winning convictions for bombings and assassinations that stretched from Manhattan to Miami, including the 1980 murder of Cuban diplomat Félix García Rodríguez.[284]

In 1984 Cuban intelligence uncovered what appeared to be a plot by right-wing extremists to assassinate President Reagan during a campaign stop in North Carolina. On a Saturday in early October, Cuban diplomat Néstor García called the U.S. UN Mission to warn the head of security, Robert Muller. Reluctant to bother Muller on a weekend, the duty officer asked whether it was important. "The counselor of the Cuban Mission is calling on a Saturday for the chief of security of the U.S. Mission," García replied. "Don't you think it must be important?" Later that day, García passed along the Cuban intelligence to both Muller and U.S. Secret Service agents. The following Monday, García received word the conspirators had been arrested (albeit not for threatening the president). A few days later, Muller treated García to lunch to express U.S. appreciation for Cuba's assistance.[285]

Faced with the 1997 hotel bombings, Castro took the initiative to reach out to Washington. After the April 12 bombing at the Melia Cohiba, Cuban security officials drafted a report on thirteen "terrorist acts" between 1992 and 1997 against tourist destinations in Cuba, alleging that CANF had financed some of them. Castro then enlisted former senator Gary Hart, who was visiting Havana in early May, to secretly deliver the report to President Clinton.[286] Following the quadruple bombings on September 4, and the death of Fabio Di Celmo, the Clinton administration finally responded. Late on the evening of October 1, the chief of the U.S. Interest Section, Michael Kozak, phoned the Cuban Foreign Ministry (MINREX) and shared urgent U.S. intelligence that another bombing on a tourist facility might take place within twenty-four hours. As Castro recalled, Kozak said "he couldn't confirm this information but he wanted us to know about it." The next morning, the Cubans summoned Kozak to MINREX to "thank him officially for having passed [the intelligence] on."[287]

Six months later, on March 7, 1998, Kozak again passed an intelligence tip on a plot to detonate explosives somewhere in Cuba within the next forty-eight hours. Two days later, Foreign Minister Roberto Robaina met with Kozak to tell him that Cuban authorities had intercepted two Guatemalans carrying the same type of C-4 explosives that had been used in previous attacks. Their plot had been thwarted, and Cuba appreciated the U.S. support and collaboration. "These criminal acts are extremely serious and affect not only Cuba and the United States but also other countries in the region," Robaina said. "We have a duty to prevent such acts. . . . This would not be difficult if Cuba and the United States coordinated . . . the fight against such actions." As Cuba had done in counter-narcotics collaboration, Robaina noted, fighting terrorists would be handled with "complete seriousness and discretion." Kozak congratulated the Cubans on the arrests and suggested that Cuba share information with U.S. authorities that might lead to identifying the masterminds behind the attack. U.S. officials, Kozak told the foreign minister, "understood the importance of working together in this area."[288]

García Márquez's Mission

At this point, Castro decided to raise the profile of counterterrorism collaboration. He enlisted his trusted, experienced, and esteemed secret emissary, Gabriel García Márquez, who was on his way to Washington, to carry an urgent message to President Clinton. Rather than send a direct letter to the U.S. president, Castro personally drafted his secret communication as a memorandum entitled "Summary of Issues that Gabriel García Márquez May Confidentially Transmit to President Clinton."

First and foremost, Castro wanted Clinton to know that Cuban intelligence had uncovered a "sinister terrorist plan" that involved placing a bomb on a jetliner carrying tourists to or from Cuba—a modern-day version of bombing of Cubana flight 455 in 1976. The United States, according to the message, possessed "enough reliable information on the main people responsible" to take action to prevent "this new modality of terrorism." Castro also took the opportunity to offer his thoughts on a half-dozen other issues in U.S.-Cuban relations, among them the Brothers to the Rescue shoot-down.[289] In addition, Castro entrusted García Márquez with two additional unwritten questions to pose to Clinton—"if the circumstances were propitious."[290]

On May 1, García Márquez arrived in Washington. Originally he had asked UN ambassador Bill Richardson to set up a private meeting with Clinton to discuss Colombia; now as a special emissary from Cuba, he was forced to tell

Richardson that he was carrying "an urgent message" for the president. Word came back that Clinton would be on the West Coast for six days and that García Márquez would have to give his message to National Security Advisor Sandy Berger. "I didn't feel authorized to accept of my own volition the alternative of Berger receiving me instead of the President, above all because I was bringing him a very sensitive message that wasn't even mine," García Márquez wrote in his trip report. "My personal opinion was that I should only deliver it directly into Clinton's hands."[291]

As he waited for a response from the White House on whether Clinton would see him after he returned, the Nobel Prize–winning writer occupied himself by working on his memoirs in his hotel room. After a few days, he was fortuitously invited to a private dinner at the house of the former president of Colombia, César Gaviria, along with one of Clinton's top foreign policy advisors, Thomas "Mack" McLarty. "The occasion seemed providential," García Márquez believed. He arrived an hour early to consult Gaviria—"a great friend and a smart counselor"—on the secret message he was carrying and whether to discuss it with McLarty. Gaviria urged him to share the information and arranged to leave García Márquez alone with McLarty at the end of dinner to talk privately.

"McLarty and I were like two old friends," García Márquez would report.

McLarty agreed. "I think we managed to establish a good rapport and had a reasonably good exchange," he recalled. But "he made it clear that he had a communiqué from Castro and that obviously sent up a red flag."[292]

At the White House the next day, McLarty consulted with both Berger and NSC Latin America specialist James Dobbins on how to handle this delicate diplomatic situation. "We went a little back and forth," he remembered, as to "whether we would have the meeting in the White House or have a more informal meeting . . . you know, just kind of as a private citizen, a person of considerable standing but . . . still a private citizen." Two days later, they invited García Márquez to the West Wing. On May 6, at 11:15 A.M., McLarty, Dobbins, counterterrorism czar Richard Clarke, and the NSC's Cuba specialist Jeff DeLaurentis sat down with the writer and his interpreter, Patricia Cepeda. "We are at your disposal," McLarty told Castro's emissary.

"This is not an official visit," García Márquez stated for the record. "They all nodded in agreement and their unexpected solemnity I found amazing," he wrote later.

Then, in a simple way and a rather colloquial narrative, I related to them when, how and why I had the conversation with Fidel that gave rise to the informal notes that I should deliver to President Clinton. I handed them to Mack McLarty in the closed envelope and I asked him to please read them so that I could comment on them. . . . He read it to himself, apparently with the fast reading method that President Kennedy had made fashionable, but his changing emotions showed on his face as light in the water.

After McLarty was done with the memo, he passed it to Dobbins who read it and passed it to Clarke. The conversation focused on the "terrorist plan," when García Márquez posed the first unwritten question that Fidel had given him: "Wouldn't it be possible for the FBI to contact their Cuban counterpart for a joint struggle on terrorism?"

Clarke responded that this was a "very good idea" if Cuba assured the FBI that the cases would be handled discreetly; he suggested that the United States would take "immediate steps" to begin. Dobbins indicated that the White House would instruct the U.S. Interests Section in Havana to coordinate the effort.

García Márquez introduced Fidel's second unwritten question as an assertion: if the United States and Cuba could cooperate on these security issues, perhaps a political climate would be created that would allow for the full and free travel of U.S. citizens to Cuba. But this suggestion departed from the major focus of the meeting, and he received no real response. It was clear, he later reported back to Fidel, "that they did not have, or do not know, or didn't want to reveal any immediate intention to resume American travels to Cuba."

Nevertheless, from the perspective of both sides, the White House meeting was a success—a significant stepping-stone toward a real collaboration on Cuba's number one security issue, terrorism, and the revival of a serious high-level U.S.-Cuban dialogue more than two years after the shoot-down of the Brothers to the Rescue planes. A key part of Castro's communiqué spoke directly about the incident. "It seemed to me to be the first kind of serious overture about the shoot-down," McLarty said. "I wouldn't say [he] apologized, that's not the right characterization—but he took responsibility. . . . He did express regret that it had caused such a reaction in the United States and for the president. So the tone of it was quite positive and appropriate."

As the meeting concluded, the four U.S. officials assured García Márquez that they appreciated the information that Cuba had brought to their attention, that it would be taken seriously, and U.S. agencies would follow up accordingly. "I think we implied that this would move through channels appropriately," McLarty said, "and that President Clinton would be made aware of it." As the meeting broke up, McLarty paid García Márquez the ultimate compliment: "Your mission was in fact of utmost importance, and you have discharged it very well."[293]

The FBI Delegation

In the days following the West Wing meeting, McLarty and DeLaurentis took the issue of counterterrorism collaboration through the interagency process and eventually to National Security Advisor Sandy Berger. Berger then authorized a delegation of FBI and counterterrorism specialists to travel secretly to Cuba—an unprecedented step forward in U.S.-Cuban cooperation on this sensitive security issue. "We stood against terrorism. And we took it seriously," McLarty later explained the decision. The message García Márquez had transmitted "was a concrete signal" that the Cubans were serious about cooperation, "and that, I think, changed the dynamic from our standpoint." The NSC "reached out to the FBI" to support the Cuban effort to thwart further bombings and identify and arrest those behind the terrorist attacks.[294]

A team of FBI agents and Justice Department officials arrived in Havana on June 15, 1998, for three days of confidential briefings by high-level Cuban intelligence officials on Posada's operations and the wealthy exiles in Miami who allegedly financed him. The Interior Ministry turned over reports and dossiers stamped CONFIDENCIAL to U.S. investigators, including surveillance reports on Posada's movements, summaries of phone conversations between Posada and his colleagues, transcripts of telephone calls between the arrested bombers and their handler in El Salvador, and forensic analysis of bomb fragments recovered by investigators.[295] The meetings and information sharing seemed to go well. "They were very professional," a Cuban official later said of the U.S. investigators, and "very interested in what we had to show them."[296]

The meetings portended a new era of U.S.-Cuban cooperation on security issues and a potential turning point in the long history of violence against the island emanating from the United States. Cuban officials believed the United States now had the evidence, some of it based on material gathered by the Wasp Network spies, to detain Posada's financial backers. That expectation was raised further in mid-July when the *New York Times* published an extensive front-page series on Posada. In a recorded interview with *Times* reporters, Posada not only explicitly took credit for the bombings but implicated

Jorge Mas Canosa and CANF as his longtime financial benefactors. Over the years Mas Canosa had given him $200,000 for his operations—with the proviso that Posada not tell him what he was doing with it. The money would come with a message, Posada stated: "This is for the church."[297]

But no arrests of CANF members, Posada associates, or Posada himself took place in the summer of 1998. Instead, on September 12, the FBI launched a coordinated raid against the Wasp Network, rounding up ten of the fourteen Cuban spies. Four agents managed to escape back to Cuba; five eventually pleaded guilty and cooperated with U.S. authorities in return for leniency. The final "Cuban Five"—Antonio Guerrero, Fernando González, Gerardo Hernández, René González, and Ramón Labaniño—were charged with a range of offensives, from acting as unregistered agents of a foreign power to conspiracy to commit espionage and conspiracy to commit murder (for the Brothers to the Rescue shoot-down). Prosecuted in Miami, the five were convicted and sentenced to prison terms ranging from thirteen years to life.

The arrests stunned Castro and his top officials. They had entrusted U.S. authorities with intelligence gathered by their spies in the belief that Cuba and the United States were engaged in a common enterprise—the fight against international terrorism. Instead of using the information to detain the terrorists, the FBI arrested Cuba's counterterrorism agents. The belief that the FBI used the intelligence information shared by Cuba to unmask the Wasp Network became a staple of the Cuban public relations campaign to free the Cuban Five, but it was fundamentally flawed. The FBI detected and began surveillance on the Wasp Network in 1995, long before the hotel bombings had begun.[298]

Nevertheless, the sense of betrayal in Cuba was real, and the impact on U.S.-Cuban relations enduring. As Cuba built a worldwide solidarity movement around the battle cry of freedom for the "Cuban Five," their continuing imprisonment became yet another obstacle to better relations with Washington.

Elián

No event of the Clinton years prompted more sustained diplomatic interaction between the United States and Cuba than the saga of Elián González—the five-year-old boy found floating in an inner tube in the Florida Strait on Thanksgiving Day 1999. The diplomatic dialogue that ensued over the next seven months was also unusual because it was collaborative rather than antagonistic. For once, former U.S. diplomat Wayne Smith observed, "the two governments found themselves on the same side of the issue."[299]

Two fishermen rescued Elián, whose mother and ten others drowned when their small smugglers' boat capsized en route from Cuba to Miami. The Immigration and Naturalization Service (INS) released the boy into the custody of his great uncle Lazaro González in Miami—a spur of the moment decision the Clinton administration would soon regret.

At the U.S. Interests Section in Havana, Vicki Huddleston had arrived as chief of mission only a few months before. Dagoberto Rodríguez, from the Cuban Foreign Ministry, called her on November 27, to tell her that a small child had landed in the United States and had to be returned to Cuba. "I don't know anything about it, but I'll certainly inform my government," she replied. When she contacted the State Department, no one there knew anything about the case either. "That's how it started for us," Huddleston recalled. "Of course, we learned who Elián was pretty quickly."[300]

Although she was new to the Interests Section, Huddleston was not new to Cuba. She served for four years as deputy coordinator and then coordinator for Cuban Affairs in the State Department in the early 1990s—the post she held when she first met Fidel Castro. On that occasion, Huddleston was part of a U.S. delegation to Havana following the agreement that ended the Angolan conflict. "Fidel Castro offers this opulent reception at the Palacio de la Revolución, and the only two women there are me and the Soviet ambassador's wife," Huddleston told a journalist. "Fidel immediately comes over to our table, looks at me and says, 'And who are you? Someone's spouse?'" The diminutive but indignant Huddleston straightened herself up to confront the towering *Comandante* and declared, "No, I'm the director of Cuban affairs."

"Oh, I thought I was," quipped Fidel, echoing exactly his retort to State Department official William Wieland forty years earlier.[301]

Huddleston began her assignment as head of the Interests Section under difficult conditions. Although she regarded herself as a moderate in favor of greater engagement with Cuba, the Cubans thought she was a "hardliner" because of her strained relationship with the head of the Cuban Interests Section in Washington, Alfonso Fraga-Pérez. Shortly after her arrival in Havana, Huddleston hosted a visit by Illinois governor George Ryan. As Ryan prepared to leave, Huddleston needed to speak with him, but Cuban guards barred her from the airport protocol room where Ryan was waiting for his plane. "I was really mad, and I just pushed on the door. Well, the door flew open—it wasn't hooked or anything. And I just stumbled right into the room," she explained. "And there is Alarcón and there is Ryan . . . They were all horrified, and I was furious."[302]

"She almost knocked me over," said Ricardo Alarcón, recalling Huddleston's dramatic entrance. He was so annoyed he told his secretary, "Anytime she calls, I am not available." One day, however, the message from Huddleston was "Please call back—it is about Elián." So Alarcón did, and it was the beginning of an intense, constructive, and mutually respectful working relationship. "We met hundreds of times—almost daily, in person or by phone," Alarcón told the authors. "Vicki showed a lot of sensitivity. She was very professional."[303]

The battle for Elián González commenced almost as soon as the boy came ashore. His father in Cuba, Juan Miguel González, wanted his son back; the "Miami relatives," as they came to be known, refused to give him up. Elián became an icon to the Cuban American community—the "miracle boy" saved by divine intervention, the symbol of Cuba's youth, of Cuba's future. To most members of the community, Elián's future belonged in the United States. That this small boy should be returned to Castro's tyranny, to the Cuba of socialism-or-death, was unthinkable. A *Miami Herald* poll found that 91 percent of Cuban Americans in south Florida believed Elián should stay in the United States.[304]

In Cuba, the refusal to return "the Boy" became a symbol of the Miami community's hatred of their homeland, a hatred so intense they would take a child away from his loving father. Ordinary Cubans could identify immediately with Juan Miguel; his plight galvanized the sympathy and anger of the entire nation. "Every Cuban—the human rights activists, the man on the street, it didn't matter—they wanted Elián back. He was their child," Huddleston said, describing the atmosphere. "It was terrible propaganda against us, more effective than 40 plus years of Fidel's propaganda."[305]

Inside the Clinton administration, the instinct of most officials was to return Elián to his father, so long as he proved to be a fit parent. "I immediately felt the kid should return, because this is his only parent," said Huddleston. "The inclination was in that direction in the State Department from the very beginning."[306] But before Juan Miguel could reclaim his son, he had to prove he was a good father by providing documentary evidence and submitting to a face-to-face interview. Deeply suspicious of U.S. officialdom and increasingly angry at what he regarded as the kidnapping of his son, he refused to cooperate. The deadlock was broken when State Department official William R. Brownfield came to Havana in mid-December for the scheduled consultations on immigration. "When Bill came down, he said to Alarcón, basically our commitment is we'll do our best to return Elián," Huddleston explained. "We'll have to proceed legally, but that's our commitment, if we can do the interview. So that's when they agreed to the interview."[307]

An officer from the INS and a political officer from the U.S. Interests Section met with Juan Miguel and Elián's paternal grandparents at Juan Miguel's house. The interview went well. On the basis of sworn statements from Elián's doctor, his teachers, his neighbors, and his grandparents, there appeared to be no doubt that Juan Miguel remained a devoted father.[308] After a second interview, the INS ruled on January 5 that Elián should be returned to his father's custody.[309]

Angry Republicans on Capitol Hill introduced legislation to give Elián U.S. citizenship, accusing the Clinton administration of wanting to "appease the Castro regime."[310] The legal maneuvering in Miami and Washington made Cuban officials suspicious. "My meetings with Alarcón became more and more intense during the long period of the legal trials," Huddleston recalled.[311] As the legal wrangling dragged into March, it became clear that Juan Miguel needed his own attorney. After consulting with the White House and Department of State, Gregory B. Craig, who had defended President Clinton in his impeachment trial before the Senate, agreed to take the job.[312] When a federal district court affirmed the INS decision granting custody to Elián's father, the issue became how Elián and Juan Miguel would be reunited. Cuban Americans demanded that Juan Miguel come to the United States, thereby giving him the opportunity to defect. At first, Juan Miguel refused. Huddleston did her best to convince her Cuban counterparts that such a trip was essential: "I kept saying: 'You send Juan Miguel to Miami and it'll solve the problem, so why don't you just do that.' They said, 'No, you send Elián back, that's the right thing to do.'"

Then Greg Craig weighed in. "He really did play an absolutely key role," Huddleston said, recalling their collaboration. "He was able to eventually convince them that the way to resolve this was that Juan Miguel go [to the United States]."[313] Juan Miguel González came to the United States in April, but despite Janet Reno's promise to return Elián to him forthwith, the Miami relatives fought a seemingly interminable rearguard legal battle. They won an injunction in federal court preventing Elián from leaving the United States until the relatives' custody claim could be heard on appeal, and they ignored a federal order to surrender Elián. For more than a week, Justice Department officials negotiated with the relatives, trying to get them to give up the child peacefully.

Meanwhile, the relative's house in Miami turned into a shrine to Elián, surrounded by a gaggle of press and a phalanx of Cuban American

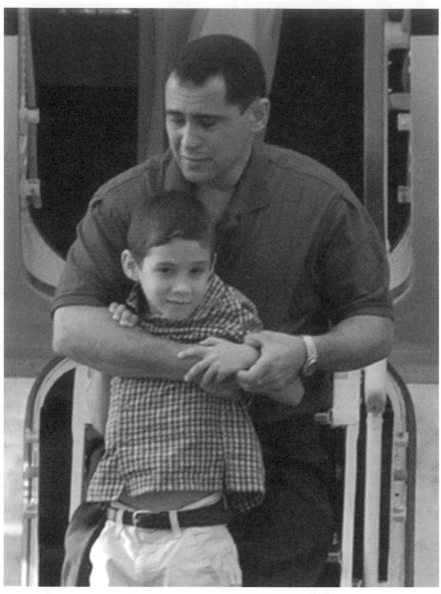

Elián González arrives at Havana's José Martí international airport carried by his father Juan Miguel González, June 28, 2000. (AP Photo/Ricardo Mazalan)

demonstrators threatening to physically block any federal attempt to recover the boy. Local Cuban American authorities added fuel to the fire by declaring that local law enforcement would not cooperate if federal marshals tried to take Elián by force.[314] Reno herself took over negotiations with the Miami relatives, speaking with them by telephone. "On Good Friday evening," President Clinton wrote in his memoir, "I talked to Reno at midnight and they were still negotiating, but she was running out of patience." The talks went on into the early hours of the morning, but the relatives remained intransigent, refusing even to recognize Juan Miguel's custody rights.[315] At 5:15 A.M., an INS SWAT team broke into the house and spirited Elián away while other officers held off demonstrators with mace and pepper spray. Elian was reunited with his father, but they were required to stay in the United States for another two months while the Miami relatives appealed their custody claim all the way to the U.S. Supreme Court, which rejected their appeal. Finally, on June 28, Elián returned to Cuba.

For many Cuban Americans, the forcible removal of Elián from his Miami relatives and his return to Cuba produced a deep sense of betrayal. In a paroxysm of rage, rioters smashed store windows, lit fires in the streets, and trampled the American flag, denouncing their adopted homeland in front of the television cameras. Anglo counterdemonstrators threw bananas at Miami's city hall to symbolize their anger at living in a "banana republic."[316]

Although the controversy over Elián González built significant trust between U.S. and Cuban officials, it also had the paradoxical effect of stalling Clinton's strategy of crafting new openings to the island. "Basically what the Clinton administration did was put everything on hold when Elián began," Huddleston explained. "It was sort of like, well if we do anything that's forthcoming with the Cubans, then that would indicate that we're on their side, that we're not impartial." As a result, the process of gradually increasing people-to-people contact "just stopped with Elián . . . the policy of opening became frozen." Among the frozen measures Clinton had been considering was lifting the travel ban.[317]

After Elián returned home, political considerations blocked the road to further progress. At the NSC, Sandy Berger had tasked Fulton Armstrong to develop a paper on threats, opportunities, and options for possible scenarios, but Vice President Gore's political staff prevented any further initiatives from the NSC or elsewhere in the administration during the months leading up to the presidential election. When the election outcome turned into a political crisis, the idea of doing anything during the transition was shelved.[318]

The seizure of Elián had done enormous damage to Al Gore's presidential ambitions, notwithstanding his lame attempt to distance himself from the decision. In November, Al Gore won only 18 percent of the Cuban American vote (compared to Clinton's 22 percent in 1992 and 35 percent in 1996), losing Florida, and the election, to George W. Bush by 537 votes.[319] "I had worked for eight years to strengthen our position in the state and among Cuban Americans . . . and the Elián case had wiped out most of our gains," Clinton wrote later.[320]

Clinton was also frustrated that he was unable to make more progress in improving U.S.-Cuban relations. "The president himself cared about this issue," Sandy Berger told the authors. "I never had to convince him to do more; he wanted to do more. It's always a question of priorities of course. But his instincts were toward more liberalization."[321]

Clinton's Cuba policy was deeply ambivalent, torn between the policy wonk's recognition that hostility no longer made sense in a post–Cold War world and the natural politician's instinct to break the Republicans' electoral lock on Florida. The strategies of calibrated response and parallel positive steps were aimed at gradually changing the policy without setting off alarms in Miami. When squaring that circle proved impossible, the president subordinated the policy to the politics. Thus Clinton missed the opportunity presented by the end of the Cold War to fundamentally change U.S.-Cuban relations for the better. By signing the Helms-Burton legislation, he foreclosed not only his own ability to enter into a dialogue with Havana to normalize relations but the ability of every succeeding president.

Nevertheless, the Clinton era produced several lasting achievements in U.S.-Cuba relations. The successful negotiation of 1994 and 1995 accords normalized migration, ending the periodic crises that had plagued relations since Camarioca in 1965. In his second term, Clinton's strategy of engaging the Cubans on issues of mutual interest led to significant, albeit limited, cooperation to combat drug trafficking and international terrorism. The expansion of people-to-people linkages—opening educational travel and cultural exchanges, easing restrictions on Cuban American travel and remittances—rebuilt bridges between U.S. and Cuban societies, even as the two governments remained estranged.

"I think it's a good story," Sandy Berger reflected. "I feel as if we pushed things in the right direction for the right reasons. I would have liked to have done more, [but] I think we made some progress—not enough, but I think we laid the foundations for things that came later."[322]

8. **GEORGE W. BUSH**
Turning Back the Clock

We opted for change even if it meant chaos. The Cubans had had too much stability over decades. . . . Chaos was necessary in order to change reality.

—Roger Noriega, Assistant Secretary of State for Western Hemisphere Affairs

In June 2003, the director of the U.S. occupation authority in Iraq, retired general Jay Garner, met with President George W. Bush in the Oval Office to report on progress. At the close of the upbeat meeting, Bush asked, "Hey Jay, you want to do Iran?"

"Sir, the boys and I talked about that and we want to hold out for Cuba." Garner replied. "We think the rum and the cigars are a little better. . . . The women are prettier."

"You got it," Bush laughed. "You got Cuba."[1]

They were joking, of course, but just a few days later, Bush drew the comparison more seriously at a campaign event in Miami. "Under the current leadership in Cuba, there will never be freedom," he declared. "One thing we believe in America is freedom, for everybody. We love it for the people of Cuba, we love it for the people of Iraq, we love it for the people of Afghanistan."[2] Of the three, only Cuba had not yet come under U.S. military occupation in the name of freedom.

As the war in Iraq turned into a quagmire, the possibility of "doing Cuba" ceased to be a feasible option. But "regime change" remained the unwavering objective of U.S. policy during Bush's presidency. Convinced that stepped-up economic pressure and aid to Cuban dissidents would collapse the regime despite fifty years of experience to the contrary, Bush's foreign policy team had no interest in dialogue with a government they were confident they could eliminate. Talking with the enemy, after all, represented a tacit acknowledgment of his de facto legitimacy. Even the most routine discussions between Havana and Washington would wither in the heat of this self-righteousness. The task of sustaining engagement with the island over the next eight years would fall to others.

Bush's uncompromising policy was rooted not only in the messianic Wilsonianism of his foreign policy but also in his close ties to Miami's most conservative Cuban Americans. They voted 82 percent Republican in 2000, punishing Democrats for returning Elián González to his father in Cuba. Florida's governor, George's brother Jeb, counted the Cuban American right as a key element of his political base. "We have an insurance policy in George W. Bush," said Lincoln Diaz-Balart (R-Fla.). "You're not going to see George W. Bush betray the Cuban-American community."[3] President Bush appointed more Cuban Americans to senior positions than any president before him. They held key posts on the National Security Council staff, at the State Department, the U.S. Agency for International Development (USAID), and the Foreign Claims Settlement Commission. In almost every agency, conservative Cuban Americans manned the front lines of Bush's policy toward Latin America.

9/11: An Opportunity for Counterterrorism Cooperation

On September 11, 2001, Cuba was one of the first countries to express condolences to the United States and offer help. As airports closed all across the country, Cuba offered its runways to any U.S. flight needing a place to land.[4] The tone of Cuba's response shifted from sympathy to worry after Bush's speech to the Congress in which he declared, "Either you are with us, or you are with the terrorists. From this day forward, any nation that continues to harbor or support terrorism will be regarded by the United States as a hostile regime."[5] While reiterating Cuba's opposition to terrorism, Castro spoke out vigorously against a unilateral U.S. military response. Bush's speech to Congress, he warned, signaled a U.S. strategy to act "under the exclusive rule of force, irrespective of any international laws or institutions." Cuba, he worried, could be a target of such unilateralism.[6]

In the ensuing months, Cuba sought to demonstrate its good faith by signing all twelve international protocols against terrorism. Havana did not even object when the United States decided to use the Guantánamo naval base as a detention center for Al Qaeda and Taliban prisoners. Raúl Castro praised the pragmatic cooperation between U.S. and Cuban military forces facing each other at the base, suggesting this as a model for cooperation in other areas: "There is room, within the current framework of relations . . . for greater cooperation with regard to the drug problem, disorganized migration and the fight against terrorism."[7]

In November 2001, Cuba gave the State Department an aide-mémoire including draft cooperative agreements on those three issues. In December, when U.S. and Cuban diplomats convened for their semiannual meeting on migration issues, Ricardo Alarcón presented the same proposals to the U.S. delegation. The U.S. diplomats insisted that their mandate extended only to discussing migration and that the proposals should be submitted through regular diplomatic channels. On March 12, 2002, Cuba again presented the draft agreements to the State Department. Washington did not respond, except to say that relations with Cuba would improve only if Cuba held free elections.[8]

Fidel Castro was still the bête noire of the hard-liners running Bush's Latin America policy. They seized on terrorism as the rationale for a more confrontational policy, hoping to fend off congressional pressure to relax the embargo. Cuba, the hard-liners pointed out, had been on the State Department's list of state sponsors of terrorism since 1982, and it maintained friendly relations with other states on the list. As soon as Bush appointed him assistant secretary of state for Western Hemisphere affairs, Otto Reich launched a review of policy toward Cuba with the aim of seeking new ways to promote "a rapid and peaceful transition to democracy."[9]

Despite these efforts, the September 11 attacks made the Cuban threat look puny by comparison. Not even the Pentagon believed Cuba still posed any significant threat to the United States.[10] Richard Nuccio had tried in vain to get Cuba dropped from the terrorist list during the Clinton administration because there was no evidence that the Cubans were engaged in or supporting international terrorism. No one in the intelligence community disputed the facts, according to Nuccio, but no one in the Clinton White House had been willing to weather the political firestorm sure to be unleashed if Cuba was dropped from the list.[11]

When the State Department's new list was released in May 2002, Cuba was still on it. Cuba had "vacillated over the war on terrorism," the report charged, because Castro had denounced U.S. military action in Afghanistan as excessive.[12] Castro complained bitterly, pointing out that 3,478 Cubans had died in terrorist attacks launched from the United States, many with U.S. government complicity, and some of those responsible still resided openly in Miami.[13]

The State Department report on terrorism was quickly eclipsed by the furor that erupted when John R. Bolton, under secretary for arms control and international security, accused Cuba of developing biological weapons. In a May 6, 2002, speech to the conservative Heritage Foundation, entitled "Beyond the

Axis of Evil," Bolton elevated "rogue states" Libya, Syria, and Cuba to Evil's second tier because of their alleged efforts to acquire weapons of mass destruction. "The United States believes that Cuba has at least a limited offensive biological warfare research and development effort," he asserted.[14]

U.S. concerns about Cuba's biotechnology industry dated to the early 1990s, because the advanced technology Cuba used to produce commercial pharmaceuticals was also capable of producing biological weapons. The charge that Cuba was producing such weapons gained currency in Miami in the late 1990s, when defector Alvaro Prendez claimed that Cuba had Soviet medium-range missiles armed with biological warheads aimed at south Florida. A State Department official dismissed such charges as unfounded. "We get lots of reports from defectors and others, but when we go to check them out it's always second and third hand, and the stuff doesn't check out."[15]

Bolton's speech seemed to announce that Cuba had launched a weapons program. Actually, he was simply repeating the conclusion of a 1999 National Intelligence Estimate (NIE) but omitting the NIE's cautionary language reflecting the intelligence community's uncertainty about the Cuban program. When Bolton circulated a draft of his Heritage speech for clearance, both the State Department's intelligence specialist on biological weapons Christian Westermann and the CIA's National Intelligence Officer for Latin America Fulton Armstrong objected that Bolton's claims went beyond the available intelligence. Bolton's response was to demand that they both be fired.[16]

Castro denounced Bolton's claim as a "diabolical fabrication" and an "infamous slander." He offered any international agency the right to come inspect Cuban biotechnology facilities.[17] In 2005 the State Department quietly acknowledged that Bolton's claims had been overblown; a new intelligence estimate concluded that it was "unclear whether Cuba has an active biological weapons effort now, or ever had one in the past."[18] Why had Bolton taken the equivocal conclusion of a 1999 NIE and, three years later, cast it as major policy declaration accompanied by a big media splash? Perhaps because Jimmy Carter was going to Cuba.

Jimmy Carter Tries to Build Bridges

Jimmy Carter first met Fidel Castro in Caracas in 1989 at the inauguration of Venezuelan president Carlos Andrés Pérez. Beforehand, Carter convened a group of academic specialists on Cuba to discuss bilateral relations and meeting with Cuban American leaders in Miami.[19] Late in the evening of February 3, Castro met Carter in his Caracas hotel room for a wide-ranging discussion.

"Castro was exceedingly polite and eager to please," recalled Robert A. Pastor, Carter's senior assistant on Latin America. "He clearly wanted to talk expansively on a long agenda, including Ethiopia, Angola, the Cuban Missile Crisis, Mariel." In a forty-five-minute conversation, the two discussed the conflict in Nicaragua, the negotiations then under way on southern Africa, TV and Radio Martí, and Cuban American travel.[20]

A decade later, lining up as honorary pallbearers at the funeral of former Canadian prime minister Pierre Elliot Trudeau in 2000, Carter and Castro found themselves face to face again. "I outlined the health programs that the Carter Center has around the world and he outlined the health programs Cuba has around the world," Carter recalled. "And we agreed that we would sometime in the future share ideas. So that really planted in my mind an idea of an actual visit to Cuba."[21]

In January 2002, Castro followed up his informal invitation with a formal one, and Carter accepted. When word of the impending trip became public, Ileana Ros-Lehtinen (R-Fla.) and Lincoln Diaz-Balart (R-Fla.) wrote to President Bush asking him to deny Carter a license to travel on the grounds that he was "seeking to appease anti-American dictators."[22] The White House was not so foolish as to deny the former president a license but made clear its lack of enthusiasm. "If President Carter were to travel to Cuba," said Press Secretary Ari Fleischer, "the president hopes that his message would be a very direct and straight-forward message: It's important for Fidel Castro to allow democracy to take root, to stop the repression and to stop the imprisonments, to bring freedom to the people of Cuba."[23]

Given Carter's commitment to human rights, there was no doubt he would speak out in support of democracy. But neither was there any doubt about his disdain for Bush's policies, which were "completely counterproductive," he declared. "We alienate the Cuban people, make a hero of Castro. We let him blame all of his self-imposed problems on the United States." Carter hoped to rebuild some of the bridges Bush had torn down. "We'll be exploring ways within the law we can improve relations between the American people and the people of Cuba."[24]

When Jimmy and Rosalynn Carter stepped off a private jet at José Martí International Airport on May 12, 2002, Fidel Castro was waiting to greet them. Gone were Fidel's olive green fatigues, replaced by a double-breasted charcoal gray pinstripe suit and black leather sneakers. Fidel brought a bouquet of white carnations and roses for Rosalynn. "The band is going to play your national anthem," Fidel advised. "Excuse them if they are a little rusty." He escorted the Carters down a red carpet to a podium on the tarmac, flanked

President Fidel Castro greets former U.S. president Jimmy Carter at his arrival at the Palace of the Revolution, May 12, 2002. Carter was the first U.S. president to visit Cuba since the 1959 revolution. (AP Photo/Jose Goita)

by the Cuban and U.S. flags, and the band struck up two national anthems. As the final strains of the *Star Spangled Banner* faded, Fidel leaned to Carter and quipped, "It's been a long time since that happened."[25]

In his televised welcome speech, Castro praised Carter as the only U.S. president since 1959 who made a serious effort to improve U.S.-Cuban relations.[26] Carter expressed his appreciation for the opportunity to visit Cuba "and to discuss ideals that Rosalynn and I hold dear . . . peace, human rights, democracy and the alleviation of suffering." The brief ceremony concluded, Castro and the Carters climbed into a black Zil armored limousine—a gift from Soviet premier Leonid Brezhnev in the 1970s. "It's about a hundred years old," Castro confided as they walked to the limo, "but it's the most comfortable we have."[27]

Behind the pleasantries lay "tough negotiations" over the details of the trip, according to Carter. "I laid down some very stringent requirements: If I go down, I demand to have unlimited opportunities to meet with any of your leaders and any of the opposition that I choose, and to be able to speak as I please to the public media. And then I wanted to have time on television." The Cubans agreed to a live broadcast of Carter's speech to the nation but scheduled it in the middle of the afternoon when most people would be working. "I demanded that it be later in the evening when people would be watching TV," Carter told the authors. When he discovered that his address would be carried only on television, not radio, he appealed directly to Castro. "As I was riding in from the airport to the downtown hotel with Fidel, I told him that I was a little bit disturbed about not being on radio, and he said, 'Well, we'll include radio, too.'"[28]

The evening of his arrival, Carter joined Fidel at the Palace of the Revolution for a state dinner and the first of two private conversations. Having been warned that Carter liked to retire early, Fidel discarded his normal modus operandi of chatting into the early hours of the morning. "He would look at his watch constantly and he would always make sure I left the meeting in time to get back to my hotel by midnight," Carter recalled gratefully. They talked about U.S.-Cuban relations and reminisced about the days when they faced one another as adversaries in the midst of the Cold War.[29]

The next morning, Carter met for breakfast at his hotel with two of Cuba's most prominent dissidents—Elizardo Sánchez and Oswaldo Payá. Just two days before Carter's arrival, Payá delivered to the National Assembly a petition calling for greater political liberty signed by 11,020 Cuban voters. Delivery of the petition marked the culmination of the Varela Project, named for Father Félix Varela, hero of Cuba's nineteenth-century independence movement. Under Article 88(g) of Cuba's Constitution, 10,000 voters could, by petition, place legislation on the agenda of the National Assembly. Payá's petition called upon the Assembly to authorize a referendum on a draft law guaranteeing freedom of expression, association, religion, and private enterprise.

To most observers, the Varela Project appeared a quixotic venture when Payá began collecting signatures in 1996, but it gathered momentum after Pope John Paul II's 1998 visit to Cuba. By 2002, Payá had enlisted the support of more than one hundred dissident groups and accumulated more than enough verified signatures to meet the constitutional requirement. The brilliance of Payá's strategy lay in combining a radically dissident stance with a mechanism clearly within the bounds of existing law.[30] The Varela Project disproved the conventional wisdom that Cuba's dissidents were too fragmented to cooperate, too few to have any impact, and too isolated to reach beyond their own immediate circle of family and friends. Payá's success came as a shock to most observers. It must have come as an even greater shock to Cuba's leaders.

After meeting with the dissidents, Carter toured Cuba's Center of Genetic Engineering and Biotechnology—and fired back at Bolton's claim that Cuba was developing biological weapons. Convinced that Bolton's speech was timed to distract attention from his trip and blunt its impact, Carter noted that in the intelligence briefings he received before departing for Havana, no one mentioned biological weapons or Cuban support for terrorism.[31]

The trip's main event was Carter's Tuesday evening televised speech to the nation. "The Cubans were annoyed that we wouldn't give them a copy of Carter's speech in advance," recalled Shelley McConnell, associate director of the Carter Center's Americas program. "They really pressured us." Carter harbored some anxiety about the speech, too. Would Castro sit passively while Carter criticized Cuba's human rights record and called for greater liberty? As the two leaders walked toward the University of Havana's Aula Magna (Great Hall), Carter ventured that perhaps he would not answer questions after the speech as originally planned.

Fidel stopped in his tracks. "Why not?"

"I'm afraid you'll jump up and start to debate me," Carter answered. "I'm no expert in Cuban law—you're the lawyer."

"I will be silent," Fidel promised. And he was.[32]

Speaking in Spanish, Carter began his address by recounting the troubled history of U.S.-Cuban relations from the Platt Amendment to Cuba's alignment with the Soviet Union during the Cold War. "Our two nations have been trapped in a destructive state of belligerence for 42 years, and it is time for us to change our relationship. . . . Because the United States is the most powerful nation, we should take the first step." He called on Congress to lift the travel ban and end the embargo. "The embargo freezes the existing impasse, induces anger and resentment, restricts the freedoms of U.S. citizens, and makes it difficult for us to exchange ideas and respect." Then he forthrightly criticized Cuba's lack of democracy. "Your Constitution recognizes freedom of speech and association, but other laws deny these freedoms to those who disagree with the government." It was time, Carter said, for Cuba to join the "community of democracies."

To the irritation of Castro loyalists in the audience, Carter endorsed the Varela Project's call for a referendum on civil liberties. "When Cubans exercise this freedom to change laws peacefully by a direct vote, the world will see that Cubans, and not foreigners, will decide the future of this country."[33] It was fitting that Carter should mention the Varela Project by name, since the urn holding the remains of Father Félix Varela was interned there in the Aula Magna where Carter was speaking. Student and faculty leaders consumed much of the question and answer period denouncing the Varela Project as a subversive scheme of the United States, but the national broadcast gave it unprecedented prominence.[34]

Although Carter had not forewarned Fidel that he would talk about the Varela Project and expected him to be upset, Castro seemed to take no offense. At the session's conclusion, Fidel said simply, "Good speech. Let's go to a baseball game." Until then, the Cubans had not confirmed Fidel's attendance, presumably waiting to see just what Carter would say on the air.[35]

At Latin American Stadium—where the Baltimore Orioles had played the Cuban national team in 1999—Cuba's eastern all-stars were taking on the west. Carter had the honor of throwing out the first pitch, and to assure a good outing, he had practiced with his Secret Service team on the roof of his hotel. Before Carter took the field, Castro made a request. "I would like for you and me to walk to the pitcher's mound without any of my security officers or your Secret Service." The unhappy chief of Carter's Secret Service detail pointed out that none of the people in the ballpark had been screened for weapons, and all of them knew exactly where Carter would be standing. Confident that Castro had not brought him to Cuba to have him assassinated in front of thousands of baseball fans, Carter agreed to Fidel's request.[36] By leaving his security behind, Carter demonstrated confidence in his host and respect for him. This, as much as anything, was what Fidel Castro had been seeking from U.S. presidents since 1959.

The next day, Carter and Castro spent two hours in private discussing the state of U.S.-Cuban relations and Cuba's future. Carter pressed Fidel to take some initiative, offering a list of actions that might improve the climate for relations with Washington, including "some suggestions for opening up his closed political and economic system." Castro replied that unilateral concessions would be seen in Washington as a sign of weakness by an administration "that is still attacking us." Emerging from the meeting, Carter encountered his advisors, Bob Pastor and Jennifer McCoy. Carter just shook his head, Pastor recalled. Castro had rejected all of Carter's proposals.[37]

Carter had no leverage. As *former* president, he could commit the United States to nothing. If John Bolton's political salvo on biological warfare did not suffice to signal the Bush administration's disdain for Carter's trip, other officials pointedly told the press that the *current* president was preparing to harden U.S. policy toward Havana, not relax it.

On Carter's last full day on the island, he met with two dozen dissidents. They were thrilled that Carter had publicly criticized the government's lack of democracy and endorsed the Varela Project. To Carter's surprise, the Cuban daily, *Granma*, had published the complete transcript of his speech in that morning's edition. Although the dissidents expressed divided views about the U.S. embargo, they were unanimous in their support for freer travel to Cuba. They opposed Washington's harsh rhetoric because when the bilateral climate deteriorated, their situation grew more tenuous. Significantly, they were also opposed to U.S. government funding for opposition activities inside Cuba, something Bush had pledged to increase. "They expressed deep concern about any assistance that was identified as coming directly or indirectly from the U.S. government, or any declaration by the U.S. government that official funds were being channeled to them," Carter told the press. Such funding created an "undeserved stigma" that they were "subservient" to Washington—exactly the charge that Cuban officials routinely leveled against Payá and the Varela Project.[38]

At the departure ceremony the following morning, Fidel personally bid the Carters farewell. If it was significant, as Carter believed, that Fidel wore civilian clothes throughout his visit, perhaps it was equally symbolic that he arrived at the departure wearing his traditional olive green fatigues.[39] The Carter visit had been a friendly interlude, but it did not produce any lasting change in U.S.-Cuban relations, or Castro's preferred attire.

Carter had approached his trip with modest aims. "I recognized far in advance that after forty-three years of misunderstanding and animosity, that one brief trip could not change basic relationships between people," he said at the press conference just before returning to the United States.[40] Later, in private, he was even more pointed: "I didn't have any dreams that my visit would change the policies in Washington," he told the authors. But by opening a dialogue with Castro and speaking out to the Cuban people, he hoped to foster a better climate for future relations.[41] Nevertheless, Castro's unwillingness to respond to any of Carter's suggestions disappointed him. He had imagined that Fidel might play a role like Deng Xiaoping in China, catalyzing reform. Their conversations convinced him otherwise.

Immediately upon his return, Carter traveled to Washington to brief a bipartisan congressional group before being invited to brief President Bush. Carter urged Bush to expand cultural and scientific exchanges and academic travel as gestures toward better relations. Castro was offering to cooperate with the United States on environmental protection, counter-narcotics operations, and counterterrorism issues, the former president related. But Carter found Bush deaf to any alternative thinking about Cuba. Emerging from the meeting, Carter and his principal Latin American advisor, Jennifer McCoy, were surprised that Bush seemed so uninformed about Cuba.[42]

Rather than engage the Cuban government, Bush aimed to replace it. Just three days after Carter's trip, on May 20, Cuban Independence Day, Bush announced his "Initiative for a New Cuba," setting regime change as the necessary condition for normalizing U.S.-Cuban relations and committing the United States to "accelerate freedom's progress in Cuba in every way possible." He promised to strengthen TV and Radio Martí, intensify enforcement of travel restrictions, increase support for Castro's internal opponents, and hold firm against efforts to relax the embargo. To cheers from a Cuban American audience in Miami, Bush described Castro as "a brutal dictator who cares everything for his own power and *nada* [nothing] for the Cuban people . . . [who] clings to a bankrupt ideology that has brought Cuba's workers and farmers and families nothing—nothing—but isolation and misery."[43]

Just as George Bush ignored Carter's advice to engage Cuba, Fidel Castro ignored his advice to accept the Varela Project's referendum. Castro did not take Oswaldo Payá's challenge lightly, however. Shortly after Carter's departure, Castro called upon Cuban citizens to sign petitions for a constitutional amendment declaring socialism "untouchable." The government's mobilization was framed not as a response to the Varela Project, however, but as a response to George Bush's "Initiative for a New Cuba." The drive was launched with patriotic speeches and rallies on the 101st anniversary of the Platt Amendment. In a spectacular show of organizational muscle, the government turned out more than 8 million people in just a few days to sign Castro's petition. The National Assembly tabled the Varela proposal and amended the constitution as Castro proposed.

You Can't Get There from Here

President Bush had no faith in people-to-people exchanges and ended most of them. A key element of Bush's policy was to curtail travel from the United States in order to reduce the flow of hard currency to the Cuban government. Travel to Cuba, both legal and illegal, had been growing since the end of the Cold War. By most estimates, the total number of Americans visiting annually was 150,000 to 200,000, most of whom were Cuban Americans. Some 30,000 others traveled legally under approved licenses, and the rest—somewhere between 20,000 and 50,000—traveled illegally.[44] Bush stepped up enforcement of the travel ban, bringing thousands of enforcement actions against travelers, among them a seventy-five-year-old grandmother who unwittingly took an illegal bicycle trip and an evangelical Christian who went to Cuba to distribute bibles. The Treasury Department's Office of Foreign Assets Control (OFAC) had nearly two dozen people working on enforcement of the embargo against Cuba, compared to just two investigating Osama Bin Laden's finances.[45]

In March 2003 Bush promulgated new regulations abolishing the people-to-people exchanges initiated by Bill Clinton, the largest category of legal travelers who were not Cuban Americans. During the 2004 presidential campaign, he restricted academic exchanges so severely that only a few of more than thirty study abroad programs between U.S. and Cuban universities survived. Bush cut Cuban American travel from one trip annually to only one trip every three years. The new regulations also restricted the support Cuban Americans could provide to family on the island through remittances and gift packages.[46] The 2003 and 2004 regulations cut travel by U.S. residents in half, reduced humanitarian assistance from some $10 million annually to $4 million, and shrank remittances from $1.25 billion annually to about $1 billion.[47]

Travel in the opposite direction—Cubans visiting the United States—was virtually eliminated by Bush's invocation of a moribund Reagan-era presidential executive order banning entry to anyone employed by the Cuban government. In a centrally planned economy, that meant almost everyone. Cuban officials seeking to meet with U.S. businessmen to legally buy food and medicine were denied U.S. entry. Visas for Cuban musicians were held up so long that twenty-two of them missed the 2002 Grammy Awards ceremony. The Bush administration's rationale for these tougher sanctions was the unabashed aim of subverting the Cuban government by economic strangulation—to "bring about an expeditious end to the Castro dictatorship."[48]

Bush's antipathy to travel had a political as well as an economic dimension. Returning travelers demystified Cuba and made it more difficult to demonize Fidel Castro. The travel section of every major newspaper ran stories about Cuba as an attractive tourist destination, and every bookstore featured travel guides to Cuba from all the major publishers. As more and more people went and recounted their experiences to family and friends, Cuba seemed more and more like just another tropical island, albeit a little threadbare—not the evil archenemy of Bush's rhetoric. The Cubans themselves were well aware of this dynamic and encouraged it by welcoming American tourists.

"Each one who comes, goes back to the United States and tells the truth about Cuba." said Foreign Minister Felipe Pérez Roque. "They say they have been to hell, but hell is not as hot as it had been depicted."[49]

The Migration Talks

President Bush had little use for state-to-state dialogue either, even on issues of mutual interest. Ronald Reagan laid the foundation for U.S.-Cuban cooperation on migration with the 1984 agreement. Bill Clinton built on that foundation with agreements in 1994 and 1995 and bequeathed to George W. Bush a consultative mechanism—semiannual talks to resolve problems in implementing the existing migration agreements and to avoid another migration crisis. But the migration talks did not take place in a vacuum; as the animosity between Washington and Havana intensified, the consultations could not withstand the pressure.

Cuba used the talks as a forum to articulate its long-standing complaint about the unwillingness of the United States to either prosecute or extradite Cubans who hijacked boats and planes. Former foreign minister Ricardo Alarcón, who represented Cuba in the early rounds, routinely expressed Cuba's dismay with the Cuban Adjustment Act, which enabled Cubans reaching U.S. territory illegally to become permanent residents after a year. Together, the lack of prosecution and the fast track to residency constituted—in Cuba's view—an open invitation to illegal departures facilitated by violence.[50] It was the same argument Fidel had made to Jimmy Carter's diplomats twenty years earlier on the eve of the Mariel exodus.

The U.S. side refused to discuss the Cuban Adjustment Act, and the Cuban side refused to discuss issues on the U.S. agenda. The talks fell into a predictable pattern of charges and countercharges, each delegation repeating set positions at six month intervals, with no visible movement. "I cannot say we have advanced," Alarcón acknowledged in 2001. "We are in the same place we were six months ago."[51] Both sides downgraded their diplomatic representation. Alarcón, who negotiated the 1994 and 1995 accords, led the Cuban delegation during the first half-dozen rounds, even though Washington never sent anyone more senior than a deputy assistant secretary of state. In December 2001 the State Department's Cuba desk officer led the U.S. delegation. At the next consultative meeting in 2002, Cuba sent Rafael Dausa, the Foreign Ministry director for North American Affairs.

A rash of hijackings in early 2003 threatened a new migration crisis and brought the issue to a head. The slump in international tourism after

September 11, 2001, tipped the Cuban economy into recession for the first time since 1994. Cuba's tourist industry suffered, and the recession in Florida reduced Cuban Americans' remittances. In the past, economic hardship had been a harbinger of discontent and increased migration. The Mariel boatlift of 1980 was preceded by recession and a rash of hijackings, as was the rafters crisis of 1994.

The 1994 and 1995 migration agreements eased emigration pressure by providing for the orderly departure of twenty thousand Cubans annually. In 2002–3, however, U.S. processing of visas for Cuban emigrants slowed dramatically. Five months into the year, only 505 had been processed, compared with more than 7,000 the year before. The State Department explained the delays as a result of more elaborate immigration screening after September 11. The Cubans were convinced that Washington was delaying the visas to shut off the migration safety value, in the hope that discontent on the island would boil over.[52]

At the same time it slowed visa approvals, the Bush administration warned Cuba that a migration crisis like 1980 or 1994 would be regarded as "an act of war."[53] Nevertheless, Cubans who stole or hijacked boats and planes to get to Florida were still being routinely paroled into the community rather than prosecuted. To Castro, it appeared that the Bush administration was intentionally creating the conditions for a migration crisis that could then be used as "a pretext for a military aggression against Cuba."[54]

A wave of hijacking attempts in early 2003 indicated that discontent and migration pressures were rising as the economy declined. The hijackings prompted a brief moment of U.S.-Cuba cooperation—one of the few during eight years of the Bush presidency. When an armed hijacker seized control of a Cuban civilian airliner in March, hoping to fly to Florida, U.S. Interests Section chief James Cason helped Cuban authorities try, unsuccessfully, to talk the hijacker into surrendering. Cason even went out to the plane on the tarmac to speak to the hijacker in person. Two days later, when armed men hijacked a civilian ferry, Cason provided Cuban television with a statement warning that hijackers would be prosecuted in the United States and barred from residency.[55] Anxious to halt the hijackings, the Cuban government took the drastic step of executing three young men who tried to hijack the ferry— the first executions in Cuba in more than a decade.

The United States did arrest and prosecute the plane hijacker with whom Cason tried to negotiate, and in July the U.S. Coast Guard returned fifteen people who stole a boat in exchange for a Cuban promise of mild sentences for them. Cason issued another statement to the Cuban media reiterating

Washington's strong opposition to any form of hijacking and urging Cubans to use the available legal mechanisms to emigrate.[56]

Cooperation proved short-lived, however. In January 2004, Washington rejected Cuba's request to schedule the next round of migration consultations, suspending the talks because the Cubans would not address issues on Washington's agenda. The Cubans called cancellation of the talks "irresponsible." The immigration consultations did not resume for the remainder of the Bush presidency.[57] In 2007, the migration agreements came close to collapse when Washington failed to comply with its core commitment: processing a minimum of twenty thousand Cuban emigrants for entry visas. The Interests Section fell about five thousand visas short. A statement from the Foreign Ministry complained that Washington's failure to honor its "basic obligation" would encourage illegal migration. If Washington hoped to provoke instability, the ministry warned, that "would surely also affect the United States."[58]

Democracy Promotion

The State Department claimed it fell short of processing immigrant visas because Cuba refused to allow the Interests Section to fill vacancies in staff positions needed for immigrant screening and blocked the importation of needed materials.[59] The Cubans blocked the new staff and materials because the Interests Section had taken on major responsibility for delivering U.S. assistance to Cuban dissidents. In 2005 Interests Section staff delivered 155,000 pounds of material to more than twenty-five hundred Cuban recipients—three times the amount distributed in 2000.[60]

Overt U.S. support for "democracy promotion" in Cuba began under President Bill Clinton, but most of the funding stayed in the United States, going to nongovernmental organizations that produced or distributed critical commentary about Cuba for global audiences.[61] Under Bush, the funding for these programs rose from an annual budget of $3.5 million in FY2000, to a peak of $45.7 million in FY2008, and more of the money went into Cuba, supporting Cuban human rights activists, independent journalists, independent trade unionists, and former political prisoners.[62]

The U.S. Interests Section in Havana spearheaded this expanded support for regime opponents. The post served as a vehicle for delivering material assistance, a haven for collective planning by dissidents, and a megaphone amplifying their message. Support for the dissidents supplanted diplomatic communication as the Interests Section's principal mission. Shortly after

Bush's inauguration, Vicki Huddleston, who had been the chief U.S. diplomat in Havana since late 1999, began handing out shortwave radios to dissidents with whom she met periodically, describing her efforts as a new, "robust" outreach policy made possible by the new administration in Washington. "Now I'm really able to push the envelope," she explained.[63]

Cuban officials protested that her behavior was improper, but to no avail. "This is sheer intervention in our internal affairs," complained one official. "They did that in Eastern Europe, and they think they have a right to do it in Cuba. We won't allow it."[64] When private protests brought no surcease, Castro himself publicly reproached the diplomats. "The U.S. government is also making a mistake if it expects that people who work as hired hands of a foreign power will go unpunished," he warned. U.S. diplomats were acting in ways inconsistent with their diplomatic status. "We are not willing to allow our sovereignty to be violated or to allow the norms that govern diplomatic behavior to be flouted in a humiliating manner." He threatened to close the Interests Section.[65] One measure of Castro's annoyance: he never invited Huddleston to meet with him. The first time they met face to face after she was assigned to the Interests Section came during the arrival ceremony for the Carter delegation. "He just look relieved I didn't give him a little radio!" she joked.[66]

In September 2002 James Cason replaced Huddleston and took an even more aggressive public stance in support of the dissidents, meeting with them frequently and offering them the use of the U.S. mission and his residence for meetings. He attended meetings in their homes, including some to which the international press was invited.[67] Huddleston thought the tactics a mistake: "You can't do anything in Cuba that's effective if it's [too] public. You cannot be in the face of the government." She tried to explain this to Cason, advising him that he shouldn't try to push any harder on support for the dissidents because she had already "pushed right up to the line of what the Cubans would stand for, and maybe a little beyond it." Cason and his bosses in the State Department, however, had a different agenda: "They wanted to show how tough they were."[68]

On March 6, in a speech to the National Assembly, Castro publicly condemned Cason's disparaging remarks about the Cuban government made at a press conference at the home of prominent dissident Marta Beatriz Roque, calling it a "shameless and defiant provocation." He repeated his threat to close the Interests Section. "Cuba can easily do without this office, a breeding ground for counterrevolutionaries and a command post for the most offensive subversive actions against our country." But he also speculated that perhaps the Bush administration was intentionally trying to provoke him into severing diplomatic ties.[69]

He was right. Provoking Castro was exactly Cason's aim, as Bush's assistant secretary of state for Western Hemisphere affairs Roger Noriega later admitted: "We told our friend James Cason that if only he could provoke the Cuban regime to expel him from the country, we could respond by closing the Cuban Interests Section in Washington."[70]

Rather than strike at the diplomatic mission, Castro struck at the dissidents. On March 18, 2003, State Security began rounding them up. Seventy-five of the accused were found guilty of working with the United States to subvert the Cuban government and sentenced to long terms in prison, ranging from six to twenty-eight years. The U.S. Interests Section's public posture in aiding them enabled prosecutors to portray the defendants as U.S. agents, thereby branding dissent as treason. Washington responded by expelling fourteen Cuban diplomats from the UN mission in New York and the Cuban Interests Section in Washington—the largest mass expulsions since diplomatic relations were broken in 1961.[71]

Castro's crackdown reflected his fear that Washington planned to foment disorder on the island as an excuse for intervention. The United States had articulated a doctrine of preemptive war and invaded Iraq on the grounds that dictator Saddam Hussein supported terrorism and was developing weapons of mass destruction. Exactly the same charges had been leveled against Cuba. Arresting the dissidents not only broke up their internal network but also projected an image of strength and implacable determination to resist U.S. pressure. "This new preemptive-strike policy of yours puts us in a new ball game," a Cuban official said to former diplomat Wayne Smith after the U.S. invasion of Iraq. "And in that new game, we must make it clear that we can't be pushed around."[72]

Commission for Assistance to a Free Cuba

In October 2003 President Bush appointed a Commission for Assistance to a Free Cuba to "plan for Cuba's transition from Stalinist rule to a free and open society, to identify ways to hasten the arrival of that day."[73] It issued its first report on May 6, 2004, just as the presidential campaign was heating up, and recommended a menu of policy options, most of which had been circulating among conservative think tanks for years. Bush promptly accepted them all. The unabashed aim of the recommendations was subversion: "to bring about an expeditious end to the Castro dictatorship."[74] By constricting the flow of hard currency, the United States would cripple the economy, stoke popular discontent, and thereby precipitate Castro's collapse—the same rationale for imposing the original embargo in 1962.

The Cuban government's reaction to the new measures was immediate and intense. "This is the plan for Cuba's annexation and the return to the fake republic of the Platt Amendment," declared the Central Committee of the Communist Party.[75] On May 14, a million Cubans marched past the U.S. Interests Section in Havana to protest the new measures, and Castro declared himself ready "to die fighting in defense of my homeland."[76]

As relations deteriorated, the U.S. Interests Section became ever more isolated. Although James Cason was never expelled, he was for all intents and purposes persona non grata. A Cuban cartoonist caricatured him as a pink fairy who magically turned free clinics into private ones, only to be chased away by loyal Cuban citizens as he metamorphosed into a rat. Delighted, Cason had a pink fairy costume made and had his picture taken in it, declaring, "I've become like an icon." He was none too diplomatic, either. He called Castro a "power-hungry egomaniac" and referred to Ricardo Alarcón, president of Cuba's National Assembly, as "Alacrán" (scorpion). In the backyard of his residence, he built a model of a Cuban prison cell to show visitors.[77]

Antagonism reached a Fellini-like apogee in December 2004, when Cason supplemented the Interests Section's Christmas decorations of Frosty the Snow Man, Santa Claus, and candy canes, with a large neon sign reading "75" to commemorate the convicted dissidents. Twice the Foreign Ministry summoned him to demand that the decorations be taken down. Twice he refused. In retaliation, the Cubans erected a billboard just across the coastal highway, depicting photographs of U.S. soldiers abusing Iraqi prisoners in Abu Ghraib prison, overwritten with a swastika and the words "Fascists," and "Made in the USA." Cuban artists painted a two-story-high caricature of Cason as Santa Claus riding in a sleigh full of bombs pulled by soldiers.[78]

The atmosphere did not improve much when Michael E. Parmly replaced Cason in late 2005. At first, Parmly appeared intent on toning down the bombast. "I didn't intend to bring Jim Cason's attitude to the job," Parmly explained.[79] But after being upbraided by Washington hard-liners, he adopted the same confrontational rhetoric as his predecessor. Parmly, like Cason before him, saw U.S. support for the dissidents as essential preparation for the regime's imminent demise. While serving in the U.S. Embassy in Romania, he had witnessed the fall of Nicolae Ceauşescu and was convinced Castro would meet the same fate. He foresaw "revolt spreading like wildfire in the streets," and although he could not predict exactly when, he said, "I am pretty sure it is coming."[80]

In January 2006, Parmly went on the offensive in the psychological war, erecting a three-foot-high scrolling electronic news billboard, running the length of the fifth floor of the Interests Section. The screen displayed excerpts from the Universal Declaration of Human Rights, the works of Martin Luther King, and sundry other messages meant to inspire Castro's opponents and annoy Cuban authorities. It certainly annoyed Fidel Castro. He mobilized a million Cubans to rally in "Anti-Imperialist Plaza" next to the Interests Section, where he denounced the Bush administration for "its insolence and its rubbish." Parmly could not resist turning on the billboard, which scrolled: "Only in totalitarian societies do governments talk and talk at their people and never listen."[81] After the rally, the Cubans erected 138 black flags outside the U.S. mission to commemorate more than three thousand Cubans killed by U.S. covert operations—and to obscure the billboard. "I realized that by turning the billboard on, we were plunging the relationship into a deep hole." Parmly said later. From then on, the Cuban government "only talked to us if they absolutely had to."[82]

There were a handful of exceptions. Communications between the U.S. Coast Guard liaison and his Cuban counterpart remained professional and productive. Another area of cooperation, surprisingly, was counterterrorism. In 2006 the FBI sent another team to Havana to investigate Luis Posada Carriles's role in the 1997 hotel bombings. They were able to interview witnesses, examine forensic evidence, and visit crime scenes, which they had been unable to do previously.[83] "It was all about respect." Parmly recalled. "If you respected the Cubans, they respected you."[84]

Disaster Diplomacy

Humanitarian disaster relief was one area in which Cuba and the Bush administration came close to cooperating but ultimately failed for lack of trust. Cooperation on hurricane tracking and prediction dated back to the early twentieth century and continued even after 1959. Scientists working at the U.S. National Hurricane Center and the U.S. Weather Bureau in Miami stayed in contact with their Cuban colleagues, exchanging information on developing storms, despite the ups and downs of bilateral relations.[85] Cooperation in hurricane tracking was not matched by cooperation on hurricane relief, however.

An unusually large number of tropical storms battered Cuba during the Bush administration, leading to some unexpected initiatives. In November 2001 Hurricane Michelle, a Category 4 storm, did $2.8 billion in damage on the island. Washington responded by offering condolences, a disaster assess-ment team, and the possibility of humanitarian aid to be channeled through nongovernmental organizations. Cuban foreign minister Felipe Pérez Roque declined, but in surprisingly polite fashion. The "kindly offered" assistance would not be needed, he explained, but instead Cuba asked to be able to make a one-time purchase of food to replenish its reserves destroyed by the storm. The Trade Sanctions Reform and Export Enhancement Act of 2000 (TSRA) had exempted food sales from the embargo, so there was no legal impediment to granting Havana's request. U.S. and Cuban diplomats quickly agreed on the terms of the sale, and the necessary licenses were granted to U.S. suppliers. The "one-time" purchase turned into a continuing commer-cial relationship, and over the next decade, Cuba purchased $4.3 billion of U.S. agricultural products.[86]

U.S. offers of humanitarian assistance (always on the condition that the aid be channeled through nongovernmental organizations) became more or less routine thereafter, as did Cuban refusals. Then, in 2005, it appeared that Hurricane Wilma might break this stalemate. As usual, Washington of-fered to deploy an assessment team, and this time, instead of rejecting it, Castro accepted the offer conditionally. He proposed widening the scope of the team's mission to include a discussion of regional cooperation on disas-ter preparation and relief. Cuba wanted to be treated as an equal partner, not a supplicant for assistance. The Bush administration rejected Castro's proposal and withdrew the offer to send a team, charging that the Cubans "wanted to make this into some sort of political show."[87]

In 2008 Cuba was hit by the worst hurricane season in its history: five major storms wracked the island, inflicting more than $5 billion in damage. At first the United States simply repeated its routine offer to send $100,000 in disaster relief via private charities. But as the scope of the damage became clear, even Cuban American members of Congress, usually unanimous in their opposition to any engagement with Cuba, urged the White House to find a way to help. In response, the administration increased the offer of bilateral assistance to $6.3 million and agreed to provide $5 million directly to the Cuban government without preconditions—an unprecedented offer.[88] But Cuban officials could not bring themselves to take U.S. help. Instead, they countered with a request analogous to what they had done in 2001 after Hurricane Michelle—they asked that the embargo be lifted, at least for six months, so that Cuba could buy construction materials to rebuild dam-aged homes.[89] President Bush was not willing to allow another chink in the embargo.

Havana saw Washington's offers of aid as an attempt to appear beneficent while continuing to promote regime change through economic strangulation. Fidel Castro, in particular, was unwilling to be seen as chasing after Yanqui dollars—an image of Cuban subservience that had obsessed him since his first trip to the United States as Cuba's leader in April 1959. Washington could have treated Cuba's willingness to accept a disaster assessment team in 2005 as a breakthrough and understood Havana's desire to expand the agenda as face-saving. Instead, the administration treated the proposal as a trick to gain political advantage. Cuba could have treated Washington's 2008 offer of government-to-government assistance as a significant change in U.S. policy, which it was, and accepted the badly needed aid. Instead, it rejected the offer out of pride. Washington could have temporarily lifted the embargo on construction materials, establishing a precedent for future cooperation. Instead, the White House chose to keep the embargo intact. Each time one side made a gesture, suspicion prevented a positive response.

Succession

The announcer on Cuban TV looked grim—shaken, but struggling to maintain his composure—as he read Fidel Castro's July 31, 2006, announcement that illness required him to temporarily hand power to his brother Raúl and a leadership team of six others. In the forty-seven years since the triumph of the revolution, Fidel had never before surrendered the mantle of leadership. Clearly, the emergency intestinal surgery that sidelined him in July 2006 was serious, and its complications would prove more debilitating than anyone could foresee.

In Miami, conservative Cuban Americans danced in the streets when they got word of Castro's illness. Many assumed he must be dead already or soon would be, and—they hoped—his regime would quickly follow the old man to the grave.[90] In Washington, uncertainty prevailed. Was Castro dead or dying? Would the team of successors be able to hold the regime together? And most importantly, would Cubans by the tens of thousands take to the streets—or to rafts? Publicly, the Bush administration reacted cautiously, not wanting to set off a migration crisis. White House Press Secretary Tony Snow disparaged Raúl Castro as Fidel's "prison-keeper." But the United States remained committed to legal channels of migration, he added. "We encourage people not to get into the water."[91]

In Cuba, reaction to Castro's illness was muted. His age and prior health problems—he fainted during a speech in June 2001 and tripped as he stepped off a stage in October 2004, breaking his knee and arm—had put the issue of succession on the public agenda. But faced with the possibility of losing the only leader 70 percent of Cubans had ever known, the public's predominant emotion was quiet concern and uncertainty about the future. There were no riots, no celebrations, and no rush to exodus.

On August 18, Cuba's major daily, *Granma*, published Raúl Castro's first public statement since assuming the presidency. After reassuring everyone that the government was functioning smoothly, he spent most of the interview talking about relations with the United States. He ridiculed Washington's assumption that it had the right and ability to disrupt Cuba's leadership transition, "as if they were the rulers of the planet." The Bush administration would get nowhere with "impositions and threats," he affirmed, but Cuba remained open to "normal relations on an equal plane." He then read a passage from Fidel's speech to the 1986 Congress of the Cuban Communist Party: "Cuba is not remiss to discussing its prolonged differences with the United States and to go out in search of peace and better relations between our people. . . . This would be possible only when the United States decides to negotiate with seriousness and is willing to treat us with a spirit of equality, reciprocity and the fullest mutual respect." In the twenty years since Fidel's address, this had been Cuba's position and remained so, Raúl said.[92] In response to Raúl's offer to negotiate, the State Department insulted him, calling him "Fidel's baby brother" and "Fidel Lite." U.S. policy remained committed to promoting regime change, and the administration would "do everything we can to hasten that day," said spokesman Tom Casey.[93]

On December 2, 2006, Cuban armed forces day, Raúl Castro gave a major national address, explicitly repeating his offer of dialogue, "based on the principles of equality, reciprocity, non-interference and mutual respect."[94] To be sure that Washington understood that the offer was not just rhetorical, the Cubans asked the Swiss ambassador in Havana to carry a private message affirming it to the State Department. The Interests Sections in Havana and Washington were still technically extensions of the Swiss embassies, even though they had been staffed by U.S. and Cuban diplomats since 1977. That the Cubans felt compelled to send a message through the Swiss, rather than use either of the Interests Sections, reflected just how much the lines of communication between the two governments had deteriorated.[95]

The administration dismissed the Cuban initiative as "nothing new," Assistant Secretary for Western Hemisphere Affairs Thomas Shannon told the press. Washington had no interest in dialogue until the Cuban regime changed.[96] Castro's illness and prolonged disappearance from public life heightened expectations in Washington that the long-awaited moment of regime change might finally be at hand. "Ultimately, this transfer won't work," Shannon predicted. "There is no political figure inside of Cuba who matches Fidel Castro." From there, Shannon let wishful thinking get the better of him. "You have to understand that authoritarian regimes are like helicopters. There are single fail point mechanisms. When a rotor comes off a helicopter, it crashes. When a supreme leader disappears from an authoritarian regime, the authoritarian regime flounders. . . . And I think that's what we're seeing at this moment."[97]

The core assumption underlying Bush's policy was that the Cuban government, solidly in power for nearly half a century, was actually fragile and vulnerable, dependent on Fidel Castro's charismatic authority. U.S. officials appeared convinced that when Fidel Castro finally passed from the political scene, the regime would simply collapse. Since his death was inevitable, albeit unpredictable, they saw no reason to negotiate with a regime that had a life expectancy no better than that of its octogenarian founder. Planning for the moment of Fidel's demise had been the focal point of U.S. policy since the first report of the Commission for Assistance to a Free Cuba in 2004. A second report from the Commission in July 2006, just before Castro's illness, recommended spending $80 million over two years on "democracy promotion," with $31 million specifically slated for dissidents.[98] The report also included a classified annex, which presumably outlined covert operations to complement the overt policy of subversion. Shortly after Raúl Castro assumed the presidency, the State Department established a "war room" to plan for the Cuban collapse.[99]

Fidel Castro remained gravely ill throughout the rest of Bush's presidency, but succession did not auger transition; the Cuban regime continued to function normally. Bush bet that Fidel's demise would lead to a quick collapse, catapulting to power the dissidents in whom Washington had invested so much. "The dissidents of today will be the leaders of tomorrow," Bush declared in October 2007.[100] When that outcome failed to materialize, however, Bush was left with a policy from the 1960s: unmitigated hostility incapable of either removing the regime or exercising any constructive influence over it.

When Raúl Castro gave the annual July 26 speech in 2007 on the anniversary of the attack on Moncada barracks, he did not bother to yet again offer an olive branch to the Bush administration, which he called "erratic and dangerous." Instead, he offered it to the next U.S. president, reaffirming Cuba's "willingness to discuss on equal footing the prolonged dispute with the government of the United States. . . . Otherwise," he added, "we are ready to continue confronting their policy of hostility, even for another 50 years, if need be."[101]

9. **OBAMA**

A New Beginning?

The United States seeks a new beginning with Cuba. I know there's a longer journey that must be traveled to overcome decades of mistrust, but there are critical steps we can take toward a new day.

—President Barack Obama, at the Summit of the Americas, April 17, 2009

"We've been engaged in a failed policy with Cuba for the last 50 years, and we need to change it," declared presidential candidate Barack Obama in August 2007, at a political rally in Miami's Little Havana, the citadel of Cuban American conservatism. Obama promised to end restrictions on remittances and family travel for Cuban Americans, resume "people-to-people" educational and cultural exchanges, and engage Cuba in talks on issues of mutual interest. Engagement, he argued, offered the best hope for promoting "a democratic opening in Cuba," which would be "the foremost objective of our policy."[1]

While Obama's opponents, Hillary Clinton and John McCain, followed the tried and true path of lambasting Cuba to appeal to conservative Cuban American voters, Obama aimed to win over moderates—a growing segment of the community according to opinion polls. In May 2008 Obama was warmly received in Miami by the Cuban American National Foundation, the most prominent political group in the community. The foundation's own journey from extremism to relative moderation reflected the political evolution of its constituency.[2]

Advocating engagement proved to be a winning strategy. Obama received 35 percent of the Cuban American vote compared to just 25 percent for John Kerry in 2004, and he carried Florida, proving that a Democrat could take a moderate stance on Cuba and still make inroads with this solidly Republican constituency.[3] Having defied conventional wisdom that only a "get tough on Cuba" platform would sell in south Florida, Obama changed the domestic political dynamics of the issue, making new thinking about Cuba politically feasible. As the new president took the oath of office, conditions for a rapprochement between Cuba and the United States appeared more propitious than at any time in a half century. "We saw this as the best opportunity in a generation to break the logjam in U.S.-Cuban relations," said a former senior administration official.[4]

Reconnecting

In Latin America, hopes ran high that Obama would finally tackle this anachronistic Cold War policy that symbolized a bygone era of U.S. hegemony. Several heads of state—foremost among them Brazilian president Luiz In ácio Lula da Silva—called for ending U.S. sanctions against Cuba, even as they congratulated Obama on his victory.[5] Just days before the hemisphere's heads of state convened at the Fifth Summit of the Americas in Trinidad and Tobago in April 2009, Obama fulfilled his pledge to lift travel and remittance restrictions on Cuban Americans. He also authorized U.S. telecommunications companies to contract with Cuba to provide improved television, radio, telephone, and Internet access.[6] Latin American presidents applauded Obama's actions but still pressed him, making Cuba a litmus test of Obama's declared desire to forge a new "equal partnership" with the region. One after another they spoke in the plenary session of the need to reintegrate Cuba into the inter-American community. Obama tried to assuage their concerns, reiterating his commitment to engagement. "The United States seeks a new beginning with Cuba," he promised. His pledge, however, was short on specifics.[7]

Two months later, at the Thirty-Ninth General Assembly of the Organization of American States, Latin American states moved to repeal the 1962 resolution that suspended Cuba's membership—the symbolic cornerstone of Washington's policy of excluding Cuba from the hemispheric community. At first, the United States opposed the repeal, but faced with the prospect of humiliating defeat, Secretary of State Hillary Clinton agreed to compromise. The United States supported repeal in exchange for language that required Cuba to accept "the practices, purposes, and principles of the OAS," including, implicitly, the commitment to democracy embodied in the Santiago Declaration of 1991.[8]

Although Cuba foreswore any interest in rejoining the OAS, hopes also ran high in Havana—both in the government and on the street—for a change in U.S.-Cuban relations. Raúl Castro repeated his offer, first made when he assumed Cuba's presidency in 2006, to open a dialogue with Washington. Just before the Summit of the Americas, he declared, "We have let the American government know both in private and in public," that Cuba was willing to open a dialogue on all issues, including human rights, political prisoners, and political freedoms—"everything they would like to talk about, but on an equal footing, with absolute respect for our sovereignty and for the right of the Cuban people to their self-determination."[9]

At the Interests Section in Havana, U.S. diplomats turned off the streaming electronic news billboard that so annoyed Cuban officials, and the Cubans replaced the phalanx of black flags erected to obscure the billboard with Cuban flags. With the billboard gone, the Foreign Ministry resumed midlevel diplomatic contacts with the Interests Section.

Obama also moved to restore the cultural and academic linkages that the Bush administration worked so assiduously to sever. Many Cuban scholars who had been denied permission to travel to the United States for a decade were granted visas, and cultural exchanges flourished once again. The Miami-based musician Juanes gave a concert to a million young Cubans in Havana's Plaza de la Revolución in September, and Cuban singer Silvio Rodríguez played in Daughters of the American Revolution (DAR) Constitution Hall the following May. "We are no longer denying visas on policy grounds," explained a State Department official, but the policy changes were being made "below the radar" to avoid stirring up political controversy on Capitol Hill.[10]

In May 2009 the State Department proposed to Havana a resumption of the bilateral consultations on migration suspended by President Bush in 2004. Havana accepted, and the talks resumed in July. Cuban deputy foreign minister Dagoberto Rodríguez, heading the Cuban delegation, presented the U.S. side with a draft accord to curb people smuggling and indicated Cuba's interest in expanding the talks to include cooperation on counterterrorism, counter-narcotics operations, and hurricane preparedness. Although no formal agreements came out of the meeting, both sides judged it a good first step.

In September, Deputy Assistant Secretary of State (DAS) Bisa Williams traveled to Cuba for talks on restoring direct mail service, suspended since 1963. She was given "unprecedented access," according to the report by U.S. Interests Section chief Jonathan Farrar. Over five days, she met with Cuban officials in the Justice, Agriculture, Health, and Interior ministries, academics at the University of Havana, and a pantheon of bloggers and dissidents. She traveled outside Havana (which U.S. diplomats had not been allowed to do since 2003), visiting the hurricane-damaged region of Pinar del Rio and the Latin American School of Medicine for foreign scholarship students (including some from the United States)—the first time a U.S. diplomat had been allowed to visit the school.

In extensive discussions with Vice Minister Rodríguez, Williams came away with the clear impression that the Cubans were serious about wanting better relations. Rodríguez told her that, by according her such positive treatment, "we meant to show our readiness to move forward in our relationship." To be sure, progress would require "confidence building," but, "even within the existing diplomatic constraints, we see a way forward."

"It is hard to overstate just how markedly improved were our dealings with the Cuban Government and GOC [Government of Cuba] institutions" during Williams's visit, Farrar concluded his report. "There are a number of action items from the various meetings that provide opportunity for us to test the GOC's willingness to continue to make progress on issues of interest."[11]

Making Up Is Hard to Do

Despite this promising start, there were clouds on the horizon suggesting that President Obama might not move as fast as expected—or as promised—to change fifty years of failed U.S. policy. When he rolled back restrictions on Cuban American travel and remittances, he passed up the opportunity to also roll back the restrictions President Bush placed on "people-to-people" educational exchanges. For another two years, travel to Cuba would remain far less open than it was under President Clinton for everyone except Cuban Americans. In April 2009, when the State Department released its annual country reports on terrorism, Cuba was still included as a "state sponsor of terrorism," despite a dearth of supporting evidence (although the narrative was far more balanced than it had been previously, making the discrepancy between evidence and conclusion all the more stark).[12] Obama's 2009 and 2010 foreign aid budgets both included $20 million for USAID's semicovert "democracy promotion" program targeting Cuba—exactly the same funding Bush had requested in 2008.[13] Among the programs the Obama administration inherited and continued was the Cuba Democracy and Contingency Planning Program, which, according to USAID internal records, was "expressly designed to hasten Cuba's peaceful transition to a democratic society"—in other words, to facilitate regime change.[14]

By December 2009, the initial flurry of U.S. gestures had subsided, and relations were already slipping back into business as usual. As so often happened with Cuba policy, Obama's caution was born of political calculation.

Senator Robert Menendez, the senior Cuban American Democrat in Congress, vehemently opposed any opening to Cuba. With the Democrats holding just sixty seats in the Senate (before Edward Kennedy's death), and Republicans determined to filibuster every significant Obama initiative, Menendez's vote took on unusual importance. In March 2009 he signaled his willingness to defy both his president and his party to get his way, voting with Republicans to block passage of a $410 billion Omnibus Appropriations bill needed to keep the government running because it relaxed the requirement that Cuba pay in advance for purchases of food from U.S. suppliers.[15] To get Menendez to relent, Treasury Secretary Timothy Geithner had to promise in writing that the administration would interpret the law in the narrowest possible way and would consult Menendez on any change in U.S. policy toward Cuba.[16]

After lifting restrictions on Cuban Americans, debating Latin American heads of state at the Summit, and supporting repeal of the 1962 OAS resolution, the members of Obama's foreign policy team felt that they had "done" Cuba, even though they had not come close to "re-setting" relations with Havana in the way they "re-set" relations with Moscow. Administration officials had an inflated opinion of just how dramatically they had changed policy. Hillary Clinton called it "a completely new approach," and Obama called it "the most significant changes to my nation's policy towards Cuba in decades."[17] But, in fact, Obama's policy at the end of 2009 was still more restrictive than Bill Clinton's or Jimmy Carter's.

Having "done" Cuba, the administration moved on to other issues. Cuba, unlike Russia, could not command sustained attention from the president and his senior aides, who confronted an imposing array of international problems: wars in Iraq and Afghanistan, nuclear proliferation in Iran and North Korea, China's growing economic might, and turmoil in the Middle East. Even in the Western Hemisphere bureau at the Department of State, Cuba was not at the top of the agenda. Taking office in November 2009, Arturo Valenzuela, Obama's new assistant secretary, faced more urgent issues: repairing the diplomatic damage done by Washington's equivocal response to the military coup in Honduras; working with Mexico to counter the surge in drug violence along the border; and coordinating relief efforts in the wake of Haiti's devastating earthquake. "Every day you are bombarded by a thousand things," explained a former U.S. official who worked on Latin America. In short, Cuba was not a problem so urgent or acute that it demanded policy makers' attention.

Moreover, Obama regarded lifting restrictions on Cuban American travel as a major concession to Havana. For both policy reasons and domestic political ones, he wanted to see some significant Cuban response before doing more. "Cuba has to take some steps, send some signals that when it comes to human rights, when it comes to political rights, when it comes to the ability of Cubans to travel," the president told CNN en Español on the eve of the 2009 Summit of the Americas.[18] The president was under no illusion that improving bilateral relations would be quick or easy:

> What you saw [with the relaxation of restrictions on Cuban Americans] was a good-faith effort, a show of good faith on the part of the United States that we want to recast our relationship. Now a relationship that effectively has been frozen for 50 years is not going to thaw overnight. And so having taken the first step, I think it's very much in our interest to see whether Cuba is also ready to change. We don't expect them to change overnight. That would be unrealistic. But we do expect that Cuba will send signals that they're interested in liberalizing in such a way that not only do U.S.-Cuban relations improve, but so that the energy and creativity and initiative of the Cuban people can potentially be released. . . . There are a range of steps that could be taken on the part of the Cuban government that would start to show that they want to move beyond the patterns of the last 50 years.[19]

Asked by a reporter if this meant that the "ball is now in their [Cuba's] court," Secretary Clinton replied affirmatively. "We do expect Cuba to reciprocate. . . . We would like to see Cuba open up its society, release political prisoners, open up to outside opinions and media, have the kind of society that we all know would improve the opportunities for the Cuban people and for their nation. So I think it is fair to say . . . that we would like to see some reciprocal recognition by the Cuban Government for us to continue to engage in this dialogue and take further steps."[20] The same message was conveyed privately. In discussions with their Cuban counterparts, U.S. officials repeatedly emphasized that "the key to normalizing relations . . . was not to be found solely in the degree of bilateral engagement between the United States and Cuba, but in the Cuban Government's efforts to engage its own people and to respond to their wishes."[21]

The demand for reciprocity did not go over well in Havana, nor did Washington's expectation that Cuban leaders should restructure their political system to accommodate the United States. Cuban officials did not give Obama much credit for his early initiatives. His rhetoric at the Summit of the Americas and Washington's grudging support for repealing the 1962

OAS resolution were written off by Cuban officials as forced on him by Latin America. Ending restrictions on Cuban Americans was seen as a campaign debt he owed to Miami, not as a signal of goodwill toward Havana. Moreover, while U.S. officials portrayed it abroad as a concession to Cuba, the White House justified it domestically as a way of undermining the Cuban government, "creating independence, creating space for the Cuban people to operate freely from the regime . . . the kind of space, in our view, that is necessary to move Cuba forward to a free and democratic Cuba."[22]

Raúl Castro acknowledged that the U.S. measures were "positive," but they were of limited scope. "The blockade remains intact. . . . Cuba has not imposed any sanction on the United States or its citizens. . . . Therefore, it is not Cuba that should make gestures." Cuba's offer to negotiate with the United States rested on the sole condition that the talks be conducted on the basis of equality. Raúl spelled out exactly what he meant: "We are willing to discuss everything with the United States government, on equal footing; but we are not willing to negotiate our sovereignty or our political and social system, our right to self-determination or our domestic affairs."[23]

Cyber War

One reason for the Cuban leadership's disenchantment with Obama was his continuation of George W. Bush's democracy promotion programs—especially what the Cubans referred to as Washington's "cyber war." U.S. efforts to use computer technology to undermine the Cuban regime traced back to the very first democracy promotion grant that President Bill Clinton gave to Freedom House in October 1995, which provided $500,000 for the purchase of computer equipment, copiers, and fax machines for Cuban dissidents.[24] The Internet was also an important component of George W. Bush's plans to foster regime change. Unfettered Internet access would allow dissidents to communicate with one another and with a global audience through sites in the United States (some of which were also funded by the democracy promotion program).[25] The 2006 report of Bush's Commission for Assistance to a Free Cuba recommended spending $24 million "to provide communications technologies to activists in Cuba," the *Miami Herald* reported. "Officials say Internet access, YouTube videos and cell phone text messages propelled movements to challenge governments in places like Tibet and Burma."[26]

Cuban authorities also recognized the political power of the Internet. While acknowledging that digital technology was essential for Cuba's economic development, Minister of Communications and Information Ramiro

Valdés warned that it also provided the United States with powerful new tools to "bring the destabilizing power of the empire to threatening new levels." Cyberspace, he argued, had to be understood as a "battlefield in the struggle against imperialism." The Internet, "the wild colt of new technologies, can and must be controlled."[27]

A U.S. initiative begun in the second Bush administration sought to create a series of secure, clandestine wireless networks in Cuba that could communicate directly via satellite with Internet access points in the United States, circumventing Cuban government servers and surveillance. Various USAID contractors, including the International Republican Institute (IRI), Freedom House, and Development Alternatives Incorporated (DAI), won contracts to provide selected Cubans with Internet technology enabling them to communicate through protected networks.[28] In a confidential meeting in August 2008 at USAID headquarters, a top USAID official advised DAI representatives that the democracy program "wants to provide the technology and means for communicating the spark which could benefit the population" and "provide a base from which Cubans can 'develop alternative visions of the future.'" The program was "an operational activity" that demanded "continuous discretion."[29]

Despite Obama's promise to take a "new approach" to Cuba, these covert programs did not subside; they grew.[30] Obama and Hillary Clinton made "Net Freedom" a global foreign policy priority. "The freedom to connect," Clinton argued, "is like the freedom of assembly, only in cyberspace." Moreover, the social networks of cyberspace were also a powerful tool for popular mobilization for collective action—"an accelerant of political, social, and economic change," in places like Iran, Tunisia, and Egypt.[31]

Cuban officials regarded Washington's plans to create secure telecommunications networks among dissidents as the latest variation in Washington's fifty-year project to destabilize the government. Cuba's nascent community of bloggers, some of them critical of the regime, was seen as part of this strategy. Washington did not create Cuba's bloggers, but it embraced them enthusiastically as more appealing and effective challengers to Cuban authority than the aging, disputatious dissident movement. "Younger individuals, including bloggers, musicians, and performing and plastic artists do not belong to identifiable organizations, though they are much better at taking 'rebellious' stands with greater popular appeal," U.S. Interests Section chief Jonathan Farrar cabled Washington in April 2009.[32] When Bisa Williams traveled to Havana in September, she made a point of meeting with a group of bloggers, including Yoani Sánchez, whose "Generación Y" blog offered an

acerbic look at daily life in Cuba, winning Sánchez international acclaim—
and the hostility of Cuban officialdom, which she regularly lampooned.

After Sánchez was awarded Spain's Ortega y Gasset prize for journalism
and was named by *Time* magazine as one of the world's one hundred most
influential people in 2008, U.S. officials began lauding her at every opportunity. Sánchez's growing notoriety brought increasing pressure from Cuban
authorities. Fidel Castro himself criticized her for providing fodder to "imperialism's mass media" in order to undermine the revolution.[33] The government intermittently blocked access to her website, and authorities warned
her that she had "transgressed all the limits of tolerance with your closeness
and contact with elements of the counterrevolution."[34] In November 2009,
plainclothes police forced her and a friend into an unmarked car, roughed
them up, and, before releasing them, warned them to stop their counterrevolutionary activity.[35]

The White House condemned the assault, and two weeks later, President
Obama surprised Sánchez by sending her written responses to a series of
interview questions she had submitted. "It is telling that the Internet has
provided you and other courageous Cuban bloggers with an outlet to express
yourself so freely," Obama wrote, "and I applaud your collective efforts to
empower fellow Cubans to express themselves through the use of technology."[36] Two weeks later, on December 3, 2009, Cuban State Security arrested
Alan Gross.

The Case of Alan Gross

Working as a contractor for the consulting firm DAI on a project funded by
USAID's democracy promotion program, Alan Gross traveled to Cuba five
times—all on tourist visas—to surreptitiously provide advanced satellite
communications technology, laptop computers, disks, flash drives, and cell
phones, to independent nongovernmental organizations in Cuba's Jewish
community.[37] "A wireless network where none previously existed was developed and made operational in three target group communities. Network
usage by target groups can now be tracked. Direct communications between
target communities and the US are generated on a regular basis," Gross reported to DAI after the first, four-trip phase of his "Para La Isla" project. In
the second phase, aborted when he was detained, Gross intended to "improve
security tactics and protocols" in order "to impede [Cuba's] ability to track
or detect specific aspects of the non-terrestrial transmitted signals." He also
planned to provide a "fixed package of telecommunications system"—what

he called "telco-in-a-bag"—to an additional three "beneficiaries" to be approved by USAID.[38]

At the U.S. Interests Section, officials speculated that Gross's arrest had been prompted by the Cuban government's growing concern about bloggers and Washington's promotion of them. In a SECRET cable to Washington, Farrar wrote:

> The conventional wisdom in Havana is that GOC [Government of Cuba] sees the bloggers as its most serious challenge, and one that it has trouble containing in the way that it has dealt with traditional opposition groups. The "old guard" dissidents mostly have been isolated from the rest of the island. The GOC doesn't pay much attention to their articles or manifestos because they have no island-wide resonance and limited international heft. For a while, ignoring the bloggers too seemed to work. But the bloggers' mushrooming international popularity and their ability to stay one tech-step ahead of the authorities are causing serious headaches in the regime. The attention that the United States bestowed on [Yoani Sánchez], first by publicly complaining when she was detained and roughed up and later by having the President respond to her questions, further fanned the fears that the blogger problem had gotten out of control.[39]

Obama's continuation of Bush's democracy promotion program led Raúl Castro to conclude that Washington's claim to want a new relationship with Cuba was nothing but "a huge propaganda campaign staged to confuse the world." In fact, he told Cuba's National Assembly on December 20, 2009, two weeks after Gross's arrest, "The truth is that the instruments for the policy of aggression to Cuba remain intact and that the U.S. government does not renounce its efforts to destroy the Revolution. . . . The enemy is as active as ever," he continued. "Proof of that is the detention in recent days of an American citizen . . . who engaged in the illegal distribution of sophisticated means of communications." In March 2011 Gross was convicted of subversive "acts against the independence or territorial integrity of the state" and sentenced to fifteen years in prison.[40]

Washington insistently denied that Gross had done any wrong and declared that no further progress in U.S.-Cuba relations could be made until he was released. U.S. officials speculated that his arrest and conviction signaled Cuba's disinterest in better relations. "It is my personal belief that the Castros do not want to see an end to the embargo and do not want to see normalization with the United States," Secretary of State Hillary Clinton declared.[41]

Author Peter Kornbluh (right) visits USAID subcontractor Alan Gross in Havana, November 28, 2012. Gross's December 2009 arrest and subsequent conviction for subversion stalled President Obama's policy of engagement with Cuba. (Courtesy of Peter Kornbluh)

But Gross's arrest prompted congressional Democrats—especially John Kerry (D-Mass.), chair of the Senate Foreign Relations Committee, and Howard Berman (D-Calif.), chair of the House Foreign Affairs Committee— to take a close look at USAID's Cuba democracy program. They were shocked by what they found. Although the program was not classified, it was run as a covert operation; even USAID did not know who in Cuba was receiving assistance from some of the project's contractors. Senior USAID officials were uncomfortable with this legacy of Bush's regime change policy. In a series of meetings with congressional staff, they worked out a plan to downsize the Cuba program and reorient it toward supporting genuine links between U.S. and Cuban societies—to "decontaminate it," in the words of Fulton Armstrong, who had retired from the CIA and was working for Senator Kerry.

For a few months in 2010, it appeared that Gross might be released in exchange for restructuring the USAID program. With the State Department's approval, Armstrong briefed Cuban diplomats about the impending changes, asking whether this would smooth the way for Gross's release. The Cubans responded that it would. In October 2010 Senator Kerry met with Cuban foreign minister Bruno Rodríguez in New York to discuss the democracy program and Alan Gross; the informal deal seemed to be on track. Back in Washington, however, Senator Menendez called the White House demanding that the Cuba program be left intact. Obama's team did not have the stomach to wage a political fight with Menendez, so they scuttled the proposed changes in the program. From this, the Cubans concluded that the Obama administration's word could not be trusted.[42]

Expanding Travel

Frustrated that President Obama had left in place the restrictions on people-to-people travel imposed by President Bush, freedom-to-travel advocates launched a major legislative campaign to lift the travel ban in 2010. With large Democratic majorities in both the House and Senate, hopes for success ran high. Opponents blasted the freedom-to-travel coalition as venal for putting dollars ahead of human rights. Senator Menendez denounced businessmen who "only care about padding their profits by opening up a new market."[43] But it was hard to make the case that travel advocates were insensitive to human rights when seventy-four of Cuba's prominent dissidents and human rights advocates, including Yoani Sánchez, supported lifting the ban.[44] In August 2010, Cuba's Cardinal Jaime Ortega came to the

United States, met with administration officials, and quietly urged members of Congress to allow freer travel, following Pope John Paul II's 1998 injunction that "Cuba . . . open itself to the world and . . . the world open itself to Cuba."[45]

The principal obstacle faced by supporters of the travel bill was not the opposition of Cuban American Republicans but opposition from moderate and conservative Democrats. In the Senate, Menendez threatened to filibuster the travel bill. In the House, Debbie Wasserman Schultz, a rising star of the party from south Florida, organized opposition within the Democratic caucus. When supporters of the travel bill first rolled it out with 178 cosponsors, Wasserman Schultz recruited 53 House Democrats to write a letter to Speaker Nancy Pelosi declaring their determination to vote against it—a formidable number that foreshadowed a nasty battle inside the Democratic caucus if the bill went to the House floor.[46]

But the most frustrating obstacle facing advocates of free travel was the indifference displayed by President Obama. The White House could have tipped the balance by endorsing the travel legislation or even by lobbying quietly behind the scenes. Instead, the administration did nothing. Freedom-to-travel advocates could not collect the votes necessary to get their bill out of the House Foreign Affairs Committee, where it died.

Meanwhile, the Obama administration had its own, more limited travel initiative. Advocates of greater engagement with Cuba, especially Obama's appointees in the State Department's bureau of Western Hemisphere Affairs, argued from the outset that the president ought to roll back Bush's restrictions on academic and educational travel. The bureau developed a package of regulations that restored "people-to-people" educational travel and made academic exchanges even easier than they had been under Bill Clinton. The bureau then began the laborious process of pushing them through the executive branch bureaucracy. Blocked by Obama's political advisors in the White House, the new regulations won approval only when Secretary of State Clinton took the issue directly to the president in August.

But when the administration briefed congressional Democrats on the impending policy change, some pushed back hard. Senator Menendez released a public statement opposing the new measures.[47] Florida Democrats, led by Wasserman Schultz, warned that any easing of the travel regulations would hurt their prospects in the midterm elections.[48] The White House shelved the new regulations until January 2011 and then announced them late Friday before a holiday weekend to attract as little attention as possible.[49] Cuba's

Foreign Ministry called the new measures "positive," though they "have a very limited scope and do not change the policy against Cuba."[50]

Spain's Good Offices

One element of Obama's new approach to Latin America was to partner with Spain, especially when dealing with Cuba and Venezuela. "They recognize our ability to pass along messages and to mitigate diplomatic incidents, big and small," said the Spanish ambassador to the United States, Jorge Dezcallar de Mazarredo. When Obama met with Spanish prime minister José Luis Rodríguez Zapatero just a few weeks after inauguration, they talked about how Spain might assist U.S. overtures to Cuba.[51]

By the fall of 2009, the White House was frustrated that Cuba had done nothing significant in response to Obama's relaxation of restrictions on Cuban American travel and remittances. When Obama met Zapatero again on October 13, the president asked that Foreign Minister Miguel Angel Moratinos carry a back-channel message to Raúl Castro. "We're taking steps, but if they don't take steps, too, it will be very difficult for us to continue," Obama explained. "Tell Raúl that if he doesn't take steps, neither can I." The president understood the process would take time. "Tell the Cuban authorities that we understand that things can't change overnight, but down the road, when we look back, it should be clear that this was the moment when changes began."[52]

Moratinos delivered Obama's message to Havana the following week. In reply, Raúl Castro proposed the creation of an ongoing "secret channel of communication" to the White House, through which the two sides could discuss Cuban steps that would meet U.S. concerns. Washington, however, was not interested in opening a high-level dialogue. If Havana wanted to talk with Washington, it "should engage seriously through the existing channels," Moratinos was informed.[53]

As U.S. efforts to engage Cuba stalled, Spain decided to go forward on its own. "We have been traditionally ahead of you in engaging with Cuba," a Spanish diplomat told his U.S. colleague in Havana, and Madrid was not about to wait to see how U.S. policy unfolded.[54] With Spain's encouragement, Raúl Castro and Cardinal Jaime Ortega entered into discussions about the release of political prisoners. Castro's dialogue with the church began in May 2010, when Ortega appealed for the government to lift a ban on public demonstrations by the Ladies in White, female relatives of political prisoners. Castro agreed, and the dialogue turned to the broader issue of prisoners.

In early July, Moratinos came to Havana to join the discussion. On July 7, after a meeting among Raúl Castro, Ortega, and Moratinos, the cardinal's office announced that the government would release 52 political prisoners, including everyone arrested in 2003 who was still imprisoned. Those who wished to go into exile would be welcomed by Spain.[55] Over the course of the next few weeks, the government agreed to release even more prisoners, with the total eventually reaching 127, including almost everyone classified by Amnesty International as a prisoner of conscience.[56] The Cuban government's willingness to treat the Catholic Church as a legitimate party in a dialogue on human rights was unprecedented. As Ortega said, the government had "recognized the role of the Church as an interlocutor" with civil society in a way that it never had before.[57]

Although the United States played no role in the discussions that led to the prisoner release, Spanish diplomats and Cardinal Ortega kept Washington well-briefed. In late June, just before the prisoner release was announced, Ortega traveled quietly to Washington to meet with administration officials and members of Congress. According to the Spanish daily *El Pais*, the consultations were part of the agreement the church reached with the Cuban government and "were designed . . . to pressure U.S. political leaders to respond with other gestures of goodwill toward Cuba." Cuban officials felt that the coming prisoner release was a major concession, and they expected some reciprocal action.[58]

Ortega also reaffirmed Raúl Castro's hope for better relations with Washington. "He repeated to me on several occasions that he is ready to talk to the United States government directly, about every issue," Ortega said during a follow-up trip in August. It would be a mistake, Ortega implied, for Washington to maintain the status quo until Cuba became a democracy. "Everything should be step by step," he said. "It's not realistic to begin at the end. This is a process. The most important thing is to take steps in the process."[59]

But with Alan Gross still in jail, Obama was not disposed to take any new steps. Many constructive things could happen in U.S.-Cuban relations, a senior U.S. official told the cardinal, but only after the case of Alan Gross was resolved. When the prisoner releases were announced, Secretary Clinton called it a "positive sign," but the White House was completely silent, in contrast to Obama's outspoken defense of Yoani Sánchez in November 2009 and his condemnation of Cuba's "clenched fist" repression in March 2010 after the death of hunger striker Orlando Zapata Tamayo.[60] Obama's silence was especially ironic, since in 2009, when specifying what Cuba needed to do to prompt better relations with the United States, he had listed releasing political prisoners and allowing greater freedom of religion.[61] Now, when the Cuban government took significant steps in these areas, Washington did nothing in response.

With progress in U.S.-Cuban relations stalled, Assistant Secretary of State Arturo Valenzuela proposed a bold and politically risky move: a meeting with Foreign Minister Rodríguez at the United Nations in New York. It would be the highest-level diplomatic contact between the two countries since the Clinton years. Valenzuela hoped that, face-to-face, the two diplomats might be able to move U.S.-Cuban relations off dead center. Other administration officials opposed the idea, but Valenzuela was able to win Secretary Clinton's approval.

Through diplomatic channels, the administration proposed a meeting to the Cubans on the condition that Havana give some indication it was serious about moving forward, especially regarding Alan Gross. Havana agreed to the meeting, but as it drew near, Cuba had not responded with an agenda, despite entreaties from both Washington and Madrid. With no Cuban response, Valenzuela felt compelled to cancel the meeting. The Cubans then appealed to Spanish diplomats, who convinced senior U.S. officials to re-schedule it.

From this inauspicious beginning, things went downhill quickly. Rodríguez opened the meeting at the Waldorf Astoria Hotel with a lengthy recitation of Cuba's historical grievances against the United States—something Cuba diplomats often do in their encounters with U.S. officials before they get down to serious dialogue. Instead of arguing about the past, Valenzuela tried to shift the focus toward the future, but Rodríguez did not engage on that basis. In the end nothing positive came out of the ninety-minute encounter. "It was a terrible meeting," Valenzuela later confided to colleagues. "The result was zero."[62]

Governor Richardson's Private Diplomacy

In August 2009 New Mexico governor Bill Richardson, a diplomatic trouble-shooter who carried messages between Havana and Washington during the Clinton administration, headed to Havana to promote New Mexico's agricultural exports. In light of Richardson's close relationship with Obama (he broke with longtime ally Bill Clinton to endorse Obama over Hillary in 2008), and his many exploits as a high-level envoy (he had secured the release of prisoners in Cuba, North Korea, Iraq, and Sudan), many observers wondered if Obama had tapped Richardson for some secret diplomacy with Cuba.

"I'm not an envoy of the administration. I'm carrying no message." he insisted, but adding, "Obviously I do plan to submit my impressions to the administration after I conclude."[63] Having used Richardson as a channel for communicating with the Clinton White House in 1996, the Cubans took advantage of the opportunity to use him again.[64] Richardson came away with the strong impression that Cuban leaders wanted to move forward. "I found the atmosphere of the Cubans good," he said upon returning. "They like President Obama. They like the new tone." Richardson conveyed Obama's impatience with Cuban inaction. "I told the Cubans, 'You need to do something. . . . You've got to reciprocate with some gestures.'"[65]

The Cubans did not agree. A few days after Richardson's departure, Foreign Minister Bruno Rodríguez made it clear that Cuba would not make any concessions to win better relations with Washington and certainly not concessions of the sort Obama was seeking. "Cuba is not going to negotiate its internal affairs with anyone, neither the United States nor any government or group of countries," Rodríguez reaffirmed. "The [embargo] policy is unilateral and should be lifted unilaterally."[66]

A year later, in August 2010, Richardson returned to Havana to open another round of trade talks and to try to get Alan Gross out of prison. "I am here not as an administration envoy," Richardson again insisted. "I'm trying to sell chili, salsa, green chili to the Cuban government." But he admitted that the State Department had asked him to use his good offices to seek Gross's release. "I'm going to be working very hard today to see if we can get Mr. Gross out," he told CNN.[67] Richardson urged Foreign Minister Rodríguez to release Gross as "a humanitarian gesture," and he came away encouraged. "After my intervention, there is some progress in the case. . . . I believe I've made some inroads."[68] But when Richardson returned to the United States, Alan Gross did not come with him.

A few weeks later, on October 27, Richardson was invited to New York to meet with Foreign Minister Rodríguez, who was in town for the annual UN General Assembly debate on the U.S. embargo. Rodríguez had a message he wanted Richardson to deliver to "the highest authorities of the U.S. Government."[69] Rodríguez had just met with Assistant Secretary Valenzuela, but the meeting had not gone well, he told Richardson. Valenzuela would only talk about Alan Gross, Rodríguez claimed. To the Cubans, Gross was merely a symptom of the troubled relationship, not the heart of it.[70]

Rodríguez noted that Cuba had encouraged its supporters in the General Assembly to tone down their criticism of President Obama in the debate that led to a vote of 187-2 in support of Cuba's demand that the embargo be lifted—a gesture that he said indicated Cuba's desire to improve relations. "Foreign Minister Rodríguez several times affirmed that President Raúl Castro had made the political decision to improve ties with the U.S.," Richardson wrote in his report on the meeting, "but that Cuba perceived that the U.S. Government and the Obama Administration did not reciprocate the sentiment." Rodríguez dismissed Obama's relaxation of restrictions on Cuban Americans as insignificant, suggesting instead that if the administration was serious about gestures, it should ease the embargo to allow agricultural credits and disaster relief. He also noted Washington's failure to respond to the Cuban government's dialogue with the Catholic Church and the release of more than one hundred political prisoners.

Rodríguez acknowledged the importance of the Alan Gross case but at the same time "wants the U.S. to recognize the importance the Cuban Five case holds for them," Richardson wrote in his notes. "In response to a question, he said he wasn't linking the two, but was specifying that there must be progress on both fronts simultaneously." Richardson delivered the message to the White House, along with a public exhortation for Obama to use his executive authority to take new initiatives to jump-start the diplomatic process. His efforts had no noticeable effect on policy, but he was not discouraged and he was not done trying.

Jimmy Carter Returns

In March 2011 Jimmy Carter made a surprise trip to Cuba at the invitation of Raúl Castro. Carter had been looking for an opportunity to encourage better U.S.-Cuban relations and to get a feel for the changes under way since Fidel's retirement. His first trip in 2002 failed to improve ties between the two governments; neither George W. Bush nor Fidel Castro was disposed to take any initiative to change the atmosphere of animosity. Now, however, new leaders in both capitals professed a desire to escape the legacy of a half century of hostility. With the diplomatic process begun by Obama in 2009 stalled, Carter felt it was a propitious moment to provide a catalyst to get things moving again.

Word of Carter's trip sparked immediate speculation that he might be on a mission to free Alan Gross. Just a few months earlier, Carter had traveled to North Korea and won the release of a U.S. citizen imprisoned for entering the country illegally. Moreover, many observers thought it unlikely that the Cuban government would have invited Carter or that Carter would have accepted without some expectation that he could obtain Gross's release. But this hope was quickly dashed. "The Cuban officials made it very clear to me before I left my home that the freedom of Alan Gross would not be granted," he later revealed.[71] Carter decided to make the trip anyway. It was brief—just three days, half the length of his 2002 trip—but it was a whirlwind of activity. He met with Cardinal Ortega to discuss the church's dialogue with the government. He visited the Patronato Jewish center and Temple Beth Shalom to meet with leaders of the Jewish community. He had breakfast with a group of dissidents, former prisoners, and bloggers, including Yoani Sánchez. He also met with relatives of the Cuban Five, and he had a long meeting with Alan Gross.

While Cuban officials understood that Washington politics made an explicit exchange of the Cuban Five for Alan Gross problematic, they nevertheless saw the two cases as linked (as Foreign Minister Rodríguez had told Bill Richardson). Each side could simply agree in advance to a release on humanitarian grounds, publicly justified on its own merits rather than as part of a trade. Carter himself had established the precedent. In 1979, when Carter requested the release of four imprisoned CIA agents, Fidel suggested a parallel release of four Puerto Rican nationalists. Without any formal agreement between the two sides, Carter granted the Puerto Ricans clemency, and Castro released the CIA prisoners. Accompanying Carter on this trip, Bob Pastor, the architect of the 1979 deal, was reminded by Cuban colleagues of the success of the "non-trade trade" and asked if it could be repeated.

Carter spoke twice with Foreign Minister Rodríguez, who argued that Obama's rhetoric about improving relations was belied by escalating U.S. sanctions against international banks doing business with Cuba and the ongoing democracy promotion program. Carter had lunch with National Assembly president Ricardo Alarcón, who briefed him on the economic reforms to be discussed at the upcoming Sixth Congress of the Communist Party. He visited Fidel at home, where they reminisced about old times.

Carter's meeting with Raúl Castro lasted three hours, after which they adjourned for dinner in colonial Havana. Carter emphasized that Gross's detention was a serious obstacle to improving relations and urged Raúl to consider releasing him on humanitarian grounds. Castro demurred, hinting that there was no consensus in the Cuban government about how to handle the Gross case. Raúl repeated his oft-stated willingness to engage Washington in wide-ranging talks, without preconditions, so long as those talks were undertaken "on equal terms . . . with full respect for our independence and sovereignty." Any topic could be discussed, he affirmed. "We are ready."[72]

In both a televised interview and a press conference before his departure, Carter reiterated two themes from his first trip to Cuba in 2002: the United States ought to fully normalize relations with Cuba immediately, and Cuba ought to allow full freedom of speech, assembly, travel. Specifically, he called for an end to the U.S. embargo, removal of Cuba from the terrorism list, release of the Cuban Five, and release of Alan Gross. In response to Carter's statement, Raúl Castro quipped, "I agree with everything President Carter said."[73]

Upon his return to the United States, Carter received a cool reception from the Obama administration. Secretary Clinton gave him a polite hearing, and then the administration returned to business as usual. The day after Carter's return, the administration notified Congress it would request $20 million in new funding for the "democracy promotion" program that had landed Alan Gross in jail in the first place—the same level of funding requested by the Bush administration.

Issues of Mutual Interest: Coast Guard Cooperation

From the outset, a key difference between the Obama and Bush administrations was Obama's willingness to talk to the Cuban government about issues of mutual interest. The decision to resume the migration talks was emblematic of that commitment. Cuba's agenda also included cooperation to counter terrorism and narcotics trafficking. In 2001, shortly after the September 11 terrorist attacks, Cuban diplomats submitted draft agreements on these three issues to the State Department, but the Bush administration never replied. When Obama resumed the migration talks, the Cubans hoped to reopen discussions on these other issues and added disaster preparedness as well.

Alan Gross's arrest drastically reduced the possibility of progress, however. Washington was unwilling to engage Cuba very deeply or sign any formal accord while Gross was imprisoned. Topics like migration, counternarcotics operations, and Coast Guard search and rescue were "areas where it behooves us to talk to the Cuban government," the Coordinator for Cuban Affairs Peter Brennan acknowledged, but "we've told the Cubans that we will not move on issues X, Y, and Z, until Alan Gross is released."[74]

Even without formal agreements, there were a few islands of cooperation that could not only be expanded to the benefit of both governments but also pursued with a very low profile so as not to stir up trouble on Capitol Hill. One was Coast Guard cooperation. The Clinton administration was the first to station a U.S. Coast Guard liaison officer (referred to as the "Drug Interdiction Officer," or DIS) at the U.S. Interests Section in Havana. Over time, the relationship between the DIS officers and their Cuban counterparts became increasingly respectful and productive. During the Bush years, when U.S. diplomats were cut off from any communication with the Cuban government, the Coast Guard liaison was the only point of official contact that remained intact.

The Cubans routinely used the Coast Guard liaison as an informal channel to convey messages to the U.S. government. In June 2009, during a routine repatriation of Cubans picked up at sea by the U.S. Coast Guard, a Ministry of Foreign Relations official told the U.S. officer that Cuba was interested in using the semiannual migration talks to open a dialogue on counter-narcotics operations, counterterrorism, and natural disaster response. "He stated that the aforementioned forums for engagement are a launching point, or segue, to further talks on larger issues," Jonathan Farrar reported to Washington.[75] In September the Cubans used the liaison officer to let the United States know that Cuba might be willing to accept hurricane relief assistance if it were offered—something Cuba had always rejected during the Bush years.[76]

Coast Guard cooperation, already "the most effective and closest [area] of U.S.-Cuba engagement," according to Farrar, improved after Obama took office.[77] During Bisa Williams's visit in September 2009, "the GOC pushed hard for increased law enforcement cooperation, especially in counter-narcotics," Farrar reported. "The top drug fighter at the Interior Ministry, Colonel Jorge Samper, commented that . . . the GOC would like to be able to work more closely with the United States in sharing information about trafficking patterns in the region."[78] In November, U.S. Coast Guard officials met with Cuban counterparts to share technical information on "counter smuggling tactics and procedures."[79] By 2011, increased cooperation had significantly reduced people smuggling and narcotics trafficking in the Florida Strait.[80] A senior regional Coast Guard commander in Florida described cooperation with Cuba on search and rescue and counter-narcotics operations as "second to none."[81] Nevertheless, the formal agreement Cuba proposed on counter-narcotics cooperation remained "under review," even though the State Department admitted that concluding such an agreement "could advance the counter-narcotics efforts undertaken by both countries" and "would likely lead to increased interdictions and disruptions of illegal trafficking."[82]

Law Enforcement Cooperation

The Obama administration had an opportunity to renew counterterrorism cooperation with Cuba when it tried to bring an infamous terrorist to justice.

On January 10, 2011, the U.S. Justice Department finally put Luis Posada Carriles on trial in El Paso. Despite a long career of political violence—blowing up a civilian airliner with seventy-three passengers in 1976; orchestrating a string of hotel bombings in Havana that wounded eleven people and killed an Italian businessman in 1997; and plotting to blow up an auditorium full of people in order to assassinate Fidel Castro in Panama City in 2000—Posada was prosecuted only for the crimes of immigration fraud and perjury. Nevertheless, at eighty-three years of age, the trial represented the best chance to put Posada behind bars for the rest of his life.

Arrested in Miami in May 2005, Posada was initially incarcerated in El Paso for illegal entry. U.S. Immigration and Customs Enforcement (ICE) went through the motions of trying to deport him, but no country would take him. The United States refused to extradite him to the one country that had a legitimate claim to him—Venezuela (where the bombing of the Cuban airliner was planned). Only after the immigration court decided to release him on bail did ICE officially identify him as a terrorist: Posada's "long history of criminal activity and violence in which innocent civilians were killed," ICE wrote, meant that his "release from detention would pose a danger to both the community and the national security of the United States."[83]

Yet, after holding him for twenty months as "a danger," in January 2007 U.S. prosecutors indicted Posada only for making "false statements" about how he entered the United States. Four months later, Judge Kathleen Cardone dismissed all charges against him and set him free on the grounds that the government had engaged in "fraud, deceit and trickery" to gather evidence. Eventually, an appeals court overturned that ruling, and in the spring of 2009 the Justice Department counterterrorism division indicted Posada on additional charges for lying about his role in the bombing of Cuba's hotels and discotheques in 1997 and 1998.

Prosecuting Posada on those charges required the support of Raúl Castro's government. Setting aside their suspicions that the U.S. judicial system appeared to be treating "the Osama bin Laden of Latin America" with kid gloves, Cuban officials offered substantial cooperation. Teams of Justice Department lawyers and investigators traveled to Havana at least four times to interview witnesses and review evidence. FBI agents were allowed to question and depose Posada's accomplices incarcerated in Cuba. The Cuban government provided video footage of the crime scenes and more than fifteen hundred pages of investigative reports on the hotel bombings. As the trial progressed into the early spring of 2011, the Cuban government sent two police investigators to El Paso to testify about the forensic evidence they had found.[84]

Washington and Havana engaged in an extensive, protracted, and substantive effort to finally bring Luis Posada Carriles to justice and thereby foster broader counterterrorism collaboration. But like so many other good-faith efforts, this one ended in insult and outrage for the Cubans. After a three-month trial, the El Paso jury took less than three hours to find Posada "not guilty" on all counts, and he went free. The Cuban Foreign Ministry promptly accused the U.S. government of supporting and sheltering an international terrorist. As Ricardo Alarcón declared, "The stupid and shameful farce is over."[85]

Disaster Diplomacy

Natural disasters tend to elicit humanitarian empathy by reminding us that we are all vulnerable in the face of catastrophe, and they create opportunities for cooperation that can build bonds of trust even between adversaries. The earthquake that devastated Port-au-Prince, Haiti, on January 12, 2010, offered an opportunity for Cuba and the United States to cooperate on a purely humanitarian mission to alleviate extraordinary human suffering. The United States moved quickly to provide emergency assistance and to coordinate worldwide offers of relief. Cuba had a well-established medical mission in Haiti of four hundred doctors, nurses, and paramedics who immediately began providing emergency aid to the injured. Hundreds more Cuban doctors soon joined them.

Cooperation began with Cuba granting U.S. planes the right to fly through Cuban airspace as they evacuated the injured to medical facilities abroad, an offer that garnered a public expression of appreciation from Secretary Clinton.[86] Two high-level diplomatic meetings ensued to discuss ways in which Washington and Havana could extend their cooperation. In January, Secretary Clinton's chief of staff, Cheryl Mills (coordinating Haiti relief efforts at State) and Julissa Reynoso (from the Western Hemisphere Affairs bureau) met in Santo Domingo with senior Cuban Foreign Ministry and Health Ministry officials.[87] Two months later, Mills met with Cuban foreign minister Bruno Rodríguez in New York at a United Nations donor conference. The discussion, according to Rodríguez, focused on how to rebuild Haiti's heath system. "Some cooperative activities have taken place between Cuba and the United States, in the effort to provide emergency care," he explained, and more were expected to follow.[88] Although no one at the State Department wanted to draw too much attention to it, U.S. relief workers on the ground in Haiti were providing medical supplies to the field hospitals the Cuban doctors set up.[89] Southcom's deputy commander Lieutenant General Ken Keen, who directed U.S. disaster relief operations in Haiti, was so impressed with the Cuban response that he recommended more sustained, long-term U.S.-Cuban cooperation. "We've had an unprecedented level of coordination with Cuba in providing aid to Haiti," Arturo Valenzuela said in October 2010. "We've worked very closely with Cuban authorities in Haiti."[90]

The bilateral meetings produced an idea for a joint project: the United States would provide $30 million to build a new hospital in rural Haiti, to be staffed in part by Cuban medical personnel. The two sides were near agreement when the Cubans asked that in light of this cooperation, Washington end its Cuban Medical Professional Parole program. The program, designed by the Bush administration, had enticed almost 1,600 Cuban doctors and other medical personnel serving abroad into defecting to the United States by promising them automatic entry. After the Obama administration refused to halt the program, Havana proposed that Washington fund a second medical facility in the capital, Port-au-Prince. Again, the administration refused, and the talks broke off.[91] "We have not produced any agreements," lamented Jorge Bolaños, head of the Cuban Interests Section in Washington after a third meeting, but he reaffirmed Cuba's continued willingness to cooperate.[92]

The explosion of the Deepwater Horizon oil rig in the Gulf of Mexico on April 20, 2010, focused new attention on U.S.-Cuban environmental cooperation. As the spill spread eastward toward the Florida Strait, experts warned that the Gulf Stream could carry the slick onto Cuba's northern beaches and even to Florida's Atlantic Coast. In mid-May, almost a month after the blowout, the State Department formally notified Cuba of the environmental hazard posed by the spill, as required by international law, and began "low, technical" bilateral talks about its spread.[93] Havana gave permission for a National Oceanic and Atmospheric Administration vessel to enter Cuban waters to monitor the spill.[94]

In the end, Cuba's coasts were spared. But the debate over U.S.-Cuban cooperation on energy, oil, and environmental protection was just beginning. The U.S. Geological Survey estimated Cuban oil reserves in the Gulf at about 4.6 billion barrels, enough to make the island a medium-sized exporter.[95] The Cuba government had already leased blocks in the commercial zone for exploration by companies in Russia, China, India, Malaysia, Vietnam, Angola, Norway, Brazil, Venezuela, and Spain. The Deepwater Horizon accident prompted people to ask what would happen if a Cuban well suffered a similar accident. The answers were unsettling. "The existing trade embargo prohibits U.S. assistance for containment, clean up, drilling a relief well, or capping the well," warned Brian Petty, from the International Association of Drilling Contractors, the main industry trade association. "Absolutely no U.S. resources can be committed to containment or clean up."[96]

As former oil executive Jorge Piñon explained, all the companies cooperate when an accident happens—but not if the accident was at a Cuban well. "That's not the case with Cuba given the embargo, so days would go by as the bureaucratic paperwork was shifted from agency to department, and in the meantime the oil would be moving towards Key West and South Beach."[97] Piñon argued vigorously for a proactive U.S. approach that would remove all obstacles to an immediate U.S. response in the event of a Cuban accident, including preapproval of licenses to deploy equipment, technology, and personnel; regular exchanges of scientific and technical information to enhance Cuban safety; and joint U.S.-Cuban exercises to practice containment and cleanup of a spill.[98] The International Association of Drilling Contractors (IADC) echoed Piñon's recommendations.[99]

The Obama administration took some small steps toward cooperation. Before the Deepwater Horizon disaster, when the IADC had requested a license to send a delegation to Cuba to discuss offshore drilling safety, the Treasury Department denied it. When IADC reapplied after the accident, the license was granted. "Senior [Cuban] officials told us they are going ahead with their deepwater drilling program," said IADC president Lee Hunt upon his return. "They are utilizing every reliable non-U.S. source that they can for technology and information, but they would prefer to work directly with the United States in matters of safe drilling practices."[100]

In the low-level technical discussions between U.S. and Cuban officials during the Deepwater Horizon crisis, Cuba proposed a bilateral protocol for cooperation in handling an accident. Cuban diplomats submitted a draft document to the State Department, but no formal agreement resulted. Former senator Bob Graham of Florida, co-chair of the U.S. National Commission on the BP Deepwater Horizon Oil Spill, suggested using Mexico as an intermediary to discuss safety standards for drilling in the Gulf: "This is not a capitulation to Castro; rather it is something in our self-interest to ensure that anything that relates to drilling have high safety standards."[101] Graham's co-chair, William Reilly, traveled to Mexico to encourage authorities there to take on the intermediary role. [102]

But when the Department of the Interior hosted a twelve-nation conference in April 2011 on the lessons learned from the Deepwater Horizon accident, Cuba was excluded, even though Secretary Ken Salazar acknowledged that the prospect of imminent drilling in Cuban waters was "an issue of concern." Michael Bromwich, director of the U.S. Bureau of Ocean Energy Management, Regulation and Enforcement, agreed that reaching an agreement with Cuba on safety standards "would certainly be desirable." However, he added, "finding the mechanism to do that is tricky and needs to be explored further."[103]

The administration refused to directly engage with Cuba to formulate a coordinated response plan of the sort that the Coast Guard had developed with Mexico in the Caribbean and Russia in the Aleutians. The "tricky mechanism" the administration settled on was to deal indirectly with Cuba, under the cover of multinational initiatives. This, officials seemed to hope, would provide a margin of safety for the environment while blunting the political furor that would result from engaging the Cubans directly. In December 2011 U.S. officials participated in a multilateral conference with delegations from the Bahamas, Jamaica, Mexico, and Cuba to discuss offshore drilling safety. U.S. participants "were impressed with the Cuban delegation's professionalism and the country's emergency spill response plan," according to the trade publication, *Oil Daily*.[104] The meeting concluded with an agreement that each government would compile and share an "authorities matrix" identifying the officials responsible for various aspects of safety, regulation, and accident response. By early 2013, both Cuba and the United States had submitted their matrices.[105] In April 2012 another multilateral meeting conducted a tabletop response exercise based on a hypothetical accident at a Cuban well. The Cuban delegation discussed notification protocols and the facilitation of international assistance and expressed its willingness to share with the United States its safety plans on future deepwater drilling. The two delegations met together informally during the conference.[106]

On the U.S. side, the Coast Guard was assigned to take the lead in managing any offshore spill in the Caribbean and was given the necessary licenses from the Department of the Treasury to work directly with the Cuban government.[107] The Department of Commerce began licensing firms in advance to transfer equipment and expertise to Cuba in the event of an accident. "I'm confident that once we get through this process, the United States will be able to respond to an accident quickly," Coordinator for Cuban Affairs Peter Brennan affirmed.[108] Industry professionals were less sanguine about the adequacy of this strategy. Paul Schuler from Clean Caribbean, which had already run the gauntlet of getting a license from the Treasury Department, had his doubts. Coping with a major spill would require drawing on resources from dozens of companies, he pointed out. Most would not have preapproved licenses; they would have to go through the licensing process, "which, in my experience has not been quick."[109]

Bill Richardson Rides Again

After he failed to win Alan Gross's release on his 2010 trip to Cuba, Governor Bill Richardson did not give up hope. He stayed in touch with Ambassador Bolaños at the Cuban Interests Section in Washington, and on June 20, 2011, Bolaños called to invite Richardson to meet with him at the Cuban mission. According to Richardson's aide Gilbert Gallegos, Bolaños read the governor a diplomatic note that "basically said that after the judicial process ended the Cubans were ready to talk to him about Gross."[110] The ambassador urged Richardson to hold off on another trip to the island until the Cuban Supreme Court ruled on Gross's appeal. After the court upheld Gross's fifteen-year sentence on August 5, Bolaños and Richardson met for lunch to discuss plans for a trip in September. Richardson left convinced that the purpose of his trip was to begin a dialogue about the terms on which Gross might be released. "We were going to negotiate," Richardson recalled. "There was not a commitment that I would get Gross, but that we would talk about it."[111]

Before Richardson departed for Havana, State Department officials briefed him on the status of the Gross case and gave him a list of ten things the United States was prepared to do to improve relations if Gross was pardoned. The list covered a range of issues of interest to Havana, but most were framed as possibilities rather than pledges: Washington would review Cuba's inclusion on the State Department's list of state sponsors of terrorism; it would reduce (but not eliminate) USAID's democracy promotion program and "change" it in unspecified ways; it would look at the possibility of allowing U.S. companies to invest in Cuba's telecommunications infrastructure; it would seek to restore Cuba's ownership of the *Havana Club* trademark, which U.S. courts had awarded to Bacardi; it would seek the extradition of Luis Posada Carriles, wanted in Venezuela and Cuba for terrorist bombings; and it would encourage the Department of Justice to allow René González, the one member of the Cuban Five who had completed his prison sentence, to return home rather than forcing him to stay in Florida on parole for three more years.[112]

The items on Richardson's list that were promised unequivocally were, for the most part, things the administration had already publicly announced as U.S. policy: restoring postal relations; allowing U.S. companies to provide spill-mitigation services to Cuba's offshore oil drilling rigs; and vetoing congressional efforts to rollback Obama's policy of allowing unlimited Cuban American family travel. The one new item was a pledge to end the program encouraging Cuban doctors abroad to defect, which would have cleared the way for cooperation in Haiti.

Richardson understood the tenuous nature of the U.S. list. "There was no deal that if Gross is released, we will do these things," he acknowledged. Rather, what Washington was offering was "not a commitment but a process. You give us Alan Gross and we can talk about a number of issues."[113]

Richardson's September trip got off to a bad start when he leaked word of it to Wolf Blitzer at CNN, who reported that the governor was "invited by the Cuban government for the specific mission of trying to negotiate the release of Gross."[114] To the Cubans, this looked like an attempt to force their hand. "I think maybe the Cubans felt a little pressured by all the press attention," Richardson admitted later, acknowledging his misstep.[115]

During his meeting in Cuba with Foreign Minister Rodríguez, Richardson presented the State Department's list of things that could happen if Gross was released and told Rodríguez that a military plane was standing by in Florida to take Gross home. The foreign minister did not react well to the list or to Richardson's presumptuousness. "Rodríguez told me three things," Richardson recalled: "One, you won't get Gross; two, you won't see Raúl; and three, you won't even see Gross."

"Is that it?" Richardson asked.

"Yes, this is it."

"I'll have to talk with the press," Richardson warned, in light of all the hype surrounding his trip.

"You do what you have to do," Rodríguez replied evenly.[116]

When the foreign minister reported to his subordinates how badly the meeting had gone, they convinced him to reconsider his decision to deny Richardson a meeting with Gross. Almost every U.S. visitor who asked was being allowed to see Gross; it would be an enormous insult to bar Richardson. But as Vice Minister Dagoberto Rodríguez was on his way to tell Richardson that he could see Alan Gross after all, he received word of Richardson's statement to the press.

Richardson left his meeting with Rodríguez angry and puzzled. The Cubans had invited him to discuss releasing Gross, and now that he was here, with negotiating terms, they would not even talk to him. That evening, he vented his frustration to Associated Press reporter Paul Haven at the Hotel Nacional. "My mission here as a private citizen is to secure the release of Alan Gross, an American hostage," he said. "I've been informed by the Cuban government that I would not be allowed to see Alan Gross during my visit." The following day, Richardson held a press conference at the hotel, declaring that he would not leave Cuba until he was allowed to see Gross.[117]

Calling Gross a "hostage" effectively ended Richardson's mission. The Cuban Foreign Ministry issued a press statement declaring that Alan Gross's release was "never on the table" and that this "had been made clear to Richardson as soon as he raised it." Richardson's request to see Gross "became impossible due to his slanderous statements to the press in which he described Gross as a 'hostage' of the Cuban government and his attempt to pressure by affirming publicly that he would not leave Cuba until he had achieved this goal. We explained to Mr. Richardson that Cuba is a sovereign country which does not accept blackmail, pressure or posturing."[118]

Despite Richardson's vow to stay in Cuba until he was allowed to visit the prisoner, Cuban officials would have nothing more to do with him. After a few days, he gave up and came home. "I am very disappointed and surprised," he told reporters on his departure." Unfortunately after this negative experience, I don't know if I could return here as a friend."[119] Back in Washington, Richardson lamented "this dramatic snub of me" on air with Wolf Blitzer. "I'm still scratching my head because I was invited by the Cubans," Richardson mused. "My message to the Cubans was, look, I'm a private citizen. I'm not representing the administration. But if you free Alan Gross, a whole host of issues that you disagree with the United States can be discussed, human rights, environmental, commercial. And they shut the door."[120]

Therein lay the problem. As a private citizen, Richardson could promise nothing that would bind the Obama administration. Indeed, as Richardson sat in his hotel room hoping to eventually see Alan Gross, President Obama reiterated the governor's lack of authority to deal. "Richardson is acting as a private citizen on an humanitarian mission to try to free Gross," the president told reporters. "Anything to get Mr. Gross free we will support, although Mr. Richardson does not represent the U.S. government in his actions there."[121] The list of potential U.S. actions itself was poorly framed; if Cuba released Gross, the United States would consider things, or attempt to do things, or open talks about doing things. But there was precious little that Washington promised to actually do.

The Cubans had heard promises like this many times before; if only they would make concessions up front on an issue of interest to the United States, better relations would follow. More than once, the Cubans had taken the deal, but never did they see any payoff. Fidel Castro freed U.S. prisoners in 1963 after hints that their release could lead to a process of reconciliation; he ended the 1980 Mariel migration crisis when Washington promised broader bilateral talks; he signed the 1984 migration accord when U.S. negotiators suggested that Cuban concessions would lead to better relations; Cuba contributed to a diplomatic settlement in southern Africa in exchange for an explicit U.S. promise that Havana's cooperation would open the door to wider talks; and Castro ended the 1994 rafters migration crisis when President Clinton promised negotiations on the embargo. In none of these cases did the United States make good on its commitment. A nonbinding, informal proposal from a private citizen who himself admitted he could not make a firm commitment was not, for the Cubans, a credible offer.

A Second-Term President

In 1994, Fidel Castro told a group of former U.S. ambassadors that he needed a two-term U.S. president to normalize relations with Cuba because no first-term president would have the political courage to do it.[122] Barack Obama's surprisingly strong showing among Cuban Americans in the 2012 election positioned him well to be that president. Obama won half the Cuban American vote in Florida—far more than any Democrat before him.[123] His success resulted from a realignment among Cuban Americans rather than just Mitt Romney's weakness. A decade of polling by Florida International University (FIU) chronicled gradual attitudinal changes in the Cuban American community—changes that finally began to manifest themselves in voting behavior.[124] When FIU began polling in 1991, 87 percent of respondents favored continuing the embargo. By 2011, support had fallen to 56 percent. In 1993, 75 percent opposed the sale of food to Cuba and 50 percent opposed the sale of medicine. By 2011, solid majorities (65 and 75 percent respectively) supported both. These changes in attitude were produced by demographic shifts. Exiles who arrived in the United States in the 1960s and 1970s came as political refugees opposed to the socialist direction of the revolution. Those who arrived in the Mariel exodus of 1980 and after were more likely to have left for economic reasons and were far more likely to retain ties with family on the island and favor better U.S.-Cuban relations.

At first, these attitudinal changes did not manifest themselves at the polls, where the early arrivals composed a disproportionately larger share of the Cuban American electorate. Over 90 percent of those who arrived before 1985 were registered to vote. For those who arrived after the end of the Cold War, the registration rate was only 60 percent—if they were citizens. But with every passing year, the cohort of early exiles became a smaller proportion of the community as natural mortality took its toll, and new immigrants arrived at a rate of some thirty thousand annually.

Obama's success in Florida, and the fact that he would not have to stand for reelection, gave him more freedom of action on Cuba than any president in recent decades. Yet many of the same forces that prevented Obama from taking a truly new approach to U.S.-Cuban relations during his first term were still operative. Opponents like Marco Rubio (R-Fla.) and Robert Menendez in the Senate were still determined to fight a legislative guerrilla war against the president's Cuba policy by holding up nominations and threatening to filibuster must-pass legislation in order to block any new initiative. Major policy changes that require a significant expenditure of political capital rarely happen unless the urgency of the problem forces policy makers to act.

At first, it seemed like the president was intent on trying to resume the forward momentum of Cuba policy. His new secretary of state, John Kerry, had tried to reform USAID's democracy promotion program toward Cuba when he served in the Senate, and the new secretary of Defense, Chuck Hagel, had called the U.S. embargo an "outdated, unrealistic, irrelevant policy."[125] In private, senior administration officials expressed their desire for an opening to Cuba but lamented the tricky politics of the issue and the demands of other priorities.

Alan Gross's imprisonment had impaled the administration on the horns of a dilemma. U.S. officials wanted to get Gross out of jail for humanitarian reasons but also because his imprisonment blocked movement on issues of mutual interest. To move on these issues while Gross remained behind bars would invite conservative charges of appeasement. At the same time, administration officials could not bring themselves to acknowledge publicly that Gross had done anything wrong. By insisting on Gross's innocence, the administration gave fuel to conservative charges that Gross was a hostage, making it harder to broker a deal with Havana to win his release.

Alan Gross himself realized that U.S.-Cuban relations were mired down over his incarceration and would have to improve before he had any chance of freedom. During a four-hour meeting with author Peter Kornbluh just days after Obama's reelection, Gross suggested that Washington and Havana "sit down and talk *tachlis*—truthfully—without preconditions" and sign a nonbelligerency pact as a step toward normalization. Once there was a momentum to advance bilateral ties, he said, Washington and Havana could address and resolve his case.[126]

Early in the second term, the Obama White House initiated some quiet, below-the-radar actions to see if it could find a way out of the corner into which it had painted itself. In May the Department of Justice dropped its opposition to allowing René González, a member of the Cuban Five, to serve out his probation in Cuba rather than forcing him to remain in Miami. Shortly thereafter, Cuba granted Alan Gross's request to be examined by his own doctor.[127]

In May, the Cuban Foreign Ministry official in charge of relations with the United States, Josefina Vidal, met with Assistant Secretary of State for Western Hemisphere Affairs Roberta Jacobson. While their conversation covered a range of issues, they spent much of the time discussing Alan Gross.[128] Shortly thereafter, the State Department announced the resumption of bilateral talks on immigration (suspended since January 2011 because of Gross's arrest), and talks on the reestablishment of direct postal service. Working-level diplomats were given "a green light" to make progress where possible on issues of mutual interest. The two sides quickly resolved most points of disagreement on a postal accord, a Coast Guard search-and-rescue accord, and an oil spill containment protocol—though the U.S. side was loathe to use the word "agreement" lest it stir up trouble in Congress.

Although Cuba was once again listed as a sponsor of terrorism in the State Department's annual report in May, the rationale read more like a justification for removing Cuba from the list. Every reason cited for Cuba's inclusion was followed by an explanation of how Cuban behavior had changed for the better.[129] Nevertheless, when the administration sent its annual budget request for FY2014 to Capitol Hill in late May, it again requested $20 million for democracy promotion in Cuba.[130]

Although U.S. policy appeared to no longer be completely paralyzed by the predicament of Alan Gross, it remained tentative, cautious, and incremental—far from the bold stroke that Fidel Castro was hoping for from a second-term president. Real change in U.S.-Cuban relations would require vision and courage—qualities Obama had displayed in his push for comprehensive health care and immigration reform. Escaping fifty years of hostility between the United States and Cuba would by no means be easy or cost-free for the president. But, as Lyndon Johnson replied when warned that taking on civil rights would be too difficult and politically risky, "Well, what the hell's the presidency for?"[131]

The More Things Change, the More They Remain the Same

Good intentions notwithstanding, eighteen months into Obama's second term, U.S. relations with Cuba were not much different from what they had been under his ten predecessors. To be sure, Obama's approach contrasted sharply with President George W. Bush's. The previous president's policy was premised on a "big bang" theory of change in Cuba. Convinced that Cuban leaders would never allow significant change, Bush officials sought to ratchet up economic pressure and fuel the internal opposition until the regime collapsed. Obama embraced the "soft power" instruments of people-to-people exchange and diplomatic engagement in the hope of fostering gradual, incremental change. If Washington responded positively to Cuban economic or political liberalization, it might set in motion a self-reinforcing virtuous circle of change in Cuba and improvement in bilateral relations. This strategy was less innovative than Obama's team imagined. Jimmy Carter's 1977 decision to improve relations by negotiating a series of "reciprocal and sequential steps" and Bill Clinton's policy of "calibrated response" and, after Helms-Burton, parallel positive steps, were all variations on the same theme.

Despite being cloaked in the rhetoric of change, however, Obama's approach shared two premises common to U.S. policy since the end of the Cold War: (1) significant progress in bilateral relations would come only if Cuba began to dismantle its political and economic systems, replacing them with a multiparty electoral democracy and a free-market economy; and (2) even the smallest U.S. steps toward a reduction in tension would have to be met by reciprocal steps from the Cuban side. Under Obama, the goal of U.S. policy was not phrased as confrontationally as it was under George W. Bush, but neither was it fundamentally different.

At first, Obama's team hoped it could maintain principled support for democracy and human rights in Cuba without letting those commitments be an obstacle to improving bilateral relations. Eventual normalization of relations and lifting the embargo would still depend on domestic change in Cuba (unless and until the Helms-Burton law was repealed), but a lot could be accomplished short of that. However, Obama's insistence on quid pro quo reciprocity, defined in terms of Cuban domestic policy change, tied progress in bilateral relations directly to concessions the Cuban government was least willing to make. "We have made it very clear that we could not do much more in dealing with Cuba unless Cuba changes," said Secretary Clinton after Obama's 2009 initiatives. "The political prisoners need to be released. Free and fair elections need to be held. . . . So we are opening up dialogue with Cuba, but we are very clear that we want to see some fundamental changes within the Cuban regime."[132]

Even on issues in which the United States had important interests of its own at stake, the administration proved surprisingly timid. Progress was sparse due to a mixture of hope that going slow would provide some leverage to gain freedom for Alan Gross and fear of being pilloried on Capitol Hill for engaging with Cuba at all. Even those in the Obama administration who were genuinely interested in improving relations with Cuba had to fight a war on two fronts: they were exasperated with Cuban American members of Congress for making any policy change so hard and with the Cuban government for not doing anything to make it easier.

The only area in which the administration was willing to chance bold action was in the realm of people-to-people engagement. Obama went almost as far as he could under existing law by allowing all sorts of "purposeful" travel to Cuba—everything except pure tourism, which was prohibited by the Trade Sanctions Reform and Export Enhancement Act of 2000. One major advantage of people-to-people programs was that Washington could pursue them unilaterally, without engaging the Cuban government at all. Thus Obama's policy evolved, especially after the arrest of Alan Gross, very much in the pattern of Bill Clinton's policy after the 1996 shoot-down of the Brothers to the Rescue planes. With the opportunity for significant bilateral negotiations largely foreclosed, attention turned to people-to-people programs in the hope that they would build bonds between Cuban and U.S. civil society (a good thing in itself) and—in the best-case scenario—"create a foundation to later go forward with other things," as a State Department official working on Cuba explained.[133]

A year and a half into his second term, Barack Obama had yet to free himself from the core assumptions that had locked U.S.-Cuban relations into an impregnable pattern of mutual recrimination and animosity for more than half a century. As a result, he was stuck in the same impasse as his predecessors: sanctions against Cuba had produced nothing positive, but he was unwilling to run the political risk of trying something truly new. Ten presidents before him had tried in vain to untie this Gordian knot. Whether Obama could summon the courage to cut it during his second-term remained an open question.

10. INTIMATE ADVERSARIES, POSSIBLE FRIENDS

We both made mistakes, but it is time to put the past behind us.

—President Raúl Castro to U.S. congressional delegation led by Senator Patrick Leahy, February 19, 2013

"Mr. President, I am Castro," Raúl said as he reached out to shake hands with the president of the United States.

"I know," Barack Obama replied, smiling. Their encounter lasted just a few seconds, but it was historic—the first time since 1959 that a U.S. president met publicly with the president of Cuba. Neither government was willing to say that the handshake implied any warming of relations, but the sheer normalcy of this simple gesture was itself unusual in a relationship long fraught with tension and distrust. Its symbolism was underscored by the occasion; the two leaders met at the December 10, 2013, memorial service for Nelson Mandela, where Obama praised the spirit of forgiveness and reconciliation Mandela exemplified. "We can choose a world defined not by our differences, but by our common hopes," Obama intoned. "We can choose a world defined not by conflict, but by peace and justice and opportunity."[1]

Cuba had been on Obama's mind of late. At a fundraising dinner in Miami a few weeks earlier, he acknowledged that important changes were under way on the island and expressed his frustration with the policy stalemate. "We have to be creative and we have to be thoughtful and we have to continue to update our policies," he told his listeners. "Keep in mind that when [Fidel] Castro came to power I was just born, so the notion that the same policies that we put in place in 1961 would somehow still be as effective . . . in the age of the internet, Google and world travel, doesn't make sense."[2]

Returning from South Africa, Raúl too expressed his hope that Cuba and the United States might "establish civilized relations," and reiterated his offer to

U.S. president Barack Obama shakes hands with Cuban president Raúl Castro at the memorial service for former South African president Nelson Mandela, December 10, 2013. The handshake between the leaders of two Cold War enemies came during a ceremony focused on Mandela's legacy of reconciliation. (AP Photo)

open "a respectful dialogue" with Washington. "If we really want to make progress in bilateral relations," he told Cuba's National Assembly, "we must learn to mutually respect our differences and get used to coexisting peacefully."[3]

As the remarks by both presidents suggested, beneath the complex knot of conflict between Cuba and the United States lies a rich vein of mutual concerns, shared culture, and common humanity. Across half a century, their turbulent relations have been marked by the interplay of interests in conflict and interests in common. Since 1959, Washington has tried everything except direct intervention to force Cuba back into the political and economic orbit of the United States. Cuba has done everything to maintain the independent, socialist path Fidel Castro charted in 1959–60. Nevertheless, there has always been a countervailing impetus toward rapprochement. The very same closeness that made the conflict so intense also created an incentive in both capitals to find ways to cooperate—especially when coercion and defiance alone simply prolonged the conflict rather than resolving it. These "closest of enemies," as retired U.S. diplomat Wayne Smith called Cuba and the United States, needed each other's cooperation to deal effectively with a range of issues important to them both.[4] Yet for more than fifty years, Cuba and the United States have not been able to consummate a reconciliation. The two nations remain stuck in a relationship of hostility that is both a relic of the Cold War and an impediment to the national interests of both. Why hasn't there been more progress toward better relations after half a century?

First, real conflicts of interest lie at the heart of the dispute. By severing Cuba's economic and political dependence on the United States, Fidel Castro did serious harm to U.S. economic interests on the island and to U.S. political interests across the hemisphere. Cuba's alliance with the Soviet Union challenged U.S. security interests, symbolized most obviously by the 1962 missile crisis, but also manifested in Cuban efforts to extend its revolutionary socialist model abroad. As the State Department explained in 1964, "The primary danger we face in Castro is . . . in the impact the very existence of his regime has upon the leftist movement in many Latin American countries. . . . The simple fact is that Castro represents a successful defiance of the U.S., a negation of our whole hemispheric policy of almost a century and a half."[5]

On the Cuban side, Washington's policy of economic strangulation and covert subversion threatened the revolution's very existence. Havana built its security around a strategic alliance with the Soviet Union to deter U.S. attack and the promotion of socialism abroad to expand the community of like-minded states willing to stand shoulder to shoulder with Cuba. These core principles were not open for discussion, as Fidel Castro said repeatedly in both public and private. When Washington pressed Cuba to abandon the whole architecture of its foreign policy as the price of better relations with the United States, Castro refused.

With the end of Cold War, U.S. security interests dissipated, giving way to political ones. Washington's long-standing conditions for improving relations—that Cuba reduce military ties with Moscow and stop supporting revolution abroad—were replaced by the demand that Cuba repudiate the core tenets of the revolution by restoring capitalism and adopting a multiparty liberal democracy. "We keep moving the goal posts," observed

Wayne Smith.[6] For Cuba, the core ideological conflict with the United States has always been the revolution's adamant nationalism in the face of U.S. efforts to return Cuba to its pre-1959 dependency, a fear reinforced after the end of the Cold War by Washington's preoccupation with how Cuba runs its internal affairs.

Ironically, the end of the Cold War made reconciliation harder rather than easier. The real security issues at stake when Cuba served as an ally of the Soviet Union gave Washington an incentive to pursue coexistence. Absent compelling security interests, that incentive was much reduced. The most serious U.S. attempts to normalize relations took place during the Cold War, under Gerald Ford and Jimmy Carter. (Kennedy's 1963 initiative could be counted as well, though it was just getting under way when it was cut short by his assassination.) No president since has made a comparable effort. Bill Clinton and Barack Obama tried to improve relations, but nevertheless insisted that full normalization would have to await fundamental changes in Cuba's internal political and economic order. Ronald Reagan, George H. W. Bush, and George W. Bush were openly committed to regime change, not reconciliation, though even they found reason to talk with Havana about a range of common interests. The absence of compelling foreign policy reasons to normalize relations with Havana also opened the way for domestic politics—that is, the Cuban American lobby in Florida—to hold greater sway. As Brent Scowcroft, national security advisor to Presidents Gerald Ford and George H. W. Bush admitted: "Cuba is a domestic issue for the United States and not a foreign policy issue."[7]

Does Cuba Want Better Relations?

One of the most striking things about the long history of antagonism between Cuba and the United States is how often the Cubans have tried to find a way to bridge the divide. Although Fidel Castro professed to believe that the imperialist United States could never accept Cuban socialism, every time a new president took office in Washington, Castro held out an olive branch to see if the administration—no matter how conservative or antagonistic—might be open to better relations.

To be sure, Fidel Castro made a successful political career at home and abroad portraying himself as David in battle with the imperialist Goliath. As Che Guevara told Richard Goodwin in 1961, the Bay of Pigs proved to be a political bonanza, allowing Fidel to wrap the revolution's socialist agenda in the flag of Cuban nationalism. Castro himself was more blunt. "The Revolution has to fight; combat is what makes revolutions strong," he told an audience in early 1961. "A revolution that is not attacked is probably not a true revolution. A revolution that does not confront an enemy runs the risk of falling asleep, of growing weak. . . . Like armies hardening themselves, revolutions need to confront an enemy!" Decades later, a more philosophical Fidel acknowledged that battling the United States had its political advantages, even as he argued for an end to the confrontation. The United States would benefit more than Cuba from normal relations, he argued. "If the United States makes its peace with us, it will take away a little of our prestige, our influence, our glory."[8]

At certain moments, other Cuban interests clearly outweighed better relations with the United States. Castro calculated that Cuba had more to gain in its relations with Moscow and its standing in the Third World by intervening in Africa in the 1970s. Those interventions, which happened at moments when Washington was sincerely interested in moving toward normalization, led some observers to conclude that Castro did not really want better relations. "Six former U.S. presidents tried to negotiate Cuba into accommodation; all failed," the CIA concluded in 1982. "The very nature of the Castro regime precludes anything but an adversary relationship between Havana and Washington. . . . This adversary relationship will not change as long as Castro is in power."[9]

This notion was reinforced by the shoot-down of the Brothers to the Rescue planes in 1996, at a time when Clinton was hoping to at least improve relations if not normalize them. "It almost appeared that Castro was trying to force us to maintain the embargo as an excuse for the economic failures of his regime," Bill Clinton concluded in his memoir.[10] The arrest of Alan Gross in 2009 after Obama had announced his intention to improve relations turned the idea that Cuba did not want better relations into a truism among U.S. officials. "If you look at any opening to Cuba, you can almost chart how the Castro regime does something to try to stymie it," Secretary of State Hillary Clinton argued after the Gross arrest.[11]

On the other side of the historical ledger, however, substantial evidence indicated that Castro was, in fact, serious about wanting normal relations. Although he declared early on that Cuba would never negotiate while the embargo remained a "a dagger at our throat," he soon backed off that absolutist position to negotiate the release of the Bay of Pigs prisoners and a wide variety of other agreements over the next five decades.

Whenever Havana and Washington engaged in talks on narrow issues, Castro tried to parlay them into negotiations about the core issue of the embargo. He first raised the idea of dialogue about normalizing relations to James Donovan as they finished negotiating the release of the Bay of Pigs prisoners. Over the years, U.S. negotiators certainly thought Cuba was serious about normalization because they repeatedly offered to expand talks on narrow issues into negotiations about the embargo as a way of enticing Cuba to make concessions up front. In 1980 Peter Tarnoff offered Fidel new negotiations on normalization in Carter's second term if Castro would end the Mariel migration crisis. In 1984 Washington hinted that Cuban concessions on migration would lead to better relations and a broader dialogue, and then reneged once the migration agreement was signed. In 1988 the State Department explicitly promised that Cuban cooperation in the southern African negotiations would lead to a broader dialogue on bilateral issues, and Washington reneged again. In 1994 Clinton promised Castro that Cuban concessions to end the rafters crisis would lead to a broader dialogue about the embargo. Cuba made the concessions, but Clinton never followed through.

Over the years, there has been a long trail of broken commitments from Washington. If anything, the historical record suggests that the Cubans have been too eager to negotiate and too gullible in believing U.S. promises, which, time after time, were made but not kept. If U.S. officials could point to evidence that Havana did not really want reconciliation, Cuban officials could just as easily point to evidence that Washington was disingenuous in offering it.

Finally, Raúl Castro is not Fidel. Whereas Fidel took a certain satisfaction in defying the United States and exploited U.S. hostility to rally nationalist sentiment, Raúl has focused on Cuba's domestic problems. Anti-U.S. diatribes feature much less prominently in his speeches, and he blames Cuba's economic problems on the shortcomings of Cuban policy rather than the embargo. If Fidel was motivated to maintain an acrimonious relationship with Washington for domestic political reasons, Raúl is not. The end of the Cold War strengthened Cuba's incentive to seek normal ties with its northern neighbor. Lifting the embargo would benefit the Cuban economy, and normal diplomatic recognition would reduce the security threat posed by the United States. U.S. presidents arguably have had a greater domestic political incentive—electoral votes in Florida—to maintain hostile relations than Cuban leaders have.

Lessons from the Past, Prospects for the Future

President Obama's second term appeared to offer usually favorable conditions for improving U.S.-Cuban relations. With no need for the president to worry about reelection and the Cuban American electorate embracing more moderate policies, domestic politics posed less of an obstacle than at any time since the end of the Cold War. Moreover, with every passing year, the United States has paid a growing diplomatic price for its static Cuba policy, especially in Latin America.

In Cuba, historic economic reforms were moving the island toward a mixed economy akin to Vietnam's, and incipient political decompression allowed more space for open debate and a more robust civil society. These changes, undertaken in response to domestic necessity rather than U.S. demands, were nevertheless moving Cuba in directions long cited by Washington as necessary for better relations. To exert any positive influence on the trajectory of Cuba's evolution, however, Washington needed to engage, not just with Cuban society but with Cuba's government.

Eager to put Cuba on a more solid footing before passing the torch to the next generation of leaders, Raúl Castro not only initiated an ambitious reform program but also offered unconditional talks with Washington. After Raúl Castro steps down in 2018, when his current term as president ends, it may well be harder for new, untested leaders who lack the legitimacy of the revolutionary regime's founders to make peace with Washington. Just as only Nixon could go to China, only a Castro can come to Washington.

As President Obama and his successors consider whether and how to engage with Cuba, the experience of ten presidents before them offers some useful lessons. The discontinuity from one administration to the next has made these lessons difficult for U.S. policy makers to recognize. Eager to promote the new president's agenda, every foreign policy team looks forward, not back. Ricardo Alarcón, who led Cuban delegations negotiating with the United States from the 1980s to 2003, remarked on how little institutional memory the State Department seemed to carry over from one administration to the next. During his years as negotiator, he noted wryly, the only person on the Cuban delegation who changed was the translator; on the U.S. side, the only person who remained the same was the translator. With the benefit of more than fifty years of hindsight, we can identify a number of lessons from past dialogues that can guide future ones.

LESSON 1. Even at moments of intense hostility, there have always been reasons and opportunities for dialogue. The intensity of hostility between Washington and Havana has waxed and waned, ranging from concerted efforts to fully normalize relations to actions that nearly eradicated any sort of dialogue. But every U.S. president since Eisenhower has seen fit to negotiate with the Cuban government to some extent. In the midst of the missile crisis, Kennedy sought to open a channel of communication with Castro. Despite Cuban interventions in Africa, both Ford and Carter were willing to continue a dialogue. At the height of the wars in Central America, Reagan sent secret envoys to test Cuba's willingness to deescalate. Indeed, sometimes the very intensity of conflict and the imminent threat of violent confrontation was the catalyst for communication.

LESSON 2. Although Cuban leaders have always been willing to talk, they instinctively resist making concession to U.S. demands. During the Cold War, Washington had three core requirements for normalizing relations, all focusing on Cuban foreign policy. Cuba had to reduce if not eliminate its military relationship with the Soviet Union, stop supporting revolution in Latin America, and withdraw its military forces from Africa. When the end of the Cold War resolved all these issues, George H. W. Bush demanded that Cuba change the nature of its social and political system, accepting a free-market economy and multiparty liberal democracy.

During the 1970s, Fidel Castro repeatedly refused to negotiate Cuban solidarity with ideological comrades in Latin America or Africa. To Castro, proletarian internationalism was a foundational principle of Cuban foreign policy, not something to be negotiated away in return for some quid pro quo from Washington. The most he ever conceded was that if Cuba and the United States had normal relations, that relationship would constrain Cuba's actions abroad. When U.S. demands about Cuban foreign policy were replaced by demands about Cuba's internal affairs, Fidel, and later Raúl Castro, reacted with even greater indignation. As Che Guevara told Kennedy aide Richard Goodwin in 1961, Cuba would never abandon the "type of society" the revolution was building. Fifty years later, Raúl Castro was still sending Washington that same message.

LESSON 3. Nevertheless, Cuba has been willing to take steps responsive to U.S. concerns so long as those steps come at Havana's own initiative, not as explicit concessions. "I can assure you that we would never decide anything as a function of a precondition imposed by the United States," Carlos Rafael Rodríguez said to Peter Tarnoff in 1978. "The pride of small countries, which can even push them to make the wrong decision at times, and their feelings of dignity and sensitivity must be borne in mind."[12]

Yet, even on internal issues they regarded as sacrosanct, Cuban leaders were willing to respond to U.S. concerns so long as Washington did not pose them as explicit demands. Castro released more than three thousand political prisoners in response to Carter's human rights policy, though just twelve months earlier he had publicly rejected any such concession when Carter posed it as a condition of normalization.[13] Similarly, Raúl Castro unilaterally released most of Cuba's remaining political prisoners in 2010, knowing that this was an issue that Obama cared about. However, when Washington has demanded linkage between Cuban concessions and U.S. steps toward normalization, Havana has rejected them.

Rather than linkage, a more successful approach has been parallel positive steps—a strategy first recommended by Ambassador Viron "Pete" Vaky in 1968.[14] The United States takes a unilateral positive action and suggests to Cuban officials what steps they could take that would be regarded favorably in Washington. Such reciprocal steps have proved successful in building trust and cooperation in areas of mutual interest such as people-to-people exchanges, hurricane prediction and tracking, counter-narcotics operations, and environmental protection. This sort of confidence building may be necessary to set the stage for a constructive dialogue, but will not by itself lead to major change in the relationship. Gradual reciprocal actions can lead to diplomatic reconciliation only if both sides have the political will to reconcile—political will that has thus far been lacking.

LESSON 4. **Small successes do not necessarily lead to big ones.** Successful talks between Washington and Havana have been about relatively narrow issues. Sometimes they were straightforward, bilateral issues on which both sides had a clear interest in cooperation—migration, fishing and maritime boundaries, antihijacking, Coast Guard search and rescue, counter-narcotics operations, for example. But even complex, multilateral issues like those involving southern Africa were amenable to agreement. Nevertheless, successful talks have always been narrower in scope and less complex than the issue of full normalization.

Policy makers in both Havana and Washington have shared the presumption that progress on issues of mutual interest could provide a bridge to progress toward normalizing relations. Che Guevara was the first to broach the concept of using "secondary issues" as a starting point for dialogue, as a way to build mutual confidence. Fidel said the same thing when he was negotiating with James Donovan. Carter began his approach to Cuba with talks about fishing boundaries and Coast Guard cooperation. Clinton began with immigration. Obama's pledge to pursue a new policy of engagement began with a dialogue about migration, narcotics control, and educational exchange. Despite significant successes on narrow issues, the two sides have never been able to translate the momentum of these tertiary agreements into real progress toward normalization. This avenue, like the avenue of positive parallel actions, can lead to normalization only if both sides have requisite political will.

LESSON 5. Cuban leaders have had a hard time distinguishing between gestures and concessions. "Tell the President that he should not interpret my conciliatory attitude, my desire for discussions as a sign of weakness," Castro advised in a secret message to Lyndon Johnson in early 1964. The Cubans, as the CIA pointed out in a July 1975 intelligence assessment of Castro's negotiating posture, worry that even small steps on their part may be misinterpreted in Washington as "exploitable" concessions. Thus Cuba wants the United States to take not just the first step toward reconciliation but the first several. Whenever Cuba engaged in talks with the United States, Castro was at pains to make it clear that he was doing so from a position of strength. In fact, at times he seemed to go out of his way to be defiant—for example, stepping up Cuba's advocacy of Puerto Rican independence in 1975 during Kissinger's secret dialogue, despite U.S. sensitivity on the issue. Announcing the 1984 migration agreement to the Cuban people, he ended by saying, "We are not in a hurry to discuss any other problems. We are calm, serene, firm, and strong. We are not going to plead for anything from anyone. Our constructive, positive, and receptive attitude does not imply an eagerness to negotiate."[15]

To make matters worse, Havana discounts U.S. gestures that serve U.S. interests. When Kissinger decided not to oppose the OAS lifting sanctions against Cuba in 1975, hoping Cuba would take this as a gesture of good faith, Havana instead saw it as Washington merely trying to cut its diplomatic losses in Latin America, where sanctions were increasingly unpopular—an "empty gesture," Cuban diplomat Ramón Sánchez-Parodi called it.[16] In 2009, when Obama decided not to oppose the OAS repeal of the 1962 resolution suspending Cuba, Havana had exactly the same interpretation. When he lifted limits on Cuban American travel, Cuban leaders regarded it as a political debt to the Cuban American community, not a gesture to Cuba.

Washington, for its part, has wanted Cuba to take significant steps to give the White House political cover from domestic critics by showing that a policy of engagement pays dividends. When U.S. gestures fail to elicit significant reciprocal steps from Havana, the White House risks looking soft. This worry preoccupied Kissinger, Carter, Clinton, and Obama, making them reluctant to undertake dramatic moves toward Cuba that might have broken the Alfonse-Gaston stalemate. "It is a question of domestic politics," Kissinger conceded as far back as 1974. "We need something we can use to explain [better relations] domestically."[17]

LESSON 6. Timing is everything. There has never been a moment when both sides wanted to normalize relations on terms acceptable to the other. At key moments when Washington was motivated to reconcile, Cuba subordinated its desire for normal relations to its policies in Africa and Latin America. At moments when Cuba's interest in normalization was strongest, U.S. presidents were either uninterested or intimidated by the Cuban American lobby.

Of late, Havana has been more interested in improving relations than has Washington. Since assuming the presidency in 2006, Raúl Castro has repeatedly offered to open a dialogue with Washington on all issues dividing the two countries. The economic benefits from normalizing relations are substantial at a time when the Cuban economy is undergoing major restructuring. In the areas of disaster response, medical cooperation, and environmental protection, the Cuban side has been consistently interested in extending and deepening cooperation, while the U.S. side has been reluctant. Other areas such as counter-narcotics, counterterrorism, and migration show a similar pattern. The United States has been content to live with "perpetual antagonism" toward Cuba because the costs have been relatively low; and changing the policy entails domestic political risks that successive presidents have judged too high. Obama, while acknowledging that the policy of hostility has been futile, has been no more willing than his predecessors to break this impasse.

LESSON 7. An incremental approach to normalization has not worked. Kissinger tried it. Carter tried it. Clinton thought about trying it, albeit without much enthusiasm. Obama started to try it, but set unrealistic conditions. In his secret talks with the Cubans, Kissinger proposed a "package deal"—a series of discrete, reciprocal steps leading to normalization, and actually took a few initial ones. The process stalled when Cuba failed to reciprocate and sent troops to Angola instead. Carter directed his government to move toward normalizing relations by negotiating "reciprocal and sequential steps," but after Cuba sent troops to Ethiopia, the president insisted that Havana had to withdraw from Africa for the process to move forward.[18] Clinton announced a policy of "calibrated response," in which Washington would respond to incremental positive steps by Cuba with positive steps of its own, but the Helms-Burton legislation eviscerated that approach.[19] Obama took some initial positive steps and then called for Cuban reciprocity, but insisted that Cuban steps had to be movements toward democracy, which Havana rejected. History has demonstrated that the quid pro quo approach does not work.

Incrementalism has three fatal flaws. First, it is slow, and confounding issues are likely to arise that disrupt the process of building mutual confidence, making further progress difficult—Angola under Ford; Ethiopia and the Mariel migration crisis under Carter; the rafters migration crisis and Brothers to the Rescue shoot-down under Clinton; the arrest of Alan Gross under Obama. Second, incremental steps do not fundamentally change the relationship and are therefore easily reversed. Ford lifted the embargo on trade with Cuba by subsidiaries of U.S. corporations in third countries; the 1992 Cuban Democracy Act reimposed it. Carter lifted the ban on travel to Cuba; Reagan reimposed it. Clinton relaxed restrictions on people-to-people exchanges; George W. Bush reimposed them. Obama relaxed them again, and then faced congressional efforts to reimpose them.

Finally, although gradualism seems politically safe because each incremental step is small and therefore ought to be less controversial, in fact, an incremental approach prolongs the political fight with domestic opponents, who are no less vociferous in opposing small steps than large ones. They, like policy makers, understand that small steps can lead down the slippery slope, building momentum for normalization, so they battle to derail the process at every juncture. Every incremental step gives them a new opportunity to halt the process, and they only need to win once. With U.S. congressional elections every two years and presidential elections every four, an incremental approach inevitably becomes fodder for electoral politics. The alternative is a bold stroke that fundamentally changes the relationship (even if it does not resolve every issue) and leaves opponents facing a fait accompli. Nixon's trip to China is the paradigmatic example.

LESSON 8. Domestic politics is always an issue on both sides. Major policy changes always require aligning policy options with politics. A brilliant policy solution is worthless if you cannot assemble a winning political coalition behind it. Fifty years of failure for the policy of hostility toward Cuba is not, in itself, sufficient reason to change it when there are significant domestic political costs and no pressing foreign policy reasons compelling change. From the beginning, there have been people in both capitals interested in improving U.S.-Cuban relations and those opposed. Domestic opposition has been a tougher obstacle in Washington than in Havana because the U.S. political system is a democracy with many veto points designed to make policy change difficult. From Philip Bonsal's losing battle with Eisenhower conservatives like Thomas Mann, to Cyrus Vance's bitter rivalry with Zbigniew Brzezinski, to Chester Crocker's outflanking Elliot Abrams on the southern Africa talks, advocates of rapprochement have always had to fend off domestic opponents while maneuvering to start and sustain a dialogue. In the sixties and seventies, opposition to improving relations with Cuba came mostly from Cold Warriors inside the foreign policy bureaucracy. In the eighties, nineties, and beyond, it came mostly from conservative Cuban Americans. The end of the Cold War reduced the first obstacle; changing demographics in the Cuban American community have gradually eroded the second, as demonstrated by Obama's success in the 2008 and 2012 elections. But for the foreseeable future, any U.S. president who contemplates changing relations with Havana will have to pay a political price, in Congress if not in Florida.

In Havana, decision making was less complex. Fidel by himself could make the decision to warm relations with Washington or plunge them back into the deep freeze. But even Fidel did not operate in a political vacuum. In 2001 Raúl Castro hinted that others in the revolutionary leadership saw significant risk in normalization. "It would be in imperialism's interest to try to normalize relations as much as possible during Fidel's life," he said, because afterward "it will be more difficult."[20] As the second-most-powerful "historic" leader of the revolution, Raúl effectively established his own authority in Cuba's collective leadership after Fidel retired, and he continued to push for better relations with Washington. But Raúl has announced his intention to step down as president in 2018, passing the torch to a new generation of leaders, none of whom will have the dominant authority or freedom of action enjoyed by Fidel and Raúl.

LESSON 9. Neither side really comprehends the other's bureaucracy, so the opportunities for misunderstanding abound. The secret dialogue initiated by Kissinger had a Rashomon quality—each side saw in the slow responses of the other reason to doubt its seriousness. The Department of Justice's slow processing of former political prisoners for entry to the United States during the Carter years convinced Castro that Washington was deliberately trying to destabilize Cuba by stranding the ex-prisoners. That set the stage for the Mariel migration crisis. When Cuban officials complained repeatedly about Brothers to the Rescue violating Cuban airspace, they assumed

Clinton would put a stop to the provocations. When the flights continued, the Cubans regarded it a deliberate provocation, rather than a by-product of the convoluted federal bureaucracy. When George W. Bush's "democracy promotion" programs targeting Cuba continued into the Obama administration, the Cubans concluded that Obama's rhetoric about a new Cuba policy was insincere, rather than recognizing that bureaucratic momentum carries established programs forward despite changes in administrations.

At moments when the Cubans were willing to make significant concessions, Washington sometimes missed the signals. During the marathon secret talks in the Carter years, the Cubans steadfastly refused to negotiate away their support for African allies, but they hinted they would work with the United States to find diplomatic solutions that would enable them to bring their troops home—thus accomplishing Washington's main objective. Brzezinski did not recognize this as an opening, and it took Chester Crocker months to convince the Reagan administration to seize the opportunity. When it did, Cuba helped broker a southern African peace accord. Havana made similar suggestions to both Reagan and Bush on peace proposals in Central America. When Bush officials finally decided to explore the Cuban offer, their effort was cut short by the advent of TV Martí and the defeat of the Sandinistas in the 1990 Nicaraguan election.

U.S. diplomats have to listen carefully to how their Cuban counterparts frame issues, alert for oblique hints of flexibility, even on issues that the Cubans have sworn publicly never to negotiate.

LESSON 10. Cuba wants to be treated as an equal, with respect for its national sovereignty. Like the Melians during the Peloponnesian War, Cubans refuse to accept the idea that Great Powers, especially the United States, should be able to play the game of international politics by different rules from everyone else's. Washington, on the other hand, has long felt entitled to do whatever realpolitik demands, especially in Latin America, its "own backyard." This "hegemonic presumption," as scholar Abraham F. Lowenthal termed it, has been especially strong with regard to Cuba, a virtual possession of the United States for the first half of the twentieth century.[21] That very idea inflamed Cuban nationalism, laying one of the ideological cornerstones for the revolution in 1959.

"Perhaps it is because the United States is a great power, it feels it can do what it wants," Castro said to Peter Tarnoff and Robert Pastor in 1978. "Perhaps it is idealistic of me, but I never accepted the universal prerogatives of the United States. I never accepted and never will accept the existence of a different law and different rules."[22]

Carlos Rafael Rodríguez made the same point to Al Haig when they met in Mexico in 1981. "Frankly speaking, we do not understand why the United States, merely because it happens to be, at the present time, one of the most powerful states, can have a right which we, being a small country, do not have," Rodríguez said. "I believe that it is irrational to hold such a position."[23] Irrational or not, Washington's position has long echoed Athens: the strong do what they will; the weak suffer what they must.

In late 1959, Havana responded to a diplomatic protest from Washington with a long recitation of the history of U.S. domination of the island, concluding, "The Cuban Government and the Cuban people are anxious to live in peace and harmony with the Government and the people of the United States . . . but on the basis of mutual respect and reciprocal benefits."[24] This theme has echoed across half a century of U.S.-Cuban relations. In 1986, Fidel told the delegates to the Third Congress of the Cuban Communist Party:

> As we have demonstrated many times, Cuba is not remiss to discussing its prolonged differences with the United States and to go out in search of peace and better relations between our people. But that would have to be on the basis of the most unrestricted respect for our condition as a country that does not tolerate shadows on its independence, for whose dignity and sovereignty entire generations of Cubans have fought and sacrificed themselves. This would be possible only when the United States decides to negotiate with seriousness and is willing to treat us with a spirit of equality, reciprocity and the fullest mutual respect.[25]

In his first public statement after assuming the presidency in 2006, Raúl Castro quoted this passage and reiterated its continuing relevance. Over the next five years, he repeated the same point over and over. Cuba's offer to negotiate with the United States rested on the sole condition that the talks be conducted "in a spirit of equality, reciprocity and the fullest mutual respect."[26]

Yet treating Cuba with the respect due a sovereign nation was the hardest thing for Washington to do. The long history of Cuba's subordination to the United States before 1959 has weighed on the minds of policy makers on both sides of the Florida Strait. Successive U.S. presidents could not reconcile themselves to Fidel Castro's apostasy—his rejection of the American

Way of Life and with it, U.S. influence. They held fast to John Quincy Adams's belief that Cuba was, by geography and by destiny, a natural partner of the United States that would eventually return to the U.S. orbit. Cuba's revolutionary leaders feared nothing so much as the possibility that Washington would succeed in reclaiming dominion over the island, thwarting their determination to secure Cuba's sovereign independence, just as the United States thwarted José Martí a century earlier.

To finally end the animosity and fear that has characterized U.S.-Cuban relations since 1959, policy makers in Washington need to accept that Cuba in the twenty-first century will never again be the dependent, semi-sovereign Cuba that it was in the nineteenth and early twentieth. In that regard, the revolution of 1959 has proved irreversible. Policy makers in Havana need to trust that reconciliation with the United States is possible without putting at risk Cuba's national independence, which Cubans made a revolution to secure.

The closeness of Cuba and the United States, which has been the source of so much of their antagonism, has also provided the impetus for cooperation and reconciliation. In a century when the most pressing problems transcend national boundaries, near neighbors cannot afford perpetual hostility. With every passing day, Cuba and the United States become ever more closely intertwined—as Cubans buy wheat from U.S. farmers in the Midwest, as Cuban and U.S. citizens travel more freely back and forth, and as Cubans and Cuban Americans knit back together the cultural, financial, and family ties severed by the revolution in 1959.

The history of dialogue between Cuba and the United States since 1959 demonstrates that it is not only possible to replace sterile hostility with reconciliation but preferable for the national and international interests of both nations. José Martí, whose eloquently expressed suspicions about U.S. imperial designs on Cuba inspired a young Fidel Castro's nationalism, nevertheless saw the possibility of a relationship between the United States and Cuba based on equality. "There is that other America, North America, that is not ours, and whose enmity it is neither wise nor viable to encourage," Martí wrote a few months before his death. "However, with firm propriety and an astute independence, it is not impossible—and indeed it is useful—to be friends."[27]

NOTES

Abbreviations Used in the Notes

AP	Associated Press
Carter Library	Jimmy Carter Library and Museum, Atlanta, Ga.
CIA FOIA	U.S. Central Intelligence Agency, Freedom of Information Act Electronic Reading Room
DDRS	Declassified Documents Reference System, Gale Cengage Learning
Discursos Archive	Discursos e intervenciones del Comandante en Jefe Fidel Castro Ruz, Government of Cuba, Havana
Donovan Papers	James B. Donovan Papers, 1919–1976, Hoover Institution Archives, Stanford University, Stanford, Calif.
FAA	Federal Aviation Administration
FBIS	Foreign Broadcast Information Service
FOIA	Freedom of Information Act
Ford Library	Gerald R. Ford Presidential Library and Museum, Ann Arbor, Mich.
FRUS	U.S. Department of State, Office of the Historian, *Foreign Relations of the United States*
Johnson Library	LBJ Presidential Library, Austin, Tex.
Kennedy Library	John F. Kennedy Presidential Library and Museum, Boston, Mass.
LAT	*Los Angeles Times*
LOC, Bonsal Papers	Library of Congress, Manuscript Division, Washington, D.C., Philip W. Bonsal Papers, 1914–1992
MH	*Miami Herald*
NARA	National Archives and Records Administration
NARA-MD, RG 59	National Archives and Records Administration, College Park, Md., General Records of the Department of State (Record Group 59)
NARA-MD, RG 84	National Archives and Records Administration, College Park, Md., Records of the Foreign Service Posts of the Department of State (Record Group 84)
Nixon Library	Nixon Presidential Library and Museum, Yorba Linda, Calif.
NSA Cuba Collection	National Security Archive, U.S.-Cuba Diplomacy Collection
NYT	*New York Times*
PPP	*Public Papers of the Presidents of the United States*, American Presidency Project, University of California, Santa Barbara
USINT	U.S. Interests Section, Havana

WP   *Washington Post*
WWC   Woodrow Wilson Center Digital Archive, International History
        Declassified, Woodrow Wilson International Center for Scholars,
        Washington, D.C.

Introduction

1. Transcript of Donovan's oral report to Miskovsky, reel 4, pp. 13–14, NSA Cuba Collection.

2. Ibid.

3. Castro and Ramonet, *Fidel Castro: My Life*, 262.

4. Bigger, *Negotiator*, 154, 155.

5. Kornbluh and LeoGrande, "Talking with Castro."

6. The characterization is from Pérez-Stable, *Cuba and the United States: Intimate Enemies*.

7. Memorandum, Shlaudeman to Kissinger, "Normalizing Relations with Cuba", March 27, 1975, NSA Cuba Collection.

8. "Raul Castro Says U.S. Team's Visit Is Step Forward," *NYT*, April 9, 1977.

Chapter One

1. Azicri, "Could the War Have Been Avoided?," *NACLA Report on the Americas* 24, no. 3 (November 1990): 22–23; Letter, Stevenson to Bonsal, April 22, 1959, LOC, Bonsal Papers, box 1, folder 7, Geographical File, Cuba, 1959, Jan.–July.

2. *FRUS, 1958–1960*, VI, doc. 286.

3. *FRUS, 1958–1960*, VI, doc. 280.

4. *FRUS, 1958–1960*, VI, doc. 286.

5. Ibid.; Geyer, *Guerrilla Prince*, 225.

6. Franqui, *Family Portrait with Fidel*, 32; Geyer, *Guerrilla Prince*, 225.

7. Letter from John Quincy Adams, U.S. Secretary of State, to Hugh Nelson, American Minister in Madrid, April 23, 1823, in Gott, *Cuba: A New History*, 326.

8. Pérez, *On Becoming Cuban*, 282, 174.

9. José Martí, "Letter to Manuel Mercado," in *José Martí: Selected Writings*, 347.

10. For a good history of U.S.-Cuban relations before 1959, see Pérez, *Cuba and the United States: Ties of Singular Intimacy*.

11. For U.S. financial and commercial interests in Cuba, see Benjamin, *The United States and Cuba: Hegemony and Dependent Development, 1880–1934*.

12. The best account of the 1933 revolution is Aguilar, *Cuba 1933*.

13. On the evolution of U.S. policy during the 1950s, see Morley, *Imperial State and Revolution*, 40–71.

14. Paterson, *Contesting Castro*, 89.

15. Castro, *History Will Absolve Me*, 195.

16. Ibid.

17. Paterson, *Contesting Castro*, 110–11.

18. E. W. Kenworthy, "U.S. Said to Pick Envoy to Havana," *NYT*, January 14, 1959; "A Foe of Dictatorships: Philip Wilson Bonsal," *NYT*, January 22, 1959.

19. Bonsal, *Cuba, Castro, and the United States*, 29.

20. Ibid., 28.

21. Paterson, *Contesting Castro*, 110–14; "Special National Intelligence Estimate," *FRUS, 1958–1960*, V, doc. 188.

22. Caribbean and Central American Chiefs of Mission Meeting, San Salvador, April 9–11, 1959, NARA-MD, RG 59, Central Decimal File, 1955–1959, box 509, file: 120.1416/59; *FRUS, 1958–1960*, V, doc. 118; Bonsal, *Cuba, Castro, and the United States*, 58–59.

23. U.S. Senate, Committee on the Judiciary, Subcommittee to Investigate the Administration of the Internal Security Act and Other Internal Security Laws, *Communist Threat to the U.S. through the Caribbean, Part 1*, 871.

24. William L. Ryan, "Rebels Executed Batista Aides," *WP*, January 8, 1959; R. Hart Phillips, "Military Court in Cuba Dooms Fourteen for 'War Crimes,'" *NYT*, January 13, 1959; Thomas, *Cuba*, 1076–77.

25. Franqui, *Family Portrait with Fidel*, 18–19.

26. Phillips, "Military Court in Cuba."

27. "Events in Oriente-Reaction (Jan. 6–14, 1959)," *FRUS, 1958–1960*, VI, doc. 225.

28. Discurso Pronunciado por Fidel Castro, en el Palacio Presidencial, el 21 de Enero de 1959, Discursos Archive.

29. Bonsal, *Cuba, Castro, and the United States*, 51.

30. Bonsal's meeting with Castro is described in Bonsal's memoir, ibid., 53; and his report to Washington, *FRUS, 1958–1960*, VI, doc. 258. The description of the setting is based on a series of photographs taken by Andrew St. George, held at Yale University Library Manuscripts and Archives.

31. Suarez, *Cuba: Castro and Communism, 1959–1966*, 47; "Cuba: One-Man Court," *Time*, March 16, 1959.

32. Szulc, *Fidel*, 503; Lockwood, *Castro's Cuba*, 159.

33. U.S. Senate, Committee on the Judiciary, Subcommittee to Investigate the Administration of the Internal Security Act and Other Internal Security Laws, *Communist Threat to the U.S. through the Caribbean, Part 1*, 700.

34. Morley, *Imperial State*, 79.

35. Lockwood, *Castro's Cuba*, 211. The fullest account of this trip is McPherson, "The Limits of Populist Diplomacy: Fidel Castro's April 1959 Trip to North America."

36. Casuso, *Cuba and Castro*, 208.

37. "Crowd Hails Castro as He Reaches U.S. for 11-Day Visit," *NYT*, April 16, 1959; Philip Benjamin, "Castro Gets a Noisy Reception Here," *NYT*, April 22, 1959; AP, "10,000 Hear Castro at Harvard," *WP*, April 26, 1959.

38. "Castro Hops Rails at Bronx Zoo to Greet Lion, Tiger," *Chicago Tribune*, April 25, 1959.

39. Bogenschild, "Dr. Castro's Princeton Visit, April 20–21, 1959"; Brinkley, *Acheson: The Cold War Years*, 155.

40. Fursenko and Naftali, *One Hell of a Gamble*, 10–11; Bird, *The Color of Truth*, 148–49.

41. For example: E. W. Kenworthy, "Castro Declares Regime if Free of Red Influence," *NYT*, April 18, 1959; Robert C. Albright, "Castro Is Quizzed by Senators, Denies Any Link with Reds," *WP*, April 18, 1959; Dana Adams Schmidt, "Castro Rules Out Role as Neutral; Opposes Reds," *NYT*, April 20, 1959.

42. Franqui, *Family Portrait with Fidel*, 31–32; *FRUS, 1958–1960*, VI, doc. 292.

43. "Visitor from Cuba," *NYT*, April 25, 1959.

44. Eisenhower, *Waging Peace*, 523.

45. Fidel Castro, "Reflections by the Commander in Chief: Submission to Imperial Politics," August 27, 2007, Discursos Archive.

46. *FRUS, 1958–1960*, VI, doc. 272.

47. López-Fresquet, *My 14 Months with Castro*, 106.

48. Thomas, *Cuba*, 1208–10; Edward T. Folliard, "Red Label Is Rejected by Castro," *WP*, April 18, 1959.

49. López-Fresquet, *My 14 Months with Castro*, 170; Morley, *Imperial State*, 79.

50. Morley, *Imperial State*, 79.

51. Casuso, *Cuba and Castro*, 212.

52. Franqui, *Family Portrait with Fidel*, 32.

53. Letter, Stevenson to Bonsal, April 22, 1959, LOC, Bonsal Papers, box 1, folder 7, Geographical File, Cuba, 1959, Jan.–July.

54. Memorandum of Conversation, Richard M. Nixon and Fidel Castro, April 19, 1959, NSA Cuba Collection; Nixon, *Six Crises*, 351–53; Bonsal, *Cuba, Castro, and the United States*, 93; Wyden, *Bay of Pigs*, 29–30.

55. López-Fresquet, *My 14 Months with Castro*, 169.

56. Wyden, *Bay of Pigs*, 28.

57. "Reflections of President Fidel Castro: World Tyranny; The Basics of the Killing Machine," *Granma International*, July 9, 2007.

58. López-Fresquet, *My 14 Months with Castro*, 110.

59. Paterson, *Contesting Castro*, 64, 105–6; Szulc, *Fidel*, 428–29.

60. Transcript, panel one, Bay of Pigs Forty Years Later conference, Havana, Cuba, March 22–24, 2001, NSA Cuba Collection.

61. CIA, "Official History of the Bay of Pigs Operation," vol. III, "Evolution of CIA's Anti-Castro Policies, 1951–January 1961, December 1979: 8, NSA Cuba Collection.

62. Ibid., 12–13.

63. Andrew St. George, "Castro Seeking U.S. Talks On Cuban Political Issues," *NYT*, December 11, 1958.

64. Szulc, *Fidel*, 490; Hunt, *Give Us This Day*, 24.

65. Wyden, *The Bay of Pigs*, 31; CIA briefing memorandum for NSC, May 8, 1959, National Security Archive, *Bay of Pigs 40 Years Later*.

66. López-Fresquet, *My 14 Months with Castro*, 110. Although the CIA was unaware of it, Fidel and his inner circle were already meeting secretly with top Popular Socialist Party leaders about the future course of the revolution. Szulc, *Fidel*, 471–75.

67. *FRUS, 1958–1960*, VI, doc. 292.

68. The radicals, it seems, were not so pleased with the trip. Raúl called his brother in the middle of it to say that Fidel's carefully conciliatory remarks were being interpreted in Cuba to mean he had "sold out" to the Americans. Casuso, *Cuba and Castro*, 216.

69. Thomas, *Cuba*, 1209.

70. "The PSP [Popular Socialist Party] had men who were truly revolutionary, loyal, honest and trained," Castro told Herbert Matthews. "I needed them." Matthews, *Castro: A Political Biography*, 162.

71. Thomas, *Cuba*, 1216–17.

72. *FRUS, 1958–1960*, VI, doc. 311; Bonsal, *Cuba, Castro, and the United States*, 72–73.

73. "U.S. Informs Cuba of Views on Agrarian Reform Law," *Department of State Bulletin* 40, no. 1044 (June 29, 1959): 958–59.

74. *FRUS, 1958–1960*, VI, doc. 320.

75. Szulc, *Fidel*, 476–78.

76. Rubottom Oral History, Princeton University, 73–74. Rubottom takes credit for the change in U.S. policy in a letter to Robert D. Murphy, March 21, 1969, in Papers of Robert D. Murphy, Hoover Institution Archives, Stanford University, correspondence, box 122, folder 39.

77. Notes from the OCB meeting quoted in U.S./Cuban Relations—January 2, 1959, to January 3, 1961, p. 49, DDRS. This is a highly critical, never completed, assessment of U.S. policy drafted in 1964 by NSC staff assistant Gordon Chase.

78. Rubottom Oral History, Princeton University, 75–76. In the oral history, Rubottom mistakenly places this meeting in the fall, but his own contemporary notes place it in June (*FRUS, 1958–1960*, VI, doc. 416). The dates of the two meetings with Murphy and Allen Dulles are in Murphy's appointment books, Papers of Robert D. Murphy, Hoover Institution Archives, Stanford University, box 5, folder 5.

79. "Secretary Herter last July agreed that we could no longer work with the Cuban Government." *FRUS, 1958–1960*, VI, doc. 419.

80. *FRUS, 1958–1960*, VI, doc. 423.

81. Memorandum of Conversation, "Matters Discussed at Assistant Secretary Rubottom's Luncheon in Honor of Cuban Minister of State Raúl Roa," June 20, 1959, NARA-MD, RG 59, Records of the Bureau of Inter-American Affairs, Office of the Coordinator of Cuban Affairs, Subject Files 1960–1963, box 6, lot 63D91, file: Efforts at Negotiation with Cuba.

82. Letter from Wieland to Bonsal, June 19, 1959, NARA-MD, RG 84: Records of the Foreign Service Posts of the Department of State, Cuba, Havana Embassy: Classified General Records, 1959–1961, box 5 [should be in box 4], file: 350 Cuba (July–Sept.) 1959.

83. Bonsal, *Cuba, Castro, and the United States*, 74, 87–88; *FRUS, 1958–1960*, VI, doc. 323; doc. 342.

84. *FRUS, 1958–1960*, VI, doc. 423.

85. *FRUS, 1958–1960*, VI, doc. 336.

86. Thomas, *Cuba*, 1229–30; U.S. Senate, Committee on the Judiciary, Subcommittee to Investigate the Administration of the Internal Security Act and Other Internal Security Laws, *Communist Threat to the U.S. through the Caribbean, Part 1*.

87. "Castro Asserts U.S. Interferes in Cuba," *NYT*, July 13, 1959; *FRUS, 1958–1960*, VI, doc. 332:556–57; doc. 334.

88. Thomas, *Cuba*, 1232–33.

89. Embassy Telegram to State from Bonsal, No. 281, July 31, 1959, NARA-MD, RG 59, 1955–1959 Central Decimal File, box 2473, folder 611.37/4-159, doc. 611.37/7-73159; Embassy Telegram to State from US Emb Havana, Bonsal, No. 354, August 10, 1959, NARA-MD, RG 59, General Records of the Department of State 1955–1959 Central Decimal File, box 2473.

90. Bonsal, *Cuba, Castro, and the United States*, 89; *FRUS, 1958–1960*, VI, doc. 359.

91. *FRUS, 1958–1960*, VI, doc. 364.

92. Memorandum to Mr. Rubottom from Mr. Wieland, "Summary of Discussion Regarding Nature of Instructions Ambassador Bonsal Might Take Back with Him," October 1, 1959, NARA-MD, RG 59, Bureau of Inter-American Affairs, Records of the Special Assistant on Communism, 1958–1961, box 4, file: Planning and NSC Briefings 1960.

93. *FRUS, 1958–1960*, VI, doc. 362.

94. *FRUS, 1958–1960*, VI, doc. 365.

95. Memorandum to Mr. Rubottom from Mr. Wieland, "Summary of Discussion Regarding Nature of Instructions Ambassador Bonsal Might Take Back with Him," October 1, 1959 (details in note 79).

96. Memorandum of Conversation, Bonsal and Roa, "General Attitude toward the U.S.," October 6, 1959, and Telegram, Bonsal to State, Havana 814, October 14, 1959, NARA-MD, RG 59, Records of the Bureau of Inter-American Affairs, Office of the Coordinator of Cuban Affairs, Subject Files 1960–1963, box 6, lot 63D91, file: Efforts at Negotiation with Cuba.

97. Bonsal, *Cuba, Castro, and the United States*, 99; AP, "U.S. Bids Britain Deny Jets to Cuba," *NYT*, October 17, 1959.

98. British Foreign Office Cable, "From Washington to Foreign Office," November 24, 1959, No. 2455, National Security Archive, *Bay of Pigs 40 Years Later*.

99. López-Fresquet, *My 14 Months with Castro*, 130–31.

100. Díaz Lanz had been the most senior military defector prior to Matos, but as chief of the rebel air force, clandestinely ferrying supplies to the guerrillas in the sierra, he had not fought with them on the ground. One of the best accounts of the Matos trial is Quirk, *Fidel Castro*, 266–79.

101. R. Hart Phillips, "Cuban Crowds Assail U.S. after Attack by Terrorists," *NYT*, October 23, 1959.

102. R. Hart Phillips, "Castro Charges Planes from U.S. Bombed Havana," *NYT*, October 24, 1959; R. Hart Phillips, "300,000 Rally to Back Castro; He Condemns 'Raids' from U.S.," *NYT*, October 27, 1959.

103. *FRUS, 1958–1960*, VI, doc. 377.

104. "Text of U.S. Statement on Envoy's Protest against Accusations by Premier Castro," *NYT*, October 28, 1959.

105. Discussion Paper, "U.S. Policy towards Cuba," drafted by J. C. Hill. NARA-MD, RG 59, Records of the Bureau of Inter-American Affairs, Office of Caribbean and Mexican Affairs (CMA), Subject Files 1957–1962, lot 63D67, box 2, folder: Cuba, General 1959, 2 of 2.

106. *FRUS, 1958–1960*, VI, doc. 387.

107. *FRUS, 1958–1960*, VI, doc. 376.

108. *FRUS, 1958–1960*, VI, doc. 423.

109. Kornbluh, *Bay of Pigs Declassified*, 67; Discussion Paper, "Pedro Diaz Lanz," July 7, 1959, NARA-MD, RG 59, Records of the Bureau of Inter-American Affairs, Office files of William P. Snow, 1956–1959, box 1 of 2, lot 61D411, file: ARA Deputy, Cuba 1959.

110. CIA Memorandum, "Cuban Problems," [Request for Approval of Recommended Actions against the Cuban Government], December 11, 1959, National Security Archive, *Bay of Pigs 40 Years Later*.

111. Letter to Bonsal from Rubottom, November 20, 1959, LOC, Bonsal Papers, box 1, folder 8, Geographical File, Cuba, 1959, Aug.–Dec.

112. Letter to Rubottom from Bonsal, December 2, 1959, LOC, Bonsal Papers, box 1, folder 8, Geographical File, Cuba, 1959, Aug.–Dec.

113. *FRUS, 1958–1960*, VI, doc. 393; Telegram to US Embassy Havana from Herter, December 2, 1959, No. 732, NARA-MD, RG 84, Records of the Foreign Service Posts of the Department of State, Cuba, Havana Embassy: Classified General Records, 1959–1961, box 3, file: U.S.-Cuba 1959.

114. "Nixon Warns Cuba on Alienating U.S.," *NYT*, January 17, 1960; *FRUS, 1958–1960*, VI, doc. 424.

115. *FRUS, 1958–1960*, VI, doc. 430.

116. *FRUS, 1958–1960*, VI, doc. 436.

117. "Statement by the President Restating United States Policy toward Cuba," January 26, 1960, *PPP Eisenhower*.

118. *FRUS, 1958–1960*, VI, doc. 437. In his memoirs, Bonsal denies that the Amoedo initiative was undertaken at U.S. request, presumably because the U.S. government had not yet acknowledged the initiative publicly.

119. *FRUS, 1958–1960*, VI, doc. 439.

120. Julio A. Amoedo, "Negotiating with Fidel Castro," *New Leader*, April 27, 1964, pp. 10–12; Letter to Ambassador Philip W. Bonsal from Daniel M. Braddock [Chargé], February 9, 1960, NARA-MD, RG 59, Records of the Bureau of Inter-American Affairs, Office of the Coordinator of Cuban Affairs, Subject Files 1960–1963, box 4, lot 62D442, file: Bonsal, Amb. Philip W.

121. Over the next few weeks, the State Department was struck by the "notable absence of anti-American statements." *FRUS, 1958–1960*, VI, doc. 460.

122. Amoedo, "Negotiating with Fidel Castro."

123. *FRUS, 1958–1960*, VI, doc. 440.

124. *FRUS, 1958–1960*, VI, doc. 448:780–81; doc. 449:782; doc. 455.

125. *FRUS, 1958–1960*, VI, doc. 467.

126. Bonsal, *Cuba, Castro, and the United States*, 128.

127. *FRUS, 1958–1960*, VI, doc. 467.

128. Thomas, *Cuba*, 1269.

129. Transcript, panel one, Bay of Pigs Forty Years Later conference, Havana Cuba, March 22–24, 2001, NSA Cuba Collection.

130. This was the first time Castro used the famous slogan with which he would close every speech from then on. Palabras Pronunciadas . . . en las Honras Funebres de las Victimas de la Explosión del Barco "La Coubre," el 5 de Marzo de 1960, Discursos Archive (author's translation).

131. *FRUS, 1958–1960*, VI, doc. 469; "Cuba Rejects Herter's Protest," *WP*, March 9, 1960.

132. *FRUS, 1958–1960*, VI, doc. 470; Letter to Bonsal from Braddock, March 8, 1960, LOC, Bonsal Papers. box 1, folder 9, Geographical File, Cuba, 1960, Jan.–Apr.

133. Fursenko and Naftali, *One Hell of a Gamble*, 11, 26–29.

134. Lévesque, *The USSR and the Cuban Revolution*, 8–14.

135. Transcript, panel one, Bay of Pigs Forty Years Later conference, Havana Cuba, March 22–24, 2001, NSA Cuba Collection.

136. López-Fresquet, *My 14 Months with Castro*, 174. In Lazo's brief account of this feeler, he claims it was his idea alone and that he was not acting on behalf of the U.S. government

(Lazo, *Dagger in the Heart*, 224). Lazo suggested the initiative to the embassy in February, and Deputy Chief of Mission Braddock referred the query to Washington, but there is no record of Washington's reply. *FRUS, 1958–1960*, VI, doc. 446.

137. The conversation took place on February 17, 1960. Berle, *Navigating the Rapids*, 703.

138. *FRUS, 1958–1960*, VI, doc. 481.

139. On Amoedo dinner: Telegram, Bonsal, US Emb Havana to Department of State, May 12, 1960, No. 3209, NARA-MD, RG 84: Records of the Foreign Service Posts of the Department of State, Cuba, Havana Embassy: Classified General Records, 1959–1961, box 5, file: 350 Argentine Ambassador to Cuba 1960. On Roa: Bonsal, *Cuba, Castro, and the United States*, 138. On photo: Letter to Roy R. Rubottom Jr., from Philip W. Bonsal, March 21, 1960, NARA-MD, RG 59, Records of the Bureau of Inter-American Affairs, Office of the Coordinator of Cuban Affairs, Subject Files 1960–1963, box 4, lot 62D442, File: Bonsal, Amb. Philip W; Letter to Rubottom from Bonsal, May 2, 1960, LOC, Bonsal Papers, box 2, folder 1, Geographical File, Cuba, 1960, May–June; Letter to Robert A. Stevenson, CMA, from Philip W. Bonsal, U.S. Embassy, Havana, May 5, 1960, NARA-MD, RG 59, Records of the Bureau of Inter-American Affairs, Office of the Coordinator of Cuban Affairs, Subject Files 1960–1963, box 4, lot 62D442, File: Bonsal, Amb. Philip W.

140. Letter from Bonsal to Rubottom, April 22, 1960, LOC, Bonsal Papers. box 1, folder 9, Geographical File, Cuba, 1960, Jan.–Apr.

141. Bonsal, *Cuba, Castro, and the United States*, 6, 117.

142. *FRUS, 1958–1960*, VI, doc. 414.

143. Bonsal, *Cuba, Castro, and the United States*, 134; Edward T. Folliard, "Kennedy Asks Nixon Explain Cuba 'Disaster,'" *WP*, October 16, 1960.

144. *FRUS, 1958–1960*, VI, doc. 328; doc. 409; Memorandum to Rubottom from Mallory, "Some Difficulties Which Would Arise from Premature Application of U.S. and/or Inter-American Economic Sanctions against Cuba," January 25, 1960, NARA-MD, RG 59, Bureau of Inter-American Affairs, Records of the Special Assistant on Communism, 1958–1961, box 3, file: Cuba, 1960.

145. *FRUS, 1958–1960*, VI, doc. 743 Tab D.

146. Eisenhower, *Waging Peace*, 535.

147. Bonsal, *Cuba, Castro, and the United States*, 29, 39–42.

148. *FRUS, 1958–1960*, VI, doc. 526.

149. Ibid.

150. *FRUS, 1958–1960*, VI, doc. 421; R. Hart Phillips, "Castro Orders Seizure—Also Bitterly Attacks U.S. Sugar Bill," *NYT*, June 30, 1960.

151. *FRUS, 1958–1960*, VI, doc. 536; doc. 410; Jack B. Pfeiffer, *Official History of the Bay of Pigs Operation*, DCI-8, vol. III, Central Intelligence Agency, December 1979, p. 262.

152. "Statement by the President upon Signing Bill and Proclamation Relating to the Cuban Sugar Quota," July 6, 1960, *PPP Eisenhower*.

153. "Castro Forces Carry Out Seizure of U.S. Properties," *NYT*, August 8, 1960.

154. E. W. Kenworthy, "U.S. Puts Embargo on Goods to Cuba; Curbs Ship Deals," *NYT*, October 20, 1960; "Castro Takes Over 167 Additional U.S. Firms," *LAT*, October 26, 1960; "Text of U.S. Announcement of Embargo," *NYT*, October 20, 1960.

155. Khrushchev's letter is in *FRUS, 1958–1960*, VI, doc. 549. His private assessment is in Shevchenko, *Breaking with Moscow*, 137.

156. Harrison E. Salisbury, "Russian Goes to Harlem, Then Hugs Cuban at U.N.," *NYT*, September 21, 1960.

157. *FRUS, 1958–1960*, VI, doc. 562; doc. 564:1027; doc. 565; Telegram from Dillon, Dept. of State, to US posts, Circular 791, November 29, 1960, NARA-MD, RG 84: Records of the Foreign Service Posts of the Department of State Cuba, Havana Embassy: Classified General Records, 1959–1961, box 3, file: International Political Relations between United States and Cuba, 1960.

158. Letter to Bonsal from Mann, September 27, 1960, LOC, Bonsal Papers, box 2, folder 2, Geographical File, Cuba, 1960, July–Sept.

159. Smith, *Closest of Enemies*, 65.

160. "Statement by the President on Terminating Diplomatic Relations with Cuba," January 3, 1961, *PPP Eisenhower*.

161. Smith, *Closest of Enemies*, 66–67.

162. Castro talks about his goals in Castro and Ramonet, *Fidel Castro: My Life*, 100, 151–52.

163. Embassy Telegram to State from US Emb Havana (Braddock), No. 869, January 22, 1959, NARA-MD, RG 59, 1955–1959 Central Decimal File, box 2473, folder 611.37/1-159, doc. 611.37/1-22-59.

164. "U.S./Cuban Relations—January 2, 1959 to January 3, 1961," draft report attached to Memorandum, Chase to Bundy, "Plank/Chase Cuban Project." February 3, 1964, DDRS.

165. *FRUS, 1958–1960*, VI, doc. 420.

166. Letter from Bonsal to Schlesinger, November 13, 1962, LOC, Bonsal Papers, box 2, folder 4, Cuba, 1961–1964.

167. "U.S./Cuban Relations—January 2, 1959 to January 3, 1961," DDRS.

168. Sean Penn, "Conversations with Chávez and Castro," *Nation*, December 15, 2008.

169. Smith, *Closest of Enemies*, 144–45.

Chapter Two

Some documents cited in this chapter were first declassified pursuant to a Mandatory Declassification Review request by Peter Kornbluh to the John F. Kennedy Library for a secret file entitled "Contacts with Cuban Leaders." The National Security Archive has created a special set of these and other records, referred to herein as the NSA Cuba Collection.

1. Blight, Allyn, and Welch, *Cuba on the Brink*, 237.

2. Jean Daniel was interviewed for a Discovery Times Channel documentary, "Kennedy and Castro: The Secret History," first broadcast in November 2003. This account is based on that interview and Daniel's articles: Daniel, "Two Interviews: Castro's Reply to Kennedy Comments on Cuba," *NYT*, December 11, 1963; Daniel, "Unofficial Envoy: An Historic Report from Two Capitals," *New Republic*, December 14, 1963, pp. 15–20; Daniel, *Le temps qui reste*, 149–69.

3. "Text of Statement by Kennedy on Dealing with Castro Regime," *NYT*, October 21, 1960; E. W. Kenworthy, "U.S. Will Reject Cuba Mediation," *NYT*, March 7, 1961.

4. "The President's News Conference," April 21, 1961, *PPP Kennedy*. The literature on the Bay of Pigs is massive, but the best account is still Wyden, *Bay of Pigs*.

5. U.S. Senate, Select Committee to Study Governmental Operations with Respect to Intelligence Activities, *Alleged Assassination Plots Involving Foreign Leaders*, 142.

6. CIA Inspector General, "Report on Plots to Assassinate Fidel Castro," p. 94, reprinted in *CIA Targets Fidel*, 90.

7. Bundy interview, March 22, 1996, NSA Cuba Collection.

8. Ibid.

9. Memorandum, Gordon Chase to Mr. Bundy, "Cuba—Policy," April 11, 1963, NSA Cuba Collection.

10. Goodwin has told this story in many venues. This version, unless otherwise indicated, was told to Peter Kornbluh and the Discovery Times Channel, August 28, 2003. See also Goodwin, "Cigars & Che & JFK"; Goodwin, "Annals of Politics"; and Goodwin, *Remembering America*, 195–205.

11. Goodwin, *Remembering America*, 199.

12. Goodwin, "Conversation with Commandante Ernesto Guevara of Cuba," *FRUS, 1961–63*, X, doc. 257. The conversation was also recorded in a telegram from Ambassador Barbosa to the Brazilian Foreign Ministry, "Cuba, Information for the Interview of the President of the Republic with the Minister of Economics of Cuba, Mr. Guevara," August 19, 1961, obtained by Professor James Hershberg, NSA Cuba Collection.

13. *FRUS, 1961–63*, X, doc. 257.

14. Barbosa, "Cuba, Information for the Interview of the President of the Republic with the Minister of Economics of Cuba, Mr. Guevara."

15. Word of the meeting did leak, through the Argentine press. Goodwin was attacked by conservatives and investigated by the Senate Foreign Relations Subcommittee on Latin America for allegedly violating the Logan Act. See "U.S. Aide Backed on Guevara Chat," *NYT*, September 1, 1961.

16. The president was alluding to the possibility the cigars could have been poisoned. It is not clear if Kennedy was aware that, among several CIA assassination schemes aimed at Castro, one was to lace Castro's favorite cigars with a toxic substance. U.S. Senate, Select Committee to Study Governmental Operations with Respect to Intelligence Activities, *Alleged Assassination Plots Involving Foreign Leaders*, 73.

17. Goodwin's recommendations on Cuba policy are contained in his August 22, 1961, cover memorandum to the president for his Memorandum of Conversation with Che Guevara, *FRUS, 1961–63*, X, doc. 256.

18. *FRUS, 1961–63*, X, doc. 258.

19. Goodwin, "Cigars & Che & JFK."

20. Goodwin, *Remembering America*, 185–86.

21. Smith, "Negotiating with Fidel Castro." Smith provides a comprehensive account of the Tractors-for-Freedom Committee negotiations with Cuba, and much of the following account draws on his research.

22. FBIS, "Castro Hails Agrarian Reform Gains," *Latin America Daily Report*, May 18, 1961.

23. FBIS, "Castro Says History Dooms Imperialists," *Latin America Daily Report*, May 22, 1961; FBIS, "Castro Statement on Prisoners Exchange," *Latin America Daily Report*, May 22, 1961.

24. Johnson, *The Bay of Pigs*, 271.

25. FBIS, "Castro's Message to the Tractor Committee," *Latin America Daily Report*, June 8, 1961.

26. Smith, "Negotiating with Fidel Castro," 79.

27. Letter from Tad Szulc to Arthur Schlesinger Jr., June 23, 1961, NSA Cuban Missile Crisis Collection.

28. Testimony of Tad Szulc, June 10, 1975, JFK Assassination Records, Record no. 157-10005-10255, NARA-MD. This conversation is better known for the president's discussion with Szulc about pressure Kennedy was receiving to authorize the assassination of Fidel Castro.

29. Eisenhower, *The Wine Is Bitter*, 287, 290.

30. Johnson, *The Bay of Pigs*, 261–63, 267–68.

31. Goodwin to Bundy, "Actions on Cuban Prisoners," March 29, 1962, NSA Cuba Collection.

32. *FRUS, 1961–63*, X, doc. 327.

33. Johnson, *The Bay of Pigs*, 291.

34. Bigger, *Negotiator*, 287.

35. Ibid., 107.

36. This summary was recovered from Donovan's private papers and published in Pérez-Cisneros et al., *After the Bay of Pigs*, 71–72. Donovan's papers, including a lengthy typed diary/chronology of his efforts in Cuba, are archived at the Hoover Institution, James B. Donovan Papers, 1919–1976, box 39.

37. Bigger, *Negotiator*, 109–12.

38. Ibid., 114; Johnson, *The Bay of Pigs*, 303.

39. The information on McCone's briefing is contained in a TOP SECRET Defense Department memorandum for the Assistant Secretary of Defense, "Release of Cuban Prisoners," October 8, 1962, NSA Cuba Collection.

40. Schlesinger, *Robert Kennedy and His Times*, 534–35; Pérez Cisneros et al., *After the Bay of Pigs*, 128–30.

41. Hershberg, "The United States, Brazil . . . Parts 1 and 2." Unless otherwise noted, details in this section are drawn from Professor Hershberg's groundbreaking research.

42. *FRUS, 1961–63*, XII, doc. 146.

43. Hershberg, "The United States, Brazil . . . Part 1," 15–16.

44. *FRUS, 1961–63*, XII, doc. 226.

45. *FRUS, 1961–63*, X, doc. 335.

46. Fursenko and Naftali, *One Hell of a Gamble*, 221–22; Merle, *Ben Bella*, 136–37.

47. Hershberg, "The United States, Brazil . . . Part 2," 6.

48. "Letter to Mr. F.C.," October 17, 1961. This letter was discovered among the newly declassified papers of Robert Kennedy at the John F. Kennedy Presidential Library by Peter Kornbluh.

49. "Transcript of the Second Executive Committee Meeting, October 16, 1962," in Chang and Kornbluh, *The Cuban Missile Crisis, 1962*, 103.

50. Chang and Kornbluh, *The Cuban Missile Crisis, 1962*, 119–20.

51. Hershberg, "The United States, Brazil . . . Part 2."

52. "Radio and Television Report to the American People on the Soviet Arms Buildup in Cuba," October 22, 1962, *PPP Kennedy*.

53. Hershberg, "The United States, Brazil . . . Part 2," 22.

54. "Executive Committee Record of Action, October 25, 1962, 10:00 A.M.," in Chang and Kornbluh, *The Cuban Missile Crisis, 1962*, 167–71.

55. State Department Memorandum, "Political Path," October 25, 1962, NSA Cuban Missile Crisis Collection.

56. ExComm transcript, October 26, 1962, 10:00 A.M., in May and Zelikow, *The Kennedy Tapes*, 458–62.

57. *FRUS, 1961–63*, XI, doc. 81; Hershberg, "The United States, Brazil . . . Part 2," 29–30.

58. Embassy Telegram 902, Gordon to Rusk, October 28, 1962, cited in Hershberg, "The United States, Brazil . . . Part 2," 38.

59. Hershberg, "The United States, Brazil . . . Part 2," 42.

60. Embassy Telegram 915, Gordon to Rusk, October 31, 1962. Albino's report was transmitted to Gordon by Prime Minister Lima, NSA Cuban Missile Crisis Collection. See also Hershberg, "The United States, Brazil . . . Part 2," 44–48.

61. Embassy Telegram 915, Gordon to Rusk, October 31, 1962. See also Hershberg, "The United States, Brazil . . . Part 2," 44–48.

62. "Brazilian Reports Success in Cuban Conciliation Talks," *NYT*, November 2, 1962.

63. Hershberg, "The United States, Brazil . . . Part 2," 51, 52.

64. For a discussion of the pressures put on Kennedy not to sign a UN accord to formally end the missile crisis, see Chang and Kornbluh, *The Cuban Missile Crisis, 1962*, pp. 245–47.

65. *FRUS, 1961–63*, XI, doc. 261. On the CIA's pessimism, see Fursenko and Naftali, *One Hell of a Gamble*, 199.

66. Paper Prepared by the Bureau of Inter-American Affairs of the Department of State, "Future Relations with Castro," June 20, 1963, NSA Cuba Collection.

67. These quotes are from a chronology that Donovan kept on the negotiations; see "Chronology of Cuban Prisoner Release Negotiations," undated, p. 6, box 39, folder 5, Donovan Papers.

68. *FRUS, 1961–63*, XI, doc. 178; Bigger, *Negotiator*, 134–35.

69. Bigger, *Negotiator*, 147–48.

70. Ibid., 150.

71. Nolan has told this story often, including in an interview with the authors, New York City, April 29, 2004.

72. Quoted in Pérez-Cisneros et al., *After the Bay of Pigs*, 158.

73. Ibid., 175.

74. *FRUS, 1961–63*, XI, doc. 275.

75. Ibid.

76. See source note in ibid., 687.

77. This five-page CIA document was drafted in February 1963 and declassified in May 2002, NSA Cuba Collection.

78. Ibid., 3.

79. Ibid., 5.

80. Memorandum, Chase to Bundy, "Mr. Donovan's Trip to Cuba," March 1, 1963, NSA Cuba Collection.

81. Chase Memorandum for the Record, "Mr. Donovan's Trip to Cuba," March 4, 1963, NSA Cuba Collection.

82. "Negotiating Instructions," undated. This secret U.S. government memorandum is among the Donovan Papers, box 48, folder 3.

83. Samuels, "How Metadiplomacy Works."

84. Donovan-Miskovsky Tape, reel 4, pp. 9, 10, NSA Cuba Collection.

85. Samuels, "How Metadiplomacy Works," 302.

86. Donovan-Miskovsky Tape, reel 4, pp. 13, 14.

87. Ibid., reel 4, p. 11.

88. Ibid., reel 4, p. 14.

89. Ibid., reel 1, p. 5.

90. Ibid., reel 4, p. 9.

91. Martin Arnold, "Molina and 3 Others Free in Exchange with Cuba," *NYT*, April 23, 1963.

92. "TV's First Lady of Sin," *People Today*, April 22, 1953.

93. "No One Dodges Lisa," *Time Magazine*, October 25, 1963.

94. Ibid.

95. Lisa Howard note to Cuban UN Mission, NSA Cuba Collection.

96. Donovan, unpublished memoir, pp. 752, 753, Donovan Papers, boxes 39 and 40.

97. "May 10, 1963—Lisa Howard Interviews Fidel Castro in Cuba," transcript from the original program press packet, NSA Cuba Collection.

98. Lisa Howard, "Castro's Overture," *War/Peace Report*, September 1963.

99. Draft letter to Fidel Castro, April 27, 1963, NSA Cuba Collection.

100. Howard's debriefing in Miami is referred to in a May 2, 1963, letter from Acting CIA director Marshall S. Carter to McGeorge Bundy and Attorney General Robert Kennedy. *FRUS, 1961–63*, XI, doc. 332.

101. Helms to McCone, "Interview of U.S. Newswoman with Fidel Castro Indicating Possible Interest in Rapprochement with the United States," May 1, 1963, NSA Cuba Collection. The SECRET memo has a blue handwritten lettering on the top right hand corner, "PSAW," meaning President Saw.

102. McCone's objections are contained in a letter signed by Acting CIA Director Marshall S. Carter to McGeorge Bundy, May 2, 1963, *FRUS, 1961–63*, XI, doc. 332.

103. Gordon Chase Memorandum to Mr. Bundy, "Cuba—Policy," April 11, 1963, NSA Cuba Collection.

104. *FRUS, 1961–63*, XI, doc. 320.

105. The sources included the Yugoslav ambassador, a Latin American engineer working in Havana, and several Cubans. See Helms to McCone, "Reported Desire of the Cuban Government for Rapprochement with the United States," June 5, 1963, NSA Cuba Collection.

106. Minutes of the Special Group, June 6, 1963, NSA Cuba Collection.

107. Helms to McCone, "Reported Desire of the Cuban Government for Rapprochement with the United States," June 5, 1963, NSA Cuba Collection.

108. *FRUS, 1961–63*, XI, docs. 322 and 344.

109. *FRUS, 1961–63*, XI, docs. 350, 351.

110. *FRUS, 1961–63*, XI, docs. 349, 322.

111. Bohning, *The Castro Obsession*, 157–60.

112. Attwood, *The Reds and the Blacks*, 144; Attwood, *Twilight Struggle*, 258–59; Atwood Memorandum to Gordon Chase, November 8, 1963, Chronology of Events (hereafter, Attwood chronology), *FRUS, 1961–63*, XI, doc. 374.

113. *FRUS, 1961–63*, XI, doc. 367.

114. Attwood, *Twilight Struggle*, 259; Attwood testimony before a closed session of the Senate Select Committee to Study Governmental Operations with Respect to Intelligence Activities, July 10, 1975, p. 4 (hereafter Attwood testimony), NSA Cuba Collection. This TOP SECRET testimony to the Church Committee was declassified in 1994 at the request of Peter Kornbluh.

115. Lechuga, *In the Eye of the Storm*, 197–98.

116. Attwood testimony, 5–6; Attwood chronology, 3; Lechuga, *In the Eye of the Storm*, 198–201.

117. "Rapprochement with Cuba—The Testimony of William Attwood," July 9, 1975, National Archives, JFK Collection, box 74, folder 2 (also in NSA Cuba Collection).

118. Attwood testimony, 6. The attorney general remained skeptical however, arguing at a Special Group meeting on November 5 that "the U.S. must require some fundamental steps such as the end of subversion in Latin America and removing the Soviet troops in Cuba before any serious discussion can take place about a detente." *FRUS, 1961–63*, XI, doc. 373.

119. "Rapprochement with Cuba—The Testimony of William Attwood," July 9, 1975.

120. Attwood chronology, 4–5; see also Attwood, *Twilight Struggle*, 260–61.

121. Attwood chronology, 7.

122. The Kennedy tape, first obtained by Peter Kornbluh, is posted on the website of the National Security Archive, http:www.nsarchive.org. See also the Special Group's same-day discussion of Cuban "peace feelers," November 5, 1963, *FRUS, 1961–63*, XI, doc. 373.

123. Attwood testimony, 7–8.

124. *FRUS, 1961–63*, XI, doc. 377; William H. Attwood, November 8, 1965, p. 10, Kennedy Library, Oral History Program.

125. Attwood added that Vallejo's manner was "extremely cordial and he called me 'sir' throughout the conversation." See Attwood's chronology addendum, Memorandum to Gordon Chase, November 22, 1963, *FRUS, 1961–63*, XI, doc. 379.

126. Attwood testimony, 9.

127. "Address in Miami before the Inter-American Press Association," November 18th, 1963, *PPP Kennedy*.

128. Schlesinger interview.

129. Robert E. Thompson, "Kennedy Urges Cuban Revolt," *LAT*, November 19, 1963; Schlesinger, *Robert Kennedy and His Times*, 554.

130. Attwood, *Twilight Struggle*, 260.

131. Daniel was interviewed by the Discovery Times Channel for the documentary film, "Kennedy and Castro: The Secret History," which premiered in November 2003, on the fortieth anniversary of Kennedy's assassination. This account is based upon that interview and Daniel's written descriptions of his meetings with Kennedy and Castro: Jean Daniel, "Two Interviews: Castro's Reply to Kennedy Comments on Cuba," *NYT*, December 11, 1963; Daniel, "Unofficial Envoy: An Historic Report from Two Capitals"; Daniel, *Le temps qui reste*, 149–69.

Chapter Three

1. Chase to Bundy, "Cuba—Item of Presidential Interest," November 25, 1963. Kennedy Library file, "Contacts with Cuban Leaders." The same file is located at the Johnson Library,

National Security File, Central File, Cuba, box 21. This document, along with many others cited in this chapter, was first obtained through a Mandatory Declassification Review request by Peter Kornbluh. The National Security Archive has created a special file of these records, referred to here as NSA Cuba Collection.

2. Holland, *The Kennedy Assassination Tapes*, 194, 181.

3. Dumbrell, *President Lyndon Johnson and Soviet Communism*, 138.

4. Schoultz, *That Infernal Little Cuban Republic*, 214.

5. William H. Attwood, November 8, 1965, p. 10, Kennedy Library, Oral History Program.

6. Chase to Bundy, "Cuba—Item of Presidential Interest," November 25, 1963; Kennedy Library, "Contacts with Cuban Leaders," NSA Cuba Collection.

7. "Excerpts from Castro's Talk," *NYT*, November 25, 1963.

8. Chase to Bundy, "Bill Attwood Activities," December 2, 1963, Johnson Library, National Security File, Central File, Cuba, "Contacts with Cuban Leaders," box 21.

9. Ibid.

10. Chase to Bundy, "Bill Attwood's Activities," December 3, 1963, DDRS.

11. Attwood's executive session testimony before the Senate Select Committee to Study Governmental Operations with Respect to Intelligence Activities, July 10, 1975, 9, NSA Cuba Collection. This testimony, kept secret until 1994, was declassified by the Senate Foreign Relations Committee at the request of Peter Kornbluh.

12. Attwood's December 9 chronological report was titled "Latest Cuban Developments for Your Talk with President Johnson." That chronology, and two previous ones, are at the Johnson Library, National Security File, Central File, Cuba, "Contacts with Cuban Leaders," box 21.

13. Attwood, *The Twilight Struggle*, 263.

14. Memorandum for the President, TOP SECRET/SENSITIVE, "Meeting on Cuba—December 19, 1963," Johnson Library, National Security File, Central File, Cuba, box 21.

15. Ibid., 8.

16. Ibid., 17.

17. Meeting with the President, December 19, 1963, "Cuba," DDRS.

18. Chase to Bundy, "Bill Attwood Activities," January 24, 1964, Johnson Library, National Security File, Central File, Cuba, "Contacts with Cuban Leaders, box 21; Attwood, *The Reds and the Blacks*, 146.

19. Attwood, *The Twilight Struggle*, 263.

20. "Two Interviews: Castro's Reply to Kennedy Comments on Cuba," *NYT*, December 11, 1963; Jean Daniel, "When Castro Heard the News," *New Republic*, December 7, 1963; Daniel, "Unofficial Envoy," *New Republic*, December 14, 1963.

21. "Two Interviews," *NYT*, December 11, 1963.

22. Daniel, "Unofficial Envoy."

23. FBIS, "Castro on Normalization of U.S.-Cuban Relations," *Report on Cuban Propaganda*, no. 13, March 4, 1964, 14. See also the CIA's Current Intelligence Weekly, "Castro's Anniversary Speech," January 10, 1964, 19, NSA Collection.

24. Tad Szulc, "Rusk Rebuts Cuba on Kennedy View" *NYT*, January 3, 1964.

25. Richard Helms to McGeorge Bundy, "Alleged Contacts between Castro and American Government," March 4, 1964, NSA Collection.

26. The ABC *Issues and Answers* program aired on Sunday, March 22, 1964.

27. This section of the transcript of Howard's interview is reprinted in Rasky, *Nobody Swings on Sunday*, 107.

28. "Verbal Message Given to Miss Lisa Howard of ABC News on February 12, 1964, in Havana, Cuba." An original carbon copy of this document was first obtained by Peter Kornbluh from Lisa Howard's husband and published in Kornbluh, "JFK and Castro: The Secret Quest for Accommodation," *Cigar Aficionado*, September/November 1998 (also in DDRS).

29. Kornbluh, "JFK and Castro."

30. Bundy sent this untitled February 26, 1964, memorandum to White House press secretary Pierre Salinger, presidential advisor Jack Valenti, and White House aide Kenneth O'Donnell, among others. Johnson Library, National Security File, Central File, Cuba, "Contacts with Cuban Leaders," box 21.

31. Chase reported his conversation with Howard to Bundy in a five-page, single-spaced TOP SECRET/EYES ONLY memorandum titled "Mrs. Lisa Howard," March 10, 1964, DDRS.

32. Ibid.

33. Ibid.

34. Chase to Bundy, "Cuba," March 11, 1964, DDRS.

35. Chase to Bundy, "Castro," March 13, 1964, and attached paper, "Negotiations with Castro—Possible Scenario First Steps," DDRS.

36. Chase, Memorandum for the Record, "Talks with Castro," April 13, 1964, DDRS.

37. Ibid.

38. *FRUS 1964–1968*, XXXII, doc. 271.

39. The Cuban protest was delivered in person to John Crimmins by the Czech Embassy, which represented Cuban interests, Memorandum of Conversation, February 4, NARA-MD, RG 59, Central Files 1964–66, POL 33-4 CUBA-US. See also Paul W. Ward, "Castro Cuts Off Water Supply at Guantanamo," *Baltimore Sun*, February 7, 1964.

40. *FRUS, 1964–1968*, XXXII, doc. 230.

41. Bundy's report to Johnson, and Johnson's instructions to Rusk, March 6, 1964, *FRUS, 1964–1968*, XXXII, doc. 248.

42. Chase to Bundy, "Cuba-Miscellaneous," March 12, 1964. The first section addresses "Warnings to Cubans and Russians about SAM's," Johnson Library, National Security File, Cuba, Overflights, vol. II, 3/64–67.

43. *FRUS, 1964–1968*, XXXII, doc. 253.

44. Rusk to Johnson, "Warning to Cubans and Soviets against Interference with our Aerial Surveillance of Cuba," March 15, 1964, Johnson Library, National Security File, Country File, Cuba, Overflights, vol. II, 3/64–7/67.

45. Deputy Assistant Secretary Robert W. Adams to Czech Ambassador Duda, cited in footnote 2, *FRUS, 1964–1968*, XXXII, doc. 256.

46. Ibid., doc. 261.

47. Memorandum from Raford W. Herbert to Helms, "U-2 Message to Fidel Castro," May 8, 1964, NSA Cuba Collection.

48. Chase to Bundy, "Lisa Howard," May 2, 1964, DDRS.

49. Chase to Bundy, "Lisa Howard," May 15, 1964, DDRS.

50. Stevenson to the President, June 16, 1964, NSA Cuba Collection.

51. Stevenson to the President, untitled, June 26, 1964, in a collection of documents on contacts with Cuba (p. 37), DDRS.

52. Chase to Bundy, "Contact with Castro," July 6, 1964, DDRS.

53. Chase to Bundy, "Adlai Stevenson and Lisa Howard," July 7, 1964, DDRS.

54. Chase to Bundy, "Adlai Stevenson and Lisa Howard," July 7, 1964, DDRS.

55. Shenon, *A Cruel and Shocking Act*, 388–92.

56. The interview is reported in Richard Eder, "Castro Proposes Deal to Halt Aid to Latin Rebels," *NYT*, July 6, 1964, and Tad Szulc, "U.S. Aides Rebuff Castro on Peace Talk Overture," *NYT*, July 7, 1964. The assessment by the State Department's Bureau of Intelligence and Research is in Kornbluh, "JFK and Castro."

57. United Press International, "Cuba May Lift Requirements for U.S. Talks," *Chicago Tribune*, July 22, 1964.

58. Memorandum of Conversation, "Message from Castro on Exchange of Political Prisoners for Pledge by U.S. of Non-interference," March 20, 1964. NSA Cuba Collection.

59. CIA assessment, "Current Thinking of Cuban Government Leaders," March 5, 1964, NSA Cuba Collection.

60. British Embassy, Washington, NSA Cuba Collection. Watson's cable is dated July 20, but it was not transmitted to the U.S. State Department until August 10, 1964.

61. British Embassy, Havana, Dispatch number 38, August 5, 1964, NSA Cuba Collection. Whitehead's report was transferred to the United States and eventually arrived on the desk of McGeorge Bundy in Washington.

62. *FRUS 1964–1968*, XXXII, doc. 276.

63. For the text of the declaration, see "The Castro Declaration," *NYT*, July 27, 1964.

64. Keller, "A Foreign Policy for Domestic Consumption," 115.

65. "Mexico Seeks to Reunite United States and Cuba," *WP*, September 2, 1960.

66. The audio of this presidential tape can be found on the website of the National Security Archive, nsarchive.org.

67. Morley, *Imperial State and Revolution*, 191–239.

68. For a comprehensive account of the Aranzazu operation and its aftermath, see Bohning, *The Castro Obsession*, 217–18.

69. *FRUS, 1964–1968*, XXXII, doc. 289.

70. Guevara, *Che Guevara Reader*, 337.

71. Chase to Bundy, "Lisa Howard and Che Guevara," December 15, 1964, DDRS.

72. *FRUS 1964–1968*, XXXII, doc. 292.

73. Ibid.

74. Offitt interview.

75. *FRUS 1964–1968*, XXXII, doc. 293.

76. Chase to Bundy, "Che Guevera [sic] and Lisa Howard," December 17, 1964, NSA Cuba Collection.

77. *FRUS 1964–1968*, XXXII, doc. 293.

78. The Guevara visit marked Lisa Howard's last hurrah as an intermediary between Havana and Washington. In the fall of 1964, she was dismissed from ABC News for becoming prominently involved in a group called Democrats for Keating, which opposed the New York Senate bid of Robert F. Kennedy. In the spring of 1965, she suffered a miscarriage and was hospitalized with depression. She committed suicide in East Hampton, on July 4, 1965.

79. Kornbluh, "Cuban Embargo-Buster."

80. The lard documents were published by Peter Kornbluh in "Bay of Fat Free Pigs," *Harper's Magazine*, June 1999, 24–25.

81. Kennedy to Rusk, "Travel to Cuba," December 12, 1963, NSA Cuba Collection.

82. Memorandum, Abba P. Schwartz and Abram Chayes to the Acting Secretary [of State], "Travel Regulations," December 13, 1963, NSA Cuba Collection.

83. National Security Council, "Student Travel to Cuba," May 21, 1964, NSA Cuba Collection.

84. Discurso . . . del V Aniversario de los Comités de Defensa de la Revolución, el 28 de Septiembre de 1965, Discursos Archive.

85. AP, "No 'Serious' Offer from Cuba," *Chicago Tribune*, October 1, 1965.

86. Bowdler to Bundy, "Castro's Proposal on Disaffected Cubans," October 1, 1965, NSA Cuba Collection.

87. "Remarks at the Signing of the Immigration Bill, Liberty Island, New York," October 3, 1965, *PPP Johnson*.

88. Telegram to be transmitted by Swiss Embassy, Washington, to Swiss Embassy, Havana, October 6, 1965, NSA Cuba Collection.

89. "Draft Translation of Note from the Cuban Government," October 12, [1965], DDRS.

90. Bowdler to Bundy, "Cuban Refugee Problem," October 15, 1965, NSA Cuba Collection.

91. Telegram to Ambassador Stadelhofer via Swiss Embassy Washington, undated draft, DDRS.

92. "Text of a Note Delivered by the Cuban Foreign Ministry to the Swiss Embassy in Havana on October 19, 1965, in the Evening," DDRS.

93. *FRUS 1964–1968*, XXXII, doc. 308.

94. Bowdler to Bundy, "Cuban Refugee Problem," October 28, 1965, DDRS.

95. Department of State, Bureau of Public Affairs, Office of the Historian, Research Memorandum No. 1230, May 20, 1980, NSA Cuba Collection.

96. Bowdler to Moyers, "Cuban Refugee Problem," October 30, 1965, DDRS.

97. "Statement by the President on the Agreement Covering Movement of Cuban Refugees to the United States," November 6, 1965, *PPP Johnson*. The final agreement is in *Department of State Bulletin* 53, no. 1379 (November 29, 1965): 850–53.

98. *FRUS, 1964–1965*, XXXII, doc. 308.

99. *FRUS, 1964–1968*, XXXII, doc. 313.

100. *FRUS, 1964–1968*, XXXII, doc. 299.

101. *FRUS, 1964–1968*, XXXII, doc. 300.

102. Chase to Bundy, "U.S./Cuban Talks," April 24, 1964, NSA Cuba Collection. This document was obtained by Peter Kornbluh through a Mandatory Declassification Review request.

103. Paul Hoffman, "Cuba Said to Seek Spain's Aid for an 'Arrangement' with U.S." *NYT*, May 22, 1964.

104. Chase to Bundy, "Contact with Castro—Press Guidance," May 22, 1964, DDRS.

105. Cable, State to American Embassy Madrid, no subject heading, December 21, 1967, State 88198, DDRS.

106. This cable, dated November 16, 1967, and numbered 793, was discovered by Peter Kornbluh among the papers of Foreign Minister Castiella, in the archives of the Real

Academia de la Historia, Madrid. See also Cable, State to American Embassy Madrid, no subject heading, December 21, 1967, State 88198, DDRS.

107. Ibid.

108. A Spanish translation of the Kohler cable was found among the papers of Foreign Minister Castiella, Real Academia de la Historia, Madrid.

109. "Entrevista de Nuestro Enviado Especial con Fidel Castro," November 28, 1967, Papers of Fernando Castiella, Real Academia de la Historia, Madrid.

110. "Segunda Conversación de nuestro enviado especial con Fidel Castro," November 29, 1967, Papers of Fernando Castiella, Real Academia de la Historia, Madrid.

111. *FRUS, 1964–1968*, XXXII, doc. 318.

112. Memorandum of Conversation between Rusk and Castiella, "Cuba (Part 7 of 9)," July 15, 1968, DDRS.

113. Ibid.

114. Memorandum from Rostow to the President, "Death of 'Che' Guevara," October 11, 1967, NSA Cuba Collection.

115. Hughes to the Secretary of State, "Guevara's Death—The Meaning for Latin America," October 12, 1967, NSA Cuba Collection.

116. FBIS, "Fidel Castro Delivers Eulogy on Che Guevara," *Latin America Daily Report*, October 19, 1967.

117. CIA, *Castro's Cuba Today*, September 30, 1966; *Current Intelligence Weekly Special Report*, 2, 16, CIA FOIA website.

118. *FRUS, 1964–1968*, XXXII, doc. 314.

119. "National Policy Paper—Cuba: United States Policy," July 15, 1968, DDRS. Quotations over the next several pages are all from this document unless otherwise noted.

120. *FRUS, 1964–1968*, XXXII, doc. 320.

121. Editorial note, *FRUS, 1964–1968*, XXXII, doc. 322.

122. *FRUS, 1964–1968*, XXXII, doc. 324.

123. Editorial note, *FRUS, 1964–1968*, XXXII, doc. 322.

Chapter Four

1. Kissinger Telcon, April 24, 1974. Many of the documents cited in this chapter were part of a "special file" compiled by Kissinger's Assistant Secretary of State for Inter-American Affairs William D. Rogers during the secret talks with Cuba. In 1993 Peter Kornbluh and the National Security Archive assisted Rogers in obtaining an expedited declassification of the entire file. The documents are now part of the archive's special Cuba dialogue collection, referred to here as NSA Cuba Collection.

2. Interviews with Frank Mankiewicz and his two colleagues, Kirby Jones and Saul Landau. As Jones recalls, the three read the letter to Castro before they delivered it.

3. Memorandum of Conversation, "Cuba Policy: Tactics before and after San Jose," June 9, 1975, NSA Cuba Collection.

4. Kissinger, *Years of Renewal*, 771.

5. Nixon, *Six Crises*, 351–53.

6. *FRUS, 1969–1976*, vol. E-10, doc. 195.

7. Memorandum, Haig to Kissinger, "Cuba, Items to Discuss with the President," October 3, 1971, quoted in Schoultz, *That Infernal Little Cuban Republic*, 248.

8. Memorandum, Helms to Attorney General Mitchell, July 10, 1970, quoted in footnote 1 of *FRUS, 1969–1976*, vol. E-10, doc. 220.

9. *FRUS, 1969–1976*, vol. E-10, doc. 197. The Cubans told the Swiss that they were approaching the United States without informing the Russians of this initiative.

10. Memorandum, Vaky to Kissinger, March 17, 1969, quoted in footnote 1 of *FRUS, 1969–1976*, vol. E-10, doc. 197.

11. *FRUS, 1969–1976*, vol. E-10, doc. 198.

12. *FRUS, 1969–1976*, vol. E-10, doc. 199.

13. Ibid.

14. *FRUS, 1969–1976*, vol. E-10, doc. 209.

15. Memorandum of Conversation, "Cuba," September 27, 1969, NSA Cuba Collection.

16. *FRUS, 1969–1976*, vol. E-10, doc. 213.

17. *FRUS, 1969–1976*, vol. E-10, doc. 215.

18. *FRUS, 1969–1976*, vol. E-10, doc. 36.

19. *FRUS, 1969–1976*, vol. E-10, doc. 247.

20. Feste, "Reducing International Terrorism."

21. *FRUS, 1961–1963*, X, doc. 257. Castro's proposal and the U.S. rejection are described in "Airliner Returns to Miami," *LAT*, August 10, 1961; and "Editorial Note," *FRUS, 1961–1963*, X, doc. 252.

22. "Antihijacking Law Enacted by Havana" *NYT*, September 20, 1969.

23. *FRUS, 1969–1976*, vol. E-10, doc. 208.

24. *FRUS, 1969–1976*, vol. E-1 doc. 79.

25. "Havana Decries Hijacks," *WP*, November 16, 1972.

26. *FRUS, 1969–1976*, vol. E-1, doc. 135.

27. The draft agreement is attached to Memorandum from the President's Assistant for National Security Affairs (Kissinger) to President Nixon, Washington, December 3, 1972, *FRUS, 1969–1976*, vol. E-1, doc. 138.

28. The final agreement is "Cuba-United States: Memorandum of Understanding on the Hijacking of Aircraft and Vessels." *International Legal Materials* 12, no.2: 370–76.

29. Nixon tapes, February 13, conversation no. 43-66, WH Telephone, Jan. 31–Feb. 27, 1973, Nixon Library.

30. Quoted in Schoultz, *That Infernal Little Cuban Republic*, 259.

31. *FRUS, 1969–1976*, vol. E-10, doc. 209.

32. Harris Poll from February 1973. Found in Mayer, "Trends: American Attitudes towards Cuba," 600.

33. Whalen et al., "A Detente with Cuba."

34. Javits and Pell, *The United States and Cuba: A Propitious Moment*, 1–2.

35. Kornbluh and Blight, "Dialogue with Castro."

36. Memorandum of Conversation, "Meeting with Argentine Foreign Minister Vignes," September 16, 1974. Obtained through the FOIA by the National Security Archive, in National Security Archive, *Talking with Castro*.

37. Mankiewicz, along with his associate, Kirby Jones, remembered a discussion with Fidel about the protocol of this note—should it be typed, handwritten, signed, in English

or in Spanish, from Castro or from Kissinger's Cuban counterpart, Foreign Minister Raúl Roa. In the end, Castro decided to dictate the note to Roa, who wrote it by hand.

38. Mankiewicz interview.

39. Kissinger, *Years of Renewal*, 773.

40. Kornbluh and Blight. "Dialogue with Castro."

41. Memorandum of Conversation, August 15, 1974, Ford Library, National Security Advisor's Memoranda of Conversation Collection, online, http://www.fordlibrarymuseum .gov/library/guides/findingaid/Memoranda_of_Conversations.asp.

42. Memorandum of Conversation, September 13, 1974, Ford Library, National Security Advisor's Memoranda of Conversation Collection, online.

43. Memorandum of Conversation, September 21, 1974, Ford Library, National Security Advisor's Memoranda of Conversation Collection, online.

44. Sánchez-Parodi interview, August 6, 2012.

45. García interview, December 21, 2012.

46. Sánchez-Parodi interview, August 6, 2012.

47. García, *Diplomacia Sin Sombra*, 29.

48. "The United States and Cuba: A Balance Sheet," January 2, 1975, NSA Cuba Collection.

49. Memorandum, Rogers to Kissinger, "Meetings with Cuban Emissary," January 2, 1975, in National Security Archive, *Talking with Castro*.

50. Undated, unsigned aide-mémoire, obtained through the Freedom of Information Act by Peter Kornbluh. NSA Cuba Collection.

51. Memorandum, Eagleburger to Kissinger, "Meeting in New York with Cuban Representatives," January 11, 1975, NSA Cuba Collection (also DDRS).

52. García, *Diplomacia Sin Sombra*, 27–28.

53. Rogers to Maroney, no date, NSA Cuba Collection.

54. Memorandum, Robert Ingersoll, NSC Under Secretaries Committee, Memorandum for the President, "Cuba Policy—Our Constraints on US Subsidiaries," February 25, 1975, DDRS.

55. García, *Diplomacia Sin Sombra*, 33–37.

56. Kornbluh and Blight, "Dialogue with Castro."

57. Memorandum, Rogers to Kissinger, "Trip to Panama," January 22, 1975, NSA Cuba Collection.

58. Ibid.

59. Memorandum, Rogers to Kissinger, "The Mankiewicz Trip," January 20, 1975, NSA Cuba Collection.

60. Quoted in Memorandum, Rogers to Kissinger, "Cuba," January 25, 1975, NSA Cuba Collection.

61. United Press International, "Cuba Seeking Trade for 'CIA Agent,'" *WP*, January 23, 1975; Memorandum, Rogers to Kissinger, "Cuba," January 25, 1975, NSA Cuba Collection.

62. Memorandum, Rogers to Kissinger, "Cuba," February 20, 1975, NSA Cuba Collection.

63. Ibid.

64. Letter, Kuhn to Kissinger, January 14, 1975, NSA Cuba Collection.

65. Memorandum, Rogers to Kissinger, "From Rogers," February 13, 1975, NSA Cuba Collection.

66. Memorandum, Rogers to Kissinger, "Cuba," February 20, 1975, NSA Cuba Collection.

67. Memorandum, Rogers to Kissinger, "Cuba," February 24, 1975, NSA Cuba Collection.

68. Kissinger, "The United States and Latin America: The New Opportunity, March 1, 1975," *Department of State Bulletin* 72, no. 1865 (March 24, 1975): 361–69.

69. Memorandum, Shlaudeman to Rogers, "Normalizing Relations with Cuba," March 27, 1975, NSA Cuba Collection.

70. Ibid.

71. "Normalizing Relations with Cuba," cover memorandum, March 27, 1975, NSA Cuba Collection.

72. Ibid.

73. Memorandum, Rogers to Kissinger, "Cuban Policy: After the OASGA," April 25, 1975, NSA Cuba Collection.

74. Memorandum to the Files, "Telephone Conversation between Senator McGovern and Mr. Rogers," May 12, 1975, NSA Cuba Collection.

75. This dialogue is based on verbatim notes of the meeting transcribed in a SECRET Memorandum of Conversation, "Cuba Policy: Tactics before and after San Jose," June 9, 1975, NSA Cuba Collection.

76. The untitled note was found in William Rogers "Special Activities" file, attached to a report to the files on the June 21 meeting with García. NSA Cuba Collection.

77. Both Eagleburger and García related this story in interviews with the authors. García recounts the communications breakdown in, *Diplomacia Sin Sombra*, 46–48.

78. Memorandum, "WDR" [Rogers] to "WDR and nobody else," June 21, 1975, NSA Cuba Collection.

79. García, *Diplomacia Sin Sombra*, 52–53.

80. Detailed notes became the basis for a comprehensive transcript of the meeting, which was obtained by Peter Kornbluh under the Freedom of Information Act. Memorandum of Conversation, July 9, 1975, NSA Cuba Collection (also DDRS).

81. Kissinger, *Years of Renewal*, 780.

82. García, *Diplomacia Sin Sombra*, 59.

83. Memorandum of Conversation, July 9, 1975, NSA Cuba Collection (also DDRS).

84. Kissinger, *Years of Renewal*, 781.

85. García, *Diplomacia Sin Sombra*, 63.

86. James Blight et al., "United States–Cuban Detente: The 1974–76 Initiative and the Angolan Interventions," Typescript of Conversations in Havana, 14–15 December 1992, NSA Cuba Collection.

87. AP, "U.S. Ready to Open Talks on Cuba Ties," *NYT*, July 31, 1975.

88. García, *Diplomacia Sin Sombra*, 63–64.

89. AP, "Cuba Refunds Ransom in '72 Hijacking," *NYT*, August 12, 1975.

90. Memorandum of Conversation, August 7, 1975, Ford Library, National Security Advisor's Memoranda of Conversation Collection, online.

91. Memorandum, Kissinger to the President, "Third Country Sanctions against Cuba," August 19, 1975, DDRS.

92. Text of the State Department announcement is included in Leslie H. Gelb, "U.S. Relaxes Ban against Trading with the Cubans," *NYT*, August 22, 1975. The formal NSDM was signed later. "National Security Decision Memorandum 305," September 15, 1975,

Ford Library, National Security Decision Memoranda Collection, online, http://www
.fordlibrarymuseum.gov/library/document/0310/nsdm.asp. Castro's reaction is quoted in
Murrey Marder, "Castro Hails U.S. 'Gesture,'" *WP*, August 23, 1975.

93. The note is reproduced in García, *Diplomacia Sin Sombra*, Anexo I.

94. Ibid., 64–65.

95. Murrey Marder, "U.S. Visit by Brezhnev Moved Back," *WP*, September 10, 1975.

96. Transcript of conference on Cuba organized by the Center for American Policy
Development, Brown University, and held at the Rockefeller estate in Pocantico Hills, New
York, August 23, 1993, NSA Cuba Collection.

97. Jones interview; García, *Diplomacia Sin Sombra*, 66–67.

98. Eagleburger and Rogers to Kissinger, "Cuban Family Visits," January 12, 1976, NSA
Cuba Collection (also DDRS).

99. Gleijeses, *Conflicting Missions*, 9.

100. "Questions and Answers Following the Secretary's Pittsburgh Address," *Department
of State Bulletin* 73, no. 1901 (December 1, 1975): 765–69.

101. "Building an Enduring Foreign Policy, November 24, 1975," *Department of State
Bulletin* 73, no. 1903 (December 15, 1975): 841–54.

102. "The President's News Conference," December 20, 1975, *PPP Ford*.

103. Kornbluh and Blight, "Dialogue with Castro."

104. Memorandum, Eagleburger and Rogers to Kissinger, "Cuban Family Visits"; García,
Diplomacia Sin Sombra, 71–72.

105. García recounted this conversation in a filmed interview with Saul Landau for
Landau's film, "Will the Real Terrorist Please Stand Up?," March 2010.

106. Memorandum, Rogers and Eagleburger to Kissinger, "Cuban Family Visits."

107. FBIS, "Castro News Conference, January 15, 1976," *Latin America Daily Report*,
January 16, 1976.

108. Memorandum of Conversation, February 7, 1976, NSA Cuba Collection (also DDRS).

109. García, *Diplomacia Sin Sombra*, 75.

110. "Remarks at a President Ford Committee Reception in Miami," February 14, 1976,
PPP Ford; "Remarks in Miami, Florida," February 28, 1976, *PPP Ford*; Reuters, "Angry Castro
Calls Ford 'Vulgar Liar,'" *WP*, April 20, 1976.

111. Memorandum of Conversation, February 25, 1976, Ford Library, Memoranda of
Presidential Conversations collection online, http://www.fordlibrarymuseum.gov/library/
dmemcons.asp

112. Memorandum of Conversation, March 15, 1976, Ford Library, Memoranda of
Presidential Conversations collection online.

113. David Binder, "U.S. Is Reviewing Its Cuba Options," *NYT*, March 26, 1976.

114. Washington Special Action Group Meeting, Memorandum of Conversation, "Cuba,"
March 24, 1976, p. 1, NSA Cuba Collection. This document, kept secret for thirty-four
years, was declassified pursuant to a Mandatory Declassification Review request by Peter
Kornbluh.

115. Ibid., 3.

116. Ibid., 4.

117. The "Cuban Contingencies" papers—a summary, a detailed 38-page outline,
and a 27-page options paper—were obtained by Peter Kornbluh through a Mandatory

Declassification Review request to the Gerald Ford Presidential Library. They are undated but appear to have been given to Kissinger in April 1976. NSA Cuba Collection.

118. "Cuban Contingencies," Outline, p. 2.

119. Ibid., 18.

120. "Meeting with William Rogers," March 10, 1976. Jones kept detailed memos on his contacts with U.S. officials. He graciously provided the authors with access to his personal files on his involvement as an intermediary between the United States and Cuba.

121. Ibid. At the end of the meeting, Jones suggested that the next president, whether it was Ford or Reagan or a Democrat, would "probably lift the blockage anyway." Rogers disagreed. He "said that he was not so sure about that and that there might be some mistake in that thinking."

122. Kissinger, "The United States and Latin America."

123. Rogers interview.

124. AP, "McGovern's Plan Scores with Cubans," *NYT*, May 9, 1975.

125. Stanley Meisler, "Castro Signals He's Ready for U.S. Ties," *LAT*, May 9, 1975.

126. Kornbluh and Blight, "Dialogue with Castro."

127. Rogers interview.

128. CIA, Intelligence Memorandum, "Cuba's US Policy: Ready for a Change," July 23, 1975, NSA Cuba Collection.

129. Minutes of the meeting between Todor Zhivkov and Fidel Castro in Sofia, March 11, 1976, WWC, Cuban Foreign Relations Collection, http://digitalarchive.wilsoncenter.org/collection/82/cuban-foreign-relations.

130. Memorandum of Conversation, Kissinger and Boumediene, October 14–15, 1974, NSA Cuba Collection.

131. Transcript of conference on Cuba organized by the Center for American Policy Development, Brown University, and held at the Rockefeller estate in Pocantico Hills, New York, August 23, 1993, NSA Cuba Collection.

132. CIA Intelligence Information Cable, "Activities of Cuban Exile Leader Orlando Bosch during His Stay in Venezuela," October 14, 1976, NSA Cuba Collection.

133. Speech at the Memorial Service for the Victims of the Cubana Airlines Plane Destroyed in Flight on October 6, October 15, 1976, Discursos Archive.

Chapter Five

1. Presidential Directive/NSC-6, March 15, 1977, "Cuba," Carter Library, Vertical File, Presidential Directives, 1–20.

2. Carter interview.

3. Memorandum, Pastor to Brzezinski, "Cuba Policy-PRC Meeting," March 8, 1977, DDRS.

4. Mankiewicz interview.

5. U.S. Senate, Committee on Foreign Relations, *Nomination of Hon. Cyrus R. Vance to Be Secretary of State*, 17.

6. Memorandum, Pastor to Brzezinski, "Cuba Policy–PRC Meeting."

7. Graham Hovey, "Possibility Is Raised of U.S.-Cuba Meeting," *NYT*, February 4, 1977.

8. Memorandum, Pastor to Brzezinski, "Your Lunch with Senator Church: Cuba," August 1, 1977, Tab B, "US-Cuban Relations Chronology, Jan.–July 1977," Carter Library, Brzezinski Collection, Subject File, folder: "Meetings—PRC29: 8/3/77," box 24.

9. Lee Lescaze, "U.S. Allowing College Basketball Team to Go to Cuba," *WP*, March 4, 1977; "Passport Ban Dies; Americans Now Free to Travel Anywhere," *LAT*, March 19, 1977; "Last Travel Curbs Removed by Carter," *NYT*, March 10, 1977.

10. David Binder, "Carter Says Cubans May Leave Angola, Is Receptive on Ties," *NYT*, February 17, 1977.

11. "Castro Praising Carter Sees a Prospect for Ties," *NYT*, February 10, 1977; Murrey Marder, "Castro Hails U.S. 'Gesture'" *WP*, August 23, 1975.

12. Memorandum, Borg to Brzezinski, February 22, 1977, "The President's February 23 Meeting with Congressman Bingham," attachment, "Talking Points for Meeting with Congressman Bingham," Carter Library, White House Central Office Files, Subj. File Countries, CO-38 (Cuba), box CO 20, folder CO-38, 1/20/77–3/30/77.

13. "Castro Contrasts 'Idealism' of Carter and U.S. 'Reality,'" *NYT*, April 10, 1977; and Memorandum, Pastor to Brzezinski, "Cuba and the President's Meeting with Senators McGovern and Abourezk," April 20, 1977, Tab A, "President's Meeting with Senators James Abourezk and George McGovern, March 19 [*sic* (the meeting was actually in April)], 1977," Carter Library, White House Central Office Files, box 7H-4, TAI/CO-38.

14. Memorandum, Church to the President, August 12, 1977, "Visit to Cuba," Carter Library, White House Central Office Files, Subj. File Countries, CO-38 (Cuba), box CO 20, folder CO-38, 1/20/77–1/20/81 (also DDRS).

15. "Department of Agriculture Remarks and a Question-and-Answer Session with Department Employees," February 16, 1977, *PPP Carter*.

16. Ann Crittenden, "Castro Says Cuba's Role in Angola Is Not Negotiable," *NYT*, December 7, 1977. Piero Gleijeses confirms this based on Cuban archives: Gleijeses, "Moscow's Proxy? Cuba and Africa 1975–1988."

17. Pastor to Brzezinski, "President's Meeting with Senators James Abourezk and George McGovern, March 19 [*sic* (April)], 1977." Cuba offered similar assurances to Sweden, which it shared with the United States: AmEmbassy Stockholm (Smith) to State (Kissinger), Stockholm 2985, May 25, 1976, "Text of Castro Message to Palme on Angola," NARA-MD, RG 59, Central Foreign Policy Files, Electronic Telegrams, 1/1/1976–12/31/1976. Cuban vice president Carlos Rafael Rodríguez told visiting Americans on August 28, 1976, "Another Angola is unlikely." Notes of Interview with Dr. Carlos Rafael Rodríguez, provided courtesy of Abraham F. Lowenthal.

18. "Secretary Vance's News Conference of January 31," *U.S. Department of State Bulletin* 76, no. 1965 (February 21, 1977): 137–46.

19. Brzezinski interview. He was expressing skepticism to Carter as early as February: Memorandum, Brzezinski to the President, February 19, 1977, "Weekly National Security Report," DDRS.

20. CIA, "Political and Economic Impact on the US of Delay in Normalization of Relations with Cuba," April 12, 1977, NSA Cuba Collection.

21. Presidential Review Memorandum/NSC-17, Subsection on Cuba (revised version, March 11, 1977), Carter Library, Vertical File 11-35. The following discussion of the policy review is based on this document unless otherwise indicated.

22. Memorandum, Pastor to Brzezinski, "Cuba Policy-PRC Meeting," March 8, 1977, DDRS.

23. Memorandum, Luers and Lake to Vance, "March 9 PRC Meeting on Cuba," March 8, 1977, NSA Cuba Collection.

24. Todman interview.

25. Smith, *Closest of Enemies*, 105; Todman interview; Interview with Terence A. Todman, Frontline Diplomacy: The Foreign Affairs Oral History Collection, Library of Congress.

26. Smith, *Closest of Enemies*, 106–7; Todman interview.

27. Todman interview.

28. Memorandum, Brzezinski to the President, April 27, 1977, "Your Request for Comments on Senator McGovern's Memorandum on Cuba," DDRS.

29. Memorandum, Vance to the President, April 23, 1977, "Senator McGovern's Memorandum on Cuba," DDRS.

30. Todman interview.

31. Ibid.

32. The account of this meeting is from "Versión de la entrevista con el Vice-Ministro de Relaciones Exteriores de los Estados Unidos Terence Todman . . . con el Ministro de Relaciones Exteriores de Cuba Isidoro Malmierca," April 27, 1977, Ministry of Foreign Relations of Cuba, provided courtesy of Piero Gleijeses.

33. Todman interview; Luers interview; Memorandum, Pastor to Brzezinski, "Your Lunch with Senator Church: Cuba," August 1, 1977, Tab B, "US-Cuban Relations Chronology, Jan.–July 1977."

34. Todman interview; Graham Hovey, "U.S. and Cuba Reach Fishing Agreement at Talks in Havana," *NYT*, April 29, 1977.

35. "Plains, Georgia Question-and-Answer Session with Reporters," May 31, 1977, *PPP Carter*.

36. Jon Nordheimer, "Cuba Agrees to Let 84 Americans Leave with Their Families," *NYT*, August 12, 1977.

37. Abraham F. Lowenthal, "Ending the Feud with Castro's Cuba," *WP*, January 9, 1977; Pastor to Brzezinski, "Cuba and President's Meeting with Senators James Abourezk and George McGovern," April 20, 1977, and Tab A, Summary of Conversation, "President's Meeting with Senators James Abourezk and George McGovern," March 19 [*sic* (April)], 1977," Carter Library, White House Central Office Files, box 7H-4, TAI/CO-38.

38. Summary of Conversation, "President's Meeting with Senators James Abourezk and George McGovern, March 19 [*sic* (April)], 1977."

39. Memorandum, Vance to the President, April 23, 1977, "Senator McGovern's Memorandum on Cuba," DDRS. Brzezinski gave Carter similar advice: Memorandum, Brzezinski to the President, April 27, 1977, "Your Request for Comments on Senator McGovern's Memorandum on Cuba," DDRS.

40. "Senate Panel Votes to Allow Cuba to Buy U.S. Food and Medicine," *NYT*, May 11, 1977.

41. Summary of Conversation, "President's Meeting with Senators James Abourezk and George McGovern, March 19 [*sic* (April)], 1977"; Barbara Walters interview with Fidel Castro (unedited transcript), p. 10, Carter Library, White House Central Office Files, Subj. File Countries, CO-38 (Cuba), box CO 20, folder CO-38, 7/1/77 to 8/31/77.

42. Memorandum, Pastor to Brzezinski, "Your Lunch with Senator Church: Cuba," August 1, 1977.

43. Pastor interview, July 1, 2004.

44. Memorandum, Brzezinski to the President, August 5, 1977, "PRC Meeting on Cuba—August 3, 1977," DDRS.

45. Jack Nelson, "Cuba Spurns U.S. Medicine Sale as Not Enough," *LAT*, February 20, 1978.

46. Bourne interview.

47. Letter, Bourne to Todman, October 7, 1977, and attachment, Memorandum, Bourne to Pastor, October 3, 1977, "Cuba Embargo and Pharmaceutical Products," Carter Library, Special Assistant to the President: Bourne (box 32), folder: Cuba—List of Drugs 10/7/77–4/2/79; Memorandum, Pastor to Brzezinski, November 4, 1977, "The Bourne Memo-A Status Report," White House Central Office Files, Subj. File Countries, CO-38 (Cuba), box CO 20, folder CO-38, 9/1/77–12/31/77.

48. Bourne interview.

49. Memorandum, Pastor to Brzezinski, November 4, 1977, "The Bourne Memo-A Status Report"; Memorandum, Christopher to Brzezinski, December 14, 1977, "Licensing a Shipment of Medicines to Cuba," Carter Library, Special Assistant to the President: Bourne (box 32), folder: Christopher, Warren 11/16/77–12/14/77.

50. Pastor, personal communication, March 19, 2013.

51. Nelson, "Cuba Spurns U.S. Medicine Sale as Not Enough."

52. Cable, USINT (Lane) to State (Vance), Havana 2569, April 2, 1979, "Visit of U.S. Surgeon-General to Cuba," Carter Library, Special Assistant to the President: Bourne (box 32), folder: Cuba—List of Drugs 10/7/77–4/2/79.

53. Memorandum of Conversation, "US/Cuban Relations," December 2–3, 1978, DDRS.

54. David B. Ottaway, "Castro: Cubans Not Fighting in Zaire," *WP*, March 22, 1977; Gleijeses, *Visions of Freedom*, 41.

55. Sklar, *Cuba: Normalization of Relations*, Congressional Research Service Issue Brief IB75030 (1977): 18–19.

56. Gleijeses, *Visions of Freedom*, 73–76.

57. Crittenden, "Castro Says Cuba's Role in Angola Is Not Negotiable."

58. Milton R. Benjamin, "Cuba, U.S. Argue over Africa Push," *WP*, December 7, 1977.

59. Discurso pronunciado en el acto de Conmemoración del Centenario de la Protesta de Baraguá, Santiago de Cuba, 15 de Marzo de 1978, Discursos Archive. See also Castro's detailed account of the summit in the conversation with Honecker. "Transcript of Conversation between Cuban Premier Fidel Castro and East German Leader Erich Honecker, Havana, (excerpt), May 25, 1980," *Cold War International History Project Bulletin*, nos. 8–9 (Winter 1996–97): 194–207.

60. Murrey Marder, "U.S. Cautions Havana about Role in Africa," *WP*, May 26, 1977; Graham Hovey, "Cuba Military in Ethiopia Now Put at 400 by U.S., Up from 50 in May," *NYT*, November 15, 1977.

61. "Interview with the President: Remarks and a Question-and-Answer Session with a Group of Editors and News Directors," November 11, 1977, *PPP Carter*.

62. Hedrick Smith, "U.S. Sees Cuba's African Buildup Blocking Efforts to Improve Ties," *NYT*, November 17, 1977.

63. Smith interview; Smith, *Closest of Enemies*, 122–25.

64. Pastor interview, July 1, 2004.

65. Brzezinski interview.

66. Brzezinski, *Power and Principle*, 177–79.

67. Carter interview.

68. Benjamin, "Cuba, U.S. Argue over Africa Push."

69. Smith, *Closest of Enemies*, 125–26.

70. Memorandum, Tarnoff to Brzezinski, March 22, 1978, "Tom Hughes' Memorandum of Conversation on His Talk with Cuban Vice-President," Carter Library, White House Central Office Files, Subj. File Countries, CO-38 (Cuba), box CO 20, folder CO-38, 1/20/77–1/20/81 (also in DDRS).

71. Gleijeses, *Visions of Freedom*, 45.

72. Murrey Marder, "Cubans Expand Role in Ethiopia, U.S. Says," *WP*, April 1, 1978; Graham Hovey, "Brzezinski Asserts that Soviet General Leads Ethiopian Units," *NYT*, February 25, 1978.

73. Vance, *Hard Choices*, 73–74.

74. Gleijeses, *Visions of Freedom*, 47.

75. Brzezinski interview; Gleijeses, *Visions of Freedom*, 51–53.

76. Vance, *Hard Choices*, 74, 79, 87, 88.

77. Pastor interview, July 1, 2004.

78. Memorandum, Brzezinski to the President, August 5, 1977, "PRC Meeting on Cuba—August 3, 1977," DDRS; Pastor interview, July 1, 2004.

79. Smith, *Closest of Enemies*, 137; Carter interview.

80. The following account of the meeting is from Cable, USINT Havana (Lane) to State (Vance), Havana 1300, May 18, 1978, "Fidel Castro Denies Cuban Involvement in Shaba," DDRS.

81. Cable, State (Vance) to USINT Havana (Lane), State 127459, May 19, 1978, "Message for Foreign Minister Malmierca," DDRS.

82. Bernard Gwertzman, "Castro Summons a U.S. Diplomat, Denies Cuban Involvement in Zaire," *NYT*, May 19, 1978; Don Oberdorfer and Edward Walsh, "Carter Disputes Castro Account of Zaire Role," *WP*, June 14, 1978; Richard Burt, "Lesson of Shaba: Carter Risked Serious 'Credibility Gap,'" *NYT*, July 11, 1978.

83. Oberdorfer and Walsh, "Carter Disputes Castro Account"; Murrey Marder, "U.S. Keeps Options Open on Soviet-Cuban Activity," *WP*, May 20, 1978.

84. Cable, USINT Havana (Lane) to State (Vance), Havana 1346, May 20, 1978, "Response to Secretary's Message," Staff Office Files, Press Office, Powell, folder: "Cuban Troops in Zaire, 5/78–6/78," box 55.

85. Bernard Gwertzman, "Public Debate of Aides Obscures U.S. Policy," *NYT*, May 23, 1978.

86. Smith, *Closest of Enemies*, 139–40.

87. "The President's News Conference of May 25th, 1978," *PPP Carter*.

88. Sánchez-Parodi interview, May 18, 2005.

89. Salsamendi interview; Vance, *Hard Choices*, 90; Smith, *Closest of Enemies*, 140.

90. Karen DeYoung, "Carter's Charges on Zaire Role Based on 'Lies,' Cuban Tells U.N.," *WP*, May 31, 1978.

91. Karen DeYoung, "Castro Again Denies U.S. Charges Of Cuban Complicity in Zaire Raid," *WP*, June 13, 1978; Karen DeYoung, "Castro Takes His Case to U.S. Public," *WP*, June 14, 1978; Jon Nordheimer, "Castro Says Carter Was 'Deceived' on Cuban Role," *NYT*, June 13, 1978.

92. James Nelson Goodsell, "Many Relieved over Ease-Up on Accusing Castro," *Christian Science Monitor*, June 16, 1978; Burt, "Lesson of Shaba"; Karen DeYoung, "Issue of Castro's Honesty Divides Aides to Carter," *WP*, June 5, 1978; James Nelson Goodsell, "Many Doubt Carter's Claims that Cuba Trains Katangese," *Christian Science Monitor*, June 8, 1978.

93. Vance, *Hard Choices*, 90; Carter interview. Based on Cuban archives, Piero Gleijeses demonstrates conclusively that Castro was telling the truth: Gleijeses, "Truth or Credibility."

94. FBIS, "Cuba Article Analyzes Washington-Havana Rapprochement," *Latin America Daily Report*, January 28, 1994.

95. Nolan interview. Nolan and Richmond provided the White House with a detailed report of their conversation with Castro: Memorandum, Pastor to Brzezinski, January 7, 1978, "Letter to Congressman Richmond," Tab A, "Representatives Fred Richmond and Richard Nolan, Discussions with Cuban President Fidel Castro," Carter Library, White House Central Office Files, Subj. File Countries, CO-38 (Cuba), box CO 21, folder CO-38, 1/1/78–3/31/78; Crittenden, "Castro Says Cuba's Role in Angola Is Not Negotiable."

96. Nolan interview; "Representatives Fred Richmond and Richard Nolan, Discussions with Cuban President Fidel Castro."

97. Letter, Carter to Castro, November 28, 1977, Carter Library, Staff Offices, Press, Powell (box 55), folder: Cuba. Prior references are United Press International, "Cuba Seeking Trade for 'CIA Agent,'" *WP*, January 23, 1975; Barbara Walters interview with Fidel Castro (unedited transcript), p. 8, Carter Library.

98. "Representatives Fred Richmond and Richard Nolan, Discussions with Cuban President Fidel Castro."

99. Crittenden, "Castro Says Cuba's Role in Angola Is Not Negotiable."

100. Nolan interview.

101. "Representatives Fred Richmond and Richard Nolan, Discussions with Cuban President Fidel Castro"; Crittenden, "Castro Says Cuba's Role in Angola Is Not Negotiable."

102. Benjamin, "Cuba, U.S. Argue over Africa Push"; Crittenden, "Castro Says Cuba's Role in Angola Is Not Negotiable."

103. Telecon, Califano and Kissinger, June 15, 1976, 4:55 P.M., U.S. Department of State, Electronic Reading Room.

104. DeWitt Rogers and Maurice Fliess, "Coke's Austin, Castro Meet," *Atlanta Constitution*, June 10, 1977.

105. Carter, *White House Diary*, 62.

106. Louis and Yazijian, *The Cola Wars*, 285.

107. Letter, Carter to Castro, February 7, 1978, Carter Library, Brzezinski Collection, Geographical File, box 10, folder: Cuba.

108. Carter interview.

109. Carter interview; Pastor interview, October 29, 2010; Castro to Carter, February 26, 1978, Carter Library, Brzezinski Collection, Geographical File, box 10, folder: Cuba.

110. Brzezinski interview.

111. Ojito, *Finding Mañana*, 38.

112. Benes wrote a 344-page unpublished manuscript titled "3,600 Cuban Political Prisoners: My Secret Negotiations with Fidel Castro, 1977–1986," which he provided to the authors. The manuscript was later redrafted by Robert Levine and published as *Secret Missions to Cuba: Fidel Castro, Bernardo Benes, and Cuban Miami*.

113. Sánchez-Parodi interview, May 18, 2005.

114. Ojito, *Finding Mañana*, 43.

115. Benes, "3,600 Cuban Political Prisoners," 31.

116. Padrón interview.

117. Benes took copious handwritten notes of all meetings and phone conversations with Cuban and U.S. officials, which he graciously provided to the authors.

118. Benes, "3,600 Cuban Political Prisoners," 10.

119. Ibid., 14.

120. Recounted by Robert Pastor on a panel at the Brookings Institution, April 20, 2010.

121. Brzezinski interview.

122. Memorandum, Carlucci to Brzezinski, "Message from Fidel Castro," March 22, 1978, Carter Library, Geographical File, folder "Cuba, 2/78–4/78," box 10.

123. Benes describes the creation of this document in "3,600 Cuban Political Prisoners," 61–63. However, he provided Brzezinski with a more personal memorandum conveying Padrón's representations of Castro's position along with Benes's own commentary. Memo, Benes to ZB [Brzezinski], March 24, 1978, "Message from President of Cuba Fidel Castro to President Carter and/or Dr. Z.B.," DDRS.

124. Benes provided his memorandum to the authors; it is also in DDRS.

125. Benes, "3,600 Cuban Political Prisoners," 75–76.

126. Memorandum, Brzezinski to Aaron, "Cuba," March 27, 1978, DDRS.

127. Gates, *From the Shadows*, 124–25; Aaron interview.

128. Gates, *From the Shadows*, 124–25; Aaron interview; Tarnoff interview, April 29, 2004.

129. Memorandum, Aaron to Brzezinski, April 13, 1978, "Meeting with Cubans in New York," DDRS.

130. Memorandum, Brzezinski to the President, "Contact with Castro's Representative Jose Luis Padron," undated [circa July 7, 1978], DDRS.

131. Gates, *From the Shadows*, 125.

132. The Cubans' disappointment is from Tarnoff interview, April 29, 2004; and Memorandum, Dascal to Z.B. [Brzezinski], undated [circa March 24, 1978], DDRS. The date of the meeting is from Vance's appointment book. Thanks to Cesar Rodríguez, Curator, Latin American Collection, Yale University Library, for locating this in the Cyrus Vance Papers.

133. Tarnoff interview, August 10, 2007.

134. Tarnoff interview, April 29, 2004.

135. Robert Shaplen, "Profiles: Eye of the Storm III," *New Yorker*, June 16, 1980.

136. Oppenheimer, *Castro's Final Hour*, 39–40.

137. Gleijeses, *Visions of Freedom*, 107–17.

138. Newsom interview; Memorandum of Conversation, June 15, 1978, New York City, DDRS.

139. Newsom interview.

140. Ibid.

141. Memorandum, Vance to the President, June 19, 1978, "Contact with Castro's Representative Jose Luis Padron," DDRS.

142. Memorandum, Brzezinski to the President, "Contact with Castro's Representative Jose Luis Padron," undated [circa July 7, 1978].

143. Tarnoff interview, April 29, 2004.

144. Newsom interview.

145. Summary of Conversation between U.S. and Cuban Officials, July 5, 1978, Washington, D.C., DDRS.

146. Memorandum, Vance to the President, "Further Contact with Castro's Representative, Jose Luis Padron," July 7, 1978, DDRS.

147. Ibid.

148. Memorandum, Brzezinski to the President, "Contact with Castro's Representative Jose Luis Padron," undated [circa July 7, 1978], DDRS; Memorandum, Brzezinski to Vance, July 7, 1978, "Contacts with the Cubans," Carter Library, Brzezinski Collection, Subject File, folder: "Cuba—Alpha Channel: 6/78-10/78," box 10.

149. Memorandum, Brzezinski to Vance, July 13, 1978, "Discussion with Cuba," Carter Library, Brzezinski Collection, Subject File, folder: "Cuba—Alpha Channel: 6/78-10/78," box 10.

150. Memorandum, Aaron to Brzezinski, July 20, 1978, "Cuban Consultations," Carter Library, Brzezinski Collection, Subject File, folder: "Cuba—Alpha Channel: 6/78-10/78," box 10.

151. Vance, *Hard Choices*, 131.

152. Aaron interview.

153. Gleijeses, *Visions of Freedom*, 120; "Transcript of Conversation between Cuban Premier Fidel Castro and East German Leader Erich Honecker, Havana, (excerpt), May 25, 1980," *Cold War International History Project Bulletin*, nos. 8-9 (Winter 1996-97): 194-207.

154. Newsom interview.

155. Smith, *Closest of Enemies*, 149.

156. Tarnoff, Memorandum of Conversation, no subject heading, August 3, 1978, DDRS.

157. Joseph B. Treaster, "New Cuban Diplomat: At Ease in a Hot Spot," *NYT*, June 19, 1989.

158. The following account of the meeting is based on the untitled verbatim Memorandum of Conversation, August 8, 1977. NSA Cuba Collection.

159. Aaron interview.

160. Newsom interview.

161. Ibid.

162. "We were quite irritated when our comrades returned from Cuernavaca and told us that you had said, 'We are bringing some things for you but we are not going to give them to you,'" Vice President Carlos Rafael Rodríguez later complained to Peter Tarnoff. Memorandum of Conversation, December 2-3, 1978, Havana, Cuba, "U.S./Cuban Relations," DDRS.

163. This account of the meeting is based on a verbatim Memorandum of Conversation, untitled, October 28, 1968 [*sic* (actually 1978)], NSA Cuban Collection; Memorandum,

Aaron to the President, October 30, 1978, "Private Meeting with the Cubans," DDRS; and Memorandum, Christopher (Acting Secretary of State) and Brzezinski to the President, October 19, 1978, "Discussions with the Cubans," DDRS.

164. Aaron interview.

165. Van Reigersberg interview.

166. Newsom interview; Pastor interview, October 29, 2010.

167. Memorandum, Aaron to the President, October 30, 1978, "Private Meeting with the Cubans."

168. Newsom interview.

169. Summary of Conversation between U.S. and Cuban Officials, July 5, 1978, Washington, D.C., DDRS.

170. Padrón interview, November 9, 2006. The literal meaning of *philosofia boniatillo* is "sweet philosophy" but the connotation is that Benes tended to sugarcoat things, though not in a devious way. *Boniatillo* is a Cuban desert made from sweet potatoes, but in Cuban slang a *boniato* (sweet potato) is someone who is sweet and harmless.

171. "Castro Says His Regime Plans to Free 3,000 Political Prisoners," *NYT*, November 22, 1978.

172. Howell Raines, "Castro Prisoners Arrive as a Split in Exiles Rises," *NYT*, December 13, 1978. An excerpt from the agreement is in OAS Inter-American Human Rights Commission, *Sixth Report on the Situation of Political Prisoners in Cuba*, OEA/Ser.L/V/ll.48, doc. 24, December 14, 1979.

173. Levine, *Secret Missions to Cuba*, 135–39; Jacob Bernstein, "Twice Exiled Bernardo Benes Helped Free Hundreds of Cuban Political Prisoners Twenty Years Ago," *Miami New Times*, November–December 1998.

174. Frontline, "Saving Elian," transcript, http://www.pbs.org/wgbh/pages/frontline/shows/elian/etc/script.html.

175. Castro said as much to Wayne Smith, *Closest of Enemies*, 149.

176. David Binder, "Carter Aides Urge a Gesture to Cuba," *NYT*, November 12, 1978.

177. Brzezinski interview.

178. Smith, *Closest of Enemies*, 165–66.

179. Pastor interview, July 1, 2004; Newsom interview.

180. "Cuba Receives Modern MIGs," *LAT*, October 30, 1978; Don Oberdorfer, "U.S. Studies Capabilities of Migs Supplied to Cuba," *WP*, November 16, 1978. Conservative reactions: Rowland Evans and Robert Novak, "Cuba's Mig-23s," *WP*, November 15, 1978; William Safire, "The MIG's of April," *NYT*, December 4, 1978.

181. George C. Wilson, "U.S. Sends Spy Planes to Study Migs in Cuba," *WP*, November 18, 1978.

182. Smith, *Closest of Enemies*, 168.

183. Memorandum, Pastor to Brzezinski and Aaron, "The Trip to Cuba: Some Impressions," December 19, 1978, DDRS.

184. The account of the meeting with Rodríguez is from Memorandum of Conversation, December 2–3, 1978, Havana, Cuba, "U.S./Cuban Relations," DDRS.

185. Pastor interview, July 1, 2004.

186. The account of the meeting with Castro is from Memorandum of Conversation, December 3–4, 1978, Havana, Cuba, "US/Cuban Relations," DDRS.

187. Pastor interview, July 1, 2004.

188. Memorandum, Brzezinski to the President, undated [circa December 19, 1978], "Conversations in Havana," DDRS.

189. Memorandum of Conversation, December 3–4, 1978, Havana, Cuba, "US/Cuban Relations," DDRS.

190. Newsom interview.

191. John M. Goshko, "Cuba Offers U.S. a Swap of Prisoners," WP, June 14, 1978; Memorandum, Tarnoff to Brzezinski, June 20, 1978, "Authorization to Negotiate Prisoner Exchange with the Cubans," DDRS.

192. Grahman Hovey, "Final Round Is Awaited in 3-Way Prisoner Swap," NYT, April 25, 1978; Steven R. Weisman, "Congressman Seeking a Prisoner Exchange to Free Puerto Ricans," NYT, March 25, 1979.

193. Pastor interview, July 1, 2004; Memorandum, Pastor to Aaron and Brzezinski, September 26, 1978, "Lolita Lebron," DDRS.

194. Memorandum, Tarnoff to Brzezinski, May 31, 1979, "Background Paper on Cuba," NSA Cuba Collection.

195. Memorandum, Pastor to Brzezinski, July 19, 1979, "Putting the Cubes on Ice," NSA Cuba Collection.

196. Pastor interview, July 1, 2004.

197. Memorandum, Brzezinski to NSC Principals, July 26, 1979, "SCC Meeting on Cuba, July 20, 1979," DDRS.

198. Duffy, "Crisis Mangling and the Cuban Brigade," International Security 8, no. 1 (Summer 1983): 67–87.

199. Don Oberdorfer, "'Brigada': Unwelcome Sight in Cuba," WP, September 9, 1979.

200. Newsom, The Soviet Brigade in Cuba, 22; Duffy, "Crisis Mangling and the Cuban Brigade."

201. Newsom, The Soviet Brigade in Cuba, 31–34.

202. "Senator Church Charges Moscow Has a Brigade of Troops in Cuba," NYT, August 31, 1979; "2,300-Man Soviet Unit Now in Cuba," WP, August 31, 1979.

203. "Texts of Letter and Statements by Vance and Carter," NYT, September 6, 1979.

204. Don Oberdorfer, "Vance: Status Quo Unacceptable to U.S.," WP, September 6, 1979; Vance, Hard Choices, 362.

205. David Binder, "Data Long Implied Soviet Units in Cuba," NYT, September 6, 1979.

206. Newsom, The Soviet Brigade in Cuba, 42–46.

207. Duffy, "Crisis Politics," 201.

208. Brzezinski interview.

209. Memorandum, Brzezinski to the President, September 13, 1979, "NSC Weekly Report #109," Carter library, Brzezinski Collection, NSC Weekly Reports.

210. Letter, Carter to Brezhnev, September 25, 1979, DDRS.

211. Brezhnev's letter is detailed in Don Oberdorfer, "A Message from Moscow: Don't Look for Help on Cuba," WP, October 3, 1979; "Peace and National Security Address to the Nation on Soviet Combat Troops in Cuba and the Strategic Arms Limitation Treaty," October 1, 1979, PPP Carter.

212. Smith, Closest of Enemies, 186–87.

213. Ibid., 182–86.

214. "Ford Urges Immediate Soviet Withdrawal of Troops in Cuba," *LAT*, September 9, 1979.

215. Castro interview. He also told Tarnoff and Pastor that the brigade was left over from the missile crisis. Memorandum of Conversation, "Talks with Fidel Castro," January 17, 1980, DDRS.

216. Pastor, panel presentation, "U.S.-Cuba Dialogue," 2010 Congress of the Latin American Studies Association, Toronto, Canada, and Pastor interview, July 1, 2004.

217. FBIS, "Castro Comments to Newsmen on Presence of Soviet Troops," *Latin America Daily Report*, January 10, 1979.

218. Presidential Directive/NSC-52, October 4, 1979, "U.S. Policy toward Cuba," Carter Library, Vertical File, Presidential Directives.

219. Pastor interview, July 1, 2004; Memorandum, Tarnoff to Brzezinski, October 19, 1979, "Follow-Up on Presidential Directive on Cuba," and attachment 4, U.S. State Department paper "A Strategy to Counter Cuba's Ambitions as Leader of the NAM and to Preclude Cuba's Getting a Security Council Seat or Hosting UNCTAD VI," NSA Cuba Collection.

220. Karen DeYoung, "Cuba Dealt Setback in Third World," *WP*, January 11, 1980.

221. Pastor interview, July 14, 2009.

222. Carter, *White House Diary*, 391; Pastor, personal communication, March 19, 2013.

223. Memorandum of Conversation, January 16–17, 1980, "Talks with Fidel Castro," DDRS. This account of the meeting is based on this transcript except as otherwise indicated.

224. Tarnoff interview, April 29, 2004.

225. "You hope . . . to create a core of dissidents," a Cuban official charged. Smith, *Closest of Enemies*, 200.

226. Tarnoff interview, April 29, 2004.

227. Brzezinski interview.

228. Mesa-Lago, "The Economy," 113–67; Eckstein, *Back from the Future*, 50–55.

229. Pedraza, *Political Disaffection in Cuba's Revolution and Exodus*, 152, 165, 219.

230. Smith, *Closest of Enemies*, 200–201.

231. Ibid., 202–3; Cable, USINT Havana (Smith) to State (Vance), Havana 1641, February 20, 1980, "Cuban Complaints of Provocative U.S. Actions," NSA Cuba Collection.

232. Discurso en la Clausura del III Congreso de la Federación de Mujeres Cubanas el 8 de Marzo de 1980, Discursos Archive.

233. U.S. House of Representatives, Permanent Select Committee on Intelligence, Subcommittee on Oversight, *The Cuban Emigres: Was There a U.S. Intelligence Failure?*, Staff Report, 2.

234. Smith, *Closest of Enemies*, 204–5.

235. Sklar, "Cuban Exodus 1980," 339–47.

236. Smith, *Closest of Enemies*, 207.

237. "Statement by the Revolutionary Government of Cuba," *Granma Weekly Review*, April 13, 1980. The statement ran in the domestic edition of the paper on April 4.

238. Wayne Smith's conversations with Cuban officials, in Smith, *Closest of Enemies*, 208.

239. Lexie Verdon, "Thousands in Cuba Ask Peruvian Refuge," *WP*, April 7, 1980.

240. "Cuba Gives Food, Water to Thousands at Peru's Embassy," *WP*, April 8, 1980.

241. Quoted in Palmieri, "An Act of War," chap. 5:76.

242. "Caribbean/Central American Action Remarks at a White House Reception," April 9, 1980, *PPP Carter*.

243. *Granma*, April 10, quoted in Palmieri, "An Act of War," chap. 5:54.

244. "Cuba Suspends Refugee Flights," *WP*, April 19, 1980; Marlise Simons, "Cuba Approves Refugees' Departure in Florida-Chartered Flotilla of Boats," *WP*, April 22, 1980; John M. Goshko, "State Dept. Seeks to Halt Sealift," *WP*, April 24, 1980.

245. Palmieri, "An Act of War," chap. 7:18.

246. Ibid., chap. 7:27–32.

247. Smith, *Closest of Enemies*, 217–27; Marlise Simons, "Cuban Group Attacks 800 Seeking U.S. Visas," *WP*, May 3, 1980.

248. Smith, *Closest of Enemies*, 215; Marlise Simons, "Cuba Sees Opportunity to Pressure U.S.," *WP*, May 8, 1980.

249. "Cuban Refugees Remarks to Reporters Announcing Administration Policy toward the Refugees," May 14, 1980, *PPP Carter*.

250. "Cuba Rejects 3-Nation Bid for Talks on Refugee Crisis," *WP*, May 23, 1980. On the bilateral approach, see Memorandum, Muskie to the President, May 24, 1980, "Cuba," Carter Library, Plains File, box 40.

251. Memorandum of Conversation, June 17–18, 1980, DDRS.

252. Brzezinski interview.

253. Smith, *Closest of Enemies*, 215–16.

254. Memorandum of Conversation, June 17–18, 1980, DDRS.

255. Smith interview, September 10, 2004.

256. Pastor, personal communication, March 3, 2013. Arbesú later told Pastor that he had shared Pastor's comment with Castro.

257. Memorandum of Conversation, June 17–18, 1980, DDRS.

258. Draft memorandum for the President, from Tarnoff and Pastor through Edmund S. Muskie and Zbigniew Brzezinski, June 18, 1980, "Cuban Discussions, June 17, 1980 — Summary and Next Steps," DDRS.

259. Pastor interview, July 1, 2004.

260. Ibid, July 1, 2004.

261. Smith, *Closest of Enemies*, 232; Cable, USINT (Smith) to State (Muskie), Havana 5217, July 3, 1980, "Call on Rafael Rodríguez," DDRS.

262. Smith, *Closest of Enemies*, 232.

263. Rodríguez comment to Saul Landau. Landau interview, August 29, 2006.

264. Donald P. Baker and Ronald D. White, "Va. GOP Confident at Campaign Rally," *WP*, September 14, 1980.

265. Brzezinski interview.

266. Tarnoff interview, April 29, 2004.

267. Smith, *Closest of Enemies*, 234.

268. Carter, *White House Diary*, 465.

269. Tarnoff interview, April 29, 2004.

270. Carter interview.

271. Ibid.

272. Memorandum, Pastor to Brzezinski, January 7, 1978, "Letter to Congressman Richmond," Tab A, "Representatives Fred Richmond and Richard Nolan, Discussions with Cuban President Fidel Castro."

273. Memorandum of Conversation, December 3–4, 1978, Havana, Cuba, "US/Cuban Relations."

274. The phrase is Carter's, from "Address at Commencement Exercises at the University of Notre Dame, May 22, 1977," *PPP Carter*.

275. Carter interview.

Chapter Six

1. Haig, *Caveat*, 120–22, 125; Reagan and Novak, *My Turn*, 242.

2. Weinberger, *Fighting for Peace*, 26–31.

3. LeoGrande, *Our Own Backyard*, 68–69.

4. Adam Clymer, "Reagan Suggests Blockade of Cuba on Soviets' Move into Afghanistan," *NYT*, January 28, 1980.

5. Reagan, *The Reagan Diaries*, 4.

6. U.S. Department of State, "Soviet Bloc Assistance to Nicaragua and Cuba versus U.S. Assistance to Central America," *Latin America Dispatch*, October 1987. On Cuba's strategy, see Barnes, Waters, and Koppel, *Making History: Interviews with Four Generals of Cuba's Revolutionary Armed Forces*, 45, 75.

7. Smith, "Dateline Havana," 157–74; Smith, *Closest of Enemies*, 242.

8. Haig, *Inner Circles*, 132; Levine, *Secret Missions to Cuba*, 150.

9. Haig, *Caveat*, 133.

10. Michael Getler, "Bush Urges the Sandinistas to Reject Totalitarian Rule," *WP*, November 17, 1981.

11. Leslie H. Gelb, "Haig Is Said to Press for Military Options," *NYT*, November 5, 1981. Haig's 1963 plans are described in Hersh, *The Price of Power*, 56.

12. John M. Goshko, "U.S., Accusing Castro of Lying to Populace, Plans New Radio to 'Tell the Truth' to Cuba," *WP*, September 24, 1981; Shirley Christian, "Reagan Has Few Options with Cuba," *MH*, September 20, 1981.

13. Smith, *Closest of Enemies*, 245; Cable, USINT (Smith) to State, "Cuban Interest in Negotiations," Havana 4409, July 3, 1982, NSA Cuba Collection.

14. Smith, *Closest of Enemies*, 249–50.

15. Rozental interview.

16. "Transcript of Meeting between U.S. Secretary of State Alexander M. Haig, Jr., and Cuban Vice Premier Carlos Rafael Rodríguez, Mexico City, 23 November 1981," *Cold War International History Project Bulletin*, nos. 8–9 (Winter 1996–1997): 207–15.

17. Alfonso Chardy, "Cuba's Canny Old Communist," *MH*, December 18, 1983. Haig's account of the meeting is in *Caveat*, 133–36.

18. Kornbluh, "A 'Moment of Rapprochement': The Haig-Rodríguez Secret Talks," *Cold War International History Project Bulletin*, nos. 8–9 (Winter 1996–1997): 217–19.

19. Haig, *Caveat*, 136–37.

20. Smith, *Closest of Enemies*, 254.

21. Ibid., 254–56.

22. López Portillo's speech is in Bagley, Alvarez, and Hagedorn, *Contadora and the Central American Peace Process*, 101–2.

23. Alan Riding, "Mexicans Pessimistic on Talks between U.S. and Caribbean Leftists," *NYT*, May 10, 1982; Bernard Gwertzman, "Haig Is Cautious about Any Accord with Nicaraguans," *NYT*, March 16, 1982.

24. "Draft Talking Points: Approach to Cuba," February 27, 1982, NSA Cuba Collection.

25. Walters, *The Mighty and the Meek*, 150–51.

26. Ibid., 153–54; Haig, *Caveat*, 136–37; Chardy, "Cuba's Canny Old Communist."

27. "Draft Talking Points: Approach to Cuba," February 27, 1982, NSA Cuba Collection.

28. Chardy, "Cuba's Canny Old Communist."

29. Walters, *The Mighty and the Meek*, 156–57.

30. Smith, *Closest of Enemies*, 256–60; Riding, "Mexicans Pessimistic on Talks between U.S. and Caribbean Leftists"; Alan Riding, "Diplomats Say Havana Wants Wide U.S. Talks," *NYT*, March 26, 1982.

31. Rodríguez interview, April 3, 1982. Published accounts of the interview, in which LeoGrande participated, are in Bialer and Stepan, "Cuba, the United States, and the Central American Mess," *New York Review of Books*, May 27, 1982; and Leslie H. Gelb, "Cuban Calls for Talks with the U.S. and Accepts Part Blame for Strains," *NYT*, April 6, 1982.

32. Smith, *Closest of Enemies*, 258.

33. Memorandum, from Haig to the President, "Assessment of Fidel Castro's April 4 Speech and the Leslie Gelb *New York Times* Interview," April 20, 1982, NSA Cuba Collection.

34. Richard J. Meislin, "Main Air Link between U.S. and Cuba Is Stopped," *NYT*, April 17, 1982; "Treasury Rules Seek to End Most Travel from U.S. to Cuba," *Wall Street Journal*, April 20, 1982; "Second Step for U.S. Economic Pressure on Cuba Likely to Be Disclosed in Weeks," *Wall Street Journal*, April 21, 1982; AP, "Cuba Replaces Iraq on U.S. Terrorist List," *MH*, February 27, 1982.

35. CIA, Directorate of Intelligence, "Cuba: Tactics and Strategy for Central America [redacted]; An Intelligence Assessment," August 1982, DDRS.

36. Gerald F. Seib, "White House Begins Stressing Negotiations in Wake of Tough Central America Stand," *Wall Street Journal*, April 12, 1982.

37. Smith, *Closest of Enemies*, 260.

38. "Remarks on Central America and El Salvador at the Annual Meeting of the National Association of Manufacturers," March 10, 1983, *PPP Reagan*.

39. FBIS, "Fidel Castro's Press Conference on Grenada," *Latin America Daily Report*, October 26, 1983.

40. Ferch interview. The full text of the U.S. note is in FBIS, "Fidel Castro's Press Conference on Grenada."

41. Ferch interview; Cable, USINT (Ferch) to State, "Cuban Reaction to Latest US Note— Great Bitterness," Havana 6643, October 26, 1983, DDRS.

42. FBIS, "Fidel Castro's Press Conference on Grenada."

43. The text of the Cuban note is in FBIS, "Fidel Castro's Press Conference on Grenada." Ferch's account of the conversation is in Cable, USINT (Ferch) to State, "Castro Responds to USG Approach," USINT 6636, October 26, 1983, DDRS.

44. Alma Guillermoprieto, "Cuba Says Accord Reached for Return of Prisoners," *WP*, October 30, 1983; Richard J. Meslin, "As Grenada Exodus Begins, Havana Counts 27 Deaths, at Most," *NYT*, November 5, 1983.

45. Haig, *Inner Circles*, 137.

46. Smith, *Closest of Enemies*, 236.

47. Skoug, *The United States and Cuba*, 6–7.

48. Smith, *Closest of Enemies*, 263.

49. Guillermo Martinez, "New Proposal on Return of Criminals," *MH*, January 10, 1983. On linkage, see Skoug, *The United States and Cuba*, 10.

50. "Cuba Offers Talks on Return of 'Undesirables,'" *NYT*, June 28, 1983.

51. Bernard Gwertzman, "U.S. Bids Cuba Take Several Thousand of Its Exiles Back," *NYT*, May 26, 1983.

52. Skoug, *The United States and Cuba*, 11–13.

53. "Cuba Offers Talks on Return of 'Undesirables,'" *NYT*, June 28, 1983.

54. "Cuba Is Open to Talks on Ties with U.S.," *NYT*, June 17, 1983.

55. Cable, USINT (Ferch) to State, "Cubans Defer Reply to Proposal for Talks Regarding Marielitos," Havana 1628, March 27, 1984; Memorandum, from Burkhardt and Menges to McFarlane, "Possible Talks with Cuba on Mariel Excludables," May 2, 1984, NSA Cuba Collection; Robert C. Toth, "Cuba Agrees to Refugee Talks," *LAT*, June 16, 1984.

56. Skoug, *The United States and Cuba*, 59–60.

57. Faw and Sketton, *Thunder in America*, 82–83; Gerald M. Boyd, "Castro, after Talks with Jackson, Frees 22 Jailed Americans," *NYT*, June 27, 1984.

58. Gerald M. Boyd, "Jackson Lobbies for Latin Talks," *NYT*, June 30, 1984; Francis X. Clines, "Regan Contends Jackson's Missions May Violate Law," *NYT*, July 5, 1984; Lee May, "Administration Snubs Jackson," *LAT*, June 30, 1984.

59. Skoug, *The United States and Cuba*, 63–64.

60. Alarcón interview, May 20, 2005.

61. Skoug, *The United States and Cuba*, 65–67.

62. Ibid., 67.

63. Carl J. Migdial, "Why Castro Now Wants to Deal with U.S.," *U.S. News & World Report*, July 30, 1984, 47.

64. Discurso Pronunciado en el Acto Central por el XXXI Aniversario del Asalto al Cuartel Moncada, July 26, 1984, Discursos Archive.

65. "Shultz Assails Jackson's Criticism Abroad," *WP*, July 1, 1984.

66. Skoug, "Cuba as a Model and a Challenge, July 25, 1984," U.S. Department of State, *Current Policy*, no. 600, September 1984.

67. Skoug, *The United States and Cuba*, 70, 73; Joseph B. Treaster, "Radio Martí Goes on Air and Cuba Retaliates by Ending Pact," *NYT*, May 21, 1985.

68. Skoug, *The United States and Cuba*, 74–75.

69. Alarcón interview, May 20, 2005.

70. Van Reigersberg interview.

71. Skoug, *The United States and Cuba*, 75–77.

72. William R. Long, "Talks Open 'Possibility of Understanding,'" *WP*, December 15, 1984.

73. Fidel Castro, "The U.S.-Cuban Accord on Migratory Relations," in Taber, *War and Crisis in the Americas*, 38–56.

74. Ferch interview.

75. Joanne Omang, "Democratic Party Urged to Convene Hemispheric Meeting, Invite Cuba," *WP*, January 24, 1985; Joel Brinkley, "Two in Congress, Reporting on Cuba Trip, Urge Talks," *NYT*, January 31, 1985.

76. Leonard Downie Jr. and Karen DeYoung, "Cuban Leader Sees Positive Signs for Ties in Second Reagan Term," *WP*, February 3, 1985.

77. Skoug, "The United States and Cuba, December 17, 1984," U.S. Department of State *Current Policy*, no. 646, February 1985.

78. Skoug, *The United States and Cuba*, 78; "Transcript of Interview with President on a Range of Issues," *NYT*, February 12, 1985.

79. Skoug, *The United States and Cuba*, 87–93; Castro gives a similar account of these topics in FBIS, "Fidel Castro Interview with PBS' MacNeil," *Latin America Daily Report*, February 20, 1985, 12–13.

80. Skoug, *The United States and Cuba*, 96–98.

81. AP, "Cuba May Use Radio to Retaliate," *Chicago Tribune*, August 20, 1982.

82. Reagan, *The Reagan Diaries*, 287.

83. Skoug, *The United States and Cuba*, 87.

84. Edward Cody, "Cuba Revises View of U.S.," *WP*, June 5, 1985.

85. Stone, "Cuban Clout," *National Journal*, February 20, 1993, 449–53; Menges, *Inside the National Security Council*, 219.

86. Joseph B. Treaster, "After a Brief Warming, U.S.-Cuban Ties Cool Anew," *NYT*, August 20, 1985.

87. Skoug, *The United States and Cuba*, 104–5; Ferch interview.

88. Castro is quoted in Cody, "Cuba Revises View of U.S."; "Remarks at the Annual Convention of the American Bar Association," July 8, 1985, *PPP Reagan*.

89. Edward Cody, "Castro Calls Reagan 'Liar,' 'Worst Terrorist,'" *WP*, July 10, 1985; Treaster, "After a Brief Warming."

90. Skoug, *The United States and Cuba*, 113, 122.

91. Ibid., 122–24.

92. Ibid., 124–25.

93. Downie and DeYoung, "Cuban Leader Sees Positive Signs for Ties in Second Reagan Term."

94. Julia Preston, "Cuban-U.S. Ties Termed Worst in Decades," *WP*, April 19, 1987; Joseph B. Treaster, "Downward Spiral for U.S.-Cuba Ties," *NYT*, May 2, 1987; Joseph B. Treaster, "Americans in Cuba Accused of Spying," *NYT*, July 16, 1987.

95. Skoug, *The United States and Cuba*, 141–46.

96. Ibid. 166–69; Cable from USINT (Taylor) to State, September 22, 1987, Havana 03430, NSA Cuba Collection.

97. Skoug, *The United States and Cuba*, 170–72.

98. Ibid. 175.

99. Joseph B. Treaster, "U.S. Ties with Cuba in Warming Trend," *NYT*, October 4, 1987. The Cubans were explicit in their expectation that concessions on migration would lead to their admission to the talks on southern Africa. Cable from USINT (Taylor) to State, "Castro's Conflicting Objectives," November 28, 1987, Havana 04414, NSA Cuba Collection.

100. Memorandum, Haig to the President, "Summing up Pik Botha Visit," May 20, 1981, DDRS.

101. Crocker describes his strategy in *High Noon*, 58–70.

102. Ibid., 101–2, 141–42, 151, 163.

103. Ibid., 175.

104. Ferch interview.

105. Edward Cody, "Cuba Eyeing Withdrawal of Troops from Angola," *WP*, March 13, 1984.

106. Castro described these exchanges to Angolan President José Eduardo dos Santos on July 31, 1987. "Conversaciones oficiales del Comandante en Jefe Fidel Castro . . . con José Eduardo dos Santos," from the archive of the Cuban armed forces, WWC Cuba and Southern Africa Collection.

107. Crocker, *High Noon*, 204; Ferch interview.

108. Crocker, *High Noon*, 204, 211–12.

109. Gleijeses, *Visions of Freedom*, 13, 279–85.

110. Crocker, *High Noon*, 224; Shultz, *Turmoil and Triumph*, 114–16.

111. For a detailed review of these events, see Gleijeses, *Visions of Freedom*, 251–56, 262–78.

112. Jim Hoagland, "Castro Outlines Goals in Africa," *WP*, February 6, 1985; FBIS, "President Fidel Castro's Remarks at the Isle of Youth's School for Namibian Youths," *Latin America Daily Report*, May 30, 1985.

113. The feeler and the U.S. reply are detailed in "Conversaciones oficiales del Comandante en Jefe Fidel Castro . . . con José Eduardo dos Santos," WWC Cuba and Southern Africa Collection, and Crocker, *High Noon*, 355–58.

114. Gunn, "Cuba and Angola," 121–52.

115. Gleijeses, *Visions of Freedom*, 391–92.

116. Cable from State (Abrams) to USINT (Taylor), Official/Informal, October 14, 1987, State 319310, NSA Cuba Collection.

117. "Proposición para la apertura por los angolanos de la sesión de miércoles," from the archive of the Central Committee of the Cuban Communist Party, WWC Cuba and Southern Africa Collection. See also Gleijeses, *Visions of Freedom, 390*.

118. Crocker, *High Noon*, 360–61.

119. Cable from USINT (Taylor) to State (Abrams), Official/Informal, October 20, 1987, Havana 03839; and Cable from USINT (Taylor) to State (Abrams), "U.S.-Cuban Relations and Other Issues," September 28, 1987, Havana 03534, NSA Cuba Collection.

120. Cable from USINT (Taylor) to State (Skoug), Official/Informal, September 25, 1987, Havana 03509, NSA Cuba Collection; Cable from USINT (Taylor) to State (Abrams), "Cuba and Angola," October 1, 1987, Havana 03581, NSA Cuba Collection.

121. Cable from USINT (Taylor) to State (Abrams), "U.S.-Cuban Relations and Other Issues," September 28, 1987, Havana 03534; and Cable from State (Skoug) to USINT (Taylor), Official Informal No. 43, October 2, 1987, State 307785, NSA Cuba Collection.

122. Taylor interview; Text of oral interview with John J. "Jay" Taylor, Frontline diplomacy: Foreign Affairs Oral History Collection, Library of Congress.

123. "Reunión de análisis de la situación de las tropas cubanas en la RPA, November 15, 1987," archive of the Cuban armed forces, WWC Cuba and Southern Africa Collection, quoted in Gleijeses, *Visions of Freedom, 392*.

124. Gleijeses, *Visions of Freedom*, 391–92.

125. Cable from USINT (Taylor) to State (Stu Lippe), Official/Informal No. 1063, October 28, 1987, Havana 04020, NSA Cuba Collection.

126. Skoug, *The United States and Cuba*, 173; Crocker, *High Noon*, 362.

127. Cable from USINT (Taylor) to State (Skoug), "Alarcon on Angola," November 12, 1987. Havana 04204, NSA Cuba Collection.

128. Taylor interview; Text of oral interview with John J. "Jay" Taylor.

129. "Entrevista del compañero Jorge Risquet con el señor John Taylor, jefe de la SINA, 25 de diciembre, 1987," from the archives of the Central Committee of the Communist Party of Cuba, WWC Cuba and Southern Africa Collection.

130. Taylor interview; Text of oral interview with John J. "Jay" Taylor.

131. Crocker, *High Noon*, 374, 377–79.

132. The most detailed account of these meetings, based on extensive archival work, is Gleijeses, *Visions of Freedom*. Many of the Cuban delegation's summaries of these meetings, obtained by Gleijeses, are in the WWC Cuba and Southern Africa Collection. See also Crocker, *High Noon*, 392–93.

133. Taylor interview; Howard W. French, "Cuban's Exit Hints at Trouble at Top," *NYT*, September 27, 1992.

134. Crocker, *High Noon*, 400, 405, 499–501.

135. Quoted in Gleijeses, "A History Worthy of Pride."

136. Crocker, *High Noon*, 402–8.

137. Ibid., 441.

138. Paul Lewis, "Angola and Namibia Accords Signed," *NYT*, December 23, 1988; Crocker, *High Noon*, 445–46.

139. Pavlov, *Soviet-Cuban Alliance*, 220.

140. Taylor interview; Text of oral interview with John J. "Jay" Taylor.

141. Taylor interview; Text of oral interview with John J. "Jay" Taylor.

142. AP, "No Thaw with Cuba, Baker Says; Confidential Memo Sent to U.S. Diplomats," *MH*, March 29, 1989.

143. Text of oral interview with John J. "Jay" Taylor.

144. Ibid.

145. Taylor interview; Text of oral interview with John J. "Jay" Taylor.

146. Baker, *Politics of Diplomacy*, 51; Beschloss and Talbot, *At the Highest Levels*, 57.

147. Beschloss and Talbot, *At the Highest Levels*, 57, 61–62; Baker, *Politics of Diplomacy*, 58–59, 81; Oberdorfer, *The Turn*, 338–39.

148. "Notes of Main Content of Conversation between MSGorbachev and FCastro, April 3–5, 1989," NSA Cuba Collection. This Russian-language Memorandum of Conversation was obtained from the Gorbachev Foundation Archive in Moscow and has never before been translated.

149. "Notes of Main Content of Conversation between MSGorbachev and FCastro, April 3–5, 1989."

150. Soviet Memorandum of Conversation, "The Malta Summit Meeting," December 2, 1989, in Savranskaya, Blanton, and Zubok, *Masterpieces of History*, 630, 631.

151. Memorandum of Conversation, "First Restricted Bilateral Session with Chairman Gorbachev of Soviet Union," December 2, 1989, NSA Cuba Collection.

152. Beschloss and Talbot, *At the Highest Levels*, 156; Soviet Memorandum of Conversation, "The Malta Summit Meeting," December 2, 1989; Memorandum of Conversation, "First Restricted Bilateral Session with Chairman Gorbachev of Soviet Union," December 2, 1989.

153. Bush, *All the Best*, 446–47; Beschloss and Talbot, *At the Highest Levels*, 156.

154. Gorbachev, *Memoirs*, 512–13.

155. Skoug, *The United States and Cuba*, 202.

156. Joseph B. Treaster, "Cubans Are Curious to See U.S. TV," *NYT*, February 21, 1989.

157. Text of oral interview with John J. "Jay" Taylor.

158. Armstrong interview, November 12, 2004; Taylor interview.

159. Text of oral interview with John J. "Jay" Taylor.

160. The account of García Almeida's meeting is from Taylor and Armstrong (November 12, 2004) interviews.

161. Lee Hockstader, "Castro Calls TV Martí 'Outrage,'" *WP*, April 4, 1990; Armstrong interview, November 12, 2004.

162. U.S. GAO, *Broadcasts to Cuba: TV Martí Surveys are Flawed*, August 1990.

163. Taylor interview; Text of oral interview with John J. "Jay" Taylor.

164. David Dahl, "Bipartisan Caucuses Formed to Pressure Cuba for Freedom," *St. Petersburg Times*, March 1, 1990; Laura Parker, "For Miami's Cubans, New Hope of Going Home," *WP*, April 15, 1990.

165. Latell, *After Fidel*, 239.

166. Morley and McGillion, *Unfinished Business*, 24.

167. Taylor interview; Text of oral interview with John J. "Jay" Taylor.

168. Howard W. French, "Soviets' Disorder Is Felt by Cubans," *NYT*, September 3, 1991.

169. Gorbachev, *Memoirs*, 542; Beschloss and Talbot, *At the Highest Levels*, 179, 225; Pavlov, *Soviet-Cuban Alliance*, 215.

170. Gorbachev, *Memoirs*, 513, 542; Pavlov, *Soviet-Cuban Alliance*, 214.

171. Mervyn J. Bain, "Cuba-Soviet Relations in the Gorbachev Era," *Journal of Latin American Studies* 37 (2005): 769–91.

172. Baker, *Politics of Diplomacy*, 526–29.

173. Pavlov, *Soviet-Cuban Alliance*, 234–35.

174. Thomas L. Friedman, "Gorbachev Says He's Ready to Pull Troops Out of Cuba and End Castro's Subsidies," *NYT*, September 12, 1991.

175. "Cuba Will Never Let Itself Be Turned Over or Sold Out to the United States," *Granma Weekly Review*, September 14, 1991.

176. Fidel says as much in Discurso Pronunciado en el Acto Central por el XXX Aniversario del Triunfo de la Revolución, el 4 de Enero de 1989, Discursos Archive.

177. Pavlov, *Soviet-Cuban Alliance*, 173.

178. "Message on Cuban Independence Day," May 20th, 1991, *PPP GHW Bush*.

Chapter Seven

1. Styron interview, December 8, 2008.

2. Armstrong interviews, November 12, 2004, November 28, 2011.

3. Branch, *The Clinton Tapes*, 346.

4. Morley and McGillion, *Unfinished Business*, 47.

5. Center for Responsive Politics, *The Cuban Connection: Cuban-American Money in U.S. Elections, 1979–2000*.

6. Jeffrey H. Birnbaum, "Cuban-American Contributors Open Checkbooks after Torricelli Exhibits Anti-Castro Fervor," *Wall Street Journal*, August 3, 1992; Paul Anderson and Christopher Marquis, "N.J. Congressman Makes Castro's Demise His Crusade," *MH*, February 2, 1992.

7. Robert Torricelli, "How a Few Days Changed My Life—and Castro's," *Newark Star-Ledger*, August 6, 2006.

8. Anderson and Marquis, "N.J. Congressman Makes Castro's Demise His Crusade."

9. Cliff Durand, "Cuba Slips into the Third World," *Baltimore Sun*, March 7, 1994; Wayne S. Smith, "Washington's Costly Cuba Policy," *Nation*, July 3, 2000.

10. Jennifer W. Macdonald, "Putting the Squeeze on Castro," *Journal of Commerce*, June 22, 1992.

11. Peter H. Stone, "Cuban Clout," *National Journal*, February 20, 1993.

12. Morley and McGillion, *Unfinished Business*, 51.

13. Moreno, Ilcheva, and Flores, "The Hispanic Vote in Florida," 251–70.

14. John M. Goshko, "Controversy Erupts on Latin America Post," *WP*, January 23, 1993; Mimi Whitefield and Christopher Marquis, "Cuban Concerns May Threaten Lawyer's Shot at Top Latin Post," *Journal of Commerce*, January 21, 1993.

15. Susan Benesch, "Cuban Community in Miami Strongly Opposes 'Outsider' for Post," *St. Petersburg Times* (Florida), January 28, 1993.

16. Goshko, "Controversy Erupts on Latin America Post."

17. Watson interview.

18. Feinberg interview.

19. Memorandum, Rick Nuccio to AW, "Cuba Hearing" August 1, 1993, NSA Cuba Collection.

20. Richard A. Nuccio, "Non-budgetary Policy Initiatives in the First 100 Days," October 28, 1992, NSA Cuba Collection.

21. Ibid., 3.

22. Clifton Wharton, "Forging a True Partnership of the Americas," *U.S. Department of State Dispatch* 4, no. 18 (May 3, 1993): 305.

23. Christopher Marquis, "U.S. Policy toward Cuba Is Softening Despite Denials," *MH*, August 12, 1993; Carlos Batista, "Drugs: Cuba and U.S. Join Forces against Drug-Traffickers," *Inter Press Service*, June 26, 1993.

24. Feinberg interview.

25. Mimi Whitefield, "Cuba Taking Pains Not to Rap Clinton," *MH*, May 10, 1993.

26. Chuck Clark, "Threats to Invade Cuba from Florida Prompt State Department Crackdown," *Florida Sun Sentinel*, June 10, 1993.

27. Larry Rohter, "U.S. and Cuba Team Up against a Pilot," *NYT*, August 6, 1993.

28. Mimi Whitefield, "Doctors to Tackle Cuba Eye Disease," *MH*, May 20, 1993; Sandra Jacobs, "A Mystery Solved: Cuban Eye Disease Tied to Cigars, Bad Diet," *Philadelphia Inquirer*, November 12, 1995.

29. Mimi Whitefield, "U.S. Relaxes Rules on Travel to Cuba for Certain Groups," *MH*, August 7, 1993.

30. Stephen Holmes, "U.S. Studies Expansion Of Phone Links to Cuba," *NYT*, May 29, 1993.

31. Douglas Farah, "U.S.-Cuban Ties: Slight Warming but Both Sides Doubt Massive Shift," *WP*, July 31, 1993; John Rice, "Crisis-Ridden Cuba Hopes for Better Relations," AP, August 5, 1993.

32. Howard W. French, "Cuba Gives U.S. Two Drug Suspects," *NYT*, September 20, 1993.

33. Larry Rohter, "U.S. Pact to Return Inmates to Havana Alarms Emigres," *NYT*, September 30, 1993.

34. "Castro May Weigh Ceding Power to End Embargo," *NYT*, March 7, 1993.

35. "Castro Seeks Talks with Washington," *Independent* (London), August 12, 1993.

36. Feinberg interview.

37. Ibid.

38. Memorandum, Rick Nuccio to Alexander F. Watson, "Reactions to Peters' Memo on 'Cuba Speech,'" August 29, 1993, NSA Cuba Collection.

39. Handwritten note, Watson to Nuccio, undated, NSA Cuba Collection.

40. Cuban Democracy Act, United States Code, Title 22, Foreign Relations and Intercourse, Chapter 69.

41. Author email exchange with Richard Nuccio, December 11, 2011.

42. Handwritten note, Watson to Nuccio, undated, NSA Cuba Collection.

43. Draft memorandum, "Seizing the Initiative to Promote a Soft Landing," no names, no date, NSA Cuba Collection.

44. CIA, Director of Central Intelligence, "Cuba: The Outlook for Castro and Beyond," August 1993, NIE 93-30, p. 1. This document was first declassified in July 2001 under the FOIA to Peter Kornbluh.

45. Ibid., 11.

46. Rick Nuccio to AW [Watson], "Cuba Hearing" August 1, 1993, NSA Cuba Collection.

47. Phil Peters to Alexander F. Watson, "Cuba Speech," August 27, 1993, NSA Cuba Collection.

48. Memorandum Rick Nuccio to Alexander F. Watson, "Reactions to Peters' Memo on 'Cuba Speech,'" August 29, 1993, NSA Cuba Collection.

49. U.S. House of Representatives, Committee on Foreign Affairs, Joint Hearing, *U.S. Policy and the Future of Cuba*, November 18, 1993, 17.

50. Dennis Hays to Alec Watson, "Small Group Meeting," no date (circa Sept. 1993), NSA Cuba Collection.

51. Ibid.

52. The development of these plans is described in a State Department memorandum to the files, "Contingency Plan Guide," June 20, 1995, NSA Cuba Collection.

53. Nuccio to Dennis Hays, Michael Skol, and Alexander F. Watson, "A Strategy for Broadening the Support for Administration Cuba Policy," May 26, 1994, NSA Cuba Collection.

54. Ibid.

55. Dennis Hays through Ambassador Skol to Alexander F. Watson, "Cuba Policy," no date, but states it is in response to Nuccio's memorandum of May 26, 1994, as Watson requested. NSA Cuba Collection.

56. Ibid.

57. Berger interview.

58. Feinberg to Watson, "Cuba Democracy Act—Track II," July 6, 1994, NSA Cuba Collection.

59. Anthony Lake for the President, "Implementing the Cuban Democracy Act: Track II," draft, July 6, 1994, NSA Cuba Collection.

60. Confidential interview with former NSC official, December 1, 2011.

61. Nuccio draft speech, August 29, 1994, NSA Cuba Collection.

62. CBS News Transcripts, *Face the Nation*, August 28, 1994.

63. U.S. Coast Guard data reported in *CubaINFO* 6, no. 11 (September 1, 1994): 6.

64. CIA, Directorate of Intelligence, Office of African and Latin American Analysis, "Cuba: The Rising Spector of Illegal Migration," May 11, 1994, pp. 5, 7, CIA FOIA website.

65. Tod Robberson, "Story of Tug's Sinking Incited Cubans," *WP*, 11 September 1994.

66. AP, "Castro Threatens to Unleash Refugees after Riot Follows Ferry Hijackings," *WP*, August 6, 1994.

67. Daniel Williams, "After 35 Years, Castro Still Annoys Washington," *WP*, August 13, 1994.

68. Ibid.

69. U.S. Coast Guard data reported in *CubaINFO* 6, no. 11 (September 1, 1994): 6.

70. Steven Greenhouse, "Untidy Policy Pays Off in Cuba Crisis," *NYT*, September 11, 1994.

71. Walter Pincus and Roberto Suro, "Ripple in Florida Straits Overturned U.S. Policy," *WP*, September 1, 1994.

72. Michael J. Sniffen, "Administration Says Cubans Picked Up at Sea Will Go to Guantánamo," AP, August 19, 1994.

73. Halperin interview, April 16, 2006.

74. Jim DeFede, "Back on Top . . . Jorge Mas Canosa Has Got Clout," *Miami New Times*, September 21, 1994.

75. Bardach, *Cuba Confidential*, 126.

76. Philip Brenner and Peter Kornbluh, "Clinton's Cuba Calculus," *NACLA Report on the Americas* 29, no. 2 (September–October 1995): 33–40; John Nordheimer, "Cuban Group Forges Link to Clinton," *NYT*, August 26, 1994; DeFede, "Back on Top . . . Jorge Mas Canosa Has Got Clout."

77. FBIS, "Castro Views U.S. Ties, Emigration Crisis," *Latin America Daily Report*, August 25, 1994.

78. Nuccio to Watson, "Cuba," August 21, 1994, NSA Cuba Collection.

79. U.S. Department of State, Daily Press Briefing, August, 22 1994, archived at http://dosfan.lib.uic.edu/ERC/briefing/daily_briefings/1994/9408/940822db.html; George Graham and James Harding, "U.S. Ready to Discuss Migration with Cuba," *Financial Times*, August 23, 1994.

80. Lesnick took verbatim notes on all messages from and to Guevara, and from and to Durán, and shared them with the authors. Our account of the exchanges through the phone tree derive from those notes. NSA Cuba Collection.

81. Carter, *Beyond the White House*, 75.

82. Ibid.

83. Ibid., 75–76.

84. Ibid., 76.

85. Lesnick notes, NSA Cuba Collection.

86. Carter, *Beyond the White House*, 76.

87. Ibid., 76.

88. Ibid., 76–77.

89. This never-before-published confidential memorandum was typed and signed by Carter. It is dated August 28, 1994, and addressed "To President Fidel Castro through Cuban Office at the United Nations." NSA Cuba Collection.

90. Branch, *The Clinton Tapes*, 177.

91. Tarnoff interview, January 10, 2008.

92. Salinas, *México*, 242.

93. Ibid.

94. Ibid., 243.

95. Ibid., 243–44.

96. Branch, *The Clinton Tapes*, 177.

97. Salinas, *México*, 244.

98. Ibid., 245.

99. Ibid., 245.

100. Luers interview, July 28, 2011.

101. Clinton, *My Life*, 615.

102. Salinas, *México*, 246.

103. Ibid., 246–47.

104. "Alarcón Comments on Forthcoming Immigration Talks with USA," BBC Summary of World Broadcasts, Radio Havana, September 2, 1994.

105. Daniel Williams, "U.S. Officials Warn Talks Could Collapse," *WP*, September 7, 1994.

106. Salinas, *México*, 247.

107. Ibid., 247.

108. Ibid.

109. Ibid., 248.

110. Ziegler, *U.S.-Cuban Cooperation Past, Present, and Future*, 53.

111. Tim Golden, "Cuba's Hidden Gain," *NYT*, September 10, 1994.

112. "U.S., Cuba Reach Immigration Accord," *CubaINFO*, September 22, 1994.

113. Claiborne Pell and Lee Hamilton, "The Embargo Must Go," *WP*, September 8, 1994. This opinion piece, coordinated between administration officials and Hamilton's aide, Deborah Hauger, was ghostwritten by the authors.

114. Richard Nuccio to Alexander F. Watson, "A Cuba Policy for the Second Half of the Clinton Administration," October 24, 1994, NSA Cuba Collection.

115. Watson's handwritten notes are attached to Nuccio's memorandum, "A Cuba Policy for the Second Half of the Clinton Administration."

116. V. Manuel Rocha to Anthony Lake, Richard Feinberg, and Morton H. Halperin, "A Calibrated Response to Cuban Reforms," October 3, 1994, NSA Cuba Collection.

117. George Gedda, "U.S. General Outlines Desperation of Detained Cuban Migrants," AP, May 19, 1995.

118. Halperin interview, April 16, 2006.

119. Schoultz, *That Infernal Little Cuban Republic*, 473.

120. Salinas, *México*, 253–54.

121. Landau interview, February 7, 2004.

122. Halperin interview, March 19, 2012.

123. Schoultz, *That Infernal Little Cuban Republic*, 473.

124. Tarnoff interview, January 10, 2008.

125. Alarcón interview, February 20, 2005; Halperin interview, April 16, 2006; Douglas Waller and Cathy Booth, "Clinton's Cuban Road to Florida," *Time*, October 28, 1996.

126. Halperin interview, April 16, 2006.

127. "Joint Statement with the Republic of Cuba on Normalization of Migration," May 1, 1995, *PPP Clinton*.

128. Halperin interview, April 16, 2006.

129. Larry Rohter, "U.S., Enforcing New Policy, Turns Over 13 Boat People to Cuba," *NYT*, May 10, 1995.

130. State Department, "Tarnoff Meeting with Congressional Delegation," undated Memorandum of Conversation, NSA Cuba Collection.

131. U.S. House of Representatives, Committee on International Relations, Subcommittee on the Western Hemisphere, *The Clinton Administration's Reversal of U.S. Immigration Policy toward Cuba*, May 18, 1995, 3–4.

132. Ibid., 6.

133. Ibid., 2, 118.

134. Halperin interview, December 18, 2011.

135. Interagency Task Force on Cuba, "Talking Points," June 9, 1995, NSA Cuba Collection.

136. Information Memorandum for Sandy Berger and Peter Tarnoff, "Cuba Meeting," July 17, 1995, NSA Cuba Collection.

137. Nuccio interview, March 30, 2008.

138. Tarnoff interviews, April 29, 2004; August 10, 2007.

139. Ziegler, *U.S.-Cuban Cooperation Past, Present, and Future*, 92–96.

140. Tad Szulc, "U.S. Halts Flow of Funds to Cuba at Guantanamo," *NYT*, February 8, 1964.

141. AP, "Castro Denies Plan to Kick Out U.S. Navy," *Chicago Tribune*, February 9, 1964; Reuters, "Castro Bars Haste over Guantanamo," *NYT*, February 25, 1964.

142. "U.S.-Cuban Face-off Just Daily Drudgery," *Chicago Tribune*, December 20, 1985.

143. Sheehan interview.

144. Coll interview.

145. Sheehan interview.

146. Jack Sheehan, "Across the U.S.-Cuba Divide, a Retired General Takes a Step," *WP*, May 3, 1998; Jim Hampton, "U.S., Cuban Generals Should Talk," *MH*, June 30, 1996; Dominguez, "U.S.-Cuban Relations: From the Cold War to the Colder War."

147. Steven Comarow, "Mine Removal Is Signal to Castro," *USA Today*, December 9, 1997.

148. Ziegler, *U.S.-Cuban Cooperation Past, Present, and Future*, 105–9; Raúl Castro, "Our Disagreement Is Not about Fighting Terrorism, but about the Methods Used to Fight Terrorism," *Granma International*, January 19, 2002.

149. Sheehan interview.

150. Castro, "Our Disagreement Is Not about Fighting Terrorism."

151. Memorandum for the President, "Cuba—Next Steps," October 3, 1995, NSA Cuba Collection; Waller and Booth, "Clinton's Cuban Road to Florida."

152. "Remarks at a Freedom House Breakfast," October 6, 1995, *PPP Clinton*; William L. Roberts, "Clinton Draws Mixed Reviews on Cuba Policy," *Journal of Commerce*, October 10, 1995.

153. Thomas W. Lippman, "Sanctions Move Reignites Volatile Debate on Cuba," *WP*, October 7, 1995.

154. Helms is quoted in Schoultz, *That Infernal Little Cuban Republic*, 476; Burton in Jeremy Gray, "President Agrees to Tough New Set of Curbs on Cuba," *NYT*, February 29, 1996.

155. White House, "Statement of Administration Policy on Helms/Burton Legislation," September 15, 1995, NSA Cuba Collection.

156. Jefferson Morley, "Shootdown," *Washington Post Magazine*, May 25, 1997.

157. Stephen Stock, "Docs Show Cuban Shoot Down Was Expected," CBS-4 Miami, Nov 29, 2009.

158. "Thirteen Minutes over Havana; Exile Pilot Says He Flew over Capital to Divert Cuban Authorities," *MH*, July 15, 1995; Mike Frankel, "Pilots Await News of Brothers' Fates," *Tampa Tribune*, February 25, 1996; Jefferson Morley, "Shootdown," *Washington Post Magazine*, May 25, 1997.

159. Reginald K. Brack Jr. and Joelle Attinger, "Fidel's Defense," *Time*, March 11, 1996.

160. *FRUS 1958–1960*, VI, doc. 379:642–46.

161. U.S. Department of State, "Public Announcement-Cuba," August 8, 1995, quoted in "U.S. Warns Exiles to Stay Out of Trouble," *CubaINFO* 7, no. 11 (August 28, 1995): 6.

162. Civil Aeronautics Institute of Cuba letter to FAA administrator David Hinson, August 21, 1995, NSA Cuba Collection. The FAA file on the Brothers to the Rescue shoot-down was obtained by Peter Kornbluh through the FOIA.

163. FAA, "Chronology of Events Involving Brothers to the Rescue: FAA Actions," undated; "FAA Proposes to Suspend Certificate of Pilot Who Flew Over Havana," press release, September 1, 1995, Federal Aviation Administration, U.S. Department of Transportation, Washington, D.C.

164. State Department, "Chronology of Department of State Actions on Cuban Exile Flotillas," p. 2, NSA Cuba Collection.

165. Armstrong interview, November 28, 2011.

166. Kimber, *What Lies across the Water*, 104.

167. Nuccio interview, April 28, 2004.

168. Tarnoff interview, August 10, 2007.

169. Landau interview, February 7, 2004.

170. General Tamayo's statement to the Center for Defense Information delegation was filmed by producer Glenn Baker, who provided a transcript of the statement to the authors.

171. Recounted by Ambassador White at a conference, "The United States and Cuba: Rethinking Reengagement," University of North Carolina, Chapel Hill, September 25–27, 2008.

172. Carl Nagin, "Backfire," *New Yorker*, January 26, 1998, 30–35.

173. CNN interview with Rear Admiral Eugene Carroll, "Cubans Warned They Might Shoot Down Exile Planes," February 25, 1996.

174. White interview.

175. Nagin, "Backfire."

176. Peter Bourne, "Travels with Bill," April 6, 2006. Posted on his website: www .petergbourne.co.uk.articles8.html.

177. Peter Bourne to Bill Richardson, April 9, 1996, NSA Cuba Collection.

178. Bourne interview.

179. Nagin, "Backfire."

180. Richardson interview, February 10, 2010.

181. *CBS Evening News*, April 30, 1996.

182. Reflecciones del Comandante en Jefe, "Submission to Imperial Politics," August 27, 2007, Discursos Archive.

183. Peter Bourne to Bill Richardson, April 9, 1996.

184. Waller and Booth, "Clinton's Cuban Road to Florida."

185. FAA, Capestany email, January 22, 1996, NSA Cuba Collection.

186. Nuccio email to Berger, February 24, 1996, NSA Cuba Collection.

187. Nuccio recounts this exchange in an unpublished memoir, "No Good Deed Unpunished," chap. 6. He graciously provided a copy to the authors.

188. Jefferson Morley, "Shootdown," *Washington Post Magazine*, May 25, 1997.

189. Nuccio interview, April 28, 2004.

190. Nuccio, "No Good Deed Unpunished," chap. 6.

191. Ibid., 10.

192. "Pilots' Final Words," *MH*, February 26, 1996.

193. The story of the shoot-down is told in Kimber, *What Lies across the Water*, 117–23.

194. Nuccio, "No Good Deed Unpunished."

195. Waller and Booth, "Clinton's Cuban Road to Florida."

196. Branch, *The Clinton Tapes*, 346.

197. "Remarks Announcing Sanctions against Cuba Following the Downing of American Civilian Aircraft," February 26, 1996, *PPP Clinton*.

198. Vanderbush and Haney, "Policy toward Cuba in the Clinton Administration," *Political Science Quarterly* 114, no. 3 (Autumn 1999): 404.

199. Nagin, "Backfire."

200. Clinton, *My Life*, 701.

201. Haney and Vanderbush, *The Cuban Embargo*, 113.

202. Albright, *Madam Secretary*, 331–32.

203. Berger interview.

204. Quotes from Armstrong in the next several paragraphs are from interviews on November 12, 2004, October 19, 2009, and November 28, 2011.

205. Steven Lee Myers, "Clinton Clears U.S. Media to Set Up Cuba Bureaus," *NYT*, February 13, 1997.

206. Peter Watrous, "A Song Sails Forth from Cuba," *NYT*, August 21, 1997.

207. Steven Lee Myers, "U.S. to Let 1,000 Sail From Miami to Cuba for Pope's Visit," *NYT*, August 23, 1997.

208. Richard Boudreaux and Mark Fineman, "Catholic Leaders See the Start of New Cuban Era," *LAT*, January 26, 1998.

209. Berger interview.

210. Steven Erlanger, "U.S. to Ease Curbs on Relief to Cuba and Money to Kin," *NYT*, March 20, 1998.

211. Daryn Kagan and Lucia Newman, "Cuban President Speaks about Expected U.S. Policy Changes," CNN, March 20, 1998.

212. "The President's News Conference with Prime Minister Romano Prodi of Italy," May 6, 1998; "The President's News Conference in Hong Kong Special Administrative Region," July 3, 1998, *PPP Clinton*.

213. Andrew Cawthorne, "Castro Calls Clinton 'Man of Peace' with Wrong Policy," Reuters, June 25, 1998.

214. Thomas W. Lippman, "Business-Led Coalition Urges U.S. to Relax Embargo on Cuba," *WP*, January 14, 1998; Tim Weiner, "Pope vs. Embargo," *NYT*, January 21, 1998.

215. The repeal was included in the Trade Sanctions Reform and Export Enhancement Act of 2000, 22 USC Chapter 79.

216. Andres Oppenheimer, "U.S. Poised to Act on Cuba Policy," *MH*, April 23, 1998.

217. Council on Foreign Relations, *U.S.-Cuban Relations in the 21st Century*, Independent Task Force Report, January 1999.

218. F. Armstrong interview, November 12, 2004.

219. Sweig interview.

220. Council on Foreign Relations, *U.S.-Cuban Relations in the 21st Century*.

221. "Statement on United States Policy toward Cuba," January 5, 1999, *PPP Clinton*.

222. Ricardo Alarcón, "What They Have Done Is to Inform the World that the Blockade Stays in Place, that They Will Try to Foster It, to Convince Others, to Make More Propaganda, While They Continue on That Road Doomed to Failure," *Granma International*, January 8, 1999.

223. Andres Oppenheimer, "Cuba: Back to Darkness," *MH*, March 18, 1999.

224. F. Armstrong interview, October 19, 2009.

225. Mark P. Sullivan, *Cuba: U.S. Restrictions on Travel and Legislative Initiatives*, 5.

226. "O's Owner in Cuba, Ready to Talk," Sports Illustrated/CNN.com, January 16, 1999.

227. F. Armstrong interview, August 14, 2012.

228. Letter, Kuhn to Kissinger, January 14, 1975, NSA Cuba Collection.

229. Kuhn spoke to assistant secretary of state for Latin America, William Rogers. Rogers, February 13, 1975, Memorandum of Conversation, NSA Cuba Collection.

230. "Additional Talking Points on Sending a Baseball Team to Cuba," February 19, 1975, NSA Cuba Collection.

231. Mark Asher, "Castro Challenges Yankees," *WP*, October 24, 1978. For the story of the Yankees' efforts to play in Cuba, see Jon Daly, "Hardball Diplomacy," *Hardball Times*, November 26, 2008.

232. Murray Chase, "Kuhn Reportedly Vetoes Plans for a Game in Cuba," *NYT*, January 15, 1978.

233. Schaeffer interview.

234. Landau interview, August 16, 2012.

235. Schaeffer interview.

236. Berger interview.

237. F. Armstrong interview, August 14, 2012.

238. Schaeffer interview.

239. Ibid.

240. S. Armstrong interview.

241. Peter Kornbluh, "Baseball Diplomacy," *In These Times*, May 19, 1999; Kornbluh, "Here's the Windup; Scouting a Lefty Named Castro," *Washington Post*, January 17, 1999.

242. Landau interview, February 7, 2004.

243. Remírez interview.

244. Alarcón interview, November 6, 2006.

245. S. Armstrong interview.

246. F. Armstrong interviews, October 19, 2009, and August 14, 2012.

247. Berger interview.

248. Kornbluh, *Cuba, Counternarcotics, and Collaboration*.

249. FBIS, "Castro on Mexico, USSR, U.S., Other Issues," *Latin America Daily Report*, December 21, 1988.

250. U.S. House of Representatives, Committee on Foreign Affairs, Subcommittee on Inter-American Affairs, *Foreign Assistance Legislation for FY83. (Part 6): Security Assistance Proposals for Latin America and the Caribbean*, 118–19.

251. U.S. Senate, Committee on the Judiciary, Subcommittee on Security and Terrorism, *Role of Cuba in International Terrorism and Subversion*, 144–45.

252. *United States v. Jaime Guillot Lara, et al.*, No. 82-643 (Indictment), in U.S. Senate, Committee on the Judiciary, Subcommittee on Security and Terrorism, and Committee on Foreign Relations, Subcommittee on Western Hemisphere Affairs, *Cuban Government's Involvement in Facilitating International Drug Traffic*, 100–112.

253. "Remarks at a Cuban Independence Day Celebration in Miami," Florida, May 20, 1983, *PPP Reagan*.

254. Kenneth B. Noble, "Official Ties Cuba to U.S. Drug Traffic," *NYT*, May 2, 1983.

255. Alfonso Chardy, "Cuba Cancels Pact to Halt Drug Traffic," *MH*, April 28, 1982.

256. Ferch interview, April 6, 2004.

257. Ibid.

258. Gerald M. Boyd, "Castro, after Talks with Jackson, Frees 22 Jailed Americans," *NYT*, June 27, 1984.

259. "Castro Offers to Shoot Down Drug Traffickers," United Press International, March 20, 1985.

260. Text of oral interview with John J. "Jay" Taylor.

261. Ibid.

262. For a detailed account of the Ochoa case, see Oppenheimer, *Castro's Final Hour*. Debate continues over whether de la Guardia's operation was sanctioned by higher authorities. Within months, the minister of the interior, José Abrantes, was removed and sentenced to twenty years in prison for dereliction of duty and corruption, suggesting either that he was aware of de la Guardia's actions or should have been.

263. Michael Isikoff, "Trial Uncovers Evidence of Cuban Drug-Trafficking Involvement," *WP*, July 26, 1988.

264. Castro's address to the Council of State, in *Case 1/1989*, 430–31.

265. U.S. Department of State, *International Narcotics Control Strategy Report, April 1993*; U.S. Department of State, *International Narcotics Control Strategy Report, April 1994*.

266. "A New Cuba Debate," *WP* (editorial), August 12, 1999.

267. Douglas Farah, "Cuba Wages a Lonesome Drug War," *WP*, May 25, 1999.

268. Reuters, "Cuba Cooperating to Combat Drug Trade, U.S. Official Says," *NYT*, May 8, 1999.

269. Statement on Drug Trafficking at the Commemoration of July 26, 1999, in Cienfuegos, Cuba, Discursos Archive.

270. Kornbluh, *Cuba, Counternarcotics, and Collaboration*, 8–9.

271. Christopher Marquis, "Cuba to Aid U.S. Anti-drug Effort," *MH*, August 19, 1999.

272. Juan O. Tamayo, "U.S. Officials to Visit Cuba, Discuss Cooperative Efforts in Drug War," *MH*, June 19, 1999.

273. Juan O. Tamayo, "U.S. Plans Full Review of Cuban Connections to Illegal Drug Trade," *MH*, July 23, 1999.

274. Juan O. Tamayo, "Despite Concern, Clinton Omits Cuba as Major Drug-Transit Point," *MH*, November 11, 1999.

275. U.S. Department of State, *International Narcotics Control Strategy Report, 2000* (*INCSR*).

276. Juan O. Tamayo and Gerardo Reyes, "An Exile's Relentless Aim: Oust Castro," *MH*, June 7, 1998.

277. Ann Louise Bardach and Larry Rohter, "A Bomber's Tale: Taking Aim at Castro; Key Cuba Foe Claims Exiles' Backing," *NYT*, July 12, 1998. In this interview, Posada admitted responsibility for the hotel bombings but later recanted. AP, "Jury Clears Cuban Exile of Charges that He Lied to U.S.," *NYT*, April 8, 2011.

278. Posada credited Mas Canosa with providing this assistance. Bardach and Rohter, "A Bomber's Tale." See also Bardach, *Cuba Confidential*, 180–223.

279. Gail Epstein Nieves, "Arguments Open in Trial of Five Cubans Accused of Spying," *MH*, December 6, 2000.

280. Robert Fink, "Terrorists: America Has Its Very Own Brood: CIA-Trained Cuban Exiles," *LAT*, November 6, 1977.

281. Karen DeYoung, "Castro Will Discuss U.S. Prisoners," *WP*, August 11, 1977.

282. Memorandum, Church to the President, August 12, 1977, "Visit to Cuba," Carter Library, White House Central Office Files, Subj. File Countries, CO-38 (Cuba), box CO 20, folder CO-38, 1/20/77–1/20/81.

283. Castro praised Reagan's efforts to halt exiles' attacks: FBIS, "Castro Discusses Immigration Agreement with the U.S.," *Latin America Daily Report*, December 18, 1984.

284. Jeff Stein, "U.S. Officials to Cuban Exile Groups: Stop Violence Here," *Christian Science Monitor*, October 30, 1981; Arnold H. Lubasch, "Judge Sentences Omega 7 Leader to Life in Prison," *NYT*, November 10, 1984.

285. García interview; García, *Diplomacia Sin Sombra*, 121–27.

286. In a special address to the Cuban people on May 20, 2005, Castro identified Hart only as "an outstanding political personality." See the transcript of his speech, "A Different Behavior," Discursos Archive.

287. Castro provided details of the communications with Kozak in a chronology he read at a massive rally as part of his speech, "A Different Behavior."

288. Ibid.

289. The seven points are cited in García Márquez's report on his secret diplomatic mission, which Castro read, word for word, in his May 20, 2005, speech. The next day, Castro had lunch with the authors and provided us with the actual cover memorandum

that accompanied the García Márquez report when he turned it in to Castro. Fidel explained that just a few hours before, he had called García Márquez to ask his permission to give us the cover memo.

290. García Márquez's report was also published in *Counterpunch*, May 21-22, 2005, under the title, "My Visit to the Clinton White House."

291. Ibid.

292. McLarty interview.

293. García Márquez, "My Visit to the Clinton White House"; McLarty interview.

294. McLarty interview.

295. The meetings between FBI and Cuban officials are described in Kimber, *What Lies across the Water*, 222–27. The authors thank Kimber for sharing the Cuban intelligence reports that were provided to the FBI delegation.

296. Ibid., 225.

297. Bardach, "A Bomber's Tale."

298. David Adams, "Cubans Accused of Spying on U.S. Military," *St. Petersburg Times*, September 15, 1998.

299. Lonnae O'Neal Parker, "Their Man in Washington; Cuba's Interests Section Emerges from the Shadows," *WP*, April 12, 2000.

300. Huddleston interview, August 28, 2005.

301. Huddleston has told this story on many occasions. See, for example, Larry Luxner, "Vicki Huddleston: U.S. Cuba Policy Is on the Wrong Track," *Washington Diplomat*, July 2005.

302. Huddleston interview, August 28, 2005.

303. Alarcón interview, May 20, 2005.

304. Eunice Ponce and Elaine De Valle, "Mania over Elián Rising," *MH*, January 10, 2000; Oscar Corral, "Elián Custody Case Unites Miami's Cuban Americans," *Milwaukee Journal Sentinel*, April 23, 2000.

305. Huddleston interview, August 28, 2005.

306. Ibid.

307. Ibid.

308. Karen DeYoung and Sue Anne Pressley, "Elian's Grandmothers Are Granted U.S. Visas," *WP*, January 21, 2000.

309. Neil A. Lewis, "U.S. Says It Agrees to Return Boy, 6, to Father in Cuba," *NYT*, January 6, 2000.

310. Karen DeYoung, "Elian Asylum Appeal Dismissed," *WP*, June 2, 2000.

311. Huddleston interview, August 28, 2005.

312. John M. Broder, "For Elián's Father, a Lawyer with Ties to Clinton," *NYT*, April 4, 2000.

313. Huddleston interview, August 28, 2005.

314. Rick Bragg, "Cuban Father Set to Get Boy in U.S., Castro Announces," *NYT*, March 30, 2000.

315. Clinton, *My Life*, 906.

316. Karen Branch, "Penelas Put Himself into Prominent Spot with Tough Talk," *MH*, March 31, 2000.

317. Huddleston interview, August 28, 2005; Jane Perlez, "Dispute Could Warm U.S.-Cuba Relations," *NYT*, April 25, 2000.

318. Armstrong interview, August 23, 2013.

319. The 1992 result is from Eddie Dominguez, "Clinton Courts Cuban Vote," AP, September 5, 1996. The 2000 and 1996 results are from Merico-Stephens and Schmal, "Voting," 2:270–76.

320. Clinton, *My Life*, 905.

321. Berger interview.

322. Ibid.

Chapter Eight

1. Woodward, *State of Denial*, 224.

2. "Bush Pushes 'Free Cuba' in Florida," Agence France Presse, June 30, 2003.

3. Miles A. Pomper, "Sentiment Grows for Ending Cuba Embargo, but Opponents Say Bush Will Stand Firm," *CQ Weekly Report*, February 9, 2002, 408.

4. The Cuban message is quoted in Castro's speech, "None of the Present World Problems Can Be Solved with the Use of Force," September 11, 2001, Discursos Archive.

5. "Address before a Joint Session of the Congress on the United States Response to the Terrorist Attacks of September 11," September 20, 2001, *PPP GWBush*.

6. Speech at la Tribuna Abierta de la Revolución, San Antonio de los Baños, September 22, 2001, Discursos Archive.

7. Raúl Castro, "Our Disagreement Is Not about Fighting Terrorism, but about the Methods Used to Fight Terrorism," *Granma International*, January 19, 2002.

8. "The Cuban Government Submits to the United States a Set of Proposals for Bilateral Agreements on Migratory Issues, Cooperation in Drug Interdiction and a Program to Fight Terrorism," Statement of the Ministry of Foreign Affairs, March 17, 2002; Department of State Daily Press Briefing, Richard Boucher, January 28, 2002.

9. Andres Oppenheimer and Tim Johnson, "U.S. Policy on Cuba to Receive Full Review," *MH*, March 8, 2002; Tim Johnson, "Reich Vows to Defend Cuba Embargo," *MH*, March 13, 2002.

10. Since 2001, the annual posture statement of the U.S. Southern Command has not discussed any threat posed by Cuba, other than passing mentions of the possibility of mass migration in 2007 and 2008.

11. Richard Nuccio at a panel, "Cuba's Presence on the State Department's List of Countries Supporting Terrorism," Georgetown University, Washington, D.C., October 11, 2001.

12. U.S. Department of State, Office of the Coordinator for Counterterrorism, *Patterns of Global Terrorism, 2001*.

13. Remarks at a Rally Held in General Antonio Maceo Square, Santiago de Cuba, June 8, 2002, Discursos Archive.

14. John R. Bolton, "Beyond the Axis of Evil: Additional Threats from Weapons of Mass Destruction," Remarks to the Heritage Foundation, Washington, D.C., May 6, 2002, http://www.heritage.org/research/lecture/beyond-the-axis-of-evil.

15. Juan O. Tamayo, "U.S. Downplays Rumors of Cuban Germ Missiles," *MH*, February 4, 1997; Juan O. Tamayo, "U.S. Skeptical of Report on Cuban Biological Weapons," *MH*, June 23, 1999.

16. Douglas Jehl, "Bolton's Nomination Is Questioned by Another Powell Aide," *NYT*, April 30, 2005; Sonni Efron, "U.N. Nominee, Democrats Lock Horns on His Record," *LAT*, April 12, 2005.

17. Castro responded to Bolton in two speeches: Key Address at the Open Forum Held in Sancti Spiritus Province, May 25, 2002, and Response to the Statements Made by the United States Government on Biological Weapons, May 10, 2002, Discursos Archive.

18. Warren P. Strobel, "U.S. Backs Away from Claims that Cuba Has Bioweapons Program," *San Jose Mercury News*, August 30, 2005.

19. The meeting with academics was held at the Arca Foundation's Musgrove Plantation in South Carolina in January 1989. LeoGrande was among the participants.

20. Robert Pastor, personal communication.

21. Carter interview.

22. Carol Rosenberg, "Florida Pair Asked Bush to Block Carter's Trip," *MH*, May 8, 2002.

23. Christopher Marquis, "Bush Is Likely to Approve Carter Trip to Cuba," *NYT*, March 26, 2002.

24. "Former President Jimmy Carter Discusses an Auction Being Held in Colorado to Support the Work of the Carter Center," CBS News Transcripts, *The Early Show*, February 8, 2002.

25. McConnell interview; John Rice, "Carter: U.S. Officials Said They Had No Evidence of Cuba Transferring Technology for Terrorist Uses," AP, May 13, 2002.

26. Rice, "Carter: U.S. Officials Said They Had No Evidence. . . ."

27. Kevin Sullivan, "Carter Begins Historic Cuba Visit," *WP*, May 13, 2002.

28. Carter interview.

29. Ibid.

30. David Gonzalez, "In Time for Carter's Visit, Cubans Petition Government," *NYT*, May 11, 2002.

31. David Gonzalez, "Carter and Powell Cast Doubt on Bioarms in Cuba," *NYT*, May 14, 2002.

32. McConnell interview.

33. "The United States and Cuba: A Vision for the 21st Century," Remarks by former U.S. president Jimmy Carter at the University of Havana, Cuba, May 14, 2002, The Carter Center, http://www.cartercenter.org/news/documents/doc528.html.

34. Payá insisted that he refused to accept U.S. government funds, although the National Endowment for Democracy funded an international campaign in support of the Varela Project.

35. McConnell interview; Carter, "President Carter's Cuba Trip Report," May 21, 2002, The Carter Center.

36. McConnell interview; Castro and Ramonet, *Fidel Castro: My Life*, 415–16; Carter, *Beyond the White House*, 84–85.

37. Pastor interview, July 1, 2004; Carter, "President Carter's Cuba Trip Report."

38. Carter, "President Carter's Cuba Trip Report"; Nancy San Martin, "Cuba Dissidents Split on Embargo, Oppose U.S. Sending Homeland Financial Support, Carter Report Says," *MH*, May 18, 2002; John Rice, "Carter Ends Cuba Trip Calling for Changes in US Policy, Cooperation between US and Cuban Scientists," *MH*, May 17, 2002.

39. Carter, "President Carter's Cuba Trip Report."

40. Peter McKenna, "Carter Cracked Cuba's Shell; Bush's Rants Resealed It," *Globe and Mail* (Canada), May 23, 2002.

41. Carter interview; Carter, "President Carter's Cuba Trip Report."

42. Jennifer McCoy, personal correspondence, May 1, 2014.

43. Bush gave two speeches on May 20, 2002, one in Washington and a second in Miami: "Remarks Announcing the Initiative for a New Cuba," May 20, 2002, and "Remarks on the 100th Anniversary of Cuban Independence in Miami, Florida," May 20, 2002, *PPP GWBush*.

44. Sullivan, *Cuba: U.S. Restrictions on Travel and Legislative Initiatives*, 5.

45. Max Baucus, Mike Enzi, and Jeff Flake, "Cuba Obsession Weakens U.S. Effort," *Atlanta Journal Constitution*, May 20, 2004.

46. On the Bush administrations 2003 and 2004 sanctions, see Sullivan, *Cuba: U.S. Restrictions on Travel and Legislative Initiatives*.

47. Vanessa Arrington, "Fewer Americans Travel to Cuba While Number of Fines Rise for Those Who Do, Cuba Says," AP, September 28, 2005; Gary Marx, "Tougher U.S. Policy Curtails Aid to Cubans," *Chicago Tribune*, October 13, 2005; Dalia Acosta, "Cuba-U.S.: New Transaction Fees Squeeze Family Remittances," Inter Press Service, June 9, 2006.

48. Commission for Assistance to a Free Cuba, *Report to the President, May 2004*, xii–xiv.

49. Ginger Thompson, "Cuba, Too, Felt the Sept. 11 Shock Waves, with a More Genial Castro Offering Help," *NYT*, February 7, 2002.

50. Anita Snow, "U.S. and Cuban Officials Discuss Immigrant Smuggling," AP, December 3, 2001.

51. Dalia Acosta, "Politics-Cuba/US: Havana Again Challenges U.S. Migration Policy," Inter Press Service, December 4, 2001.

52. "Press Conference by Foreign Minister of the Republic of Cuba, Felipe Pérez Roque on the Mercenaries at the Service of the Empire Who Stood Trial on April 3, 4, 5 and 7, 2003," *Granma International*, April 9, 2003.

53. Karen DeYoung, "Cuba Denounces Diplomats' Expulsions; Official Challenges U.S. to Show Evidence of Spying," *WP*, May 15, 2003.

54. Special Presentation at the Televised Roundtable on Recent Events in the Country, April 25, 2003, Discursos Archive.

55. Erikson, *The Cuba Wars*, 50–51; Anita Snow, "Top U.S. Diplomat in Cuba Warns Citizens against More Hijackings," AP, April 2, 2003.

56. Anita Snow, "U.S. Returns 15 Cubans from Allegedly Hijacked Boat," AP, July 21, 2003.

57. "Statement by the Ministry of Foreign Affairs, January 5, 2004," *Granma International*, January 7, 2004.

58. "Statement from the Ministry of Foreign Affairs," *Granma International*, July 16, 2007.

59. Pablo Bachelet and Francis Robles, "U.S. Cuba Visa Flap Swells Tensions," *MH*, July 18, 2007.

60. U.S. GAO, *U.S. Democracy Assistance for Cuba Needs Better Management and Oversight*, GAO-07-147, November 2006, 24.

61. USAID, *Evaluation of the USAID Cuba Program*, especially the chapter, "Profile of the USAID Cuba Program."

62. The budget fell back to $20 million in FY 2009 for lack of opportunities to spend the money. U.S. Department of State, *Congressional Budget Justification for Foreign Operations, FY 2003*; *FY2008*; and *FY 2009*.

63. Fred Bernstein, "Lighting Matches in Cuba on the 4th," *NYT*, July 4, 2002.

64. Kevin Sullivan, "In Havana, U.S. Radios Strike Note of Discord," *WP*, May 5, 2002.

65. Speech at the Extraordinary Session of the National Assembly of People's Power, Havana, June 26, 2002, Discursos Archive.

66. Anita Snow, "U.S. Diplomat in Cuba Walks an Often Rocky Road as Chief of Mission on Communist Island," AP, June 6, 2002.

67. Castro provides a detailed account of Cason's meetings with dissidents in Special Presentation at the Televised Roundtable on Recent Events in the Country, April 25, 2003, Discursos Archive.

68. Huddleston interviews, August 28, 2005, October 22, 2007.

69. Speech on the occasion of his inauguration as President of the Republic of Cuba, March 6, 2003, Discursos Archive.

70. Landau and Valdes, "Confessions of Roger Noriega."

71. Christopher Marquis, "Striving to Punish Cuba, U.S. Expels 14 of Its Diplomats," *NYT*, May 14, 2003.

72. Wayne S. Smith, "Why the Crackdown in Cuba?," *LAT*, April 7, 2003.

73. Edwin Chen, "Bush Steps Up Effort to Destabilize Castro's Regime," *LAT*, October 11, 2003.

74. Commission for Assistance to a Free Cuba, *Report to the President, May 2004*, xiii.

75. Central Committee of the Communist Party of Cuba, "Brutal Economic and Political Measures against Our Country and against Cubans Resident in the United States," *Granma International*, May 7, 2004.

76. Proclamation by an Adversary of the U.S. Government, May 14, 2004, Discursos Archive.

77. Vanessa Arrington, "Top U.S. Diplomat in Cuba Says Policy Will Persevere after His Departure," AP, July 6, 2005; Jacqui Goddard, "Cuba Starts Propaganda Drive after Frosty Display by American Envoy," *The Times* (London), December 24, 2004; "U.S. Diplomat Puts Prison Cell in Havana Yard to Underscore Rights," AP, September 9, 2004.

78. Goddard, "Cuba Starts Propaganda Drive. . . ."

79. Parmly interview.

80. Jim Burns, "New American Envoy Predicts Big Change in Cuba after Castro," *Human Events* online, December 19, 2005, http://www.humanevents.com/2005/12/19/new-american-envoy-predicts-big-change-in-cuba-after-castro/.

81. Frances Robles, "U.S. Uses Billboard to Jab at Castro during Mass Protest," *MH*, January 25, 2006.

82. Parmly interview.

83. Alfonso Chardy, Oscar Corral, and Jay Weaver, "FBI, Cuba Cooperating on Posada," *MH*, May 3, 2007.

84. Parmly interview.

85. For a description of U.S.-Cuban cooperation on hurricane monitoring, see Michael H. Glantz, "Climate-Related Disaster Diplomacy," *Cambridge Review of International Affairs* 14, no. 1 (2000): 233–53; Center for International Policy, *U.S.-Cuban Cooperation in Defending Against Hurricanes*, July 2011.

86. David Adams, "Storm Sows Ruin in Cuba," *St. Petersburg Times*, November 8, 2001; Christopher Marquis, "U.S. Is Reportedly Prepared to Allow Food Sales to Cuba," *NYT*, November 15, 2001; U.S.-Cuba Trade and Economic Council, "2012–2001 U.S. Export Statistics for Cuba," *Economic Eye on Cuba*, February 2013.

87. Anita Snow, "Castro Confirms His Government Will Let American Aid Officials Visit Island," AP, October 28, 2005; "U.S. Team's Visit to Cuba Put on Hold," AP, November 2, 2005; Vanessa Arrington, "Cuba Rejects Claim It Wanted to Politicize Visit by U.S. Relief Team on Hurricane Damage," AP, November 3, 2005; U.S. Department of State, Daily Press Briefing, November 4, 2005.

88. Marc Lacey, "U.S. Offers Storm Aid to Cuba Only through Relief Groups," *NYT*, September 5, 2008; Damien Cave, "In Wake of Storm Damage, Calls to Ease Cuba Embargo," *NYT*, September 11, 2008; Karen DeYoung, "U.S. Urges Cuba to Accept Aid," *WP*, September 16, 2008.

89. DeYoung, "U.S. Urges Cuba to Accept Aid"; Joshua Partlow, "Hurricanes Shift Debate on Embargo against Cuba," *WP*, September 24, 2008.

90. Peter Whoriskey, "Cubans in Miami Cheer Castro's Illness," *WP*, August 2, 2006.

91. Press Briefing by Tony Snow, August 1, 2006, Office of the Press Secretary, White House.

92. "No Enemy Can Defeat Us," *Granma Internacional*, August 18, 2006.

93. U.S. State Department Daily Press Briefing, Tom Casey, Acting Spokesman, August 18, 2006, Department of State.

94. Raúl Castro, Speech Commemorating the 50th Anniversary of the Landing of the Granma, *Juventude Rebelde*, December 2, 2006.

95. Pablo Bachelet, "Cuba Hints at Desire to Begin Formal Talks with U.S.," *San Jose Mercury News*, December 13, 2006.

96. Press Roundtable with Assistant Secretary Thomas Shannon, Assistant Secretary for Western Hemisphere Affairs, Washington, D.C., December 12, 2006, Department of State.

97. "Cuba Policy," Thomas A. Shannon, Assistant Secretary for Western Hemisphere Affairs and Cuba Transition Coordinator Caleb Charles McCarry, On the Record Briefing, Washington, D.C., August 11, 2006, Department of State.

98. Commission for Assistance to a Free Cuba, *Report to the President, July 2006*, 21.

99. Pablo Bachelet, "State Department Shifts Key Cuba Jobs," *MH*, March 19, 2007.

100. "Remarks at the Department of State," October 24, 2007, *PPP GWBush*.

101. Raúl Castro, "Speech on the 54th Anniversary of the Attack on Moncada, July 26, 2007," *Granma International*, July 27, 2007.

Chapter Nine

1. Barack Obama, "Our Main Goal: Freedom in Cuba," *MH*, August 21, 2007.

2. "Renewing U.S. Leadership in the Americas," speech by Barack Obama at the Cuban American National Foundation, May 23, 2008, http://www.barackobama.com.

3. Casey Woods, "Obama First Democrat to Win Florida's Hispanic Vote," *MH*, November 6, 2008.

4. Confidential interview.

5. Brian Wagner, "Latin American Leaders Congratulate President-Elect Obama," *Voice of America*, November 6, 2008.

6. White House, Office of the Press Secretary, "Memorandum for the Secretary of State, the Secretary of the Treasury, the Secretary of Commerce, Subject: Promoting Democracy and Human Rights in Cuba," April 13, 2009.

7. White House, Office of the Press Secretary, "Remarks by the President at the Summit of the Americas Opening Ceremony," April 17, 2009.

8. Resolution On Cuba, AG/RES. 2438 (XXXIX-O/09 June 3, 2009), in Organization of American States General Assembly, Thirty-Ninth Regular Session, San Pedro Sula, Honduras, June 2-4, 2009, *Proceedings*, 1:12.

9. Remarks by Raúl Castro at the Seventh Extraordinary ALBA Summit, Cumaná, Venezuela, April 16, 2009, http://www.cuba.cu/gobierno/rauldiscursos/index2.html. Raúl's remarks prompted press reports that Cuba was offering to negotiate its internal politics with Washington, which was not exactly what he said. Those reports then prompted Fidel to declare that Raúl's statement had been "misinterpreted" (Fidel Castro, "Obama and the Blockade," *Juventude Rebelde*, April 22, 2009). That, in turn, prompted speculation that Fidel had repudiated Raúl's offer. In fact, a close look at the full text of Raúl's original speech indicates that the initial press reports mistook his comments as a change in position.

10. Interview with a State Department official working on Cuba, July 16, 2009.

11. Cable, from USINT (Farrar) to State, "GOC Signals 'Readiness to Move Forward,'" Havana 592, September 25, 2009, Wikileaks.

12. U.S. Department of State, Office of the Coordinator for Counterterrorism, *Country Reports on Terrorism, 2008*, April 2009, 182.

13. U.S. Department of State, *Congressional Budget Justification for Foreign Operations, FY 2011, Annex: Regional Perspectives*, 679–80.

14. USAID Contract with Development Alternatives Inc., dated August 14, 2008, in Peter Kornbluh, "Our Man in Havana: Was USAID Planning to Overthrow Castro?," *Foreign Policy* (online), January 25, 2013, http://www.foreignpolicy.com/articles/2013/01/25/our_man_in_havana.

15. Shailagh Murray and Karen DeYoung, "Momentum Grows for Relaxing Cuba Policy," *WP*, March 30, 2009.

16. Letter from Geithner to Menendez, March 5, 2009, reprinted in *Congressional Record*, March 5, 2009, S2933.

17. Secretary Clinton, "Remarks with Jamaican Foreign Minister Kenneth Baugh at CARICOM, San Pedro Sula, Honduras," June 2, 2009; Secretary Clinton, "Digital Town Hall of the Americas at FUNGLODE, Santo Domingo, Dominican Republic," April 17, 2009, Department of State; "Remarks by President Obama on Latin America in Santiago, Chile," March 21, 2011, Office of the Press Secretary, White House.

18. "Interview of the President by Juan Carlos López, CNN En Español," April 16, 2009, Office of the Press Secretary, White House, April 15, 2009.

19. "Joint Press Conference with President Barack Obama and President Felipe Calderón of Mexico, Mexico City, April 16, 2009," Office of the Press Secretary, White House.

20. Secretary Clinton, "Remarks with Haitian President Rene Preval, Port-au-Prince, Haiti," April 16, 2009, Department of State.

21. Cable, from USINT (Farrar) to State, "GOC Signals 'Readiness to Move Forward,'" Havana 592, September 25, 2009, Wikileaks.

22. "Press Briefing by Press Secretary Robert Gibbs and Dan Restrepo, Special Assistant to the President and Senior Director for Western Hemisphere Affairs," April 13, 2009, Office of the Press Secretary, White House.

23. Nancy San Martin, "Raúl Castro Hints at Readiness for Dialogue with Washington," *MH*, August 19, 2006; Raúl Castro, Key Address at the Ministerial Meeting of the Non-aligned Movement, Havana, Cuba, April 29, 2009, Discursos e intervenciones del Presidente Raúl Castro Ruz, http://www.cuba.cu/gobierno/rauldiscursos/index2.html.

24. William L. Roberts, "Clinton Draws Mixed Reviews on Cuba Policy," *Journal of Commerce*, October 10, 1995.

25. Christopher Marquis, "Bush Plans to Tighten Sanctions on Cuba, Not Ease Them," *NYT*, May 15, 2002.

26. Commission for Assistance to a Free Cuba, *Report to the President, July 2006*, 20; Pablo Bachelet, "U.S. Shifting Funds Away from Miami Anti-Castro Groups," *MH*, March 30, 2008.

27. John Rice, "Cuban Official Defends Internet Controls," AP, February 13, 2007; John Rice, "Cuba Joins Other Latin Nations in Shift toward Open-Source Software," AP, February 16, 2007.

28. Marquis, "Bush Plans to Tighten Sanctions on Cuba, Not Ease Them," and Desmond Butler, "USAID Contractor Work in Cuba Detailed," AP, February 13, 2012.

29. CONFIDENTIAL "Meeting Notes from USAID CDCPP [Cuba Democracy and Contingency Planning Program] Meeting," August 26, 2008. This document entered into evidence as part of a lawsuit filed by Alan Gross against his employer, DAI, and posted on the website of the National Security Archive. http://www2.gwu.edu/~nsarchiv/NSAEBB/NSAEBB411/.

30. Mary Beth Sheridan, "Risks of Cuba Program Questioned," *WP*, December 25, 2009.

31. Secretary Clinton, "Remarks on Internet Freedom at the Newseum, Washington, D.C., January 21, 2010," Department of State; Secretary Clinton, "Internet Rights and Wrongs: Choices and Challenges in a Networked World," Remarks at George Washington University, Washington, D.C., February 15, 2011, Department of State.

32. Cable, from USINT (Farrar) to State, "The U.S. and the Role of the Opposition in Cuba," Havana 221, April 15, 2009, Wikileaks.

33. "Former President Castro Says Popular Blogger's Comments Fuel Attacks against Cuba," AP, June 19, 2008.

34. Will Weissert, "Cuba Says Blogger Ran Afoul of the Law," AP, December 5, 2008.

35. Andrea Rodríguez, "Cuban Blogger Says She Is Briefly Detained," AP, November 7, 2009.

36. Yoani Sánchez, "President Obama's Answers to My Questions," *Huffington Post*, November 19, 2009, http://www.huffingtonpost.com/yoani-sanchez/presidemt-obamas-answers_b_363553.html.

37. Butler, "USAID Contractor Work in Cuba Detailed"; "Para la Isla," proposal from Gross's consulting firm to USAID, National Security Archive website, http://www2.gwu.edu/~nsarchiv/NSAEBB/NSAEBB411/.

38. See Gross's "Proposed Expansion of Scope of Work," September 17, 2009, National Security Archive website, http://www2.gwu.edu/~nsarchiv/NSAEBB/NSAEBB411/.

39. Cable, from USINT (Farrar) to State, "U.S.-Cuba Chill Exaggerated, but Old Ways Threaten Progress," Havana 9, January 6, 2010, Wikileaks.

40. "Castro Has Some Harsh Words for US," *Miami Herald Cuban Colada Blog*, December 22, 2009; "Alan Gross Awaiting Sentence," *Granma International*, March 7, 2011.

41. Secretary Clinton, "Remarks on Nuclear Nonproliferation at the University of Louisville," Louisville, Ky., April 9, 2010, Department of State.

42. R. M. Schneiderman, "Our Man in Havana," *Foreign Affairs*, December 21, 2012, online.

43. Howard LaFranchi, "Cuba Travel Ahead for Americans? House Committee Advances Measure," *Christian Science Monitor*, June 30, 2010.

44. Will Weissert, "Cuban Dissidents Cheer Bill to End US Travel Ban," AP, June 10, 2010.

45. Johannes Werner, "Window Opens to Lift Cuba Travel Ban," *St. Petersburg Times*, July 11, 2010.

46. Mary Beth Sheridan, "Sides Gear up for Fight over U.S. Ban on Travel to Cuba" *WP*, November 19, 2009.

47. Mary Beth Sheridan, "U.S. Preparing to Expand Travel to Cuba; Measures Would Ease Cultural Exchanges, but Tourist Ban Would Go On," *WP*, August 18, 2010.

48. William Gibson, "Wasserman Shultz Defends Cuba Travel Ban," *Orlando Sentinel*, September 27, 2010.

49. White House, Office of the Press Secretary, "Reaching Out to the Cuban People," January 14, 2011.

50. "Statement of the Ministry of Foreign Affairs, January 16, 2011," *Granma International*, January 17, 2011.

51. Andrés Cala, "U.S. Reaches Out to Latin America—With Help from Spain," *Christian Science Monitor*, April 17, 2009.

52. Miguel González, "Obama a Zapatero: Decidle a Raúl que si él no da pasos tampoco yo podré darlos," *El Pais*, October 25, 2009 (author's translation).

53. Cable, from USINT (Farrar) to State, "Spain on Human Rights and Dialogue with Cuba," Havana 726, December 5, 2009, Wikileaks; Cable, from State to USINT, "Secretary Clinton's December 14, 2009 Conversation with Spanish Foreign Minister Miguel Angel," State 129362, December 18, 2009, Wikileaks.

54. Cable, from USINT (Farrar) to State, "Spain on Human Rights and Dialogue with Cuba," Havana 726, December 5, 2009, Wikileaks.

55. Marc Lacey, "Cuban Government Vows to Release 52 Prisoners," *NYT*, July 8, 2010; Will Weissert, "Cuba Agrees to Free 52 Political Prisoners," AP, July 8, 2010.

56. William Booth and Karen DeYoung, "Cuba to Release 52 Political Prisoners, Catholic Church Says," *WP*, July 8, 2010.

57. Mark Frank, "Castro in First Church Overtures," *Financial Times*, May 24, 2010.

58. Antonio Caño, "EE UU se implica en las excarcelaciones," *El País*, July 16, 2010.

59. Jackson Diehl, "Castro and the Cardinal," *WP*, August 9, 2010.

60. Weissert, "Cuba Agrees to Free 52 Political Prisoners"; Obama's March comments are in "Statement by the President on the Human Rights Situation in Cuba," March 24, 2010, White House.

61. "Interview of the President by Juan Carlos López, CNN En Español, April 15, 2009," Office of the Press Secretary, White House.

62. Confidential interview with a former U.S. official.

63. James Anderson, "New Mexico Gov. on Cuba Mission, Plans White House Report," AP, August 26, 2009.

64. Gerardo Arreola, "Discutió en Cuba plan de 'acciones recíprocas' para normalizar vínculos, dice Bill Richardson," *La Jornada* (Mexico), August 29, 2009.

65. "Gov. Bill Richardson, D-N.M., Delivers Remarks at the NDN on Cuba and on U.S.-Latin American Relations," *CQ Transcriptions*, October 9, 2009.

66. Patricia Grogg, "Cuba-US: Embargo as Usual Flies in the Face of International Opposition," Inter Press Service, September 17, 2009; Will Weissert, "Cuba Says U.S. Should Lift Embargo Unconditionally," AP, September 16, 2009.

67. "Gov. Bill Richardson, D-N.M., Is Interviewed on MSNBC," *CQ Transcriptions*, August 24, 2010; CNN, "American Morning," Interview with New Mexico Governor Bill Richardson, Federal News Service, August 26, 2010.

68. "Progress in Case of US Contractor Held in Cuba: US Governor," Agence France Presse, August 26, 2010; Will Weissert, "In Cuba, Richardson Raises Case of Jailed American," AP, August 26, 2010.

69. This account of the meeting is based on Richardson's notes, which he shared with the authors: Memorandum for the Record, October 27, 2010, Subject: Breakfast Meeting between Cuban Foreign Minister Bruno Rodríguez, Cuban Ambassador Jorge Bolaños, and Governor Bill Richardson.

70. Paul Haven, "US, Cuban Diplos Met about Jailed US Man," AP, October 18, 2010; Schneiderman, "Our Man in Havana." Rodríguez's view is from his comments to Richardson.

71. "Carter Meets Jailed American in Cuba, Calls for Release," Agence France Presse, March 31, 2011.

72. Peter Orsi, "Carter Leaves Cuba without Jailed US Contractor," AP, March 30, 2011.

73. "Trip Report by Former U.S. President Jimmy Carter, to Cuba, March 28–30, 2011," April 1, 2011, The Carter Center, https://www.cartercenter.org/news/trip_reports/cuba-march2011.html.

74. Brennan interview.

75. Cable, USINT (Farrar) to State, "From the Mouth of MINREX: Possible Insight onto US-CU Migration Talks," Havana 341, June 9, 2009, Wikileaks.

76. Cable, USINT (Farrar) to State, "Check, Please! Government of Cuba May Accept U.S. Offer of Post-Hurricane Assistance," Havana 559, September 14, 2009, Wikileaks.

77. Cable, USINT (Farrar) to State, "U.S.-Cuba Chill Exaggerated, but Old Ways Threaten Progress," Havana 9, January 6, 2010, Wikileaks.

78. Cable, from USINT (Farrar) to State, "GOC Signals 'Readiness to Move Forward,'" Havana 592, September 25, 2009, Wikileaks.

79. U.S. Department of State, *International Narcotics Control Strategy Report, 2011*, "Cuba."

80. Marc Frank, "U.S. Cuba Cooperation Cuts Illegal Migration," Reuters, January 12, 2011.

81. Senior Coast Guard Officer interview, Miami, June 2, 2011.

82. U.S. Department of State, *International Narcotics Control Strategy Report, 2011*, "Cuba."

83. David Adams, "Release of Anti-Castro Militant Stokes Debate," *St. Petersburg Times*, April 21, 2007.

84. Peter Kornbluh, "Former CIA Asset Luis Posada Goes on Trial," *Nation*, January 5, 2011.

85. "Cuba Denounces Acquittal of Former CIA Agent," *Guardian*, April 10, 2011.

86. Will Englund, "An Invasion of Mercy," *National Journal*, January 23, 2010.

87. Manuel Jimenez, "US, Cuban Officials Discuss Haiti Quake Assistance," Reuters, March 19, 2010.

88. "US, Cuba Hold Rare Meeting at UN, with Haiti Focus," Agence France Presse, April 2, 2010.

89. Secretary Clinton, "Remarks on Nuclear Nonproliferation at the University of Louisville as Part of the McConnell Center's Spring Lecture Series," April 9, 2010, Department of State.

90. Valenzuela's speech to Latin American Studies Association, Toronto, Canada, October 9, 2010.

91. Joel Millman, "New Prize in Cold War: Cuban Doctors," *Wall Street Journal*, January 15, 2011; Damien Cave, "Americans and Cubans Still Mired in Distrust," *NYT*, September 15, 2011; Randal C. Archibold, "Cuba Takes Lead Role in Haiti's Cholera Fight," *NYT*, November 7, 2011.

92. "US, Cuba Meet but Reach No Deal on Haiti Aid," Agence France Presse, April 22, 2010.

93. Paul Haven, "US and Cuba Hold Talks on Oil Spill," AP, May 19, 2010.

94. Center for Democracy in the Americas, *As Cuba Plans to Drill in the Gulf of Mexico, U.S. Policy Poses Needless Risks to Our National Interest*, 27.

95. Schenk, "Geological Assessment of Undiscovered Oil and Gas Resources of the North Cuba Basin, Cuba."

96. Petty comments at New American Foundation panel, "U.S.-Cuba Engagement in the Gulf: Lessons from the Deepwater Horizon Oil Spill," Washington, D.C., May 26, 2010.

97. Howard LaFranchi, "What If BP Oil Spill Heads for Cuba?," *Christian Science Monitor*, June 11, 2010.

98. Piñon and Muse, "Coping with the Next Oil Spill: Why U.S.-Cuba Environmental Cooperation Is Critical."

99. "From the President: Principle above Politics—Cuba, USA Need a One Gulf Strategy," *Drilling Contractor* (International Association of Drilling Contractors), November–December 2010.

100. Clifford Kraus, "Drilling Plans Off Cuba Stir Fears of Impact on Gulf," *NYT*, September 29, 2010.

101. Mary Ellen Klas, "Sen. Graham: Gulf Oil Spill a 'Wake-Up Call,'" *MH*, January 15, 2011.

102. "Offshore Drilling: U.S. Hopes to Bring Mexico—and Cuba—into Joint Effort on Oil Spills," *Greenwire*, March 9, 2011.

103. "Standards on Cuba's Offshore Drilling," *UPI Energy*, April 15, 201.

104. "US and Cuba Discuss Offshore Oil Spill Response in Bahamas," *Oil Daily*, December 15, 2011.

105. REMPEITC-Caribe, Regional OPRC Seminar to Focus on Developing National Plans for Marine Pollution Preparedness and Response Related to Offshore Units and Regional Cooperation, Nassau, Bahamas, December 30, 2011.

106. REMPEITC-Caribe, Third Regional OPRC Forum on Oil Spill Prevention, Preparedness, and Response in the Gulf of Mexico and the Caribbean, Activity Report, Kingston, Jamaica, May 27, 2012.

107. Testimony of U.S. Coast Guard Rear Admiral William Baumgartner and Rear Admiral Cari Thomas before the House Committee on Transportation and Infrastructure, Subcommittee on Coast Guard and Maritime Transportation, Regarding Offshore Drilling in Cuba and the Bahamas and Coast Guard's Oil Spill Readiness and Response Planning, January 30, 2012, Press Office, Department of Homeland Security.

108. Brennan interview.

109. U.S. Senate, Committee on Energy and Natural Resources, *Hearing to Examine the Status of Response Capability and Readiness for Oil Spills in Foreign Outer Continental Shelf Waters Adjacent to U.S. Waters.*

110. Paul Haven, "Richardson Aide Says Cuba Backtracked on American," AP, September 14, 2011; Richardson interview, October 6, 2011.

111. Richardson interview, October 6, 2011.

112. Ibid.; Damien Cave, "Americans and Cubans Still Mired in Distrust," *NYT*, September 16, 2011.

113. Richardson interview, October 6, 2011.

114. "Richardson Heads to Cuba to Discuss Release of Jailed American," *CNN Wire*, September 7, 2011.

115. Richardson interview, October 6, 2011.

116. Ibid.

117. Paul Haven, "Hopes Rise for Release of American Jailed in Cuba," AP, September 8, 2011; Paul Haven and Anne-Marie Garcia, "Ex-Gov: Cuba Denies Meeting with Jailed American," AP, September 9, 2011.

118. Portia Siegelbaum, "Cuba Accuses Bill Richardson of 'Blackmail,'" *CBS News WorldWatch*, September 14, 2011; Paul Haven, "Cuba Hits Back at Richardson over Failed Visit," AP, September 15, 2011.

119. Paul Haven, "Richardson to Leave Cuba Bitter, with No Prisoner," AP, September 14, 2011.

120. "Interview with Former New Mexico Governor Bill Richardson," *The Situation Room*, CNN, September 14, 2011.

121. Portia Siegelbaum, "Richardson Fails to Free American Jailed in Cuba," *CBS News WorldWatch*, September 13, 2011.

122. Marcus Gleisser, "Castro Set to Talk Economics with U.S. Ex-Envoy Reports," *Cleveland Plain Dealer*, May 28, 1994.

123. Two statewide exit polls showed Obama winning the Cuban American vote, 49 percent to Romney's 47 percent (Edison Research National Election Pool), or losing it narrowly, 48 percent to Romney's 52 percent (Bendixen & Amandi International). Juan O. Tamayo, "Did Obama or Romney Win the Cuban-American Vote?," *MH*, November

12, 2012; Sergio Bendixen, Comment on Brian E. Crowley, "Little Havana Turns Blue (or Maybe Not)," *Columbia Journalism Review* online, November 14, 2012, http://www.cjr.org/united_states_project/little_havana_turns_blue_or_ma.php?page=all.

124. Cuban Research Institute, "FIU Cuba Poll," http://cri.fiu.edu/research/cuba-poll/.

125. Paul Haven, "Could Kerry, Hagel Drive Reboot in U.S.-Cuba Ties?," AP, January 26, 2013.

126. Gross interview.

127. Andrea Rodríguez, "Cuban Spy Unrepentant, but Hopes for Better Ties," AP, May 6, 2013; Paul Haven, "Cuba, U.S. Try Talking, but Face Many Obstacles," AP, June 21, 2013.

128. Haven, "Cuba, U.S. Try Talking, but Face Many Obstacles."

129. U.S. Department of State, *Country Reports on Terrorism, 2012*; Paul Haven, "U.S. Keeps Cuba on State Sponsors of Terrorism List," AP, May 1, 2013.

130. For a detailed description of the request, see Tracey Eaton, "Breakdown of the $20 Million," *Along the Malecón*, May 22, 2013, http://alongthemalecon.blogspot.com/.

131. Caro, *The Passage of Power*, ix.

132. Secretary Clinton, "Interview with Leopoldo Castillo of Globovision, Washington, D.C.," July 7, 2009, Department of State.

133. Brennan interview, June 17, 2011.

Chapter Ten

1. Juan Tamayo, "What Raúl Castro said to Barack Obama," *MH*, December 19, 2013; "Remarks by President Obama at Memorial Service for Former South African President Nelson Mandela," December 10, 2013, Office of the Press Secretary, White House.

2. Jonathan Watts, "Obama and Castro Shake Hands," *Guardian*, December 11, 2013.

3. "El éxito dependerá de la inteligencia, paciencia y sobre todo la firmeza con que actuemos," *Granma*, December 23, 2013.

4. Smith, *The Closest of Enemies*.

5. Department of State Policy Planning Council, "Draft Outline: Caribbean: Cuba," February 13, 1964, DDRS.

6. Gil Klein, "Bush Lays Down His Conditions for Normal Relations with Cuba," *Washington Times*, March 20, 1990.

7. Frank Davies, "White House Considers Plan for Commission to Carry out a Bipartisan Review," *MH*, November 24, 1998.

8. Discurso Pronunciado por el Comandante Fidel Castro Ruz, en el Acto de Inauguracion de la Ciudad Escolar "Abel Santamaría," Santa Clara, el 28 de Enero de 1961, Discursos Archive; FBIS, "Castro Interview with PBS McNeil," *Latin America Daily Report, Annex*, February 20, 1985.

9. CIA, *Cuban International Activities Inimical To U.S. Interests*, November 9, 1982, 10, CIA FOIA website.

10. Clinton, *My Life*, 310.

11. Secretary Clinton, "Remarks on Nuclear Nonproliferation at the University of Louisville as Part of the McConnell Center's Spring Lecture Series," April 9, 2010, Department of State.

12. Memorandum of Conversation, December 2–3, 1978, Havana, Cuba, "U.S./Cuban Relations," DDRS.

13. Benjamin C. Bradlee, "Don't Talk to Castro about Human Rights," *WP*, March 6, 1977.

14. "National Policy Paper—Cuba: United States Policy," July 15, 1968, DDRS.

15. FBIS, "Castro Discusses Immigration Agreement with U.S.," *Latin America Daily Report*, December 18, 1984.

16. Sánchez-Parodi interview, May 18, 2005.

17. Memorandum of Conversation, Kissinger and Boumediene, October 14–15, 1974, NSA Cuba Collection.

18. Presidential Directive/NSC-6, March 15, 1977, "Cuba," Carter Library, Vertical File, Presidential Directives, 1–20.

19. "Remarks to the Cuban-American Community," June 27, 1995, *PPP Clinton*.

20. Anita Snow, "Fidel's Brother Takes Temporary Control," AP, August 1, 2006. The CIA also judged that regime "hard-liners" had "serious misgivings" about the risks normalization entailed. CIA, National Intelligence Estimate, "Cuba Changing International Role," October 16, 1975, CIA FOIA website.

21. Lowenthal, "The United States and Latin America," 199–213.

22. Memorandum of Conversation, December 3–4, 1978, Havana, Cuba, "US/Cuban Relations," DDRS.

23. "Transcript of Meeting between U.S. Secretary of State Alexander M. Haig, Jr., and Cuban Vice Premier Carlos Rafael Rodríguez, Mexico City, 23 November 1981," *Cold War International History Project Bulletin*, no. 8–9 (Winter 1996–97): 207–21.

24. "Text of Cuban Note Rejecting Protest and Calling for a Change in U.S. Policy," *NYT*, November 14, 1959.

25. "No Enemy Can Defeat Us," *Granma International*, August 18, 2006.

26. Nancy San Martin, "Raúl Castro Hints at Readiness for Dialogue with Washington," *MH*, August 19, 2006.

27. Martí, "Honduras y los extranjeros," in *José Martí: Obras Completas*, 8:35. Translation courtesy of Professor John Kirk.

BIBLIOGRAPHY

Archives

Jimmy Carter Library and Museum, Atlanta, Ga.

Declassified Documents Reference System, Gale Cengage Learning

George Bush Presidential Library and Museum, College Station, Tex.

Gerald R. Ford Presidential Library and Museum, Ann Arbor, Mich.

Government of Cuba, Havana

    Discursos e intervenciones del Comandante en Jefe Fidel Castro Ruz, Presidente
        del Consejo de Estado de la República de Cuba, http://www.cuba.cu/gobierno/
        discursos/

Hoover Institution Archives, Stanford University, Stanford, Calif.

    James B. Donovan Papers, 1919–1976

    Papers of Robert D. Murphy

John F. Kennedy Presidential Library and Museum, Boston, Mass.

LBJ Presidential Library, Austin, Tex.

Library of Congress, Manuscript Division, Washington, D.C.

    Philip W. Bonsal Papers, 1914–1992

    Frontline Diplomacy: The Foreign Affairs Oral History Collection of the Association for
        Diplomatic Studies and Training

National Archives and Records Administration, College Park, Md.

    General Records of the Department of State (Record Group 59)

    Records of the Foreign Service Posts of the Department of State (Record Group 84)

National Security Archive, George Washington University, Washington, D.C.

    Cuban Missile Crisis Collection

    U.S.-Cuba Diplomacy Collection

Nixon Presidential Library and Museum, Yorba Linda, Calif.

Princeton University, Princeton, N.J., Seeley G. Mudd Manuscript Library

    John Foster Dulles Oral History Collection

Real Academia de la Historia, Madrid, Spain

    Papers of Fernando Castiella

Ronald Reagan Presidential Foundation and Library, Simi Valley, Calif.

U.S. Central Intelligence Agency, Freedom of Information Act Electronic Reading Room,
        http://www.foia.cia.gov/

U.S. Department of State, Electronic Reading Room, http://www.state.gov/m/a/ips/c22790.htm

University of California, Santa Barbara, American Presidency Project

    Public Papers of the Presidents of the United States online at http://www.presidency
        .ucsb.edu/index.php

Wikileaks, Public Library of US Diplomacy, http://wikileaks.org/
Woodrow Wilson International Center for Scholars, Washington, D.C., Wilson Center
    Digital Archive, International History Declassified
    Cuba and Southern Africa Collection
    Cuban Foreign Relations Collection
Yale University Library, New Haven, Conn., Manuscripts and Archives
    Cyrus R. Vance and Grace Sloane Vance Papers, Manuscript Group 1664

Interviews by the Authors

Positions listed are those relevant to the person's involvement in U.S.-Cuban diplomacy.

Aaron, David, Deputy National Security Advisor. September 16, 2004.

Alarcón, Ricardo, Permanent Representative of Cuba to the UN; Vice-Minister of Foreign Relations; Minister of Foreign Relations; and President of the National Assembly. February 20, 2005; May 20, 2005; November 6, 2006.

Armstrong, Fulton, Political Officer in the U.S. Interests Section in Havana; National Security Council staff; National Intelligence Officer for Latin America; Senate Foreign Relations Committee staff. November 12, 2004; October 19, 2009; November 28, 2011; August 14, 2012; August 23, 2013; October 18, 2013.

Armstrong, Scott, journalist. August 16, 2012.

Berger, Samuel R. 'Sandy,' Deputy National Security Advisor; National Security Advisor (Clinton). October 15, 2013.

Bourne, Peter, Special Assistant to the President for Health Issues (Carter). January 17, 2007.

Brennan, Peter, U.S. Department of State Coordinator for Cuban Affairs. June 17, 2011.

Brzezinski, Zbigniew, National Security Advisor (Carter). November 22, 2004.

Bundy, McGeorge, National Security Advisor (Kennedy, Johnson). March 22, 1996.

Carter, James, President of the United States. July 23, 2004.

Castro, Fidel, President of Cuba. May 21, 2005.

Cohen, Tom, and Lisa Fuentes, private citizens. October 12, 2013.

Coll, Alberto, Deputy Assistant Secretary of Defense for Special Operations and Low Intensity Conflict. August 20, 2013.

Feinberg, Richard, Special Assistant to the President for National Security Affairs (Clinton) and Senior Director, Office of Inter-American Affairs, National Security Council. October 21, 2004.

Ferch, John, Chief of the U.S. Interests Section in Havana. April 6, 2004; October 6, 2005.

García, Néstor, First Secretary of the Cuban Mission to the UN. December 21, 2012.

Gross, Alan, USAID subcontractor. November 28, 2012, December 18, 2013.

Halperin, Morton, Special Assistant to the President (Clinton) and Senior Director for Democracy, National Security Council. April 16, 2006; December 18, 2011; March 19, 2012.

Huddleston, Vicki, U.S. Department of State Coordinator for Cuban Affairs; Chief of the U.S. Interests Section in Havana. August 28, 2005; October 22, 2007.

Jones, Kirby, businessman. April 3, 2004.

Landau, Saul, independent filmmaker. February 7, 2004; August 29, 2006; August 16, 2012.

Lechuga, Carlos, Cuba's Permanent Representative to the UN. December 1, 1994 (with Philip Brenner).

Luers, William H., Deputy Assistant Secretary of State for Inter-American Affairs. October 29, 2010; July 28, 2011.

Mankiewicz, Frank, journalist. June 5, 1994; October 29, 2010.

McConnell, Shelly, Senior Associate Director, Americas Program, The Carter Center. September 7, 2007.

McLarty, Thomas "Mack," Counselor to the President (Clinton) and Special Envoy for the Americas. September 3, 2009.

Newsom, David D., Undersecretary of State for Political Affairs. September 18, 2004.

Nolan, John E., attorney, Steptoe & Johnson. April 29, 2004.

Nolan, Richard, Member of Congress. May 12, 2006.

Nuccio, Richard A., Senior Policy Advisor to the Assistant Secretary of State for Inter-American Affairs; Special Advisor to the President and to the Secretary of State for Cuba (Clinton). April 28, 2004; March 30, 2008; January 31, 2012.

Offitt, Sidney, author. August 30, 2003; May 3, 2013.

Padrón, José Luis, special assistant to President Fidel Castro. November 9, 2006.

Parmly, Michael, Chief of the U.S. Interests Section in Havana. February 10, 2008.

Pastor, Robert A., Director, Office of Latin American and Caribbean Affairs, National Security Council (Carter); Consultant and Senior Advisor, The Carter Center. July 1, 2004; July 14, 2009; October 29, 2010.

Remírez, Fernando, First Vice Minister of Foreign Relations; Permanent Representative to the UN; Chief of the Cuban Interests Section; Head of the Department of Foreign Relations of the Central Committee of the Communist Party of Cuba. May 20, 2005.

Richardson, Bill, Member of Congress; Governor of New Mexico. February 10, 2010, October 29, 2010; October 6, 2011.

Rodríguez, Carlos Rafael, Vice-President of Cuba. April 3, 1982.

Rogers, William D., Assistant Secretary of State for Inter-American Affairs. June 16, 2005.

Rozental, Andrés, Deputy Foreign Minister of Mexico. October 1, 1996.

Salsamendi, Carlos, foreign policy advisor to Cuban vice president Carlos Rafael Rodríguez. April 1, 1982.

Sánchez-Parodi, Ramón, Chief of Cuban Interests Section in Washington; Vice Foreign Minister of Cuba. May 18, 2005; August 6, 2012.

Schaeffer, Richard, attorney and sports agent. August 17, 2012.

Schlesinger, Arthur, Jr., Special Assistant to the President (Kennedy). August 28, 2003.

Sheehan, General John J., Commander in Chief, U.S. Atlantic Command. September 19, 2013.

Smith, Wayne S., U.S. Department of State Coordinator for Cuban Affairs; Chief of the U.S. Interests Section in Havana. September 10, 2004.

Styron, Rose, author. November 12, 2008; March 23, 2012.

Sweig, Julia, Senior Fellow for Latin America, Council on Foreign Relations. January 18, 2012.

Tarnoff, Peter, Executive Secretary of the Department of State; Special Assistant to the Secretary of State; Undersecretary of State for Political Affairs. April 29, 2004; August 10, 2007; January 10, 2008.

Taylor, John J. "Jay," Chief of the U.S. Interests Section in Havana. December 20, 2004.

Todman, Terence, Assistant Secretary of State for Inter-American Affairs. July 14, 2004.

Valenzuela, Arturo, Deputy Assistant Secretary of State for Western Hemisphere Affairs; Senior Director for Inter-American Affairs, National Security Council; Assistant Secretary of State for Western Hemisphere Affairs. October 3, 2013.

Van Reigersberg, Stephanie, U.S. Department of State translator. January 15, 2007.

Watson, Alexander "Alec" F., Assistant Secretary of State for Inter-American Affairs. October 13, 2010.

White, Robert, U.S. ambassador to El Salvador. November 18, 2011.

Works Cited

Aguilar, Luis E. *Cuba 1933: Prologue to Revolution*. Ithaca: Cornell University Press, 1972.

Albright, Madeleine. *Madam Secretary: A Memoir*. New York: Miramax Books, 2003.

Amoedo, Julio A. "Negotiating with Fidel Castro." *New Leader*, April 27, 1964, 10–12.

Attwood, William. *The Reds and the Blacks: A Personal Adventure*. New York: Harper and Row, 1967.

———. *The Twilight Struggle: Tales of the Cold War*. New York: Harper & Row, 1987.

Azicri, Max. "Could the War Have Been Avoided?" *NACLA Report on the Americas* 24, no. 3 (November 1990): 22–23.

Bagley, Bruce Michael, Roberto Alvarez, and Katherine Hagedorn, eds. *Contadora and the Central American Peace Process: Selected Documents*. Boulder, CO: Westview Press, 1985.

Bain, Mervyn J. "Cuba-Soviet Relations in the Gorbachev Era." *Journal of Latin American Studies* 37 (2005): 769–91.

Baker, James A. *The Politics of Diplomacy*. New York: Putnam Adult, 1995.

Bardach, Ann Louise. *Cuba Confidential: Love and Vengeance in Miami and Havana*. New York: Random House, 2003.

Barnes, Jack, Mary-Alice Waters, and Martín Koppel, eds. *Making History: Interviews with Four Generals of Cuba's Revolutionary Armed Forces*. New York: Pathfinder, 1999.

Bendixen, Sergio. "Comment on Brian E. Crowley, 'Little Havana Turns Blue (or Maybe Not).'" *Columbia Journalism Review* online, November 14, 2012, http://www.cjr.org/united_states_project/little_havana_turns_blue_or_ma.php?page=all.

Benes, Bernardo. "3,600 Cuban Political Prisoners." Unpublished manuscript. National Security Archive, U.S.-Cuba Diplomacy Collection.

Benjamin, Jules Robert. *The United States and Cuba: Hegemony and Dependent Development, 1880–1934*. Pittsburgh: University of Pittsburgh Press, 1977.

Berle, Adolf. *Navigating the Rapids, 1918–1971, from the Papers of Adolf A. Berle*. New York: Harcourt Brace Jovanovich, 1973.

Beschloss, Michael R., and Strobe Talbot. *At the Highest Level: The Inside History of the End of the Cold War*. Boston: Little Brown, 1993.

Bialer, Seweryn, and Alfred Stepan. "Cuba, the US, and the Central American Mess." *New York Review of Books*, May 27, 1982.

Bigger, Philip J. *Negotiator: The Life and Career of James B. Donovan*. Bethlehem, Pa.: Leigh High University Press, 2006.

Bird, Kai. *The Color of Truth: McGeorge Bundy and William Bundy, Brothers in Arms; A Biography*. New York: Simon & Schuster, 1998.

Blachman, Morris J., William M. LeoGrande, and Kenneth E. Sharpe, eds. *Confronting Revolution: Security through Diplomacy in Central America*. New York: Pantheon Books, 1986.

Blight, James, Bruce J. Allyn, and David A. Welch. *Cuba on the Brink: Castro, the Missile Crisis, and the Soviet Collapse*. Boulder, Colo.: Rowman & Littlefield, 2002.

Blight, James, and Philip Brenner. *Sad and Luminous Days: Cuba's Struggle with the Russians after the Missile Crisis*. Boulder, Colo.: Rowman & Littlefield, 2003.

Blumenthal, Max. "The Other Regime Change: Did the Bush Administration Allow a Network of Right-Wing Republicans to Foment a Violent Coup in Haiti?" Salon.com, July 16, 2004.

Bogenschild, Thomas E. "Dr. Castro's Princeton Visit, April 20–21, 1959," [Princeton Program in Latin American Studies]. *PLAS Newsletter*, Fall 1998.

Bohning, Don. *The Castro Obsession: U.S. Covert Operations against Cuba, 1959–1965*. Washington, D.C.: Potomac Books, 2005.

Bonsal, Philip. *Cuba, Castro, and the United States*. Pittsburgh: University of Pittsburgh Press, 1971.

Branch, Taylor. *The Clinton Tapes: Wrestling History with the President*. New York: Simon & Schuster, 2009.

Brinkley, Douglas. *Acheson: The Cold War Years, 1953–1971*. New Haven: Yale University Press, 1992.

Brookings Institution, Florida International University, and the Cuba Study Group. "2008 Cuba/US Transition Poll." FIU website, http://www2.fiu.edu/~ipor/cuba t/.

Brzezinski, Zbigniew. *Power and Principle: Memoirs of the National Security Adviser, 1977–1981*. New York: Farrar Straus Giroux, 1983.

Bush, George. *All the Best, George Bush: My Life in Letters and Other Writings*. New York: Simon & Schuster, 2000.

Caro, Robert A. *The Passage of Power*. New York: Knopf, 2012.

Carter, Jimmy. *Beyond the White House: Waging Peace, Fighting Disease, Building Hope*. New York: Simon & Schuster, 2007.

———. "Trip Report by Former U.S. President Jimmy Carter, to Cuba, March 28–30, 2011," April 1, 2011, The Carter Center.

———. *White House Diary*. New York: Farrar Straus and Giroux, 2010.

Case 1/1989: End of the Cuban Connection. Havana: José Martí Publishing House, 1989.

Castro, Fidel. *Fidel Castro's Speeches: Cuba's Internationalist Foreign Policy, 1975–1980*. Edited by Michael Taber. New York: Pathfinder Press, 1981.

———. *History Will Absolve Me*. Havana: Editorial de Ciencias Sociales, 1975.

———. *War and Crisis in the Americas: Fidel Castro Speeches, 1984–85*. Edited by Michael Taber. New York: Pathfinder Press, 1985.

Castro, Fidel, and Ignacio Ramonet. *Fidel Castro: My Life, A Spoken Autobiography*. New York: Scribner, 2009.

Castro, Raúl. "Key Address at the Ministerial Meeting of the Non-aligned Movement, Havana, Cuba, April 29, 2009." http://www.cuba.cu/gobierno/rauldiscursos/2009/ing/r290409i.html.

———. "Speech on the 54th Anniversary of the Attack on Moncada and Carlos Manuel de Céspedes Garrisons, Camagüey, July 26, 2007." Cuban Foreign Ministry web site, http://www.cubaminrex.cu/English/Speeches/RCR/RCR_260707.htm.

Castro Mariño, Soraya M., and Ronald W. Pruessen, eds. *Fifty Years of Revolution: Perspectives on Cuba, the United States, and the World*. Gainesville: University of Florida Press, 2012.

Casuso, Teresa. *Cuba and Castro*. New York: Random House, 1961.

Center for Democracy in the Americas. *As Cuba Plans to Drill in the Gulf of Mexico, U.S. Policy Poses Needless Risks to Our National Interest*. Washington, D.C.: Center for Democracy in the Americas, 2011.

Center for International Policy. *U.S.-Cuban Cooperation in Defending against Hurricanes*. Washington, D.C.: CIP, July 2011.

Center for Responsive Politics. *The Cuban Connection: Cuban-American Money in U.S. Elections, 1979–2000*. Washington, D.C.: Center for Responsive Politics, 2001.

Chang, Lawrence, and Peter Kornbluh, eds. *The Cuban Missile Crisis, 1962*. New York: New Press, 1999.

CIA [Central Intelligence Agency]. "Cuban Support for Central American Guerrilla Groups," May 2, 1979. *Congressional Record*, May 19, 1980, 11653–55.

CIA Targets Fidel: Secret 1967 CIA Inspector General's Report on Plots to Assassinate Fidel Castro. Melbourne, Australia: Ocean Press, 1996.

Clinton, William. *My Life: Bill Clinton*. New York: Alfred Knopf, 2004.

Commission for Assistance to a Free Cuba. *Report to the President, May 2004*. Washington, D.C.: U.S. Department of State, 2004.

———. *Report to the President, July 2006*. Washington, D.C.: U.S. Department of State, 2006.

Council on Foreign Relations, *U.S.-Cuban Relations in the 21st Century*, Independent Task Force Report, January 1999. New York: Council on Foreign Relations, 1999.

Crocker, Chester A. *High Noon in Southern Africa: Making Peace in a Rough Neighborhood*. New York: W. W. Norton, 1992.

Cuban Research Institute, "FIU Cuba Poll." http://cri.fiu.edu/research/cuba-poll/.

"Cuba-United States: Memorandum of Understanding on the Hijacking of Aircraft and Vessels." *International Legal Materials* 12, no. 2 (March 1973): 370–76.

Daniel, Jean. *Le Temps qui reste: Essai d'autobiographie professionnelle*. Paris: Gallimard, 1984.

———. "Unofficial Envoy: An Historic Report from Two Capitals." *New Republic*, December 14, 1963, 15–20.

———. "When Castro Heard the News." *New Republic*, December 7, 1963, 7–9.

Dominguez, Jorge I. "U.S.-Cuban Relations: From the Cold War to the Colder War." *Latin American Politics and Society* 39 (Fall 1997): 49–75.

Duffy, Gloria. "Crisis Mangling and the Cuban Brigade." *International Security* 8, no. 1 (Summer 1983): 67–87.

———. "Crisis Politics: The Carter Administration and Soviet Troops in Cuba, 1979." Ph.D. diss., Columbia University, 1991.

Dumbrell, John. *President Lyndon Johnson and Soviet Communism*. Manchester: Manchester University Press, 2004.

Eaton, Tracey. "Breakdown of the $20 Million." *Along the Malecón* website, May 22, 2013. http://alongthemalecon.blogspot.com/.

Eckstein, Susan Eva. *Back from the Future: Cuba under Castro*. Princeton, N.J.: Princeton University Press, 1994.

Eisenhower, Dwight David. *Waging Peace, 1956–1961*. New York: Doubleday, 1965.

Eisenhower, Milton Stover. *The Wine Is Bitter*. New York: Doubleday, 1963.

Englund, Will. "An Invasion Of Mercy." *National Journal*, January 23, 2010, 12.

Erikson, Daniel. *The Cuba Wars: Fidel Castro, the United States, and the Next Revolution*. New York: Bloomsbury Press, 2009.

Faw, Bob, and Nancy Skelton. *Thunder in America*. Austin: Texas Monthly Press, 1986.

Feste, Karen. "Reducing International Terrorism: Negotiating Dynamics in the U.S.-Cuba Skyjack Crisis." Paper presented to the 19th annual conference of the Association for Conflict Management, Montreal, Canada, June 25–28, 2006.

Foreign Assistance Act of 1961 (P.L. 87-195), Sec. 620A. Prohibition on Assistance to Government Supporting International Terrorism, 22 USC § 2371.

Franqui, Carlos. *Diary of the Cuban Revolution*. New York: Viking Press, 1980.

———. *Family Portrait with Fidel: A Memoir*. New York: Random House, 1984.

"From the President: Principle above Politics—Cuba, USA Need a One Gulf Strategy." *Drilling Contractor* (International Association of Drilling Contractors), November–December 2010.

FRUS. See U.S. Department of State, Office of the Historian, *Foreign Relations of the United States*.

Fursenko, Aleksandr, and Timothy Naftali. *One Hell of a Gamble: Khrushchev, Castro, and Kennedy, 1958–1964; The Secret History of the Cuban Missile Crisis*. New York: W. W. Norton, 1998.

García Iturbe, Néstor. *Diplomacia Sin Sombra*. Havana, Cuba: Editorial de Ciencias Sociales, 2007.

Gates, Robert M. *From the Shadows: The Ultimate Insider's Account of Five Presidents and How They Won the Cold War*. New York: Simon & Schuster, 1996.

Geithner, Timothy. Letter to Robert Menendez, March 5, 2009. *Congressional Record*, March 5, 2009, S2933.

Geyer, Georgie Anne. *Guerrilla Prince: The Untold Story of Fidel Castro*. New York: Little, Brown, 1991.

Glantz, Michael H. "Climate-Related Disaster Diplomacy: A U.S.-Cuban Case Study." *Cambridge Review of International Affairs* 14, no. 1 (2000): 233–53.

Gleijeses, Piero. *Conflicting Missions: Havana, Washington, and Africa, 1959–1976*. Chapel Hill: University of North Carolina Press, 2002.

———. "A History Worthy of Pride." *Tricontinental*, no. 158 (2004): online.

———. "Moscow's Proxy? Cuba and Africa 1975–1988." *Journal of Cold War Studies* 8, no. 2 (2006): 3–51.

———. "Truth or Credibility: Castro, Carter, and the Invasions of Shaba." *International History Review* 18, no. 1 (February 1996): 70–103.

———. *Visions of Freedom: Havana, Washington, Pretoria, and the Struggle for Southern Africa, 1976–1991*. Chapel Hill: University of North Carolina Press, 2013.

González Delgado, Dalia. "El tiempo polí tico está a favor de que se elimine el bloqueo: *Granma* dialogó con Ramón Sánchez-Parodi Montoto." *Granma*, December 13, 2013.

Goodwin, Richard. "Annals of Politics." *New Yorker*, May 25, 1968, 93–95.

———. "Cigars & Che & JFK." *Cigar Aficionado*, Autumn 1996.

———. *Remembering America*. New York: Harper Collins, 1995.

Gorbachev, Mikhail. *Memoirs*. New York: Doubleday, 1996.

Gott, Richard. *Cuba: A New History*. New Haven: Yale University Press, 2004.

Guevara, Ernesto "Che." *Che Guevara Reader: Writings on Politics & Revolution*. Edited by David Deutschmann. Melbourne: Ocean Press, 2012.

Gunn, Gillian. "Cuba and Angola." In *Cuba: The International Dimension*, edited by Georges Fauriol and Eva Loser, 121–52. New Brunswick, N.J.: Transaction, 1990.

Haig, Alexander M. *Caveat: Realism, Reagan, and Foreign Policy*. New York: Macmillan, 1984.

Haig, Alexander M., and Charles McCarry. *Inner Circles: How America Changed the World; A Memoir*. New York: Grand Central Publishing, 1992.

Haney, Patrick, and Walt Vanderbush. *The Cuban Embargo*. Pittsburgh: University of Pittsburgh Press, 2005.

Hersh, Seymour M. *The Price of Power: Kissinger in the Nixon White House*. New York: Summit Books, 1983.

Hershberg, James G. "The United States, Brazil, and the Cuban Missile Crisis, 1962 (Part 1)." *Journal of Cold War Studies* 6, no. 2 (2004): 3–20.

———. "The United States, Brazil, and the Cuban Missile Crisis, 1962 (Part 2)." *Journal of Cold War Studies* 6, no. 3 (2004): 5–67.

Holland, Max. *The Kennedy Assassination Tapes*. New York: Alfred A. Knopf, 2004.

Howard, Lisa. "Castro's Overture." *War/Peace Report*, September 1963, 3–5.

Hunt, E. Howard. *Give Us This Day*. New Rochelle, N.Y.: Arlington House, 1973.

"Informational Letter on Contemporary Cuban-American Relations, April 26, 1979." *Cold War International History Project Bulletin* nos. 8–9 (Winter 1996–97): 186–90.

International Telecommunications Union. *Measuring the Information Society 2010*. Geneva: International Telecommunications Union, 2010.

Javits, Jacob K., and Claiborne Pell. *The United States and Cuba: A Propitious Moment*. A report to the Committee on Foreign Relations, United States Senate, October 1974. Washington, D.C.: Government Printing Office, 1974.

Johnson, Haynes. *The Bay of Pigs: The Leaders' Story of Brigade 2506*. New York: W. W. Norton, 1974.

Keller, Renata. "A Foreign Policy for Domestic Consumption: Mexico's Lukewarm Defense of Castro, 1959–1969." *Latin American Research Review* 47, no. 2 (2012): 100–119.

Kimber, Stephen. *What Lies across the Water: The Real Story of the Cuban Five*. Nova Scotia: Fernwood Publishing, 2013.

Kirkpatrick, Lyman B. *The Real CIA: An Insider's View of the Strengths and Weaknesses of Our Government's Most Important Agency*. New York: Macmillan, 1968.

Kissinger, Henry. "Building an Enduring Foreign Policy, November 24, 1975." *Department of State Bulletin* 73, no. 1903 (December 15, 1975): 844–54.

———. "Questions and Answers Following the Secretary's Pittsburgh Address." *Department of State Bulletin* 73, no. 1901 (December 1, 1975): 765.

———. "The United States and Latin America: The New Opportunity." *Department of State Bulletin* 72, no. 1865 (March 24, 1975): 361–69.

———. *Years of Renewal*. New York: Simon & Schuster, 1999.

Kornbluh, Peter. "Baseball Diplomacy." *In These Times*, May 19, 1999, 15–17.

———. *Bay of Pigs Declassified: The Secret CIA Report*. New York: New Press, 1998.

———. *Cuba, Counternarcotics, and Collaboration: A Security Issue in U.S.-Cuban Relations*. The Caribbean Project, Center for Latin American Studies, Georgetown University, December 2000.

———. "Cuban Embargo-Buster." *Nation*, December 13, 2001.

———. "JFK and Castro: The Secret Quest for Accommodation." *Cigar Aficionado*, September–October 1999, 86–105.

———. "A 'Moment of Rapprochement': The Haig-Rodríguez Secret Talks." *Cold War International History Project Bulletin*, nos. 8–9 (Winter 1996–97): 217–19.

Kornbluh, Peter, and James Blight. "Dialogue with Castro: A Hidden History." *New York Review of Books*, October 6, 1994.

Kornbluh, Peter, and William M. LeoGrande, "Talking with Castro." *Cigar Aficionado*, February 2009, 2–10.

Landau, Anya K., and Wayne S. Smith. "CIP Special Report on Cuba and Bioweapons: Groundless Allegations Squander U.S. Credibility on Terrorism." Washington, D.C.: CIP, July 12, 2002.

———. "Cuba on the Terrorist List: In Defense of the Nation or Domestic Political Calculation?" *International Policy Report*, November 2002.

Landau, Saul. "Of Rumors, Plots and Machinations: Fidel and The Prince." *Counterpunch*, September 5, 2003. http://www.counterpunch.org/2003/09/05/fidel-and-the-prince/.

Landau, Saul, and Nelson Valdes. "Confessions of Roger Noriega: Muscular Diplomacy or Law Breaking?" *Progreso Weekly*, September 15, 2010.

Larzelere, Alex. *The 1980 Cuban Boatlift*. Washington, D.C.: National Defense University Press, 1988.

Latell, Brian. *After Fidel: The Inside Story of Castro's Regime and Cuba's Next Leader*. New York: Palgrave Macmillan, 2007.

Lazo, Mario. *Dagger in the Heart: American Policy Failures in Cuba*. New York: Twin Circle, 1970.

Lechuga, Carlos. *In the Eye of the Storm: Castro, Khrushchev, Kennedy, and the Missile Crisis*. Boston: Ocean View Press, 1995.

LeoGrande, William M. "Cuban Dependency: A Comparison of Pre-revolutionary and Post-revolutionary International Economic Relations." *Cuban Studies* 9, no. 2 (July 1979): 1–28.

———. "Enemies Evermore: U.S. Policy towards Cuba after Helms-Burton." *Journal of Latin American Studies* 29, no. 1 (February 1997): 211–21.

———. "From Havana to Miami: U.S. Cuba Policy as a Two-Level Game." *Journal of Interamerican Studies and World Affairs* 40, no. 1 (April 1, 1998): 67–86.

———. *Our Own Backyard: The United States in Central America, 1977–1992*. Chapel Hill: University of North Carolina Press, 2000.

Lévesque, Jacques. *The USSR and the Cuban Revolution: Soviet Ideological and Strategical Perspectives, 1959–77*. New York: Praeger, 1978.

Levine, Robert M. *Secret Missions to Cuba: Fidel Castro, Bernardo Benes, and Cuban Miami*. New York: Palgrave Macmillan, 2002.

Lockwood, Lee. *Castro's Cuba, Cuba's Fidel*. New York: Vintage Giant, 1969.

López-Fresquet, Rufo. *My 14 Months with Castro*. New York: World Publishing, 1966.

Louis, J. C., and Harvey Yazijian. *The Cola Wars*. New York: Everest House, 1980.

Lowenthal, Abraham F. "The United States and Latin America: Ending the Hegemonic Presumption." *Foreign Affairs* 55, no. 1 (October, 1976): 199–213.

Martí, José. "Honduras y los extranjeros." In *José Martí : Obras Completas*, vol. 8. Havana: Editorial de Ciencias Sociales, 1975.

———. *Selected Writings*. New York: Penguin, 2002.

Matthews, Herbert L. *Castro: A Political Biography*. London: Penguin, 1969.

May, Ernest R., and Philip D. Zelikow, eds. *The Kennedy Tapes: Inside the White House during the Cuban Missile Crisis*. Cambridge, Mass.: Harvard University Press, 1997.

Mayer, William G. "Trends: American Attitudes toward Cuba." *Public Opinion Quarterly* 65, no. 4 (December 1, 2001): 585–606.

McPherson, Alan. "The Limits of Populist Diplomacy: Fidel Castro's April 1959 Trip to North America." *Diplomacy and Statecraft* 18, no. 1 (December 2007): 237–68.

Menges, Constantine. *Inside the National Security Council: The True Story of the Making and Unmaking of Reagan's Foreign Policy*. New York: Simon & Schuster, 1988.

Merico-Stephens, Ana Maria, and John P. Schmal. "Voting." In *Encyclopedia Latina: History, Culture, and Society in the United States*, edited by Ilan Stavans and Harold Augenbraum, 2:270–76. Danbury, Conn.: Grolier Academic Reference, 2005.

Merle, Robert. *Ben Bella*. London: Michael Joseph, 1967.

Mesa-Lago, Carmelo. "The Economy: Caution, Frugality, and Resilient Ideology." In *Cuba, Internal and International Affairs*, edited by Jorge Dominguez, 113–67. Thousand Oaks, Calif.: Sage Publications, 1982.

Ministry of Foreign Affairs of Cuba. "The Cuban Government Submits to the United States a Set of Proposals for Bilateral Agreements on Migratory Issues, Cooperation in Drug Interdiction and a Program to Fight Terrorism," March 17, 2002. http://www.cuba.cu/gobierno/documentos/index.html.

———. "Statement," January 16, 2011. http://www.cubaminrex.cu/english/Statements/Articulos/StatementsMINREX/2011/Statement.html.

Moore, David. "Americans Approve of U.S. Government Decision to Return Boy to Cuba." *Gallup News Service Poll Releases*, January 12, 2000.

Moreno, Dario, Maria Ilcheva, and Juan Carlos Flores, "The Hispanic Vote in Florida." In *Beyond the Barrio: Latinos in the 2004 Election*, edited by Rodolfo O. de la Garza, Louis DeSipio, and David L. Leal, 251–70. Notre Dame, Ind.: University of Notre Dame Press, 2010.

Morley, Jefferson. "Shootdown." *Washington Post Magazine*, May 25, 1997.

Morley, Morris. *Imperial State and Revolution: The United States and Cuba, 1952–1986*. Cambridge: Cambridge University Press, 1988.

Morley, Morris, and Chris McGillion. *Unfinished Business: America and Cuba after the Cold War, 1989–2001*. Cambridge: Cambridge University Press, 2002.

Nagin, Carl. "Backfire." *New Yorker*, January 26, 1998, 30–35.

National Security Archive. *Bay of Pigs 40 Years Later: Briefing Book of Declassified Documents*. Washington, D.C.: National Security Archive, 2001.

———. *Talking with Castro: Precedent and Potential for Diplomatic Dialogue between the United States and Cuba*. Washington, D.C.: National Security Archive, 2010.

Newsom, David D. *The Soviet Brigade in Cuba: A Study in Political Diplomacy*. Bloomington: Indiana University Press, 1987.

Nixon, Richard M. *Six Crises*. New York: Simon & Schuster, 1990.

Nuccio, Richard. "No Good Deed Unpunished." Unpublished manuscript. National Security Archive, U,S.-Cuba Diplomacy Collection.

Oberdorfer, Don. *From the Cold War to a New Era: The United States and the Soviet Union, 1983–1991*. Baltimore: Johns Hopkins University Press, 1998.

———. *The Turn: How the Cold War Came to an End*. New York: Poseidon Press, 1991.

Ojito, Mirta. *Finding Mañana: A Memoir of a Cuban Exodus*. New York: Penguin Group, 2005.

Oppenheimer, Andres. *Castro's Final Hour: The Secret Story behind the Coming Downfall of Communist Cuba*. New York: Touchstone, 1993.

Organization of American States, Resolution On Cuba, AG/RES. 2438 (XXXIX-O/09): Adopted at the third plenary session, held on June 3, 2009, in General Assembly, Thirty-Ninth Regular Session, San Pedro Sula, Honduras, June 2–4, 2009. *Proceedings*, 1:12.

"PAC profile: U.S. Cuba Democracy Political Action Committee." *CQ Moneyline*, published by *Congressional Quarterly*.

Palmieri, Victor H. "An Act of War: The Inside Story of the Mariel Boatlift." Unpublished manuscript, Carter Library.

Pastor, Robert. "The Carter-Castro Years: A Unique Opportunity." In *Fifty Years of Revolution: Perspectives on Cuba, the United States, and the World*, edited by Soraya M. Castro Mariño and Ronald W. Pruessen, 237–60. Gainesville: University of Florida Press, 2012.

Paterson, Thomas. *Contesting Castro: The United States and the Triumph of the Cuban Revolution*. New York: Oxford University Press, 1994.

Pavlov, Yuri. *Soviet-Cuban Alliance, 1959–1991*. Boulder, Colo.: Lynne Rienner Publishers, 1994.

Pazos, Javier. "Cuba—Was a Deal Possible in '59?" *New Republic*, January 12, 1963, 10–11.

Pedraza, Silvia. *Political Disaffection in Cuba's Revolution and Exodus*. New York: Cambridge University Press, 2007.

Pérez, Louis A., Jr. *Cuba and the United States: Ties of Singular Intimacy*. Athens: University of Georgia Press, 1990.

———. *On Becoming Cuban*. Chapel Hill: University of North Carolina Press, 2007.

Pérez-Cisneros, Pablo, John B. Donovan, and Jeff Koenreich. *After the Bay of Pigs: Lives and Liberty on the Line*. Miami: Alexandria Library, 2008.

Pérez-López, Jorge. "The Cuban Economic Crisis of the 1990s and the External Sector." *Cuba in Transition* (Association for the Study of the Cuban Economy) 8 (1998): 386–413.

Pérez-Stable, Marifeli. *Cuba and the United States: Intimate Enemies*. New York: Routledge, 2010.

Perine, Keith. "Conferees Purge Controversial Items from Treasury-Postal Service Bill." *CQ Weekly Report*, October 27, 2001, 2548.

———. "Presidents, Lawmakers Alike Caught Up in Cuba Embargo's Power to Polarize." *CQ Weekly Report*, May 18, 2002, 1270.

Peters, Phil. *Cuba, the Terrorism List, and What the United States Should Do*. Issue Brief, November 20, 2001. Arlington, Va.: Lexington Institute, 2001.

Piñon, Jorge R., and Robert L. Muse, "Coping with the Next Oil Spill: Why U.S.-Cuba Environmental Cooperation Is Critical." *U.S.-Cuba Relations at Brookings, Issue Brief No. 2*, May 2010. Washington, D.C.: Brookings Institution, 2010.

Pomper, Miles A. "Sentiment Grows for Ending Cuban Embargo, but Opponents Say Bush Will Stand Firm." *CQ Weekly Report*, February 9, 2002, 408.

Public Campaign. *Cold Hard Cash, Cold War Politics: How Cuban American Hard-Liners Influence Congress with Campaign Contributions*, November 16, 2009. Washington, D.C.: Public Campaign, 2009.

Quirk, Robert E. *Fidel Castro*. New York: Norton, 1995.

Ramírez Cañedo, Elier. "Ford, Kissinger y la normalización de las relaciones con Cuba." *Rebelión* (Havana) 23 February 23, 2011; March 8, 2011; March 12, 2011.

———. "J. F. Kennedy y la idea de la 'dulce aproximación a Cuba.'" *Rebelión*, March 24, 2010.

———. "Una historia poco conocida de las relaciones Estados Unidos-Cuba." *Rebelión*, November 25, 2011.

Rasky, Harry. *Nobody Swings on Sunday: The Many Lives and Films of Harry Rasky*. Ontario, Canada: Collier Macmillan Canada, 1980.

Reagan, Nancy, and William Novak. *My Turn: The Memoirs of Nancy Reagan*. Thorndike, Me.: Thorndike Press, 1990.

Reagan, Ronald. *The Reagan Diaries*. New York: Harper Perennial, 2009.

Rothkopf, David J. "A Call for a Post-Cold War Cuba Policy." In *Cuba: Contours of Change*, edited by Susan K. Purcell and David J. Rothkopf, 105–26. Boulder, Colo.: Lynne Rienner Publishers, 2000.

Roy, Joaquin. "The European Union's Perception of Cuba." In *A Contemporary Cuba Reader*, edited by Philip Brenner et al., 254–61. New York: Rowman & Littlefield, 2007.

Salinas de Gortari, Carlos. *México: The Policy and the Politics of Modernization*. New York: Random House, 2002.

Salinger, Pierre. "Kennedy, Cuba and Cigars." *Cigar Aficionado*, November–December 2002, online edition.

Samuels, Gertrude. "How Metadiplomacy Works: James Donovan and Castro." *Nation*, April 13, 1963.

Schenk, Joaquin. *Geological Assessment of Undiscovered Oil and Gas Resources of the North Cuba Basin, Cuba: U.S. Geological Survey Open-File Report 2010-1029*. Denver, Colo.: U.S. Geological Survey Information Services, 2010.

Schlesinger, Arthur, Jr. *Robert Kennedy and His Times*. Boston: Houghton Mifflin, 1978.

———. *A Thousand Days: John F. Kennedy in the White House*. New York: Fawcett, 1984.

Schneiderman, R. M. "Our Man in Havana: The Imprisonment of Alan Gross and the U.S. Effort to Bring Him Home." *Foreign Affairs*, December 21, 2012, online. http://www .foreignaffairs.com/articles/138693/r-m-schneiderman/our-man-in-havana.

Schoultz, Lars. *That Infernal Little Cuban Republic: The United States and the Cuban Revolution*. Chapel Hill: University of North Carolina Press, 2011.

Shaplen, Robert. "Eye of the Storm III." *New Yorker*, June 16, 1980, 44–95.

Shenon, Philip. *A Cruel and Shocking Act: The Secret History of the Kennedy Assassination*. New York: Henry Holt, 2013.

Shevchenko, Arkady. *Breaking with Moscow*. New York: Ballantine Books, 1985.

Shultz, George P. *Triumph and Turmoil: My Years as Secretary of State*. New York: Charles Scribner, 1993.

Sklar, Barry. *Cuba: Normalization of Relations*. Issue Brief. Washington, D.C.: Library of Congress, Congressional Research Service, 1977.

———. "Cuban Exodus, 1980." In *The Cuba Reader*, edited by Philip Brenner et al., 339–47. New York: Grover Press, 1989.

Skoug, Kenneth. "Cuba as a Model and a Challenge: July 25, 1984." *U.S. Department of State Current Policy*, no. 600. U.S. Department of State, Bureau of Public Affairs, Office of Public Communication, 1984.

———. *The United States and Cuba under Reagan and Shultz: A Foreign Service Officer Reports.* Westport, Conn.: Praeger, 1996.

Skoug, Kenneth, and Coleen Sussman. "The United States and Cuba: December 17, 1984." *U.S. Department of State Current Policy*, no. 646. Washington, D.C.: U.S. Department of State, Bureau of Public Affairs, 1985.

Smith, Earl E. T. *The Fourth Floor: An Account of the Castro Communist Revolution.* Madison: University of Wisconsin Press, 1962.

Smith, Thomas G. "Negotiating with Fidel Castro: The Bay of Pigs Prisoners and a Lost Opportunity." *Diplomatic History*, 19 (Winter 1995): 59–86.

Smith, Wayne S. *The Closest of Enemies: A Personal and Diplomatic Account of U.S.-Cuban Relations Since 1957.* New York: Norton, 1987.

———. "Dateline Havana: Myopic Diplomacy." *Foreign Policy*, no. 48 (1982): 157–74.

Smith, Wayne S., and Esteban Morales Dominguez. *Subject to Solution: Problems in Cuban-U.S. Relations.* Boulder, Colo.: Lynne Rienner Publisher, 1988.

"Soviet Memorandum of Conversation, The Malta Summit Meeting," December 2, 1989. In *Masterpieces of History: The Peaceful End of the Cold War in Europe, 1989*, edited by Svetlana Savranskaya, Thomas Blanton, and Vladislav Zubok, 630–31. Budapest: CEU Press, 2011.

Stone, Peter H. "Cuban Clout," *National Journal*, February 20, 1993, 452.

Suarez, Andres. *Cuba: Castro and Communism, 1959–1966.* Cambridge, Mass.: MIT Press, 1967.

Sullivan, Mark P. *Cuba: U.S. Restrictions on Travel and Remittances.* CRS Report for Congress RL31139. Washington, D.C., Congressional Research Service, 2003.

Swanson, Ian. "Hard-Line Cuba PAC Makes Inroads with House Freshmen." *The Hill*, September 18, 2007.

Sweig, Julia. *Inside the Cuban Revolution: Fidel Castro and the Urban Underground.* Cambridge, Mass.: Harvard University Press, 2004.

Szulc, Tad. *Fidel: A Critical Portrait.* New York: Post Road Press, 2000.

Taylor, Andrew. "Bush May Christen His Veto Pen on Treasury-Postal Spending Bill." *CQ Weekly Report*, July 27, 2002, 2053.

Thomas, Hugh. *Cuba: The Pursuit of Freedom.* New York: Da Capo Press, 1998.

"Transcript of Meeting between East German Leader Erich Honecker and Cuban Leader Fidel Castro, East Berlin (excerpts), April 3, 1977." *Cold War International History Project Bulletin*, nos. 8–9 (Winter 1996–97): 68–61.

"Transcript of Meeting between U.S. Secretary of State Alexander M. Haig, Jr., and Cuban Vice Premier Carlos Rafael Rodríguez, Mexico City, 23 November 1981." *Cold War International History Project Bulletin*, nos. 8–9 (Winter 1996–97): 207–21.

Turner, Stansfield. *Secrecy and Democracy: The CIA in Transition.* Boston: Houghton Mifflin, 1985.

"TV's First Lady of Sin." *People Today*, April 22, 1953, 23–25.

USAID [U.S. Agency for International Development]. *Evaluation of the USAID Cuba Program.* Washington, D.C.: USAID, 2000.

U.S.-Cuba Trade and Economic Council. "2012–2001 U.S. Export Statistics for Cuba." *Economic Eye on Cuba*, February 2013, online. http://www.cubatrade.org/CubaExportStats.pdf.

U.S. Department of State. *Congressional Budget Justification for Foreign Operations, FY 2003.* Washington, D.C.: U.S. Department of State, 2002.

———. *Congressional Budget Justification for Foreign Operations, FY 2008.* Washington, D.C.: U.S. Department of State, 2007.

———. *Congressional Budget Justification for Foreign Operations, FY 2009.* Washington, D.C.: U.S. Department of State, 2008.

———. *Congressional Budget Justification for Foreign Operations, FY 2011, Annex: Regional Perspectives.* Washington, D.C.: U.S. Department of State, 2010.

———. *Cuba's Renewed Support for Violence in Latin America: A Special Report.* Washington, D.C.: U.S. Department of State, 1981.

———. "Soviet Bloc Assistance to Nicaragua and Cuba versus U.S. Assistance to Central America." *Latin America Dispatch*, October 1987.

U.S. Department of State, Bureau for International Narcotics and Law Enforcement Affairs. *International Narcotics Control Strategy Report, April 1993.* Washington, D.C.: U.S. Department of State, 1993.

———. *International Narcotics Control Strategy Report, April 1994.* Washington, D.C.: U.S. Department of State, 1994.

———. *International Narcotics Control Strategy Report, 2000.* Washington, D.C.: U.S. Department of State, 2000.

———. *International Narcotics Control Strategy Report, 2011.* Washington, D.C.: U.S. Department of State, 2011.

U.S. Department of State, Office of the Coordinator for Counterterrorism. *Country Reports on Terrorism, 2008.* Washington, D.C.: U.S. Department of State, April 2009.

———. *Country Reports on Terrorism, 2012.* Washington, D.C.: U.S. Department of State, May 2013.

———. *Patterns of Global Terrorism, 2001.* Washington, D.C.: U.S. Department of State, May 2002.

U.S. Department of State, Office of the Historian. *Foreign Relations of the United States, 1958–1960.* Vol. V, *American Republics.* Washington, D.C.: Government Printing Office, 1991.

———. *Foreign Relations of the United States, 1958–1960.* Vol. VI, *Cuba.* Washington, D.C.: Government Printing Office, 1991.

———. *Foreign Relations of the United States, 1961 to 1963.* Vol. X, *Cuba, January 1961–September 1962.* Washington, D.C.: Government Printing Office, 1997.

———. *Foreign Relations of the United States, 1961–1963.* Vol. XI, *Cuban Missile Crisis and Aftermath.* Washington, D.C.: Government Printing Office, 1996.

———. *Foreign Relations of the United States, 1961–1963.* Vol. XII, *American Republics.* Washington, D.C.: Government Printing Office, 1996.

———. *Foreign Relations of the United States, 1964–1968.* Vol. XXXII, *Dominican Republic; Cuba; Haiti; Guyana.* Washington, D.C.: Government Printing Office, 2005.

———. *Foreign Relations of the United States, 1969–1976.* Vol. E-10, *Documents on American Republics, 1969–1972.* Department of State website.

———. *Foreign Relations of the United States, 1969–1976.* Vol. E-1, *Global Issues, 1969–1972.* Department of State website.

U.S. Department of State, Office of the Under Secretary for Democracy and Global Affairs. *Trafficking in Persons Report*. Washington, D.C.: U.S. Department of State, June 2009.

U.S. GAO [General Accounting Office]. *Broadcasts to Cuba: TV Martí Surveys Are Flawed*, August 1990.

U.S. GAO [Government Accountability Office]. *U.S. Democracy Assistance for Cuba Needs Better Management and Oversight*, GAO-07-147, November 2006, 24.

U.S. House of Representatives, Committee on Foreign Affairs. *Cuban Involvement in International Narcotics Trafficking*. 101st Congress, First Session, July 25, 27, 1989.

———. *Is It Time to Lift the Ban on Travel to Cuba?* 111th Congress, First Session, November 19, 2009.

U.S. House of Representatives, Committee on Foreign Affairs, Subcommittee on Inter-American Affairs, *Foreign Assistance Legislation for FY83. (Part 6): Security Assistance Proposals for Latin America and the Caribbean*, 97th Congress, Second Session, April 21, 1982.

U.S. House of Representatives, Committee on Foreign Affairs, Joint Hearing before the Subcommittee on Economic Policy, Trade, and Environment, Western Hemisphere Affairs, and International Operations . *U.S. Policy and the Future of Cuba: The Cuban Democracy Act and U.S. Travel to Cuba*, 103rd Congress, First Session, November 18, 1993.

U.S. House of Representatives, Committee on International Relations, Subcommittee on the Western Hemisphere. *The Clinton Administration's Reversal of U.S. Immigration Policy toward Cuba*, 104th Congress, First Session, May 18, 1995.

U.S. House of Representatives, Permanent Select Committee on Intelligence, Subcommittee on Oversight. *The Cuban Emigres: Was There a U.S. Intelligence Failure?* Staff Report, June 1980.

"U.S. Informs Cuba of Views on Agrarian Reform Law." *Department of State Bulletin* 40, no. 1044 (June 29, 1959): 958–59.

U.S. Senate, Committee on Energy and Natural Resources. *Hearing to Examine the Status of Response Capability and Readiness for Oil Spills in Foreign Outer Continental Shelf Waters Adjacent to US Waters*, 112th Congress, First Session, October 18, 2011.

U.S. Senate, Committee on Foreign Relations. *Cuba's Pursuit of Biological Weapons: Fact or Fiction?*, Hearing before the Subcommittee on Western Hemisphere, Peace Corps and Narcotics Affairs, S. Hrg. 107-736, 107th Congress, Second Session, June 5, 2002.

———. *Nomination of Hon. Cyrus R. Vance to Be Secretary of State*, 95th Congress, First Session, January 11, 1977.

U.S. Senate, Committee on the Judiciary, Subcommittee on Security and Terrorism, *Role of Cuba in International Terrorism and Subversion*, 97th Congress, Second Session, February 26, March 4, 11, 12, 1982.

U.S. Senate, Committee on the Judiciary, Subcommittee on Security and Terrorism, and Committee on Foreign Relations, Subcommittee on Western Hemisphere Affairs. *Cuban Government's Involvement in Facilitating International Drug Traffic*, Senate, S. Hrg. 98-260. 98th Congress, First Session, April 30, 1983,

U.S. Senate, Committee on the Judiciary, Subcommittee to Investigate the Administration of the Internal Security Act and Other Internal Security Laws. *Communist Threat to the U.S. through the Caribbean, Part 1*, 86th Congress, First Session, July 14, 1959.

———. *Communist Threat to the U.S. through the Caribbean, Part 11*, 87th Congress, First Session, Part 11, June 5, 1961.

U.S. Senate, Select Committee to Study Governmental Operations with Respect to Intelligence Activities (Church Committee). *Alleged Assassination Plots Involving Foreign Leaders: Interim Report*, S.Rpt. 94-465, 94th Congress, First Session, November 20, 1975.

Vance, Cyrus. *Hard Choices: Critical Years in America's Foreign Policy*. New York: Simon & Schuster, 1983.

———. "Secretary Vance's News Conference of January 31." *U.S. Department of State Bulletin* 76, no. 1965 (February 21, 1977): 137-46.

Vanderbush, Walt, and Patrick J. Haney. "Policy toward Cuba in the Clinton Administration." *Political Science Quarterly* 114, no. 3 (Autumn 1999): 387-408.

Walters, Vernon. *The Mighty and the Meek: Dispatches from the Front Line of Diplomacy*. London: St Ermin's, 2001.

Weber, Stephen, et al. *Cuba Policy and US Public Opinion*. College Park: University of Maryland, April 15, 2009.

Weinberger, Caspar. *Fighting for Peace: Seven Critical Years in the Pentagon*. New York: Warner Books, 1991.

Whalen, Charles, et al. "A Detente with Cuba." *Congressional Record*, January 29, 1973, H2506-10.

Wharton, Clifton. "Forging a True Partnership of the Americas." *U.S. Department of State Dispatch* 4, no. 18 (May 3, 1993): 305-8.

Wolfe, Kathryn A. "Mindful of Florida's Clout, Conferees Drop Cuba Travel from Transportation Bill." *CQ Weekly Report*, November 15, 2003, 2845-46.

Woodward, Bob. *State of Denial: Bush at War, Part III*. New York: Simon & Schuster, 2006.

Wyden, Peter. *Bay of Pigs: The Untold Story*. New York: Simon & Schuster, 1980.

Ziegler, Melanie M. *U.S.-Cuban Cooperation Past, Present, and Future*. Gainesville: University Press of Florida, 2007.

INDEX

26th of July Movement, 12, 19, 25, 27, 40

Aaron, David, 173, 182, 196,; and meeting at La Côte Basque, 183–86, 189, 220; criticism of State Department by, 189; and meeting in Atlanta, 190–91; and meeting in Cuernavaca, 192–94, 198
Abel, Rudolf, 51
Abourezk, James, 1, 158, 164
Abrams, Elliott, 252, 253, 254, 261, 414
Abrantes, José, 52, 469 (n. 262)
Academic travel. *See* Educational and cultural exchange
Acheson, Dean, 15
Acosta, Teofilo, 128
Adams, John Quincy, 8, 417
Afghanistan, 211, 212, 214, 219, 222, 226, 345, 347, 372
Africa, 150, 203, 205–6, 208, 220, 228, 234, 237, 409
—Cuban policy in, 151, 165, 168, 180, 188–89, 194, 203–4, 244, 260, 266, 406; Castro rejects U.S. criticism of, 201, 415
See also individual countries
Agramonte, Roberto, 23, 24, 40
Agrarian reform, 10, 13, 21, 22, 23, 24
Aguilar, Carlos, 217
Aguirre de Cárcer, Nuño, 111
Alarcón, Ricardo, 225, 362, 408; and Mariel boatlift, 217, 218, 219; and Central America, 228; and Grenada, 237; in 1984 migration talks, 240–43, 244; in 1987 migration talks, 247–48; urges talks on southern Africa, 253–55; in 1994 migration talks, 293, 294–95; in 1995 migration talks, 297–99; warnings about

Brothers to the Rescue, 308; on Clinton's 1999 measures, 319; and Baltimore Orioles-Cuban national team baseball games, 322, 324, 325; and Elián González, 340–41; in migration consultations, 347, 357; meeting with Jimmy Carter, 386; on acquittal of Posada Carriles, 390
Albino da Silva, José, 58
Albright, Madeleine K., 315, 317, 322
Aldana Escalante, Carlos, 256, 259, 261, 262–63, 328
Alderson, Sandy, 324
Algeria, 55, 152
Allende, Salvador, 123, 127
Alliance for Progress, 22, 44, 63
Alpha 66, 120, 273. *See also* Cuban Americans—paramilitary violence by
Americans for Humanitarian Trade with Cuba, 317
American Society of Newspaper Editors (ASNE), 13
Amoedo, Julio A., 30–31, 32, 34, 425 (n. 118)
Anderson, Jack, 226
Anderson, Robert B., 17, 36
Andrés Pérez, Carlos, 348
Angelos, Peter, 320, 321–22, 324
Angola, 173, 177, 196, 198, 229, 230, 291, 339, 349, 391, 413; Cuban intervention in, 145–48, 152, 153, 179, 412; as obstacle to normalization under Carter, 158–59, 160, 161, 166, 172, 223; Cuba's refusal to negotiate about, 163, 176, 184, 186–87, 191–93; tenuous security of, 168–69, 172, 176, 187, 213; Brzezinski's criticism of Cuban policy in, 169–71; Carter administration demands Cuban withdrawal from, 175–76, 184, 186, 191–93; negotiations for

Bush (G. W.) administration, 370, 387; regime change policy of, 345–47, 355; support by Cuban American conservatives, 346; tension with Cuba after September 11 attacks, 346–47; accuses Cuba of biological weapons development, 347–48, 352; and Carter's trip to Cuba, 349, 353–55; restricts people-to-people travel, 355–57; ends migration consultations, 357–60; increases support for dissidents, 359–61; support for USAID democracy promotion programs, 354, 359, 374; conflict over Interests Sections, 360–61, 362–63; and Commission for Assistance to a Free Cuba, 361, 367; response to Castro's stepping down, 365–67; rejection of Raúl Castro's offers to negotiate, 366–67; belief in imminent regime collapse, 367; counterterrorism cooperation, 363; offers disaster relief, 363–65; creates Cuban Medical Professional Parole Program, 391

Calibrated response, 115, 275–76, 278–80, 295–96, 315, 344, 400, 412
Califano, Joseph, 177
Camarioca, 103–7, 216, 248, 344
Canada, 37, 52, 108, 122, 133, 135, 349
CANF. *See* Cuban American National Foundation
Capestany, Cecilia, 312
Carazo, Rodrigo, 217
Cardone, Kathleen, 389
Carlucci, Frank C., 252
Carrillo, Antonio, 109
Carroll, Eugene, 309
Carter, Jimmy, 3, 4, 179, 202, 224; signs PD/NSC-6 to normalize relations, 155, 156; favors relations with adversaries, 155, 164; meets with Mankiewicz, 157; Castro's opinion of, 157–58, 174, 182, 217, 222; articulates conditions for normalization, 158, 410, 412; concern about reciprocity, 162; on lifting embargo on food and medicine, 164–65; halts

normalization over Cuban involvement in Africa, 166, 169–70, 172, 223; on Shaba II invasion, 172, 174, 175, 223; letter to Castro via George McGovern, 175–76; use of Austin as private emissary, 176–78; halts 1978 talks, 194, 196; and Puerto Rican nationalist prisoners, 198, 204–5; adopts policy of containment, 205; and Soviet combat brigade, 209–10; instructs Tarnoff and Pastor on talks with Castro, 212; and Mariel boatlift, 216, 217, 218, 281; attacked by Reagan, 222; briefed by Tarnoff on September 1980 talks, 223; as intermediary during 1994 rafters crisis, 285–89; trips to Cuba, 348–55, 360, 385–87
Carter, Rosalynn, 349
Carter administration, 4, 226, 227, 229, 238, 240, 255, 297, 327; decision to normalize relations, 155–56, 159–60; ends travel ban, 157; halts SR-71 overflights, 157; fishing and maritime agreement, 157, 161–63; early conditions for normalization, 158, 160–61; early concerns over Cubans in Angola, 158–59, 160, 223; Todman meeting with Malmierca, 162–64; signs Interests Sections agreement, 163; retains embargo on food and medicine, 164–65, 166–67, 168–69, 190; August 1977 policy review, 165–66; reaction to Cuban involvement in Ethiopia, 169–72, 224; reaction to Shaba invasions, 172–75; Vance meeting with Carlos Rafael Rodríguez, 173–75; use of Congressmen Nolan and Richmond as emissaries, 175–76; use of Austin as emissary, 176–78; dealings with Benes, 178–82, 184, 190, 194–95; holds 1978 secret talks, 183–94; and Nonaligned Conference, 190, 207, 210, 211, 212; meeting in Havana with Carlos Rafael Rodríguez, 196, 197–200; and MiG-23 controversy, 197; 1978 meeting in Havana with Castro, 200–203; 1979 policy review, 205–7, 210–11; reaction to Soviet combat brigade, 207–10; effort to

block Cuba from UN Security Council, 211, 212; 1980 meeting in Havana with Castro, 211–14; and Mariel boatlift, 214–23; and *Blue Fire*, 221–22; and counterterrorism cooperation, 332–33

—during Reagan administration: 226, 244; Mexican mediation, 228; meets with Walters, 231–32; on excludables, 232; on Central America, 232; and Grenada, 237–38; meets with Jackson, 240; on 1984 migration agreement, 242, 243; offers to negotiate with United States, 243; reacts to Radio Martí, 245–46; and southern Africa talks, 250, 252–53, 254, 256–57

—during G. H. W. Bush administration: meeting with Gorbachev in Havana, 260–61; on TV Martí, 261, 263; reacts to end of Soviet military aid, 265–66; attempted assassination of, in Panama, 389

—during Clinton administration, 306, 316, 324, 336; sends message to Clinton at Martha's Vineyard, 268, 290–92; calls for talks with United States, 274; eases travel for Cuban Americans, 274; opinion of Clinton, 274, 317; U.S. contingency plans for fall of, 278–79; triggers rafters crisis, 281; denounces Clinton's 1994 sanctions, 284; uses Carter as intermediary, 285–88; negotiates through Salinas, 289–90, 292–94, 297; approves 1995 migration agreement, 298–99; anger at BTTR overflights, 306, 309; meetings with Richardson, 310–11; reacts to Clinton's 1998 measures, 317; offers counter-narcotics cooperation, 326–27, 329; offers counterterrorism cooperation, 333, 334–36; meets Vicki Huddleston, 339

—during G. W. Bush administration: opposes U.S. military war on terror, 346; reacts to inclusion of Cuba on U.S. terrorism list, 347; reacts to charges of Cuban bioweapons, 348; meetings with Carter, 348–55; holds referendum on socialism, 355; on breakdown of migration agreement, 358; warns about USINT aid to dissidents, 360–61; leads protest rally at USINT, 363; and disaster assistance

from United States, 364–65; illness of, 365–67

—during Obama administration: criticizes Yoani Sánchez, 376; meets with Carter, 386

—general views of: on need for two-term U.S. president, 397; refusal to negotiate Cuban foreign policy, 404; offers talks with United States, 405, 406–7; on U.S.-Cuban antagonism, 405–6, 407; refusal to negotiate Cuban sovereignty, 415–16

Castro, Raúl, 262, 395, 409, 414; on the break in relations with United States, 1, 5, 41, 163, 402; calls for better relations with United States, 4, 5, 97, 99, 273, 366, 367, 369–70, 374, 385, 402–3, 408, 412, 416, 477 (n. 9); radicalism of, 21, 23, 33, 40, 422 (n. 68); appointed minister of FAR, 27; on relations at Guantánamo, 303–4, 346; succeeds to presidency, 365–67; criticizes U.S. policy, 367, 377; receives message from Obama via Spain, 381; dialogue with Cardinal Ortega, 381–82, 410; meets with Carter, 385, 386–87; shakes hands with Obama, 402; focuses on Cuba's economic problems, 407

Casuso, Teresa, 15, 18

Catholic Church, 381–82, 385. *See also* Ortega, Jaime

CDA. *See* Cuban Democracy Act of 1992

Center for Defense Information, 309

Central America, 158, 206, 211, 220, 241, 322; Cuban policy in, 213, 243, 244, 249, 301, 415; Reagan policy in, 225–38, 409; Bush policy in, 258–64, 409, 415. *See also* El Salvador; Nicaragua

Central Intelligence Agency (CIA), 33, 36, 73, 80, 113, 116; and Bay of Pigs, 1, 27, 29, 34, 35, 42–43, 48; attempts to assassinate Castro, 2, 29, 43, 65–66, 117; and James Donovan, 2, 50, 51–53, 62–64, 66; meeting with Castro in New York, 18–21; during Batista regime, 19–20; support for Castro's opponents, 24, 29, 34, 38, 39;

blamed by Castro for *La Coubre*, 32, 32n; covert paramilitary operations by, 43, 47, 59, 72, 83, 91, 100–101, 112, 114, 120, 122, 142, 160, 163, 266, 306, 332; facilitates secret dialogue, 47, 109, 118, 134; and missile crisis, 53, 54, 57, 59; and Howard, 70; on Cuba's interest in dialogue, 71–72, 84–85, 98, 152, 234–36, 406, 411; and Cuban threat to shoot down U-2, 91–93; cooperation with Mexico, 99–100; and death of Che Guevara, 111; in Angola, 145, 148, 251; blamed by Castro for Cubana flight 455 bombing, 154; on impact of delaying normalization, 159; and Shaba II invasion, 173; and Benes, 179, 182; assessments of migration threat, 216, 277, 280; predictions of Cuban regime collapse, 264, 276–77. *See also* CIA prisoners

Cepeda, Patricia, 290–92, 335

Chamber of Commerce, 317

Chase, Gordon, 64, 92, 109, 423 (n. 77); advocates "sweet approach," 70–71; as contact for Attwood, 74, 82, 84; on Cuba policy after Kennedy assassination, 79; advocates for reconciliation, 81–82, 84, 90, 108; as contact for Howard, 85, 88–90, 93–96, 101–3

Chile, 37, 99, 107, 123, 127, 142, 153

Chiles, Lawton, 281–83

China, 120, 126, 132, 135, 152, 254, 321, 354, 372, 391, 408, 413

Christopher, Warren, 167, 277, 280, 298, 301, 305

Church, Frank, 158, 164, 208, 332

CIA. *See* Central Intelligence Agency

CIA prisoners, 122; Donovan negotiations for release of , 61–62, 64–65, 67; negotiations for release under Ford, 131, 134–35, 140; exchange for Puerto Rican nationalists, 134, 175–76, 191, 198, 203, 204–5, 386; negotiations for release under Carter, 162, 164, 166, 167, 188, 191, 193, 196, 198, 202–3

The CIA's Secret Army, 332

Cienfuegos, Soviet submarine base at, 123, 207

Cigars, as instruments of diplomacy, 6, 20, 44, 46, 46n, 60, 119, 119n, 145, 163, 208, 223, 298, 310, 310n, 327, 428 (n. 16)

Claims, U.S. property. *See* Property claims, U.S.

Clark, William P., 250

Clark Amendment, 171, 251

Clarke, Richard, 335–36

Clean Caribbean, 393. *See also* Oil drilling safety and spill mitigation

Clinton, Bill, 301, 304, 316, 341, 407; and Mariel boatlift, 223; meeting on Martha's Vineyard, 268, 290–92; on politics of Cuba issue, 269, 275, 296, 315, 344, 411; supports Cuban Democracy Act, 269–70, 271; Castro's opinion of, 274, 317; meets Mas Canosa during rafters crisis, 283–84; uses Carter as intermediary during rafters crisis, 286, 287, 288–89; uses Salinas as intermediary during rafters crisis, 287, 289–90, 292–94, 297; fires Mort Halperin, 299; announces October 1995 measures, 304; and Richardson, 310–11, 310n, 383–84; reaction to BTTR shoot-down, 313; signs Helms-Burton legislation, 314–15; praises Cuban health and education, 317; announces January 1999 measures, 319; García Marquez's message for, 334–36; on Elián González, 343–44; wonders if Castro wants to keep embargo intact, 406

Clinton, Hillary Rodham, 275, 291; as candidate, 368, 383; at OAS, 369; views on Cuba policy, 372, 373, 377, 400, 406; support for Net Freedom, 375; support for educational travel, 380; praise for release of Cuban prisoners, 382; support for Valenzuela, 383; meeting with Carter, 387; praise for Cuban cooperation in Haiti, 390

Clinton administration, 115, 347, 383, 387; people-to-people initiatives, 268, 272, 272n, 273, 344; political calculations of,

268, 274, 314, 316, 343–44; policy of parallel positive steps, 269, 315–16; influence of Mas Canosa in, 270–71, 283–84; initial efforts to reduce tensions with Cuba, 272–74; counter-narcotics cooperation, 273, 325–31; policy of calibrated response, 275–78, 295–96, 300–301; Small Group, 278–80; rafters crisis, 280–95; 1995 migration agreement, 296–300; initiates fence line talks, 301–4; USAID programs targeting Cuba, 304, 319; and Helms-Burton legislation, 305, 314–15, 344; efforts to halt BTTR flights, 305–13; reaction to BTTR shoot-down, 313–15; licenses news bureaus in Cuba, 316; response to Pope John Paul II's visit to Cuba, 316–17; work with Council on Foreign Relations, 317–19; and baseball diplomacy, 320–25; counterterrorism cooperation, 331–38; return of Elián González, 338–43

Coast Guard. *See* U.S. Coast Guard
Coca-Cola, 176–77
Coleman, William T., Jr., 96–97
Coll, Alberto, 303
Colombia, 11, 153, 177, 211, 231, 238, 263, 326–29, 334
Commission for Assistance to a Free Cuba, 361, 367, 374
Committee of 75, 195, 214
Communist Party: Popular Socialist Party (PSP), 20, 21, 23, 33, 54, 63, 422 (nn. 66, 70); Communist Party of Cuba (PCC), 128, 190, 255, 256, 324, 325, 328, 362, 366, 386, 416
Compensation, for U.S. property. *See* Property claims, U.S.
Concilio Cubano, 313
CORU (Coordination of Revolutionary Organizations), 153–54
Costa Rica, 138, 217–19
Council on Foreign Relations, 297, 318–20
Counter-narcotics cooperation, 2, 240, 258, 334, 346, 355, 410, 412; Clinton administration discussion of, 268, 273, 274, 295,

301, 316; history of, 325–28; 1999 agreement on, 328–31, 344; during Obama administration, 370, 387–88
Counterterrorism cooperation, 125, 162, 182, 268, 316, 327, 344, 412; during Carter administration, 332–33; during Reagan and Bush administrations, 333; on hotel bombings in Havana, 331–34, 337–38, 363; and García Marquez, 334–37; Cuban proposals for, after September 11, 346, 354; during Obama administration, 370, 387, 388–90. *See also* Hijacking
Cox, Alfred, 20
Craig, Gregory B., 246, 341
Crimmins, John, 102, 108, 434 (n. 39)
Crocker, Chester A., 230, 249–57, 414, 415
Cuba: leadership succession, 5, 365–66, 408; before 1959, 8–10; agrarian reform, 10, 13, 21–22; removal of moderates from revolutionary government, 23, 25, 27–28; revolutionary goals, 39, 404
—economy of, 18, 30, 99, 117; before 1959, 8–9; ties to United States, 9, 11, 12, 13, 21, 24, 40, 165, 404; imposition of sanctions on, 29, 31, 35–37, 43, 80, 83, 100, 103, 284 (*see also* Cuban Democracy Act of 1992; Cuban Liberty and Democratic Solidarity Act; Embargo); Soviet support for, 40, 46, 122, 259, 265, 266, 270, 276–77, 279, 317; 1979–1980 recession, 214–15; Special Period, 276, 280; 2001–2002 recession, 358; updating model for, 386, 407–8, 412
—foreign relations of: in Nonaligned Movement, 174, 190, 207, 210, 211, 212; with United States, lessons of, 402–17. *See also* Educational and cultural exchange; Latin America: Cuban support for revolution in; Organization of American States; Soviet Union; *individual African and Latin American countries; individual U.S. administrations*
Cubana Airlines flight 455, 153–54, 157, 331, 332, 334, 389
Cuban Adjustment Act, 107, 215, 299, 357

Educational and cultural exchange, 312; National Policy Paper proposals for, 115; Carter proposals for, 157, 160, 166, 196, 354; Nolan and Richmond proposals for, 175; Clinton eases restrictions on, 274, 279, 301, 304, 316, 320, 344; Orioles exhibition games, 320–25; G. W. Bush imposes restrictions on, 355–56; Obama eases restrictions on, 368, 370, 371, 380, 410. *See also* Baseball diplomacy; People-to-people programs; Travel to Cuba by non–Cuban Americans

Eisenhower, Dwight D., 2, 113, 232, 266, 408; receives report from Herter on Castro, 6–7; opposes Castro's April 1959 visit, 16–17; approves policy to remove Castro, 28; offers January 1960 olive branch, 30–31; Amoedo receives photo of, 34; authorizes covert action against Cuba, 34; supports economic sanctions, 36, 37; breaks relations with Cuba, 38; on exile overflights, 306

Eisenhower, Milton, 48, 49, 50

Eisenhower administration, 4, 42, 113, 266, 408, 414; initial response to revolutionary government, 6, 10–12, 23, 26, 34, 37; and Castro's April 1959 trip to United States, 6–7, 13–21; policy toward Batista, 9–10, 19–20; and bloodbath issue, 12; Bonsal first meeting with Castro, 13–14; offer of economic aid, 17–18, 21, 26; reaction to agrarian reform, 22–23; decision to overthrow Castro, 23–24, 28–29; period of "quiet diplomacy," 24–27; support for opposition, 26, 28, 34, 35–36, 37, 39; 1960 offer to negotiate, 29–32; reaction to *La Coubre* explosion, 32–33; reaction to Mikoyan visit, 33; Lazo initiative, 33–34; imposition of economic sanctions, 35–37; rejection of third country good offices, 37; break in relations, 37–41

Electronic billboard at USINT, 363, 370

El Salvador, 213, 225–30, 232–34, 259, 337

Embargo, 2, 80, 122, 157, 177, 197, 204, 268, 294, 328, 374, 377, 398, 407; imposition

of, 35–38, 43, 103–4; U.S. conditions for lifting, 77, 115, 117, 140, 153, 161, 192–93, 201, 203, 400; U.S. allies' support for, 80, 99–100, 115, 130, 136; Cuba demands lifting of, 97, 131, 132, 133, 140, 157–58, 180, 199, 201, 384, 406; Congressional pressure to lift, 126–27, 295, 347; proposals for partial lifting of, 134, 151, 162–63, 164–65, 166, 258, 364–65, 385; Cuba demands compensation for, 140, 160, 188; lifting of on U.S. subsidiaries abroad, 143, 413; proposals to allow sales of medicine, 166–68, 193, 196, 205; in 1978 negotiations, 188, 191–92, 193, 194, 199–200, 201–2, 203; in Mariel boatlift negotiations, 220, 222, 407; tightening of by Reagan, 227; Clinton's view of, 269, 315, 406; tightening of by CDA, 270; in calibrated response debate, 274–79, 296; in rafters crisis negotiations, 281, 283–84, 287–90, 293, 301, 397, 407; Clinton pledges to maintain, 304–5; codification of by Helms-Burton, 296, 314–15; lifting of on food and medicine, 317–18, 364; Carter's view of, 352, 387; tightened by G. W. Bush, 355, 356, 362; UN condemnation of, 384–85; as obstacle to oil spill cooperation, 392–94; Cuban American opinion on, 397. *See also* Food and medicine, embargo on

Enders, Thomas O., 227, 239

Environmental cooperation, 295, 355, 391–94, 396, 399, 410, 412

Eritrea, 169

Esquipulas, 259, 262

Ethiopia, 169–73, 175, 177, 184, 191–93, 198, 213, 223–24, 229, 291, 349, 412–13

Europe, 100, 115, 116, 211, 271. *See also individual countries*

Excludables, 227, 231–32, 238–42, 247, 274

ExComm (Executive Committee), 53, 55–57. *See also* Cuban Missile Crisis

Export of revolution. *See* Latin America: Cuban support for revolution in

FAA (Federal Aviation Administration), 307–8, 312–13

Family visits. *See* Cuban Americans—family visits to Cuba by

Farrar, Jonathan, 370–71, 375, 377, 388

Farrell, Mike, 321

Fascell, Dante, 184

Federal Aviation Administration (FAA), 307–8, 312–13

Federal Bureau of Investigation (FBI), 131, 153–54, 179, 183, 191, 307; and Havana hotel bombings, 336–38, 363, 389. *See also* Counterterrorism cooperation

Feinberg, Richard, 272, 273, 275

Fence line talks, 301–4. *See also* Guantánamo Naval Station

Ferch, John, 237, 243, 244, 246, 250–51, 253, 327

Fernández, José, 325

Fischli, Alfred, 121

Fishing and maritime agreement, 157, 160–65, 234, 243, 410

Fisk, Dan, 314

Fitzgerald, Desmond, 101

Fleischer, Ari, 349

Fontaine, Roger, 226

Food and medicine, embargo on, 37, 103–4, 116, 151, 372; discussion of under Carter, 162–63, 164–65, 166–68, 190, 193, 196, 205; in Cuban Democracy Act, 270; discussion of under Clinton, 284, 296; in Trade Sanctions Reform Act, 317–18, 372; food sales, 356, 364; Cuban American attitudes on, 397

Ford, Gerald, 145, 405, 442 (n. 121); in Wednesday Group, 127; briefed by Kissinger on opening to Cuba, 130, 143; lifts embargo on U.S. subsidiary trade, 133, 143, 270, 413; in 1976 campaign, 143, 144, 148; ends opening to Cuba, 146, 148; briefed by Kissinger on military contingencies, 148–49

Ford administration: opens secret dialogue with Cuba, 119–20, 128–30; meeting at LaGuardia airport, 130–32; discusses

family visits with Cuba, 132, 140–42, 144, 146, 147–48; expands travel for Cuban diplomats, 132–33; lifts embargo on U.S. subsidiary trade, 133, 143, 270, 413; faces domestic political pressures, 134, 137, 138, 143–44, 148, 152–53; faces OAS pressure to drop Cuba sanctions, 134–35, 136–37; considers baseball diplomacy, 135–36; tries to restart stalled talks, 137–39; meeting at Pierre Hotel, 139–42; reaction to Cuban policy on Puerto Rico, 140, 143–44; votes in OAS to lift Cuba sanctions, 142; reaction to Cuban involvement in Angola, 145–46, 147; develops military contingency plans to hit Cuba, 148–50; assessment of why talks failed, 150–53

Foreign Claims Settlement Commission, 346

Fraga Pérez, Alfonso, 307, 339

Franqui, Carlos, 12, 15, 18

Frechette, Myles, 226

Free Cuba PAC, 270. *See also* Cuban American National Foundation

Freedom Flights, 106, 107, 215. *See also* Camarioca

Freedom Flotilla, 218. *See also* Mariel boatlift

Freedom House, 304, 374, 375

Freeman, Chas, 254

Frei, Eduardo, 127

Fulbright, J. William, 80

Gairy, Eric, 236

Gallegos, Gilbert, 394

García, Néstor, 130–33, 139–42, 144, 146–48, 163, 333

García Almeida, Alfredo, 259, 263

García Márquez, Gabriel, 268, 287–92, 334–37

García Rodríguez, Félix, 333

Gardner, Arthur, 9, 11

Garner, Jay, 345

Gates, Robert M., 183, 184, 220

Gaviria, César, 335

Geithner, Timothy, 372

United States seeks UN condemnation of, 247; as condition of normalization, 267; and calibrated response, 275, 278, 280; USAID funding for, 304; in Carter's speeches in Cuba, 349, 350, 352; Cuba's offer to discuss, 370; Obama on, 373, 400. *See also* Political prisoners in Cuba

Hunt, Lee, 392

Hurricane cooperation, 303, 363–64, 370, 388, 410

Hurwitch, Robert, 64

Hussein, Saddam, 310, 361

Immigration. *See* Migration entries

Interest Sections, 163–65, 247, 366. *See also* Cuban Interests Section; U.S. Interests Section

International Association of Drilling Contractors (IADC), 392

International Republican Institute (IRI), 375

Internet. *See* Cyber war

Iran, 36, 219, 222, 345, 372, 375

Iraq, 310, 345, 361, 362, 372, 383

Jackson, Everett, 205. *See also* CIA prisoners

Jackson, Jesse, 240

Jacobson, Roberta, 399

Javits, Jacob, 127

JMINDIGO, 92, 93

John Paul II (pope), 316, 351, 380

Johnson, Lyndon B., 79, 81, 91, 111, 399; appoints Warren Commission, 79–80; supports policy of hostility, 80; ends Kennedy's 1963 initiative, 82, 84, 85; Castro's message to, 87–89, 93–94, 411; and Guantánamo crisis, 91, 94, 302; Castro's opinion of, 97; and 1964 OAS sanctions, 100; supports travel ban, 104; supports Cuban immigrants, 105, 107; and Vietnam, 112

Johnson, U. Alexis, 121

Johnson administration, 4, 122; policy of hostility and economic denial, 79–80, 100, 103; support for "autonomous" exile paramilitary groups, 80, 83, 91, 100–101,

112; decision not to pursue Kennedy dialogue, 80–84; and attempts by Howard to restart talks, 84–90, 100–102; and Guantánamo crisis, 85, 90–93, 94–95; Howard carries Castro message to, 87–89, 93–94; support for OAS sanctions, 91, 99–100; concerns about Howard as intermediary, 95–96; response to Castro's July 1964 offer to negotiate, 96–99; and Che Guevara's visit to New York, 100–102; and Camarioca migration agreement, 103–6; and third country intermediaries, 107–11; produces National Policy Paper on Cuba, 111–18

Jones, Kirby, 144, 146, 150, 438 (n. 37), 442 (n. 121)

Juanes, 370

Kamman, Curtis W., 247

Katangan gendarmes, 168, 172–74, 196. *See also* Shaba Province

Kazimirov, Vladimir, 246

Keating, Kenneth, 103, 435 (n. 78)

Kennedy, Edward, 246, 372

Kennedy, John F., 40, 335; and Bay of Pigs prisoners, 1, 47–48, 50, 53, 62; considers accommodation with Castro, 2, 42, 64, 79; in 1960 campaign, 35, 68; accepts responsibility for Bay of Pigs, 42; assassination of, 42, 43, 78, 79, 80, 96–97; hostility toward Cuba, 43, 47; cigars from Che Guevara, 44, 46, 46n; meeting with Szulc, 49–50, 429 (n. 28); and missile crisis, 53–54, 55–57; meeting with Ben Bella, 55; authorizes UN dialogue, 73–75, 405; November 1963 speech on Cuba, 76; meeting with Daniel, 76–77, 78, 84; Castro's view of, 81, 84, 85

Kennedy, Robert F., 49; and Bay of Pigs prisoners, 1, 50–51, 59, 60; hostility toward Cuba, 43, 72, 432 (n. 118); instructions to Donovan, 64; on UN dialogue, 74; supports freedom to travel, 104

Kennedy administration, 4, 22, 81, 85, 86; negotiations for Bay of Pigs prisoners, 1,

Namibia, 148, 149, 184, 185, 191, 196, 199, 213, 230, 243, 249–56

National Conservative Political Action Committee (NCPAC), 208

National Front for the Liberation of Angola (FNLA), 145, 148

National Institute of Agrarian Reform (INRA), 32

National Oceanic and Atmospheric Administration (NOAA), 391

National Security Agency, 207, 298

National Union for Total Independence of Angola (UNITA), 145, 148, 169, 171, 186, 229, 249, 251, 257

Negrín, Eulalio J., 195. *See also* Committee of 75

Net Freedom, 375. *See also* Cyber war

Neto, Agostinho, 145, 168, 186

Neutrality Act, 120, 273, 332

New Jewel Movement, 236. *See also* Grenada

News bureaus, opening in Cuba, 295, 300, 304, 316

Newsom, David, 185–96, 199, 203, 204, 207–8

New York Yankees, 183, 187, 321

Nicaragua, 206, 231, 263, 264, 291, 331, 349, 415; Cuban policy toward, 112, 213, 226, 229–30, 232, 233, 243, 258–59, 262; Reagan policy toward, 226, 228, 231, 246; George H. W. Bush policy toward, 259, 261

Nixon, Richard M., 80, 127, 321, 408, 413; Castro's dislike for, 18; meeting with Castro, 18–19, 21; criticizes Cuban economic policy, 29; supports economic sanctions, 35, 36; in 1960 election, 35, 42; supports policy of hostility, 120–23, 126; resignation of, 130

Nixon administration: support for exile attacks, 120; Castro's outreach to, 121–22; and Soviet submarine base at Cienfuegos, 122; hard-line policy of, 122–23, 126; negotiates hijacking agreement, 123–26; faces pressure to improve relations with Cuba, 126–28

Nolan, John, 59–61

Nolan, Richard, 175–76

Nonaligned Movement (NAM), 174, 190, 207, 210, 211, 212

Noriega, Manuel, 262, 328

Noriega, Roger, 345, 361

North Korea, 372, 383, 385

North-South Summit, 228

Nuccio, Richard A., 310n; proposals for Clinton's first 100 days, 271–73, 275–78; and rafters crisis, 284, 295; as presidential advisor, 300–301, 304–5; and terrorism list, 301, 347; and Brothers to the Rescue, 306, 307, 312–14; resignation of, 314

OAS. *See* Organization of American States

Obama, Barack, 372, 412; declares desire for new policy toward Cuba, 4, 368–69, 373, 402, 410; appeals to Cuban American moderates, 368, 414, 482 (n. 123); at Fifth Summit of the Americas, 369, 373; political pressures on, 371–72, 380, 397, 411; writes to Yoani Sánchez, 376, 382; use of Spain as intermediary, 381; and Richardson, 383, 396; opportunities in second term, 397, 399, 401, 407; meets Raúl Castro, 402

Obama administration, 415; promises new policy, 368–69, 372–73, 400–401; ends restrictions on family travel and remittances, 369; supports repeal of 1962 OAS resolution suspending Cuba, 369; reduces restrictions on cultural exchange, 370; turns off electronic billboard, 370; migration consultations, 370, 399; opens mail talks, 370–71, 399; continues USAID democracy programs, 371, 379, 399; political calculations of, 371, 397–98; leaves Cuba on terrorism list, 371, 399; support for cyber war programs, 374–77; and Alan Gross, 376–78, 382, 387, 394–97, 398–99; restores educational and cultural travel, 380–81; collaboration with Spain, 381–82; Valenzuela meeting with Bruno Rodríguez,

383; and Richardson as emissary, 383–84, 394–97; and Coast Guard cooperation, 387–88, 393, 399; and counterterrorism cooperation, 388–90; cooperation in Haiti, 390–91; cooperation on oil spill prevention and mitigation, 391–94, 399; under pressure from Latin America to change policy, 369, 372, 374, 408, 411

Ochoa, Arnaldo, 328, 469 (n. 262)

Office of Foreign Assets Control (OFAC), 273, 356, 392–94

Office of National Drug Control Policy (ONDCP), 329

Ogaden region (Ethiopia), 169, 171, 172, 173. *See also* Ethiopia

Oil drilling safety and spill mitigation, 391–94, 399. *See also* Environmental cooperation

Oliver, Covey, 117–18

Omega 7, 333. *See also* Cuban Americans—paramilitary violence by

Operation Mongoose, 43, 47, 59

Operations Coordinating Board, Eisenhower administration, 23

Organization of American States (OAS), 24, 26, 56, 57, 116–17; imposes sanctions on Cuba, 83, 91, 99–100; ends sanctions on Cuba, 127–28, 130, 131, 135–39, 140, 142, 151, 411; repeals Cuba's suspension, 369, 372, 374, 411

Ortega, Cardinal Jaime, 379, 381–82, 386

Oswald, Lee Harvey, 79, 81

Overflights, of Cuba by U.S. reconnaissance aircraft, 53, 91–94, 157, 162, 197, 198, 201, 221–22, 247

Owens, Henry D., 117

Padrón, José Luis, 198, 199, 203, 231; background of, 178–79; meetings with Benes, 178–80, 182, 190, 195, 448 (n. 123); meets Aaron at La Côte Basque, 183–85; meets Newsom in New York, 185–87, 203; meets Newson in Washington, 188–89, 195; meeting in Atlanta, 190–92; meeting in Cuernavaca, 192–94; 1978 meeting

in Havana, 196, 197, 200; rafters crisis meetings, 219–20, 222; and Grenada, 237–38; and 1984 migration agreement, 244, 246; and southern Africa negotiations, 250–51; and counter-narcotics cooperation, 327

Palmieri, Victor H., 217, 218

Panama, 133, 153, 158, 171, 178, 179, 182, 213, 262–63, 298, 328, 389

Panama Canal, 158, 171

Panetta, Leon, 314

Parallel positive steps, 115, 268–69, 316, 344, 400, 410, 411

Parmly, Michael E., 362–63

Pastor, Robert, 155, 159, 211; on negotiating Cuban foreign policy, 165; on food and medicine sales, 165, 167; on Cubans in Africa, 170, 172; 1978 trip to Havana, 196–209; 1978 meeting with Castro, 200–204, 415, 452 (n. 215); advocates release of Puerto Rican nationalists, 204–6, 386; and Nonaligned Movement, 206, 210; advocates "cool but communicative" policy, 206–7; 1980 meeting with Castro, 212–13, 215; in Mariel boatlift negotiations, 219–20, 222, 453 (n. 256); and *Blue Fire*, 221–22; in Carter's postpresidency, 349, 353, 386

Patience and forbearance, policy of, 12, 23, 29, 39

Pavlov, Yuri, 266

Payá, Oswaldo, 351, 354–55, 473 (n. 34). *See also* Varela Project

Pazos, Felipe, 17, 40

Pell, Clairborne, 127, 295–96

Pelosi, Nancy, 380

Peña, Federico, 308, 311

Pentagon. *See* U.S. Department of Defense

People-to-people programs, 410; proposed under Johnson, 115; expanded under Clinton, 268, 270, 272–73, 272n, 312, 319–20, 324–25, 343–44, 413; ended under G. W. Bush, 355–56, 413; restored under Obama, 368, 371, 379–80, 400–401, 413. *See also* Educational and cultural

Subsidiaries of U.S. companies, embargo on trade with Cuba by, 116, 127, 133, 135, 143, 151, 270, 413

Sugar quota, 22, 29, 31, 35–37

Sullivan, Joseph, 312

Summit of the Americas, 368, 369, 370, 372, 373

SWAPO, 199, 249. *See also* Namibia

Sweig, Julia, 318

Switzerland, 97, 121, 122, 125, 157, 163, 366

Szulc, Tad, 49–50, 429 (n. 28)

Tamayo Méndez, Arnaldo, 309

Tarnoff, Peter, 301; and Benes, 184–85, 190; in Carter secret talks, 185, 187, 188, 189, 190; 1978 meetings in Havana, 196–204, 409, 415; 1980 meeting with Castro, 211–14; and Mariel boatlift, 215, 219–20, 222–23, 407; and *balsero* crisis, 284–86, 289; in wet foot–dry foot talks, 297–300; and Brothers to the Rescue, 308, 312, 314; and baseball diplomacy, 325

Task Force on Cuba: in Kennedy administration, 47; in Clinton administration, 300, 308; Council on Foreign Relations, 318–20

Taylor, John "Jay," 247, 252–55, 257–59, 261–64, 315, 328

Telecommunications service, improvement of, 273, 274, 277, 293, 369, 394

Terrorism list, state sponsors of, 234, 246, 301, 347, 352, 371, 387, 394, 399

Thompson, Tommy, 92

Tiant, Luis, 138, 151

Todman, Terence A., 161–66, 196

Torras, Pelegrín, 161, 163, 209

Torricelli, Robert, G., 270–72, 299

Torricelli bill. *See* Cuban Democracy Act of 1992

Torrijos, Omar, 179, 213

Track II, 272, 272n. *See also* Cuban Democracy Act of 1992

Tractors-for-Freedom Committee, 48–50

Trade Sanctions Reform and Export Enhancement Act (TSRA), 364, 401

Travel to Cuba by non–Cuban Americans, 115, 175, 295, 336, 352, 354; ban imposed by Johnson, 104; ban lifted by Carter, 157, 162, 177, 413; ban reimposed by Reagan, 234, 413; restrictions relaxed by Clinton, 273, 274, 279, 293, 301, 304, 316, 319–20, 343, 344, 413; restrictions tightened by G. W. Bush, 355–57, 413; restrictions relaxed by Obama, 371, 379–81, 401, 413; prohibition of, for tourism, 401. *See also* Cuban Americans—family visits to Cuba by; Educational and cultural exchange

Trinidad and Tobago, 153, 369

Trudeau, Pierre Elliot, 349

TSRA (Trade Sanctions Reform and Export Enhancement Act), 364, 401

Turner, Stansfield, 332

Turner, Ted, 316

TV Martí, 260–64, 279, 283–84, 349, 355, 415

Twenty-sixth of July Movement, 12, 19, 25, 27, 40

U-2 reconnaissance overflights, 51, 53, 91–94. *See also* SR-71 reconnaissance overflights

UNITA. *See* National Union for Total Independence of Angola

United Nations (UN), 26, 37, 109, 257, 310; as locale for Kennedy secret talks, 73–76; Cuban mission to, 128, 133, 163; Cuban policy on Puerto Rico at, 144, 188, 191; Cuba seeks Security Council seat at, 206, 211, 212; Valenzuela meeting with Bruno Rodríguez at, 383, 384; Mills meeting with Bruno Rodríguez at, 390

UN Human Rights Commission, 247

UN International Drug Control Program (UNDCP), 329

UN Resolution 435 on Namibia, 249

UN Security Council, 206, 211, 212

U.S. Agency for International Development (USAID), 116, 300, 319, 346, 371, 375–77, 379, 394, 398

U.S. Chamber of Commerce, 317

U.S. Coast Guard, 120, 358; seizure of Cuban fishing boats, 85, 91; and Camarioca migration crisis, 105, 106; and Mariel boatlift, 218; cooperation with Cuban Border Guards, 243, 327, 363; and *balsero* crisis, 280–82, 295, 305; and counter-narcotics cooperation, 301, 325–30, 387–88; and Brothers to the Rescue, 307; search and rescue cooperation, 387–88, 399, 410; and oil spill mitigation, 393, 399

U.S. Congress, 48, 74, 204, 231, 239, 296, 304, 352, 364, 372, 382, 414; and bloodbath, 12; and Cuba's sugar quota, 29, 31, 36; pushes for improving relations with Cuba, 126–27, 134, 137–38, 347; proposal to lift embargo on food and medicine, 164, 318; and Soviet combat brigade, 207–8; opposition to Radio Martí, 243; and Cuban Democracy Act, 269–70; and Helms-Burton legislation, 305, 314; slows counter-narcotics cooperation, 330; criticism of Obama's Cuba policy, 372, 399, 401, 413, 398; investigates USAID Cuba programs, 379; fails to lift travel ban, 379–80, 395

U.S. Department of Defense, 48, 91, 101, 149, 166, 227, 278, 347; Defense Intelligence Agency (DIA), 309–10

U.S. Department of Justice, 104, 132, 278; and 1964 prisoner exchange, 67; review of released prisoners, 188, 213, 414; and Puerto Rican nationalist prisoners, 205; and hijackings, 216, 273; and counter-narcotics cooperation, 326; and counterterrorism cooperation, 332–33, 337, 389; and Elián González, 341; and Cuban Five, 394, 399

U.S. Geological Survey, 391

U.S. House of Representatives, House Foreign Affairs Committee, 15, 379, 380; Subcommittee on Western Hemisphere Affairs, 270, 278, 296

U.S. Immigration and Customs Enforcement (ICE), 389

U.S. Immigration and Naturalization Service (INS), 130, 248, 339, 341, 343

U.S. Information Agency (USIA), 264

U.S. Interests Section, 168, 312; and Shaba II, 172; political prisoners seek refuge in, 218, 223; and *Blue Fire*, 221–22; during Grenada invasion, 237–38; and 1984 migration agreement, 243, 244; spying at, 247; and southern Africa, 250, 252–55; and counter-narcotics cooperation, 327, 328, 330; and counterterrorism cooperation, 333–34, 336; and Elián González, 336, 339, 341; fails to offer minimum visas in 2007, 359; serves as staging ground for dissidents, 360–62; electronic billboard at, 363, 370; on Cuban bloggers 377; DIS officer at, 387–88. *See also* Cuban Interests Section; Interests Sections

U.S. National Commission on the BP Deepwater Horizon Oil Spill, 392

U.S. National Hurricane Center, 363. *See also* Hurricane cooperation

U.S. relations with Cuba: before 1959, 8–10; lessons of, 402–17. *See also individual presidential administrations*

U.S. Senate: Committee on Foreign Relations, 15, 142, 165, 296, 305, 379, 428 (n. 15); Committee on the Judiciary, Internal Security Subcommittee, 25

U.S. Southern Command (SOUTHCOM), 329, 472 (n. 10)

U.S. Supreme Court, 343

Urrutia, Manuel, 25, 26, 40

Uruguay, 44, 99, 107

Vaky, Viron P., 113, 117, 121, 122, 124, 410

Valdés, Gabriel, 107

Valdés, Ramiro, 375

Valenzuela, Arturo, 372, 383, 384, 391

Vallejo, René, 62, 66, 67, 70, 74–76, 94

Vance, Cyrus, 168, 175; and Carter's policy of normalization, 157, 158–59; and fishing talks, 161–62; opposes lifting embargo on sugar, 164–65; conflict with